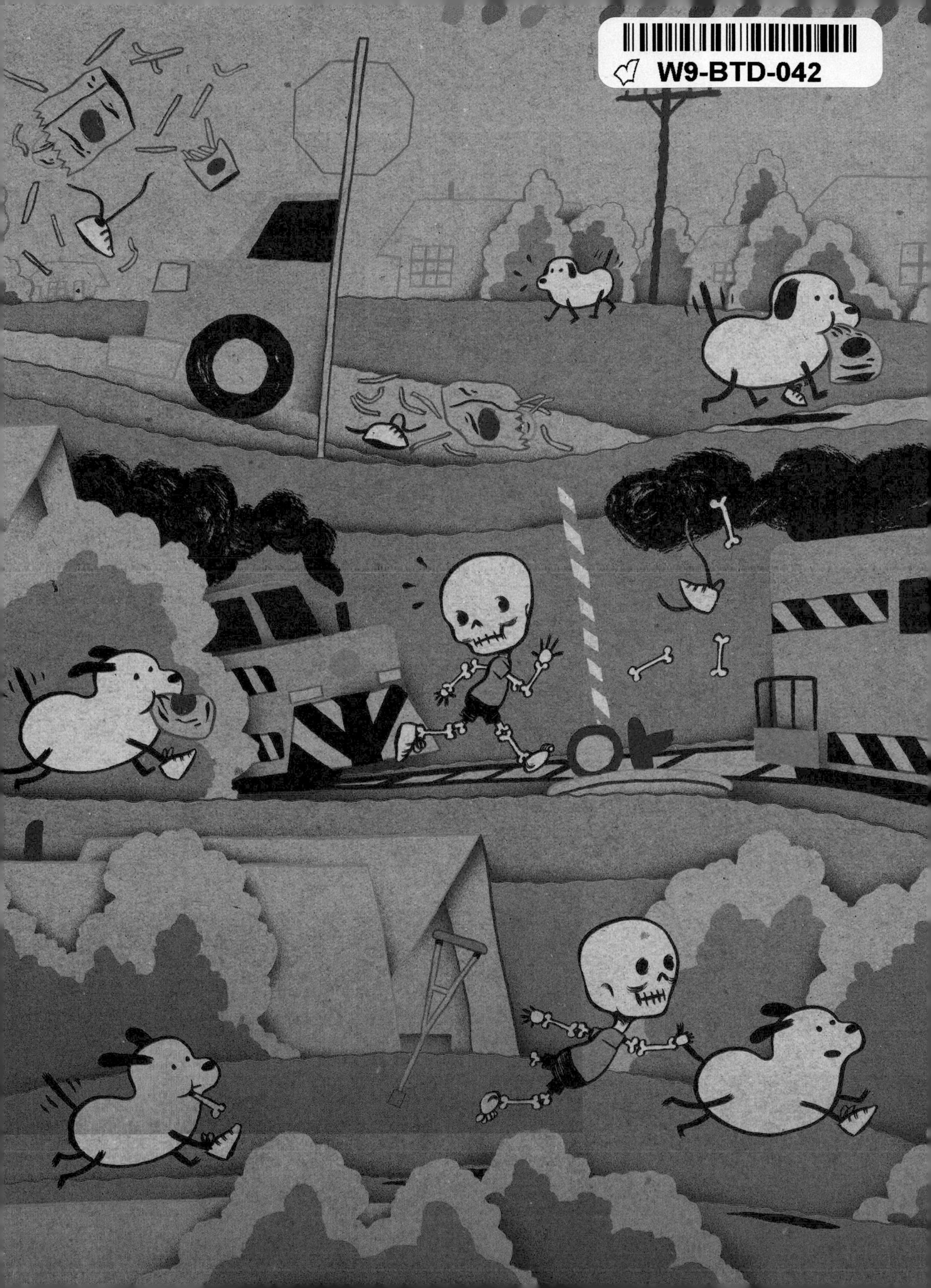

THE BEST AMERICAN

Comics 2008

GUEST EDITORS OF
THE BEST AMERICAN COMICS

2006   HARVEY PEKAR

2007   CHRIS WARE

2008   LYNDA BARRY

THE BEST AMERICAN

Comics .

2008

EDITED *and with an*

INTRODUCTION *by* Lynda Barry

JESSICA ABEL & MATT MADDEN,
series editors

HOUGHTON MIFFLIN COMPANY
BOSTON · NEW YORK   2008

www.houghtonmifflinbooks.com

ISBN 978-0-618-98976-8

Book design: Robert Overholtzer   Cover design: Eleanor Davis   Endpaper art: Joseph Lambert

PRINTED IN THE UNITED STATES OF AMERICA

DOC 10 9 8 7 6 5 4 3 2 1

Permissions credits are located on page 325

Contents

vii : JESSICA ABEL and MATT MADDEN Preface

xi : LYNDA BARRY Introduction

1 : GRAHAM ANNABLE Burden FROM *Papercutter*

16 : DAVID AXE and STEVE OLEXA War-Fix (*Excerpt*) FROM *War-Fix*

35 : T. EDWARD BAK Trouble FROM *Project: Romantic*

39 : ALISON BECHDEL Proxy War, A Terribly Civil War, Life 2.0, Scandal in the House, Who's Your Daddy?, and The Uses of Intelligence
FROM *Dykes to Watch Out For*

45 : NICK BERTOZZI The Salon (*Excerpt*) FROM *The Salon*

53 : LILLI CARRÉ The Thing About Madeline FROM *The Thing About Madeline*

75 : MARTIN CENDREDA Hopscotch FROM *Mome*

80 : SHAWN CHENG and SARA EDWARD-CORBETT The Monkey and the Crab FROM *The Monkey and the Crab*

91 : ELEANOR DAVIS Seven Sacks FROM *Mome*

103 : DERF The Bunker, Pressure, Strange Thoughts for Strange Times, The Man, and Wal-Mart FROM *The City*

108 : RICK GEARY Part II. The Benders Arrive FROM *The Saga of the Bloody Benders*

129 : MATT GROENING 'Fraid Monkeys, Daddy I Got a Haircut, Important Questions About Monsters, King of Monster Island, Movies I'm Going To Make When I Grow Up, Will and Abe's Guide to Bali, Parts I, II, and III, Will and Abe's Guide to Superheroes, Abe and Will in The Dinner Conversation, and My Class Went on a Field Trip
FROM *Will and Abe's Guide to the Universe*

140 : ERIC HAVEN Mammalogy FROM *Tales to Demolish*

156 : JAIME HERNANDEZ Gold Diggers of 1969 FROM *Love and Rockets*

167 : KAZ Underworld Strips FROM *Underworld*

177 : MICHAEL KUPPERMAN Cousin Granpa FROM *Tales Designed to Thrizzle*

181 : JOSEPH LAMBERT Turtle, Keep It Steady! FROM *Turtle, Keep It Steady!*

190 : EVAN LARSON Cupid's Day Off FROM *Project: Romantic*

198 : JASON LUTES Berlin *(Excerpt)* FROM *Berlin*

216 : CATHY MALKASIAN Percy Gloom *(Excerpt)* FROM *Percy Gloom*

231 : JOHN MEJIAS The Teachers Edition *(Excerpt)* FROM *Paping*

238 : SARAH OLEKSYK Graveyard FROM *Papercutter*

257 : KEVIN PYLE The Forbidden Zone FROM *Blindspot*

270 : SETH George Sprott (1894–1975) *(Excerpt)* FROM the *New York Times Magazine*

280 : CHRIS WARE The Thanksgiving Series FROM *The New Yorker*

290 : GENE LUEN YANG American Born Chinese *(Excerpt)* FROM *American Born Chinese*

311 : Contributors' Notes

323 : Notable Comics *from August 31, 2006, to September 1, 2007*

Preface

WHEN THE EDITOR Anjali Singh asked us to become series editors for *The Best American Comics,* we jumped at the chance. We knew we would love editing this volume; it's an extension of the way comics are woven into the fabric of our lives.

We are both first of all cartoonists, although sometimes the complexity of our lives makes that hard to remember. We teach comics in regular undergraduate courses as well as in special workshops. We have mentoring relationships with our students and other young cartoonists. We write together about making comics in our textbook. Matt writes comics criticism. Jessica writes comics. Matt is a comics editor. At a more basic level, comics are the reason we know one another; in the mid '90s, Matt lived in Austin and Jessica in Chicago, but we each made mini-comics and traded them through the mail with each other, which led to friendship, and, ultimately, marriage. Through it all, we have maintained a passion for reading and discussing comics and discovering new work. Even after twenty years of daily immersion in comics, we still get a kick wandering around comics conventions and book fairs making finds, noting trends, spotting new scenes. Whenever we travel abroad, we always keep an eye out for comics, whether we're picking up pulp weeklies at the newsstand or seeking out local mini-comics artists. So when the opportunity came along to read *yet more* comics, to be *required* to be familiar with the entire output of comics in North America, when that's what we try to do anyway, well, it was too good an opportunity to pass up.

But there's another level to our enthusiasm for this series: our belief in the value and importance of comics anthologies. As young cartoonists, anthologies had a huge influence on both of us; Jessica collected expensive imported copies of the British anthology *Deadline* and stumbled across a Rip Off Press–published volume called *Heck* that she read over and over, memorizing the linework of Julie Doucet and Mark Marek. One of Matt's earliest influences was the box of old issues of *Heavy Metal* he found in the basement of his boarding school dorm. Later, Matt sought out *Raw* magazine wherever he could find it, and then followed its trail back to *Arcade* and beyond. In the intervening years, we've looked in new comics racks and back issue bins for *Zap* and *Wimmen's Comix, Centrifugal BumblePuppy,* and *Weirdo,* as well as foreign publications like *Lapin, el Víbora,* and *Frigidaire.* Drawn & Quarterly started out publishing an anthology, as did Top Shelf. Fantagraphics has published a whole library's worth of anthology titles. Anthologies are the place where young cartoonists get a break, where they can hope to be published alongside the likes of Chris Ware and Matt Groening, and to be noticed by the likes of Lynda Barry. In fact, anthologies are where both of us got our first breaks. We both published numerous short stories in anthologies before finding publishers who would take a chance on our solo books.

The project of creating anthologies is a noble one, and for that reason also, the task of digging through the thousands of books published each year in North America looking for interesting new comics doesn't feel all that much like work, in the end.

A note on how we do our job: when we review books for consideration by the guest editor, we don't simply choose our personal favorites; rather, we try to consider each work on its own terms and ask if it is compelling or interesting in a way that makes it worth bringing to the attention of the guest editor. We encourage the guest editor to use her own, idiosyncratic judgment, but for our part we consider our job to be assembling and presenting an interesting and representative selection of the year's comics, regardless of style, format, or subject matter. It's a fact that the comics world is incredibly diverse. In no other anthology would one expect to encounter work designed for children next to genre stories, next to subtle realistic fiction, next to memoir. Our goal is to find the best examples of North American comics in a given year, but that may mean very different things to different readers, and to different creators. We try to read the work in the spirit in which it was created.

For the purposes of the anthology, we prefer complete short stories, but also consider longer works; the long form is so dominant in comics that many of the best works in a year are novel-length, and to exclude them would be to limit the picture of what is best in comics. We look at stand-alone mini-comics and single issues of ongoing series, graphic novels and nonfiction comics, as well as Web comics — and of course we scour all the anthologies that come out. Finally, the author of a work must be North American (Canadian, American, or Mexican) or make his or her permanent home here, and the work must be published in English in North America. If you'd like to submit work for consideration in a future volume, and we hope you will, you should label each submission with the artist's and/or publisher's contact information and the date of publication. If you'd like to submit your Web comic, we would love to see it, but we must ask that you do so in print form. We can't accept URLs or CDs due to the demands of reviewing so much material each year. Please label each strip with the exact date of first publication. If you're submitting newspaper strips, please make sure each is labeled with the date of first publication. Send all submissions to Jessica Abel and Matt Madden, Series Editors, Best American Comics, Houghton Mifflin Company, 215 Park Avenue South, New York, New York 10003.

We have a lot to do, but the hardest work in preparing this volume must be the effort required to narrow down all the excellent work in the year to just a few stories. The choices are agonizing, and we don't envy our guest editor that part of the job.

Working with Lynda Barry has been a treat. From our first correspondence, she infected us with her gung-ho enthusiasm and tireless energy. We bonded immediately over our mutual love of teaching and discussing the craft of comics. In fact, she was so excited about reviewing this year's comics that she finally begged us to send her every single comic we had amassed throughout the year — not just the usual 120 or so stories the series editors are supposed to send her way.

The variety of Lynda's choices pleased us a great deal, reflective as they are of her generous and individual taste. Newcomers to comics will find here a broad variety of styles of art, story subjects, and formal approaches to narrative. We think that even seasoned comics readers will find quite a few new authors in this volume. In fact, a good half of the contributors are in the early stages of their careers. Some of the creators have previously published work only in other anthologies. Others have published their work as self-produced mini-comics or online. In addition to new or undiscovered talent, we are very happy that this volume features so many examples of weekly strip comics, from Kaz's absurdist and irreverent *Underworld* to Alison Bechdel's satirical serial drama *Dykes to Watch Out For*. This format — one that Lynda helped pioneer — appearing mainly in alternative weeklies and increasingly online, often gets lost in the shuffle of the present excitement over graphic novels, Web comics, and manga. Yet it is another important current — separate, in turn, we might add, from the daily strips of the major syndicates — of this medium that readers and critics continually try to define, limit, and contain. The wonder of the comics world is that it's so big, and that it continues to grow. This volume reflects that diversity admirably.

Contributors have put together a little extra content for you as well. On our website (www.bestamericancomics.com), you'll find a few reflections on the creative process, as well as pictures of many of the artists' workspaces. Lynda suggested this idea, and we have had such fun seeing the places where the works in this book were born.

In addition to Lynda, we'd like to thank the large group of people involved in putting this volume together. We'd like to acknowledge the wonderful work of our predecessor, Anne Elizabeth Moore. Anjali Singh and her assistant, Ben Steinberg, along with the rest of their team at Houghton Mifflin, have been incredibly helpful in getting us rolling and making our work enjoyable. Finally, and to us, most importantly, we want to thank our studio assistants, Nate Doyle and Meredith Leich, who handled the grunt work of processing submissions and kept us supplied with ever more great comics to read.

JESSICA ABEL and MATT MADDEN

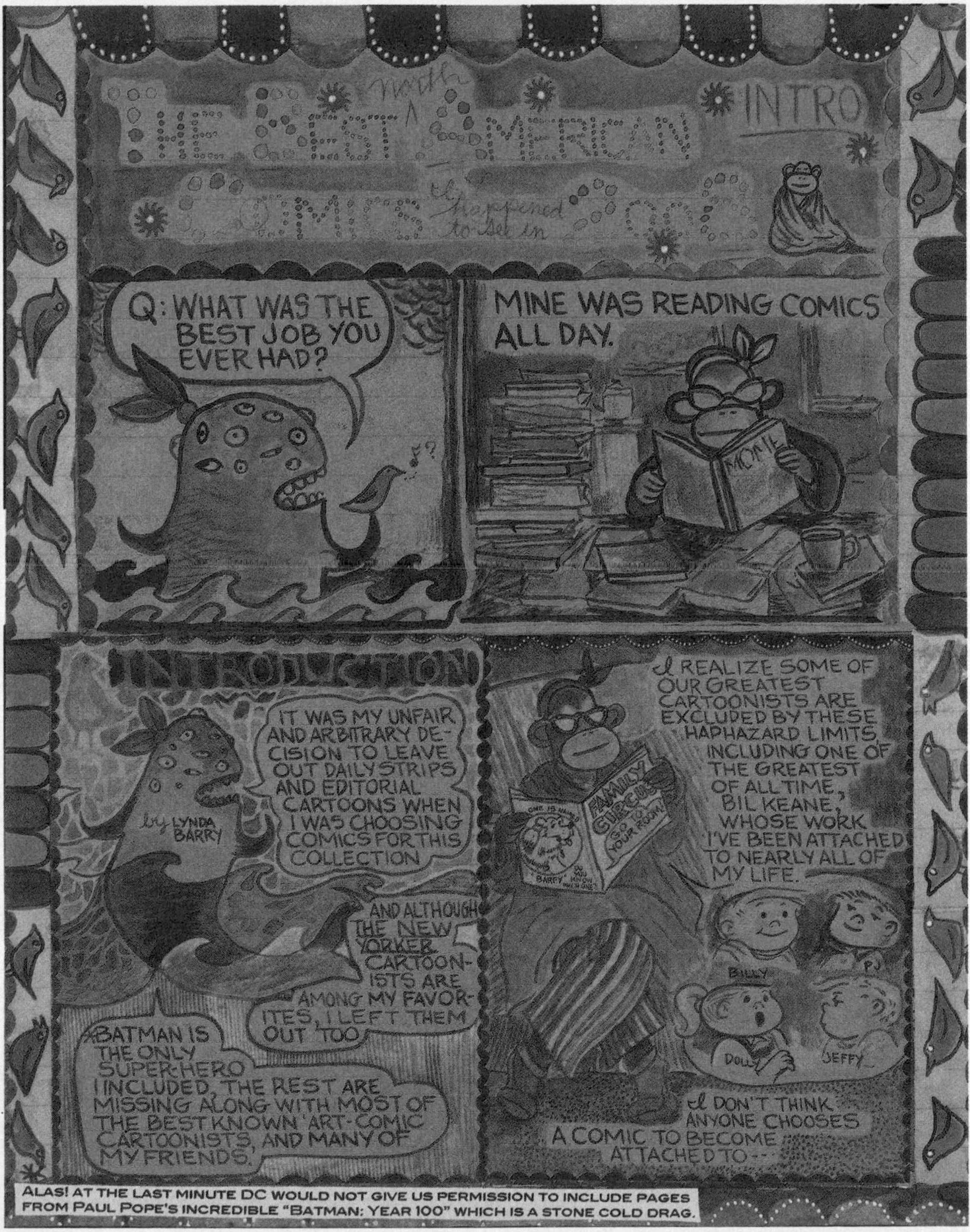
INTRO
Q: WHAT WAS THE BEST JOB YOU EVER HAD?
MINE WAS READING COMICS ALL DAY.
INTRODUCTION
by LYNDA BARRY
IT WAS MY UNFAIR AND ARBITRARY DECISION TO LEAVE OUT DAILY STRIPS AND EDITORIAL CARTOONS WHEN I WAS CHOOSING COMICS FOR THIS COLLECTION
AND ALTHOUGH THE NEW YORKER CARTOONISTS ARE AMONG MY FAVORITES, I LEFT THEM OUT TOO
*BATMAN IS THE ONLY SUPER-HERO I INCLUDED, THE REST ARE MISSING ALONG WITH MOST OF THE BEST KNOWN 'ART-COMIC' CARTOONISTS, AND MANY OF MY FRIENDS.
I REALIZE SOME OF OUR GREATEST CARTOONISTS ARE EXCLUDED BY THESE HAPHAZARD LIMITS, INCLUDING ONE OF THE GREATEST OF ALL TIME, BIL KEANE, WHOSE WORK I'VE BEEN ATTACHED TO NEARLY ALL OF MY LIFE.
FAMILY CIRCUS
GO TO YOUR ROOM!
BILLY
PJ
DOLLY
JEFFY
I DON'T THINK ANYONE CHOOSES A COMIC TO BECOME ATTACHED TO--

ALAS! AT THE LAST MINUTE DC WOULD NOT GIVE US PERMISSION TO INCLUDE PAGES FROM PAUL POPE'S INCREDIBLE "BATMAN: YEAR 100" WHICH IS A STONE COLD DRAG.

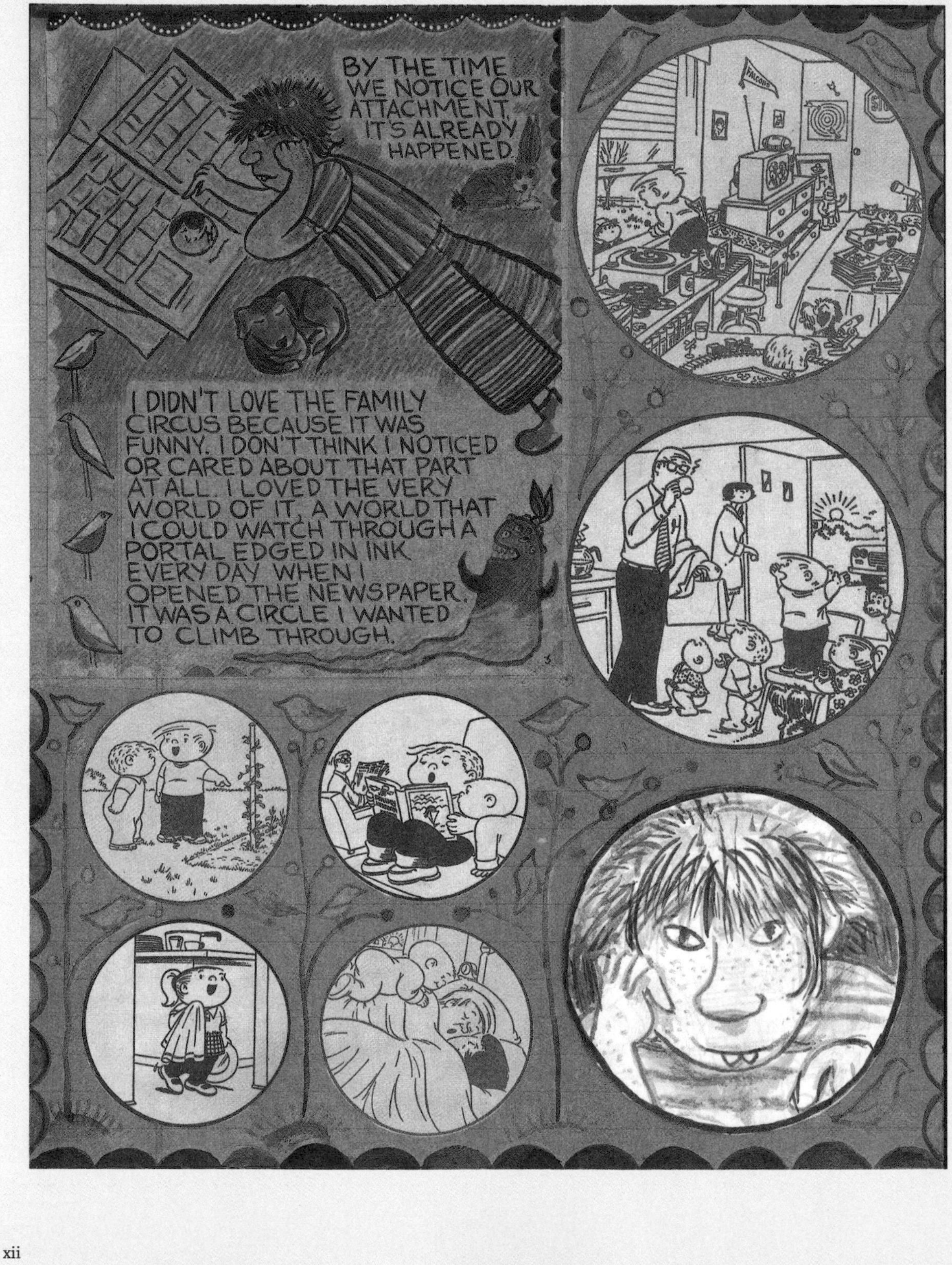
BY THE TIME WE NOTICE OUR ATTACHMENT, IT'S ALREADY HAPPENED.
I DIDN'T LOVE THE FAMILY CIRCUS BECAUSE IT WAS FUNNY. I DON'T THINK I NOTICED OR CARED ABOUT THAT PART AT ALL. I LOVED THE VERY WORLD OF IT, A WORLD THAT I COULD WATCH THROUGH A PORTAL EDGED IN INK EVERY DAY WHEN I OPENED THE NEWSPAPER. IT WAS A CIRCLE I WANTED TO CLIMB THROUGH.

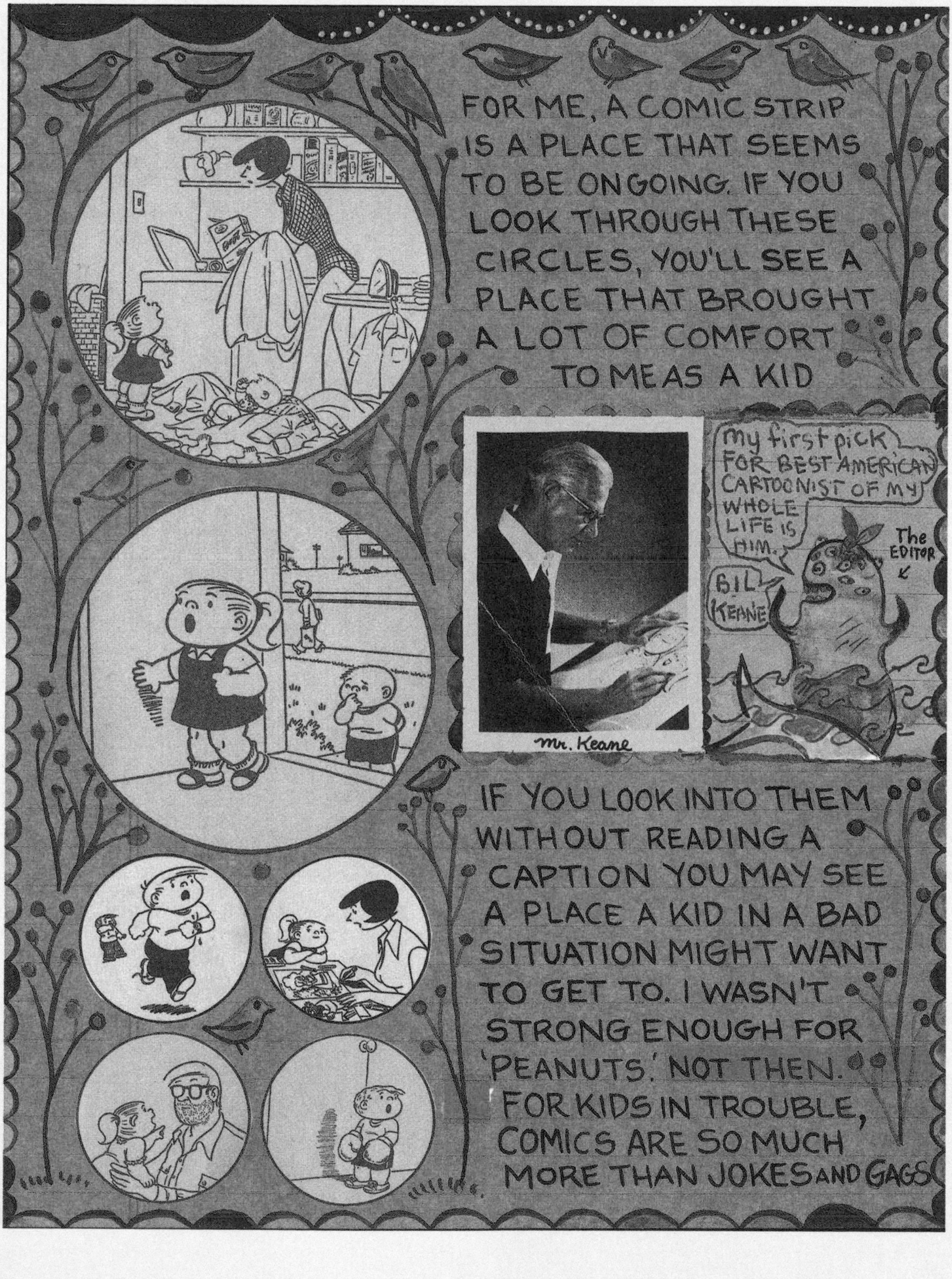
FOR ME, A COMIC STRIP IS A PLACE THAT SEEMS TO BE ONGOING. IF YOU LOOK THROUGH THESE CIRCLES, YOU'LL SEE A PLACE THAT BROUGHT A LOT OF COMFORT TO ME AS A KID
my first pick FOR BEST AMERICAN CARTOONIST OF MY WHOLE LIFE IS HIM.
BIL KEANE
The EDITOR
Mr. Keane
IF YOU LOOK INTO THEM WITHOUT READING A CAPTION YOU MAY SEE A PLACE A KID IN A BAD SITUATION MIGHT WANT TO GET TO. I WASN'T STRONG ENOUGH FOR 'PEANUTS.' NOT THEN. FOR KIDS IN TROUBLE, COMICS ARE SO MUCH MORE THAN JOKES AND GAGS

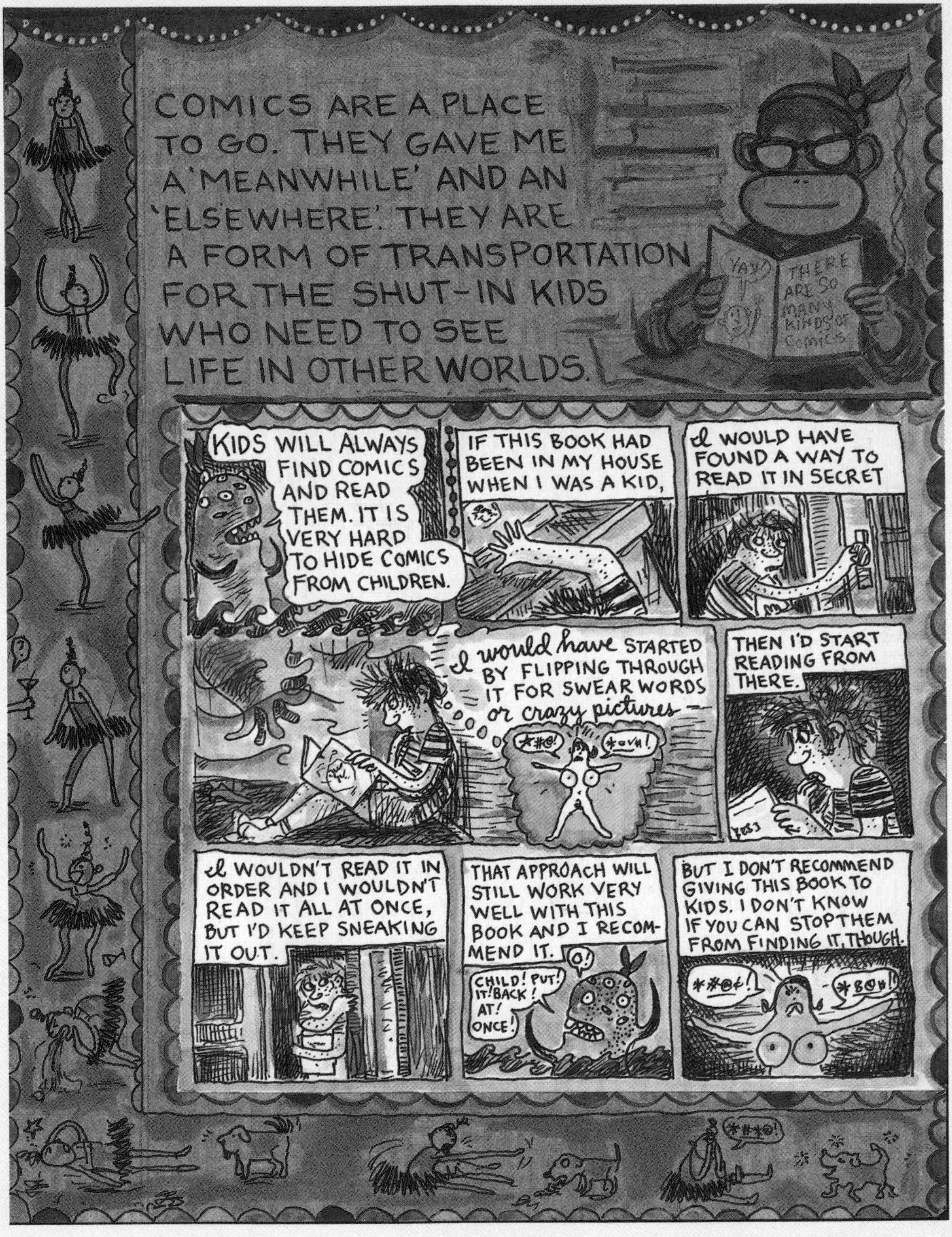
COMICS ARE A PLACE TO GO. THEY GAVE ME A 'MEANWHILE' AND AN 'ELSEWHERE'. THEY ARE A FORM OF TRANSPORTATION FOR THE SHUT-IN KIDS WHO NEED TO SEE LIFE IN OTHER WORLDS.
YAY!
THERE ARE SO MANY KINDS OF COMICS
KIDS WILL ALWAYS FIND COMICS AND READ THEM. IT IS VERY HARD TO HIDE COMICS FROM CHILDREN.
IF THIS BOOK HAD BEEN IN MY HOUSE WHEN I WAS A KID,
I WOULD HAVE FOUND A WAY TO READ IT IN SECRET
I would have STARTED BY FLIPPING THROUGH IT FOR SWEAR WORDS or crazy pictures
*#@!
THEN I'D START READING FROM THERE.
I WOULDN'T READ IT IN ORDER AND I WOULDN'T READ IT ALL AT ONCE, BUT I'D KEEP SNEAKING IT OUT.
THAT APPROACH WILL STILL WORK VERY WELL WITH THIS BOOK AND I RECOMMEND IT.
O!
CHILD! PUT! IT! BACK! AT! ONCE!
BUT I DON'T RECOMMEND GIVING THIS BOOK TO KIDS. I DON'T KNOW IF YOU CAN STOP THEM FROM FINDING IT, THOUGH.
*#@¢!
#@!

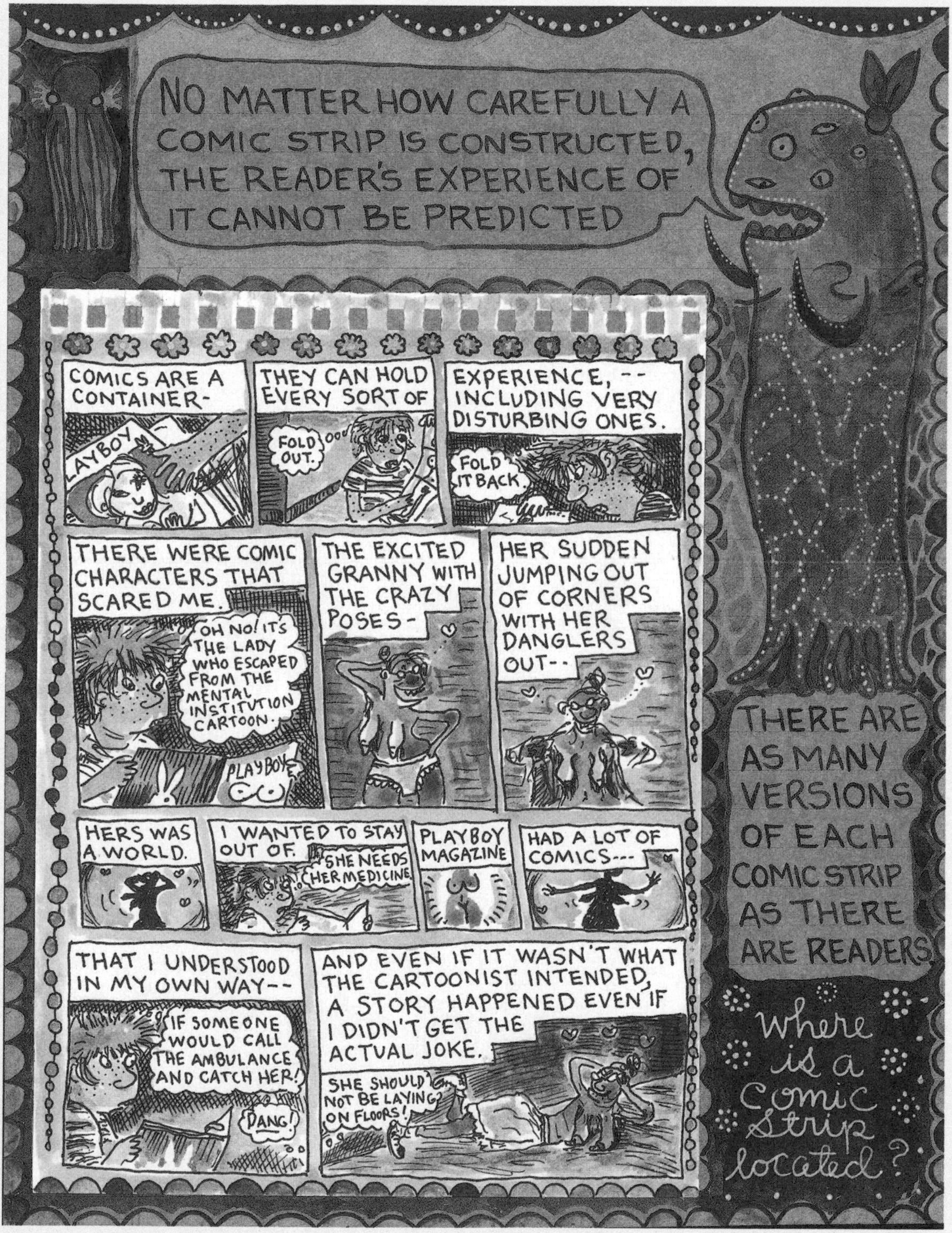

NO MATTER HOW CAREFULLY A COMIC STRIP IS CONSTRUCTED, THE READER'S EXPERIENCE OF IT CANNOT BE PREDICTED
COMICS ARE A CONTAINER-
LAYBOY
THEY CAN HOLD EVERY SORT OF
FOLD OUT.
EXPERIENCE, -- INCLUDING VERY DISTURBING ONES.
FOLD IT BACK.
THERE WERE COMIC CHARACTERS THAT SCARED ME.
OH NO! ITS THE LADY WHO ESCAPED FROM THE MENTAL INSTITUTION CARTOON.
PLAYBOY
THE EXCITED GRANNY WITH THE CRAZY POSES-
HER SUDDEN JUMPING OUT OF CORNERS WITH HER DANGLERS OUT--
HERS WAS A WORLD.
I WANTED TO STAY OUT OF.
SHE NEEDS HER MEDICINE.
PLAYBOY MAGAZINE
HAD A LOT OF COMICS---
THAT I UNDERSTOOD IN MY OWN WAY--
IF SOMEONE WOULD CALL THE AMBULANCE AND CATCH HER!
DANG!
AND EVEN IF IT WASN'T WHAT THE CARTOONIST INTENDED, A STORY HAPPENED EVEN IF I DIDN'T GET THE ACTUAL JOKE.
SHE SHOULD NOT BE LAYING ON FLOORS!
THERE ARE AS MANY VERSIONS OF EACH COMIC STRIP AS THERE ARE READERS.
Where is a Comic Strip located?

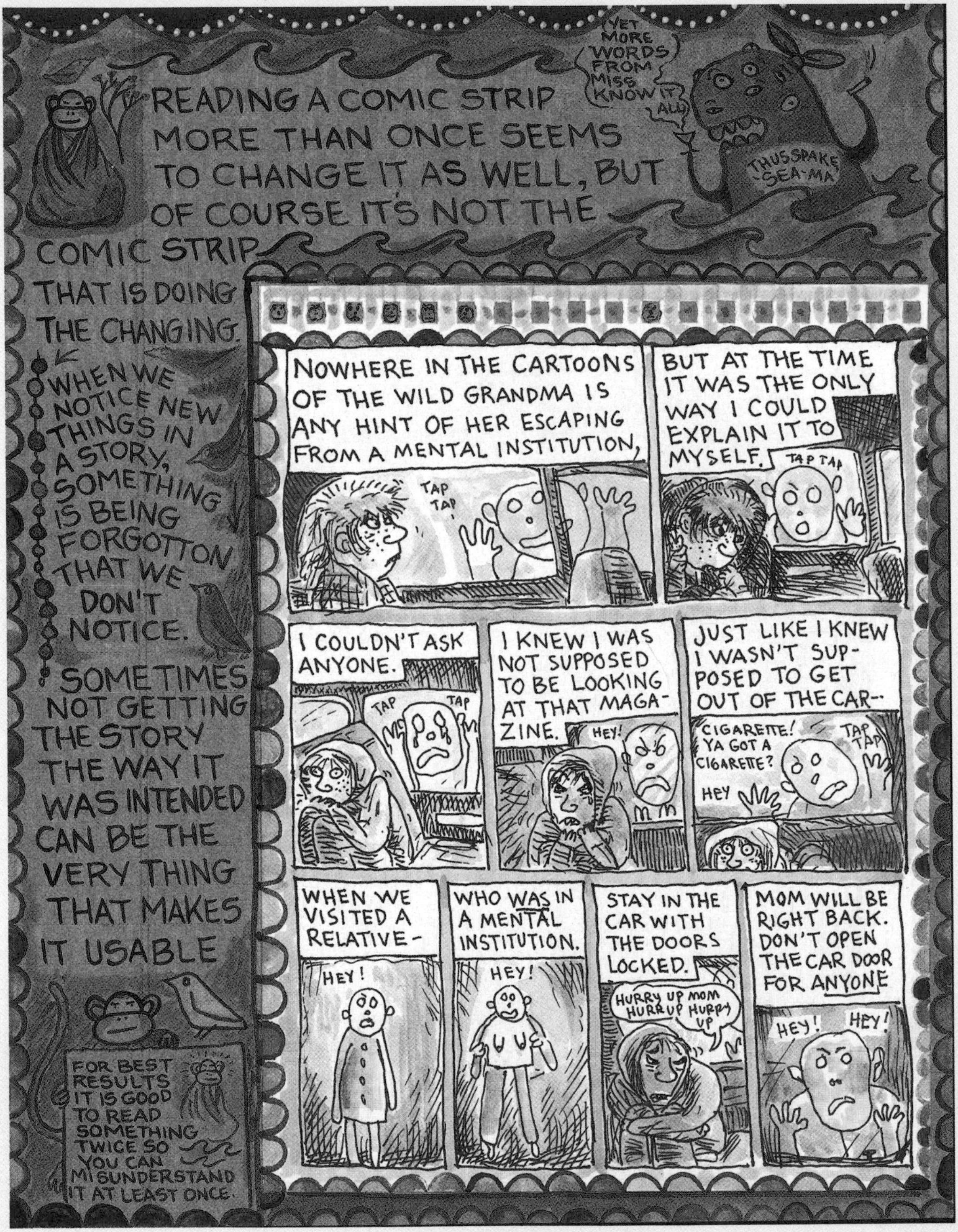
YET MORE WORDS FROM MISS KNOW IT ALL
THUS SPAKE SEA-MA
READING A COMIC STRIP MORE THAN ONCE SEEMS TO CHANGE IT AS WELL, BUT OF COURSE IT'S NOT THE COMIC STRIP THAT IS DOING THE CHANGING.
WHEN WE NOTICE NEW THINGS IN A STORY, SOMETHING IS BEING FORGOTTON THAT WE DON'T NOTICE.
SOMETIMES NOT GETTING THE STORY THE WAY IT WAS INTENDED CAN BE THE VERY THING THAT MAKES IT USABLE
FOR BEST RESULTS IT IS GOOD TO READ SOMETHING TWICE SO YOU CAN MISUNDERSTAND IT AT LEAST ONCE.
NOWHERE IN THE CARTOONS OF THE WILD GRANDMA IS ANY HINT OF HER ESCAPING FROM A MENTAL INSTITUTION,
TAP TAP
BUT AT THE TIME IT WAS THE ONLY WAY I COULD EXPLAIN IT TO MYSELF.
TAP TAP
I COULDN'T ASK ANYONE.
TAP TAP
I KNEW I WAS NOT SUPPOSED TO BE LOOKING AT THAT MAGAZINE.
HEY!
JUST LIKE I KNEW I WASN'T SUPPOSED TO GET OUT OF THE CAR--
CIGARETTE! YA GOT A CIGARETTE?
TAP TAP
HEY
WHEN WE VISITED A RELATIVE-
HEY!
WHO WAS IN A MENTAL INSTITUTION.
HEY!
STAY IN THE CAR WITH THE DOORS LOCKED.
HURRY UP MOM HURRY UP HURRY UP
MOM WILL BE RIGHT BACK. DON'T OPEN THE CAR DOOR FOR ANYONE
HEY! HEY!

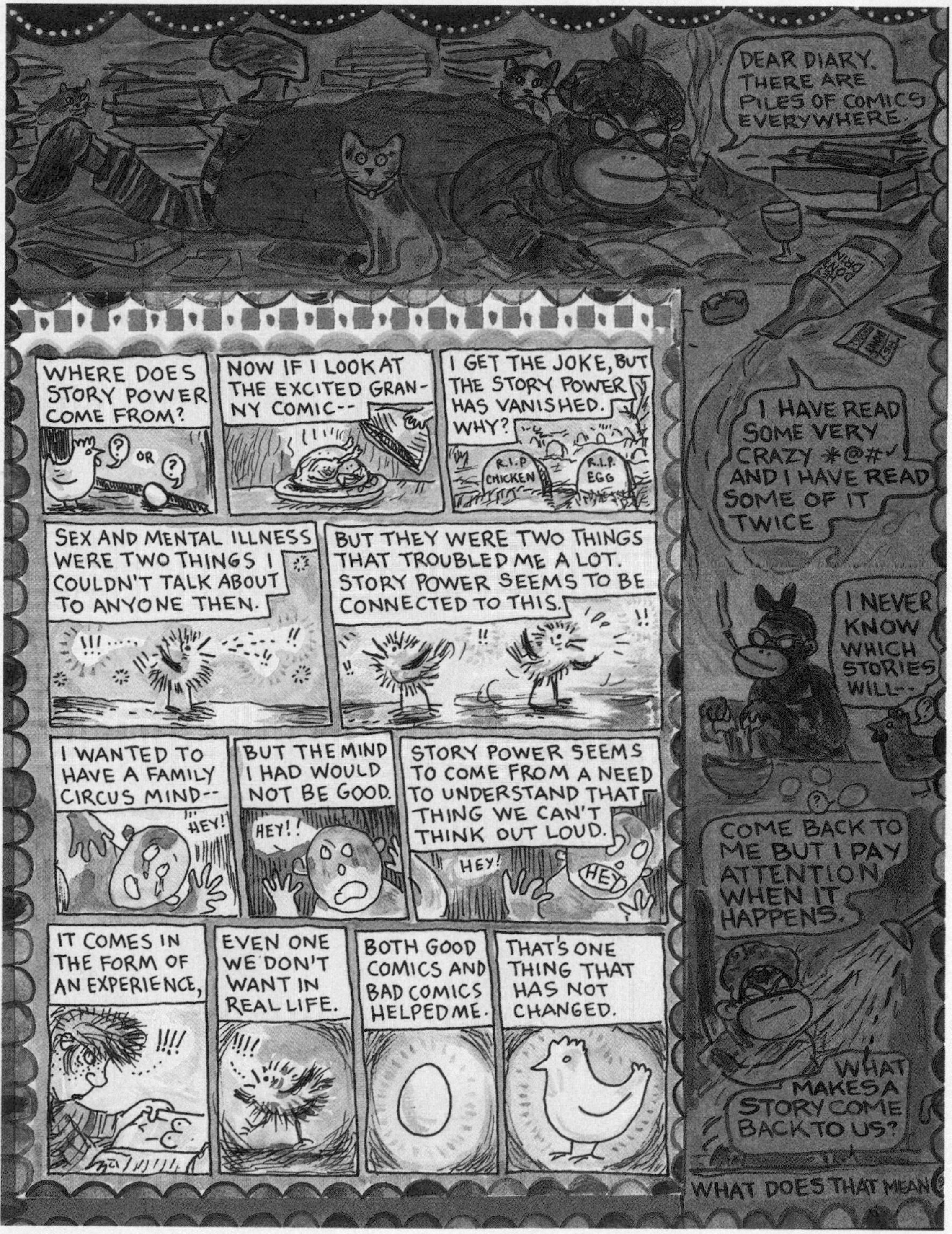
DEAR DIARY. THERE ARE PILES OF COMICS EVERYWHERE.
WHERE DOES STORY POWER COME FROM?
OR
NOW IF I LOOK AT THE EXCITED GRANNY COMIC--
I GET THE JOKE, BUT THE STORY POWER HAS VANISHED. WHY?
R.I.P CHICKEN
R.I.P. EGG
SEX AND MENTAL ILLNESS WERE TWO THINGS I COULDN'T TALK ABOUT TO ANYONE THEN.
BUT THEY WERE TWO THINGS THAT TROUBLED ME A LOT. STORY POWER SEEMS TO BE CONNECTED TO THIS.
I WANTED TO HAVE A FAMILY CIRCUS MIND--
HEY!
BUT THE MIND I HAD WOULD NOT BE GOOD.
HEY!
STORY POWER SEEMS TO COME FROM A NEED TO UNDERSTAND THAT THING WE CAN'T THINK OUT LOUD.
HEY!
HEY
IT COMES IN THE FORM OF AN EXPERIENCE,
EVEN ONE WE DON'T WANT IN REAL LIFE.
BOTH GOOD COMICS AND BAD COMICS HELPED ME.
THAT'S ONE THING THAT HAS NOT CHANGED.
I HAVE READ SOME VERY CRAZY *@#✓ AND I HAVE READ SOME OF IT TWICE
I NEVER KNOW WHICH STORIES WILL--
COME BACK TO ME BUT I PAY ATTENTION WHEN IT HAPPENS.
WHAT MAKES A STORY COME BACK TO US?
WHAT DOES THAT MEAN?

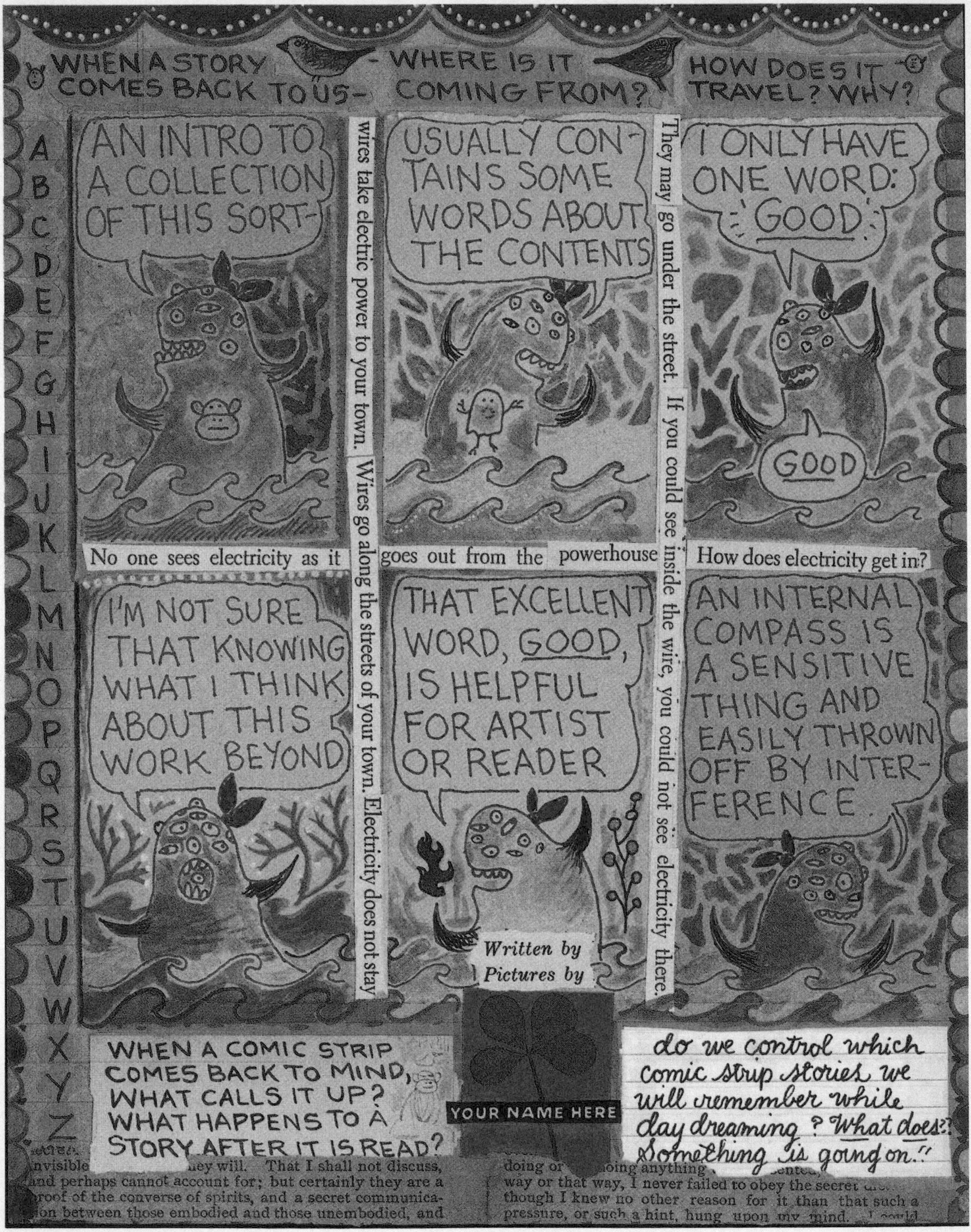

WHEN A STORY COMES BACK TO US -
WHERE IS IT COMING FROM?
HOW DOES IT TRAVEL? WHY?
A B C D E F G H I J K L M N O P Q R S T U V W X Y Z
AN INTRO TO A COLLECTION OF THIS SORT -
wires take electric power to your town.
USUALLY CONTAINS SOME WORDS ABOUT THE CONTENTS
They may go under the street. If you could see inside the wire, you could not see electricity there.
I ONLY HAVE ONE WORD: GOOD
GOOD
No one sees electricity as it
Wires go along the streets of your town. Electricity does not stay
goes out from the
powerhouse
How does electricity get in?
I'M NOT SURE THAT KNOWING WHAT I THINK ABOUT THIS WORK BEYOND
THAT EXCELLENT WORD, GOOD, IS HELPFUL FOR ARTIST OR READER
AN INTERNAL COMPASS IS A SENSITIVE THING AND EASILY THROWN OFF BY INTERFERENCE.
Written by
Pictures by
WHEN A COMIC STRIP COMES BACK TO MIND, WHAT CALLS IT UP? WHAT HAPPENS TO A STORY AFTER IT IS READ?
YOUR NAME HERE
do we control which comic strip stories we will remember while day dreaming? What does?! Something is going on!!
invisible hey will. That I shall not discuss, and perhaps cannot account for; but certainly they are a proof of the converse of spirits, and a secret communication between those embodied and those unembodied, and
doing or oing anything sented, way or that way, I never failed to obey the secret though I knew no other reason for it than that such a pressure, or such a hint, hung upon my mind.

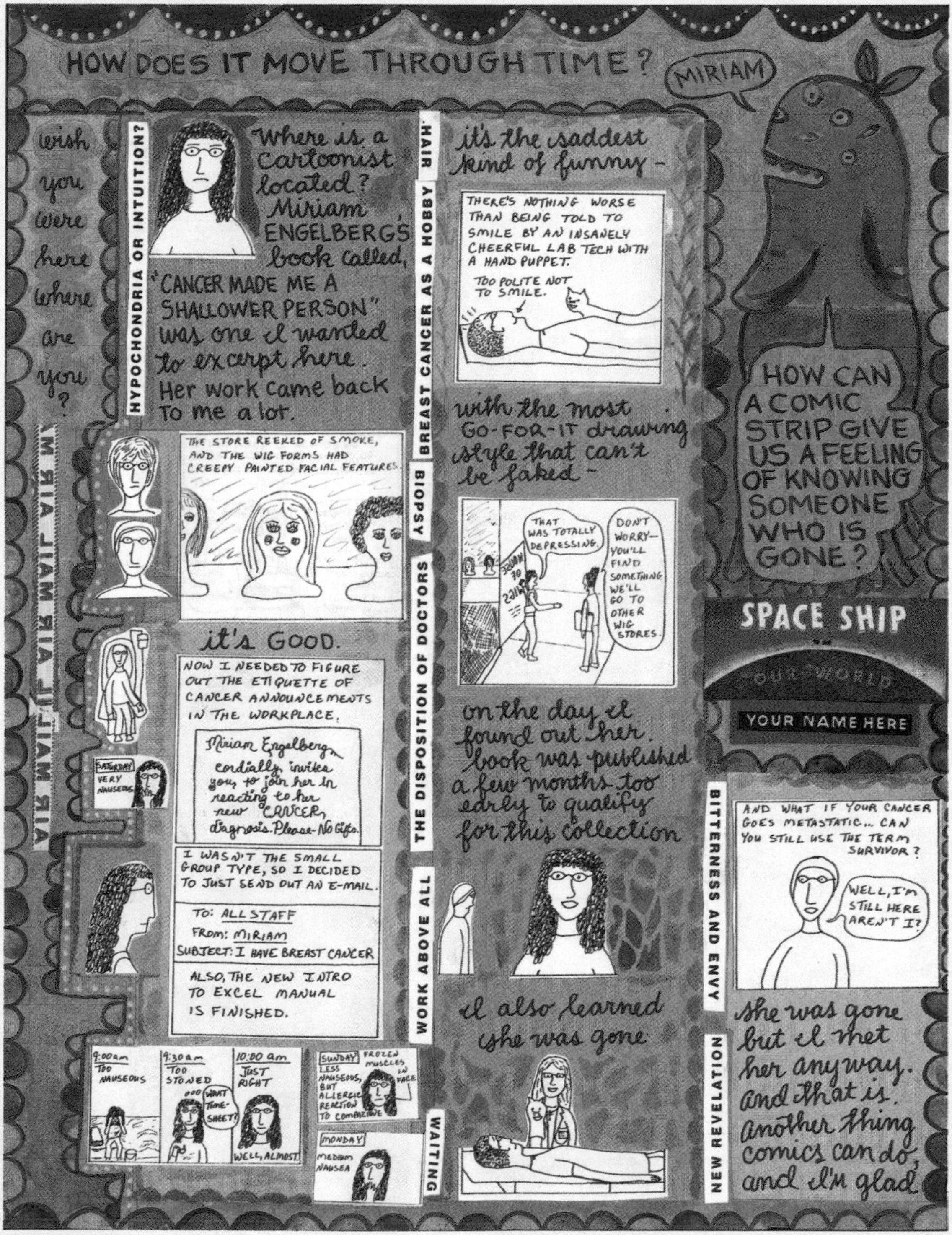
HOW DOES IT MOVE THROUGH TIME?
MIRIAM
wish you were here where are you?
HYPOCHONDRIA OR INTUITION?
Where is a cartoonist located? Miriam ENGELBERG'S book called, "CANCER MADE ME A SHALLOWER PERSON" was one I wanted to excerpt here. Her work came back to me a lot.
AIR MAIL AIR MAIL
THE STORE REEKED OF SMOKE, AND THE WIG FORMS HAD CREEPY PAINTED FACIAL FEATURES.
it's GOOD.
NOW I NEEDED TO FIGURE OUT THE ETIQUETTE OF CANCER ANNOUNCEMENTS IN THE WORKPLACE.
Miriam Engelberg cordially invites you to join her in reacting to her new CANCER diagnosis. Please - No Gifts.
SATURDAY VERY NAUSEOUS
I WASN'T THE SMALL GROUP TYPE, SO I DECIDED TO JUST SEND OUT AN E-MAIL.
TO: ALL STAFF
FROM: MIRIAM
SUBJECT: I HAVE BREAST CANCER
ALSO, THE NEW INTRO TO EXCEL MANUAL IS FINISHED.
9:00 am TOO NAUSEOUS
9:30 am TOO STONED
WHAT TIME-SHEET?
10:00 am JUST RIGHT
WELL, ALMOST.
SUNDAY LESS NAUSEOUS, BUT ALLERGIC REACTION TO COMPAZINE
FROZEN MUSCLES IN FACE
MONDAY MEDIUM NAUSEA
HAIR
BREAST CANCER AS A HOBBY
BIOPSY
THE DISPOSITION OF DOCTORS
WORK ABOVE ALL
WAITING
it's the saddest kind of funny -
THERE'S NOTHING WORSE THAN BEING TOLD TO SMILE BY AN INSANELY CHEERFUL LAB TECH WITH A HAND PUPPET.
TOO POLITE NOT TO SMILE.
with the most GO-FOR-IT drawing style that can't be faked -
THAT WAS TOTALLY DEPRESSING.
DON'T WORRY— YOU'LL FIND SOMETHING. WE'LL GO TO OTHER WIG STORES.
on the day I found out her book was published a few months too early to qualify for this collection
I also learned she was gone.
HOW CAN A COMIC STRIP GIVE US A FEELING OF KNOWING SOMEONE WHO IS GONE?
SPACE SHIP
OUR WORLD
YOUR NAME HERE
BITTERNESS AND ENVY
NEW REVELATION
AND WHAT IF YOUR CANCER GOES METASTATIC... CAN YOU STILL USE THE TERM SURVIVOR?
WELL, I'M STILL HERE AREN'T I?
she was gone but I met her anyway. And that is another thing comics can do, and I'm glad.

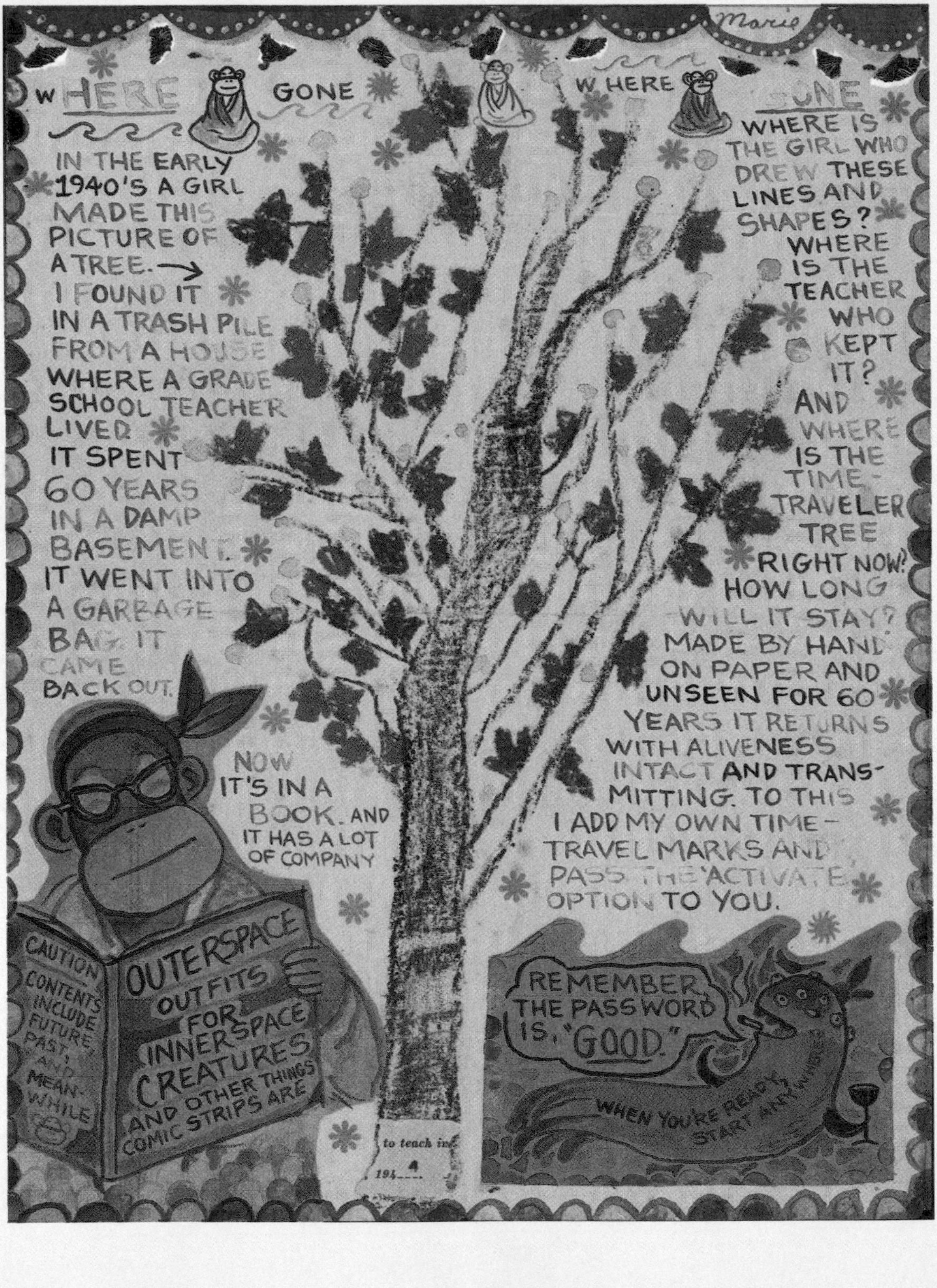
Marie
WHERE GONE
WHERE GONE
IN THE EARLY 1940'S A GIRL MADE THIS PICTURE OF A TREE. →
I FOUND IT IN A TRASH PILE FROM A HOUSE WHERE A GRADE SCHOOL TEACHER LIVED.
IT SPENT 60 YEARS IN A DAMP BASEMENT.
IT WENT INTO A GARBAGE BAG. IT CAME BACK OUT.
NOW IT'S IN A BOOK. AND IT HAS A LOT OF COMPANY
WHERE IS THE GIRL WHO DREW THESE LINES AND SHAPES? WHERE IS THE TEACHER WHO KEPT IT? AND WHERE IS THE TIME-TRAVELER TREE RIGHT NOW? HOW LONG WILL IT STAY?
MADE BY HAND ON PAPER AND UNSEEN FOR 60 YEARS IT RETURNS WITH ALIVENESS INTACT AND TRANS-MITTING. TO THIS I ADD MY OWN TIME-TRAVEL MARKS AND PASS THE 'ACTIVATE' OPTION TO YOU.
CAUTION CONTENTS INCLUDE FUTURE, PAST, AND MEAN-WHILE
OUTERSPACE OUTFITS FOR INNERSPACE CREATURES AND OTHER THINGS COMIC STRIPS ARE
REMEMBER, THE PASSWORD IS, "GOOD."
WHEN YOU'RE READY, START ANYWHERE
to teach in
194____ 4

THE BEST AMERICAN

Comics 2008

BURDEN

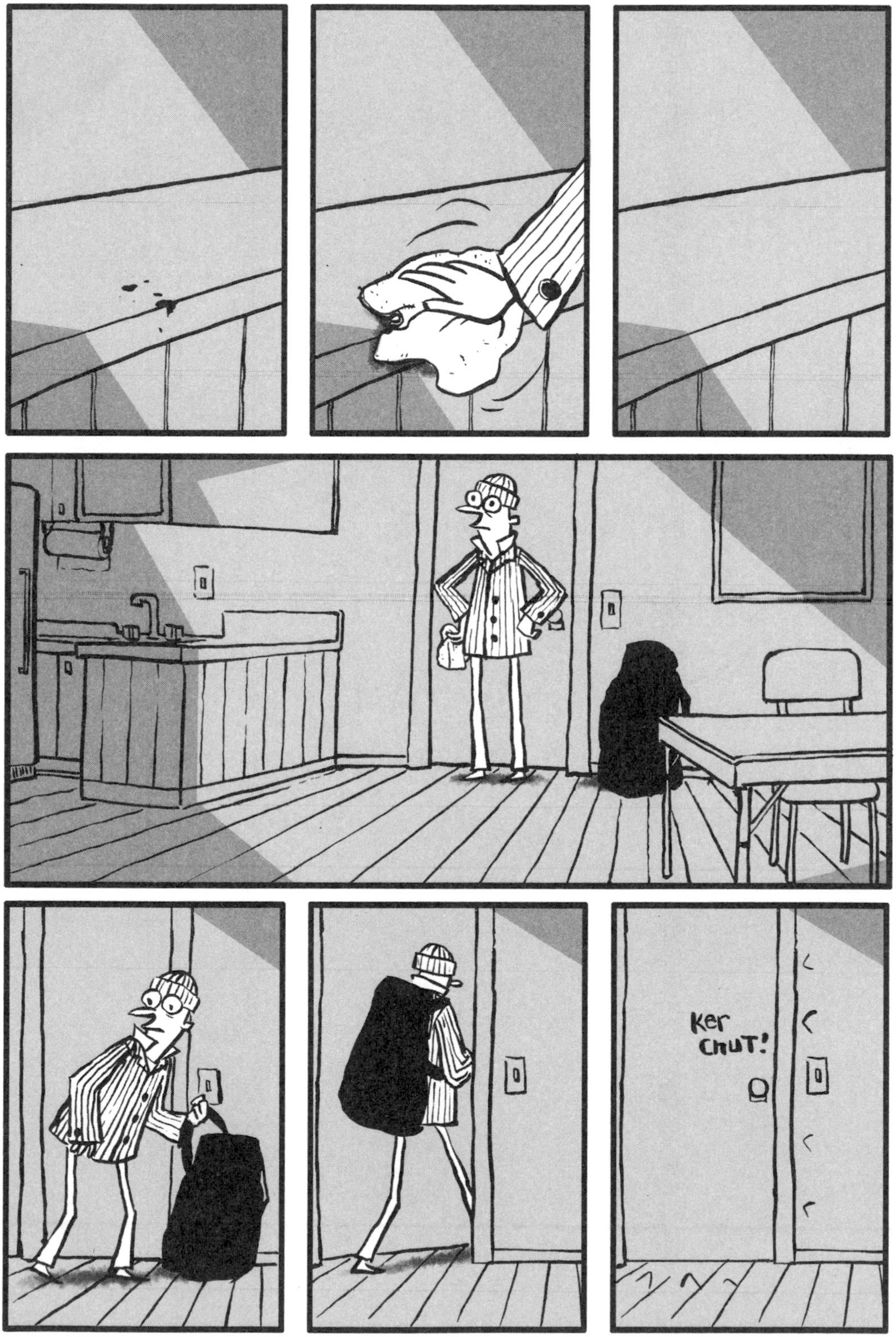
KER
CHUT!

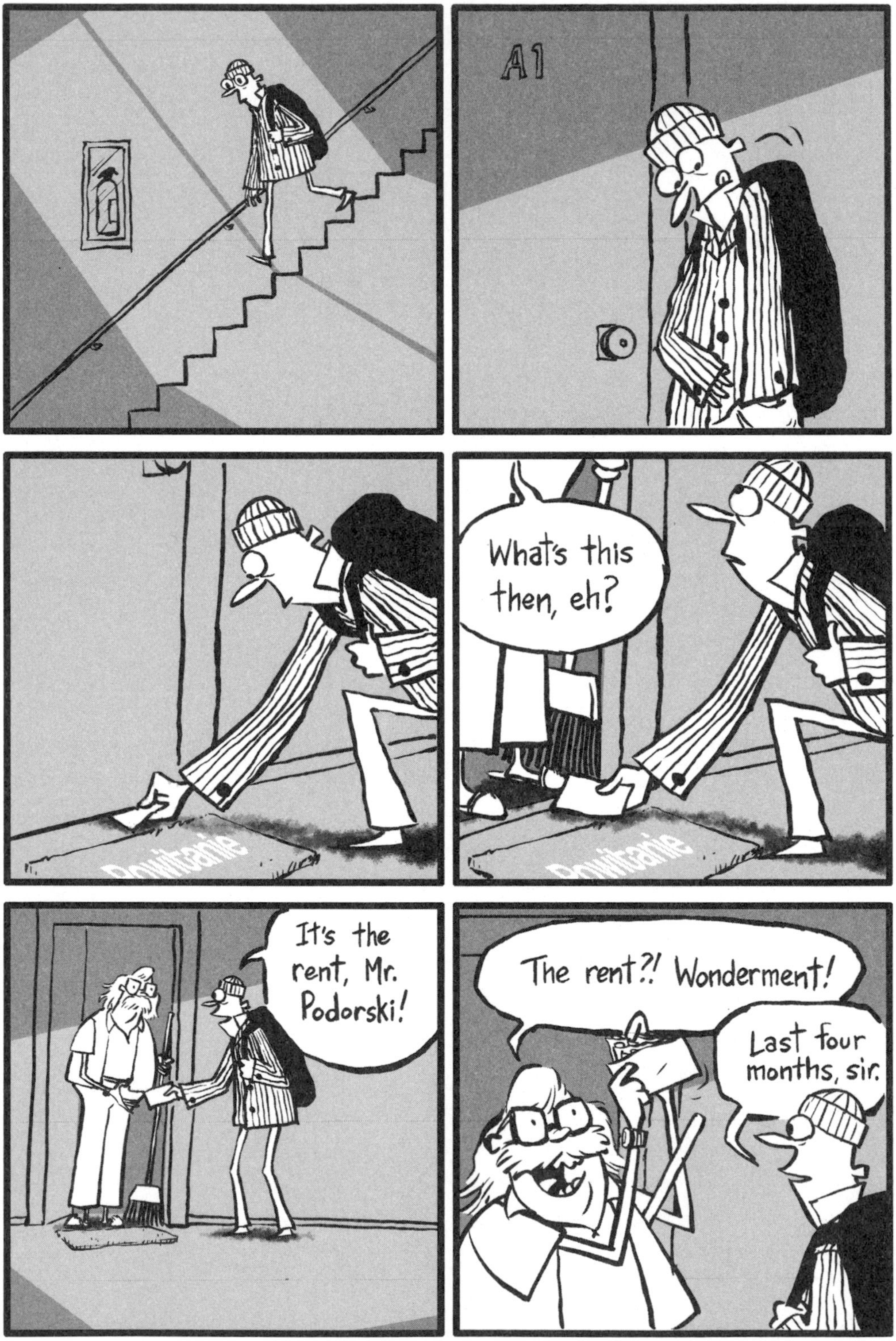
A1
Powitanie
What's this then, eh?
Powitanie
It's the rent, Mr. Podorski!
The rent?! Wonderment!
Last four months, sir.

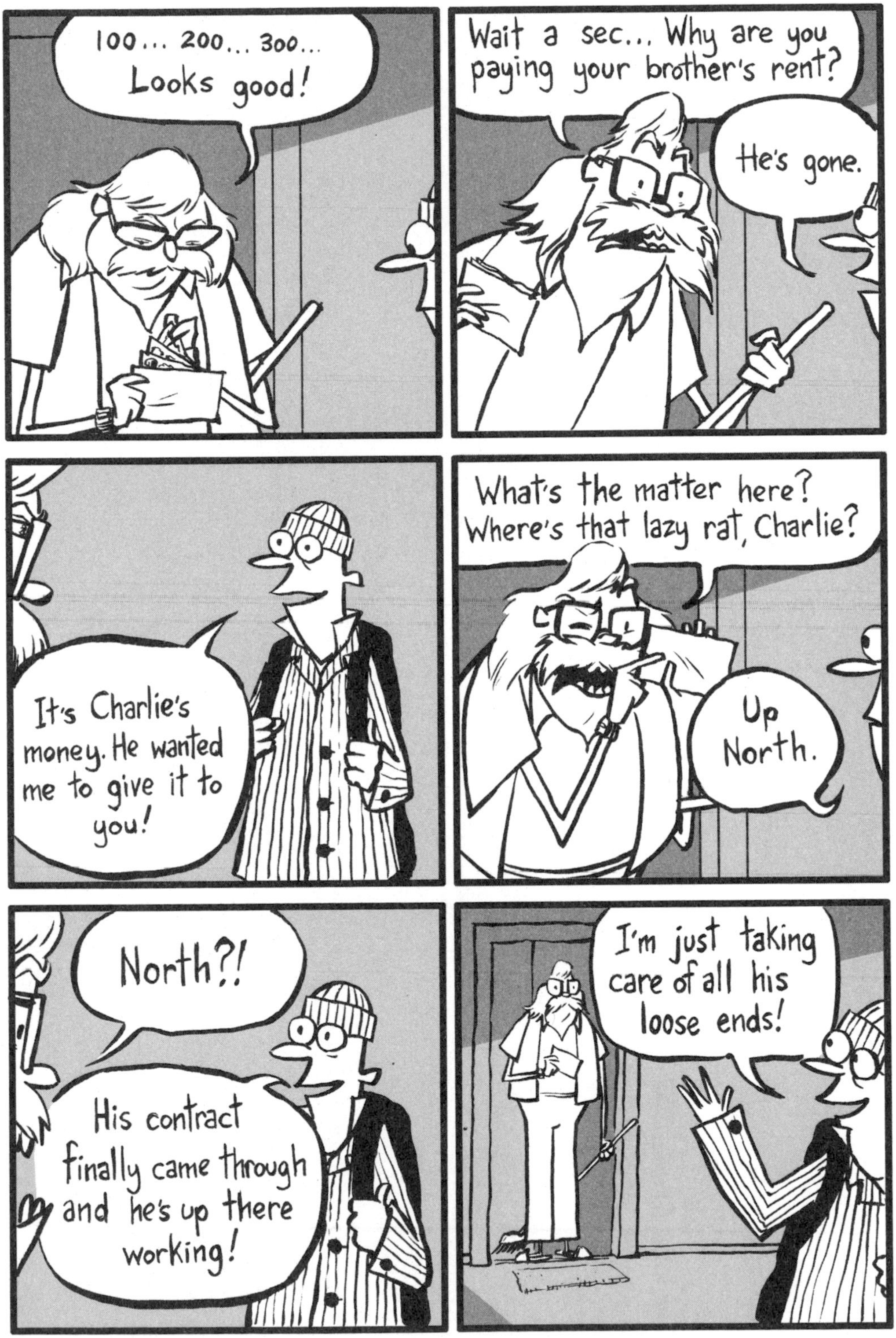
100... 200... 300... Looks good!
Wait a sec... Why are you paying your brother's rent?
He's gone.
It's Charlie's money. He wanted me to give it to you!
What's the matter here? Where's that lazy rat, Charlie?
Up North.
North?!
His contract finally came through and he's up there working!
I'm just taking care of all his loose ends!

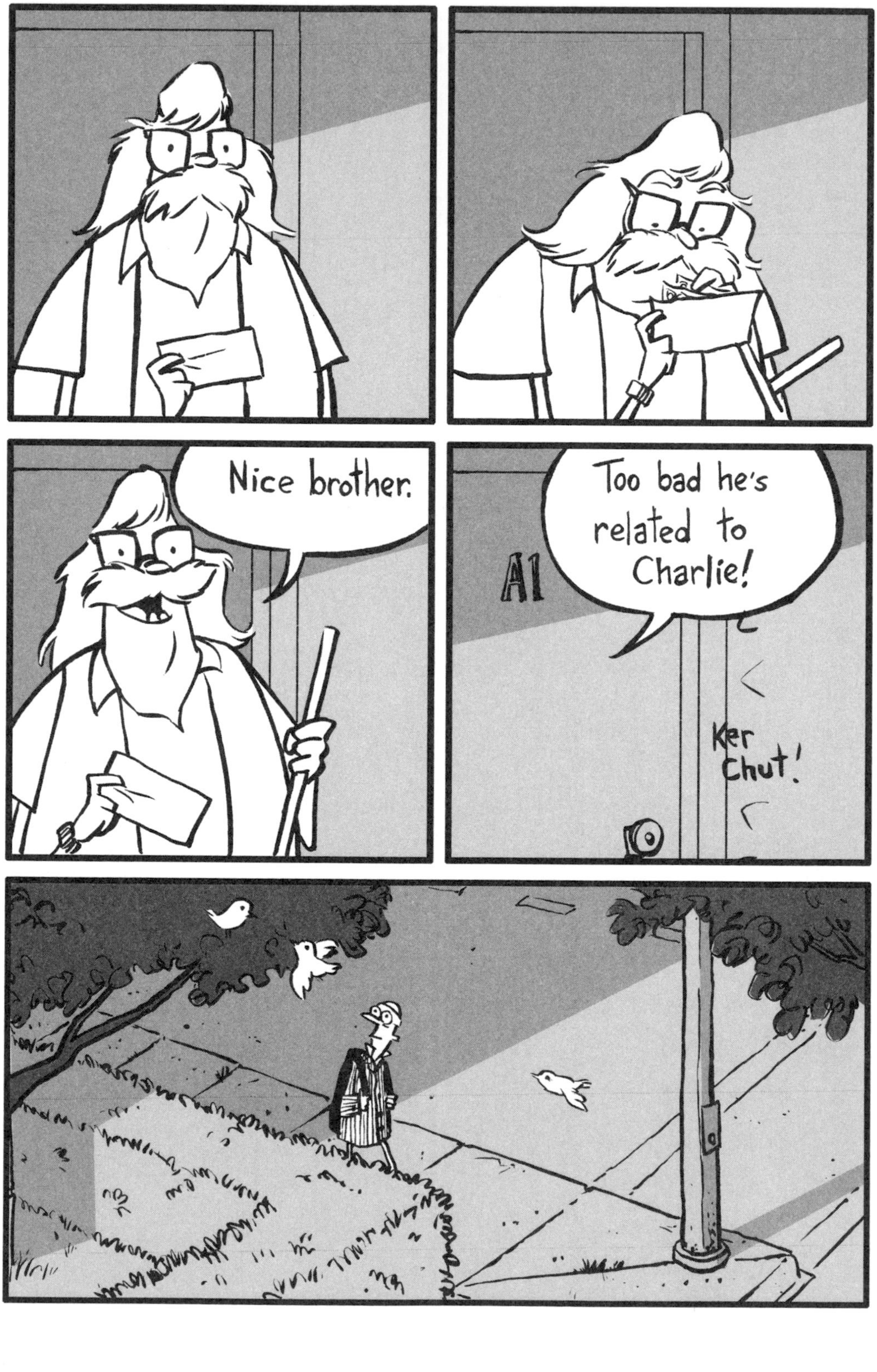
Nice brother.
Too bad he's related to Charlie!
A1
Ker Chut!

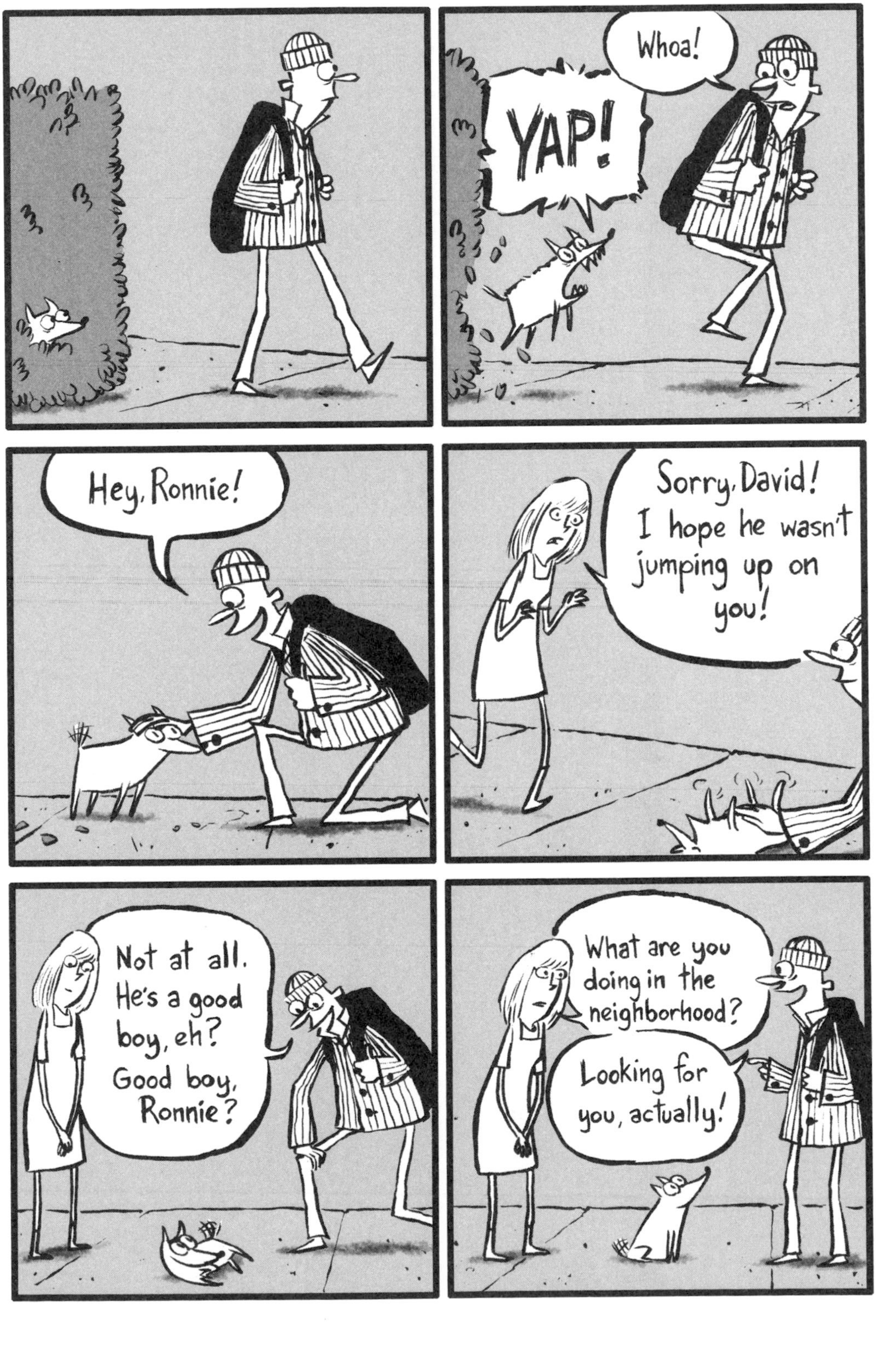
Whoa!
YAP!
Hey, Ronnie!
Sorry, David! I hope he wasn't jumping up on you!
Not at all. He's a good boy, eh? Good boy, Ronnie?
What are you doing in the neighborhood?
Looking for you, actually!

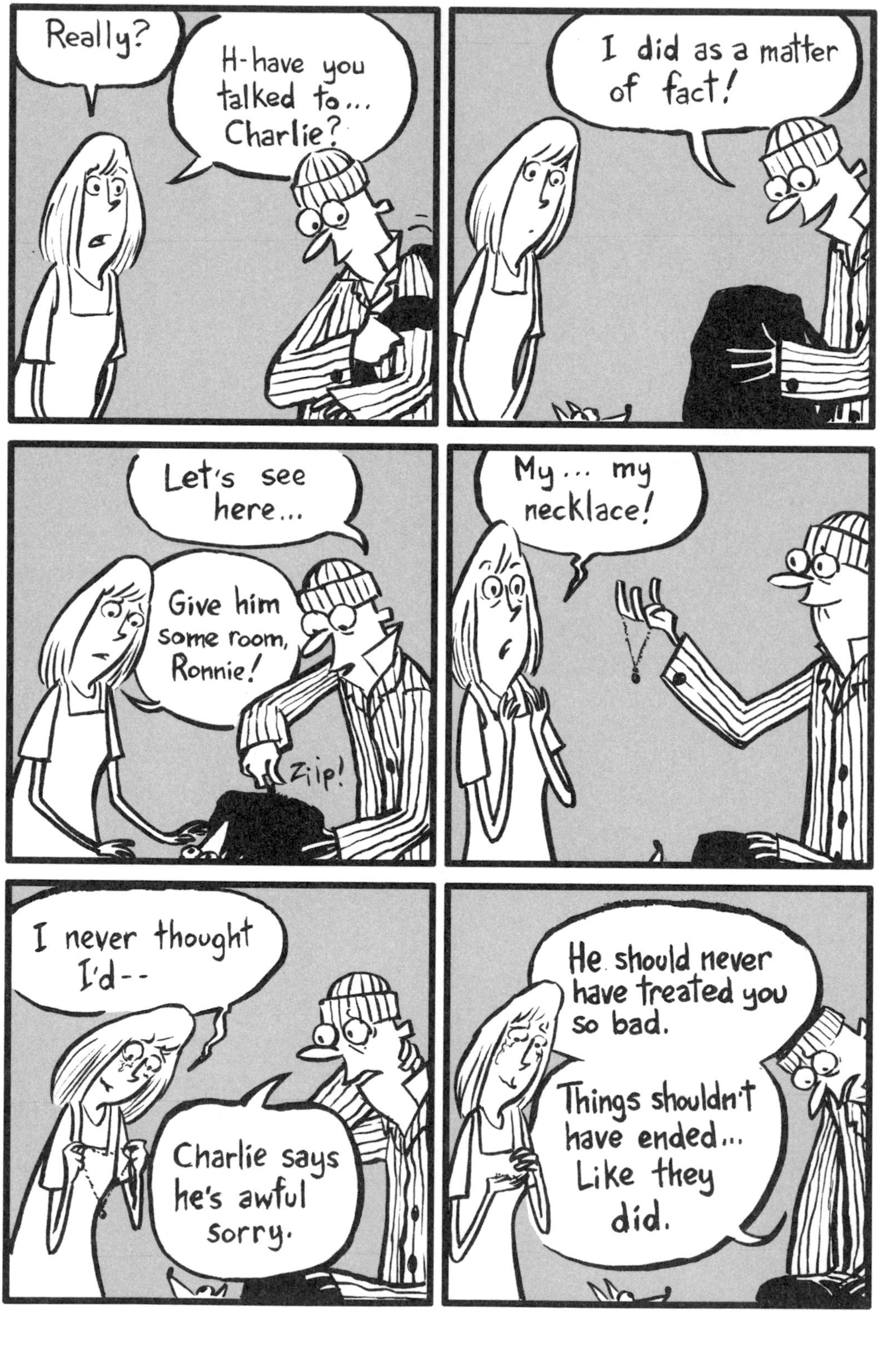
Really?
H-have you talked to... Charlie?
I did as a matter of fact!
Let's see here...
Give him some room, Ronnie!
Ziip!
My... my necklace!
I never thought I'd--
Charlie says he's awful sorry.
He should never have treated you so bad.
Things shouldn't have ended... Like they did.

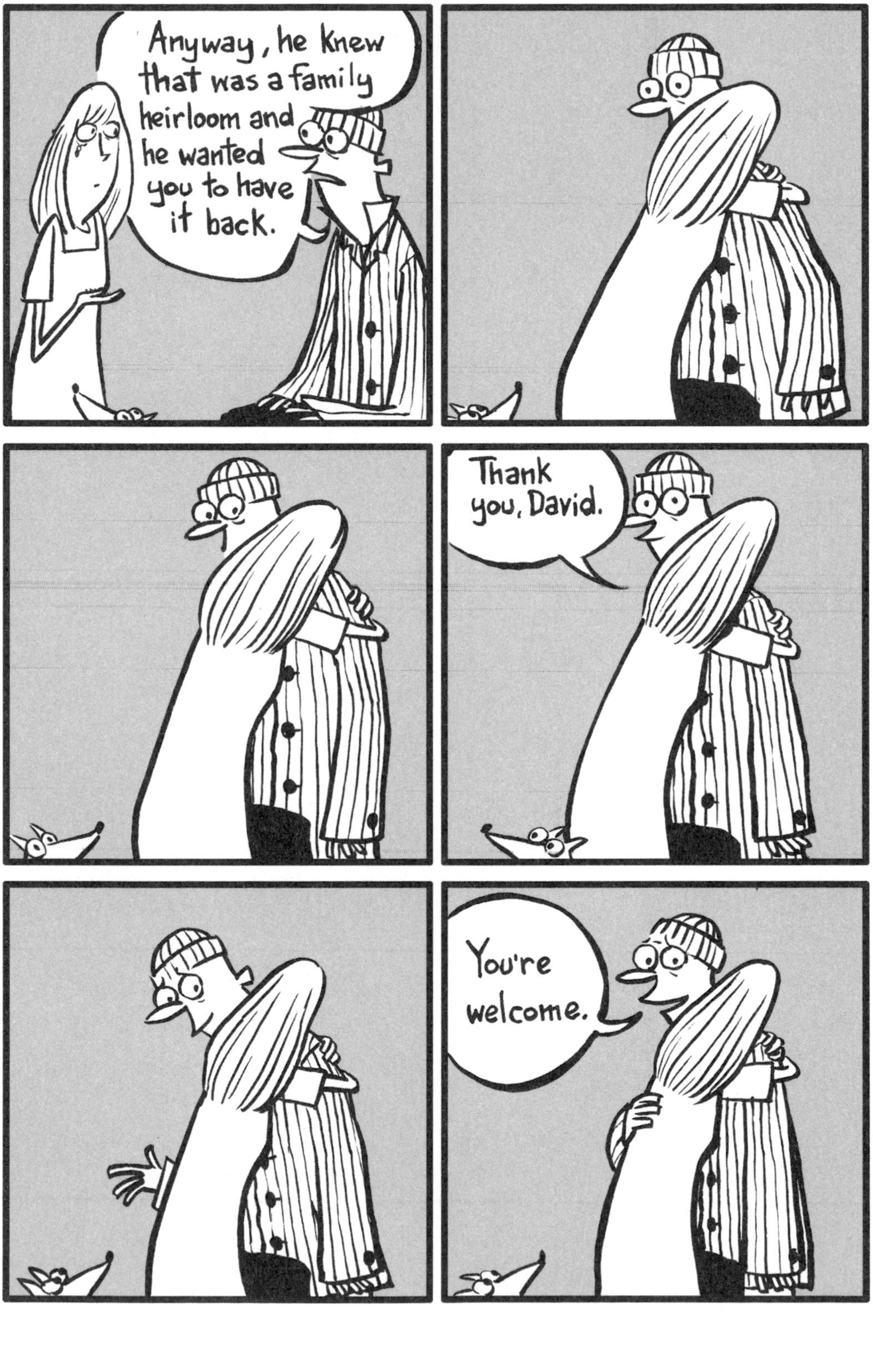
Anyway, he knew that was a family heirloom and he wanted you to have it back.
Thank you, David.
You're welcome.

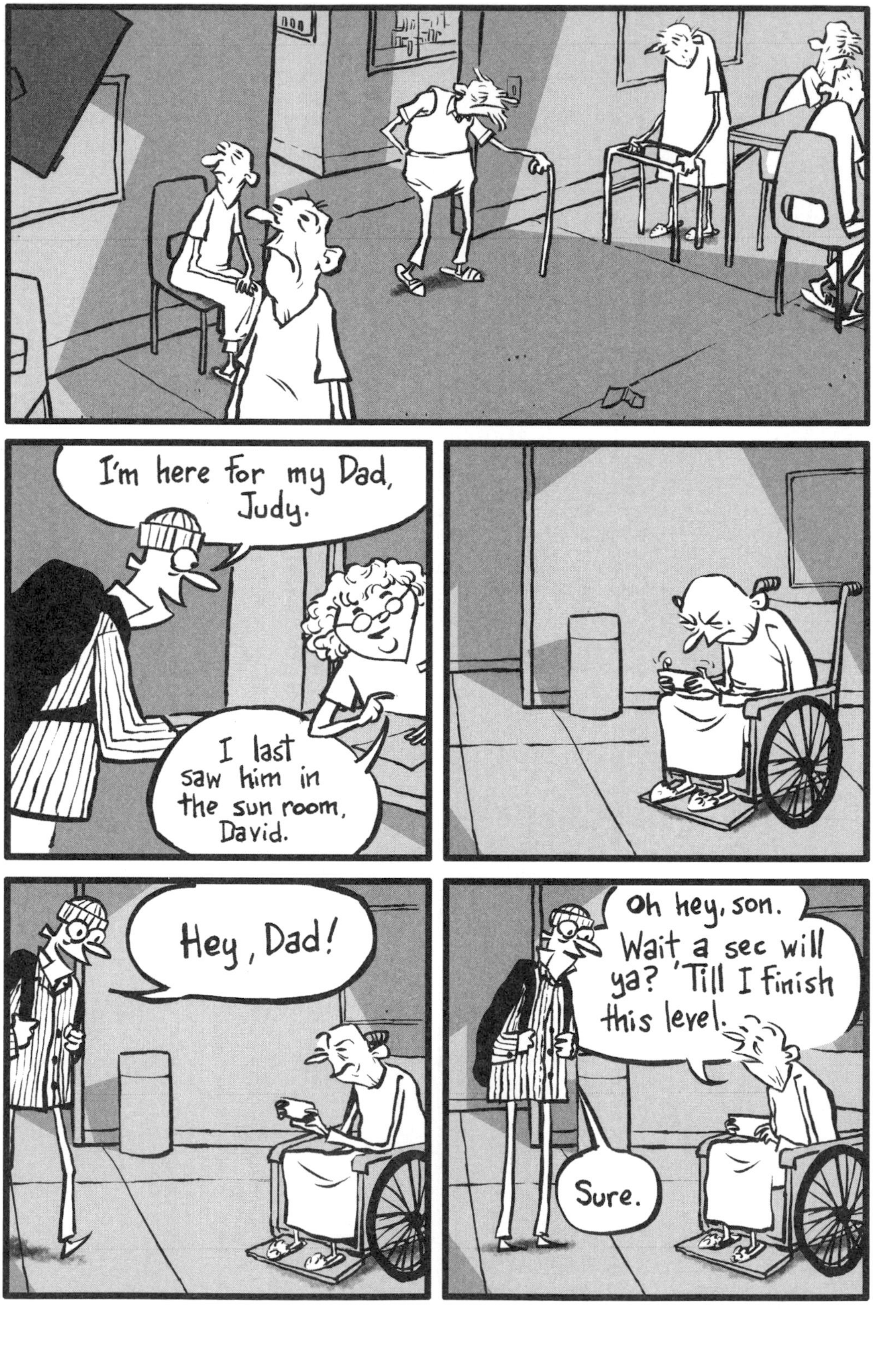

I'm here for my Dad, Judy.
I last saw him in the sun room, David.
Hey, Dad!
Oh hey, son. Wait a sec will ya? 'Till I finish this level.
Sure.

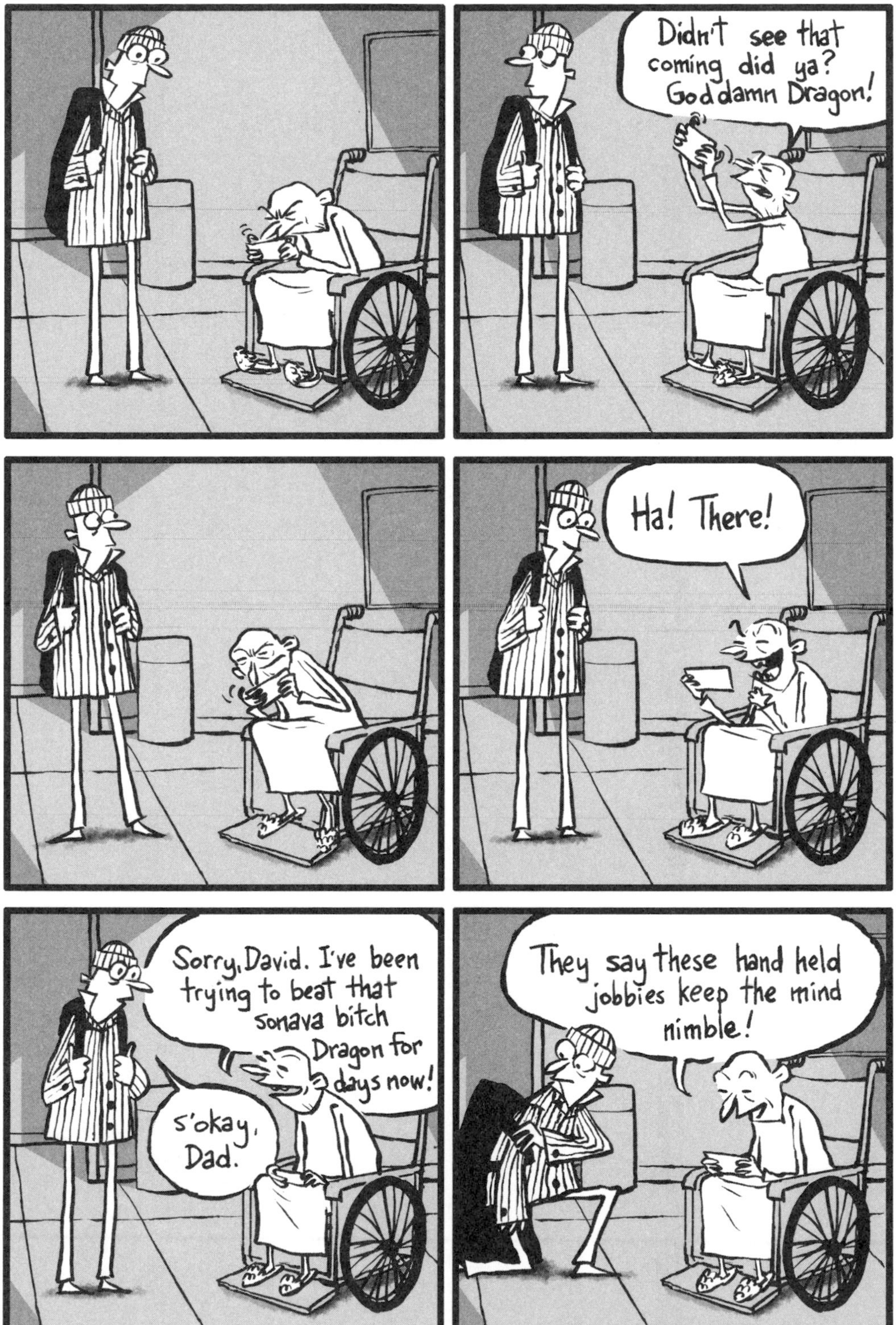
Didn't see that coming did ya? Goddamn Dragon!
Ha! There!
Sorry, David. I've been trying to beat that sonava bitch Dragon for days now!
s'okay, Dad.
They say these hand held jobbies keep the mind nimble!

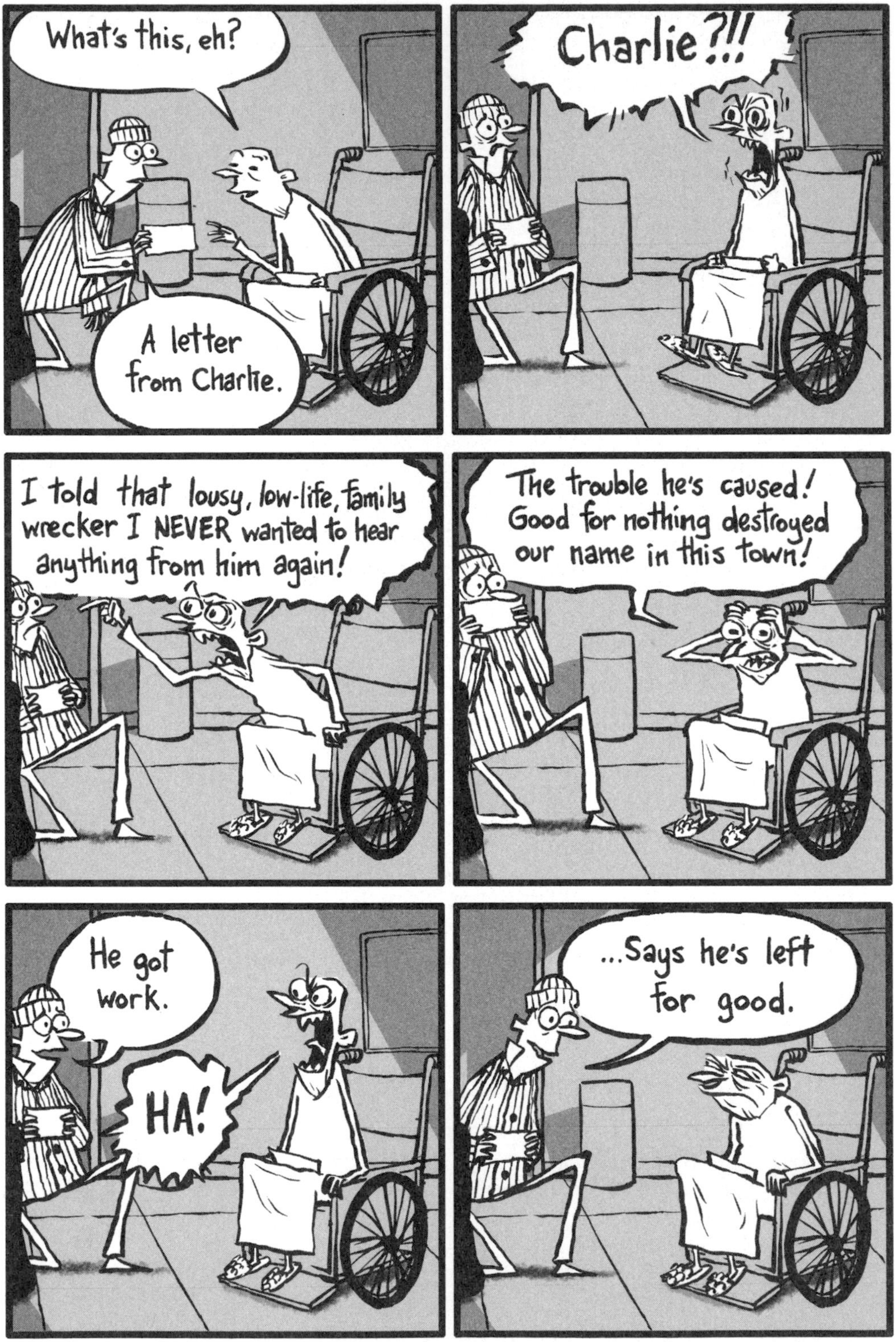
What's this, eh?
A letter from Charlie.
Charlie?!!
I told that lousy, low-life, family wrecker I NEVER wanted to hear anything from him again!
The trouble he's caused! Good for nothing destroyed our name in this town!
He got work.
HA!
...Says he's left for good.

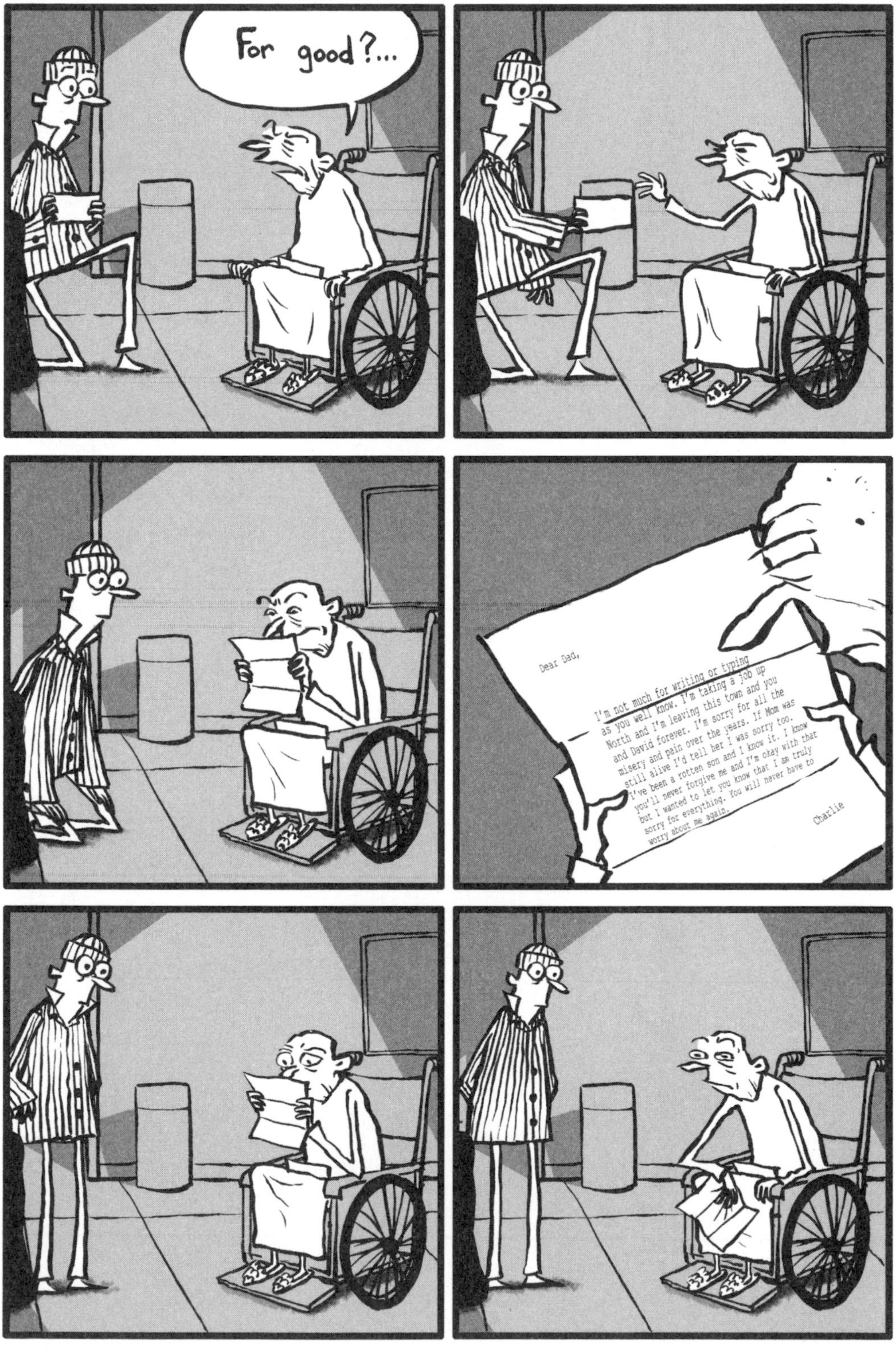
For good?...
Dear Dad,
I'm not much for writing or typing
as you well know. I'm taking a job up
North and I'm leaving this town and you
and David forever. I'm sorry for all the
misery and pain over the years. If Mom was
still alive I'd tell her I was sorry too.
I've been a rotten son and I know it. I know
you'll never forgive me and I'm okay with that
but I wanted to let you know that I am truly
sorry for everything. You will never have to
worry about me again.
Charlie

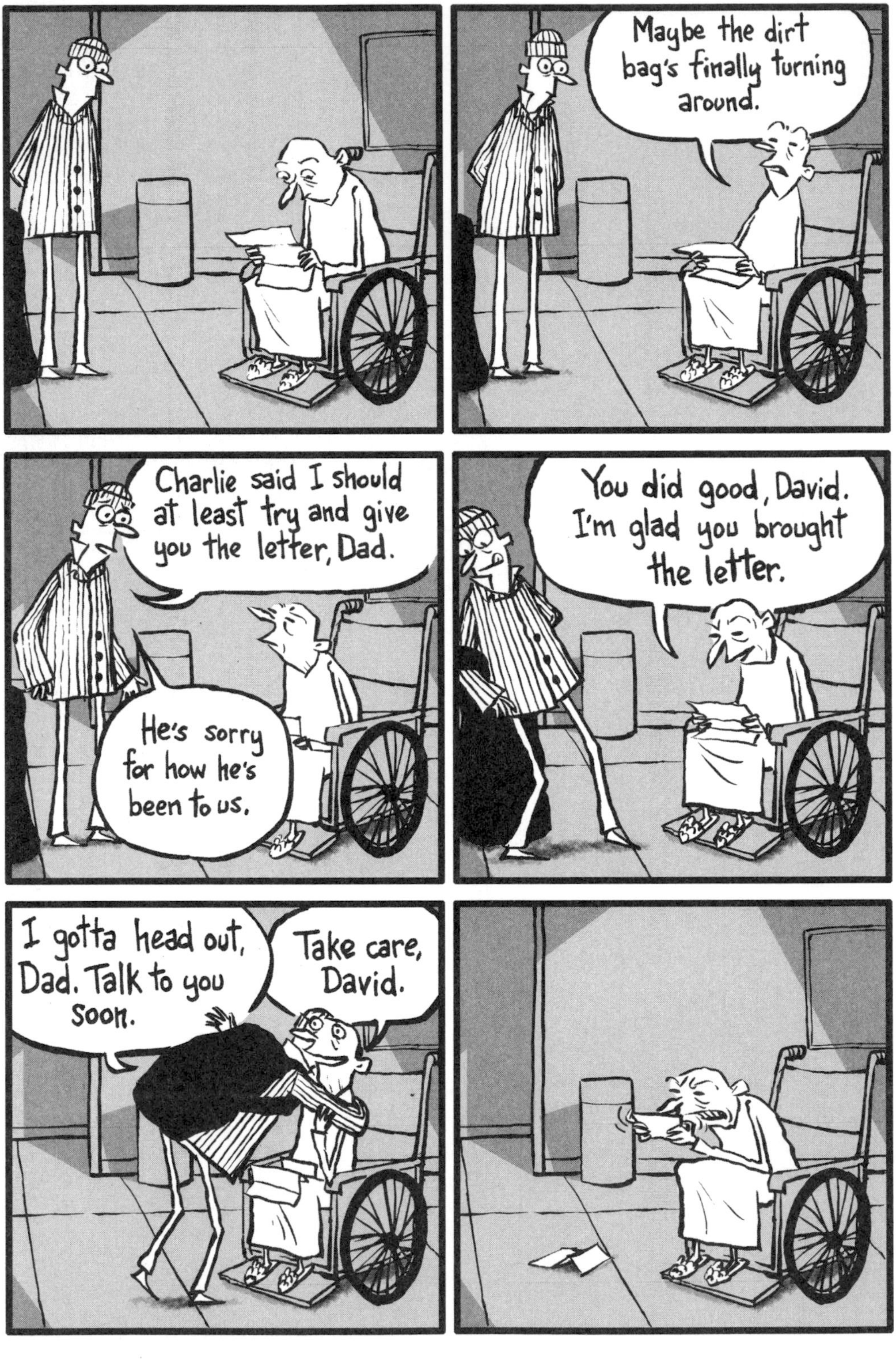
Maybe the dirt bag's finally turning around.
Charlie said I should at least try and give you the letter, Dad.
He's sorry for how he's been to us.
You did good, David. I'm glad you brought the letter.
I gotta head out, Dad. Talk to you soon.
Take care, David.

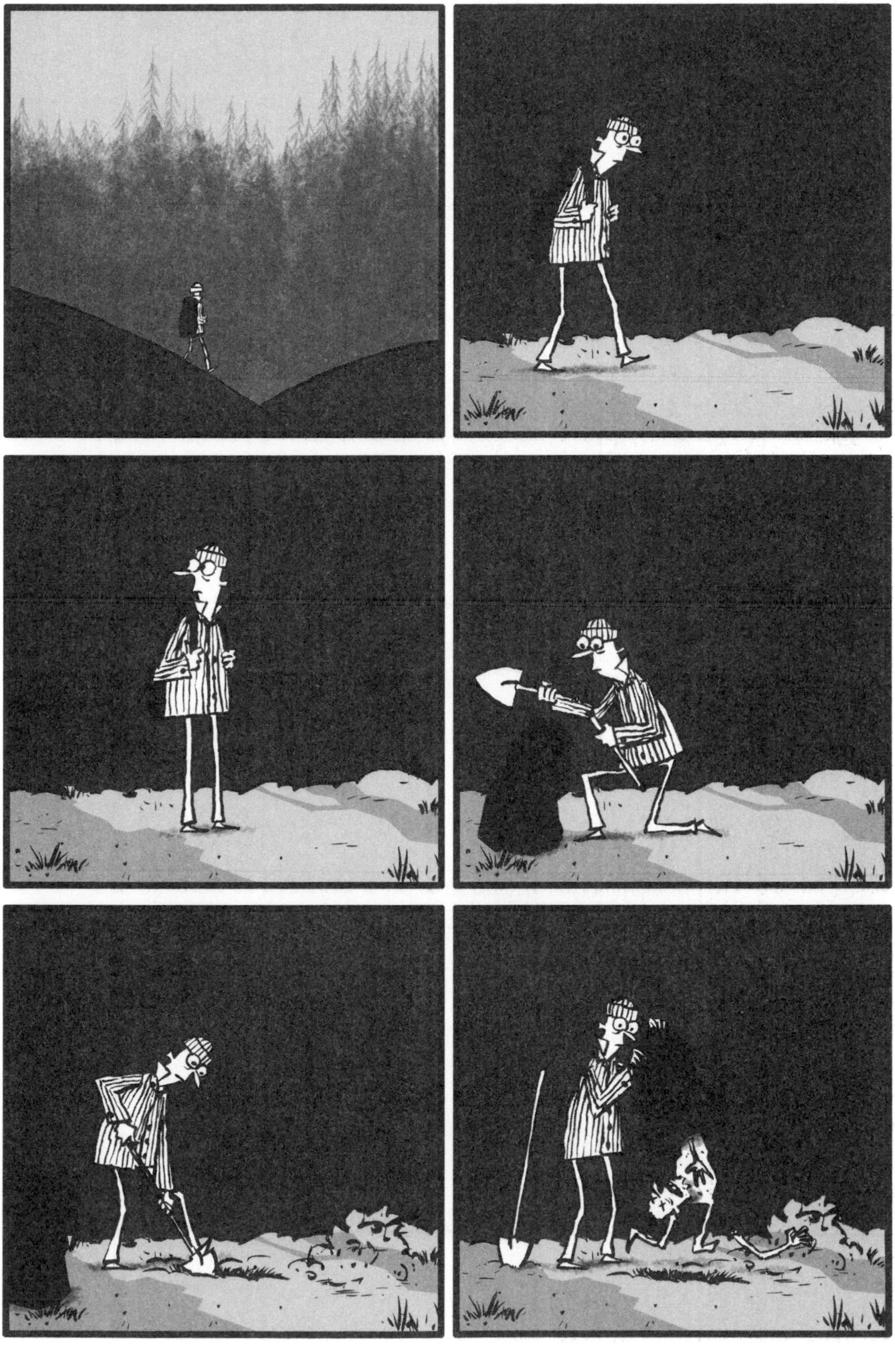

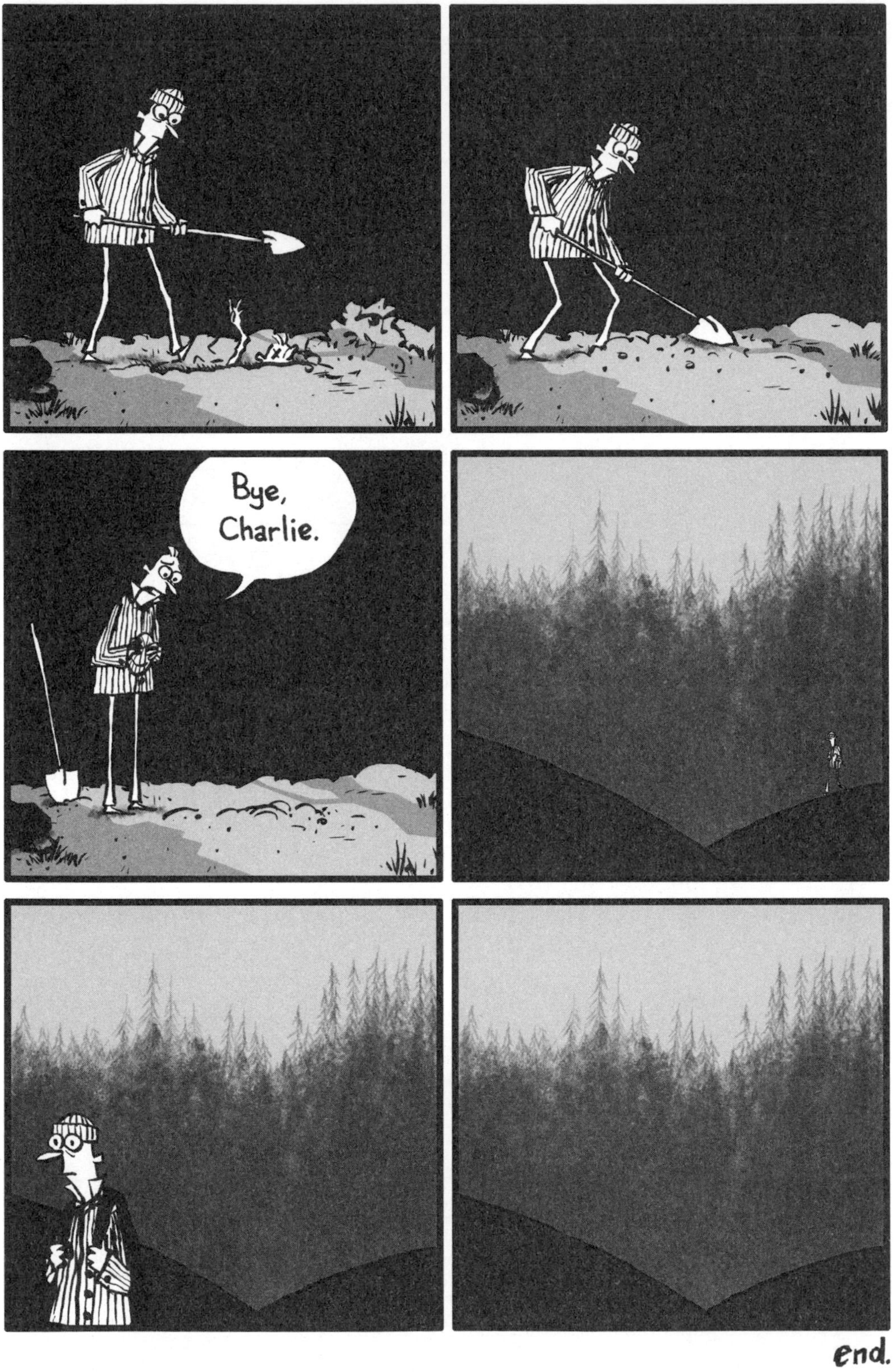
Bye, Charlie.
end.

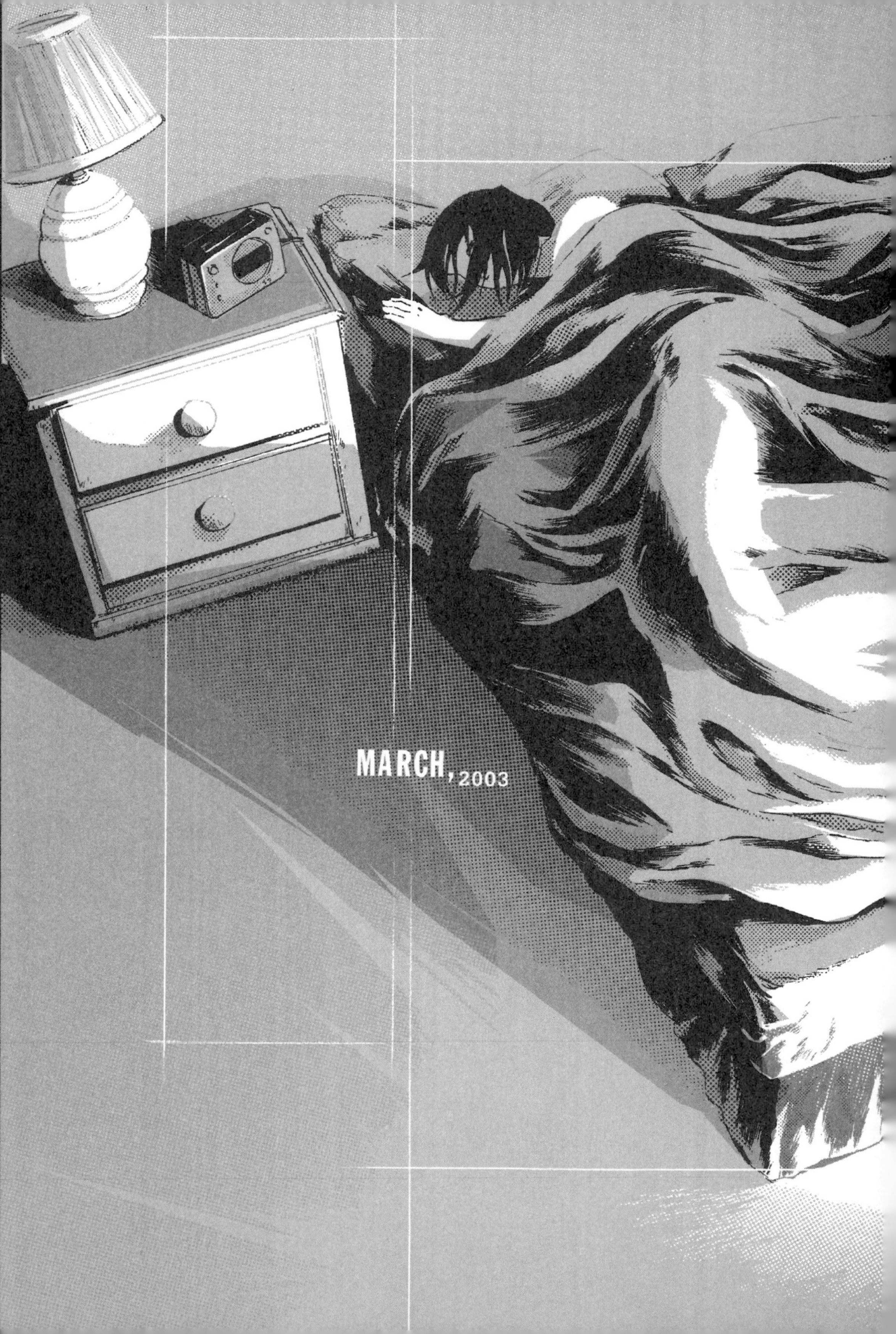
MARCH, 2003

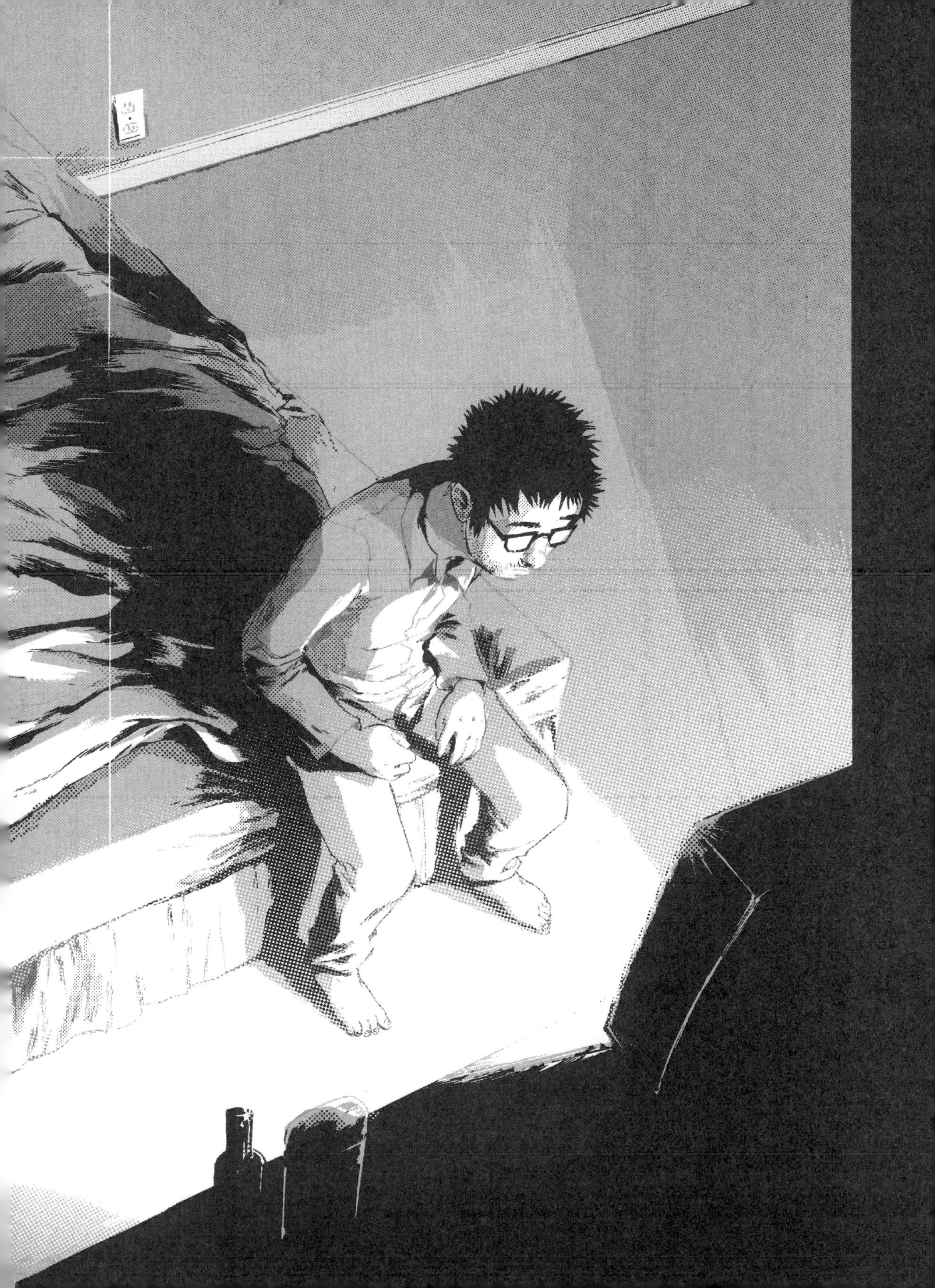

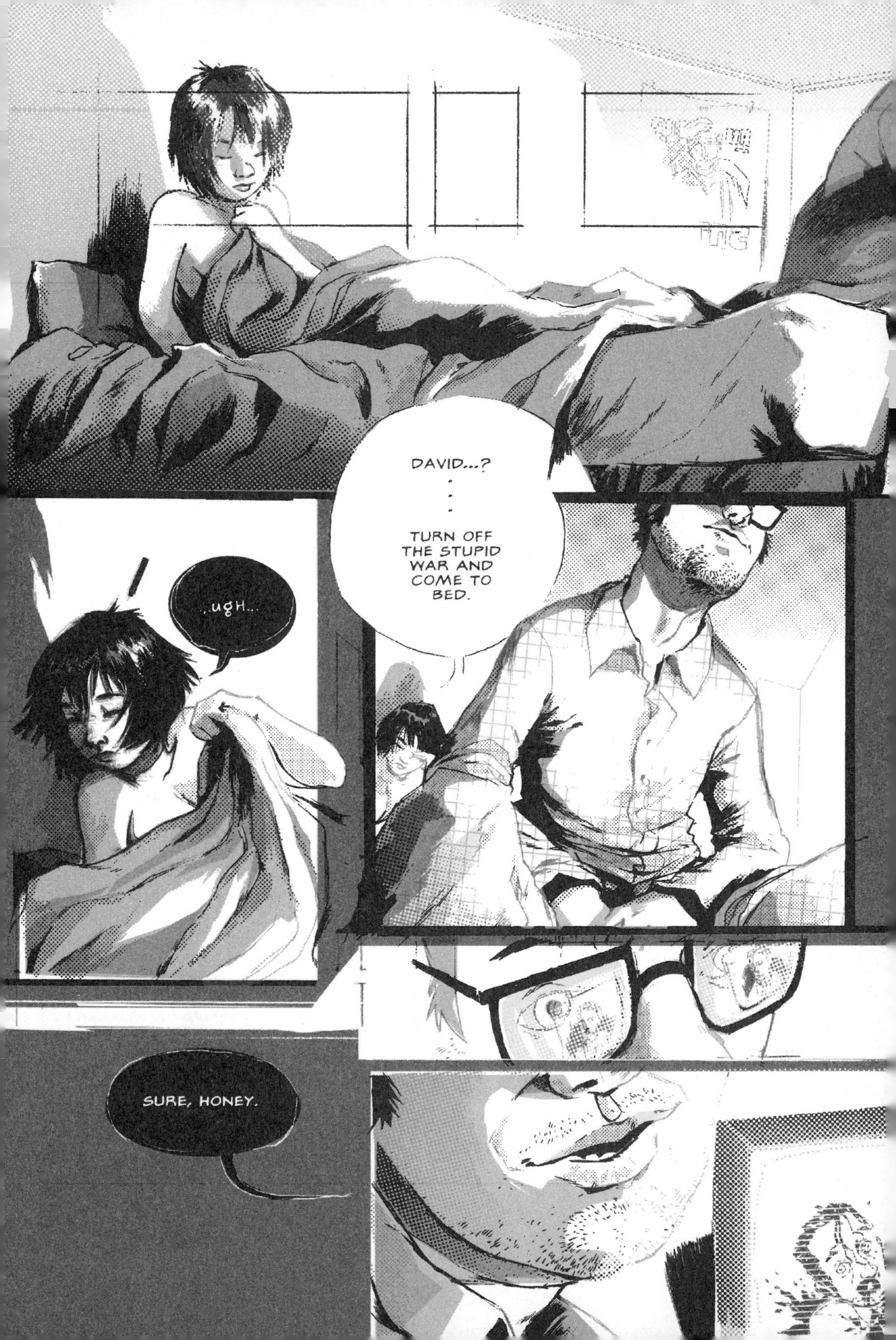
DAVID...?
. . .
TURN OFF THE STUPID WAR AND COME TO BED.
..ugh...
SURE, HONEY.

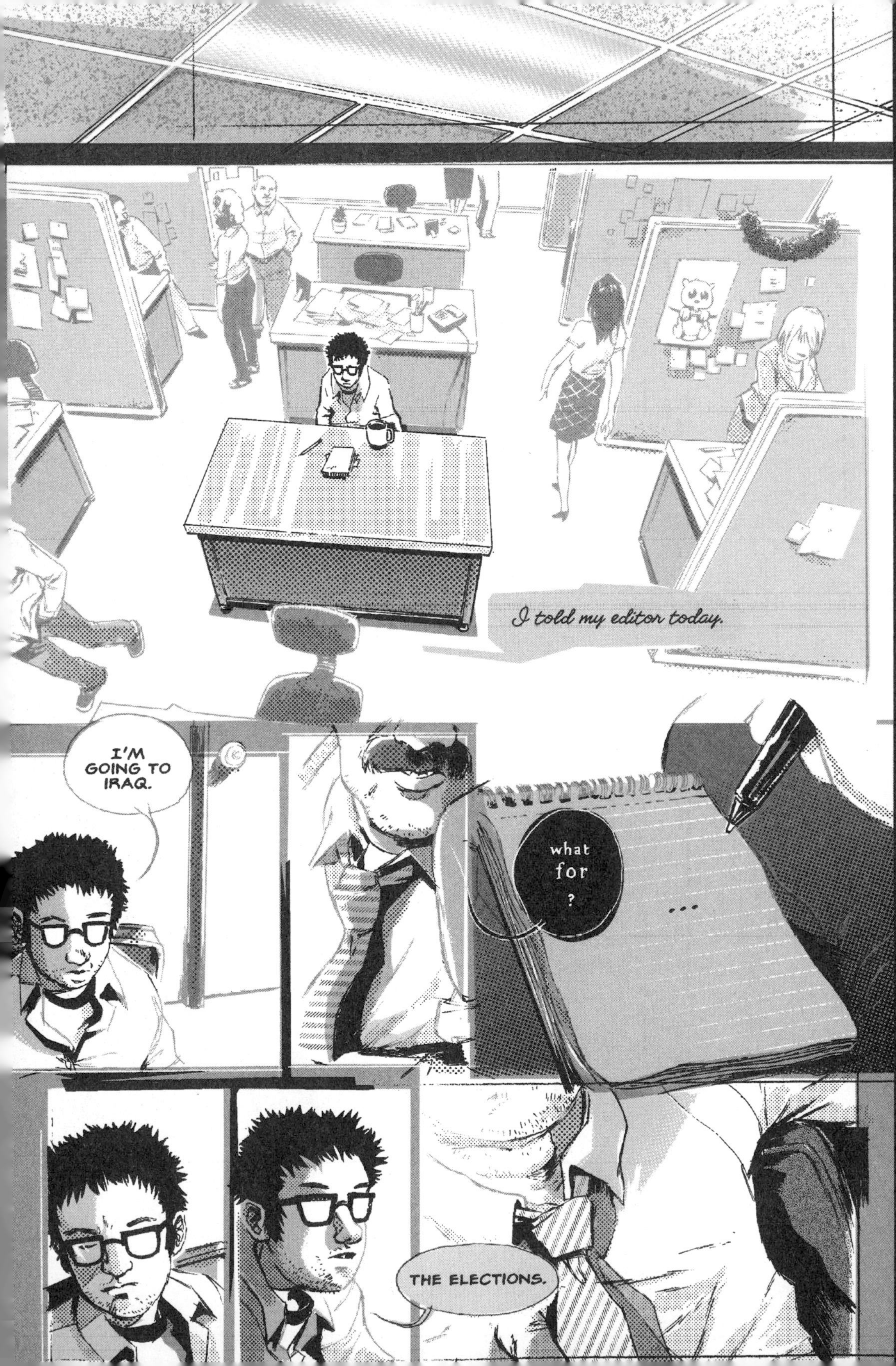
I told my editor today.
I'M GOING TO IRAQ.
what for ?
...
THE ELECTIONS.

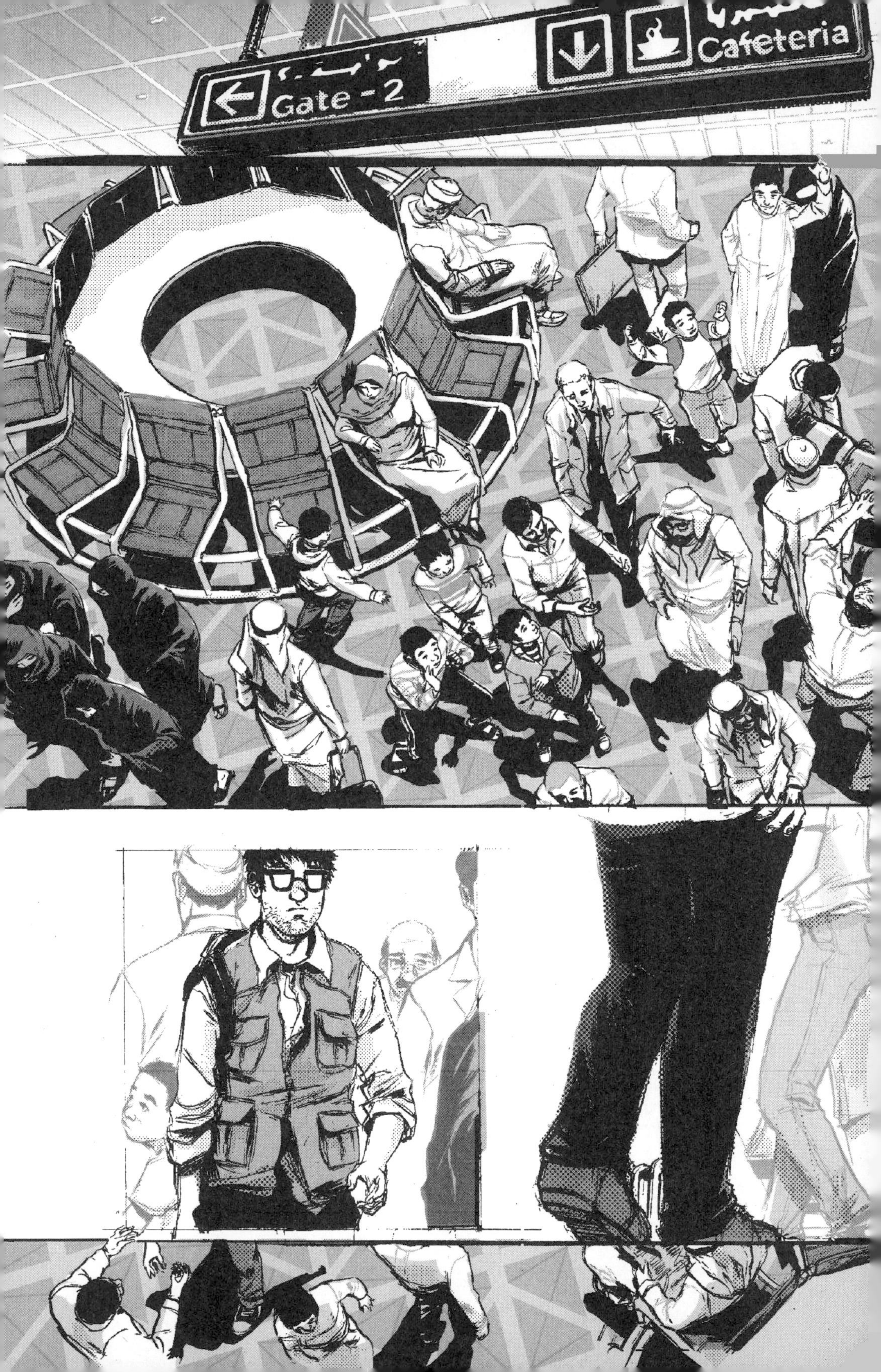
Gate - 2
Cafeteria

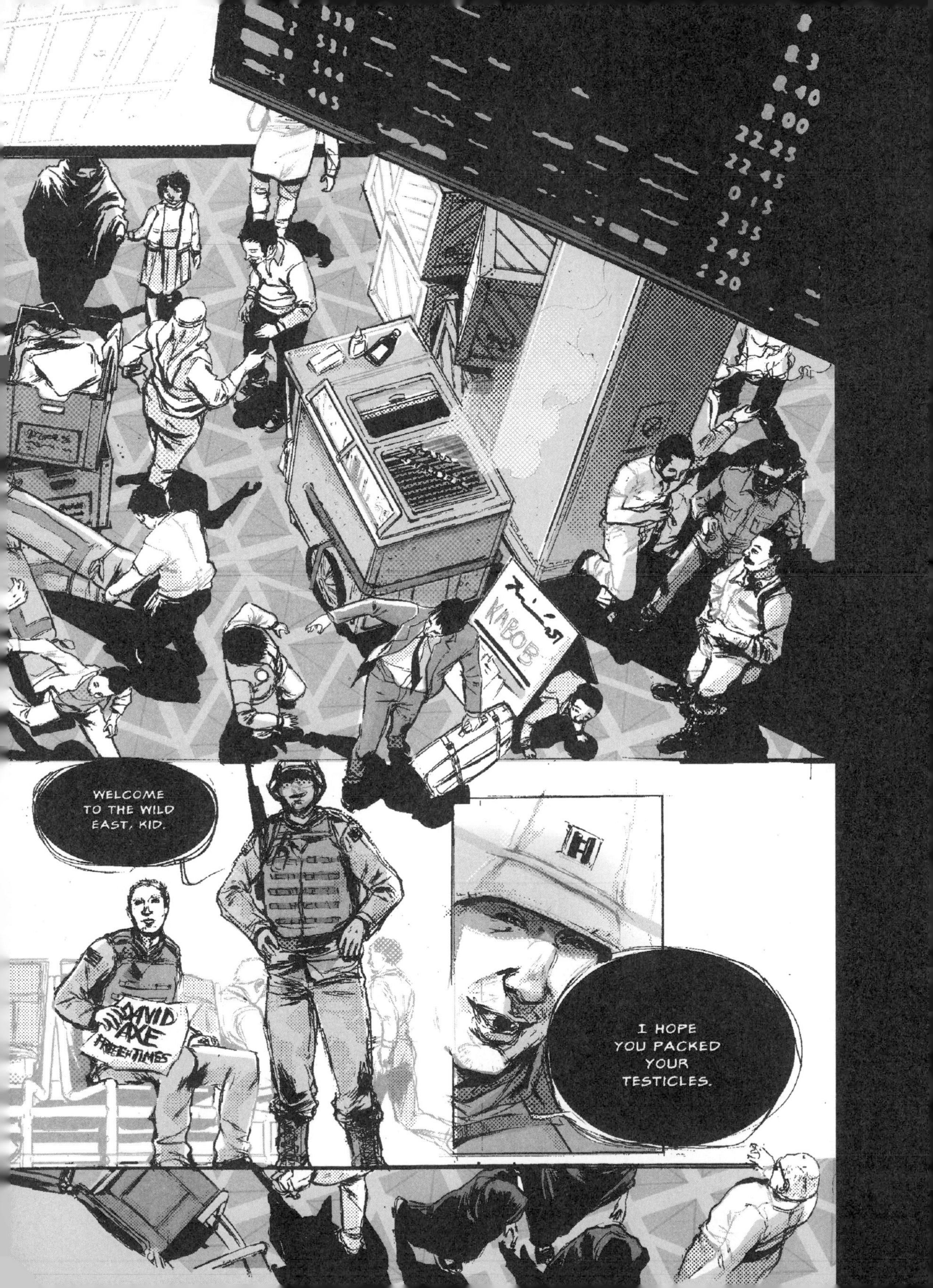
KABOB
WELCOME TO THE WILD EAST, KID.
DAVID AXE
FREE TIMES
I HOPE YOU PACKED YOUR TESTICLES.

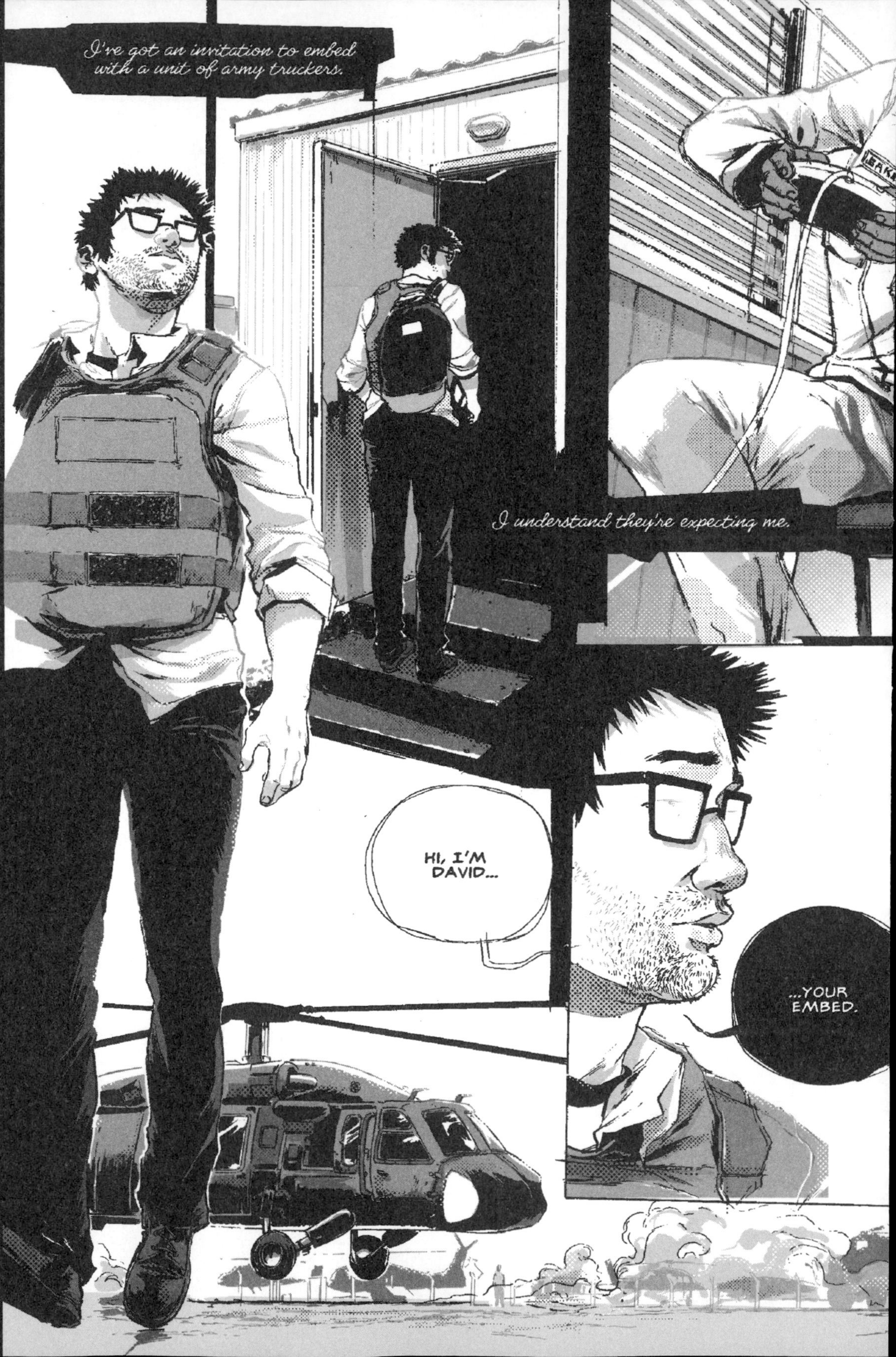
I've got an invitation to embed with a unit of army truckers.
I understand they're expecting me.
HI, I'M DAVID...
...YOUR EMBED.

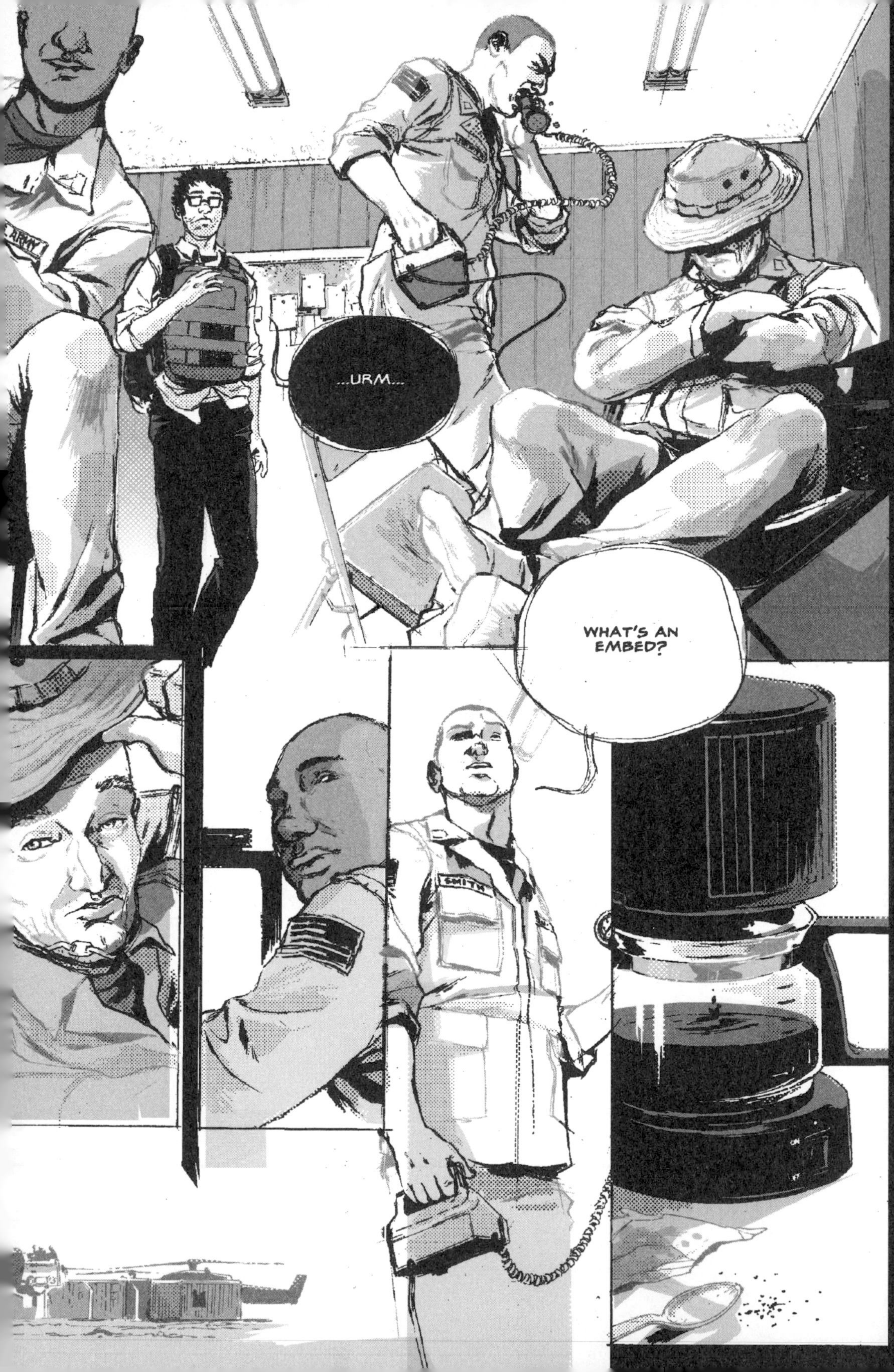
...URM...
WHAT'S AN EMBED?

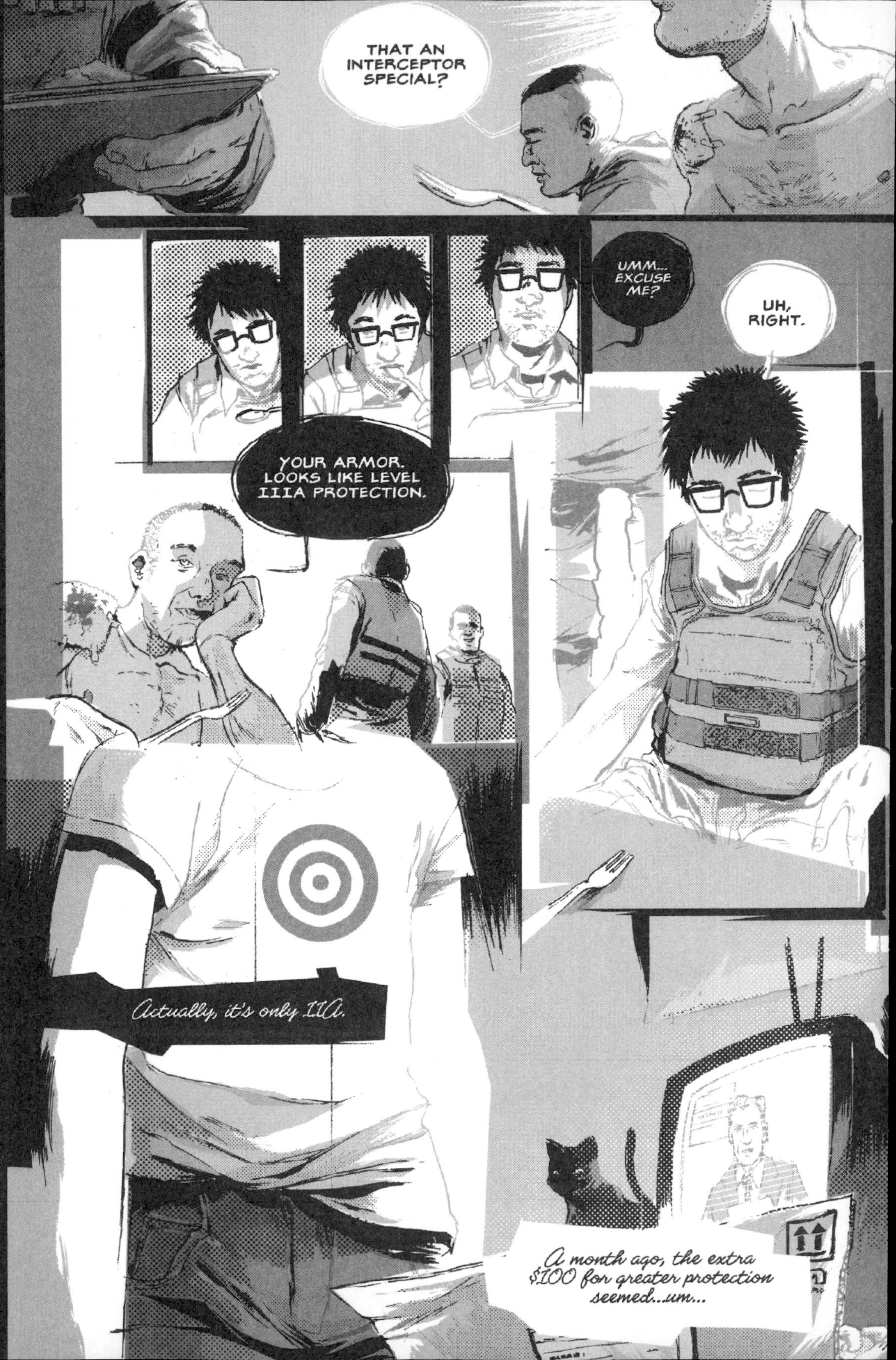
THAT AN INTERCEPTOR SPECIAL?
UMM... EXCUSE ME?
UH, RIGHT.
YOUR ARMOR. LOOKS LIKE LEVEL IIIA PROTECTION.
Actually, it's only IIA.
A month ago, the extra $100 for greater protection seemed...um...

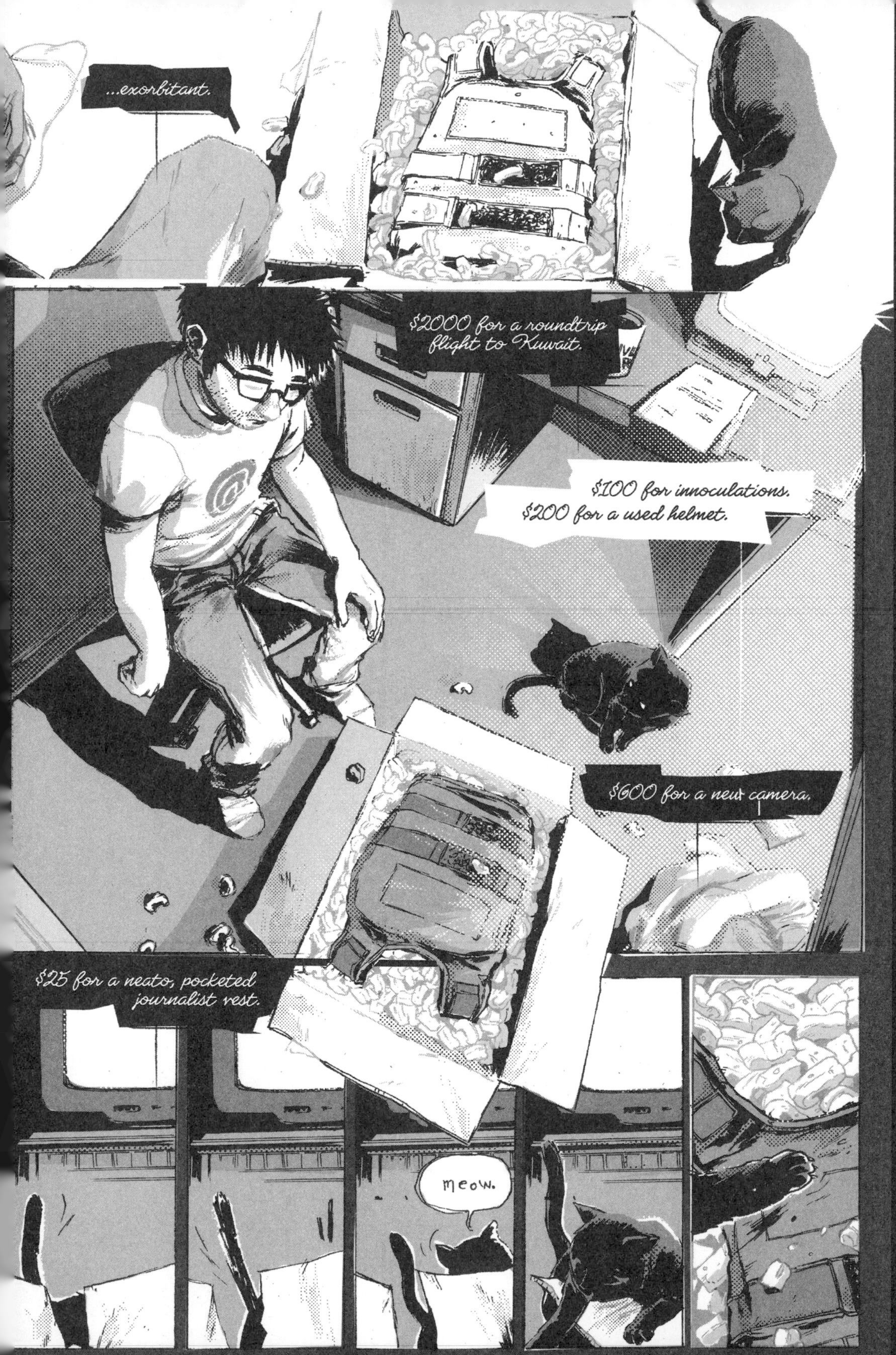
...exorbitant.
$2000 for a roundtrip flight to Kuwait.
$100 for innoculations.
$200 for a used helmet.
$600 for a new camera.
$25 for a neato, pocketed journalist vest.
meow.

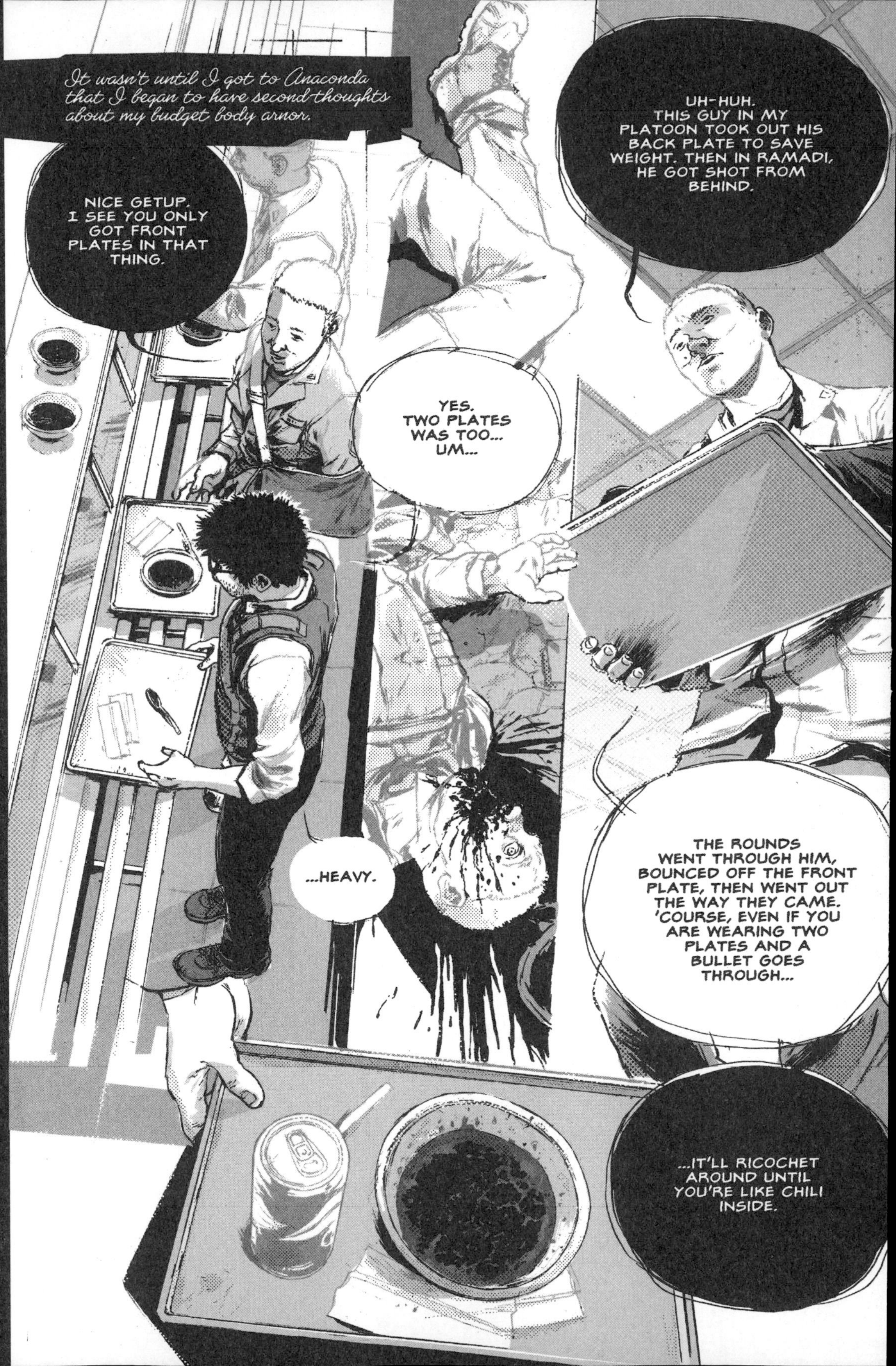
It wasn't until I got to Anaconda that I began to have second thoughts about my budget body armor.
NICE GETUP. I SEE YOU ONLY GOT FRONT PLATES IN THAT THING.
YES. TWO PLATES WAS TOO... UM...
...HEAVY.
UH-HUH. THIS GUY IN MY PLATOON TOOK OUT HIS BACK PLATE TO SAVE WEIGHT. THEN IN RAMADI, HE GOT SHOT FROM BEHIND.
THE ROUNDS WENT THROUGH HIM, BOUNCED OFF THE FRONT PLATE, THEN WENT OUT THE WAY THEY CAME. 'COURSE, EVEN IF YOU ARE WEARING TWO PLATES AND A BULLET GOES THROUGH...
...IT'LL RICOCHET AROUND UNTIL YOU'RE LIKE CHILI INSIDE.

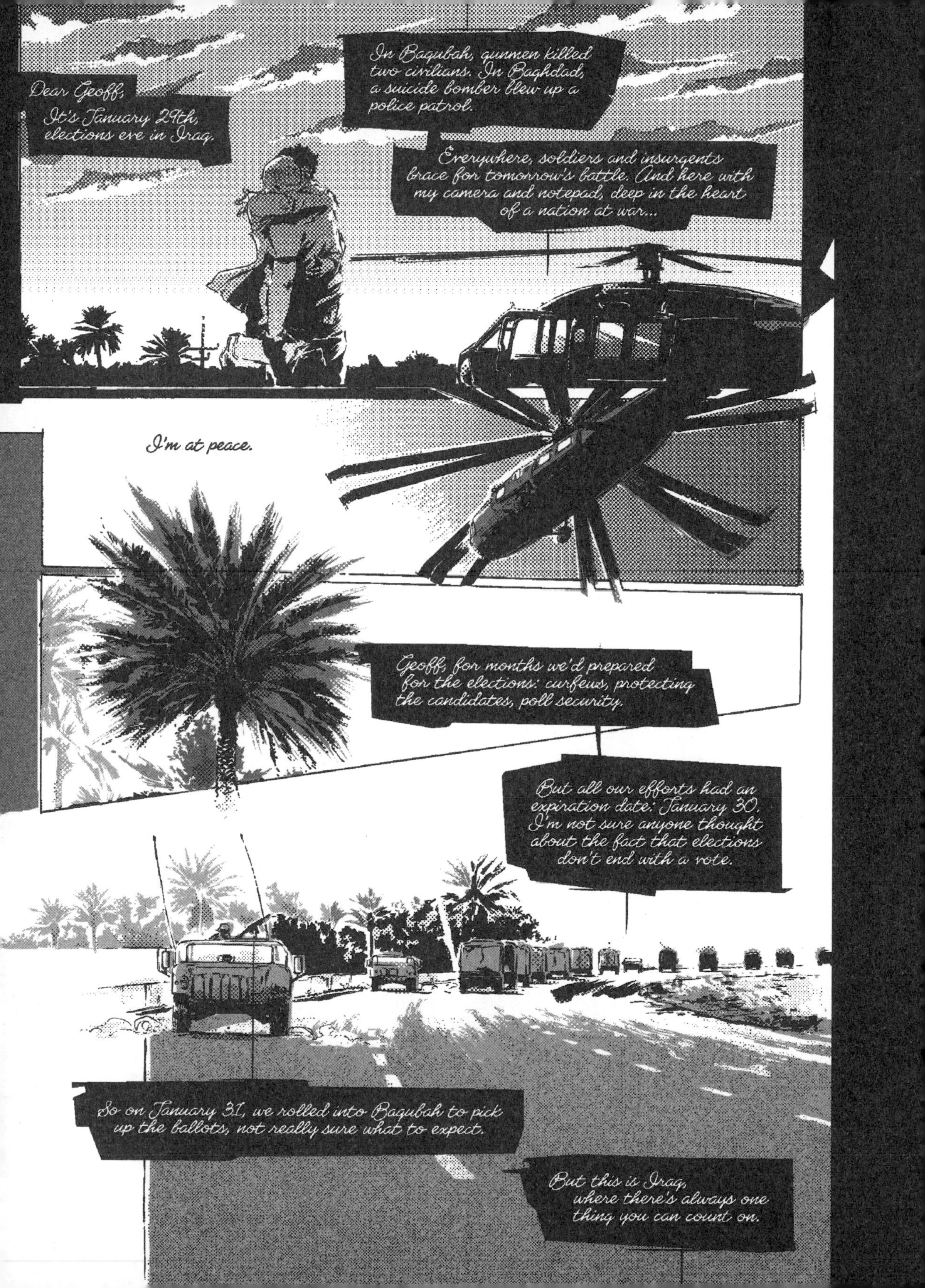
Dear Geoff,
It's January 29th, elections eve in Iraq.
In Baqubah, gunmen killed two civilians. In Baghdad, a suicide bomber blew up a police patrol.
Everywhere, soldiers and insurgents brace for tomorrow's battle. And here with my camera and notepad, deep in the heart of a nation at war...
I'm at peace.
Geoff, for months we'd prepared for the elections: curfews, protecting the candidates, poll security.
But all our efforts had an expiration date: January 30. I'm not sure anyone thought about the fact that elections don't end with a vote.
So on January 31, we rolled into Baqubah to pick up the ballots, not really sure what to expect.
But this is Iraq, where there's always one thing you can count on.

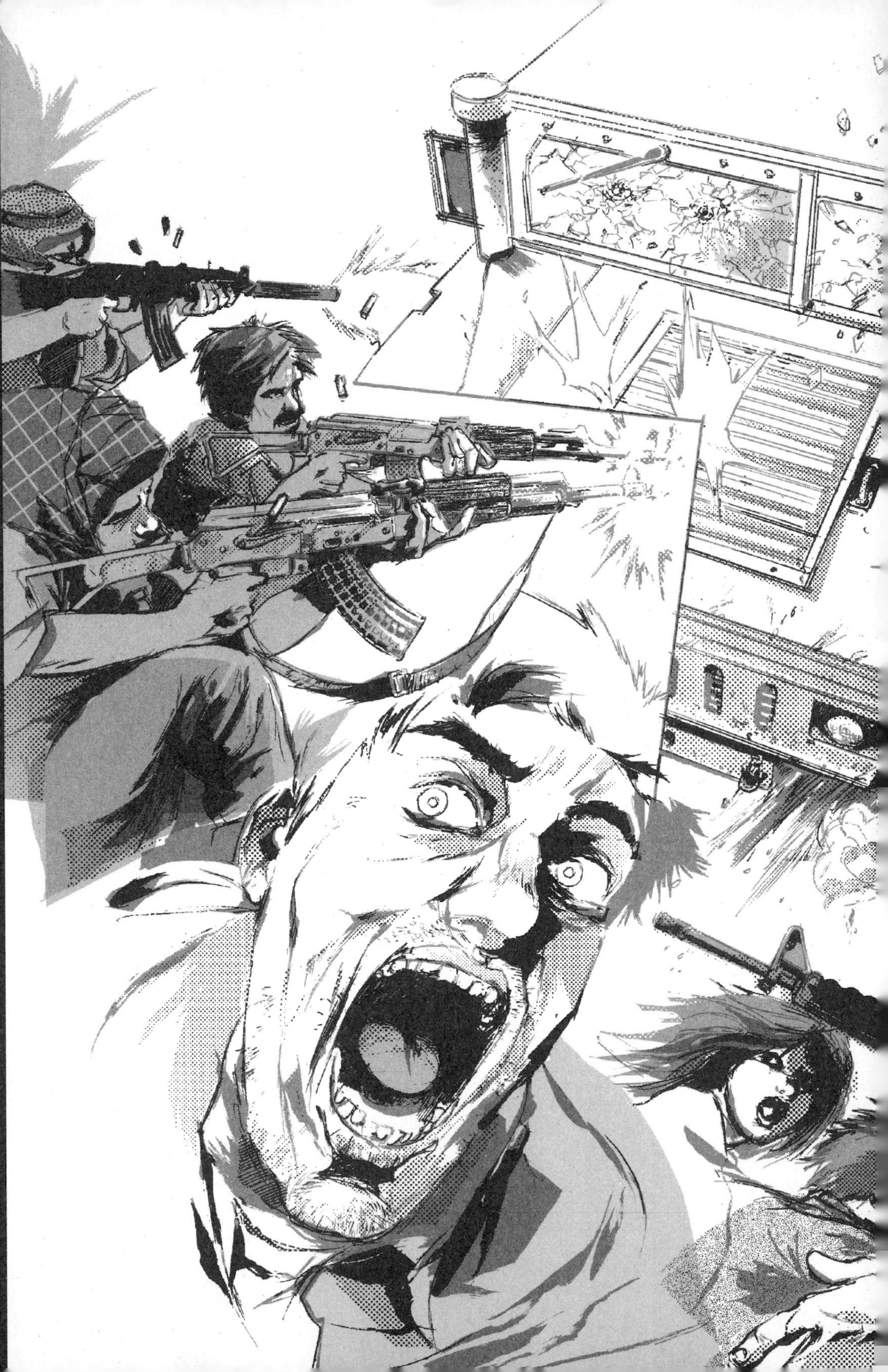

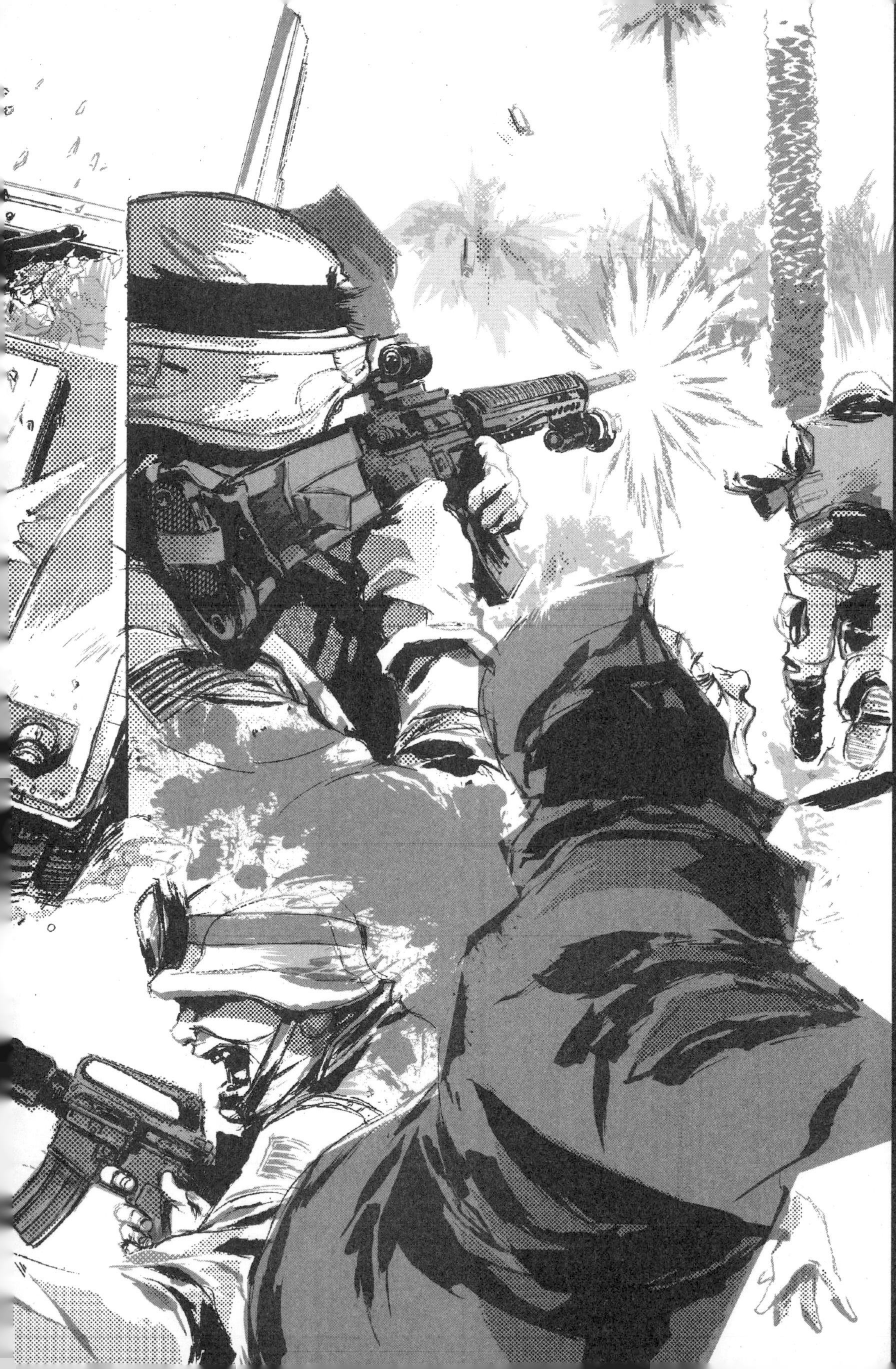

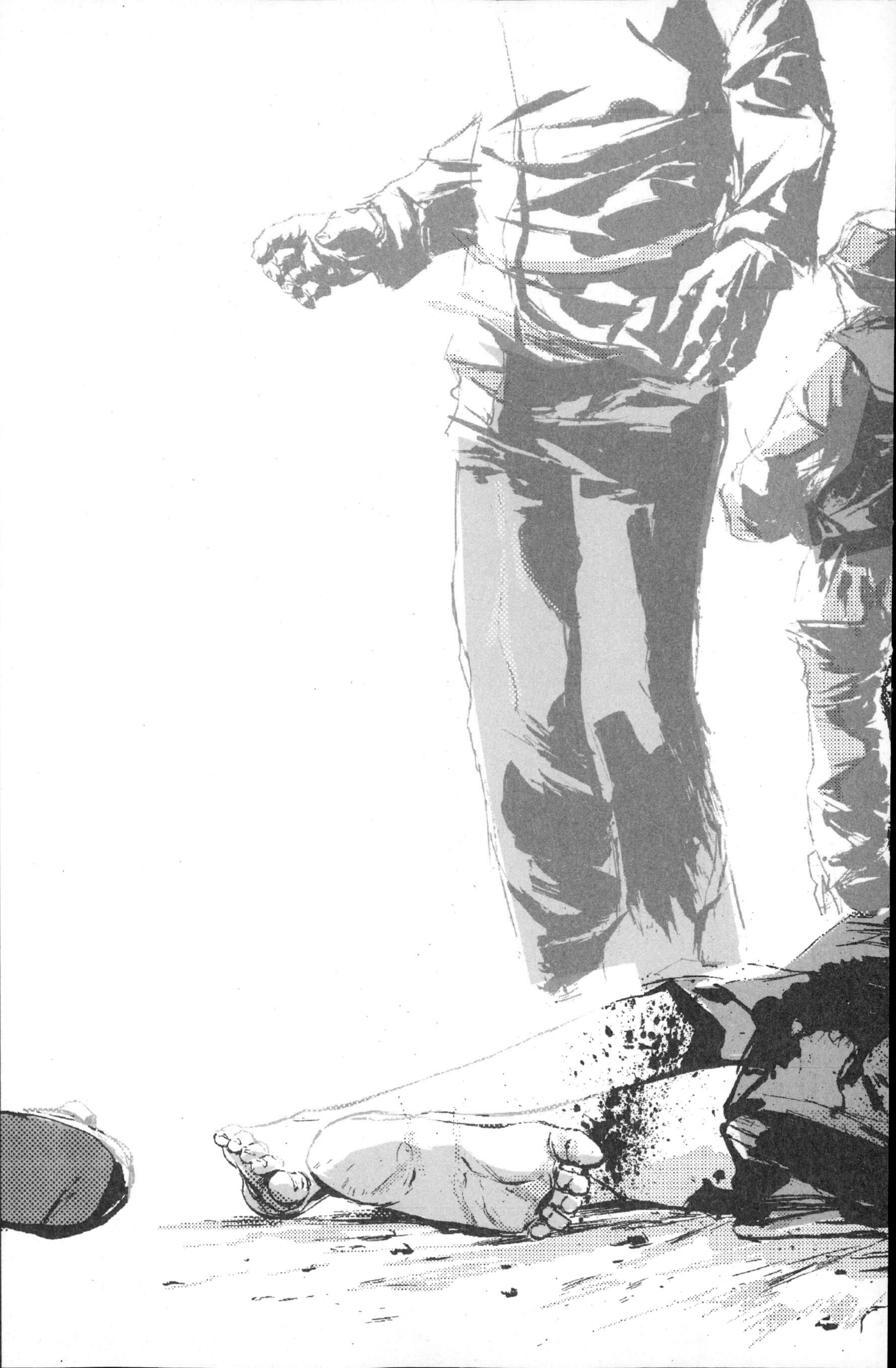

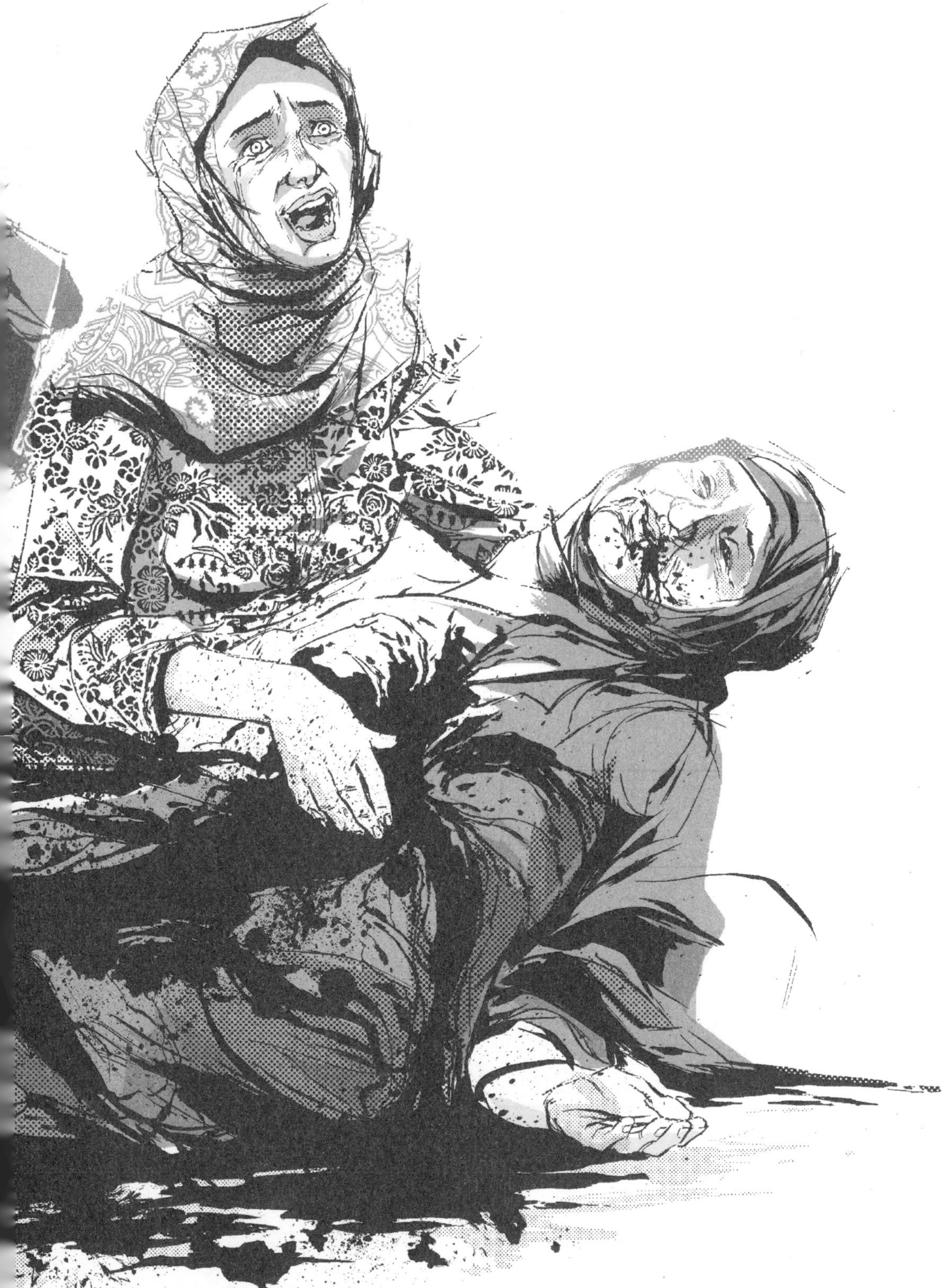

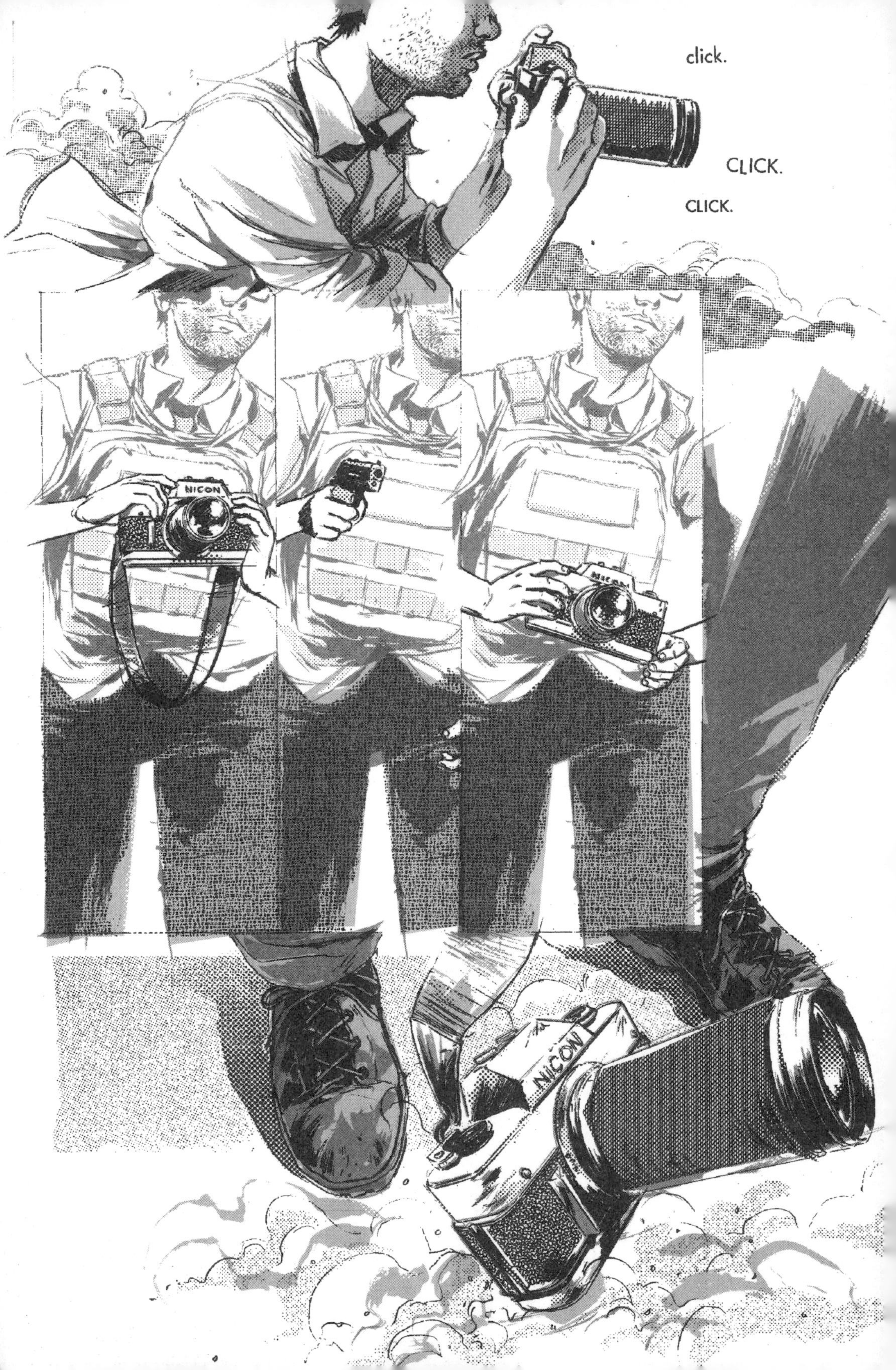
click.
CLICK.
CLICK.
NICON
NICON
NICON

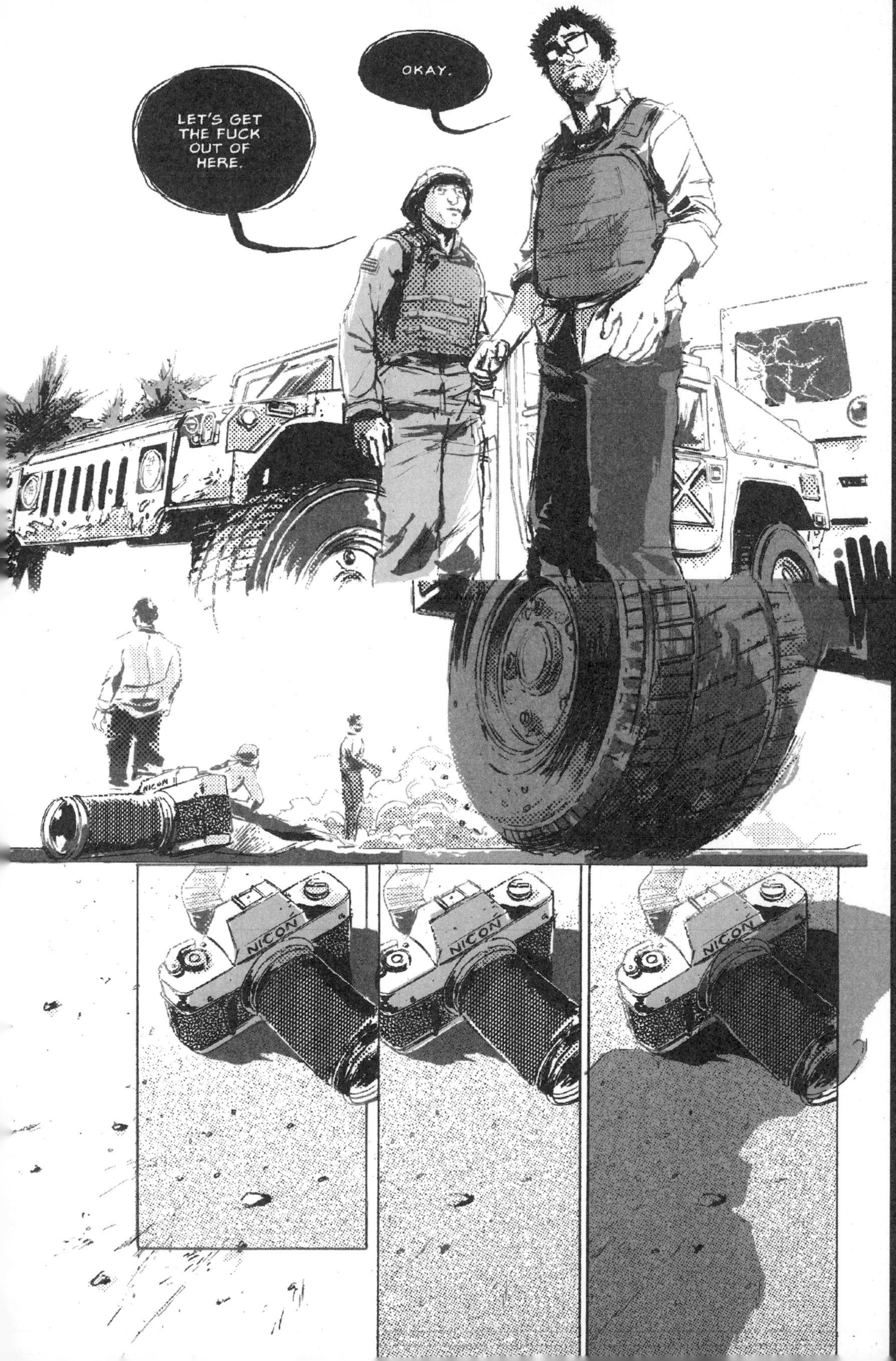
LET'S GET THE FUCK OUT OF HERE.
OKAY.
NICON
NICON
NICON

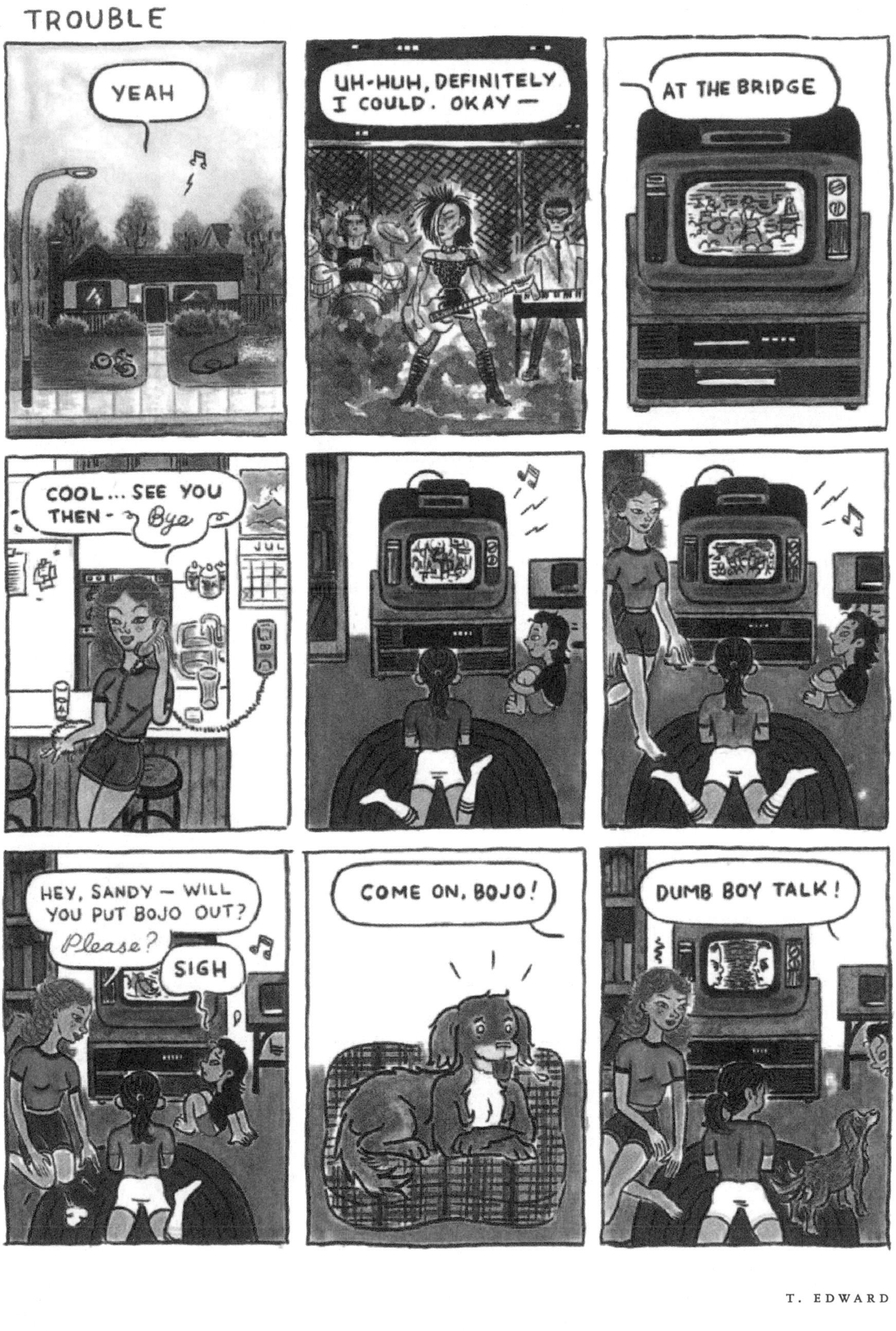
TROUBLE
YEAH
UH-HUH, DEFINITELY I COULD. OKAY —
AT THE BRIDGE
COOL... SEE YOU THEN - Bye
JUL
HEY, SANDY — WILL YOU PUT BOJO OUT? Please?
SIGH
COME ON, BOJO!
DUMB BOY TALK!

T. EDWARD BAK

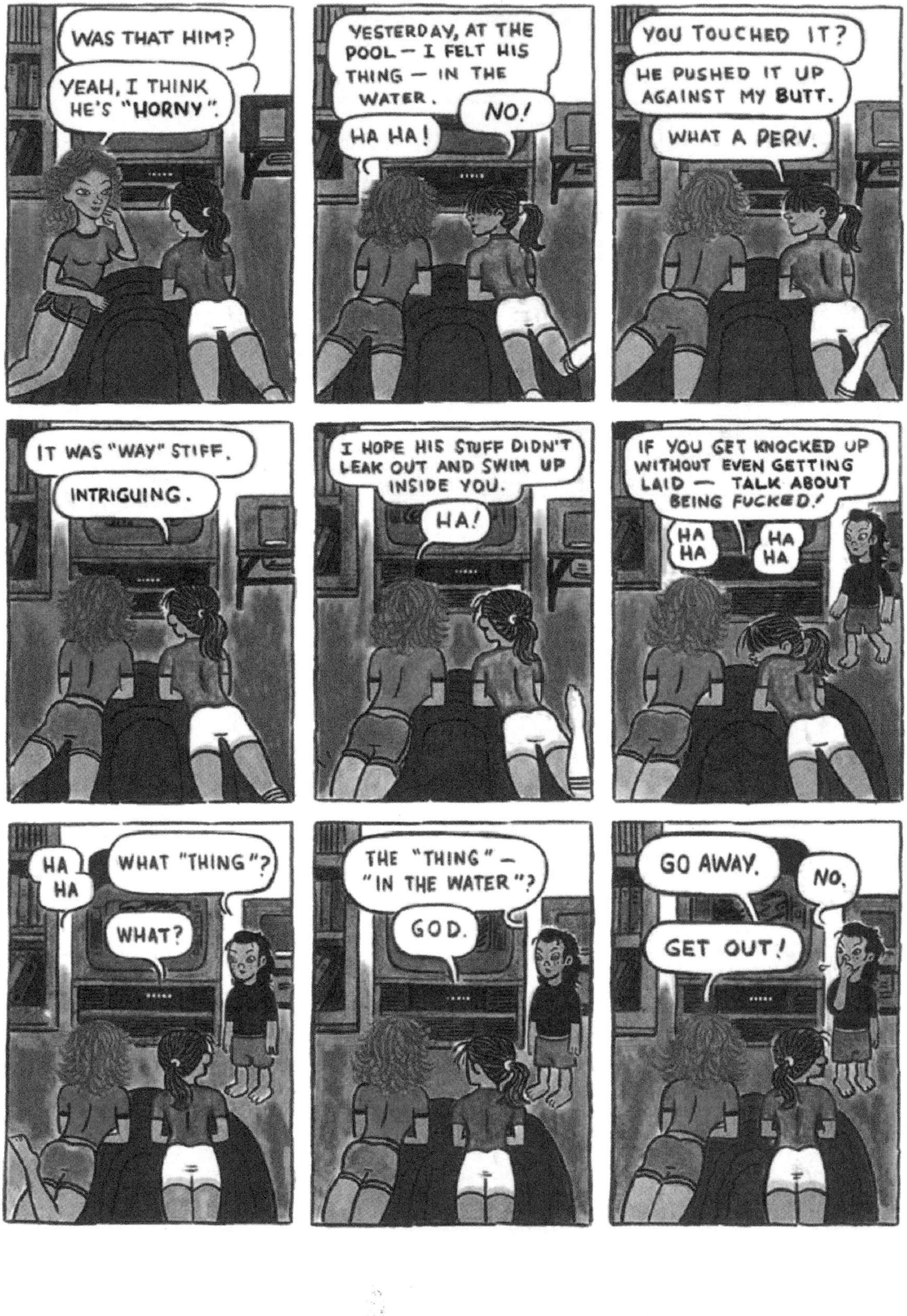
WAS THAT HIM?
YEAH, I THINK HE'S "HORNY".
YESTERDAY, AT THE POOL — I FELT HIS THING — IN THE WATER.
NO!
HA HA!
YOU TOUCHED IT?
HE PUSHED IT UP AGAINST MY BUTT.
WHAT A PERV.
IT WAS "WAY" STIFF.
INTRIGUING.
I HOPE HIS STUFF DIDN'T LEAK OUT AND SWIM UP INSIDE YOU.
HA!
IF YOU GET KNOCKED UP WITHOUT EVEN GETTING LAID — TALK ABOUT BEING FUCKED!
HA HA
HA HA
HA HA
WHAT "THING"?
WHAT?
THE "THING" — "IN THE WATER"?
GOD.
GO AWAY.
NO.
GET OUT!

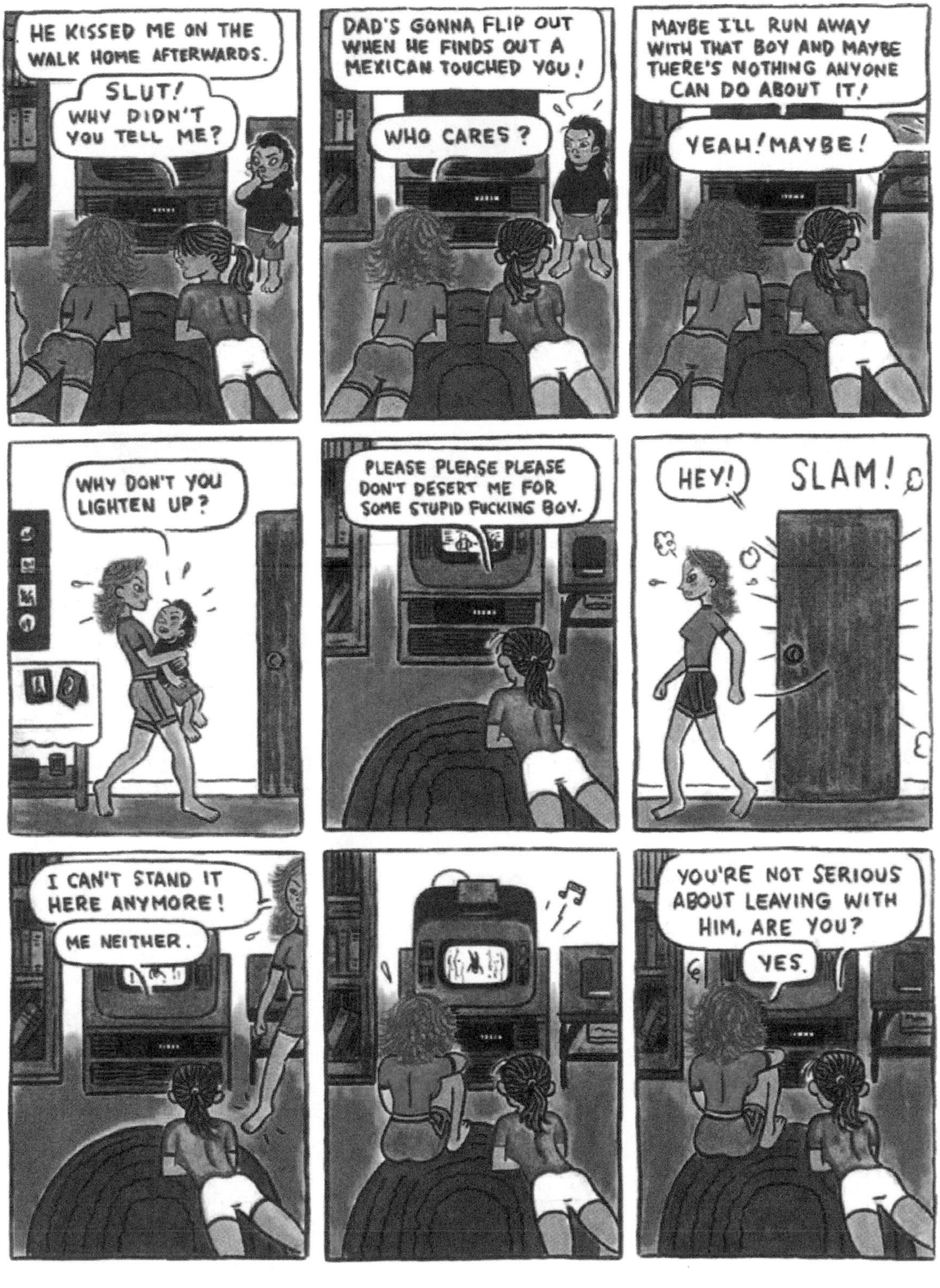
HE KISSED ME ON THE WALK HOME AFTERWARDS.
SLUT! WHY DIDN'T YOU TELL ME?
DAD'S GONNA FLIP OUT WHEN HE FINDS OUT A MEXICAN TOUCHED YOU!
WHO CARES?
MAYBE I'LL RUN AWAY WITH THAT BOY AND MAYBE THERE'S NOTHING ANYONE CAN DO ABOUT IT!
YEAH! MAYBE!
WHY DON'T YOU LIGHTEN UP?
PLEASE PLEASE PLEASE DON'T DESERT ME FOR SOME STUPID FUCKING BOY.
HEY!
SLAM!
I CAN'T STAND IT HERE ANYMORE!
ME NEITHER.
YOU'RE NOT SERIOUS ABOUT LEAVING WITH HIM, ARE YOU?
YES.

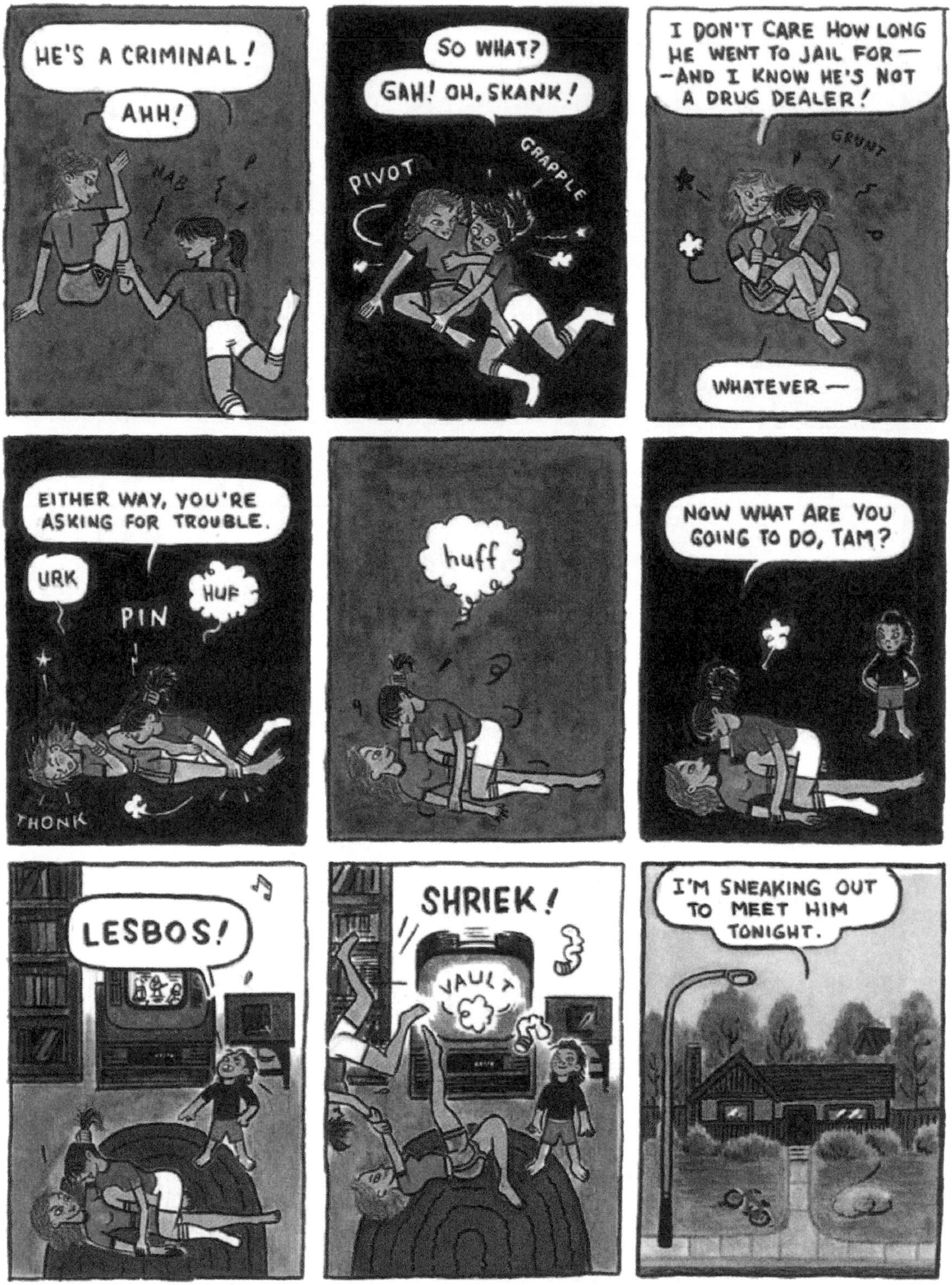
HE'S A CRIMINAL!
AHH!
SO WHAT?
GAH! OH, SKANK!
PIVOT
GRAPPLE
I DON'T CARE HOW LONG HE WENT TO JAIL FOR— —AND I KNOW HE'S NOT A DRUG DEALER!
GRUNT
WHATEVER—
EITHER WAY, YOU'RE ASKING FOR TROUBLE.
URK
HUF
PIN
THONK
huff
NOW WHAT ARE YOU GOING TO DO, TAM?
LESBOS!
SHRIEK!
VAULT
I'M SNEAKING OUT TO MEET HIM TONIGHT.

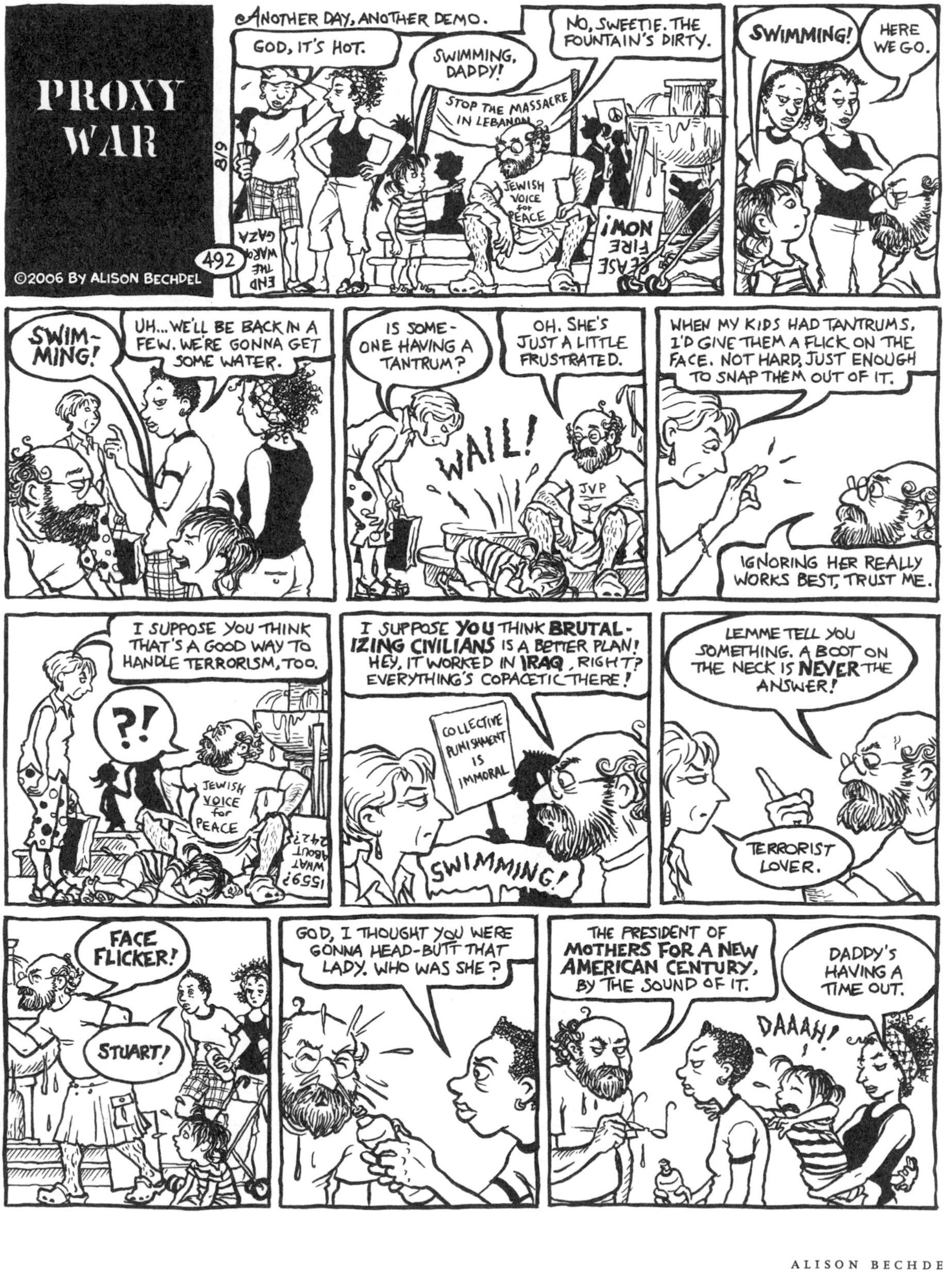

PROXY WAR
©2006 BY ALISON BECHDEL
492
8/9
ANOTHER DAY, ANOTHER DEMO.
GOD, IT'S HOT.
SWIMMING, DADDY!
STOP THE MASSACRE IN LEBANON
JEWISH VOICE for PEACE
END THE WAR ON GAZA
CEASE FIRE NOW!
NO, SWEETIE. THE FOUNTAIN'S DIRTY.
SWIMMING!
HERE WE GO.
SWIMMING!
UH...WE'LL BE BACK IN A FEW. WE'RE GONNA GET SOME WATER.
IS SOMEONE HAVING A TANTRUM?
OH. SHE'S JUST A LITTLE FRUSTRATED.
WAIL!
JVP
WHEN MY KIDS HAD TANTRUMS, I'D GIVE THEM A FLICK ON THE FACE. NOT HARD, JUST ENOUGH TO SNAP THEM OUT OF IT.
IGNORING HER REALLY WORKS BEST, TRUST ME.
I SUPPOSE YOU THINK THAT'S A GOOD WAY TO HANDLE TERRORISM, TOO.
?!
JEWISH VOICE for PEACE
1559? WHAT ABOUT 242?
I SUPPOSE YOU THINK BRUTALIZING CIVILIANS IS A BETTER PLAN! HEY, IT WORKED IN IRAQ, RIGHT? EVERYTHING'S COPACETIC THERE!
COLLECTIVE PUNISHMENT IS IMMORAL
SWIMMING!
LEMME TELL YOU SOMETHING. A BOOT ON THE NECK IS NEVER THE ANSWER!
TERRORIST LOVER.
FACE FLICKER!
STUART!
GOD, I THOUGHT YOU WERE GONNA HEAD-BUTT THAT LADY. WHO WAS SHE?
THE PRESIDENT OF MOTHERS FOR A NEW AMERICAN CENTURY, BY THE SOUND OF IT.
DAAAH!
DADDY'S HAVING A TIME OUT.

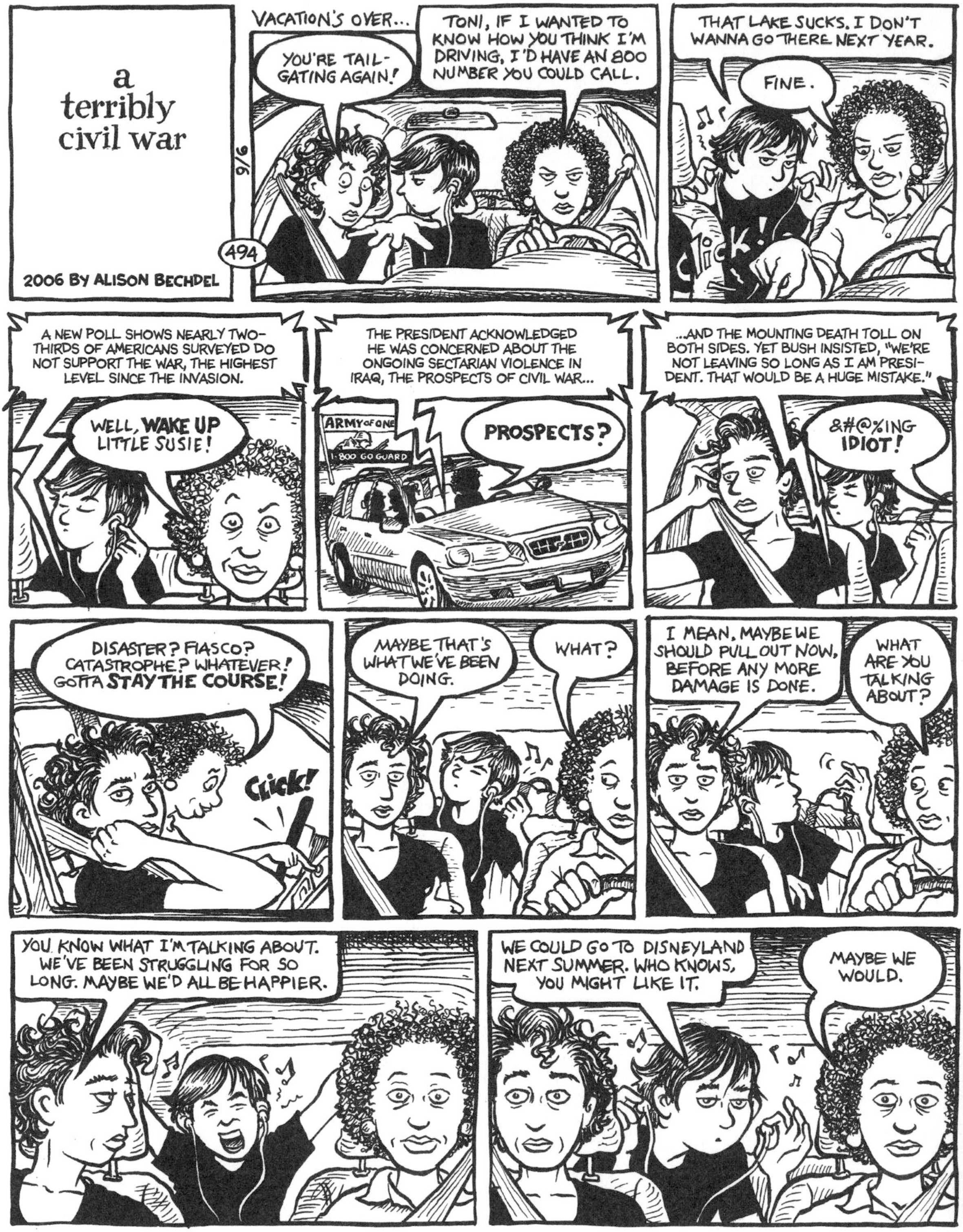
a terribly civil war
2006 BY ALISON BECHDEL
494
9/6
VACATION'S OVER...
YOU'RE TAIL-GATING AGAIN!
TONI, IF I WANTED TO KNOW HOW YOU THINK I'M DRIVING, I'D HAVE AN 800 NUMBER YOU COULD CALL.
THAT LAKE SUCKS. I DON'T WANNA GO THERE NEXT YEAR.
FINE.
CLICK!
A NEW POLL SHOWS NEARLY TWO-THIRDS OF AMERICANS SURVEYED DO NOT SUPPORT THE WAR, THE HIGHEST LEVEL SINCE THE INVASION.
WELL, WAKE UP LITTLE SUSIE!
THE PRESIDENT ACKNOWLEDGED HE WAS CONCERNED ABOUT THE ONGOING SECTARIAN VIOLENCE IN IRAQ, THE PROSPECTS OF CIVIL WAR...
ARMY OF ONE
1.800 GO GUARD
PROSPECTS?
...AND THE MOUNTING DEATH TOLL ON BOTH SIDES. YET BUSH INSISTED, "WE'RE NOT LEAVING SO LONG AS I AM PRESIDENT. THAT WOULD BE A HUGE MISTAKE."
&#@%ING IDIOT!
DISASTER? FIASCO? CATASTROPHE? WHATEVER! GOTTA STAY THE COURSE!
CLICK!
MAYBE THAT'S WHAT WE'VE BEEN DOING.
WHAT?
I MEAN, MAYBE WE SHOULD PULL OUT NOW, BEFORE ANY MORE DAMAGE IS DONE.
WHAT ARE YOU TALKING ABOUT?
YOU KNOW WHAT I'M TALKING ABOUT. WE'VE BEEN STRUGGLING FOR SO LONG. MAYBE WE'D ALL BE HAPPIER.
WE COULD GO TO DISNEYLAND NEXT SUMMER. WHO KNOWS, YOU MIGHT LIKE IT.
MAYBE WE WOULD.

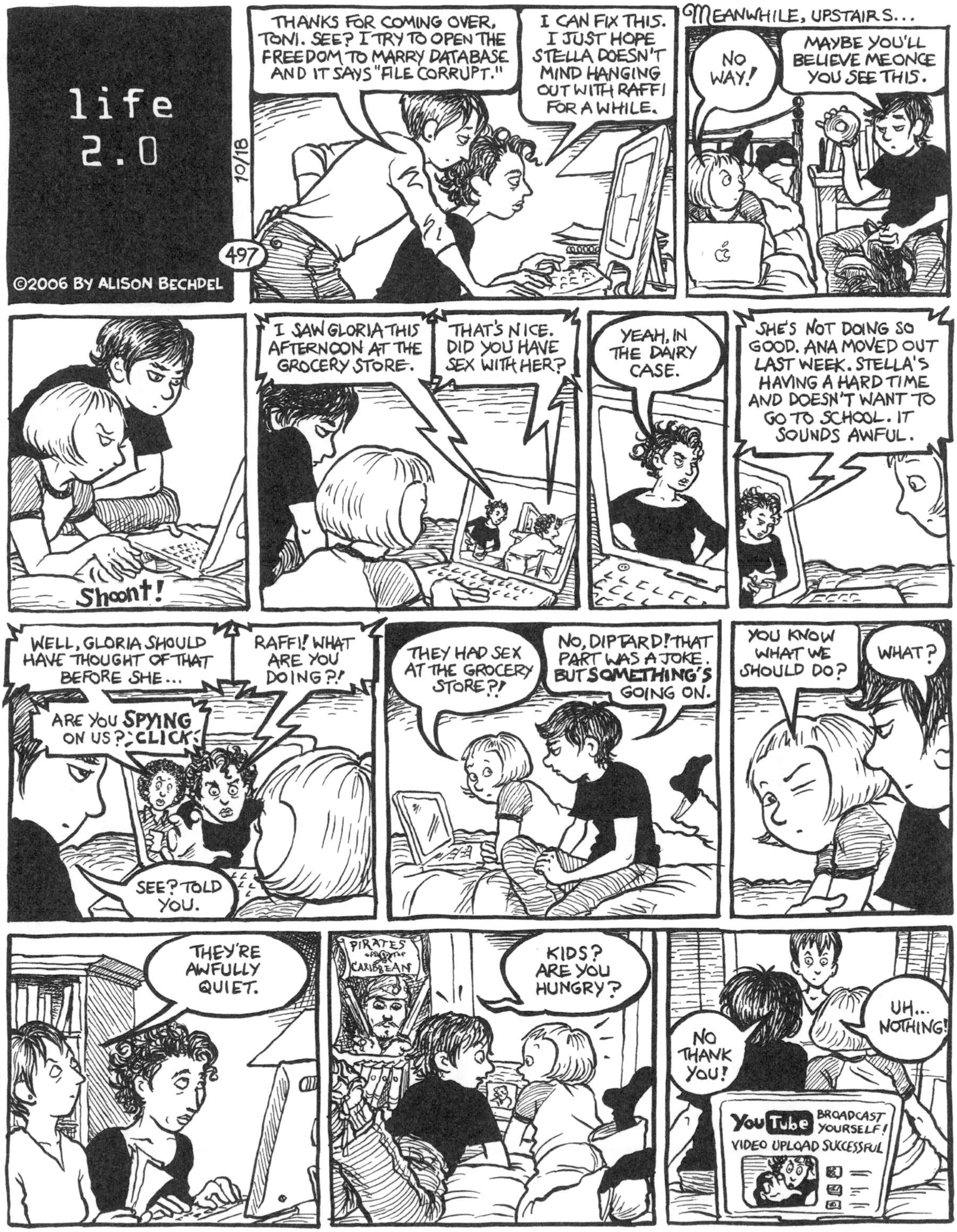
life 2.0
©2006 BY ALISON BECHDEL
10/18
497
THANKS FOR COMING OVER, TONI. SEE? I TRY TO OPEN THE FREEDOM TO MARRY DATABASE AND IT SAYS "FILE CORRUPT."
I CAN FIX THIS. I JUST HOPE STELLA DOESN'T MIND HANGING OUT WITH RAFFI FOR A WHILE.
MEANWHILE, UPSTAIRS...
NO WAY!
MAYBE YOU'LL BELIEVE ME ONCE YOU SEE THIS.
Shoont!
I SAW GLORIA THIS AFTERNOON AT THE GROCERY STORE.
THAT'S NICE. DID YOU HAVE SEX WITH HER?
YEAH, IN THE DAIRY CASE.
SHE'S NOT DOING SO GOOD. ANA MOVED OUT LAST WEEK. STELLA'S HAVING A HARD TIME AND DOESN'T WANT TO GO TO SCHOOL. IT SOUNDS AWFUL.
WELL, GLORIA SHOULD HAVE THOUGHT OF THAT BEFORE SHE...
RAFFI! WHAT ARE YOU DOING?!
ARE YOU SPYING ON US?! CLICK
SEE? TOLD YOU.
THEY HAD SEX AT THE GROCERY STORE?!
NO, DIPTARD! THAT PART WAS A JOKE. BUT SOMETHING'S GOING ON.
YOU KNOW WHAT WE SHOULD DO?
WHAT?
THEY'RE AWFULLY QUIET.
PIRATES of the CARIBBEAN
KIDS? ARE YOU HUNGRY?
NO THANK YOU!
UH... NOTHING!
YouTube BROADCAST YOURSELF!
VIDEO UPLOAD SUCCESSFUL

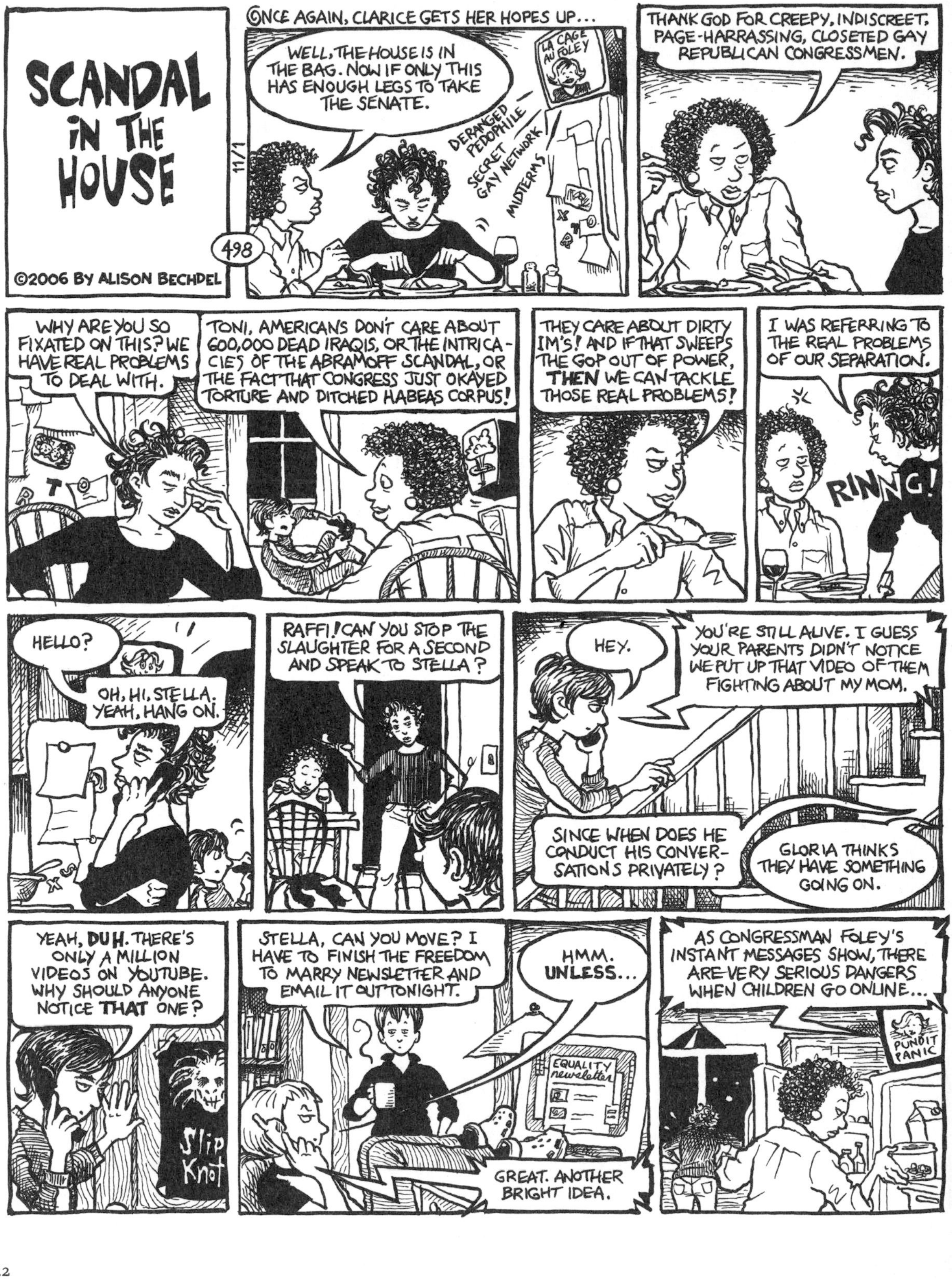

SCANDAL IN THE HOUSE
©2006 BY ALISON BECHDEL
498
11/1
ONCE AGAIN, CLARICE GETS HER HOPES UP...
WELL, THE HOUSE IS IN THE BAG. NOW IF ONLY THIS HAS ENOUGH LEGS TO TAKE THE SENATE.
LA CAGE AU FOLEY
DERANGED PEDOPHILE
SECRET GAY NETWORK
MIDTERMS
THANK GOD FOR CREEPY, INDISCREET, PAGE-HARRASSING, CLOSETED GAY REPUBLICAN CONGRESSMEN.
WHY ARE YOU SO FIXATED ON THIS? WE HAVE REAL PROBLEMS TO DEAL WITH.
TONI, AMERICANS DON'T CARE ABOUT 600,000 DEAD IRAQIS, OR THE INTRICACIES OF THE ABRAMOFF SCANDAL, OR THE FACT THAT CONGRESS JUST OKAYED TORTURE AND DITCHED HABEAS CORPUS!
THEY CARE ABOUT DIRTY IM'S! AND IF THAT SWEEPS THE GOP OUT OF POWER, THEN WE CAN TACKLE THOSE REAL PROBLEMS!
I WAS REFERRING TO THE REAL PROBLEMS OF OUR SEPARATION.
RINNG!
HELLO?
OH, HI, STELLA. YEAH, HANG ON.
RAFFI! CAN YOU STOP THE SLAUGHTER FOR A SECOND AND SPEAK TO STELLA?
HEY.
YOU'RE STILL ALIVE. I GUESS YOUR PARENTS DIDN'T NOTICE WE PUT UP THAT VIDEO OF THEM FIGHTING ABOUT MY MOM.
SINCE WHEN DOES HE CONDUCT HIS CONVERSATIONS PRIVATELY?
GLORIA THINKS THEY HAVE SOMETHING GOING ON.
YEAH, DUH. THERE'S ONLY A MILLION VIDEOS ON YOUTUBE. WHY SHOULD ANYONE NOTICE THAT ONE?
Slip Knot
STELLA, CAN YOU MOVE? I HAVE TO FINISH THE FREEDOM TO MARRY NEWSLETTER AND EMAIL IT OUT TONIGHT.
HMM. UNLESS...
EQUALITY newsletter
GREAT. ANOTHER BRIGHT IDEA.
AS CONGRESSMAN FOLEY'S INSTANT MESSAGES SHOW, THERE ARE VERY SERIOUS DANGERS WHEN CHILDREN GO ONLINE...
PUNDIT PANIC

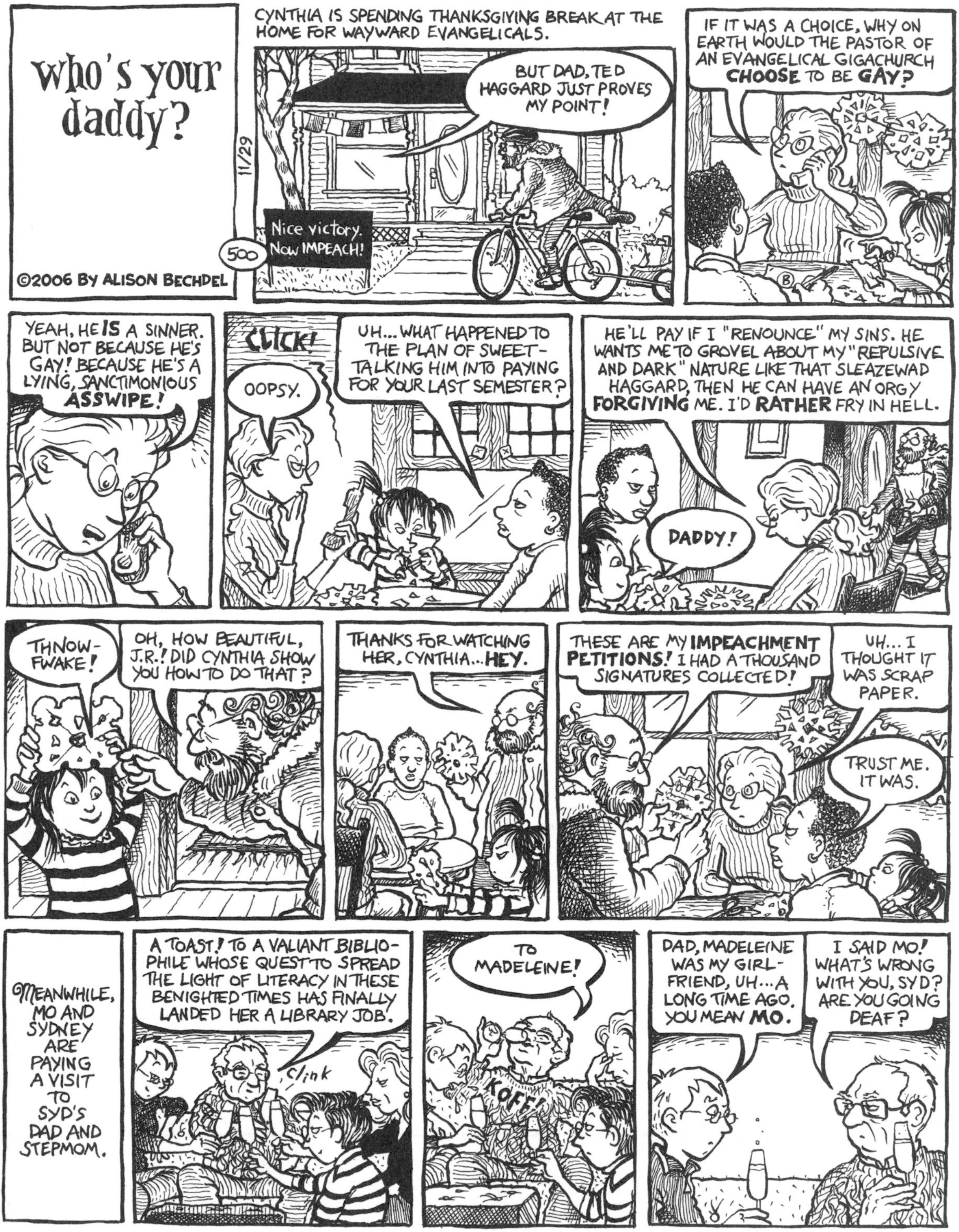
who's your daddy?
©2006 BY ALISON BECHDEL
11/29
500
CYNTHIA IS SPENDING THANKSGIVING BREAK AT THE HOME FOR WAYWARD EVANGELICALS.
BUT DAD, TED HAGGARD JUST PROVES MY POINT!
Nice victory. Now IMPEACH!
IF IT WAS A CHOICE, WHY ON EARTH WOULD THE PASTOR OF AN EVANGELICAL GIGACHURCH CHOOSE TO BE GAY?
YEAH, HE IS A SINNER. BUT NOT BECAUSE HE'S GAY! BECAUSE HE'S A LYING, SANCTIMONIOUS ASSWIPE!
CLICK!
OOPSY.
UH... WHAT HAPPENED TO THE PLAN OF SWEET-TALKING HIM INTO PAYING FOR YOUR LAST SEMESTER?
HE'LL PAY IF I "RENOUNCE" MY SINS. HE WANTS ME TO GROVEL ABOUT MY "REPULSIVE AND DARK" NATURE LIKE THAT SLEAZEWAD HAGGARD, THEN HE CAN HAVE AN ORGY FORGIVING ME. I'D RATHER FRY IN HELL.
DADDY!
THNOW-FWAKE!
OH, HOW BEAUTIFUL, J.R.! DID CYNTHIA SHOW YOU HOW TO DO THAT?
THANKS FOR WATCHING HER, CYNTHIA... HEY.
THESE ARE MY IMPEACHMENT PETITIONS! I HAD A THOUSAND SIGNATURES COLLECTED!
UH... I THOUGHT IT WAS SCRAP PAPER.
TRUST ME. IT WAS.
MEANWHILE, MO AND SYDNEY ARE PAYING A VISIT TO SYD'S DAD AND STEPMOM.
A TOAST! TO A VALIANT BIBLIOPHILE WHOSE QUEST TO SPREAD THE LIGHT OF LITERACY IN THESE BENIGHTED TIMES HAS FINALLY LANDED HER A LIBRARY JOB.
clink
TO MADELEINE!
KOFF!
DAD, MADELEINE WAS MY GIRLFRIEND, UH... A LONG TIME AGO. YOU MEAN MO.
I SAID MO! WHAT'S WRONG WITH YOU, SYD? ARE YOU GOING DEAF?

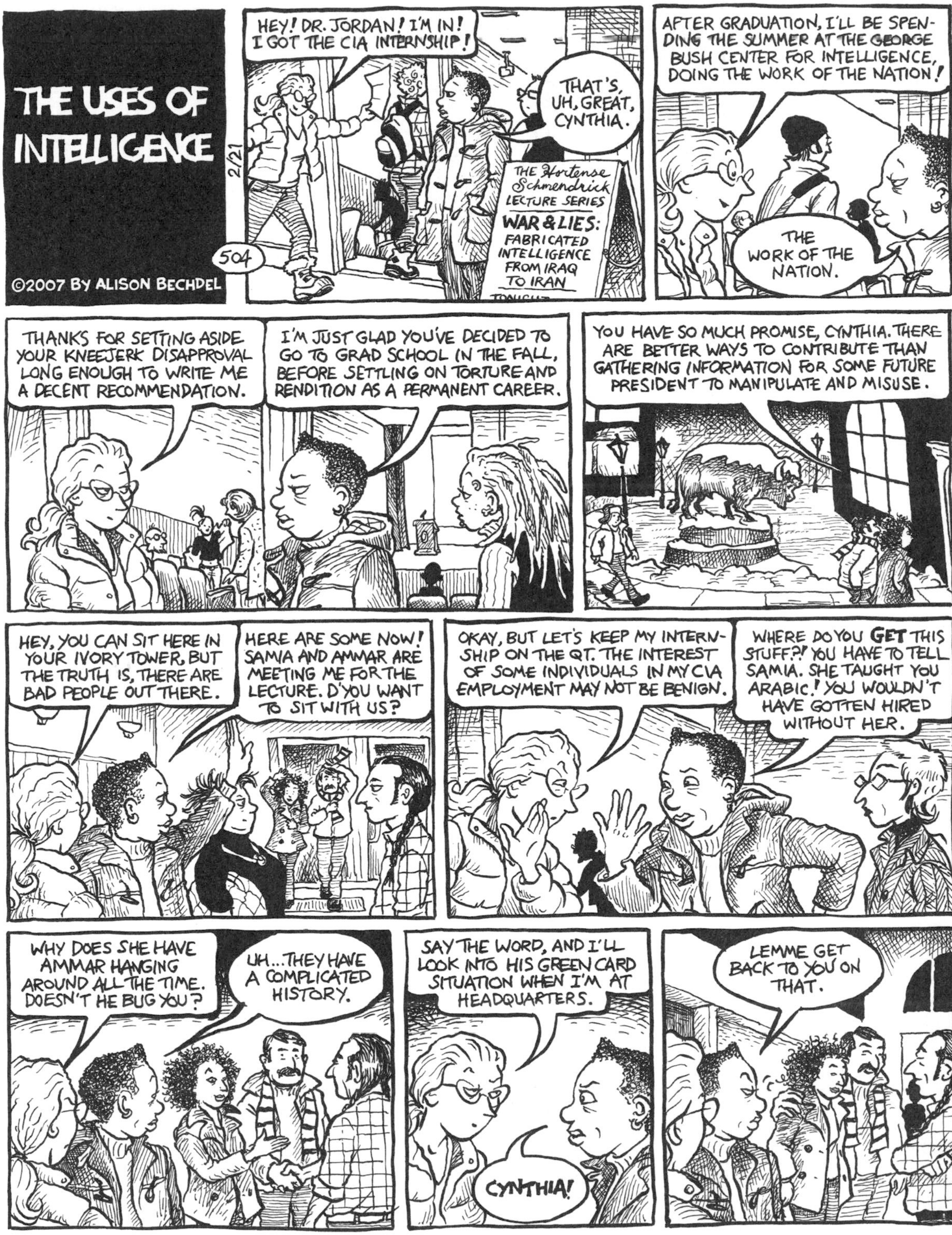

THE USES OF INTELLIGENCE
©2007 BY ALISON BECHDEL
504
2/21
HEY! DR. JORDAN! I'M IN! I GOT THE CIA INTERNSHIP!
THAT'S, UH, GREAT, CYNTHIA.
THE Hortense Schmendrick LECTURE SERIES
WAR & LIES: FABRICATED INTELLIGENCE FROM IRAQ TO IRAN
AFTER GRADUATION, I'LL BE SPENDING THE SUMMER AT THE GEORGE BUSH CENTER FOR INTELLIGENCE, DOING THE WORK OF THE NATION!
THE WORK OF THE NATION.
THANKS FOR SETTING ASIDE YOUR KNEEJERK DISAPPROVAL LONG ENOUGH TO WRITE ME A DECENT RECOMMENDATION.
I'M JUST GLAD YOU'VE DECIDED TO GO TO GRAD SCHOOL IN THE FALL, BEFORE SETTLING ON TORTURE AND RENDITION AS A PERMANENT CAREER.
YOU HAVE SO MUCH PROMISE, CYNTHIA. THERE ARE BETTER WAYS TO CONTRIBUTE THAN GATHERING INFORMATION FOR SOME FUTURE PRESIDENT TO MANIPULATE AND MISUSE.
HEY, YOU CAN SIT HERE IN YOUR IVORY TOWER, BUT THE TRUTH IS, THERE ARE BAD PEOPLE OUT THERE.
HERE ARE SOME NOW! SAMIA AND AMMAR ARE MEETING ME FOR THE LECTURE. D'YOU WANT TO SIT WITH US?
OKAY, BUT LET'S KEEP MY INTERNSHIP ON THE QT. THE INTEREST OF SOME INDIVIDUALS IN MY CIA EMPLOYMENT MAY NOT BE BENIGN.
WHERE DO YOU GET THIS STUFF?! YOU HAVE TO TELL SAMIA. SHE TAUGHT YOU ARABIC! YOU WOULDN'T HAVE GOTTEN HIRED WITHOUT HER.
WHY DOES SHE HAVE AMMAR HANGING AROUND ALL THE TIME. DOESN'T HE BUG YOU?
UH... THEY HAVE A COMPLICATED HISTORY.
SAY THE WORD, AND I'LL LOOK INTO HIS GREEN CARD SITUATION WHEN I'M AT HEADQUARTERS.
CYNTHIA!
LEMME GET BACK TO YOU ON THAT.

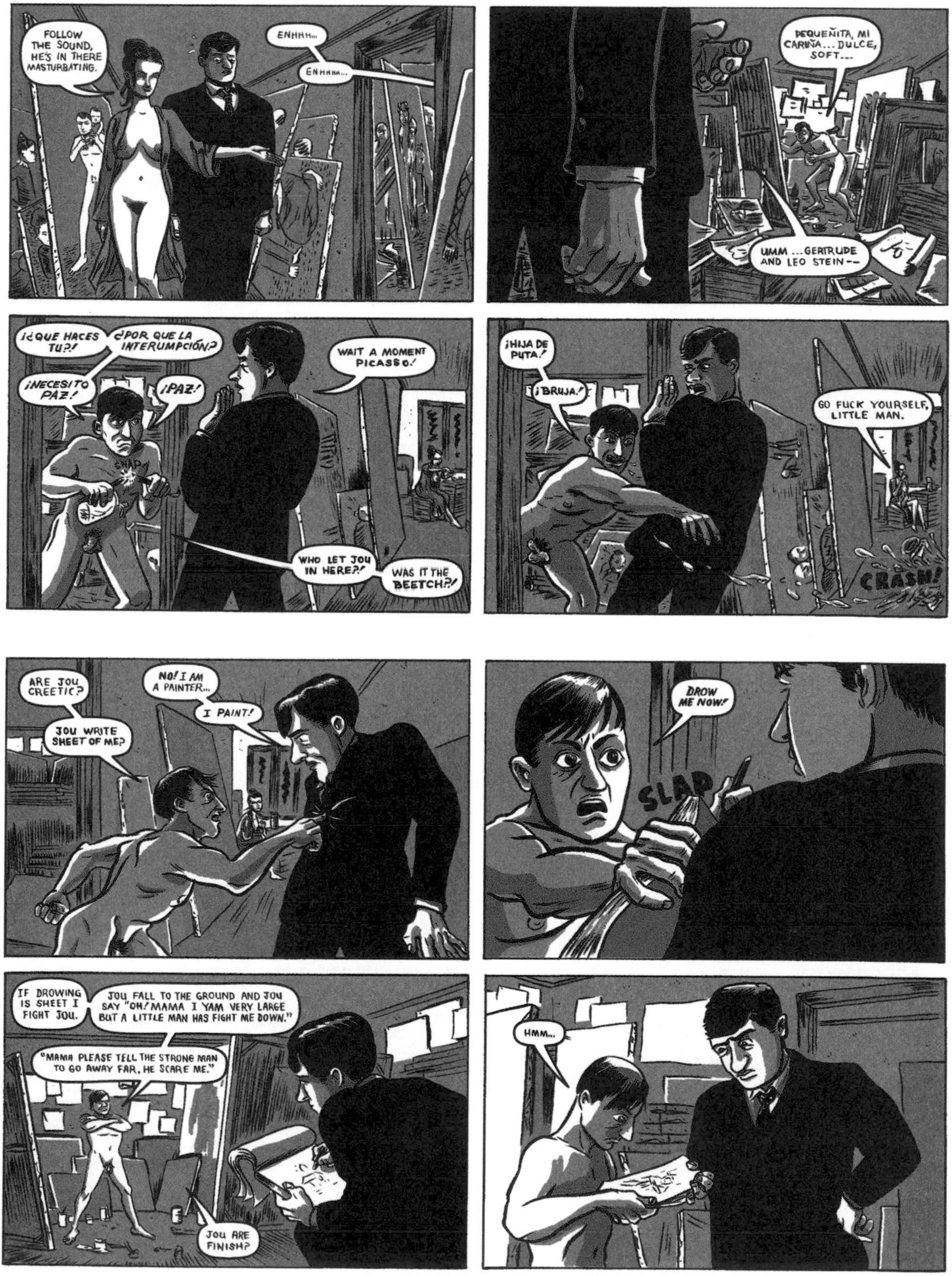
FOLLOW THE SOUND, HE'S IN THERE MASTURBATING.
ENHHH...
ENHHHH...
PEQUEÑITA, MI CARIÑA... DULCE, SOFT...
UMM ...GERTRUDE AND LEO STEIN--
¡¿QUE HACES TU?!
¿POR QUE LA INTERUMPCIÓN?
¡NECESITO PAZ!
¡PAZ!
SNAP
WAIT A MOMENT PICASSO!
WHO LET JOU IN HERE?!
WAS IT THE BEETCH?!
¡HIJA DE PUTA!
¡BRUJA!
GO FUCK YOURSELF, LITTLE MAN.
CRASH!
ARE JOU CREETIC?
NO! I AM A PAINTER...
I PAINT!
JOU WRITE SHEET OF ME?
DROW ME NOW!
SLAP
IF DROWING IS SHEET I FIGHT JOU.
JOU FALL TO THE GROUND AND JOU SAY "OH! MAMA I YAM VERY LARGE BUT A LITTLE MAN HAS FIGHT ME DOWN."
"MAMA PLEASE TELL THE STRONG MAN TO GO AWAY FAR, HE SCARE ME."
JOU ARE FINISH?
HMM...

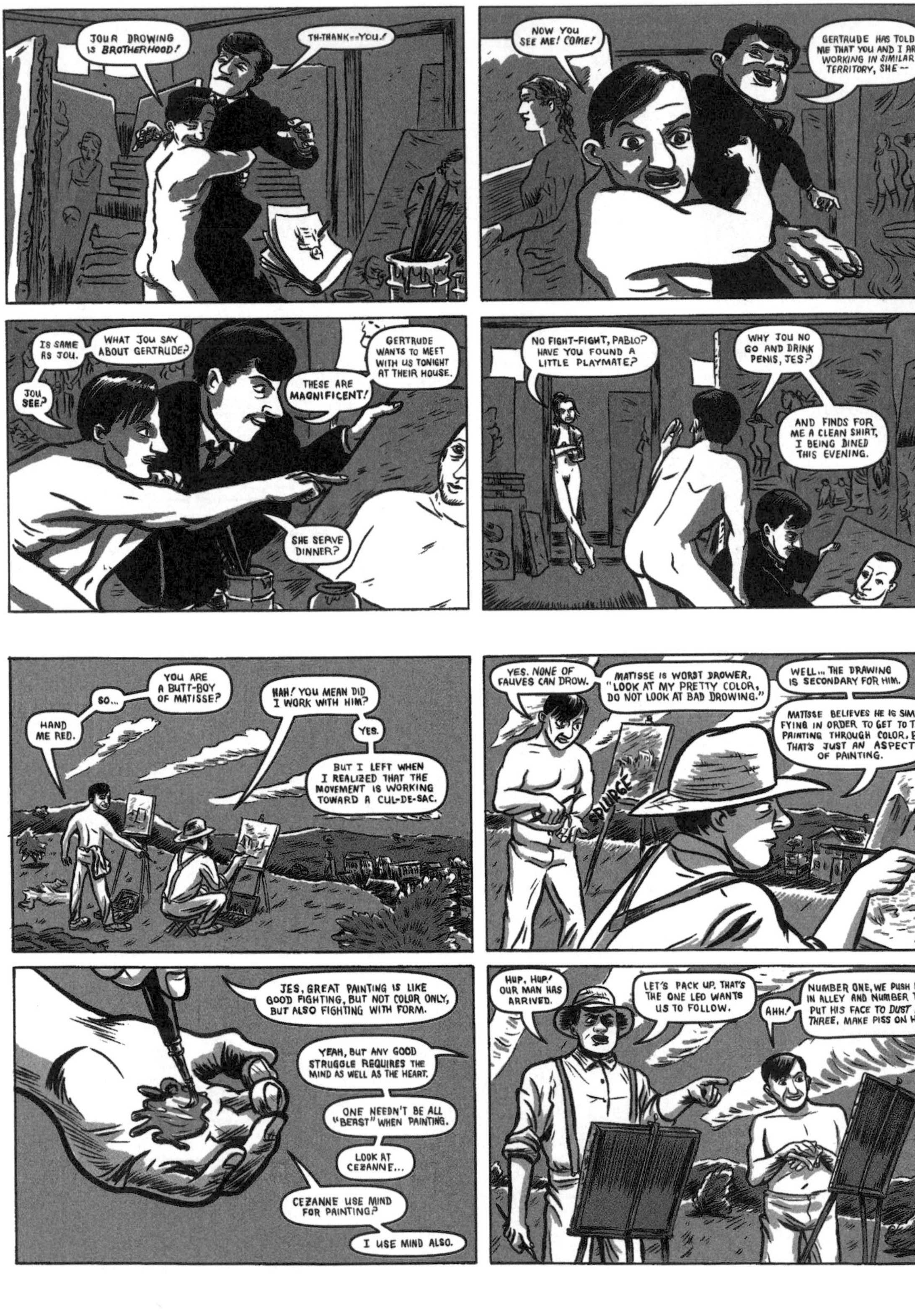
JOUR DROWING IS BROTHERHOOD!
TH-THANK--YOU!
NOW YOU SEE ME! COME!
GERTRUDE HAS TOLD ME THAT YOU AND I ARE WORKING IN SIMILAR TERRITORY, SHE--
WHAT JOU SAY ABOUT GERTRUDE?
IS SAME AS JOU.
JOU, SEE?
GERTRUDE WANTS TO MEET WITH US TONIGHT AT THEIR HOUSE.
THESE ARE MAGNIFICENT!
SHE SERVE DINNER?
NO FIGHT-FIGHT, PABLO? HAVE YOU FOUND A LITTLE PLAYMATE?
WHY JOU NO GO AND DRINK PENIS, JES?
AND FINDS FOR ME A CLEAN SHIRT, I BEING DINED THIS EVENING.
HAND ME RED.
SO...
YOU ARE A BUTT-BOY OF MATISSE?
NAH! YOU MEAN DID I WORK WITH HIM?
YES.
BUT I LEFT WHEN I REALIZED THAT THE MOVEMENT IS WORKING TOWARD A CUL-DE-SAC.
YES. NONE OF FAUVES CAN DROW.
MATISSE IS WORST DROWER, "LOOK AT MY PRETTY COLOR, DO NOT LOOK AT BAD DROWING."
WELL... THE DRAWING IS SECONDARY FOR HIM.
MATISSE BELIEVES HE IS SIMPLIFYING IN ORDER TO GET TO TRUE PAINTING THROUGH COLOR, BUT THAT'S JUST AN ASPECT OF PAINTING.
SPLURGE
JES, GREAT PAINTING IS LIKE GOOD FIGHTING, BUT NOT COLOR ONLY, BUT ALSO FIGHTING WITH FORM.
YEAH, BUT ANY GOOD STRUGGLE REQUIRES THE MIND AS WELL AS THE HEART.
ONE NEEDN'T BE ALL "BEAST" WHEN PAINTING.
LOOK AT CEZANNE...
CEZANNE USE MIND FOR PAINTING?
I USE MIND ALSO.
HUP, HUP! OUR MAN HAS ARRIVED.
LET'S PACK UP. THAT'S THE ONE LEO WANTS US TO FOLLOW.
AHH!
NUMBER ONE, WE PUSH HIM IN ALLEY AND NUMBER TWO, PUT HIS FACE TO DUST AND THREE, MAKE PISS ON HIM!

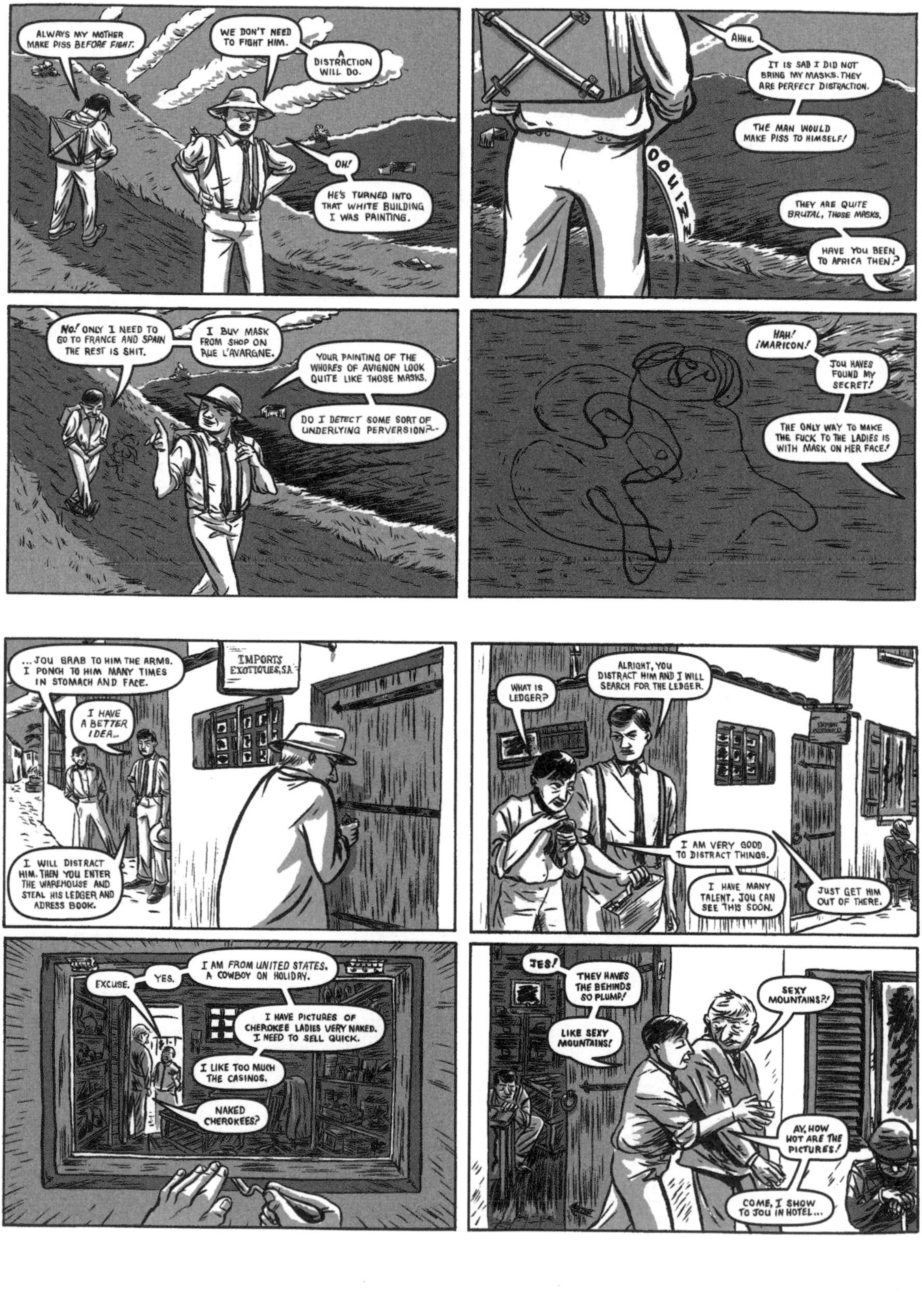

ALWAYS MY MOTHER MAKE PISS BEFORE FIGHT.
WE DON'T NEED TO FIGHT HIM.
A DISTRACTION WILL DO.
OH!
HE'S TURNED INTO THAT WHITE BUILDING I WAS PAINTING.
AHHH.
IT IS SAD I DID NOT BRING MY MASKS. THEY ARE PERFECT DISTRACTION.
THE MAN WOULD MAKE PISS TO HIMSELF!
OOUINN
THEY ARE QUITE BRUTAL, THOSE MASKS.
HAVE YOU BEEN TO AFRICA THEN?
NO! ONLY I NEED TO GO TO FRANCE AND SPAIN THE REST IS SHIT.
I BUY MASK FROM SHOP ON RUE L'AVARGNE.
YOUR PAINTING OF THE WHORES OF AVIGNON LOOK QUITE LIKE THOSE MASKS.
DO I DETECT SOME SORT OF UNDERLYING PERVERSION?-
HAH! ¡MARICON!
JOU HAVES FOUND MY SECRET!
THE ONLY WAY TO MAKE THE FUCK TO THE LADIES IS WITH MASK ON HER FACE!
...JOU GRAB TO HIM THE ARMS. I PONCH TO HIM MANY TIMES IN STOMACH AND FACE.
IMPORTS EXOTIQUES, SA.
I HAVE A BETTER IDEA...
I WILL DISTRACT HIM. THEN YOU ENTER THE WAREHOUSE AND STEAL HIS LEDGER AND ADRESS BOOK.
WHAT IS LEDGER?
ALRIGHT, YOU DISTRACT HIM AND I WILL SEARCH FOR THE LEDGER.
I AM VERY GOOD TO DISTRACT THINGS.
I HAVE MANY TALENT. JOU CAN SEE THIS SOON.
JUST GET HIM OUT OF THERE.
EXCUSE.
YES.
I AM FROM UNITED STATES, A COWBOY ON HOLIDAY.
I HAVE PICTURES OF CHEROKEE LADIES VERY NAKED. I NEED TO SELL QUICK.
I LIKE TOO MUCH THE CASINOS.
NAKED CHEROKEES?
JES!
THEY HAVES THE BEHINDS SO PLUMP!
LIKE SEXY MOUNTAINS!
SEXY MOUNTAINS?!
AY, HOW HOT ARE THE PICTURES!
COME, I SHOW TO JOU IN HOTEL...

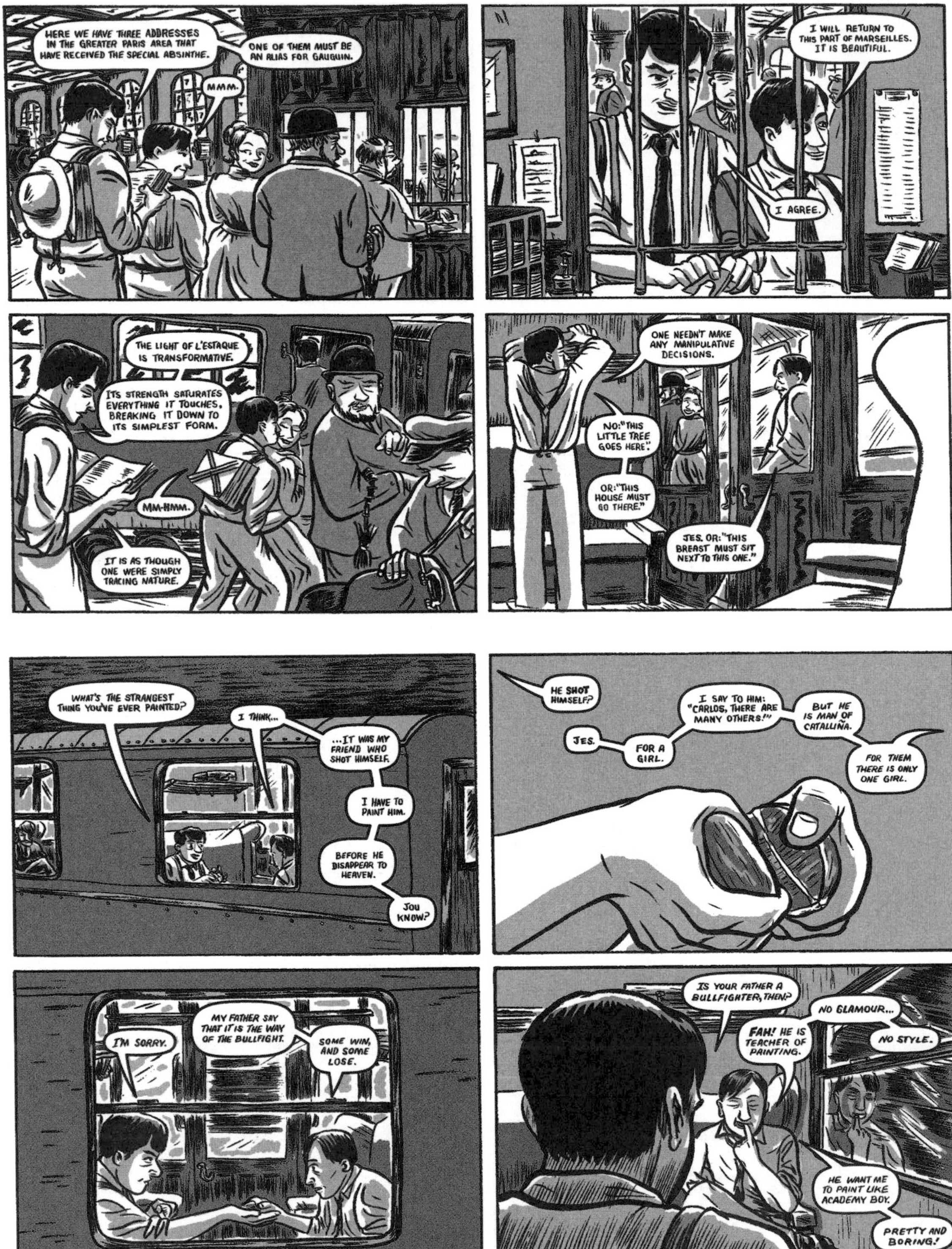
HERE WE HAVE THREE ADDRESSES IN THE GREATER PARIS AREA THAT HAVE RECEIVED THE SPECIAL ABSINTHE.
ONE OF THEM MUST BE AN ALIAS FOR GAUGUIN.
MMM.
I WILL RETURN TO THIS PART OF MARSEILLES. IT IS BEAUTIFUL.
I AGREE.
THE LIGHT OF L'ESTAQUE IS TRANSFORMATIVE.
ITS STRENGTH SATURATES EVERYTHING IT TOUCHES, BREAKING IT DOWN TO ITS SIMPLEST FORM.
MM-HMM.
IT IS AS THOUGH ONE WERE SIMPLY TRACING NATURE.
ONE NEEDN'T MAKE ANY MANIPULATIVE DECISIONS.
NO: "THIS LITTLE TREE GOES HERE".
OR: "THIS HOUSE MUST GO THERE."
JES. OR: "THIS BREAST MUST SIT NEXT TO THIS ONE."
WHAT'S THE STRANGEST THING YOU'VE EVER PAINTED?
I THINK...
...IT WAS MY FRIEND WHO SHOT HIMSELF.
I HAVE TO PAINT HIM.
BEFORE HE DISAPPEAR TO HEAVEN.
JOU KNOW?
HE SHOT HIMSELF?
JES.
FOR A GIRL.
I SAY TO HIM: "CARLOS, THERE ARE MANY OTHERS!"
BUT HE IS MAN OF CATALLIÑA.
FOR THEM THERE IS ONLY ONE GIRL.
I'M SORRY.
MY FATHER SAY THAT IT IS THE WAY OF THE BULLFIGHT.
SOME WIN, AND SOME LOSE.
IS YOUR FATHER A BULLFIGHTER, THEN?
FAH! HE IS TEACHER OF PAINTING.
NO GLAMOUR...
NO STYLE.
HE WANT ME TO PAINT LIKE ACADEMY BOY.
PRETTY AND BORING!

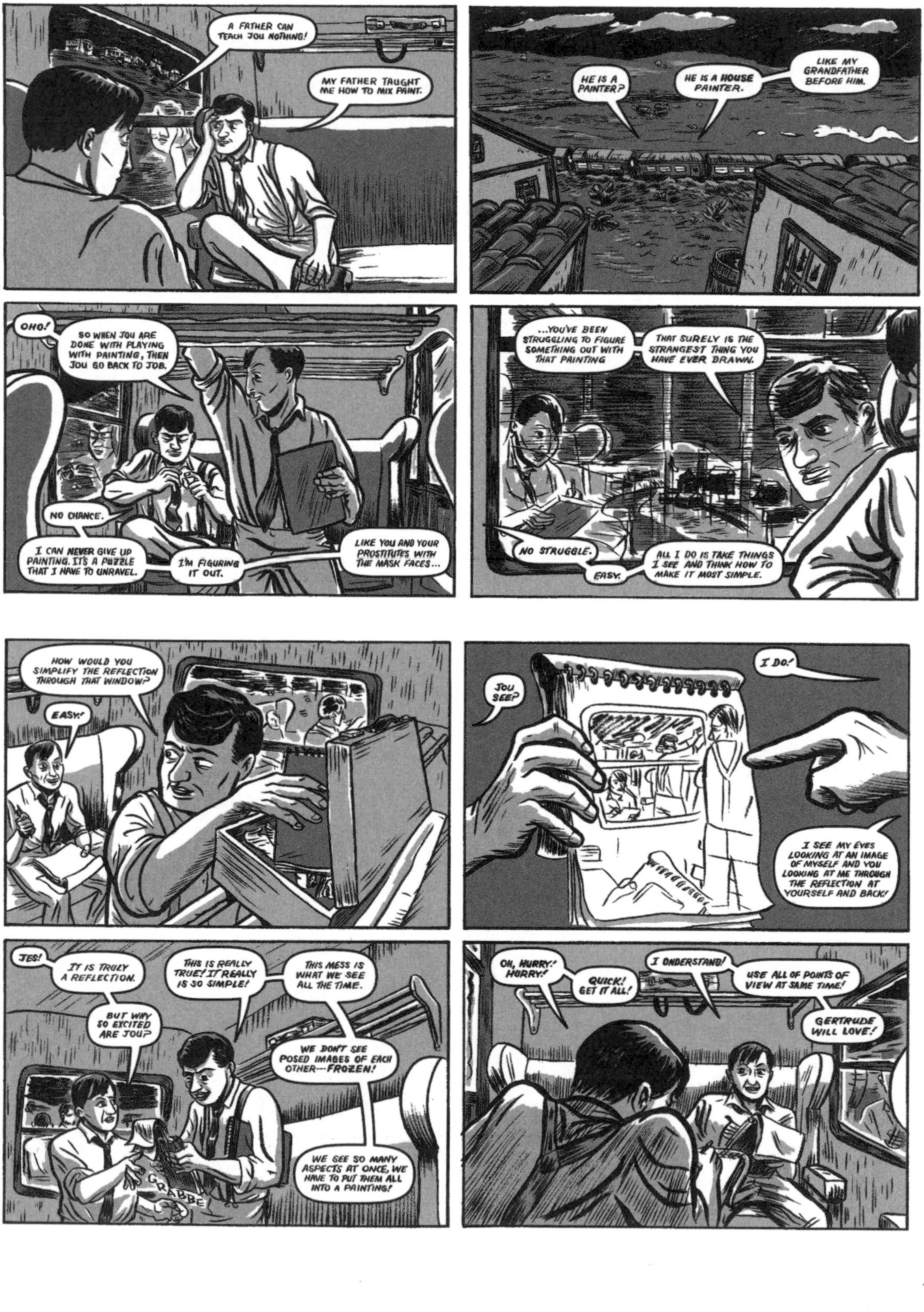
A FATHER CAN TEACH JOU NOTHING!
MY FATHER TAUGHT ME HOW TO MIX PAINT.
HE IS A PAINTER?
HE IS A HOUSE PAINTER.
LIKE MY GRANDFATHER BEFORE HIM.
OHO!
SO WHEN JOU ARE DONE WITH PLAYING WITH PAINTING, THEN JOU GO BACK TO JOB.
NO CHANCE.
I CAN NEVER GIVE UP PAINTING. IT'S A PUZZLE THAT I HAVE TO UNRAVEL.
I'M FIGURING IT OUT.
LIKE YOU AND YOUR PROSTITUTES WITH THE MASK FACES...
...YOU'VE BEEN STRUGGLING TO FIGURE SOMETHING OUT WITH THAT PAINTING
THAT SURELY IS THE STRANGEST THING YOU HAVE EVER DRAWN.
NO STRUGGLE.
EASY.
ALL I DO IS TAKE THINGS I SEE AND THINK HOW TO MAKE IT MOST SIMPLE.
HOW WOULD YOU SIMPLIFY THE REFLECTION THROUGH THAT WINDOW?
EASY!
JOU SEE?
I DO!
I SEE MY EYES LOOKING AT AN IMAGE OF MYSELF AND YOU LOOKING AT ME THROUGH THE REFLECTION AT YOURSELF AND BACK!
JES!
IT IS TRULY A REFLECTION.
BUT WHY SO EXCITED ARE JOU?
THIS IS REALLY TRUE! IT REALLY IS SO SIMPLE!
THIS MESS IS WHAT WE SEE ALL THE TIME.
WE DON'T SEE POSED IMAGES OF EACH OTHER---FROZEN!
WE SEE SO MANY ASPECTS AT ONCE, WE HAVE TO PUT THEM ALL INTO A PAINTING!
GRABBE
OH, HURRY! HURRY!
QUICK! GET IT ALL!
I UNDERSTAND!
USE ALL OF POINTS OF VIEW AT SAME TIME!
GERTRUDE WILL LOVE!

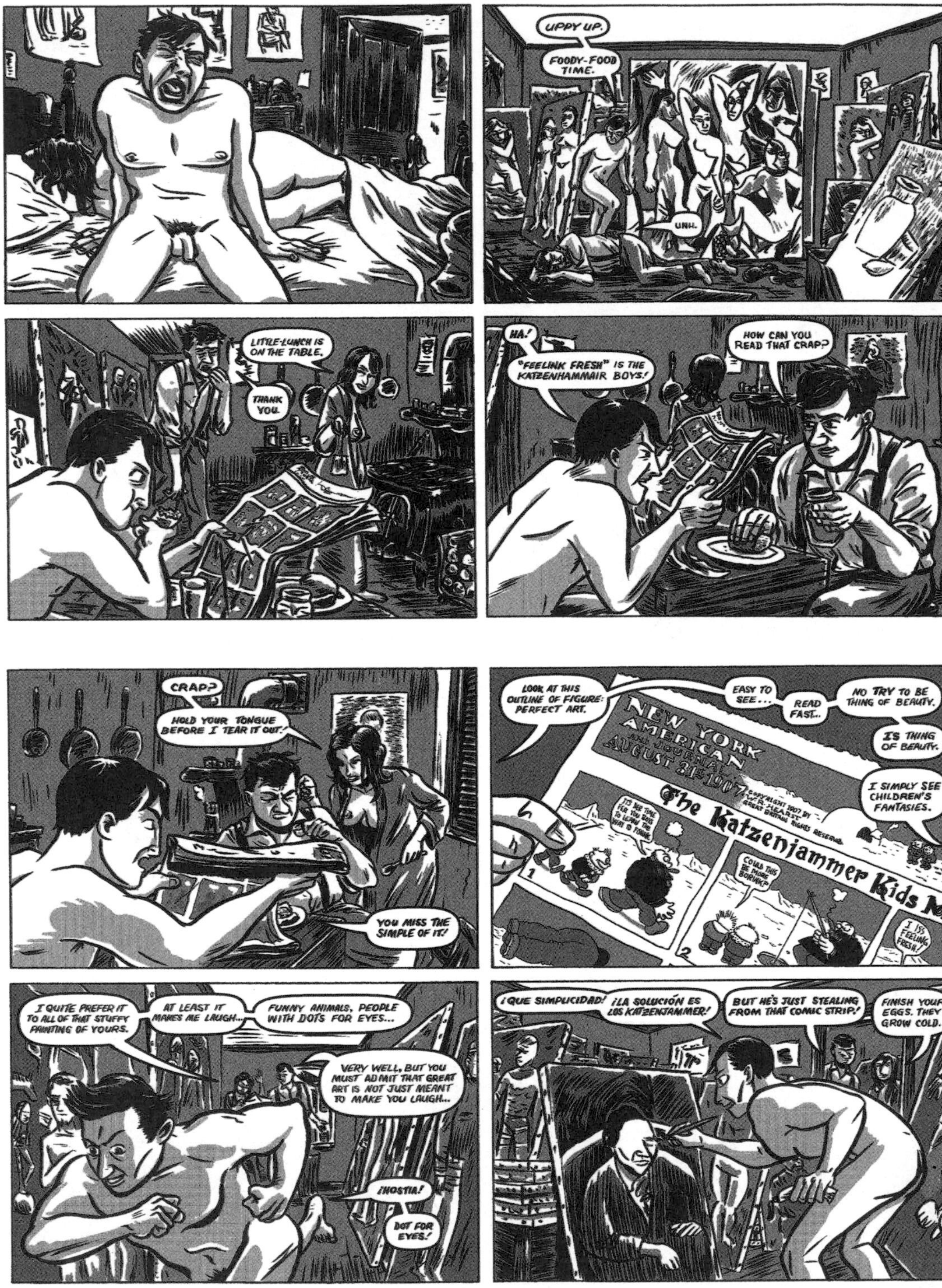
UPPY UP.
FOODY-FOOD TIME.
UNH.
LITTLE-LUNCH IS ON THE TABLE.
THANK YOU.
HA!
"FEELINK FRESH" IS THE KATZENHAMMAIR BOYS!
HOW CAN YOU READ THAT CRAP?
CRAP?
HOLD YOUR TONGUE BEFORE I TEAR IT OUT!
YOU MISS THE SIMPLE OF IT!
LOOK AT THIS OUTLINE OF FIGURE: PERFECT ART.
EASY TO SEE...
READ FAST...
NO TRY TO BE THING OF BEAUTY.
IS THING OF BEAUTY.
I SIMPLY SEE CHILDREN'S FANTASIES.
NEW YORK AMERICAN AND JOURNAL AUGUST 31ST 1907
COPYRIGHT 1907 BY W.R. HEARST GREAT BRITAIN RIGHTS RESERVED
The Katzenjammer Kids Me
COULD THIS BE MORE BORINK?
I ISS FEELING FRESH!
I QUITE PREFER IT TO ALL OF THAT STUFFY PAINTING OF YOURS.
AT LEAST IT MAKES ME LAUGH...
FUNNY ANIMALS, PEOPLE WITH DOTS FOR EYES...
VERY WELL, BUT YOU MUST ADMIT THAT GREAT ART IS NOT JUST MEANT TO MAKE YOU LAUGH...
¡HOSTIA!
DOT FOR EYES!
¡QUE SIMPLICIDAD!
¡LA SOLUCIÓN ES LOS KATZENJAMMER!
BUT HE'S JUST STEALING FROM THAT COMIC STRIP!
FINISH YOUR EGGS. THEY GROW COLD.

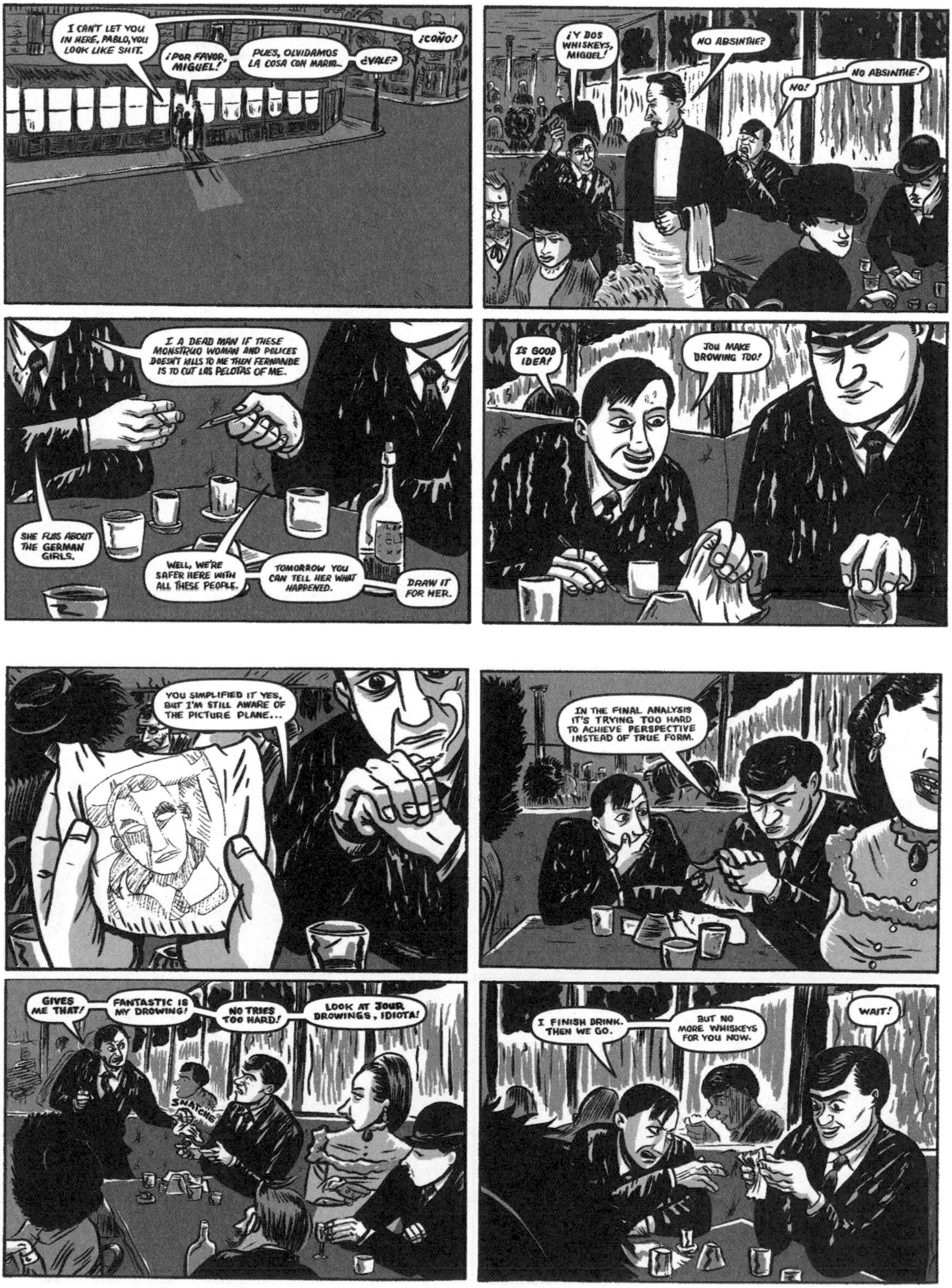
I CAN'T LET YOU IN HERE, PABLO, YOU LOOK LIKE SHIT.
¡POR FAVOR, MIGUEL!
PUES, OLVIDAMOS LA COSA CON MARIA...
¿VALE?
¡COÑO!
¡Y DOS WHISKEYS, MIGUEL!
NO ABSINTHE?
NO!
NO ABSINTHE!
I A DEAD MAN IF THESE MONSTRUO WOMAN AND POLICES DOESN'T KILLS TO ME THEN FERNANDE IS TO CUT LAS PELOTAS OF ME.
SHE FUSS ABOUT THE GERMAN GIRLS.
WELL, WE'RE SAFER HERE WITH ALL THESE PEOPLE.
TOMORROW YOU CAN TELL HER WHAT HAPPENED.
DRAW IT FOR HER.
IS GOOD IDEA!
JOU MAKE DROWING TOO!
YOU SIMPLIFIED IT YES, BUT I'M STILL AWARE OF THE PICTURE PLANE...
IN THE FINAL ANALYSIS IT'S TRYING TOO HARD TO ACHIEVE PERSPECTIVE INSTEAD OF TRUE FORM.
GIVES ME THAT!
FANTASTIC IS MY DROWING!
NO TRIES TOO HARD!
LOOK AT JOUR DROWINGS, IDIOTA!
SNATCH
I FINISH DRINK. THEN WE GO.
BUT NO MORE WHISKEYS FOR YOU NOW.
WAIT!

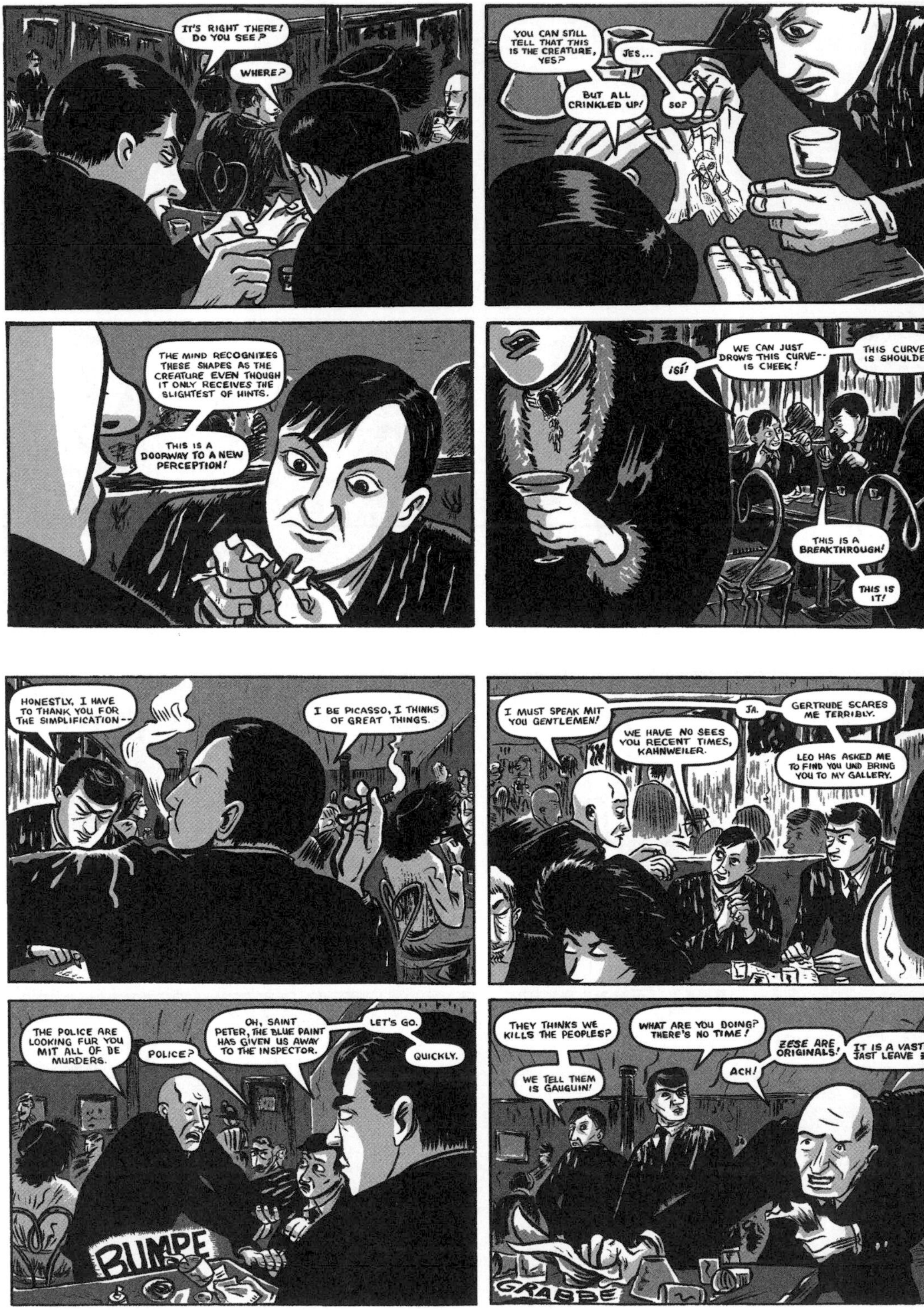
IT'S RIGHT THERE! DO YOU SEE?
WHERE?
YOU CAN STILL TELL THAT THIS IS THE CREATURE, YES?
JES...
BUT ALL CRINKLED UP!
SO?
THE MIND RECOGNIZES THESE SHAPES AS THE CREATURE EVEN THOUGH IT ONLY RECEIVES THE SLIGHTEST OF HINTS.
THIS IS A DOORWAY TO A NEW PERCEPTION!
¡SÍ!
WE CAN JUST DROWS THIS CURVE-- IS CHEEK!
THIS CURVE-- IS SHOULDER!
THIS IS A BREAKTHROUGH!
THIS IS IT!
HONESTLY, I HAVE TO THANK YOU FOR THE SIMPLIFICATION--
I BE PICASSO, I THINKS OF GREAT THINGS.
I MUST SPEAK MIT YOU GENTLEMEN!
JA.
GERTRUDE SCARES ME TERRIBLY.
WE HAVE NO SEES YOU RECENT TIMES, KAHNWEILER.
LEO HAS ASKED ME TO FIND YOU UND BRING YOU TO MY GALLERY.
THE POLICE ARE LOOKING FUR YOU MIT ALL OF BE MURDERS.
POLICE?
OH, SAINT PETER, THE BLUE PAINT HAS GIVEN US AWAY TO THE INSPECTOR.
LET'S GO.
QUICKLY.
BUMPE
THEY THINKS WE KILLS THE PEOPLES?
WE TELL THEM IS GAUGUIN!
WHAT ARE YOU DOING? THERE'S NO TIME!
ACH!
ZESE ARE ORIGINALS!
IT IS A VASTE TO JAST LEAVE ZEM!
GRABBE

The Thing About Madeline

by Lilli Carré

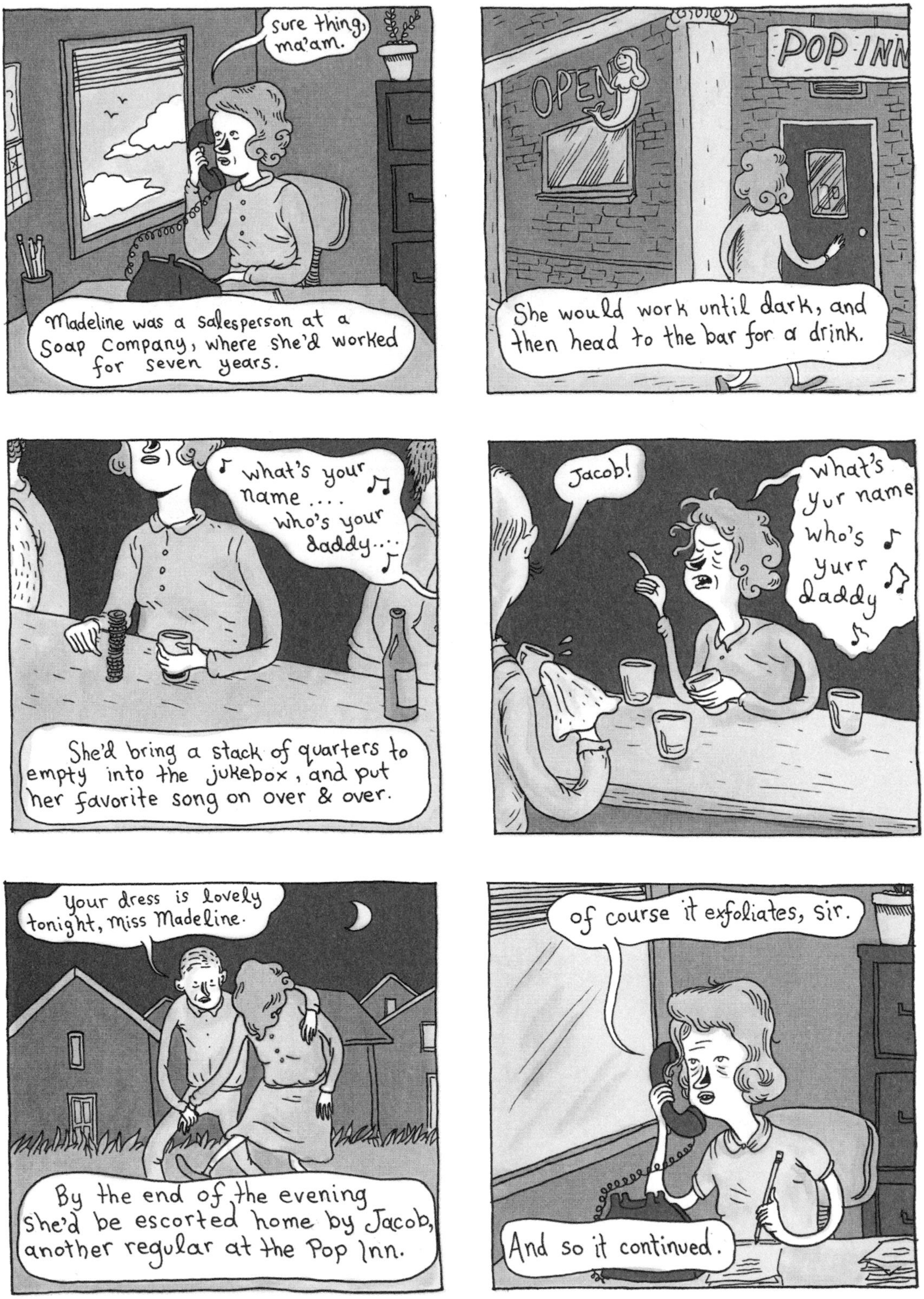
sure thing, ma'am.
Madeline was a salesperson at a Soap Company, where she'd worked for seven years.
OPEN
POP INN
She would work until dark, and then head to the bar for a drink.
what's your name .... who's your daddy....
She'd bring a stack of quarters to empty into the jukebox, and put her favorite song on over & over.
Jacob!
what's yur name who's yurr daddy
Your dress is lovely tonight, miss Madeline.
By the end of the evening she'd be escorted home by Jacob, another regular at the Pop Inn.
of course it exfoliates, sir.
And so it continued.

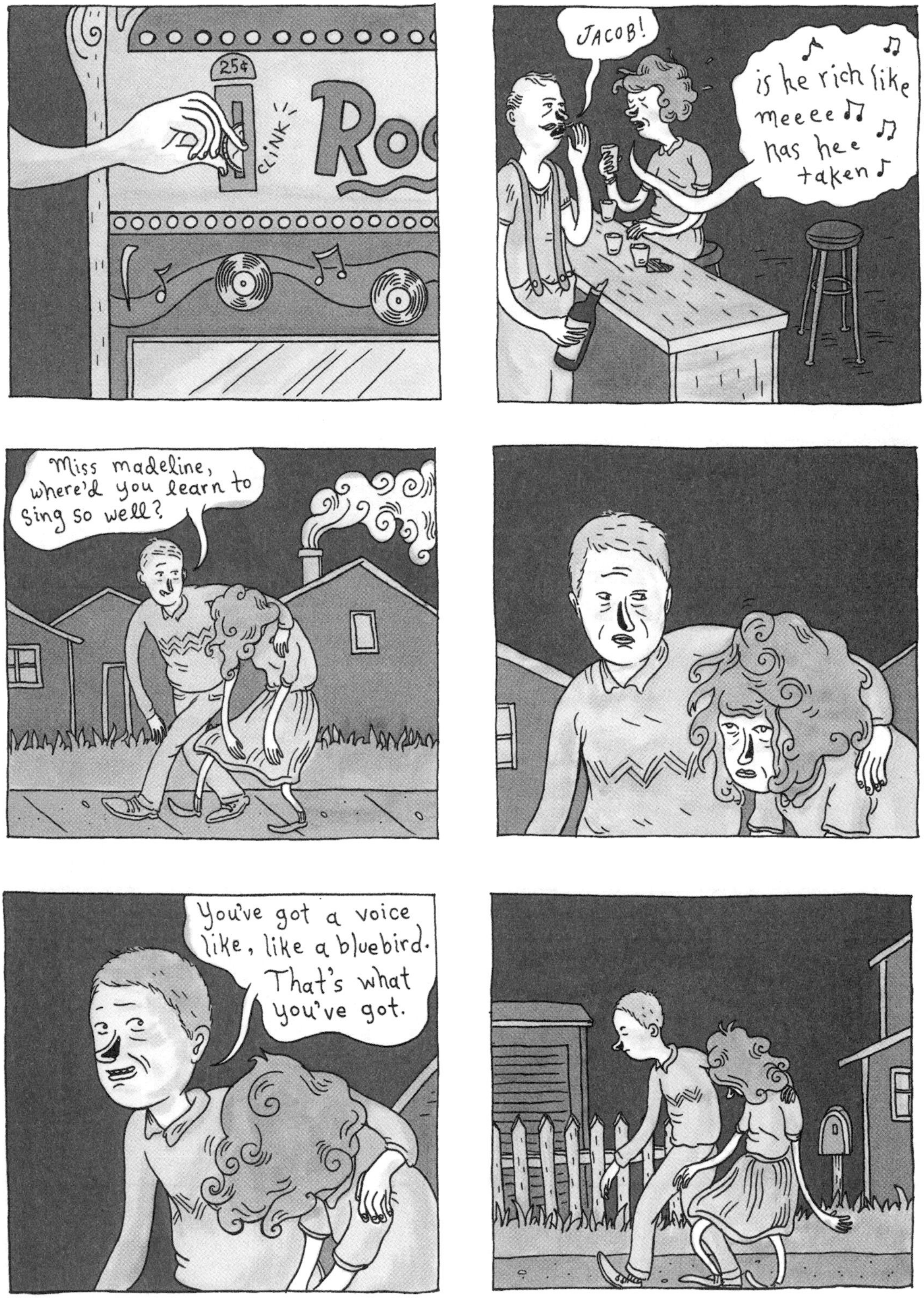
25¢
CLINK
Roc
JACOB!
is he rich like meeee has hee taken
Miss madeline, where'd you learn to sing so well?
You've got a voice like, like a bluebird. That's what you've got.

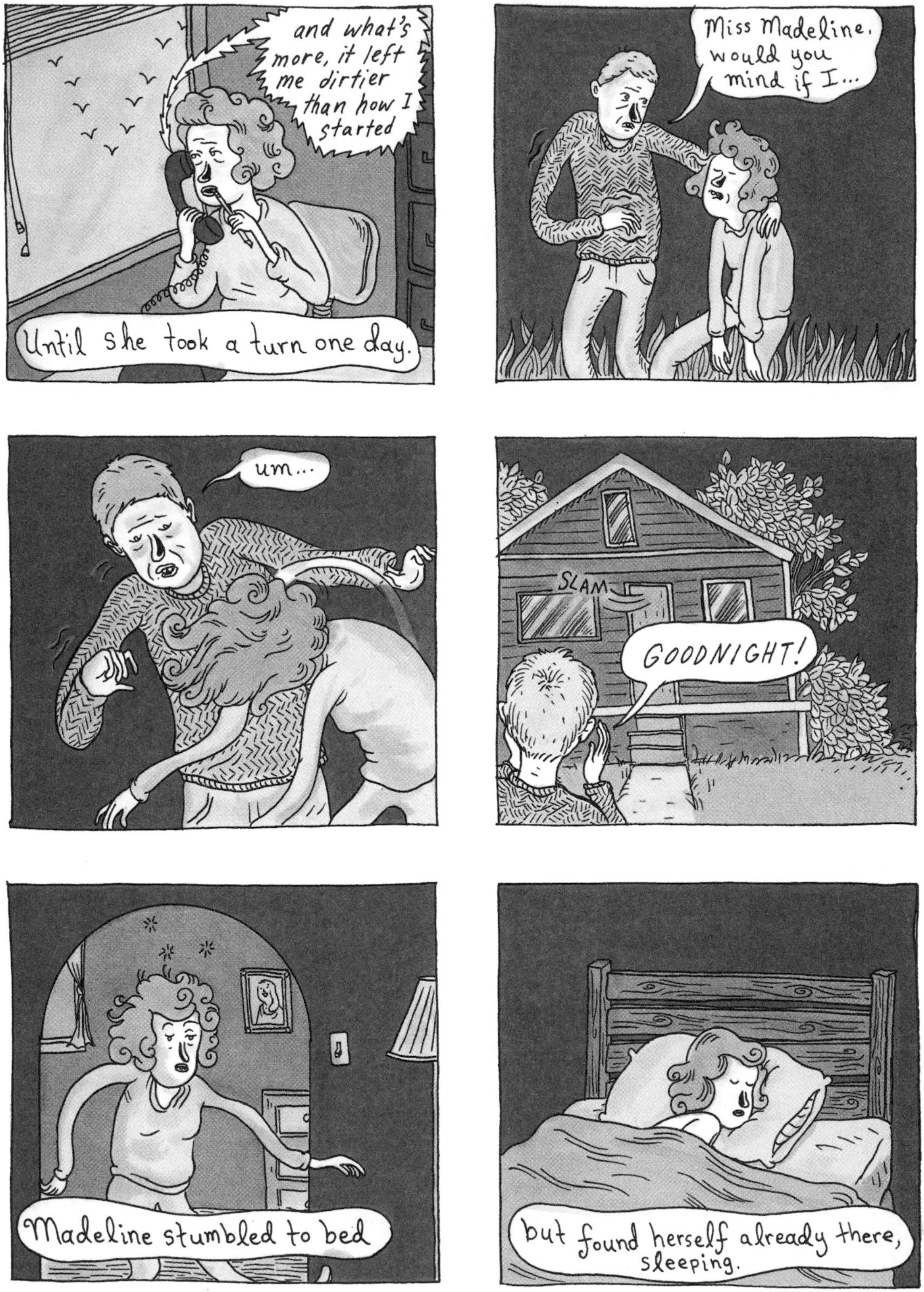
and what's more, it left me dirtier than how I started
Until she took a turn one day.
Miss Madeline, would you mind if I...
um...
SLAM
GOODNIGHT!
Madeline stumbled to bed
but found herself already there, sleeping.

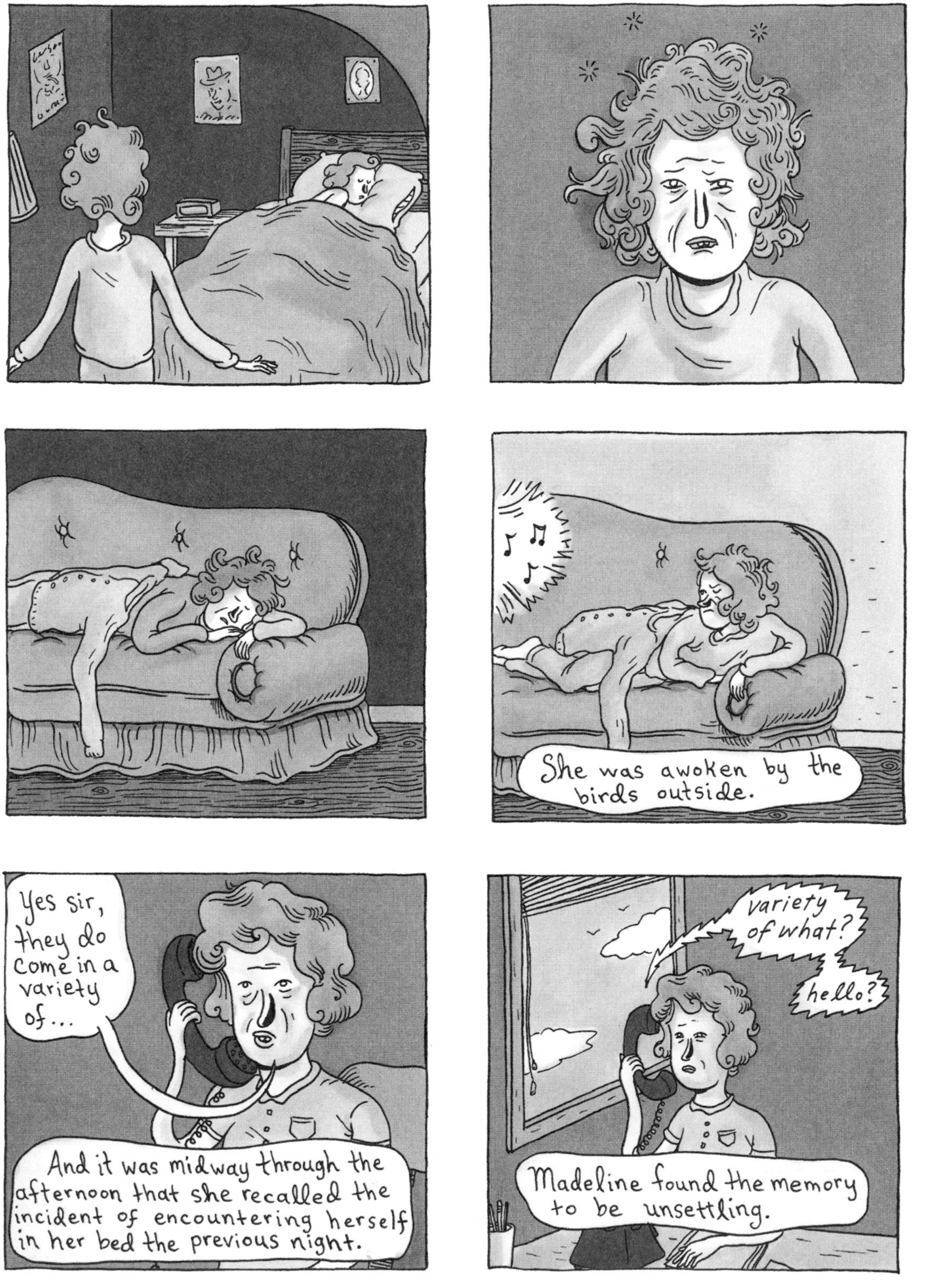
She was awoken by the birds outside.
Yes sir, they do come in a variety of...
And it was midway through the afternoon that she recalled the incident of encountering herself in her bed the previous night.
variety of what?
hello?
Madeline found the memory to be unsettling.

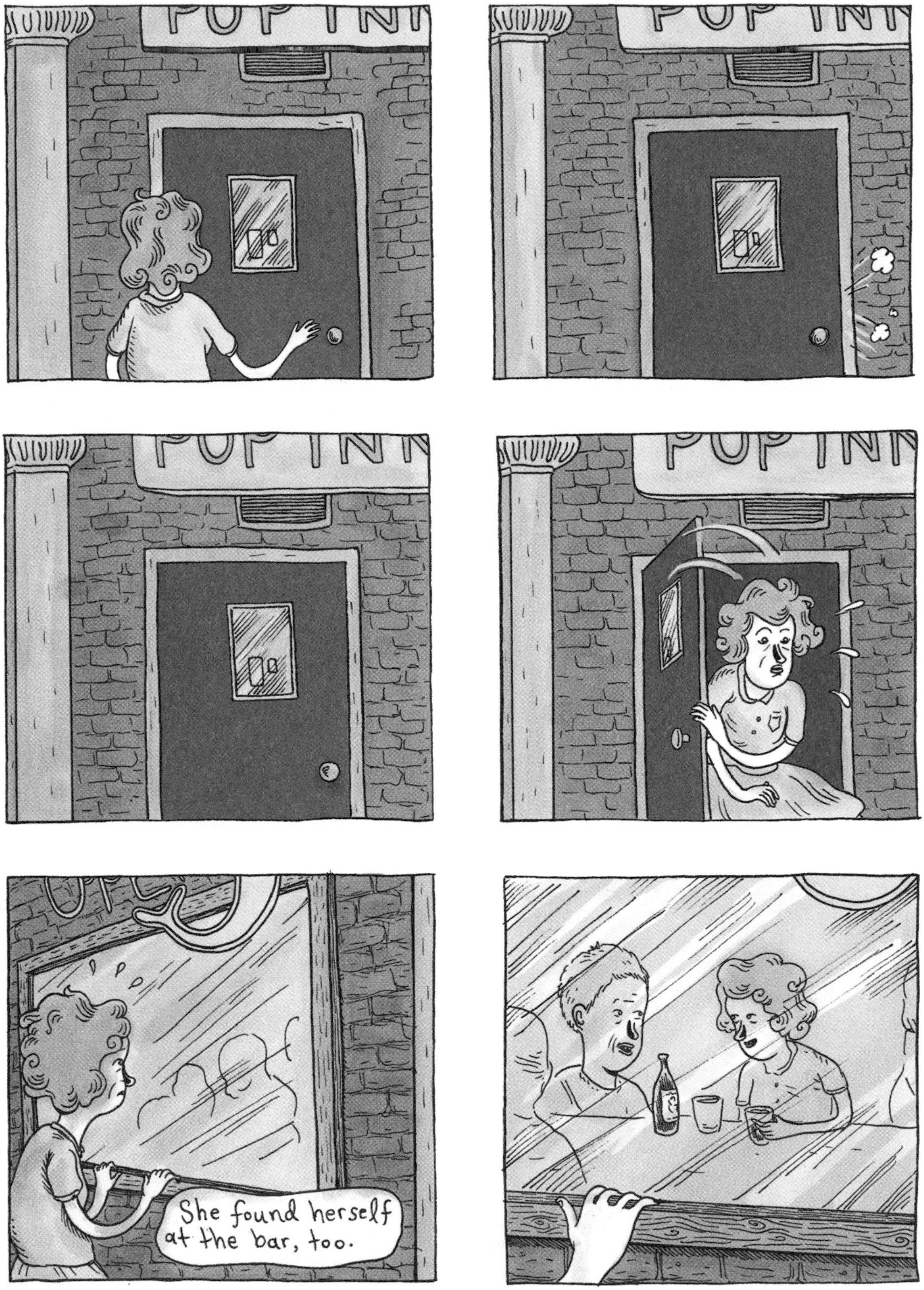
POP INN
She found herself at the bar, too.

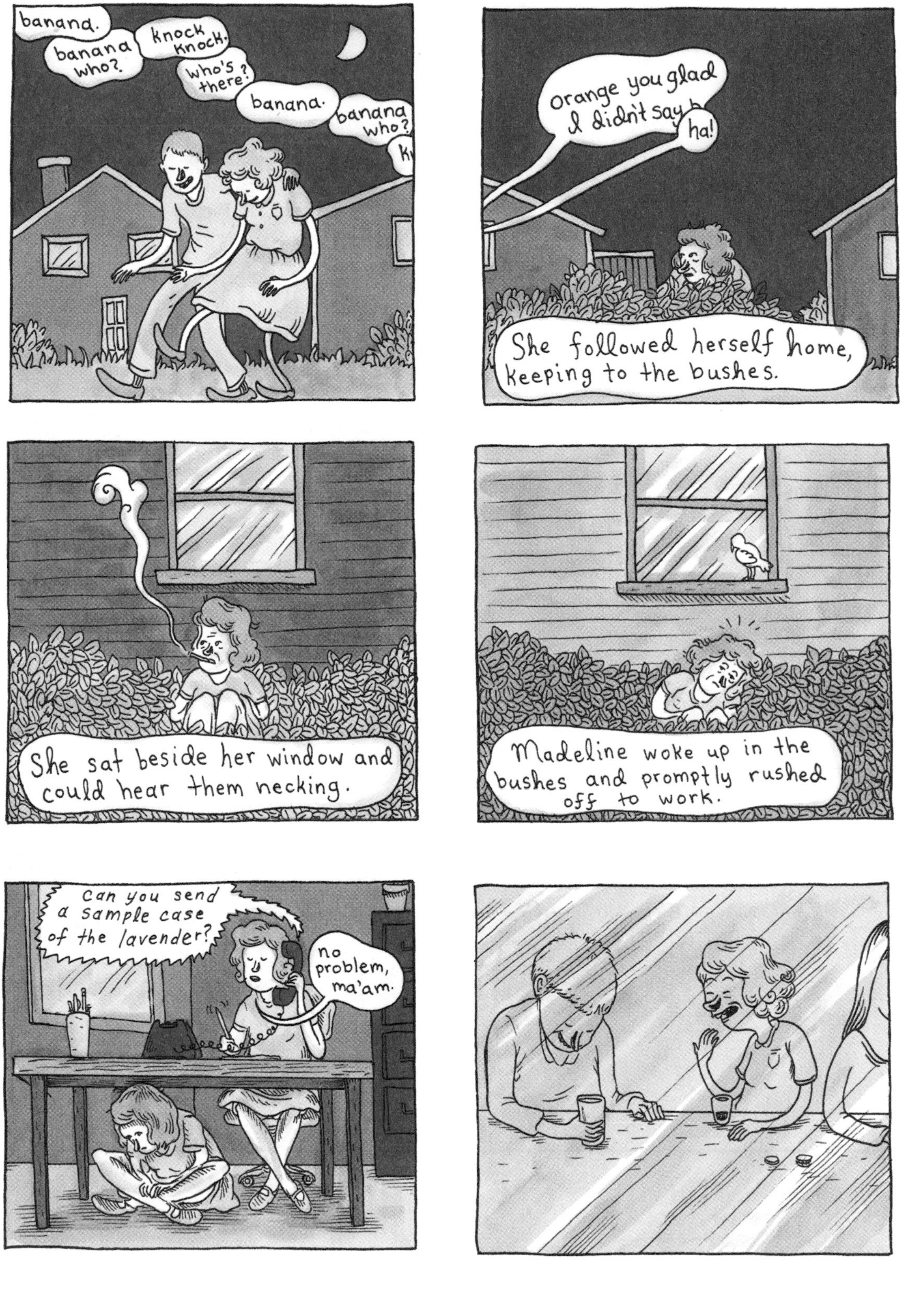
banana.
banana who?.
knock knock.
who's there?
banana.
banana who?.
Orange you glad I didn't say b
ha!
She followed herself home, keeping to the bushes.
She sat beside her window and could hear them necking.
Madeline woke up in the bushes and promptly rushed off to work.
can you send a sample case of the lavender?
no problem, ma'am.

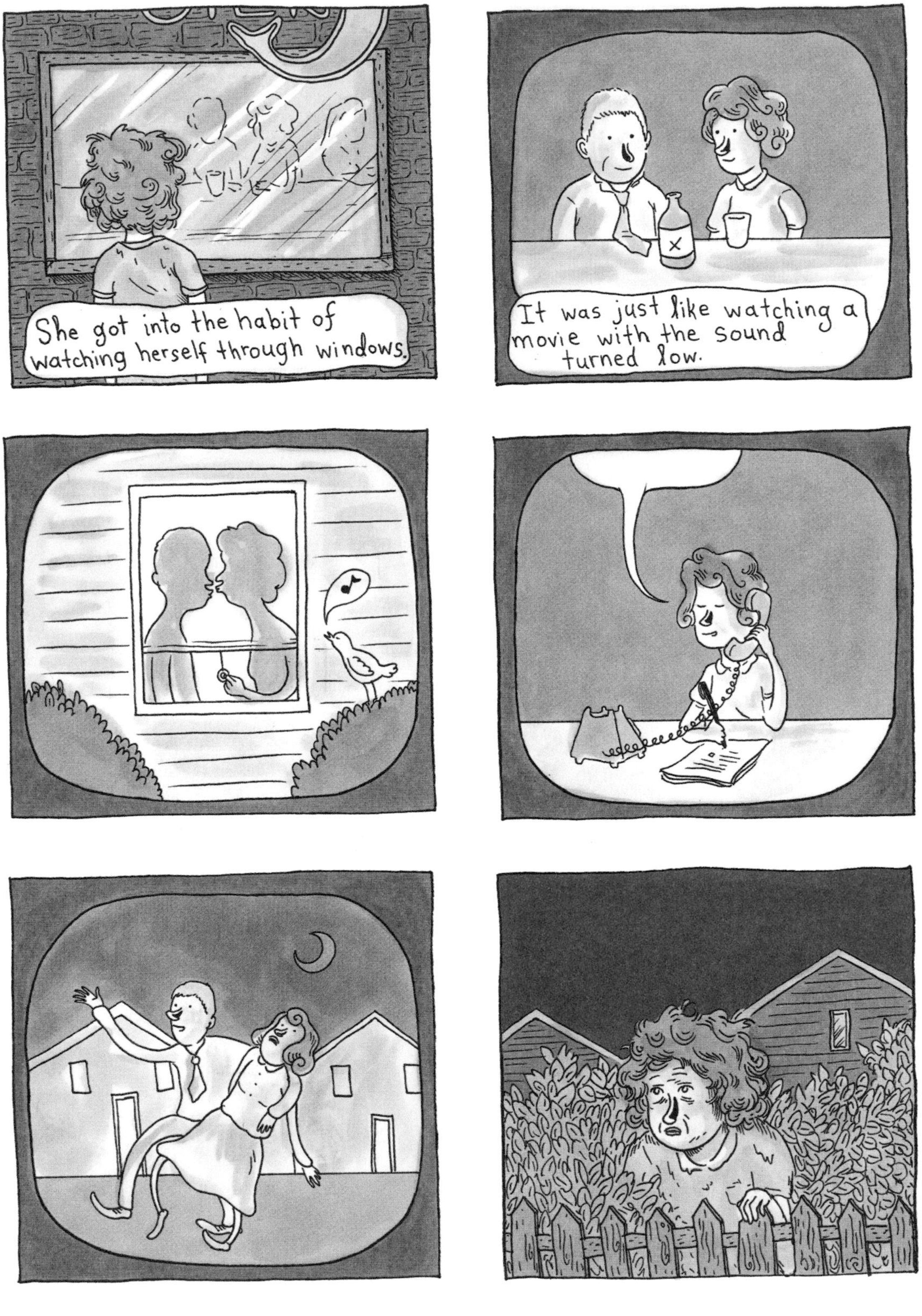
She got into the habit of watching herself through windows.
It was just like watching a movie with the sound turned low.

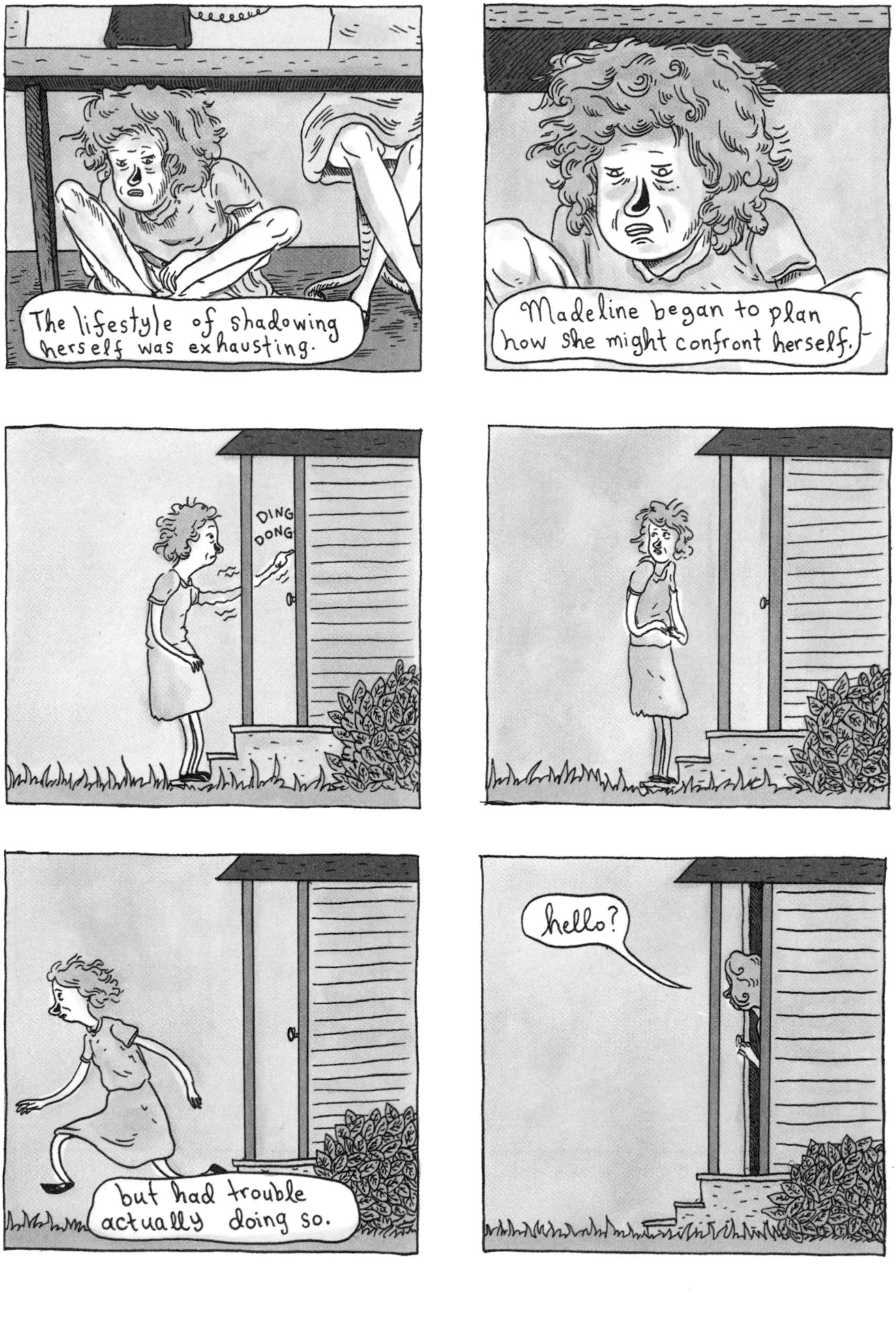
The lifestyle of shadowing herself was exhausting.
Madeline began to plan how she might confront herself.
DING DONG
but had trouble actually doing so.
hello?

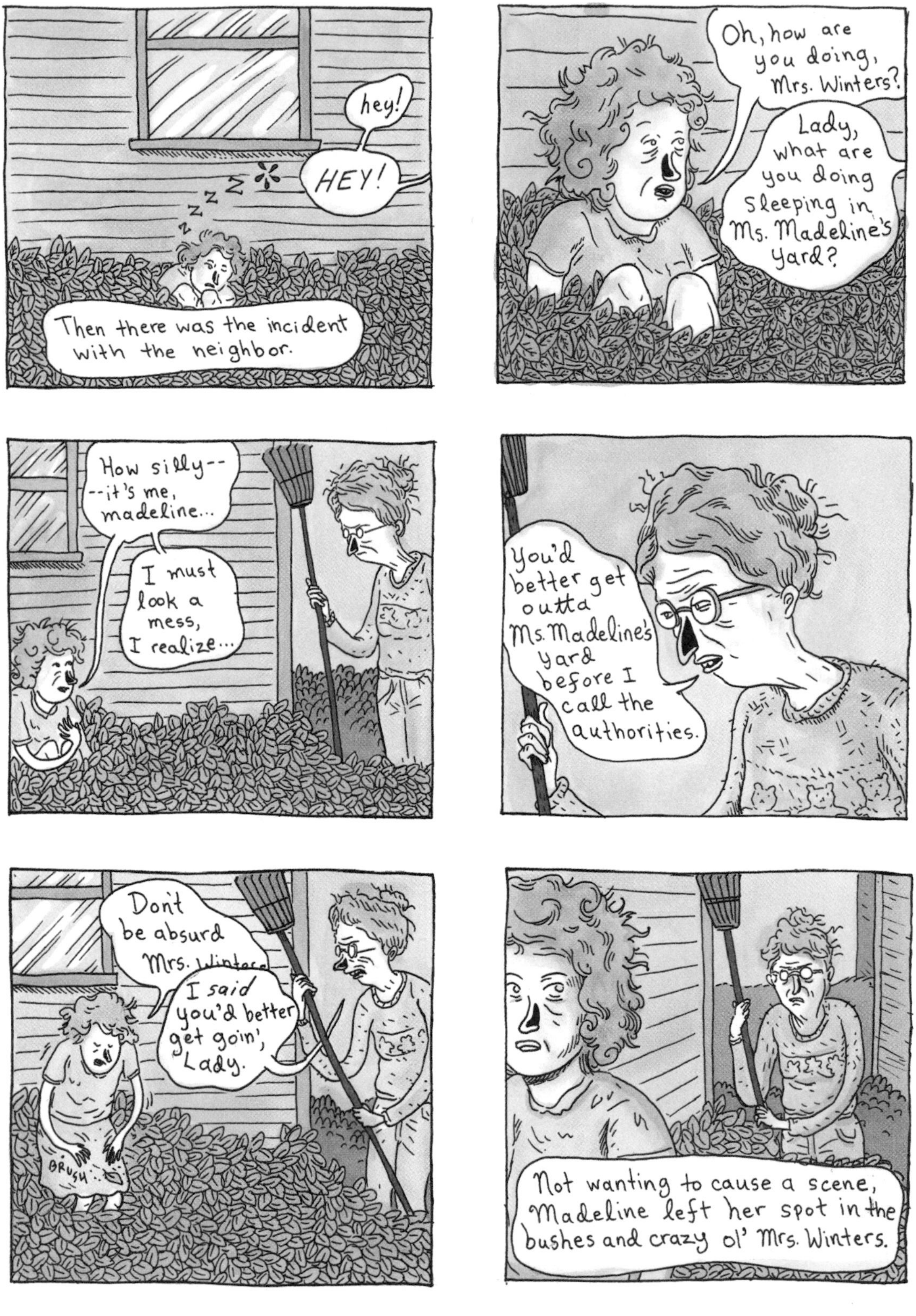

hey!
HEY!
Then there was the incident with the neighbor.
Oh, how are you doing, Mrs. Winters?
Lady, what are you doing sleeping in Ms. Madeline's yard?
How silly-- --it's me, madeline...
I must look a mess, I realize...
You'd better get outta Ms. Madeline's yard before I call the authorities.
Don't be absurd Mrs.
I said you'd better get goin', Lady.
BRUSH
Not wanting to cause a scene, Madeline left her spot in the bushes and crazy ol' Mrs. Winters.

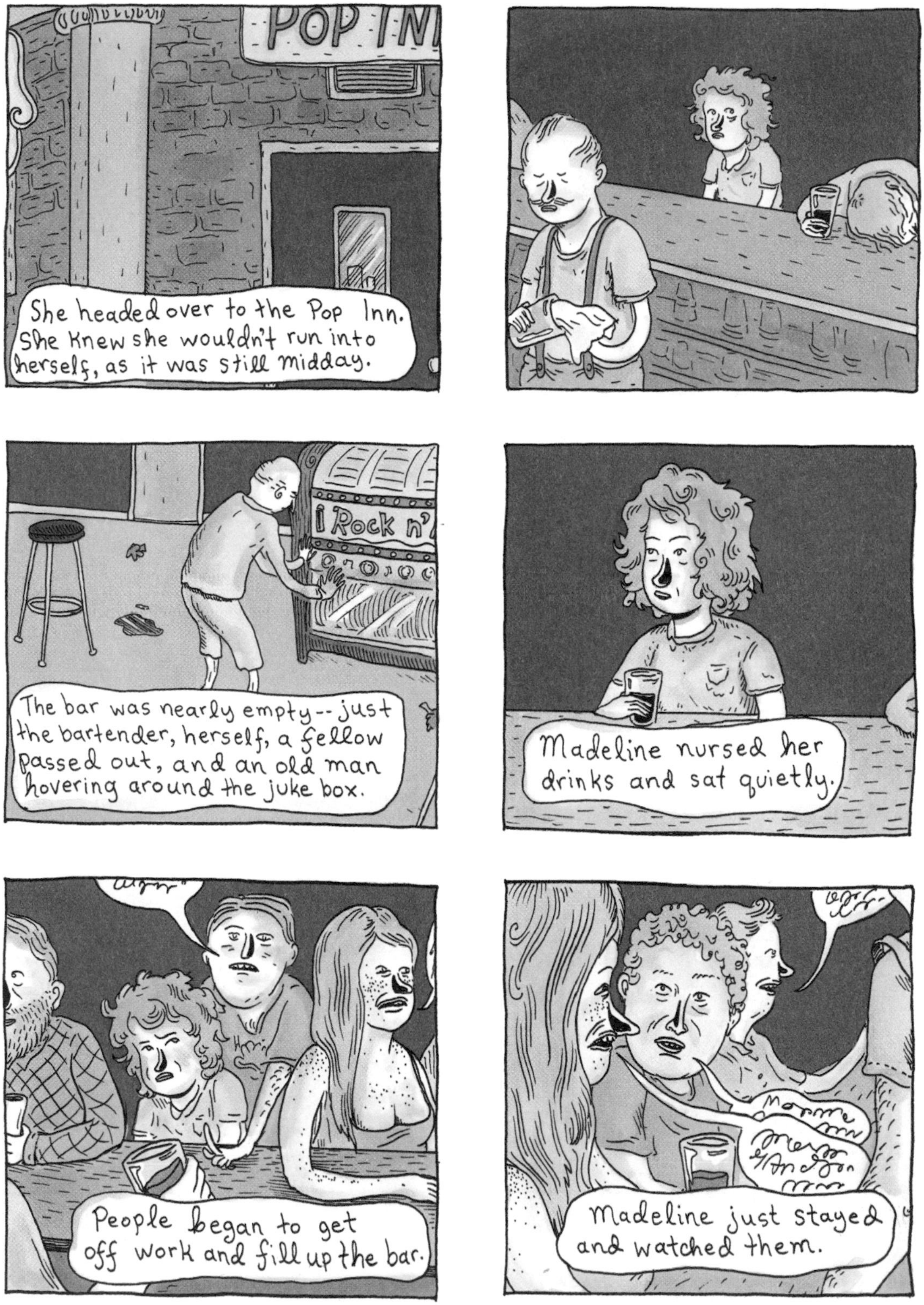
She headed over to the Pop Inn. She knew she wouldn't run into herself, as it was still midday.
The bar was nearly empty -- just the bartender, herself, a fellow passed out, and an old man hovering around the juke box.
Madeline nursed her drinks and sat quietly.
People began to get off work and fill up the bar.
Madeline just stayed and watched them.

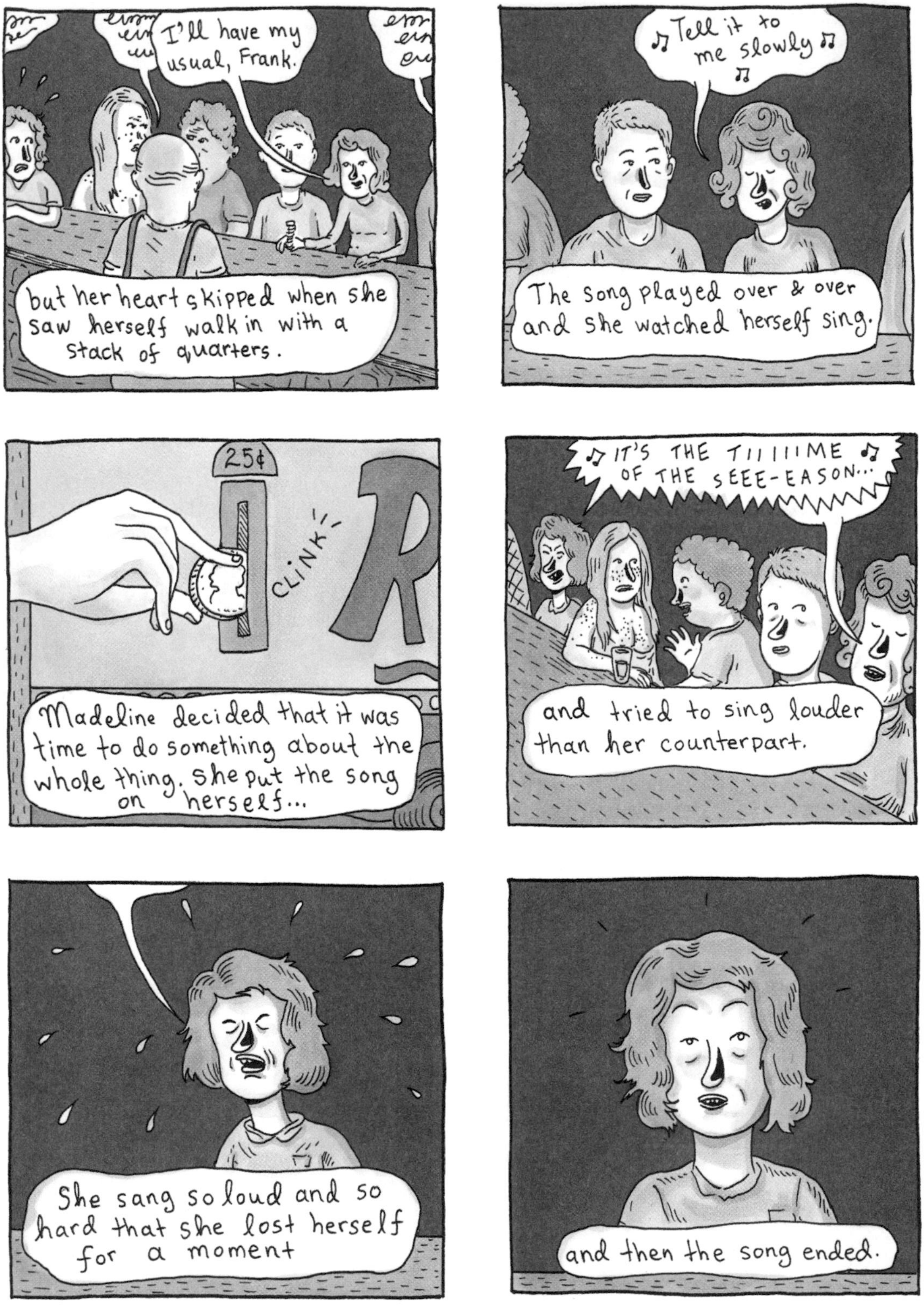
I'll have my usual, Frank.
but her heart skipped when she saw herself walk in with a stack of quarters.
♫ Tell it to me slowly ♫ ♫
The song played over & over and she watched herself sing.
25¢
CLINK
Madeline decided that it was time to do something about the whole thing. She put the song on herself...
♫ IT'S THE TIIIIIME ♫ OF THE SEEE-EASON...
and tried to sing louder than her counterpart.
She sang so loud and so hard that she lost herself for a moment
and then the song ended.

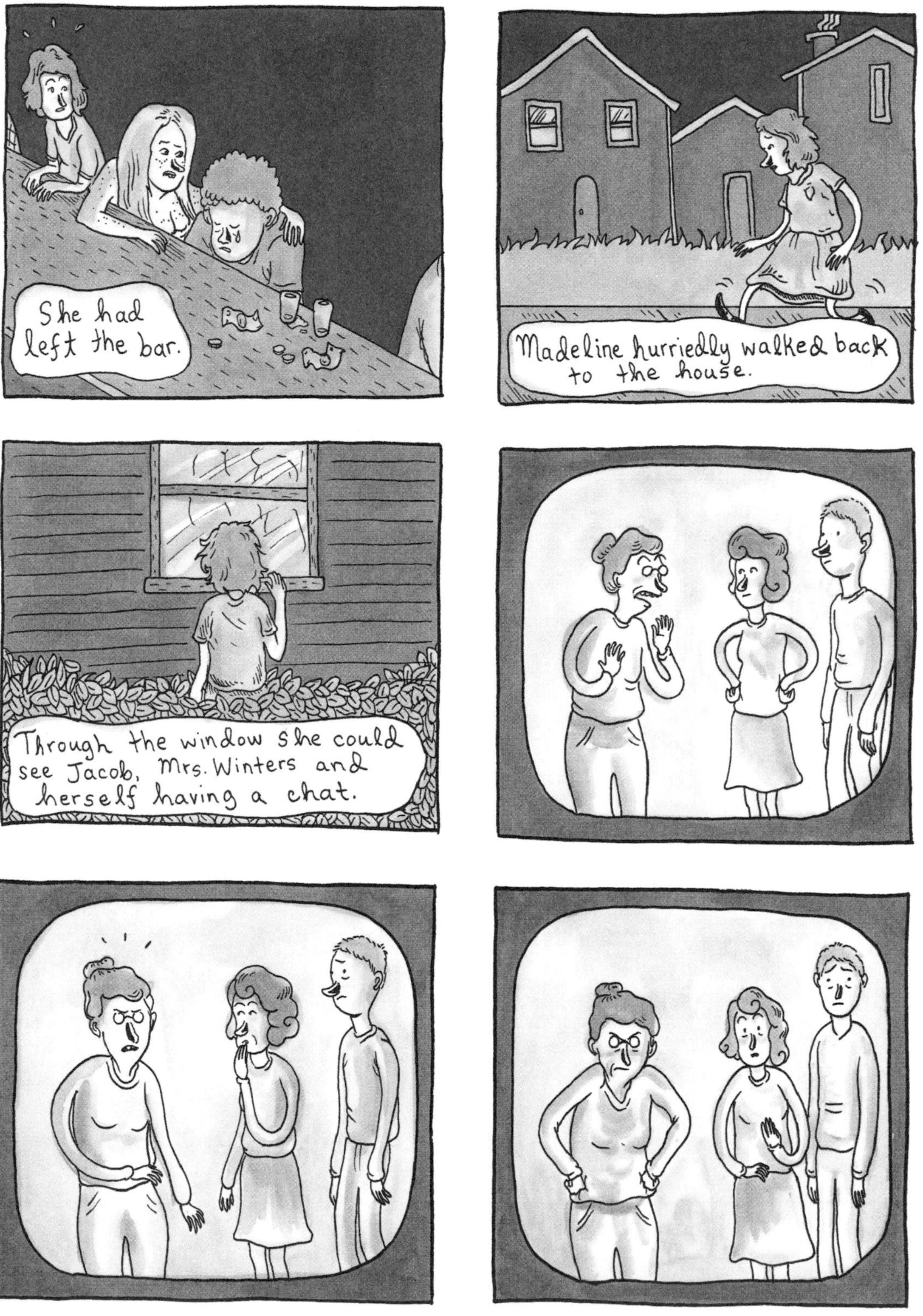
She had left the bar.
Madeline hurriedly walked back to the house.
Through the window she could see Jacob, Mrs. Winters and herself having a chat.

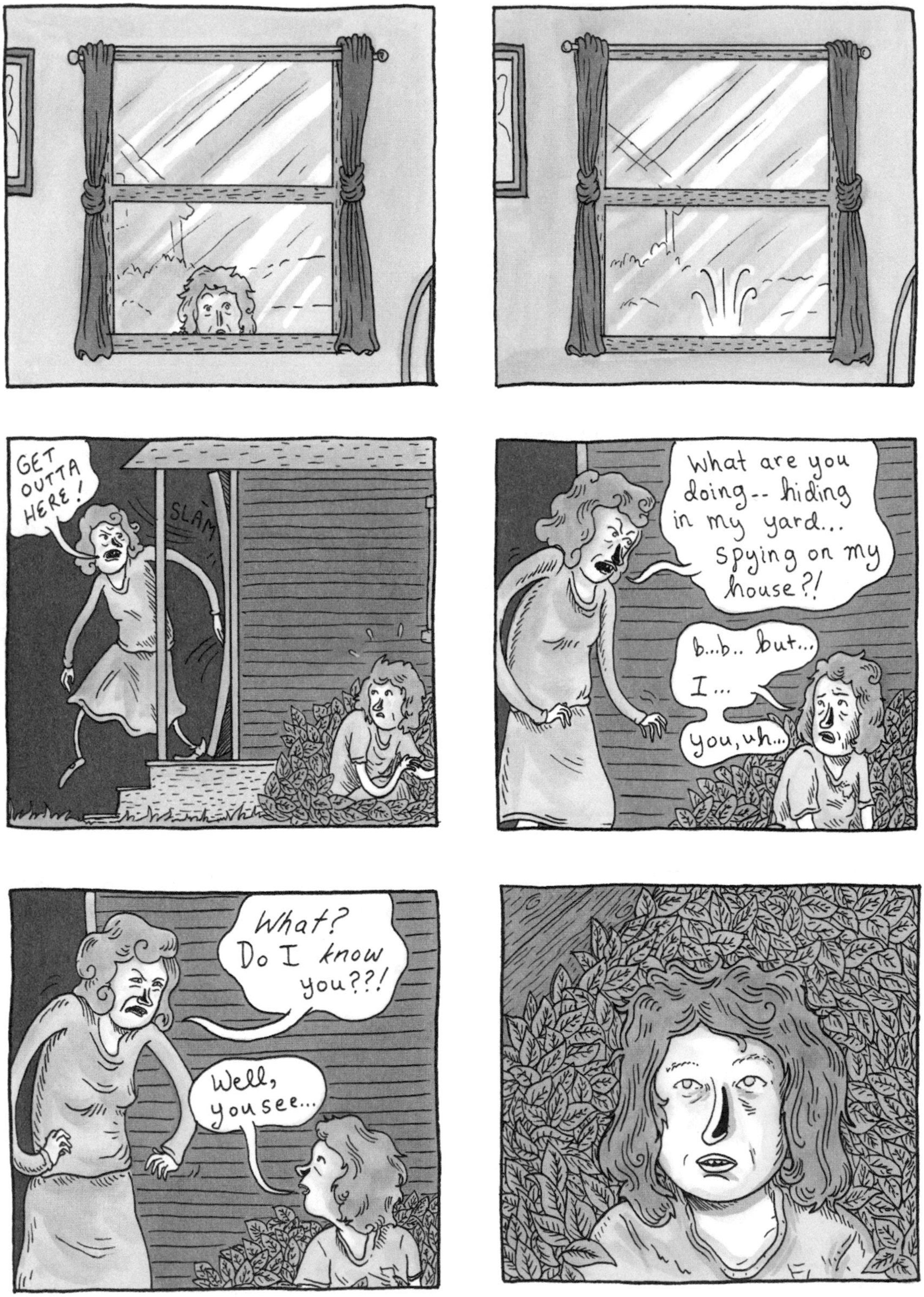
GET OUTTA HERE!
SLAM
What are you doing-- hiding in my yard... spying on my house?!
b...b.. but...
I...
you, uh...
What? Do I know you??!
Well, you see...

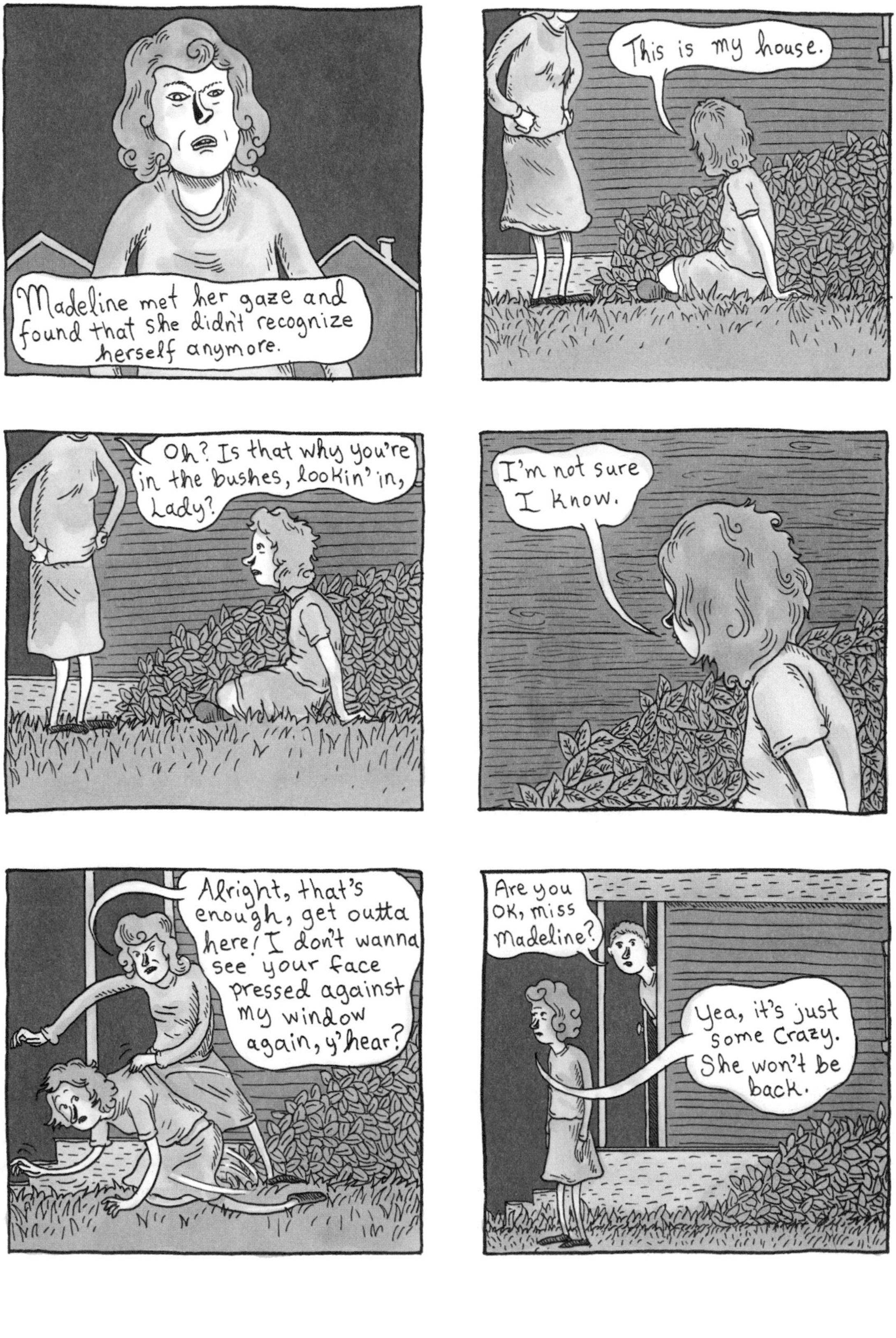
Madeline met her gaze and found that she didn't recognize herself anymore.
This is my house.
Oh? Is that why you're in the bushes, lookin' in, Lady?
I'm not sure I know.
Alright, that's enough, get outta here! I don't wanna see your face pressed against my window again, y'hear?
Are you OK, miss Madeline?
Yea, it's just some Crazy. She won't be back.

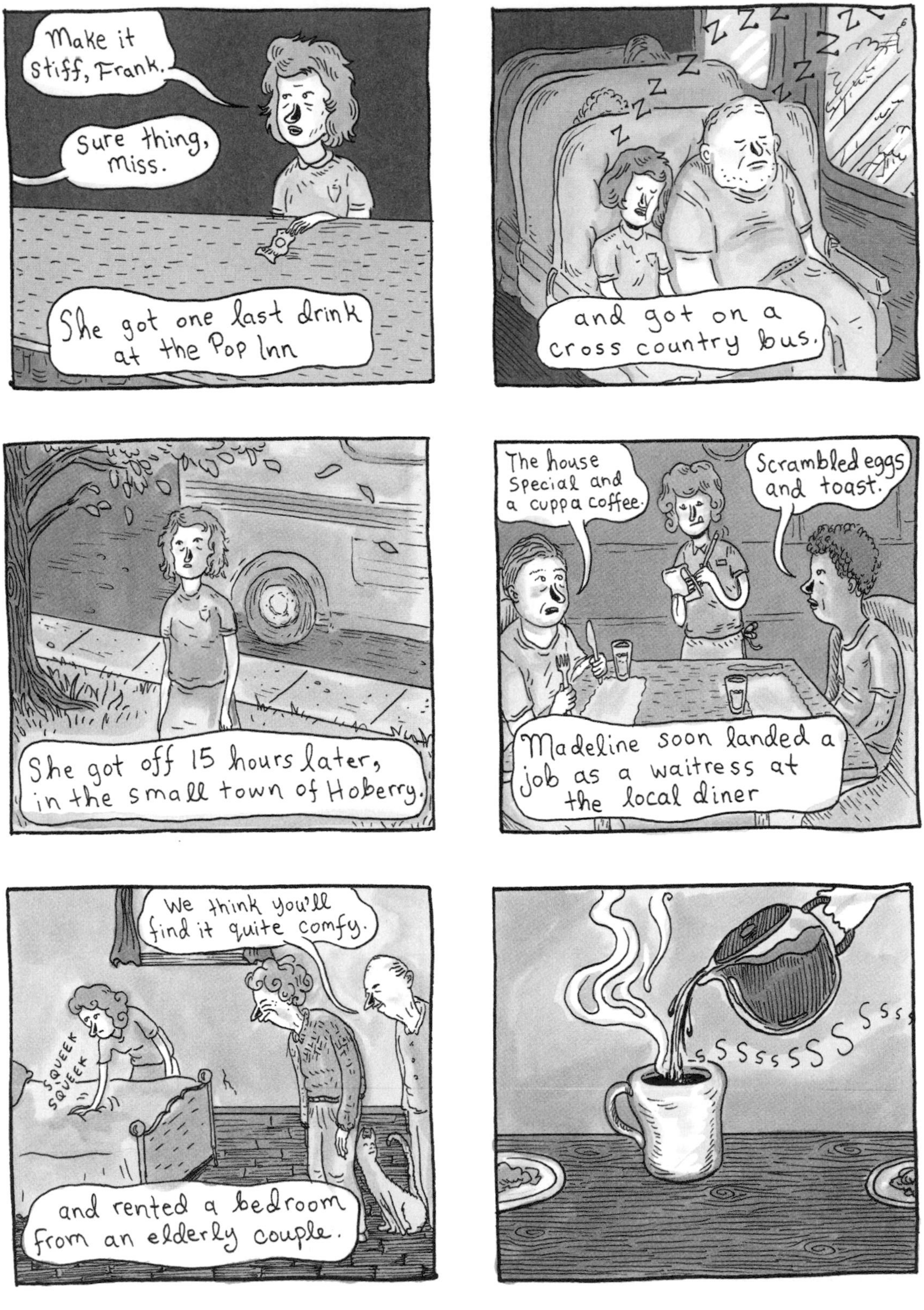
Make it stiff, Frank.
Sure thing, miss.
She got one last drink at the Pop Inn
Z Z Z Z Z Z Z Z Z Z Z
and got on a cross country bus.
She got off 15 hours later, in the small town of Hoberry.
The house Special and a cuppa coffee.
Scrambled eggs and toast.
Madeline soon landed a job as a waitress at the local diner
We think you'll find it quite comfy.
SQUEEK SQUEEK
and rented a bedroom from an elderly couple.
SSSSSSSSSSS

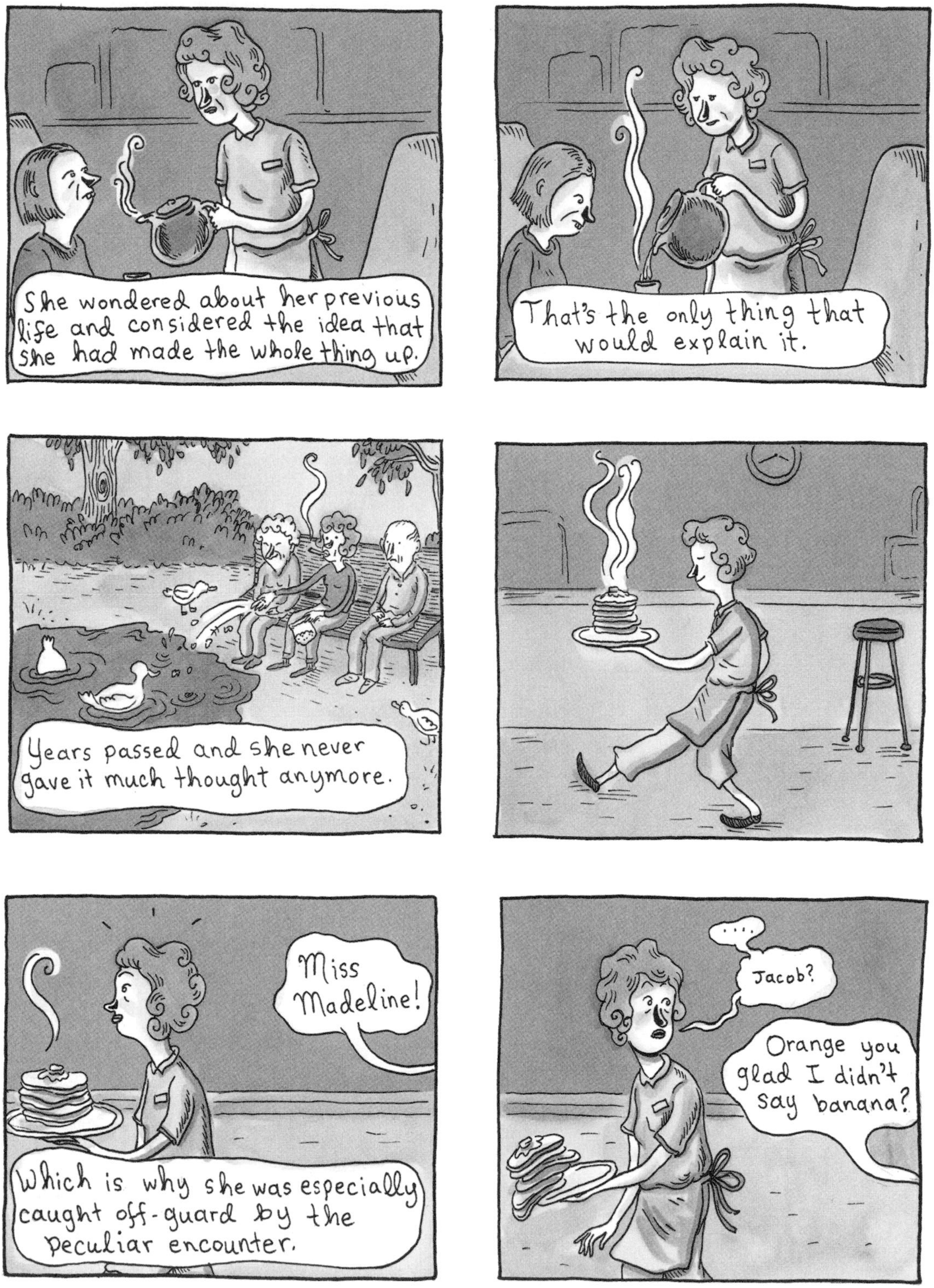
She wondered about her previous life and considered the idea that she had made the whole thing up.
That's the only thing that would explain it.
Years passed and she never gave it much thought anymore.
Miss Madeline!
Which is why she was especially caught off-guard by the peculiar encounter.
. . . .
Jacob?
Orange you glad I didn't say banana?

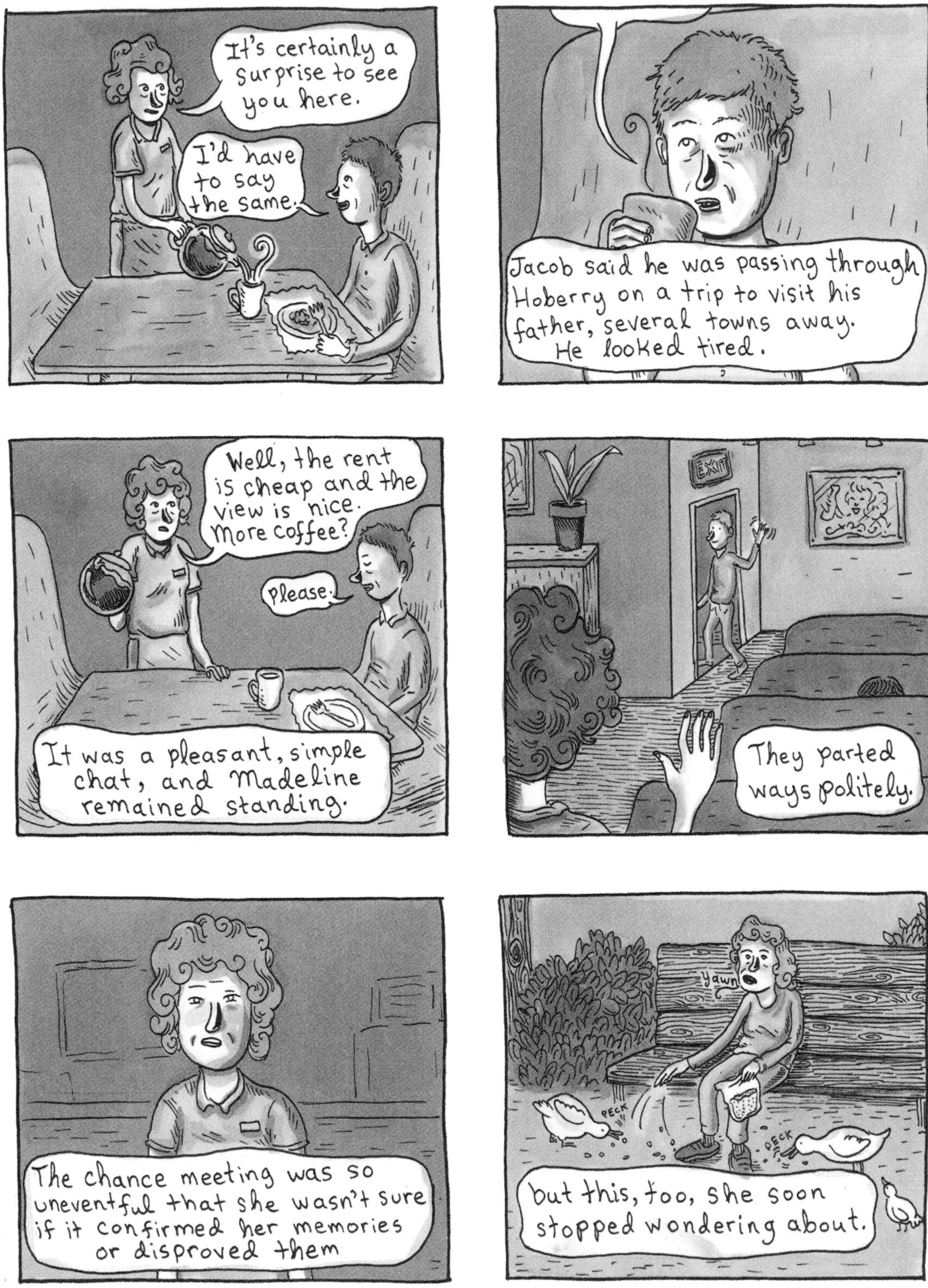
It's certainly a surprise to see you here.
I'd have to say the same.
Jacob said he was passing through Hoberry on a trip to visit his father, several towns away. He looked tired.
Well, the rent is cheap and the view is nice. More coffee?
Please.
It was a pleasant, simple chat, and Madeline remained standing.
EXIT
They parted ways politely.
The chance meeting was so uneventful that she wasn't sure if it confirmed her memories or disproved them
yawn
PECK
PECK
but this, too, she soon stopped wondering about.

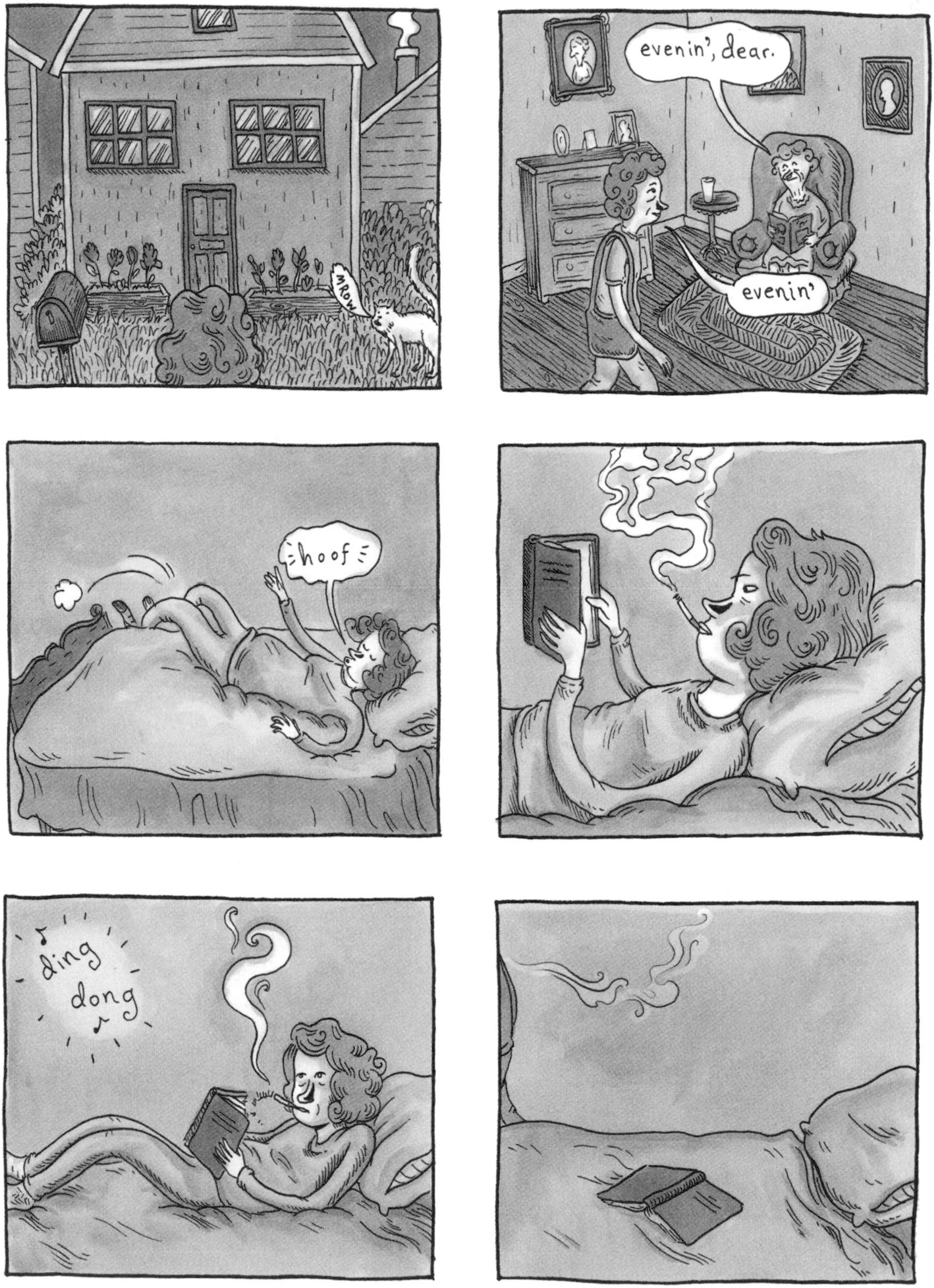
MROW
evenin', dear.
evenin'
hoof
ding dong

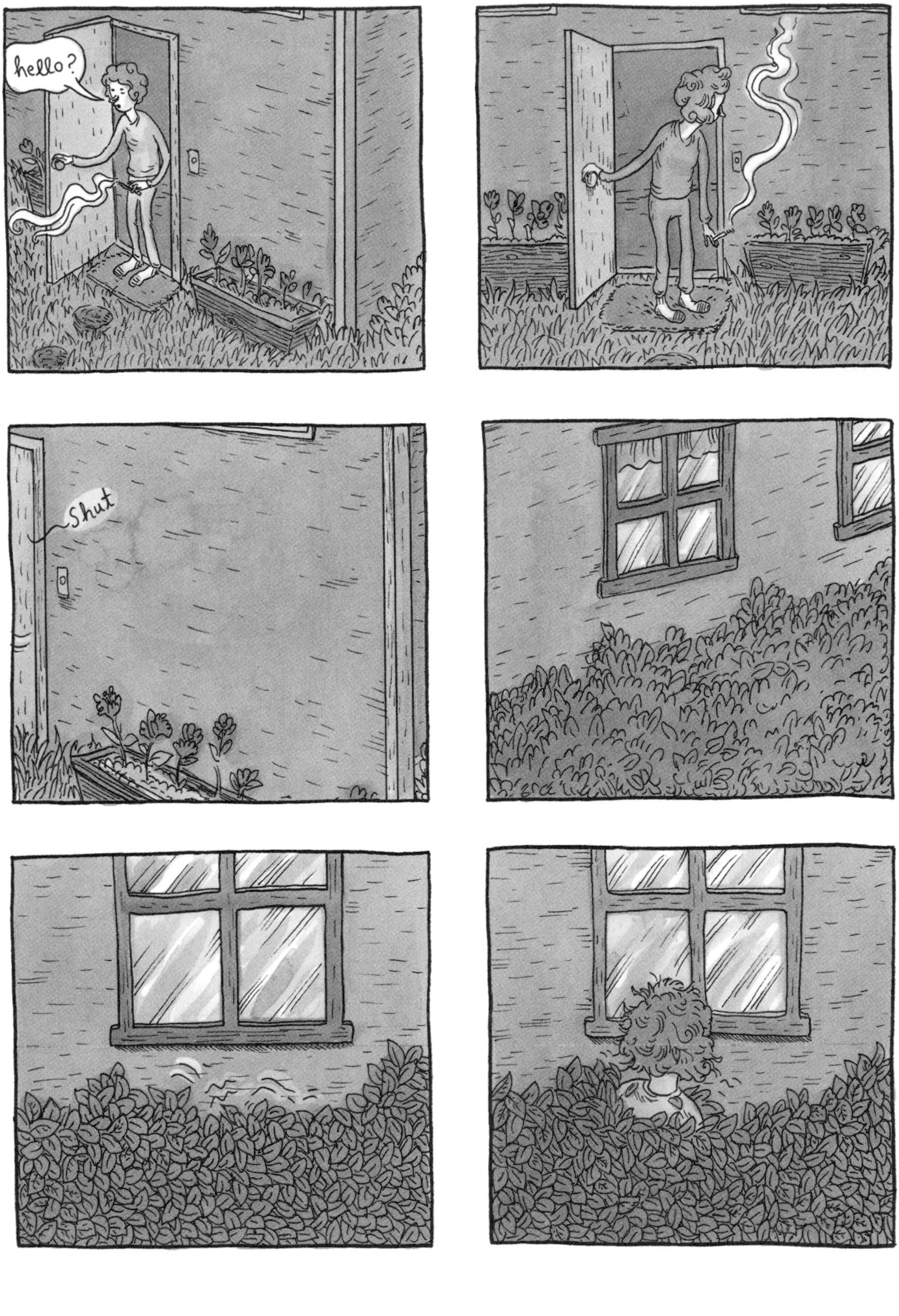
hello?
Shut

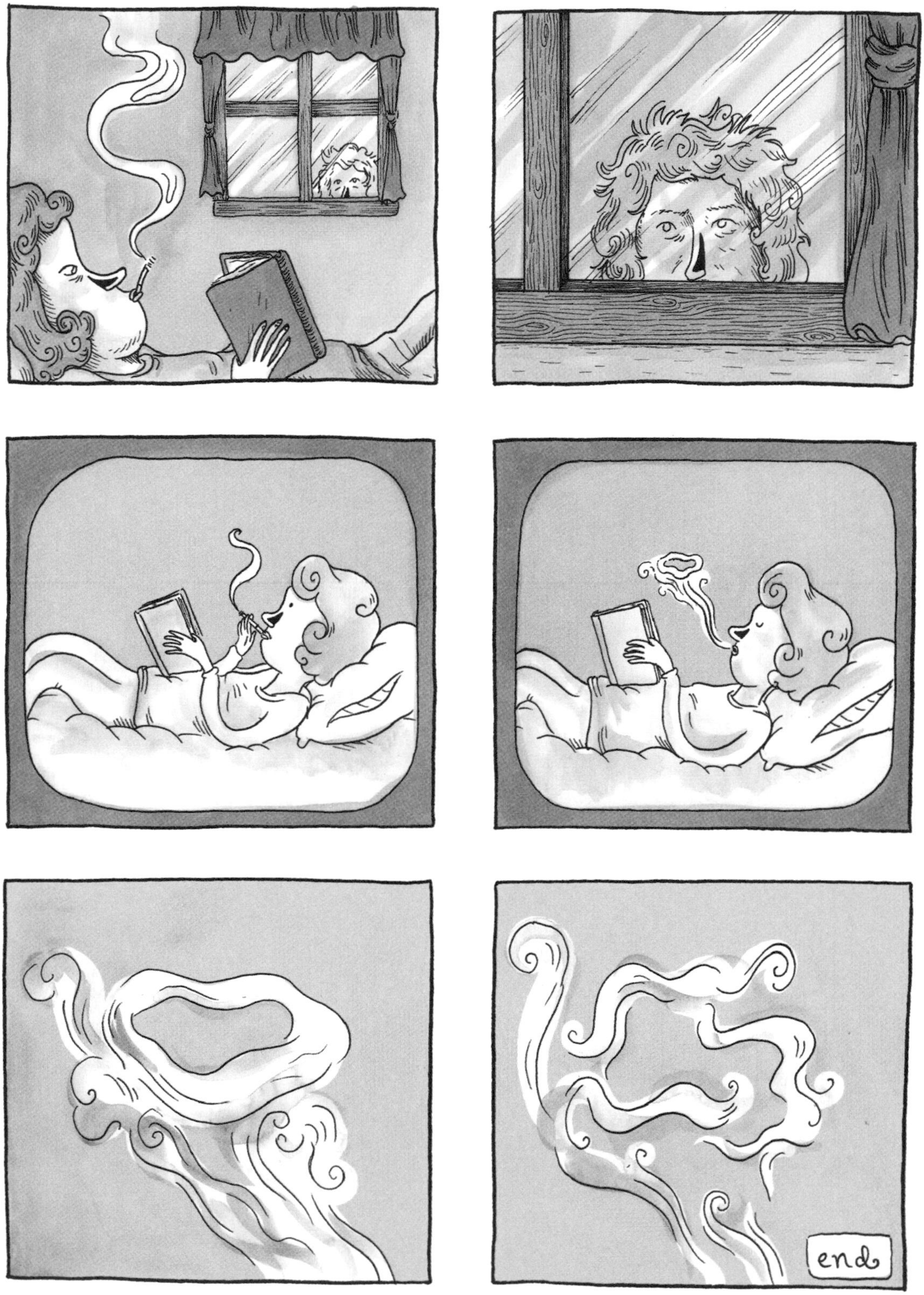
end

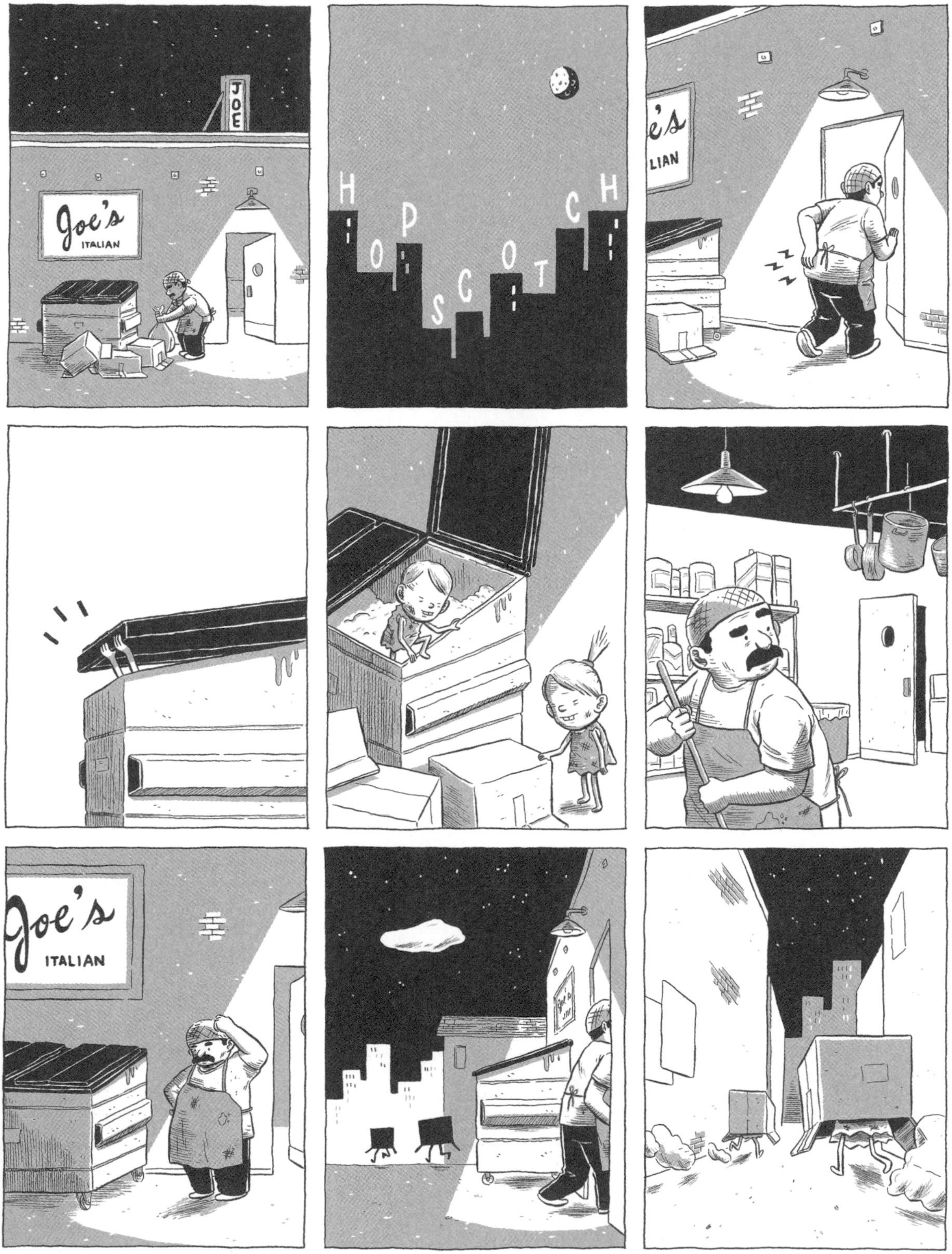
JOE
Joe's
ITALIAN
HOPSCOTCH
Joe's
ITALIAN

MARTIN CENDREDA

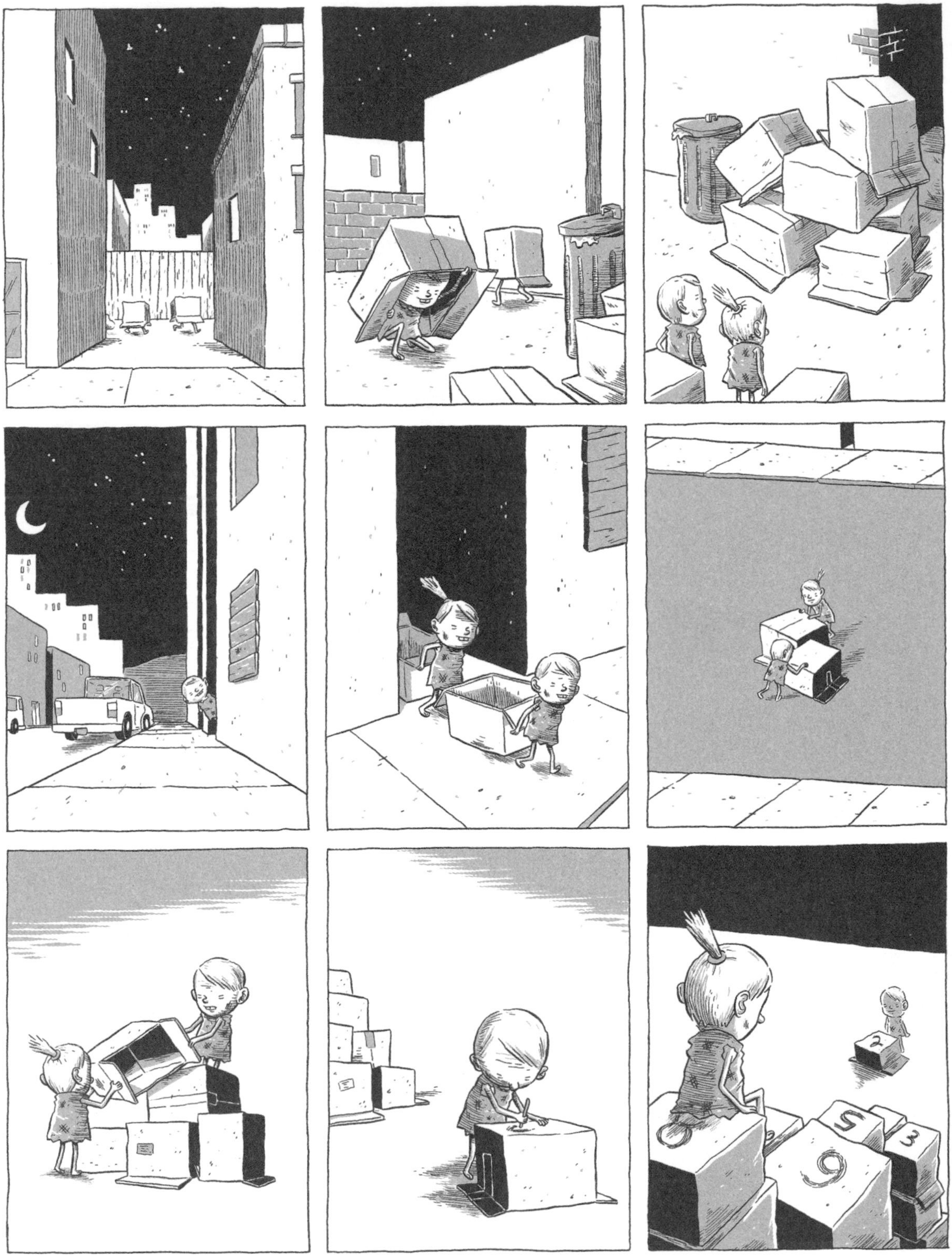

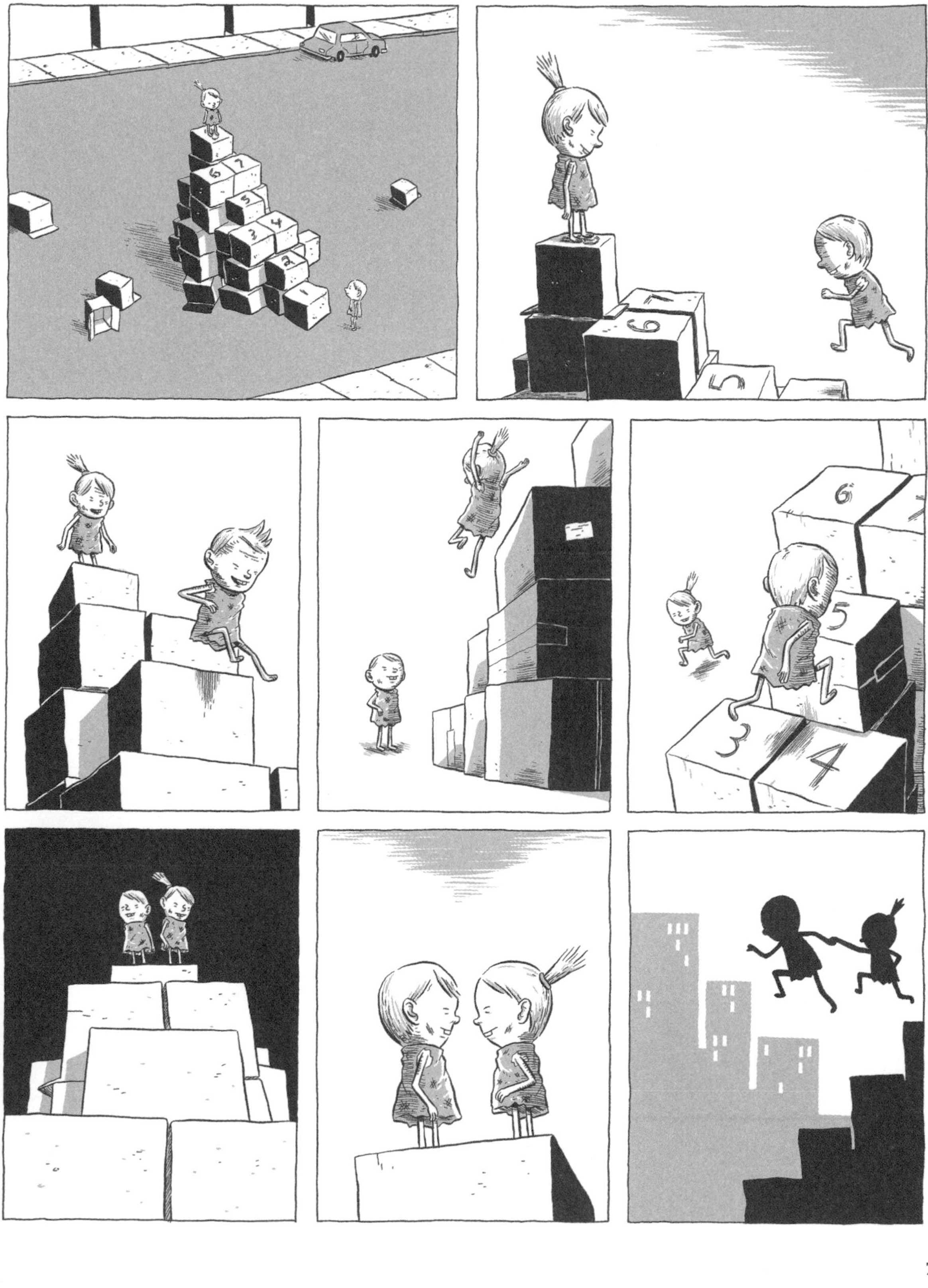

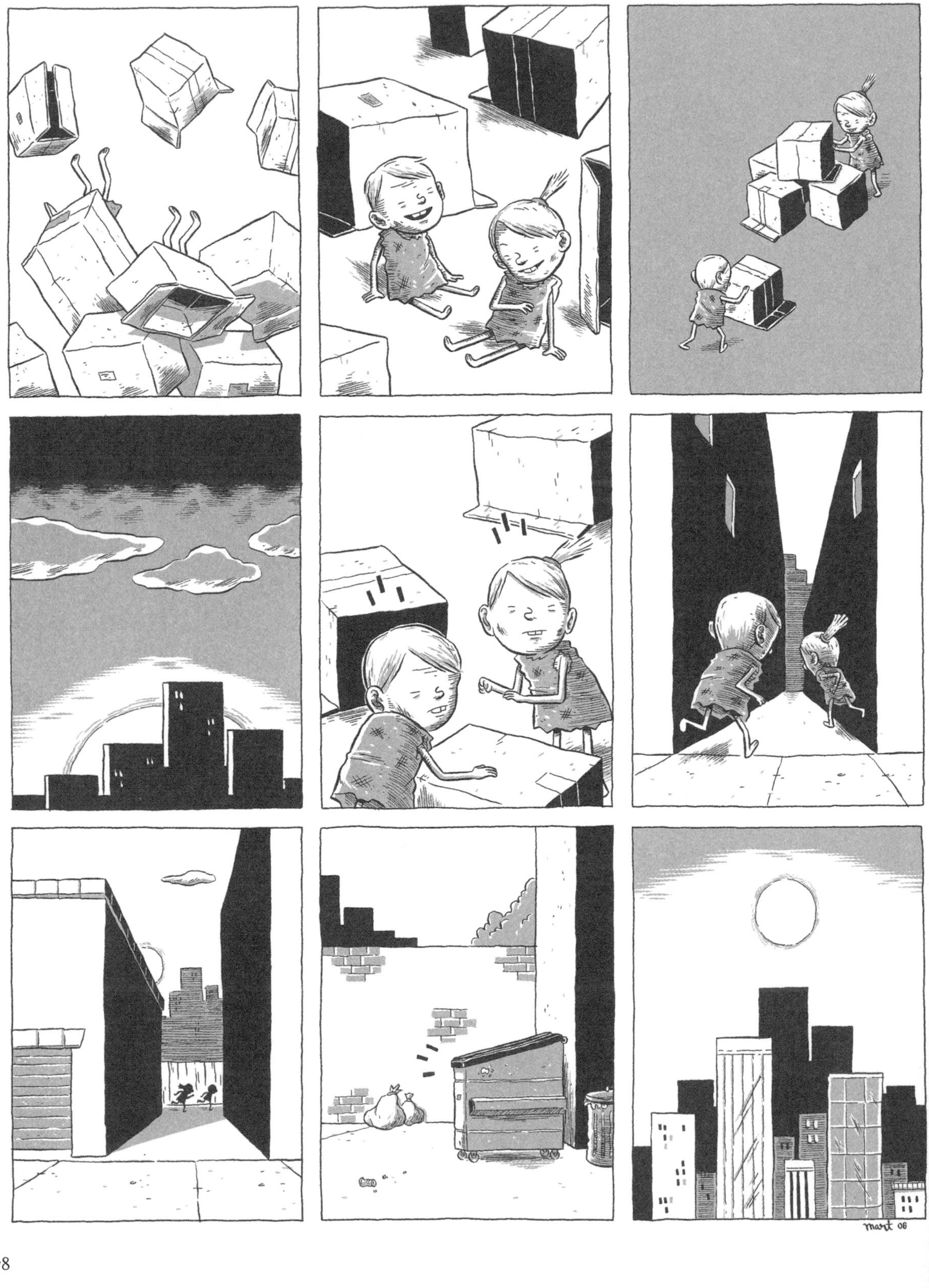
mart 06

THE MONKEY & the Crab

by Shawn Cheng & Sara Edward-Corbett

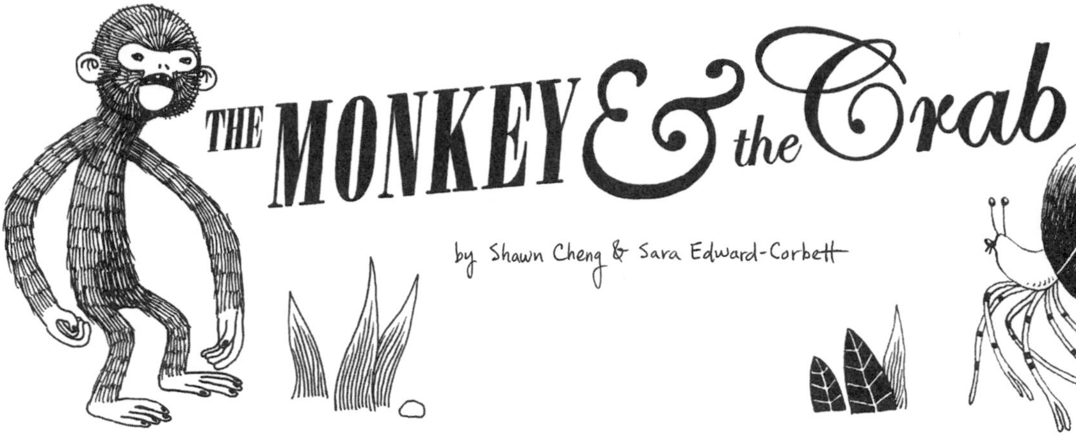

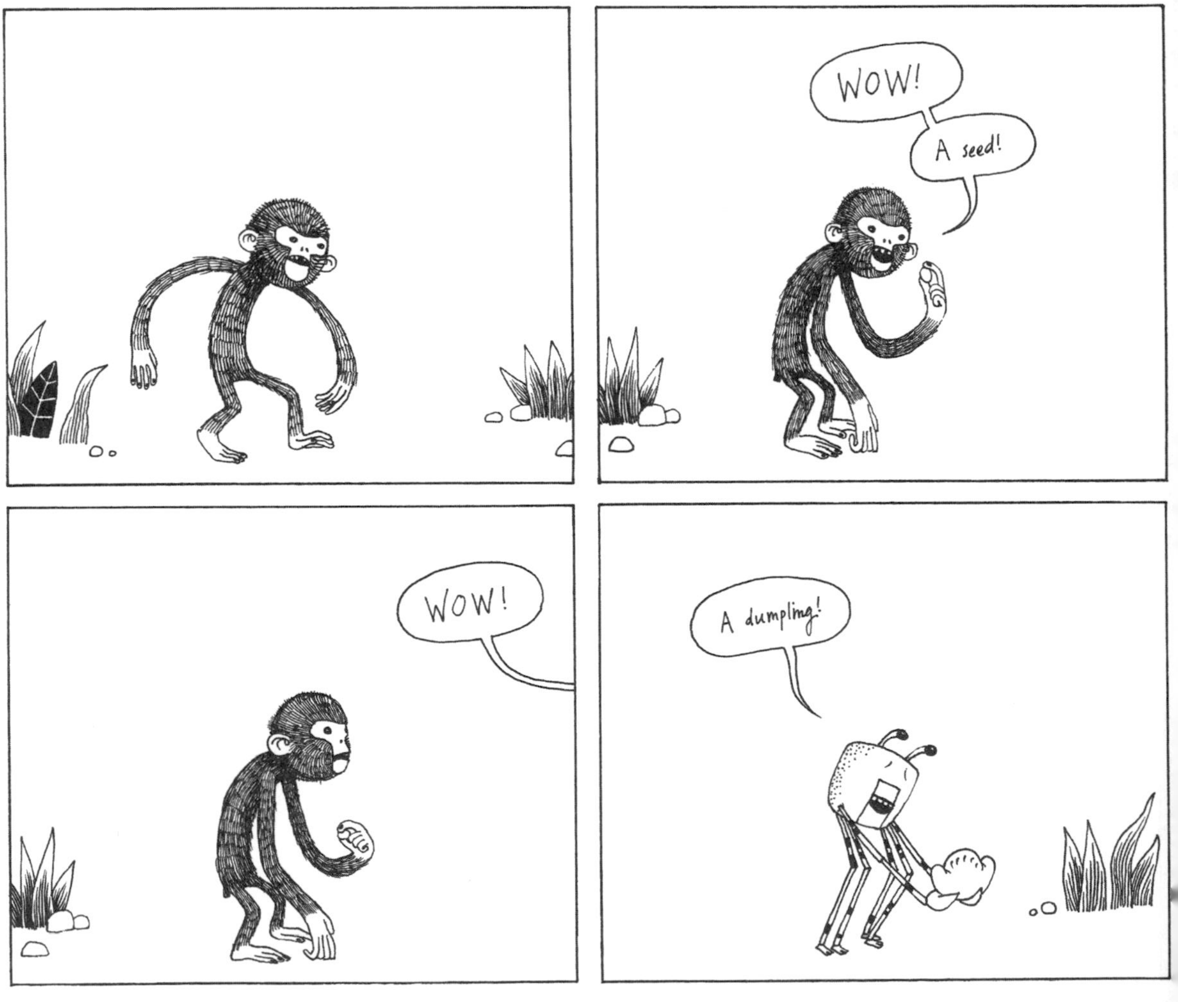
WOW!
A seed!
WOW!
A dumpling!

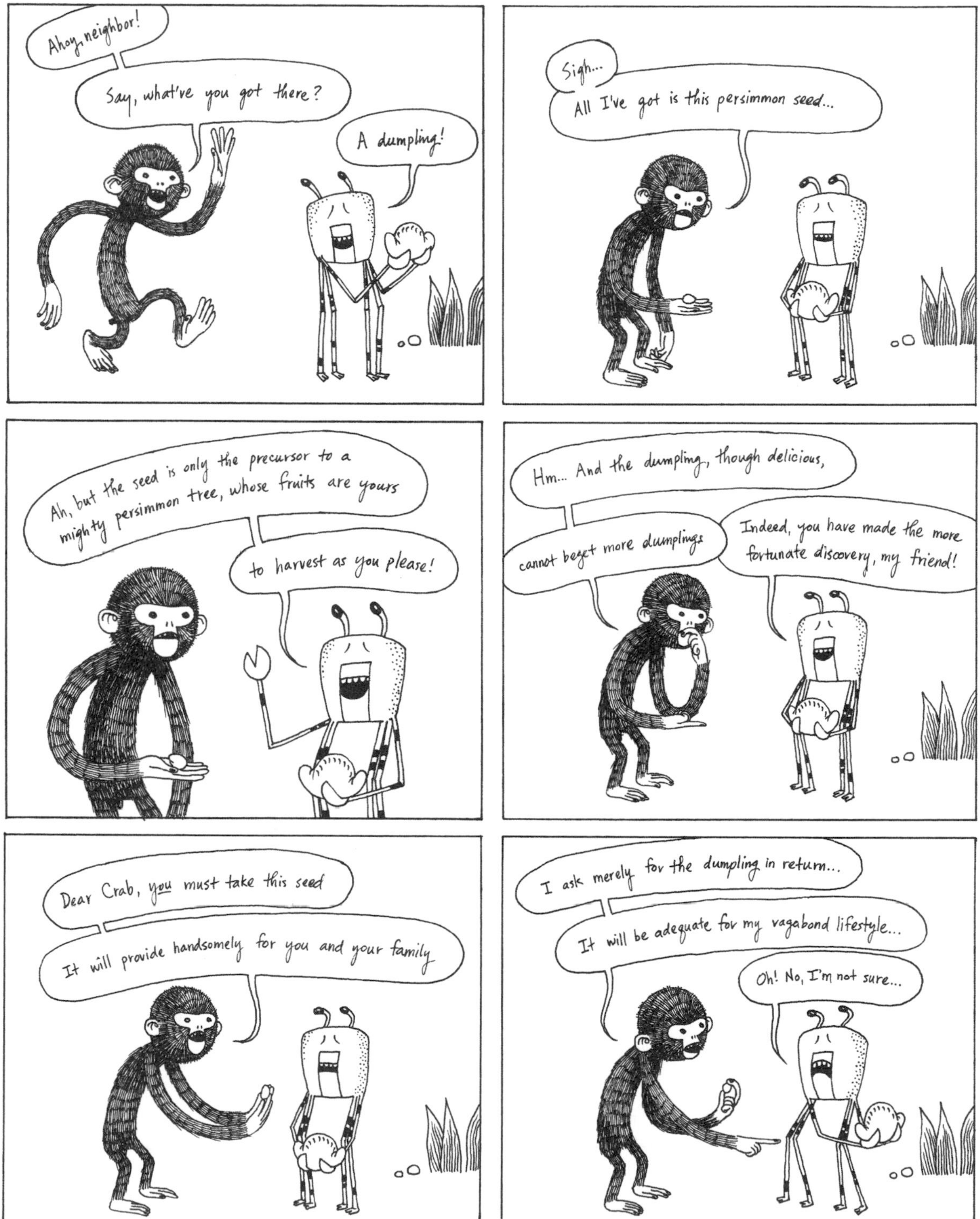
Ahoy, neighbor!
Say, what've you got there?
A dumpling!
Sigh...
All I've got is this persimmon seed...
Ah, but the seed is only the precursor to a mighty persimmon tree, whose fruits are yours
to harvest as you please!
Hm... And the dumpling, though delicious,
cannot beget more dumplings
Indeed, you have made the more fortunate discovery, my friend!
Dear Crab, you must take this seed
It will provide handsomely for you and your family
I ask merely for the dumpling in return...
It will be adequate for my vagabond lifestyle...
Oh! No, I'm not sure...

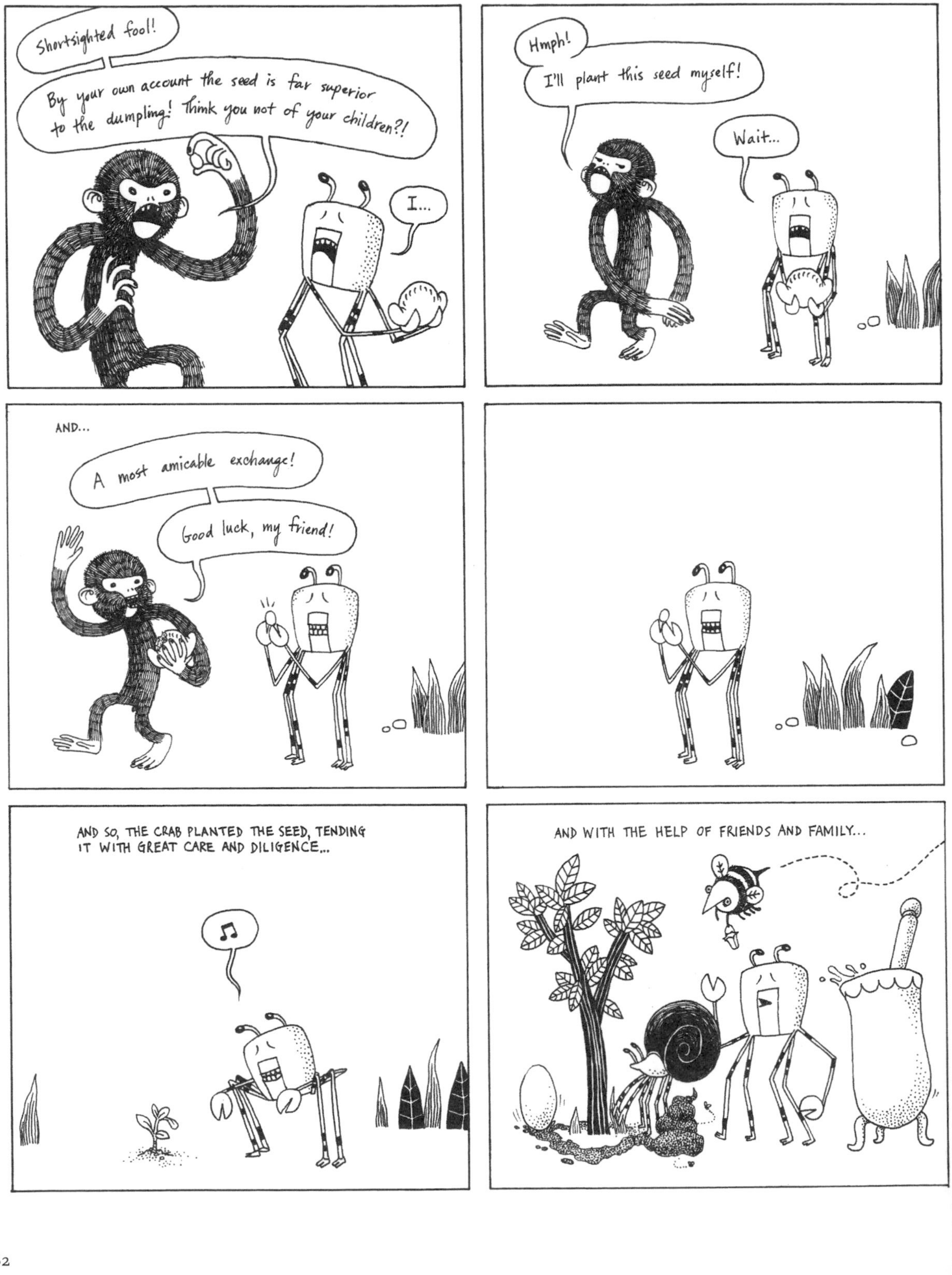
Shortsighted fool!
By your own account the seed is far superior to the dumpling! Think you not of your children?!
I...
Hmph!
I'll plant this seed myself!
Wait...
AND...
A most amicable exchange!
Good luck, my friend!
AND SO, THE CRAB PLANTED THE SEED, TENDING IT WITH GREAT CARE AND DILIGENCE...
♫
AND WITH THE HELP OF FRIENDS AND FAMILY...

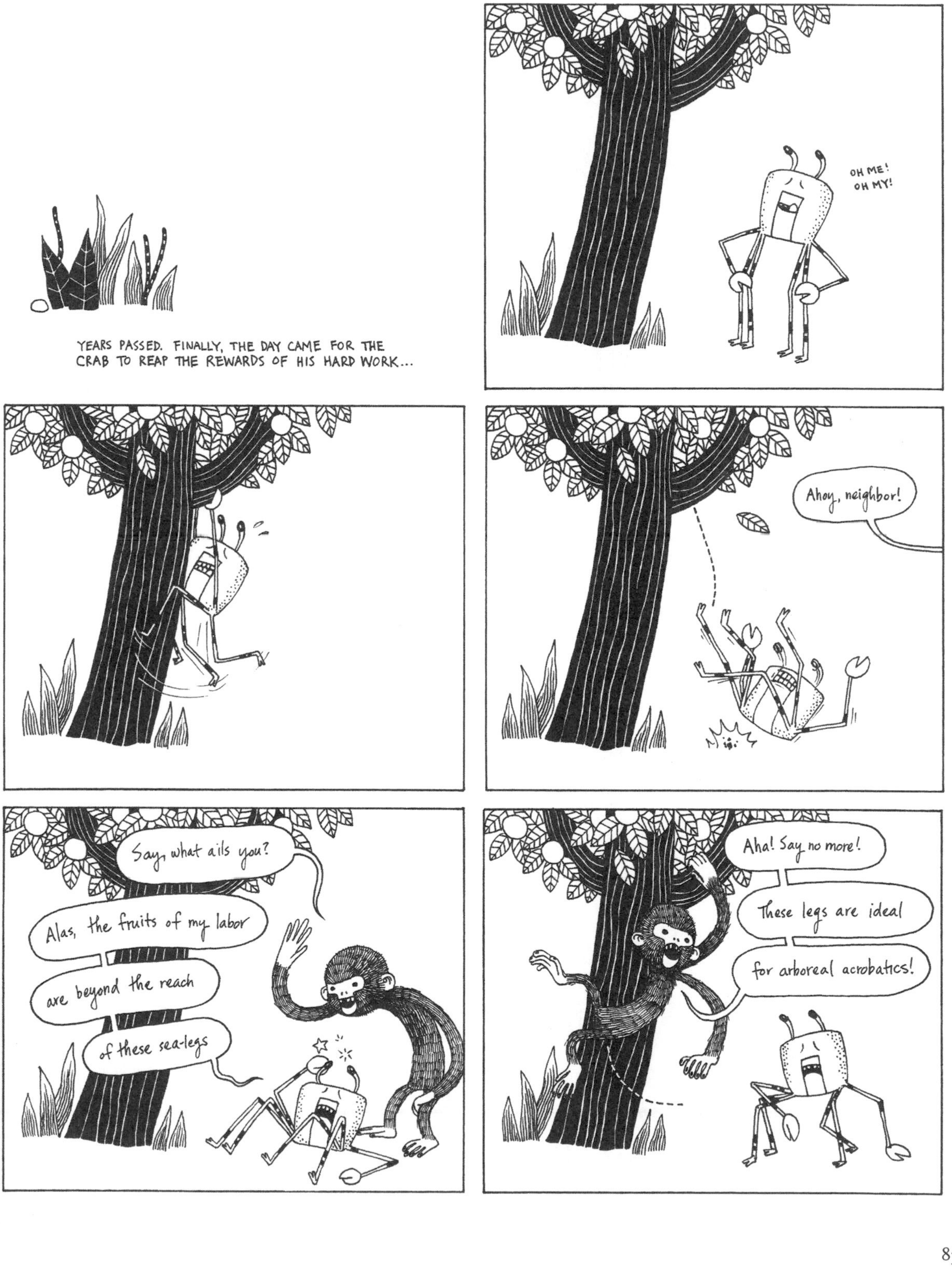
YEARS PASSED. FINALLY, THE DAY CAME FOR THE CRAB TO REAP THE REWARDS OF HIS HARD WORK...
OH ME! OH MY!
Ahoy, neighbor!
Say, what ails you?
Alas, the fruits of my labor
are beyond the reach
of these sea-legs
Aha! Say no more!
These legs are ideal
for arboreal acrobatics!

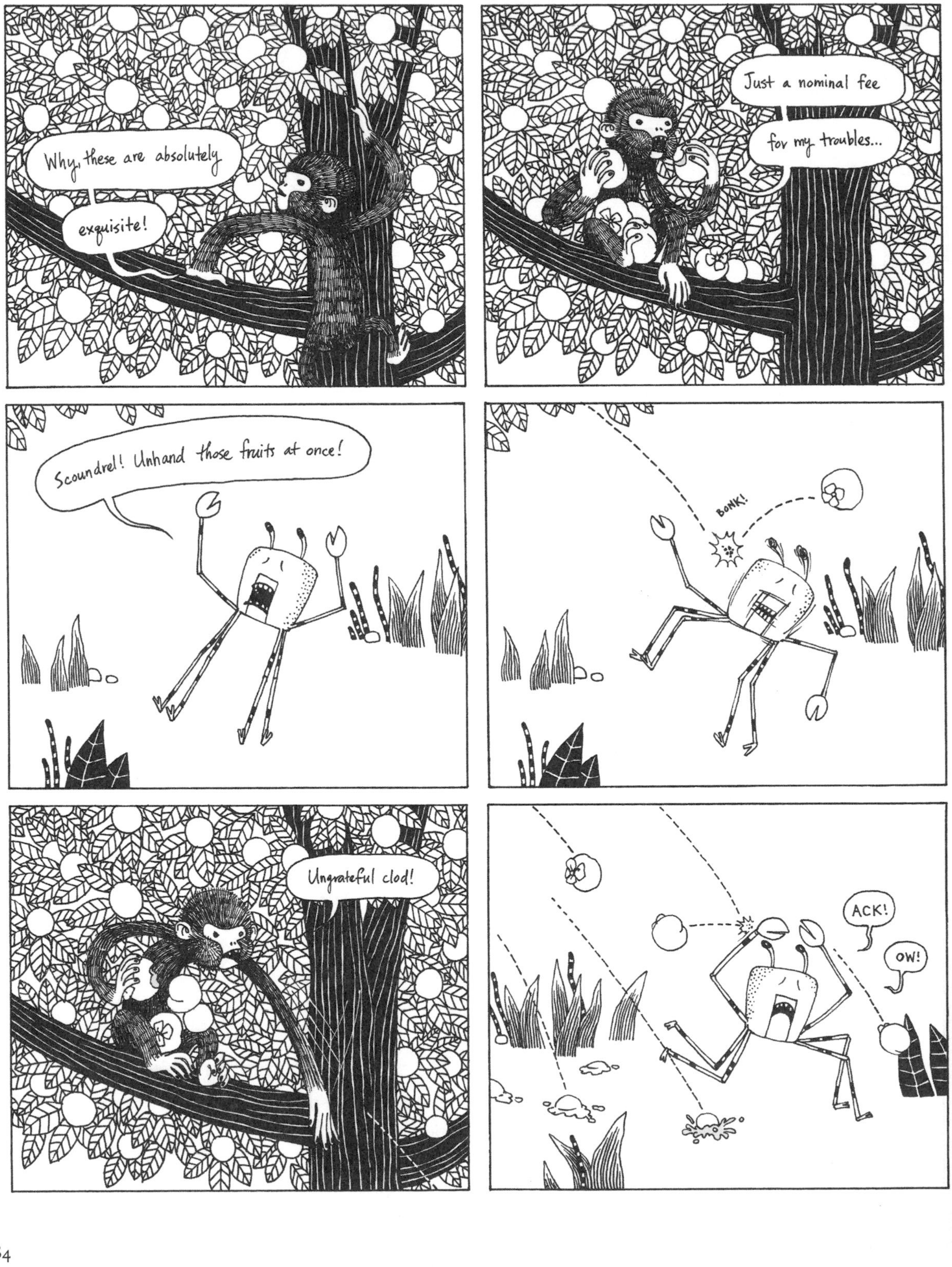
Why, these are absolutely
exquisite!
Just a nominal fee
for my troubles...
Scoundrel! Unhand those fruits at once!
BONK!
Ungrateful clod!
ACK!
OW!

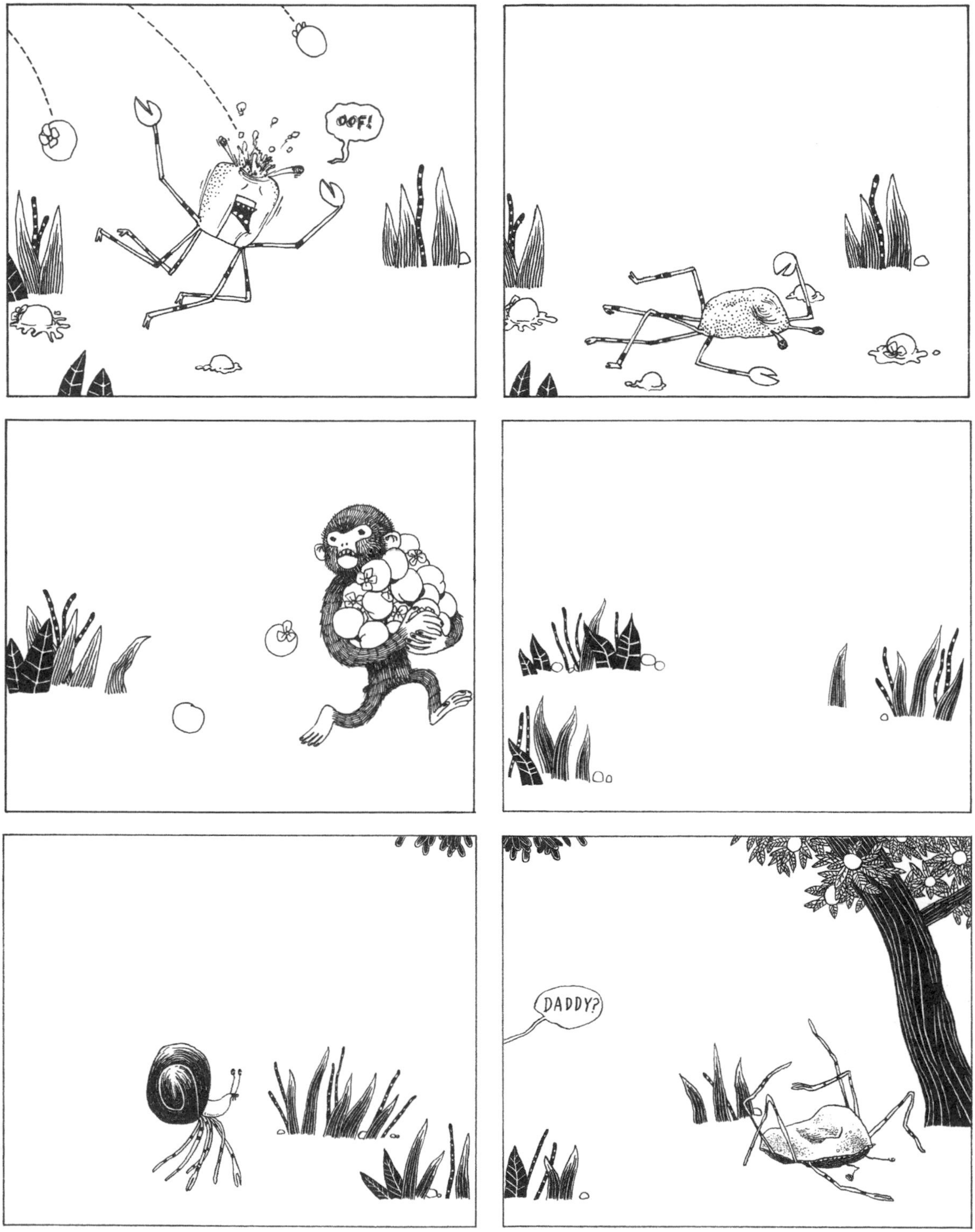
OOF!
DADDY?

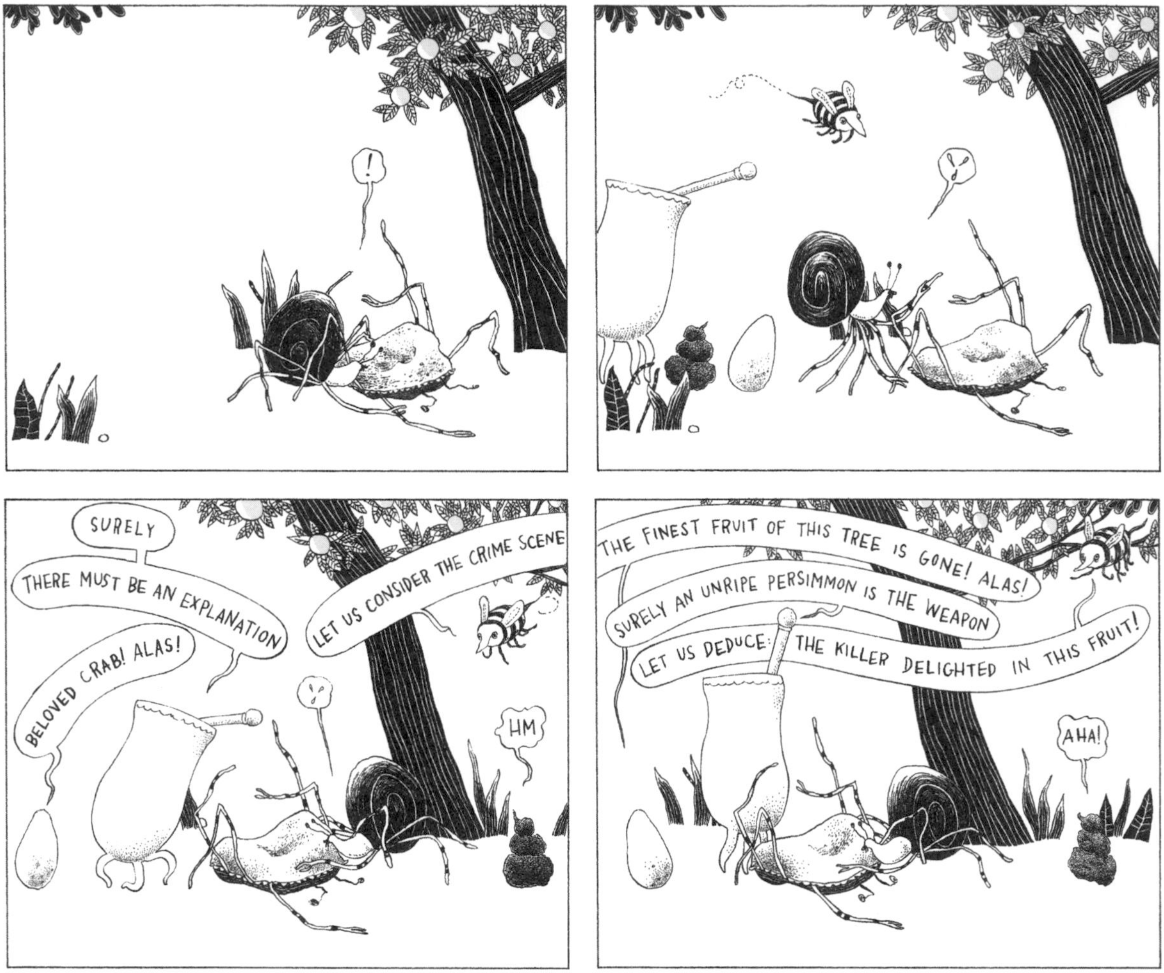
!
BELOVED CRAB! ALAS!
SURELY
THERE MUST BE AN EXPLANATION
LET US CONSIDER THE CRIME SCENE
HM
THE FINEST FRUIT OF THIS TREE IS GONE! ALAS!
SURELY AN UNRIPE PERSIMMON IS THE WEAPON
LET US DEDUCE: THE KILLER DELIGHTED IN THIS FRUIT!
AHA!

THE MONKEY ALTERNATELY DELIGHTED IN THE SUCCESS OF HIS CRIME AND SUFFERED FANCIES OF TERROR THAT HE WOULD BE FOUND OUT.

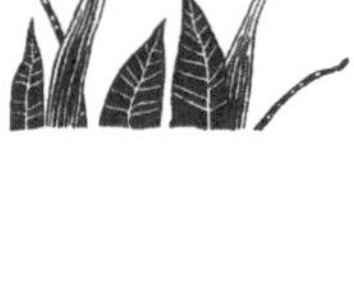

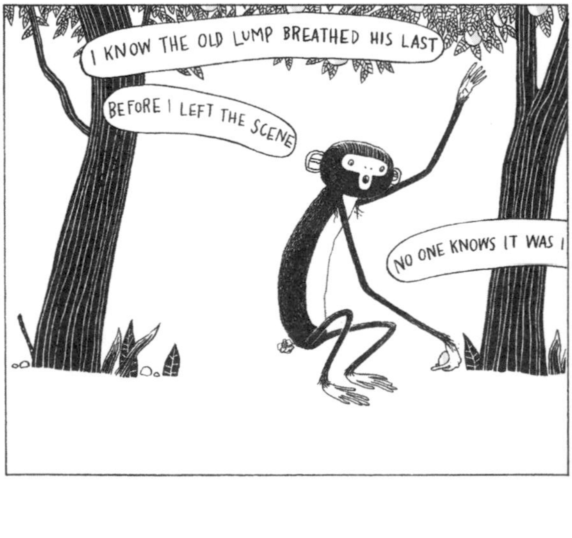
I KNOW THE OLD LUMP BREATHED HIS LAST
BEFORE I LEFT THE SCENE
NO ONE KNOWS IT WAS I

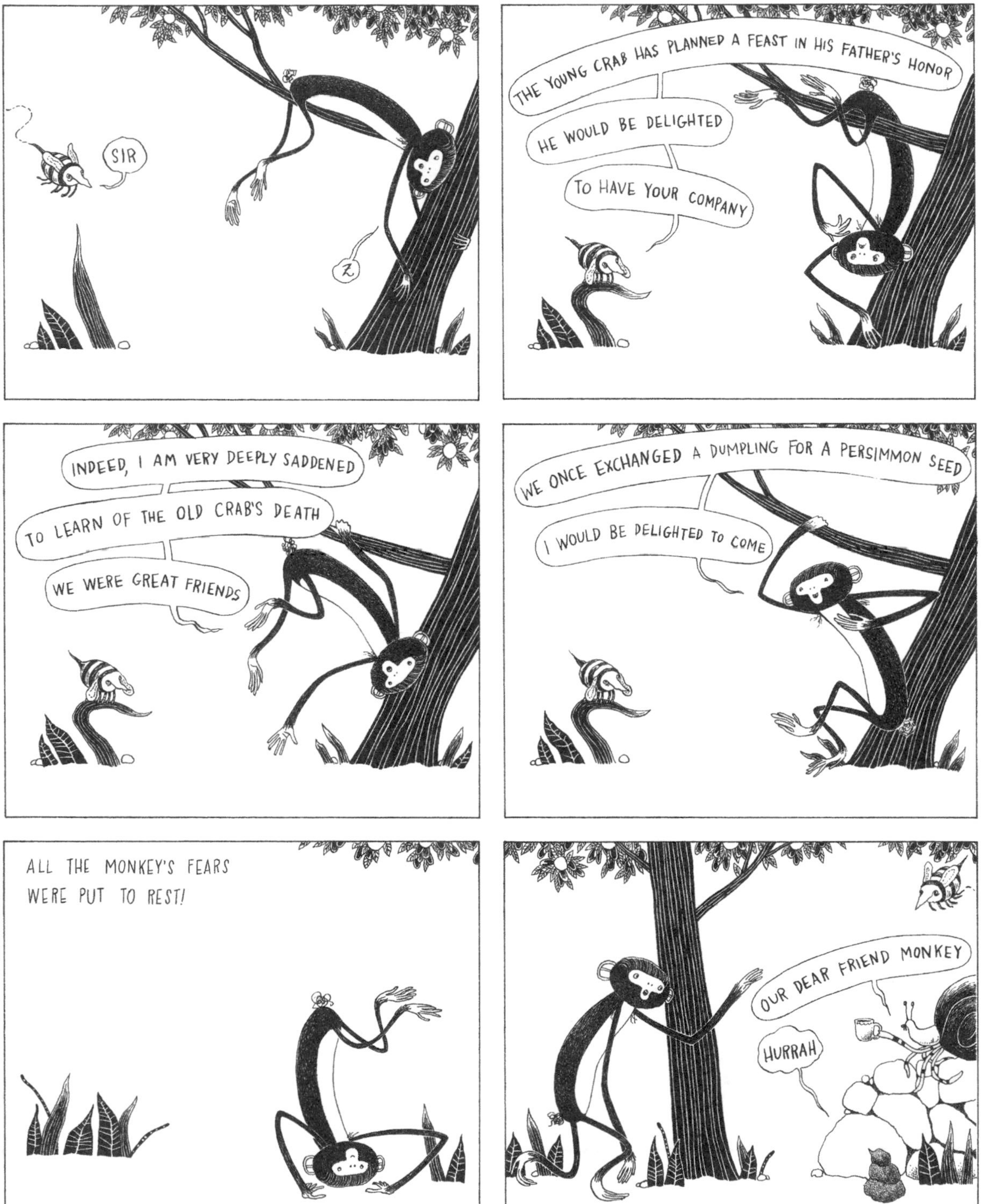
SIR
Z
THE YOUNG CRAB HAS PLANNED A FEAST IN HIS FATHER'S HONOR
HE WOULD BE DELIGHTED
TO HAVE YOUR COMPANY
INDEED, I AM VERY DEEPLY SADDENED
TO LEARN OF THE OLD CRAB'S DEATH
WE WERE GREAT FRIENDS
WE ONCE EXCHANGED A DUMPLING FOR A PERSIMMON SEED
I WOULD BE DELIGHTED TO COME
ALL THE MONKEY'S FEARS WERE PUT TO REST!
OUR DEAR FRIEND MONKEY
HURRAH

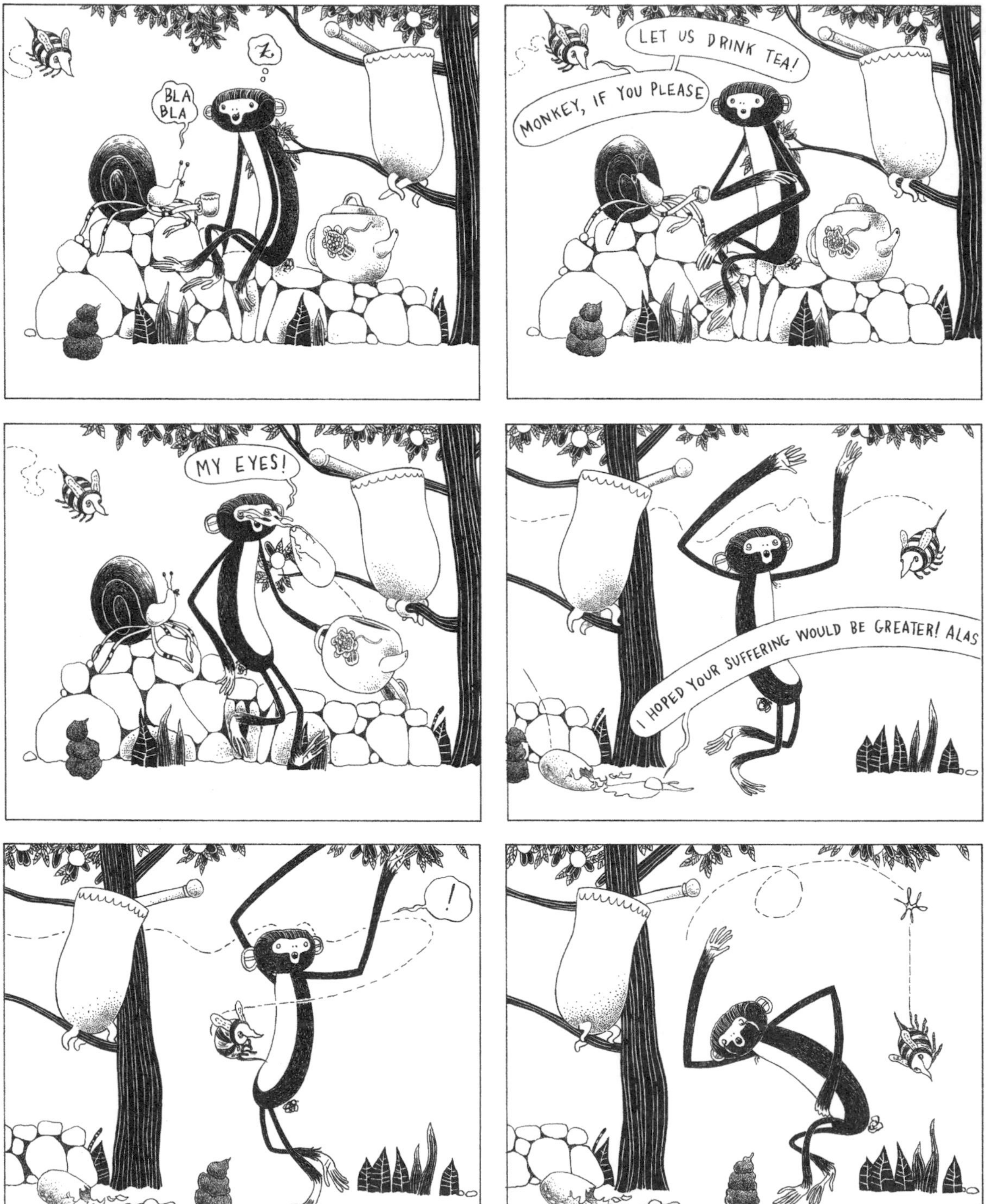
BLA BLA
Z
MONKEY, IF YOU PLEASE
LET US DRINK TEA!
MY EYES!
I HOPED YOUR SUFFERING WOULD BE GREATER! ALAS
!

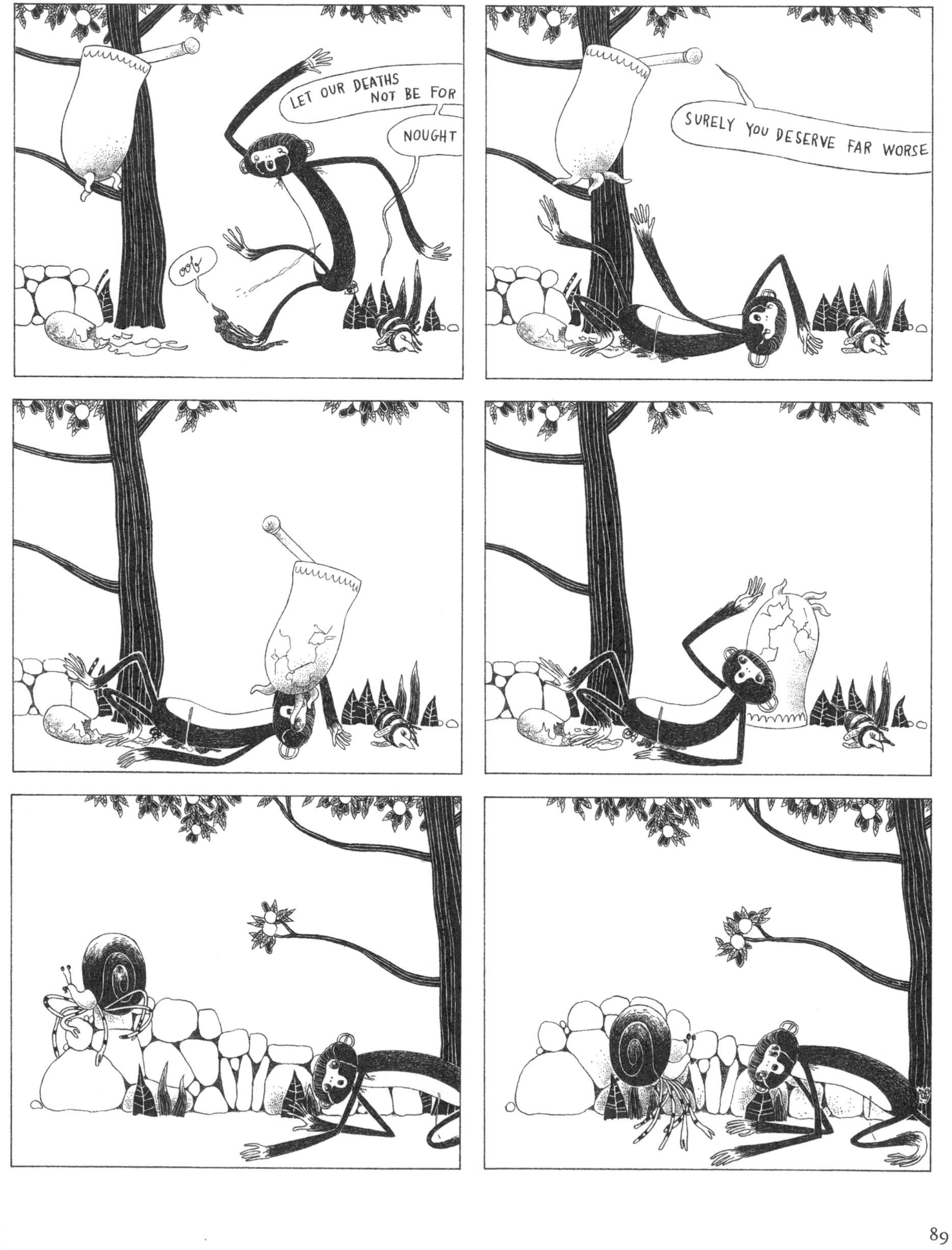
LET OUR DEATHS NOT BE FOR
NOUGHT
oof
SURELY YOU DESERVE FAR WORSE

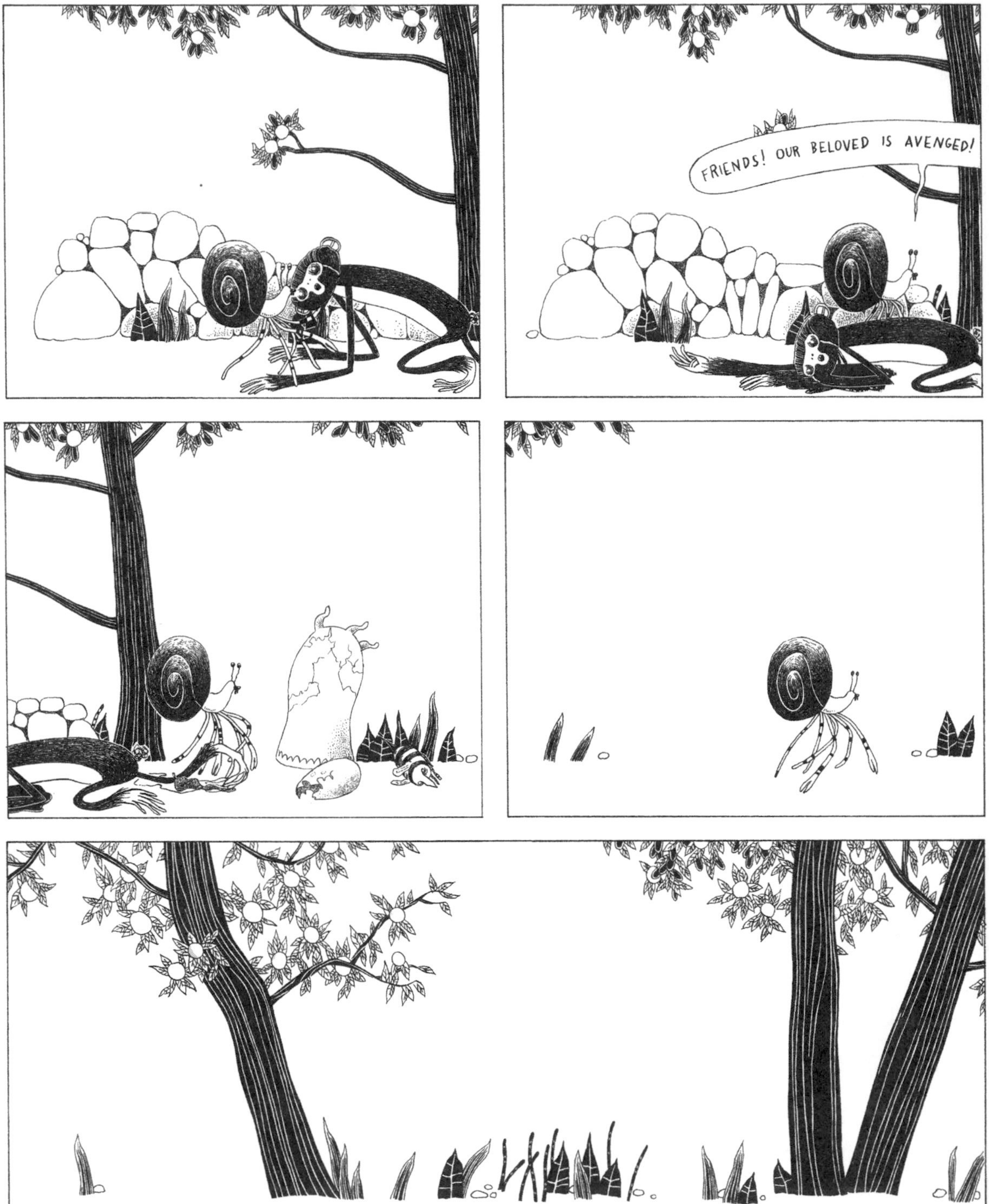
FRIENDS! OUR BELOVED IS AVENGED!

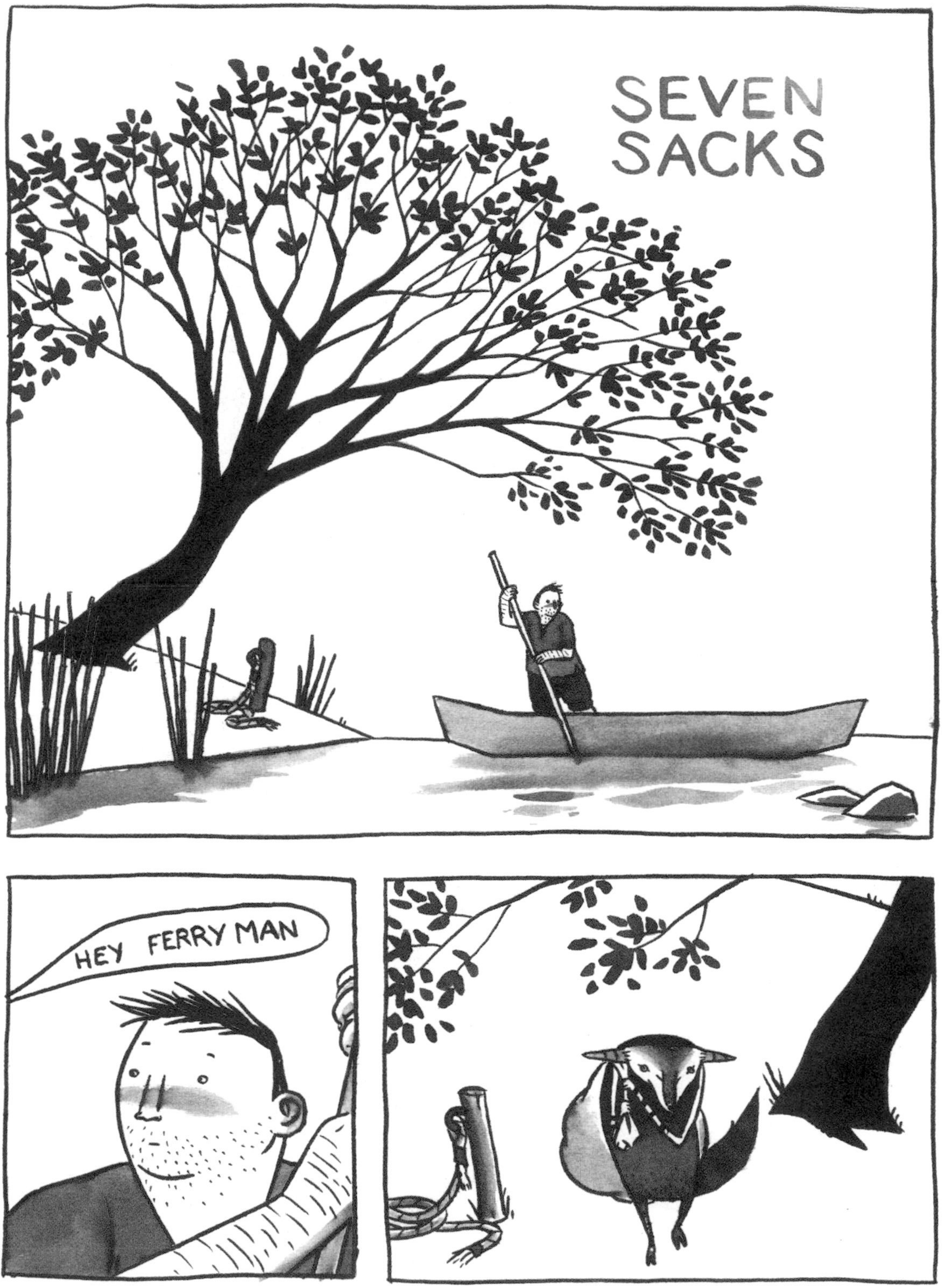
SEVEN SACKS
HEY FERRY MAN

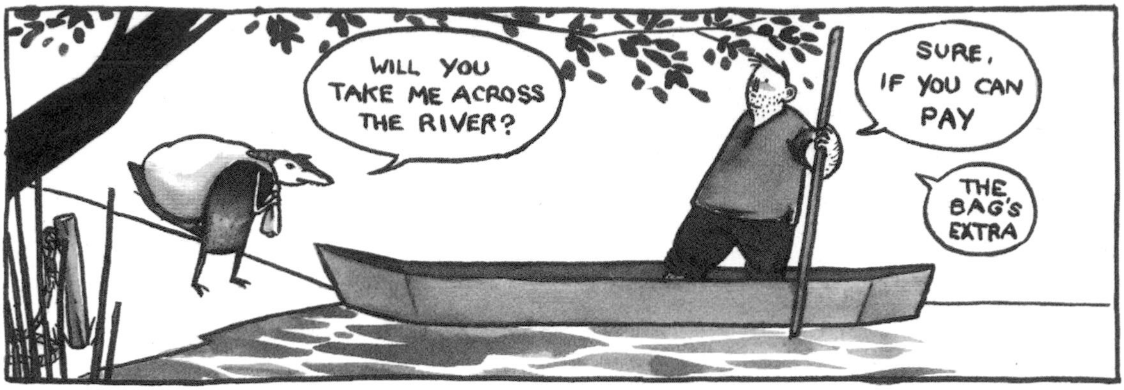
WILL YOU TAKE ME ACROSS THE RIVER?
SURE, IF YOU CAN PAY
THE BAG'S EXTRA

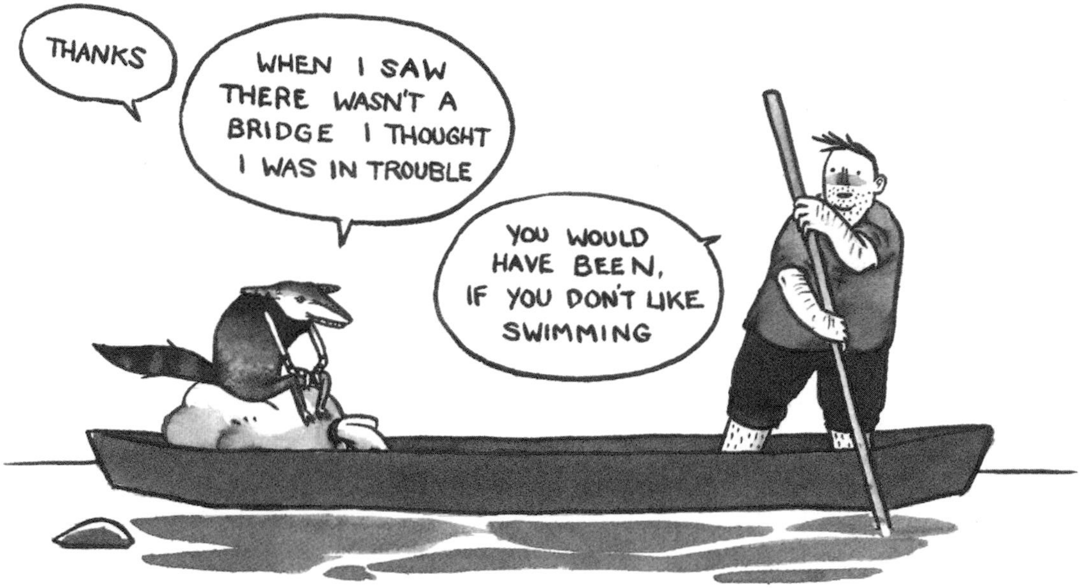
THANKS
WHEN I SAW THERE WASN'T A BRIDGE I THOUGHT I WAS IN TROUBLE
YOU WOULD HAVE BEEN, IF YOU DON'T LIKE SWIMMING

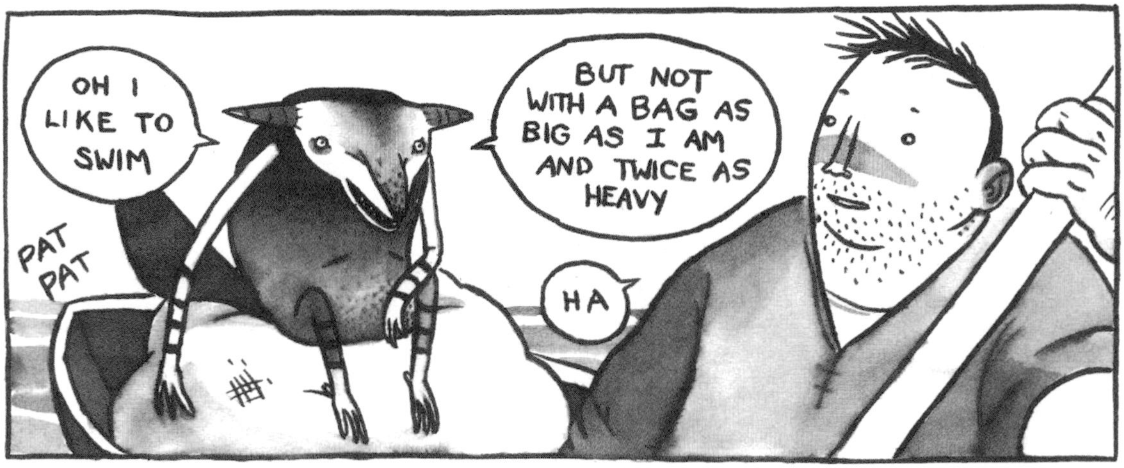
OH I LIKE TO SWIM
PAT PAT
BUT NOT WITH A BAG AS BIG AS I AM AND TWICE AS HEAVY
HA

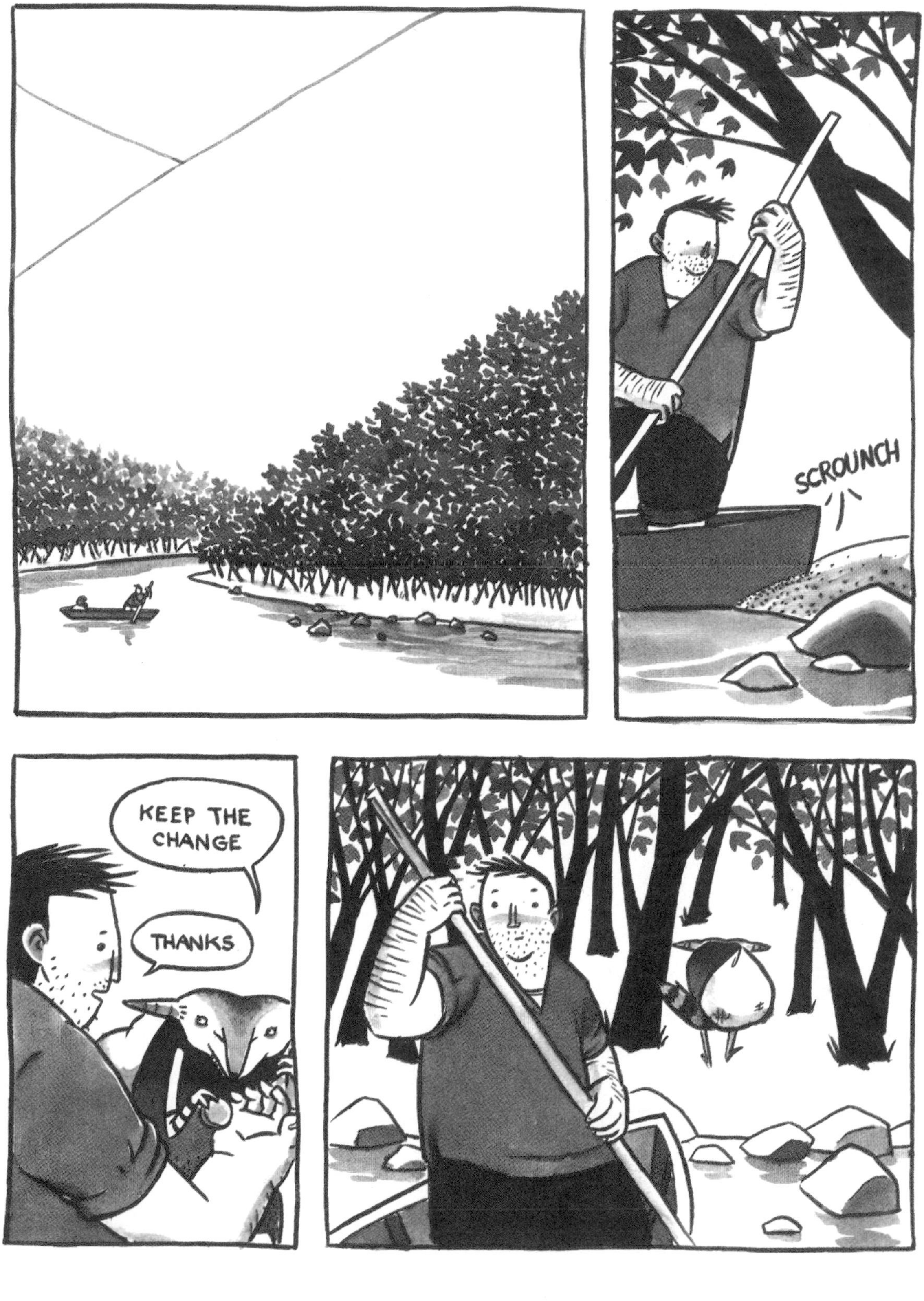
SCROUNCH
KEEP THE CHANGE
THANKS

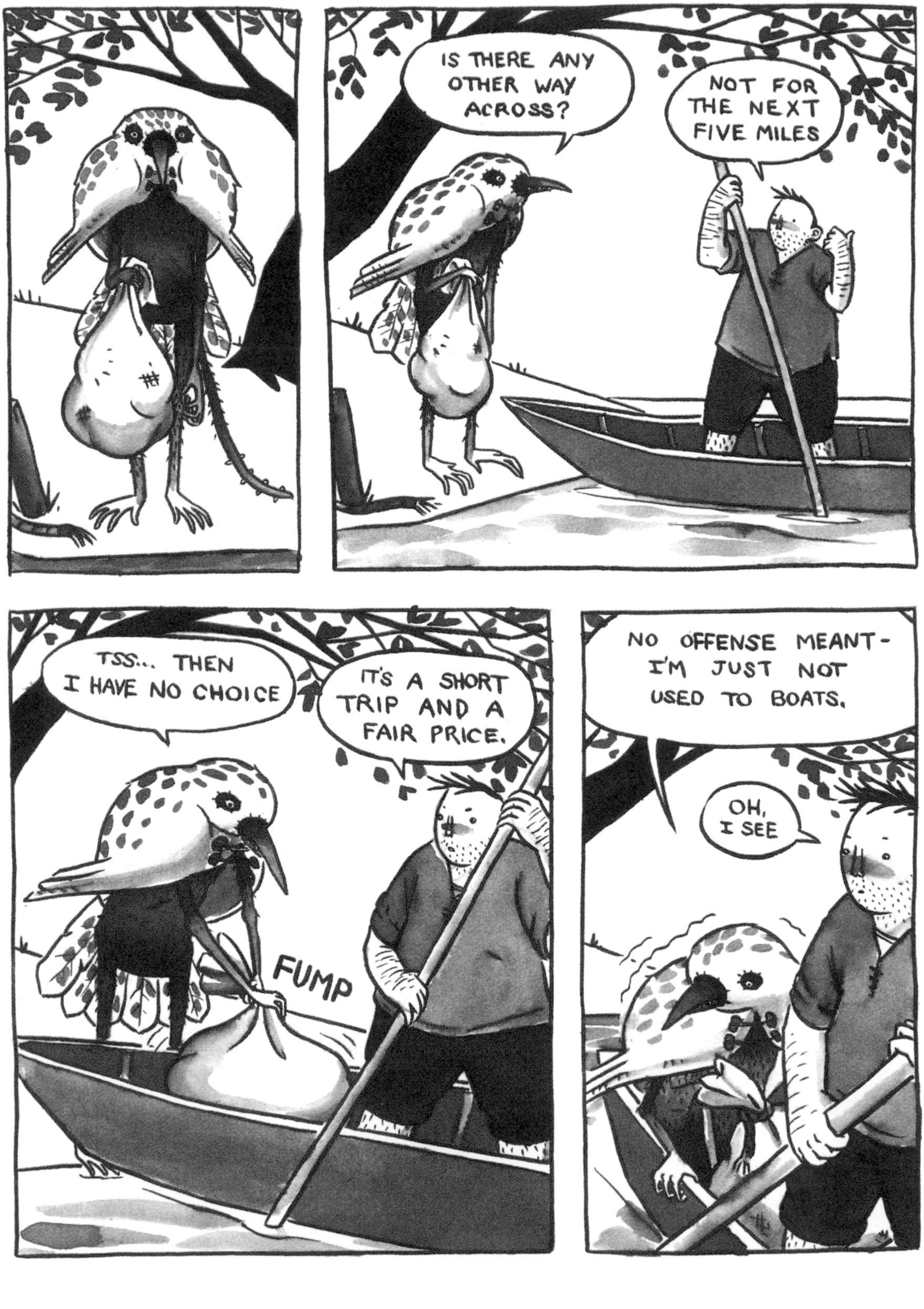
IS THERE ANY OTHER WAY ACROSS?
NOT FOR THE NEXT FIVE MILES
TSS... THEN I HAVE NO CHOICE
IT'S A SHORT TRIP AND A FAIR PRICE.
FUMP
NO OFFENSE MEANT- I'M JUST NOT USED TO BOATS.
OH, I SEE

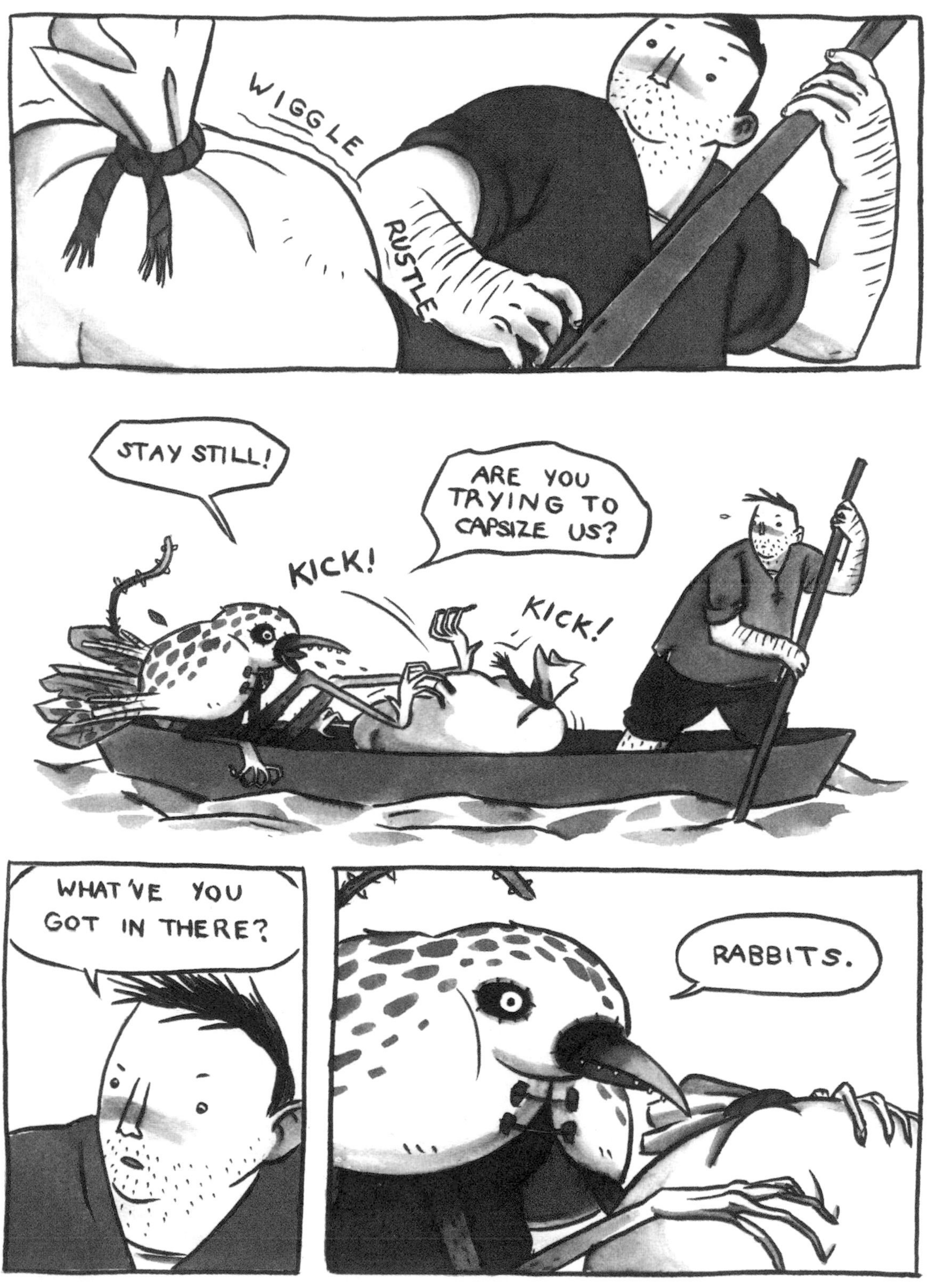
WIGGLE
RUSTLE
STAY STILL!
ARE YOU TRYING TO CAPSIZE US?
KICK!
KICK!
WHAT'VE YOU GOT IN THERE?
RABBITS.

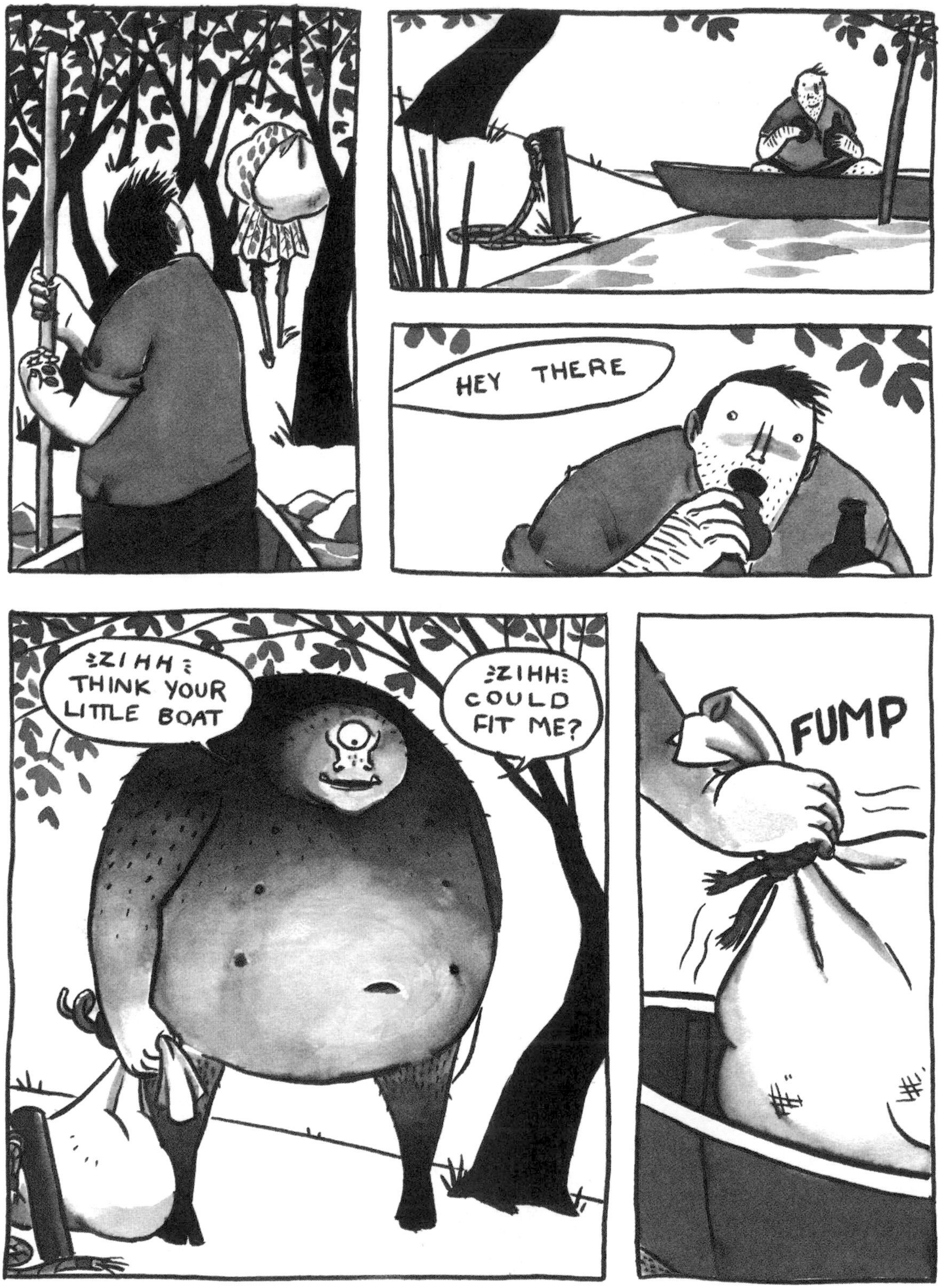
HEY THERE
ZIHH THINK YOUR LITTLE BOAT
ZIHH COULD FIT ME?
FUMP

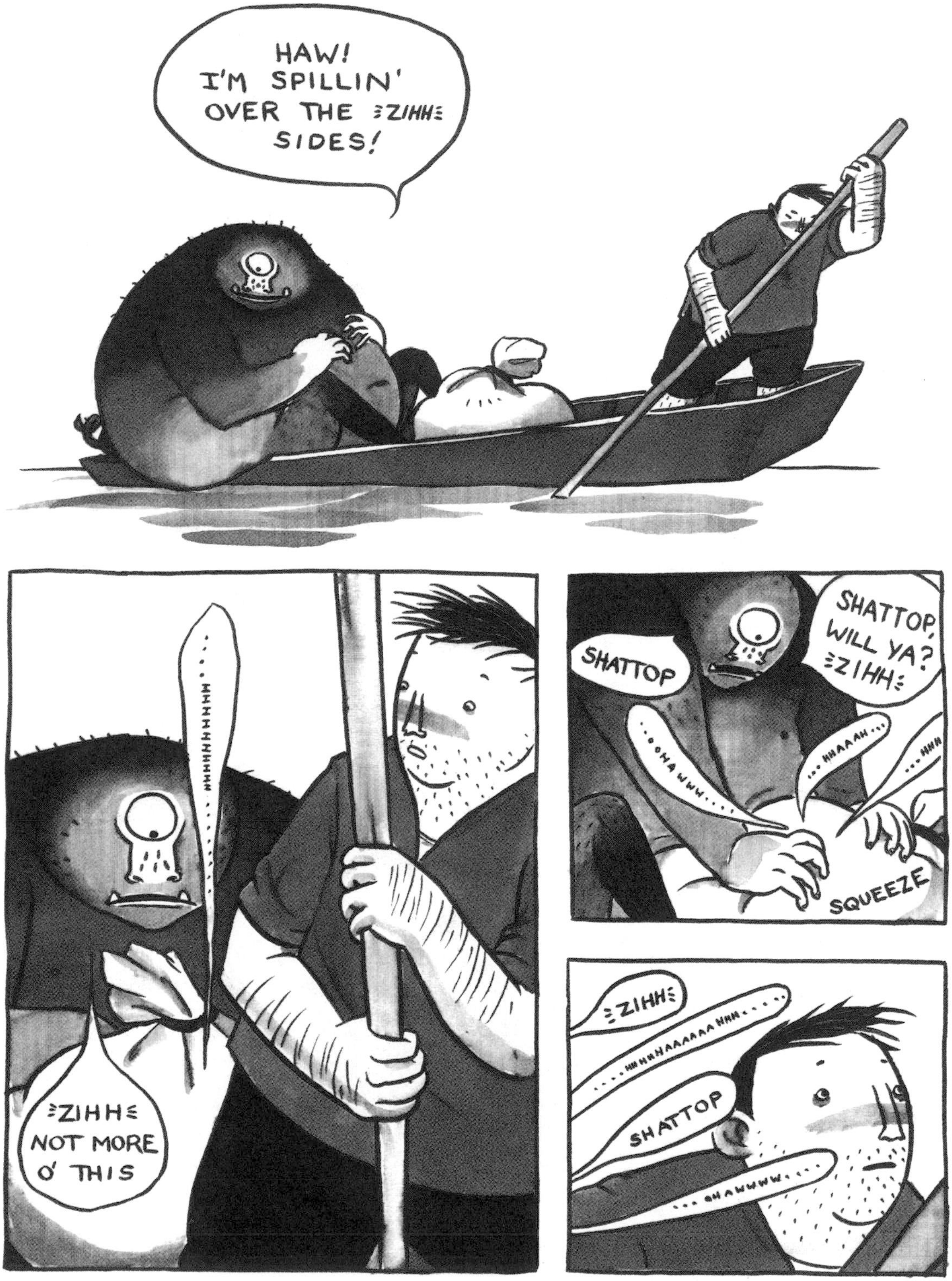
HAW! I'M SPILLIN' OVER THE ZIHH SIDES!
...MHHHHHHHH
ZIHH NOT MORE O' THIS
SHATTOP
SHATTOP, WILL YA? ZIHH
...OHAWWW...
...HHAAAH...
...HHH
SQUEEZE
ZIHH
...HHHHAAAAAAHHH...
SHATTOP
...OHAWWWW...

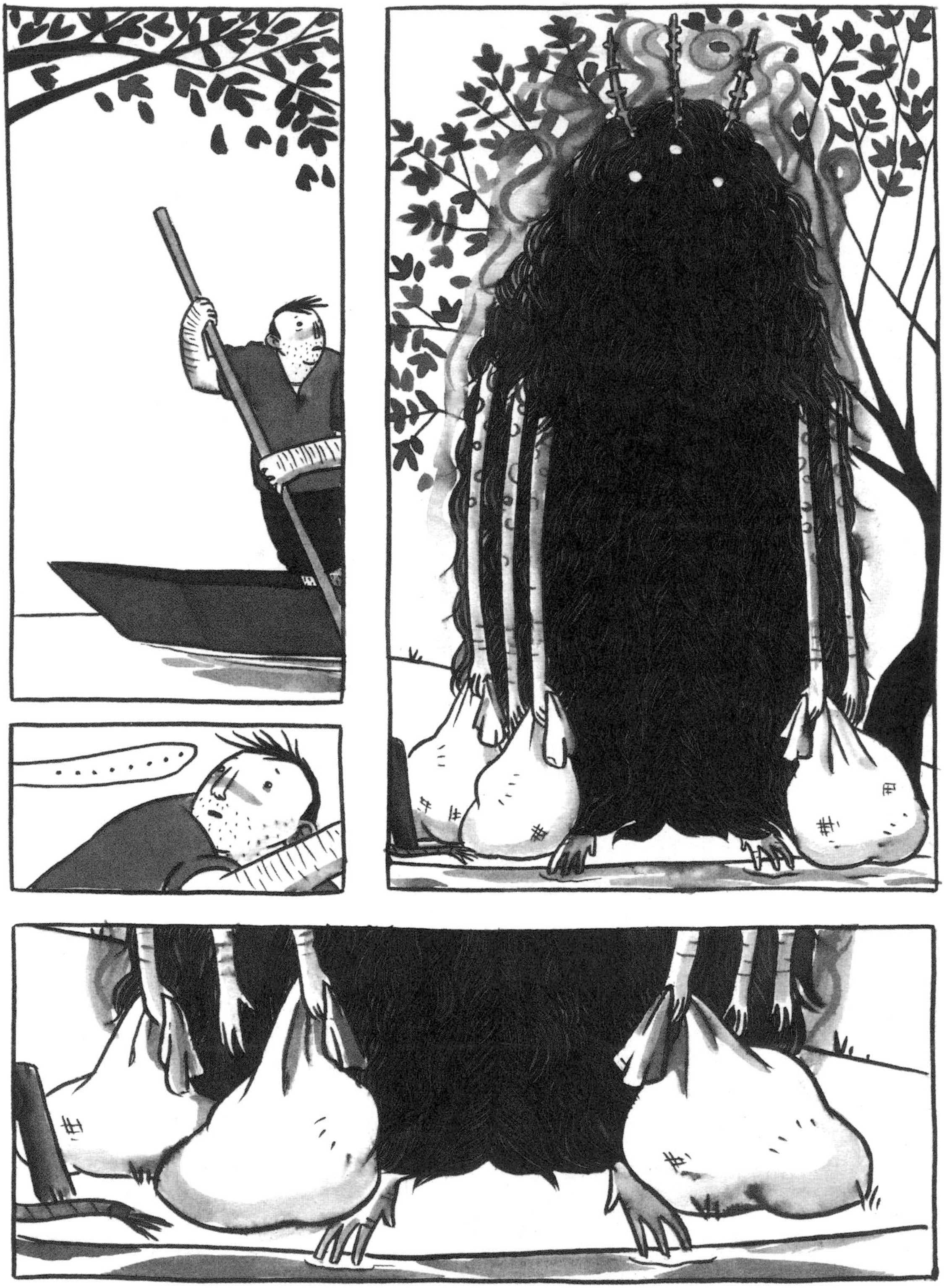

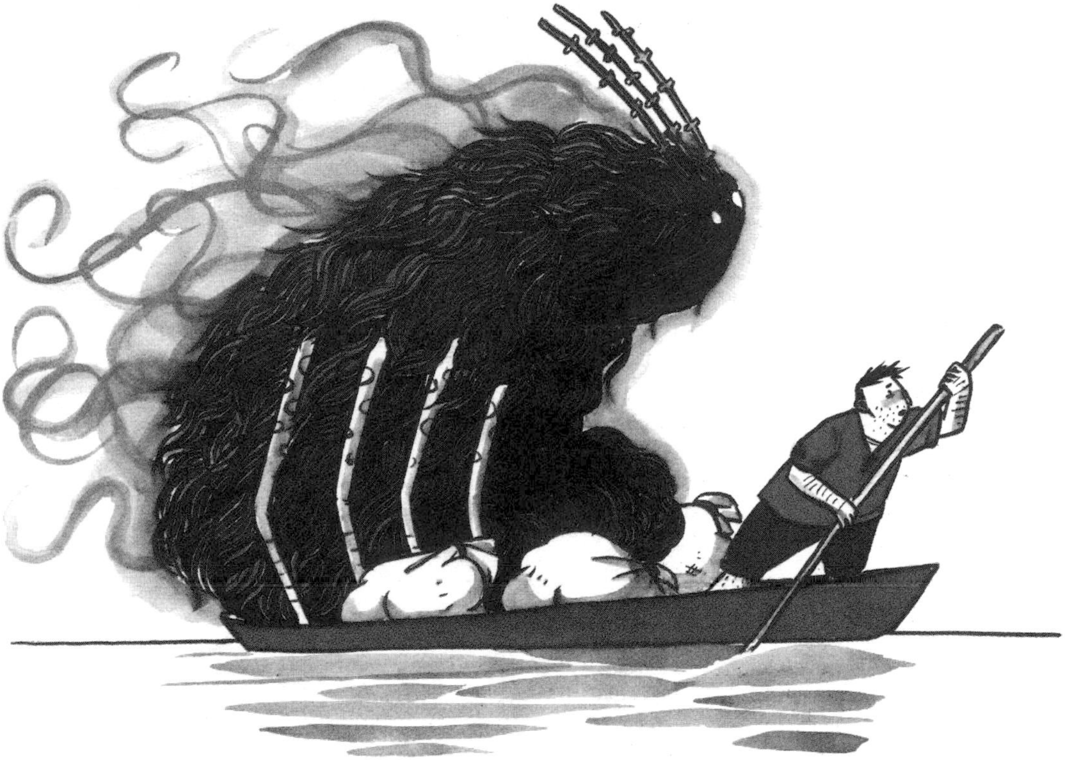

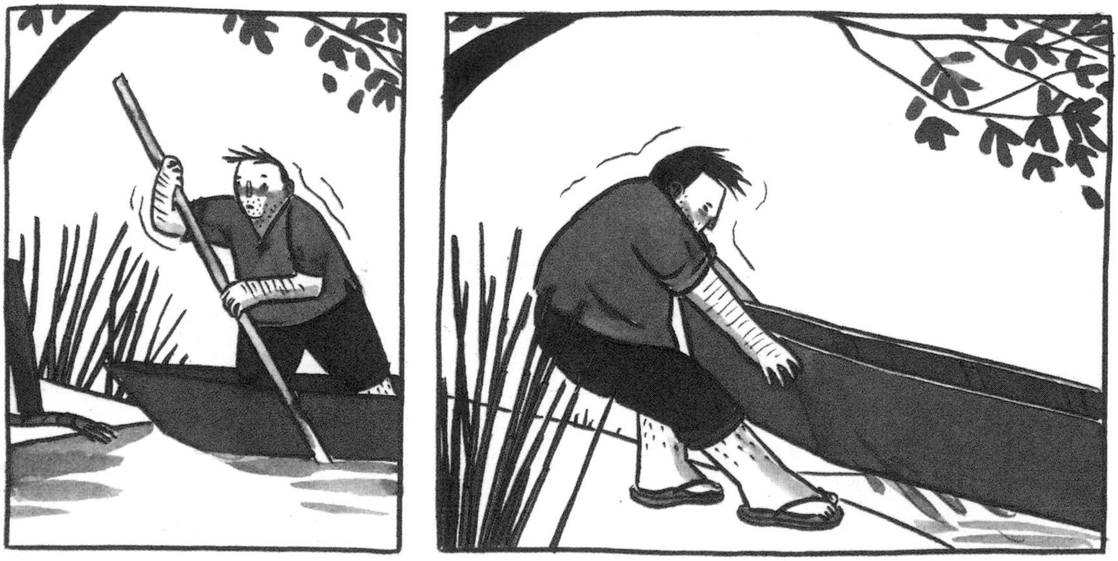

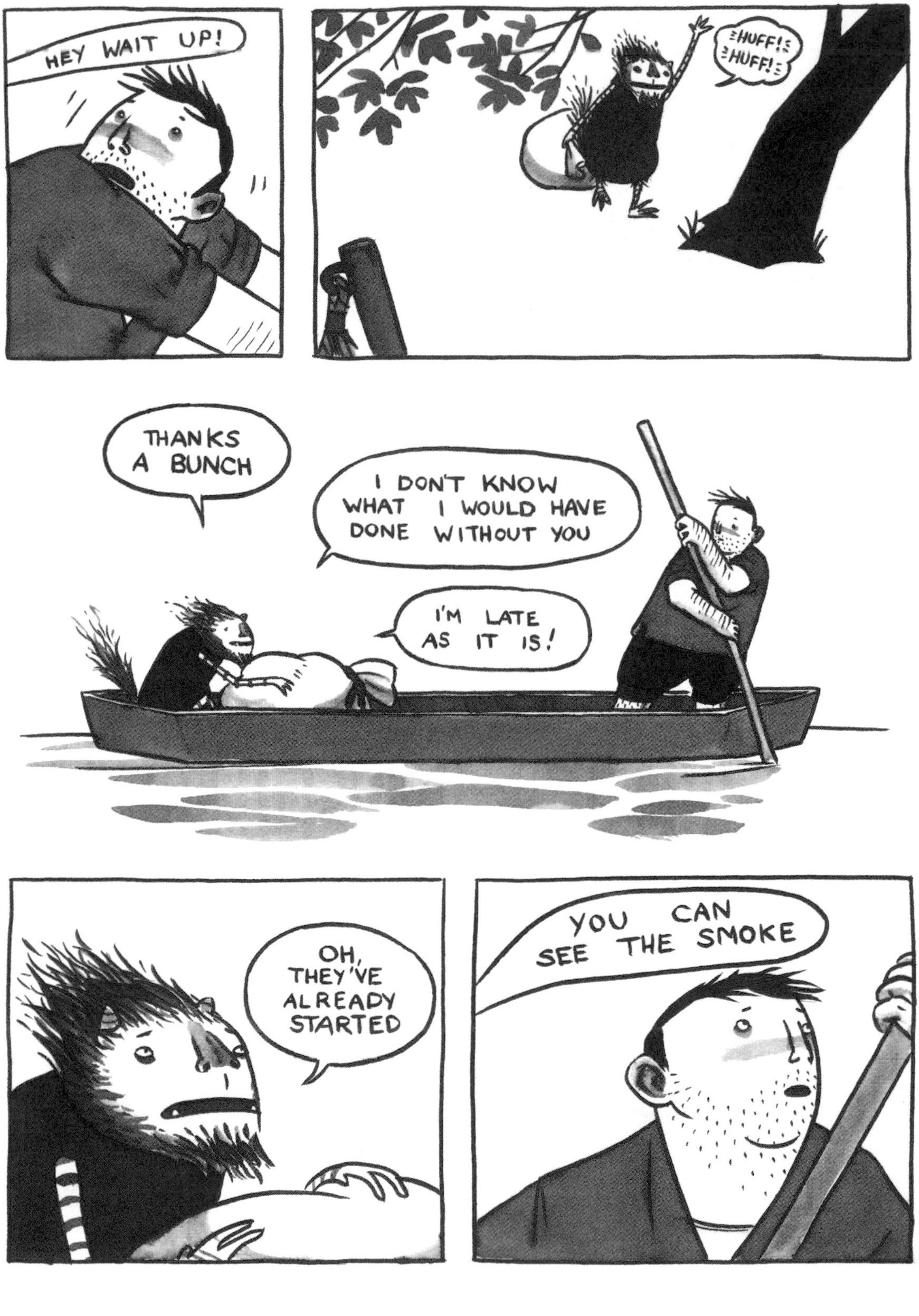
HEY WAIT UP!
HUFF! HUFF!
THANKS A BUNCH
I DON'T KNOW WHAT I WOULD HAVE DONE WITHOUT YOU
I'M LATE AS IT IS!
OH, THEY'VE ALREADY STARTED
YOU CAN SEE THE SMOKE

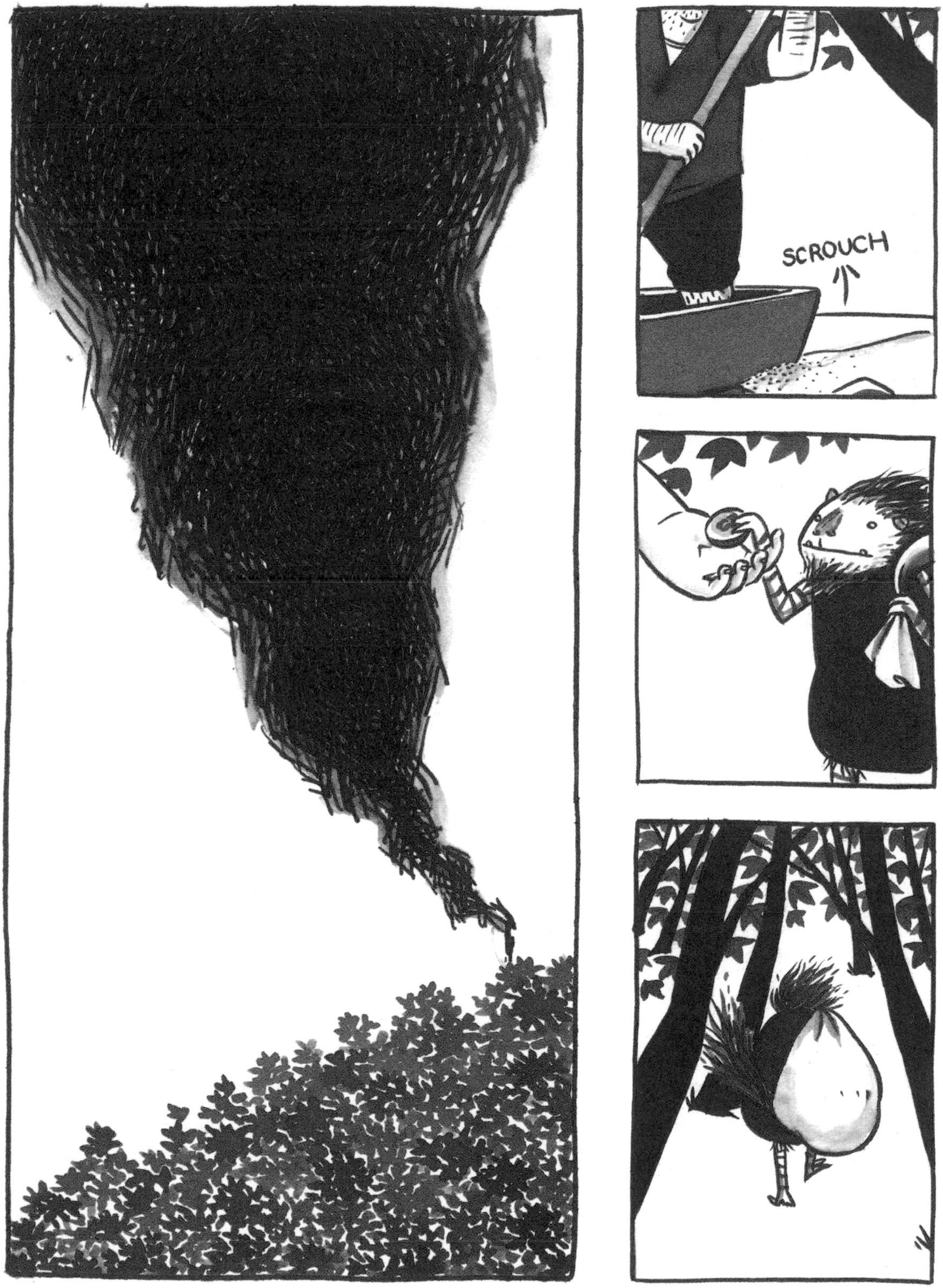
SCROUCH

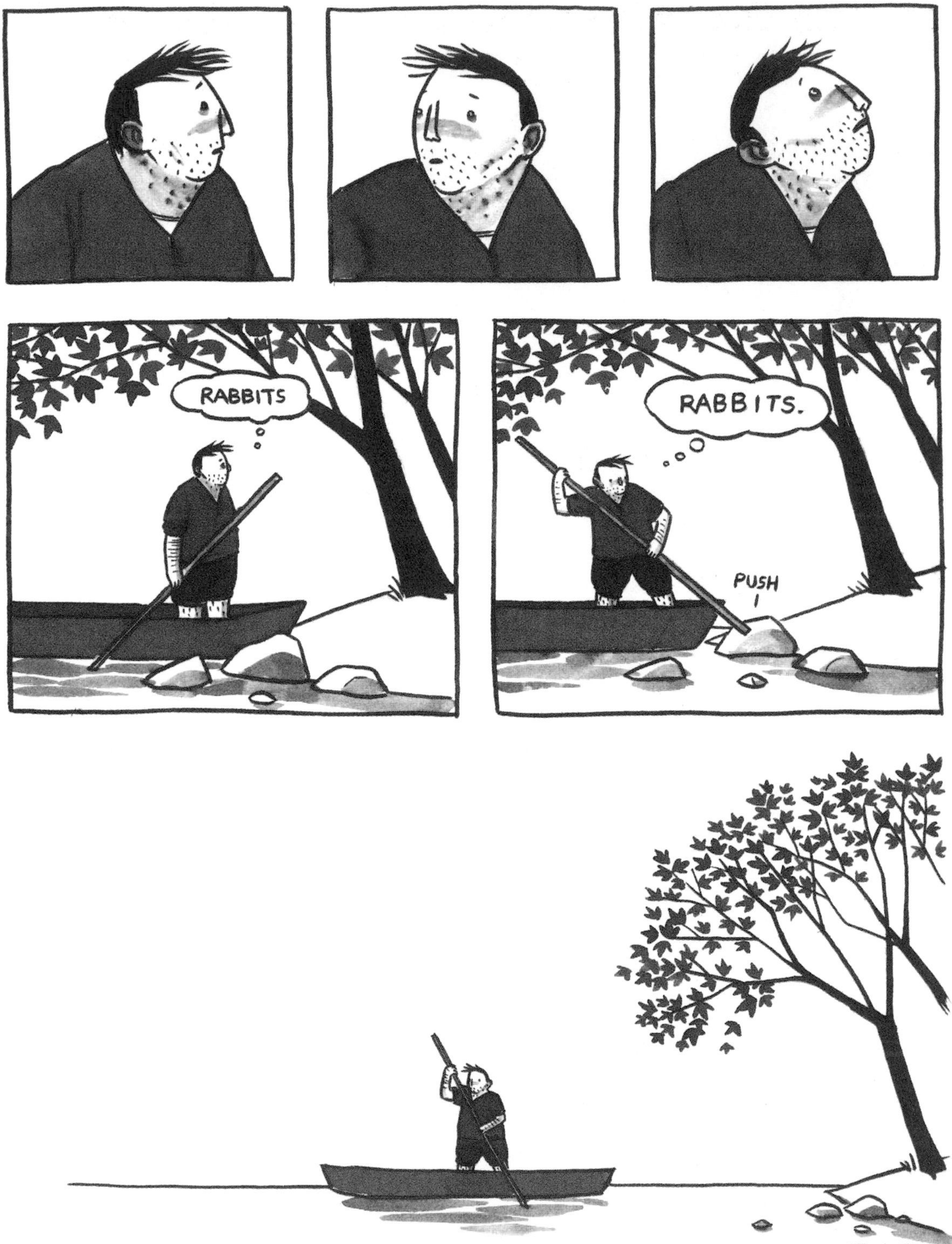
RABBITS
RABBITS.
PUSH
END

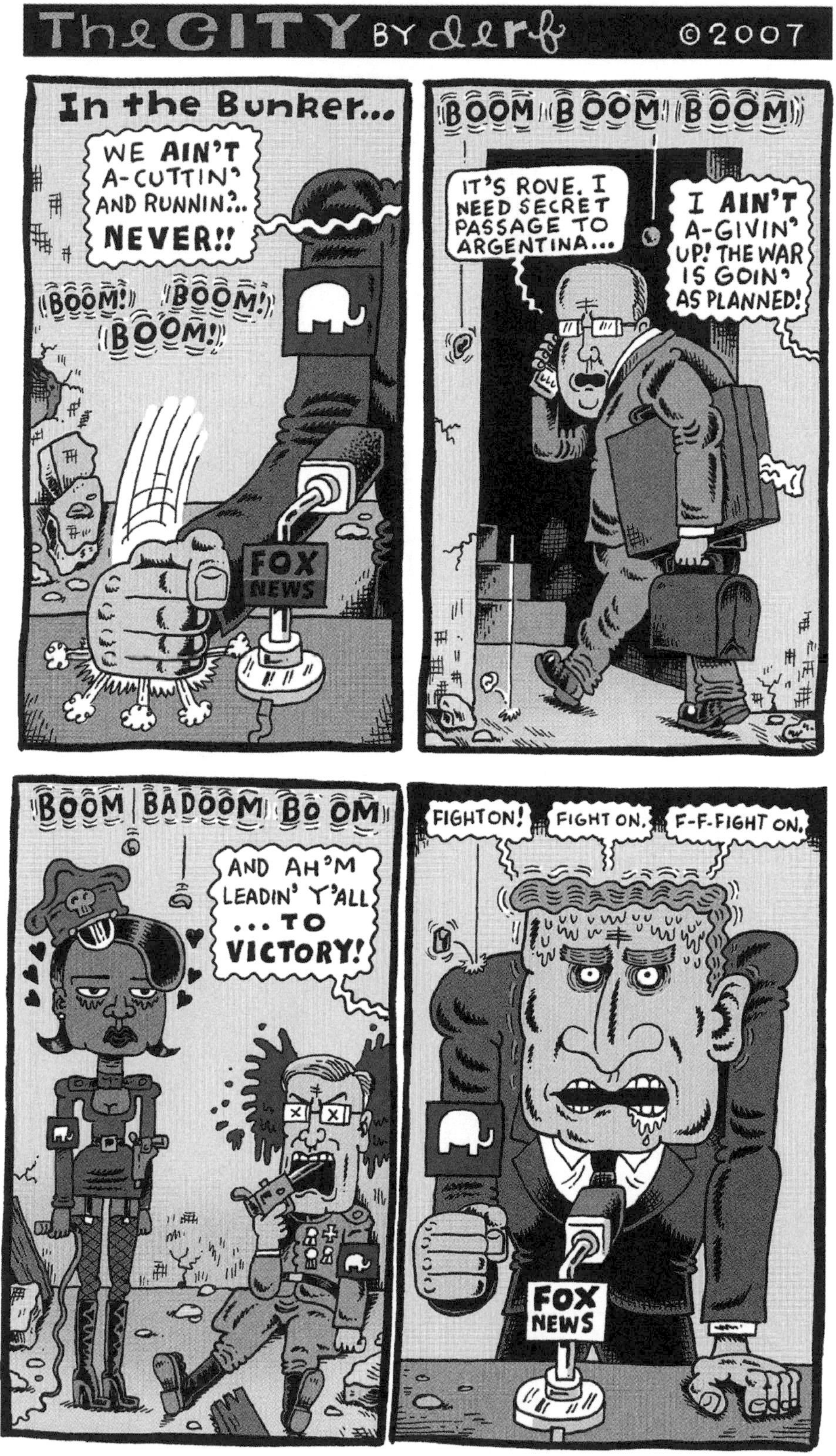
The CITY BY derf ©2007
In the Bunker...
WE AIN'T A-CUTTIN' AND RUNNIN'... NEVER!!
BOOM! BOOM! BOOM!
FOX NEWS
BOOM BOOM BOOM
IT'S ROVE. I NEED SECRET PASSAGE TO ARGENTINA...
I AIN'T A-GIVIN' UP! THE WAR IS GOIN' AS PLANNED!
BOOM BADOOM BOOM
AND AH'M LEADIN' Y'ALL ... TO VICTORY!
FIGHT ON!
FIGHT ON.
F-F-FIGHT ON.
FOX NEWS

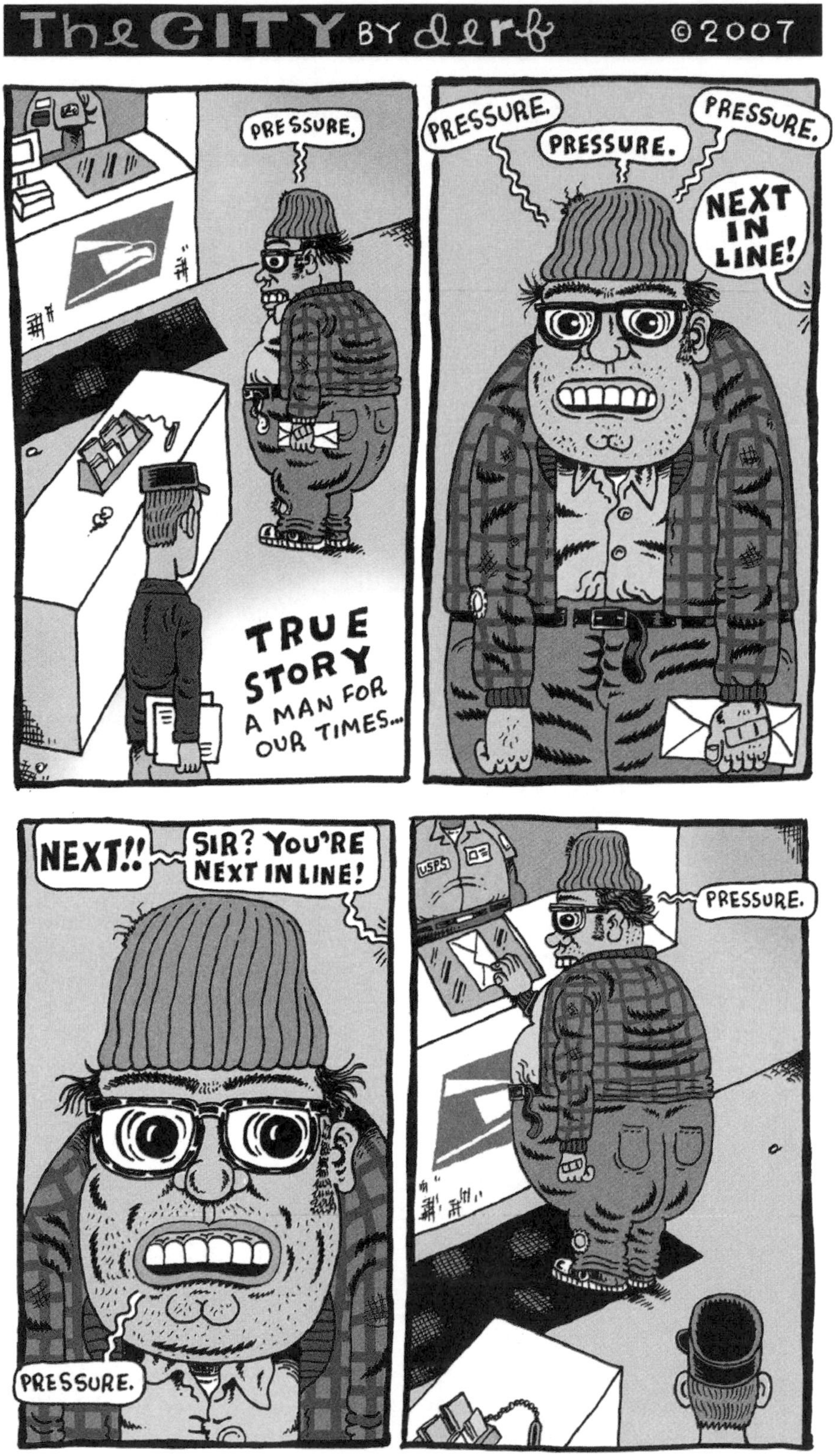
The CITY BY derf ©2007
PRESSURE.
TRUE STORY
A MAN FOR OUR TIMES...
PRESSURE.
PRESSURE.
PRESSURE.
NEXT IN LINE!
NEXT!!
SIR? YOU'RE NEXT IN LINE!
PRESSURE.
USPS
PRESSURE.

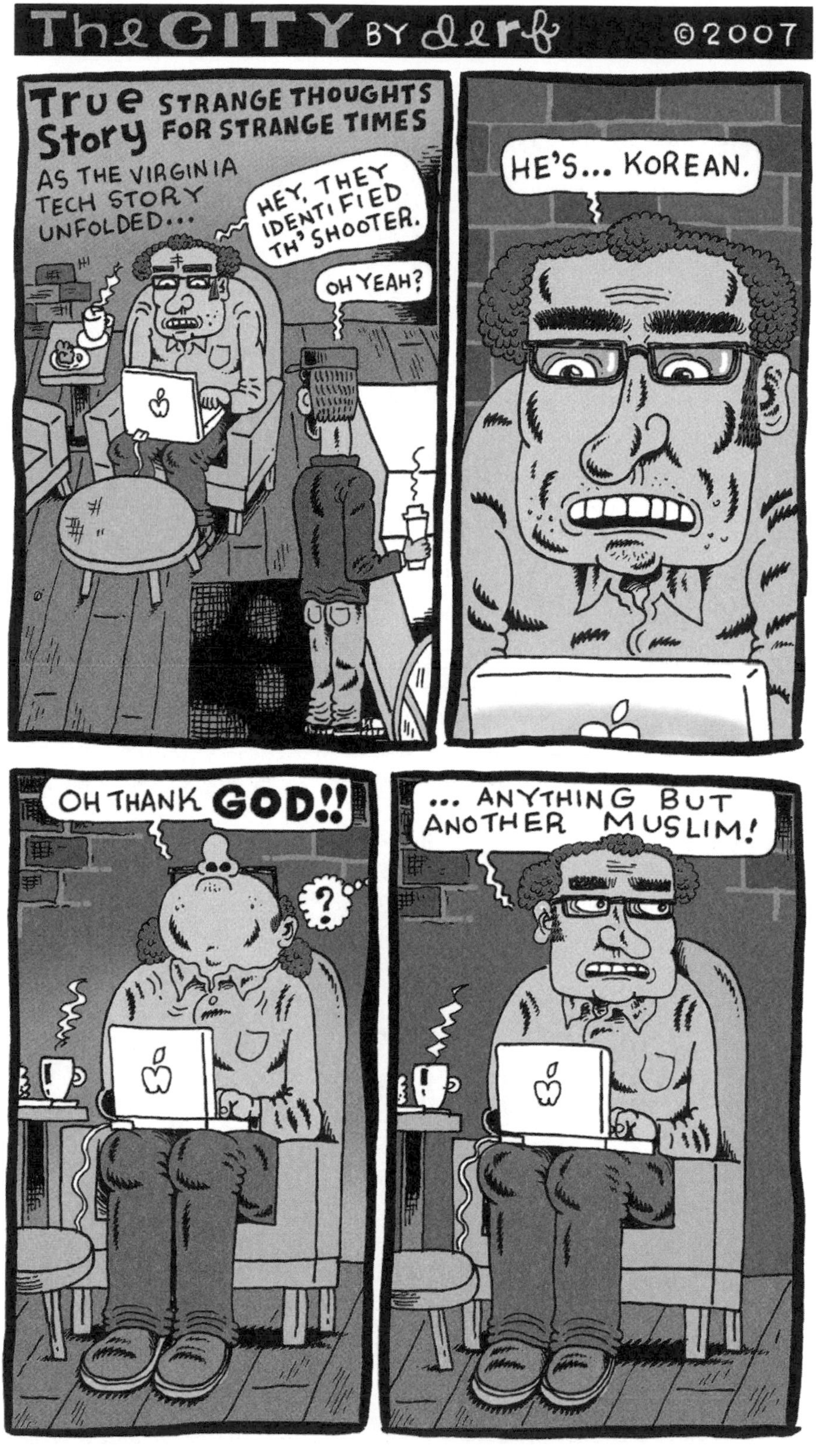
The CITY BY derf ©2007
True Story
STRANGE THOUGHTS FOR STRANGE TIMES
AS THE VIRGINIA TECH STORY UNFOLDED...
HEY, THEY IDENTIFIED TH' SHOOTER.
OH YEAH?
HE'S... KOREAN.
OH THANK GOD!!
?
... ANYTHING BUT ANOTHER MUSLIM!

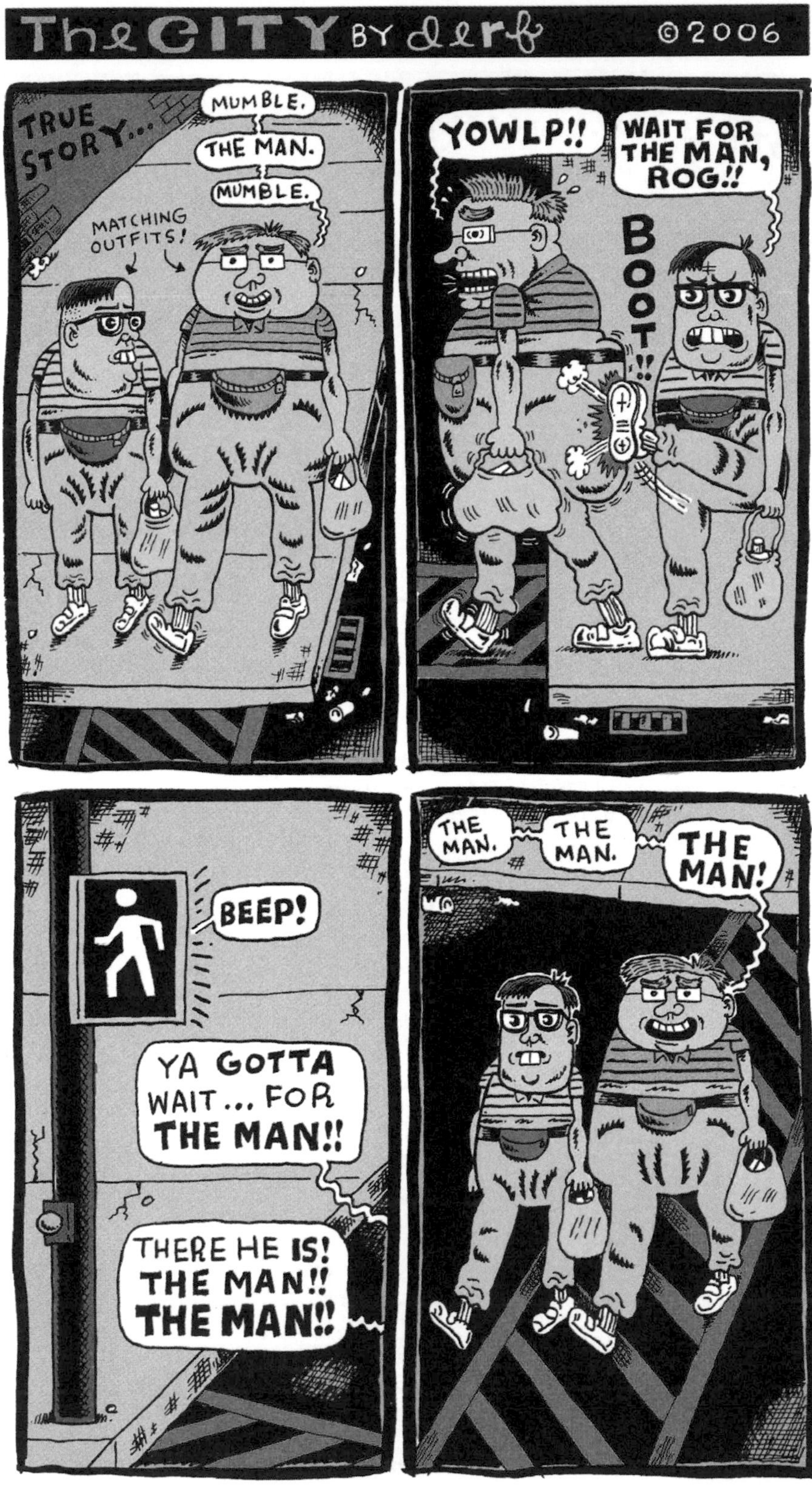
The CITY BY derf ©2006
TRUE STORY...
MUMBLE.
THE MAN.
MUMBLE.
MATCHING OUTFITS!
YOWLP!!
WAIT FOR THE MAN, ROG!!
BOOT!!
BEEP!
YA GOTTA WAIT... FOR THE MAN!!
THERE HE IS! THE MAN!! THE MAN!!
THE MAN.
THE MAN.
THE MAN!

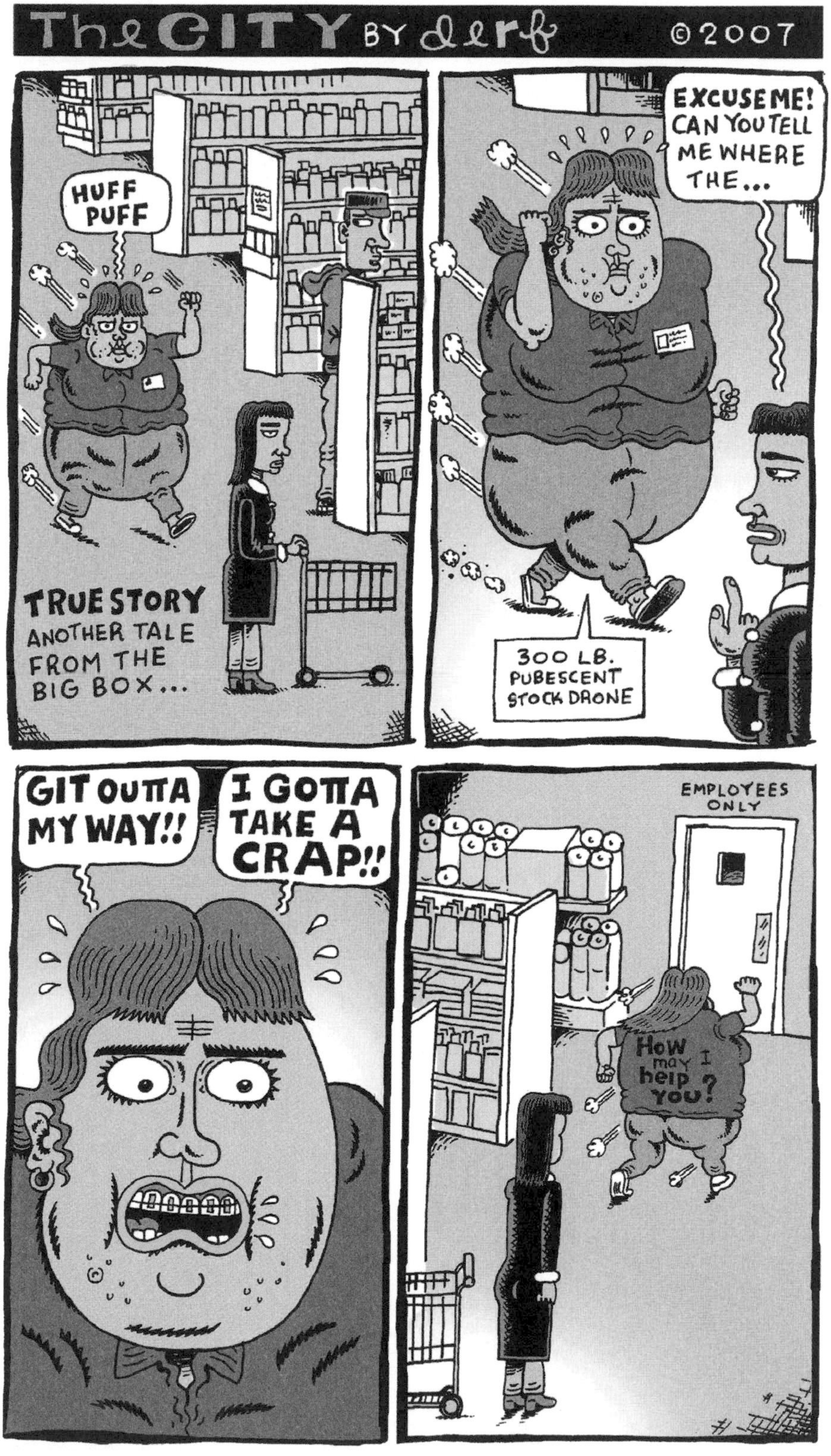
The CITY BY derf ©2007
HUFF PUFF
TRUE STORY
ANOTHER TALE FROM THE BIG BOX...
EXCUSE ME! CAN YOU TELL ME WHERE THE...
300 LB. PUBESCENT STOCK DRONE
GIT OUTTA MY WAY!!
I GOTTA TAKE A CRAP!!
EMPLOYEES ONLY
How may I help you?

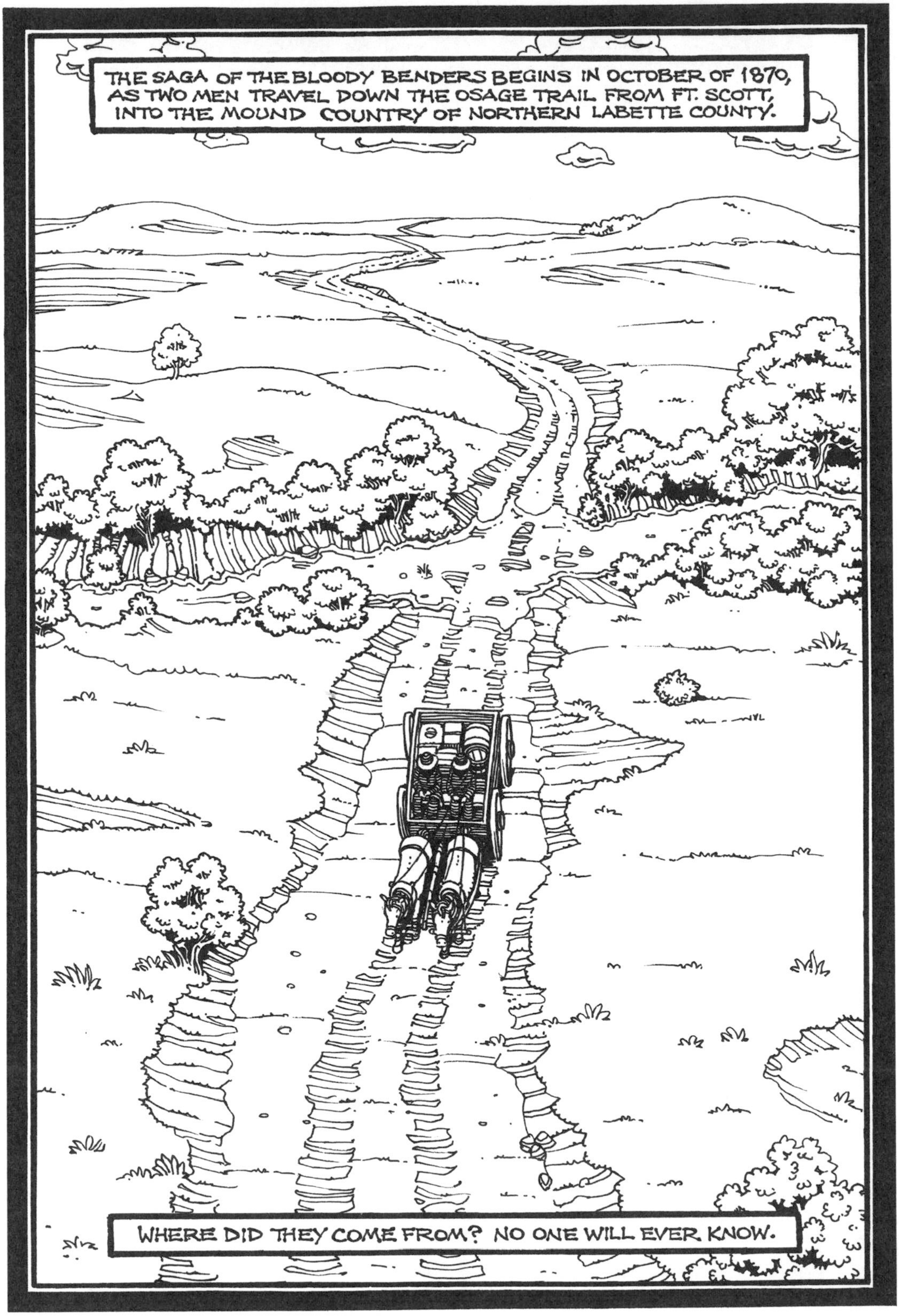
THE SAGA OF THE BLOODY BENDERS BEGINS IN OCTOBER OF 1870, AS TWO MEN TRAVEL DOWN THE OSAGE TRAIL FROM FT. SCOTT, INTO THE MOUND COUNTRY OF NORTHERN LABETTE COUNTY.
WHERE DID THEY COME FROM? NO ONE WILL EVER KNOW.

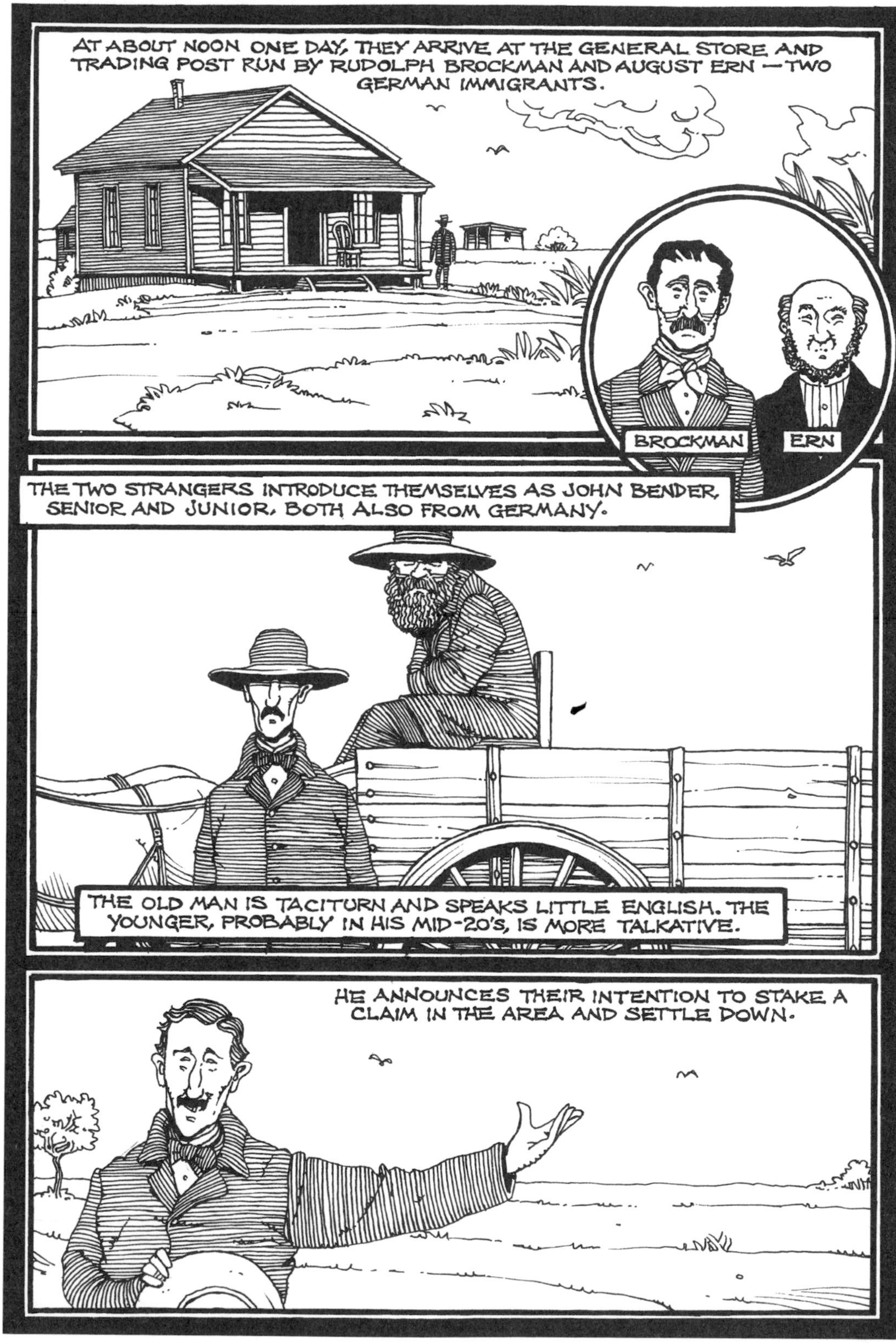
AT ABOUT NOON ONE DAY, THEY ARRIVE AT THE GENERAL STORE AND TRADING POST RUN BY RUDOLPH BROCKMAN AND AUGUST ERN — TWO GERMAN IMMIGRANTS.
BROCKMAN
ERN
THE TWO STRANGERS INTRODUCE THEMSELVES AS JOHN BENDER, SENIOR AND JUNIOR, BOTH ALSO FROM GERMANY.
THE OLD MAN IS TACITURN AND SPEAKS LITTLE ENGLISH. THE YOUNGER, PROBABLY IN HIS MID-20'S, IS MORE TALKATIVE.
HE ANNOUNCES THEIR INTENTION TO STAKE A CLAIM IN THE AREA AND SETTLE DOWN.

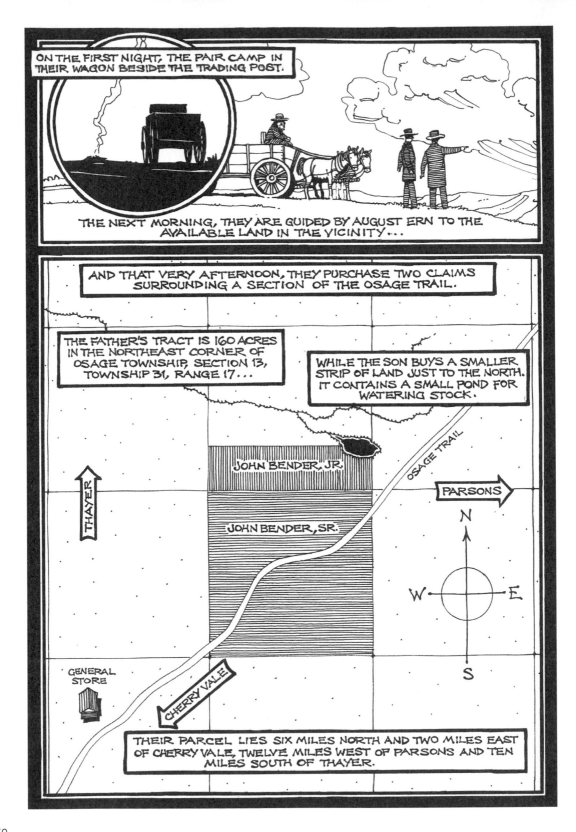

ON THE FIRST NIGHT, THE PAIR CAMP IN THEIR WAGON BESIDE THE TRADING POST.

THE NEXT MORNING, THEY ARE GUIDED BY AUGUST ERN TO THE AVAILABLE LAND IN THE VICINITY...

AND THAT VERY AFTERNOON, THEY PURCHASE TWO CLAIMS SURROUNDING A SECTION OF THE OSAGE TRAIL.

THE FATHER'S TRACT IS 160 ACRES IN THE NORTHEAST CORNER OF OSAGE TOWNSHIP, SECTION 13, TOWNSHIP 31, RANGE 17...

WHILE THE SON BUYS A SMALLER STRIP OF LAND JUST TO THE NORTH. IT CONTAINS A SMALL POND FOR WATERING STOCK.

JOHN BENDER, JR.

JOHN BENDER, SR.

OSAGE TRAIL

THAYER

PARSONS

N
W · E
S

GENERAL STORE

CHERRY VALE

THEIR PARCEL LIES SIX MILES NORTH AND TWO MILES EAST OF CHERRY VALE, TWELVE MILES WEST OF PARSONS AND TEN MILES SOUTH OF THAYER.

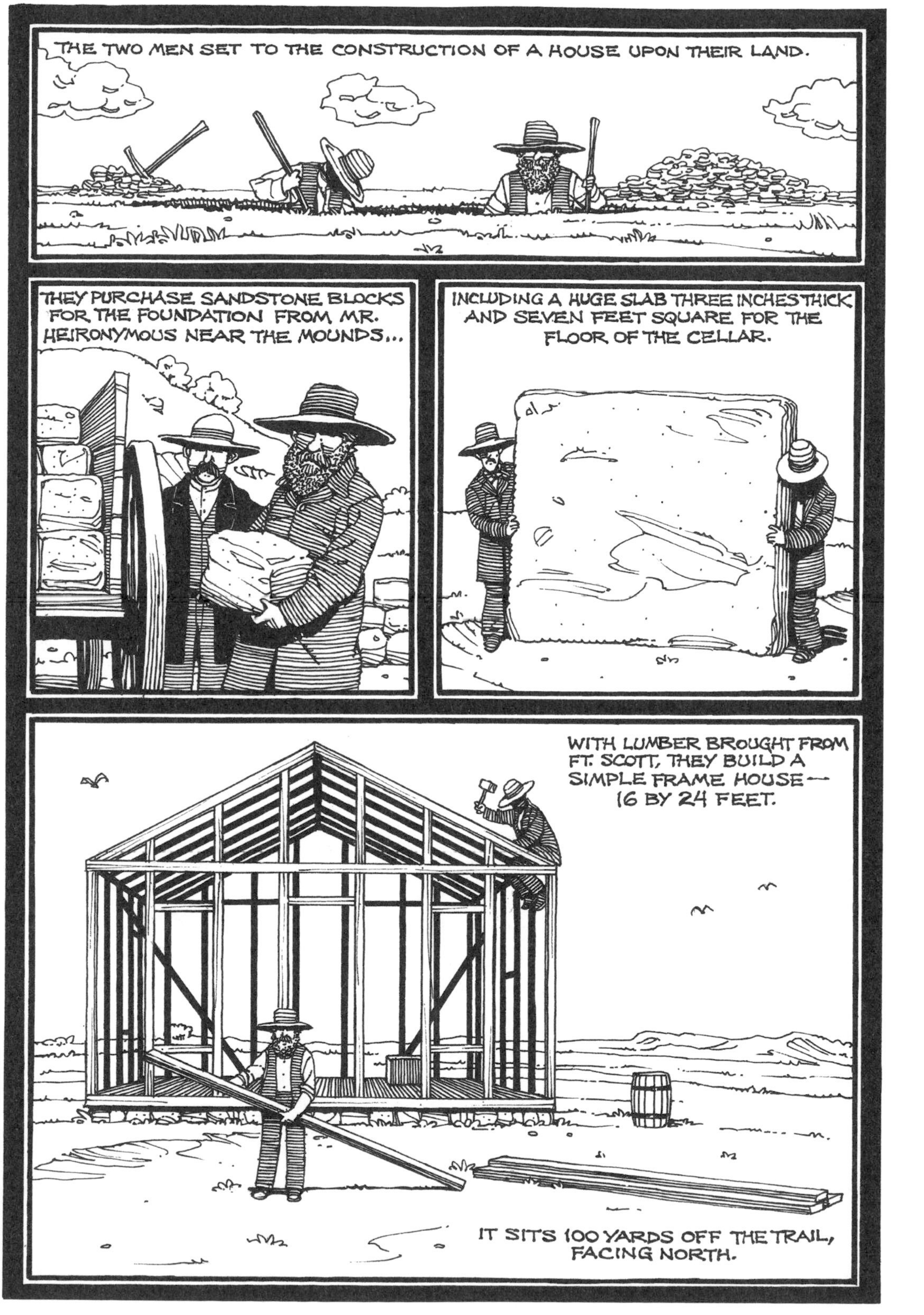
THE TWO MEN SET TO THE CONSTRUCTION OF A HOUSE UPON THEIR LAND.
THEY PURCHASE SANDSTONE BLOCKS FOR THE FOUNDATION FROM MR. HEIRONYMOUS NEAR THE MOUNDS...
INCLUDING A HUGE SLAB THREE INCHES THICK AND SEVEN FEET SQUARE FOR THE FLOOR OF THE CELLAR.
WITH LUMBER BROUGHT FROM FT. SCOTT, THEY BUILD A SIMPLE FRAME HOUSE— 16 BY 24 FEET.
IT SITS 100 YARDS OFF THE TRAIL, FACING NORTH.

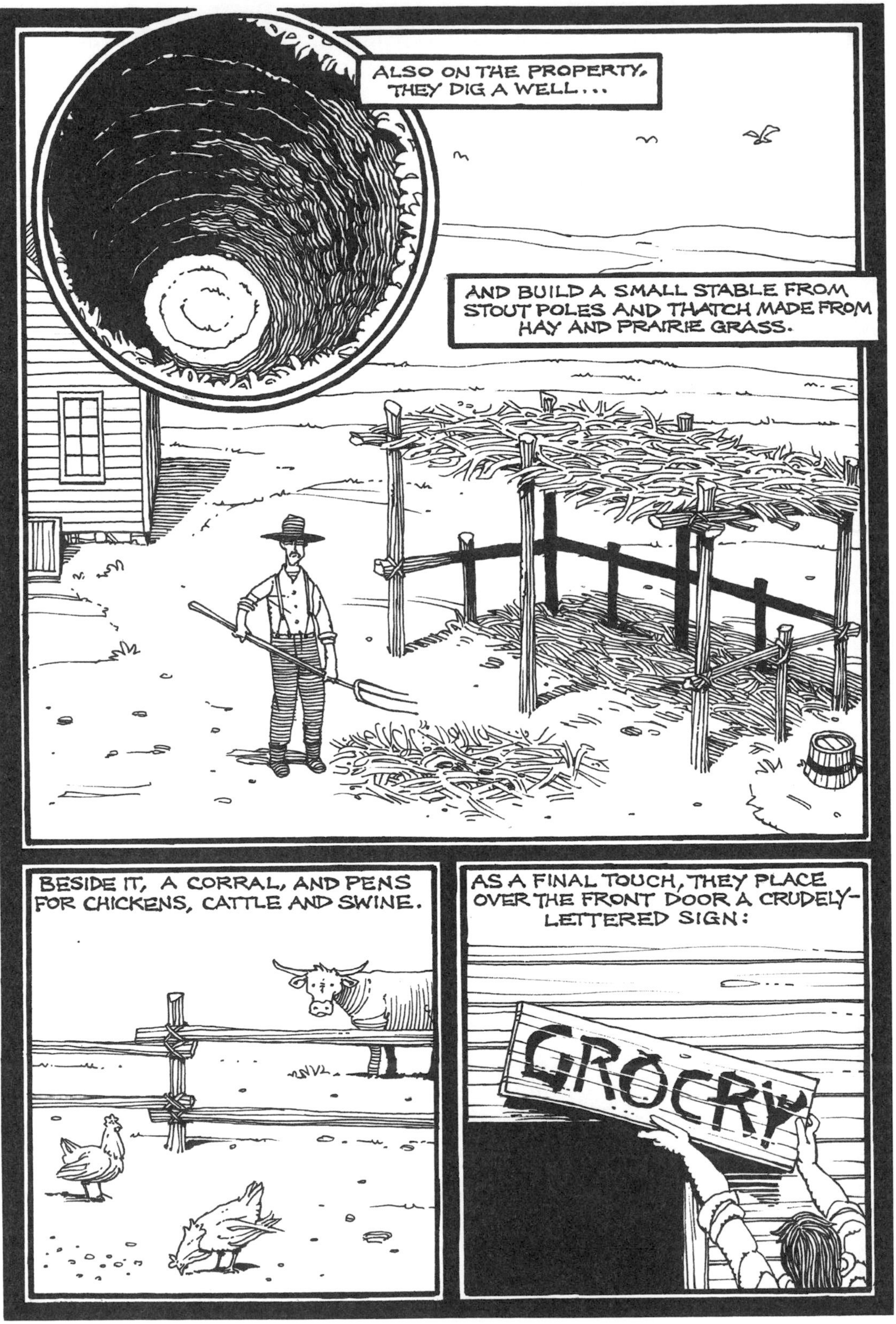
ALSO ON THE PROPERTY, THEY DIG A WELL...
AND BUILD A SMALL STABLE FROM STOUT POLES AND THATCH MADE FROM HAY AND PRAIRIE GRASS.
BESIDE IT, A CORRAL, AND PENS FOR CHICKENS, CATTLE AND SWINE.
AS A FINAL TOUCH, THEY PLACE OVER THE FRONT DOOR A CRUDELY-LETTERED SIGN:
GROCRY

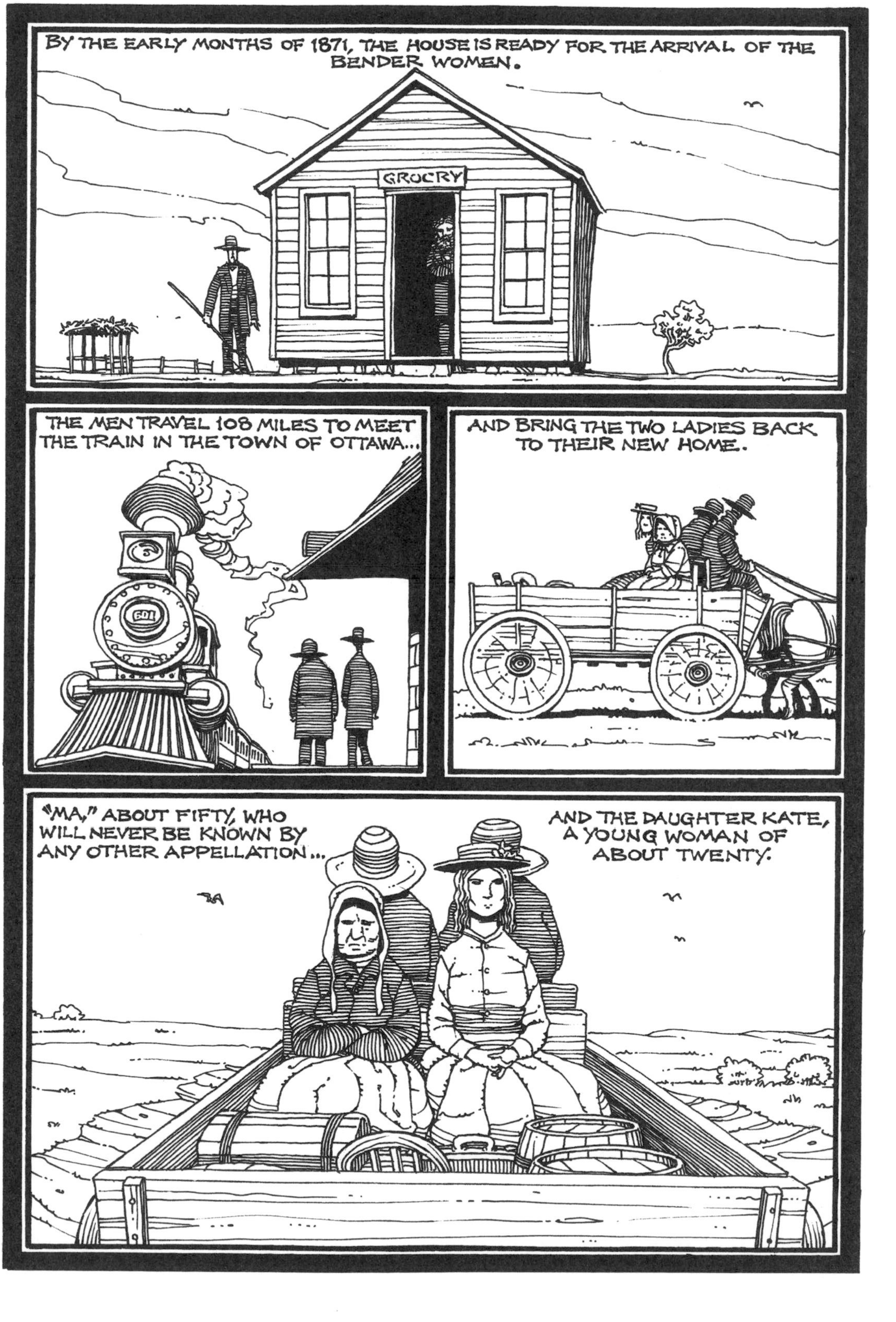

BY THE EARLY MONTHS OF 1871, THE HOUSE IS READY FOR THE ARRIVAL OF THE BENDER WOMEN.
GROCRY
THE MEN TRAVEL 108 MILES TO MEET THE TRAIN IN THE TOWN OF OTTAWA...
AND BRING THE TWO LADIES BACK TO THEIR NEW HOME.
"MA," ABOUT FIFTY, WHO WILL NEVER BE KNOWN BY ANY OTHER APPELLATION...
AND THE DAUGHTER KATE, A YOUNG WOMAN OF ABOUT TWENTY.

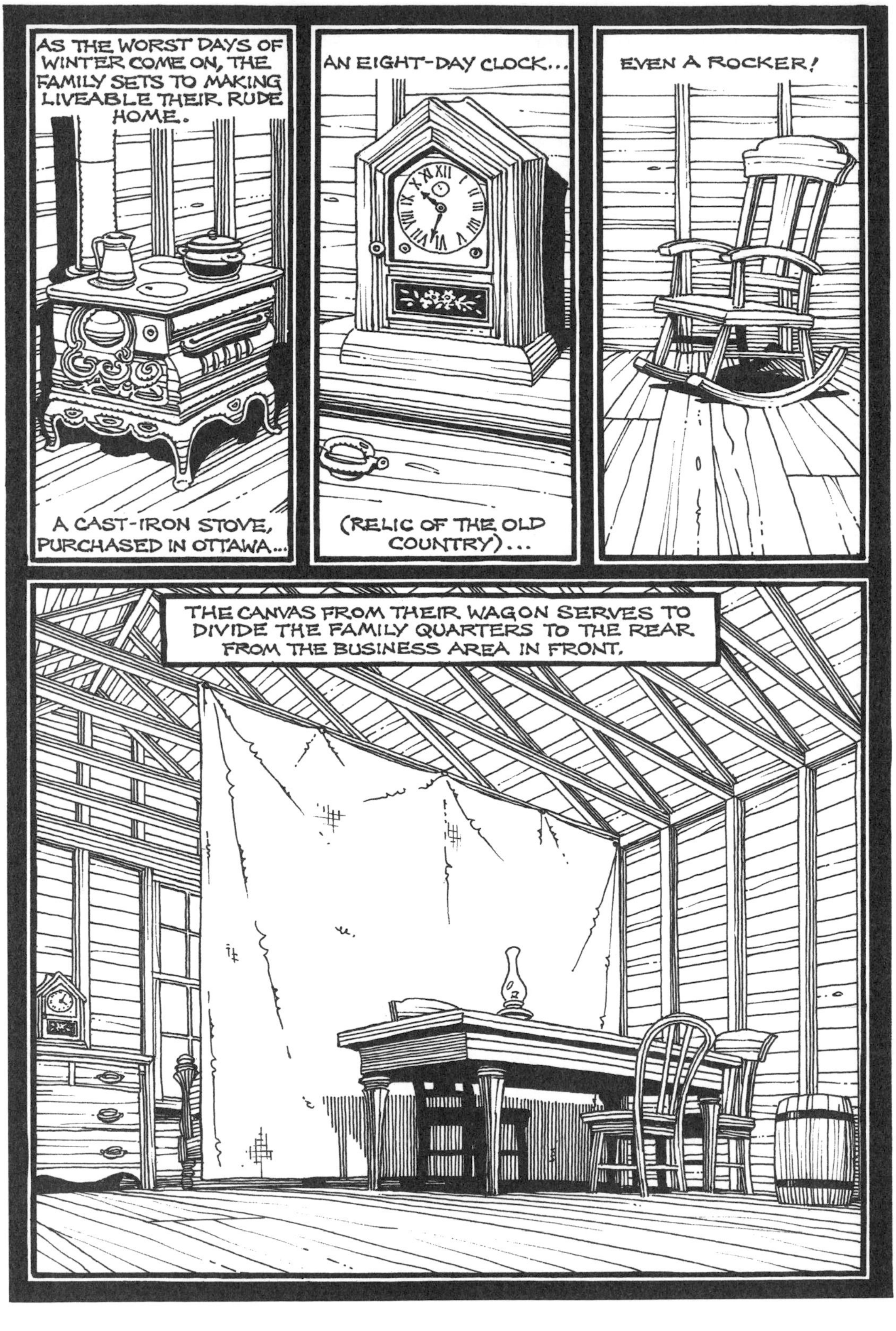

AS THE WORST DAYS OF WINTER COME ON, THE FAMILY SETS TO MAKING LIVEABLE THEIR RUDE HOME.
A CAST-IRON STOVE, PURCHASED IN OTTAWA...
AN EIGHT-DAY CLOCK...
(RELIC OF THE OLD COUNTRY)...
EVEN A ROCKER!
THE CANVAS FROM THEIR WAGON SERVES TO DIVIDE THE FAMILY QUARTERS TO THE REAR FROM THE BUSINESS AREA IN FRONT.

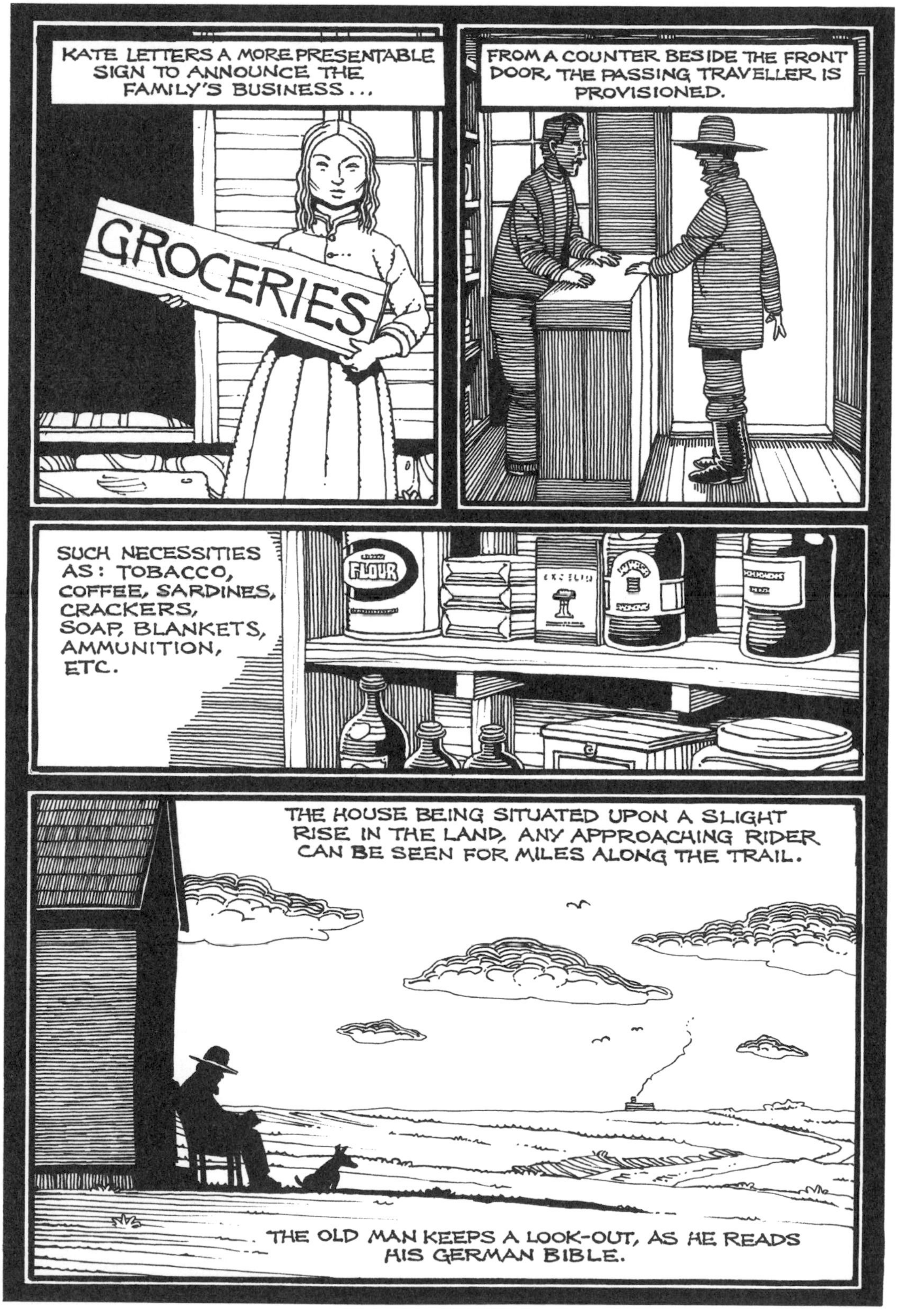
KATE LETTERS A MORE PRESENTABLE SIGN TO ANNOUNCE THE FAMILY'S BUSINESS...
GROCERIES
FROM A COUNTER BESIDE THE FRONT DOOR, THE PASSING TRAVELLER IS PROVISIONED.
SUCH NECESSITIES AS: TOBACCO, COFFEE, SARDINES, CRACKERS, SOAP, BLANKETS, AMMUNITION, ETC.
FLOUR
THE HOUSE BEING SITUATED UPON A SLIGHT RISE IN THE LAND, ANY APPROACHING RIDER CAN BE SEEN FOR MILES ALONG THE TRAIL.
THE OLD MAN KEEPS A LOOK-OUT, AS HE READS HIS GERMAN BIBLE.

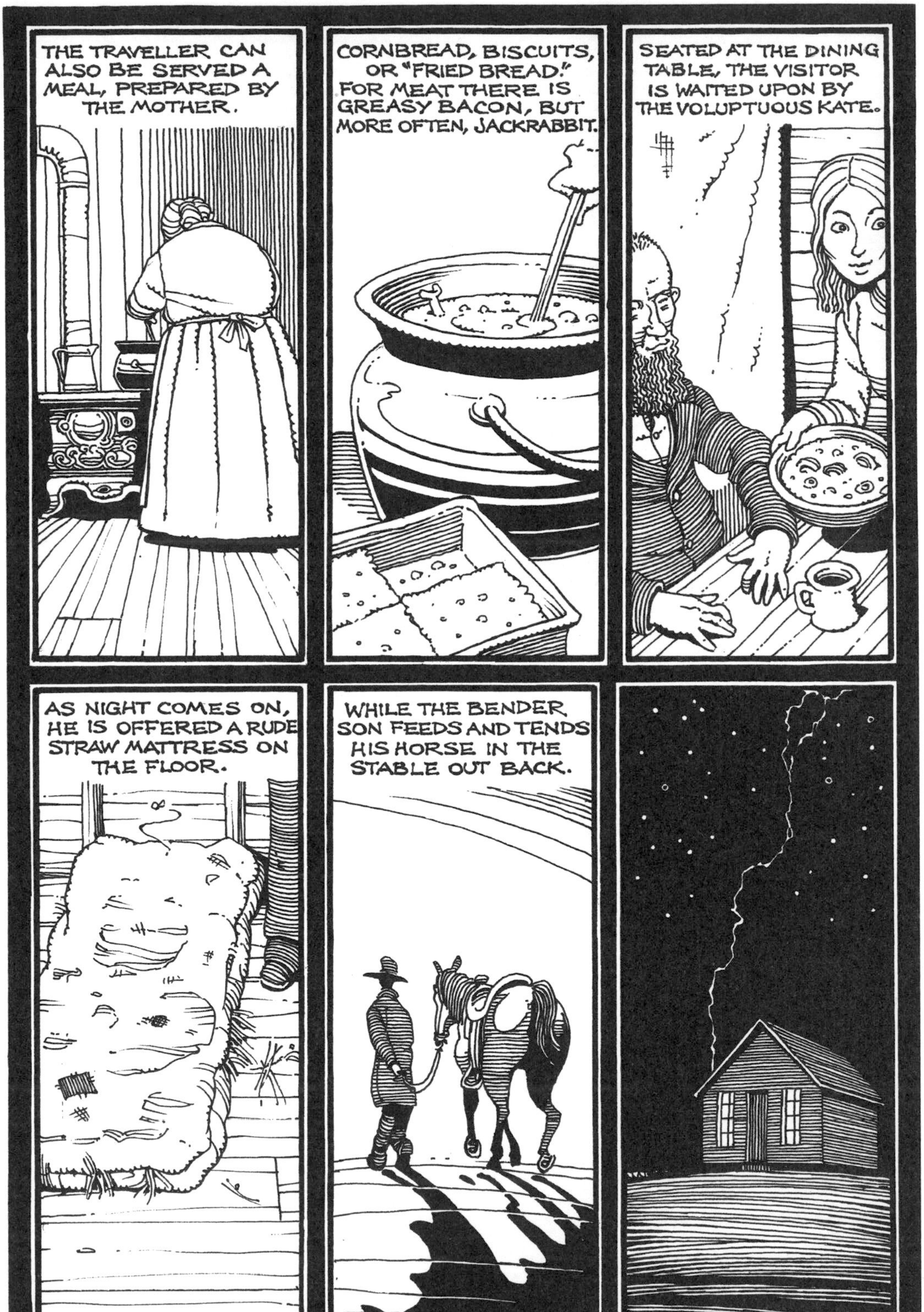
THE TRAVELLER CAN ALSO BE SERVED A MEAL, PREPARED BY THE MOTHER.
CORNBREAD, BISCUITS, OR "FRIED BREAD." FOR MEAT THERE IS GREASY BACON, BUT MORE OFTEN, JACKRABBIT.
SEATED AT THE DINING TABLE, THE VISITOR IS WAITED UPON BY THE VOLUPTUOUS KATE.
AS NIGHT COMES ON, HE IS OFFERED A RUDE STRAW MATTRESS ON THE FLOOR.
WHILE THE BENDER SON FEEDS AND TENDS HIS HORSE IN THE STABLE OUT BACK.

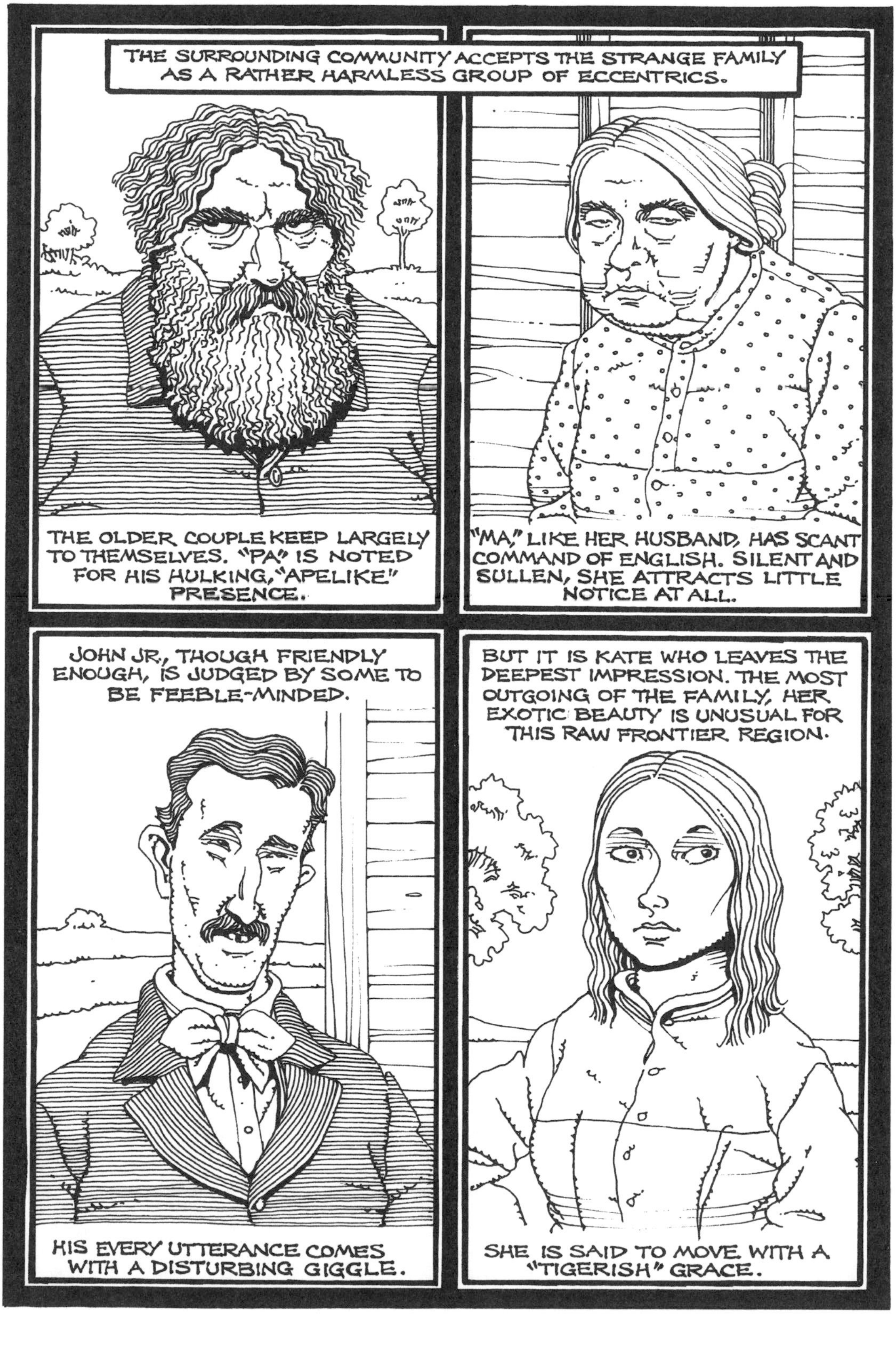
THE SURROUNDING COMMUNITY ACCEPTS THE STRANGE FAMILY AS A RATHER HARMLESS GROUP OF ECCENTRICS.
THE OLDER COUPLE KEEP LARGELY TO THEMSELVES. "PA" IS NOTED FOR HIS HULKING, "APELIKE" PRESENCE.
"MA," LIKE HER HUSBAND, HAS SCANT COMMAND OF ENGLISH. SILENT AND SULLEN, SHE ATTRACTS LITTLE NOTICE AT ALL.
JOHN JR., THOUGH FRIENDLY ENOUGH, IS JUDGED BY SOME TO BE FEEBLE-MINDED.
HIS EVERY UTTERANCE COMES WITH A DISTURBING GIGGLE.
BUT IT IS KATE WHO LEAVES THE DEEPEST IMPRESSION. THE MOST OUTGOING OF THE FAMILY, HER EXOTIC BEAUTY IS UNUSUAL FOR THIS RAW FRONTIER REGION.
SHE IS SAID TO MOVE WITH A "TIGERISH" GRACE.

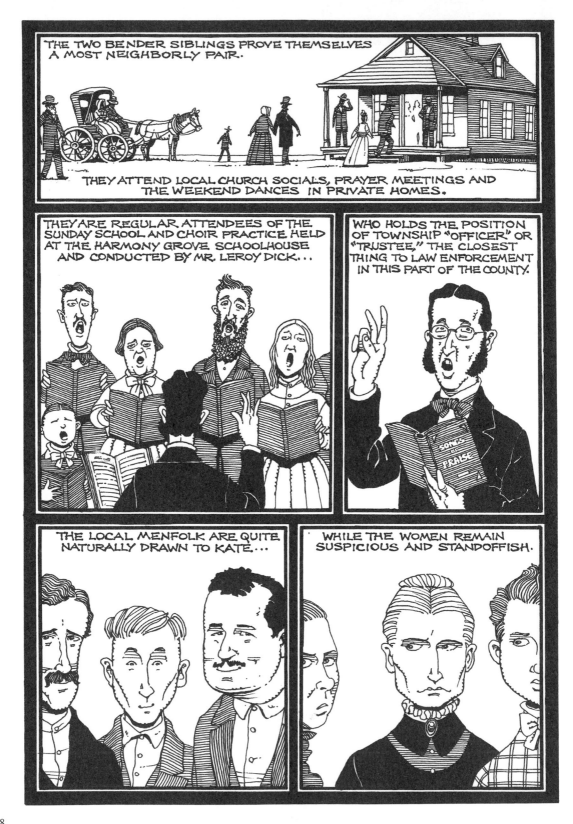

THE TWO BENDER SIBLINGS PROVE THEMSELVES A MOST NEIGHBORLY PAIR.

THEY ATTEND LOCAL CHURCH SOCIALS, PRAYER MEETINGS AND THE WEEKEND DANCES IN PRIVATE HOMES.

THEY ARE REGULAR ATTENDEES OF THE SUNDAY SCHOOL AND CHOIR PRACTICE HELD AT THE HARMONY GROVE SCHOOLHOUSE AND CONDUCTED BY MR. LEROY DICK...

WHO HOLDS THE POSITION OF TOWNSHIP "OFFICER," OR "TRUSTEE," THE CLOSEST THING TO LAW ENFORCEMENT IN THIS PART OF THE COUNTY.

THE LOCAL MENFOLK ARE QUITE NATURALLY DRAWN TO KATE....

WHILE THE WOMEN REMAIN SUSPICIOUS AND STANDOFFISH.

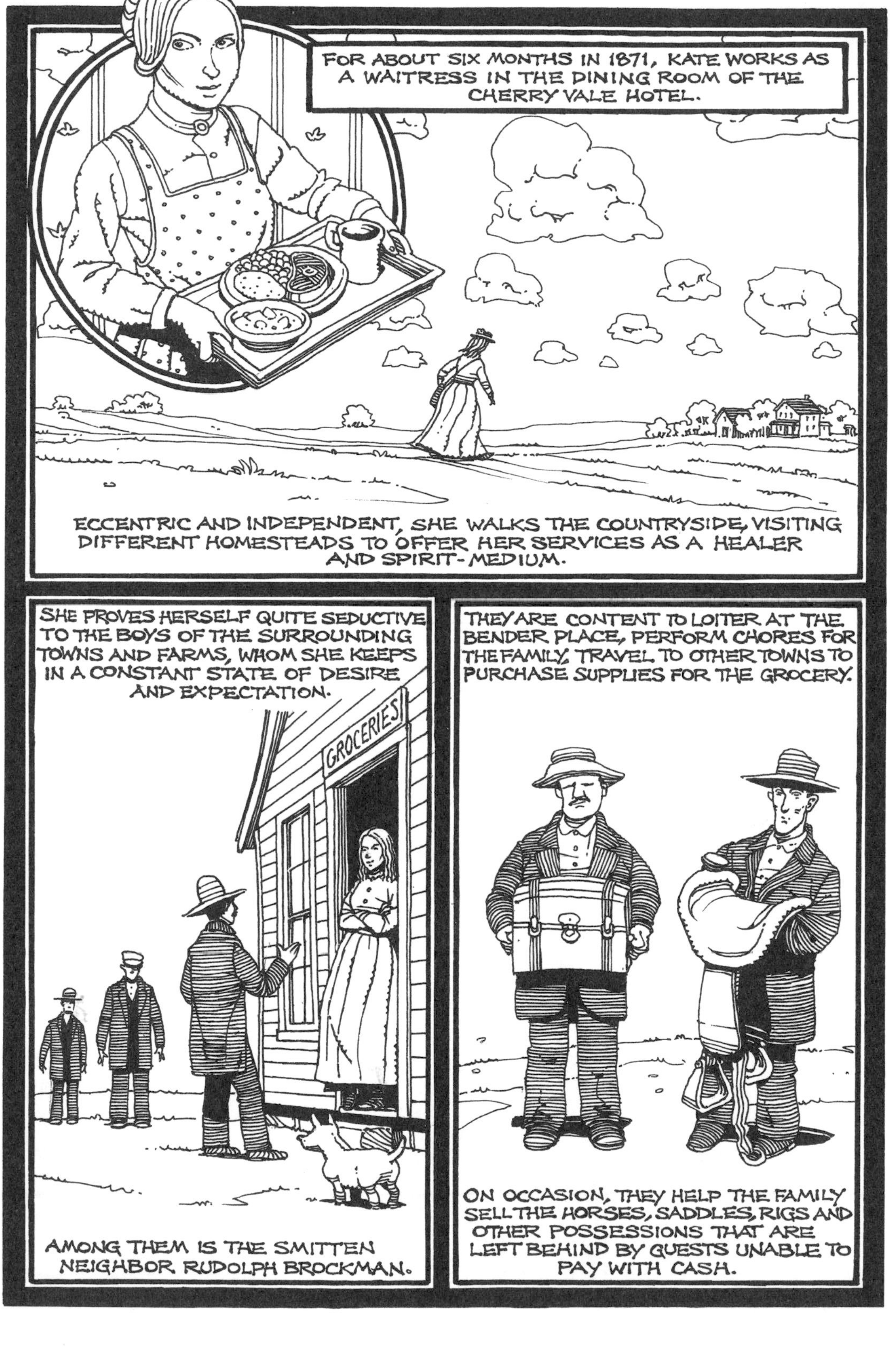
FOR ABOUT SIX MONTHS IN 1871, KATE WORKS AS A WAITRESS IN THE DINING ROOM OF THE CHERRY VALE HOTEL.
ECCENTRIC AND INDEPENDENT, SHE WALKS THE COUNTRYSIDE, VISITING DIFFERENT HOMESTEADS TO OFFER HER SERVICES AS A HEALER AND SPIRIT-MEDIUM.
SHE PROVES HERSELF QUITE SEDUCTIVE TO THE BOYS OF THE SURROUNDING TOWNS AND FARMS, WHOM SHE KEEPS IN A CONSTANT STATE OF DESIRE AND EXPECTATION.
GROCERIES
AMONG THEM IS THE SMITTEN NEIGHBOR RUDOLPH BROCKMAN.
THEY ARE CONTENT TO LOITER AT THE BENDER PLACE, PERFORM CHORES FOR THE FAMILY, TRAVEL TO OTHER TOWNS TO PURCHASE SUPPLIES FOR THE GROCERY.
ON OCCASION, THEY HELP THE FAMILY SELL THE HORSES, SADDLES, RIGS AND OTHER POSSESSIONS THAT ARE LEFT BEHIND BY GUESTS UNABLE TO PAY WITH CASH.

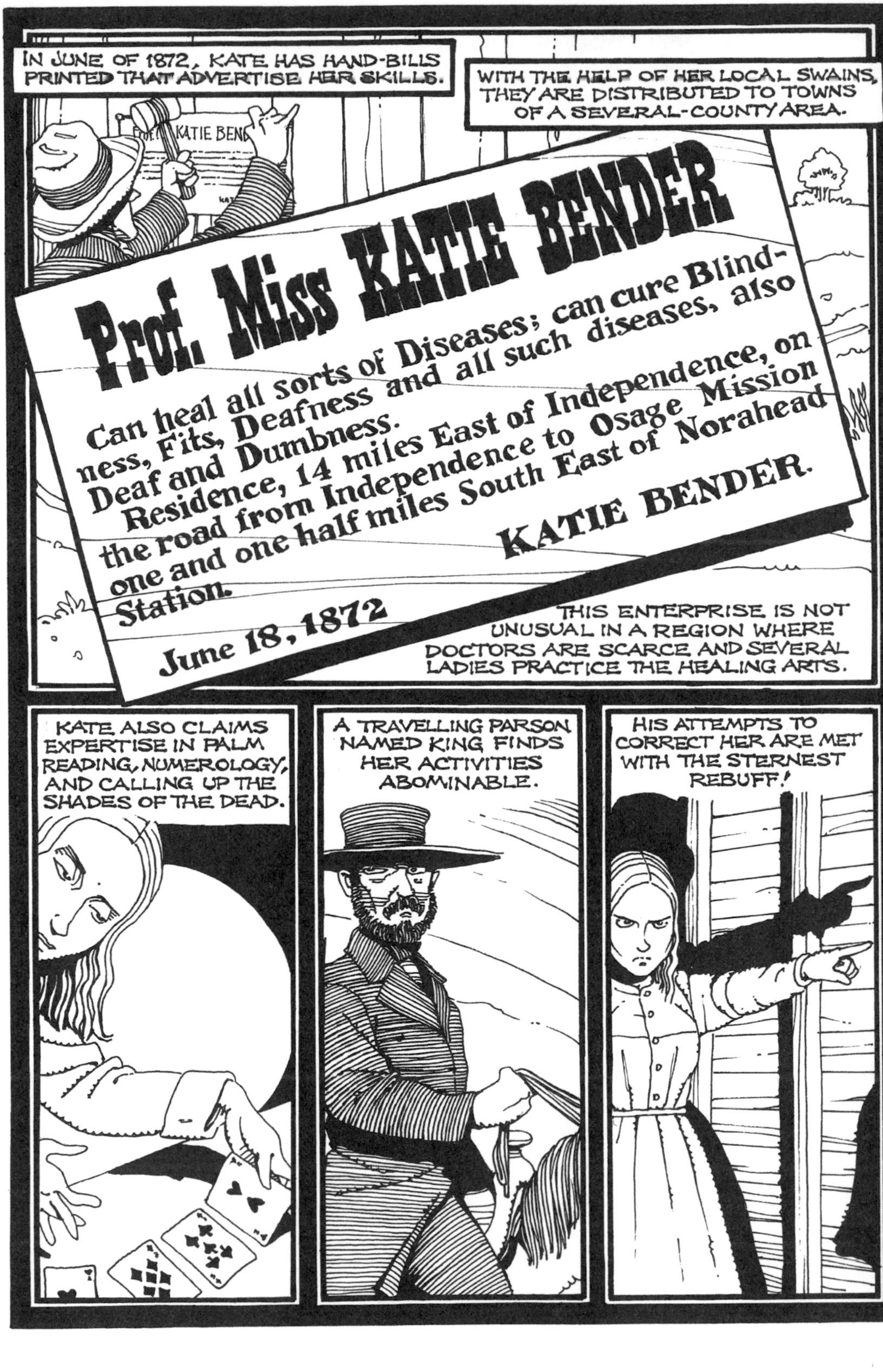
IN JUNE OF 1872, KATE HAS HAND-BILLS PRINTED THAT ADVERTISE HER SKILLS.
WITH THE HELP OF HER LOCAL SWAINS, THEY ARE DISTRIBUTED TO TOWNS OF A SEVERAL-COUNTY AREA.
Prof. Miss KATIE BENDER
Can heal all sorts of Diseases; can cure Blindness, Fits, Deafness and all such diseases, also Deaf and Dumbness.
Residence, 14 miles East of Independence, on the road from Independence to Osage Mission one and one half miles South East of Norahead Station.
KATIE BENDER.
June 18, 1872
THIS ENTERPRISE IS NOT UNUSUAL IN A REGION WHERE DOCTORS ARE SCARCE AND SEVERAL LADIES PRACTICE THE HEALING ARTS.
KATE ALSO CLAIMS EXPERTISE IN PALM READING, NUMEROLOGY, AND CALLING UP THE SHADES OF THE DEAD.
A TRAVELLING PARSON NAMED KING FINDS HER ACTIVITIES ABOMINABLE.
HIS ATTEMPTS TO CORRECT HER ARE MET WITH THE STERNEST REBUFF!

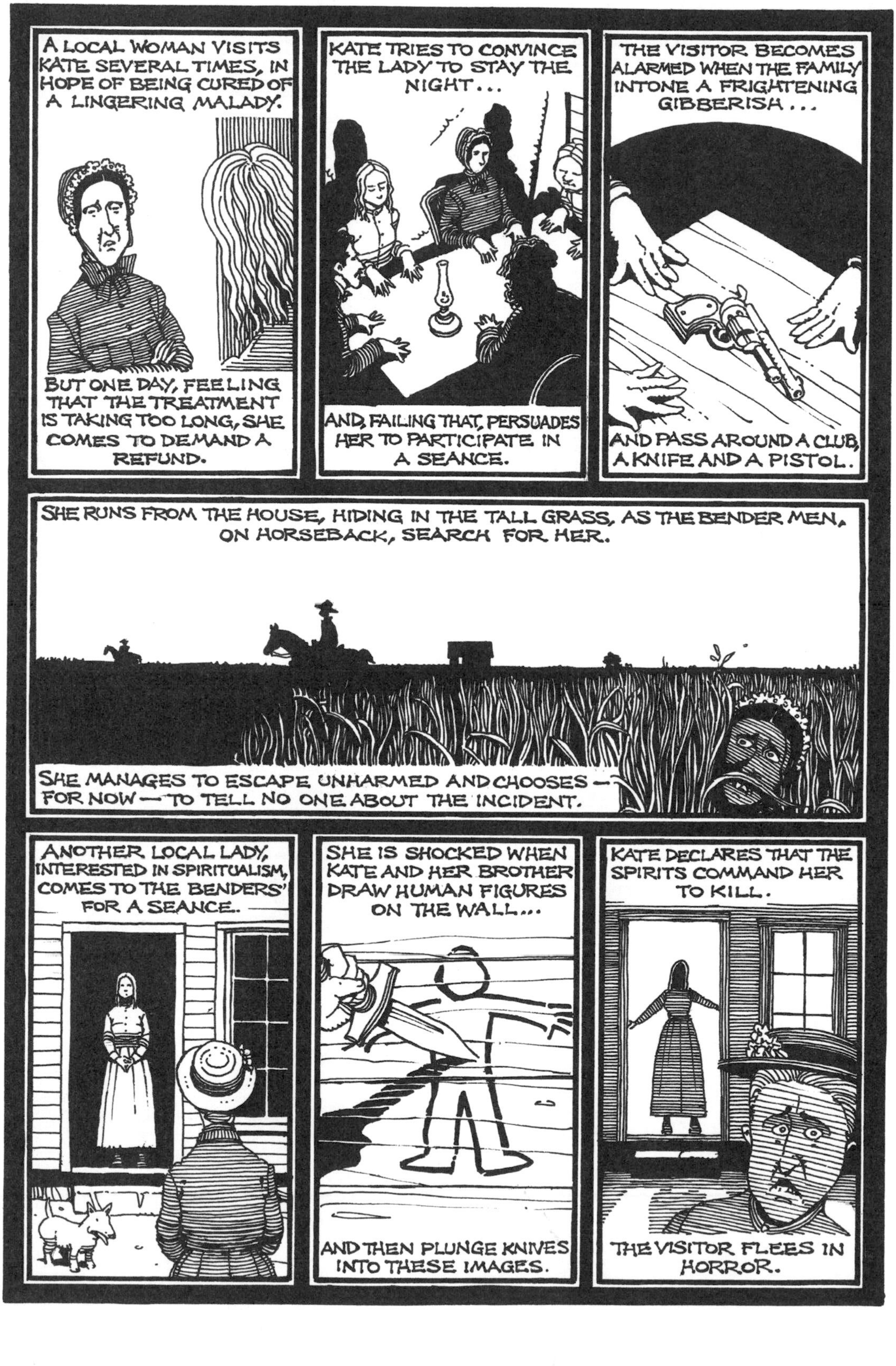
A LOCAL WOMAN VISITS KATE SEVERAL TIMES, IN HOPE OF BEING CURED OF A LINGERING MALADY.
BUT ONE DAY, FEELING THAT THE TREATMENT IS TAKING TOO LONG, SHE COMES TO DEMAND A REFUND.
KATE TRIES TO CONVINCE THE LADY TO STAY THE NIGHT...
AND, FAILING THAT, PERSUADES HER TO PARTICIPATE IN A SEANCE.
THE VISITOR BECOMES ALARMED WHEN THE FAMILY INTONE A FRIGHTENING GIBBERISH...
AND PASS AROUND A CLUB, A KNIFE AND A PISTOL.
SHE RUNS FROM THE HOUSE, HIDING IN THE TALL GRASS, AS THE BENDER MEN, ON HORSEBACK, SEARCH FOR HER.
SHE MANAGES TO ESCAPE UNHARMED AND CHOOSES — FOR NOW — TO TELL NO ONE ABOUT THE INCIDENT.
ANOTHER LOCAL LADY, INTERESTED IN SPIRITUALISM, COMES TO THE BENDERS' FOR A SEANCE.
SHE IS SHOCKED WHEN KATE AND HER BROTHER DRAW HUMAN FIGURES ON THE WALL...
AND THEN PLUNGE KNIVES INTO THESE IMAGES.
KATE DECLARES THAT THE SPIRITS COMMAND HER TO KILL.
THE VISITOR FLEES IN HORROR.

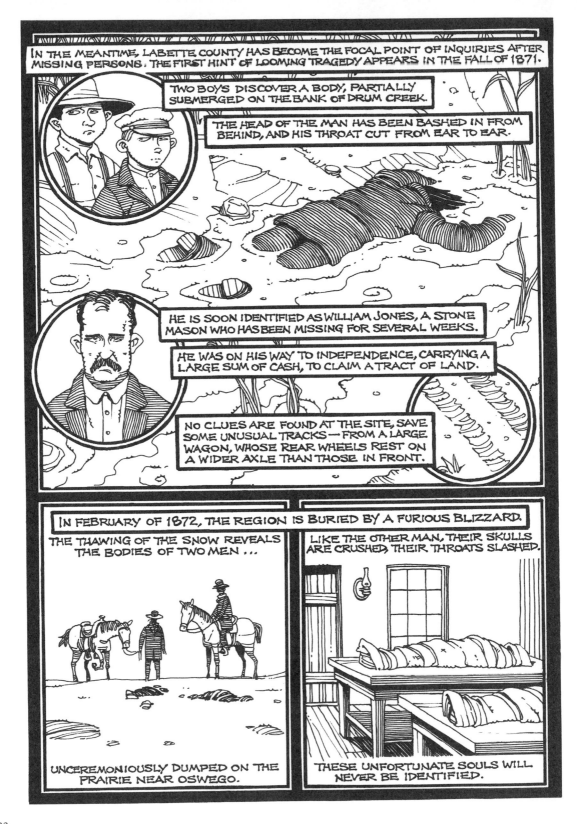

IN THE MEANTIME, LABETTE COUNTY HAS BECOME THE FOCAL POINT OF INQUIRIES AFTER MISSING PERSONS. THE FIRST HINT OF LOOMING TRAGEDY APPEARS IN THE FALL OF 1871.

TWO BOYS DISCOVER A BODY, PARTIALLY SUBMERGED ON THE BANK OF DRUM CREEK.

THE HEAD OF THE MAN HAS BEEN BASHED IN FROM BEHIND, AND HIS THROAT CUT FROM EAR TO EAR.

HE IS SOON IDENTIFIED AS WILLIAM JONES, A STONE MASON WHO HAS BEEN MISSING FOR SEVERAL WEEKS.

HE WAS ON HIS WAY TO INDEPENDENCE, CARRYING A LARGE SUM OF CASH, TO CLAIM A TRACT OF LAND.

NO CLUES ARE FOUND AT THE SITE, SAVE SOME UNUSUAL TRACKS — FROM A LARGE WAGON, WHOSE REAR WHEELS REST ON A WIDER AXLE THAN THOSE IN FRONT.

IN FEBRUARY OF 1872, THE REGION IS BURIED BY A FURIOUS BLIZZARD.

THE THAWING OF THE SNOW REVEALS THE BODIES OF TWO MEN ...

LIKE THE OTHER MAN, THEIR SKULLS ARE CRUSHED, THEIR THROATS SLASHED.

UNCEREMONIOUSLY DUMPED ON THE PRAIRIE NEAR OSWEGO.

THESE UNFORTUNATE SOULS WILL NEVER BE IDENTIFIED.

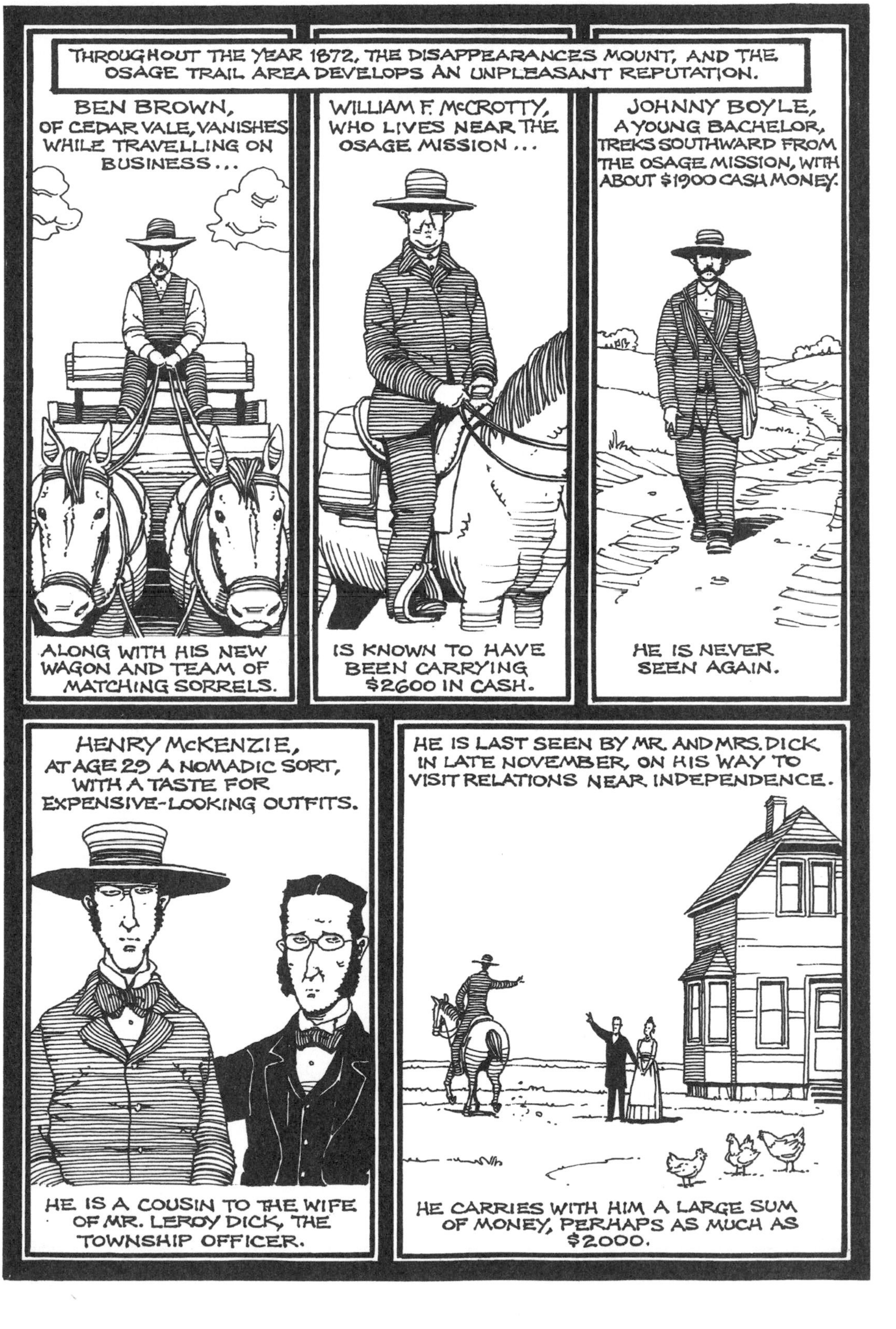
THROUGHOUT THE YEAR 1872, THE DISAPPEARANCES MOUNT, AND THE OSAGE TRAIL AREA DEVELOPS AN UNPLEASANT REPUTATION.
BEN BROWN, OF CEDAR VALE, VANISHES WHILE TRAVELLING ON BUSINESS...
ALONG WITH HIS NEW WAGON AND TEAM OF MATCHING SORRELS.
WILLIAM F. McCROTTY, WHO LIVES NEAR THE OSAGE MISSION...
IS KNOWN TO HAVE BEEN CARRYING $2600 IN CASH.
JOHNNY BOYLE, A YOUNG BACHELOR, TREKS SOUTHWARD FROM THE OSAGE MISSION, WITH ABOUT $1900 CASH MONEY.
HE IS NEVER SEEN AGAIN.
HENRY McKENZIE, AT AGE 29 A NOMADIC SORT, WITH A TASTE FOR EXPENSIVE-LOOKING OUTFITS.
HE IS A COUSIN TO THE WIFE OF MR. LEROY DICK, THE TOWNSHIP OFFICER.
HE IS LAST SEEN BY MR. AND MRS. DICK IN LATE NOVEMBER, ON HIS WAY TO VISIT RELATIONS NEAR INDEPENDENCE.
HE CARRIES WITH HIM A LARGE SUM OF MONEY, PERHAPS AS MUCH AS $2000.

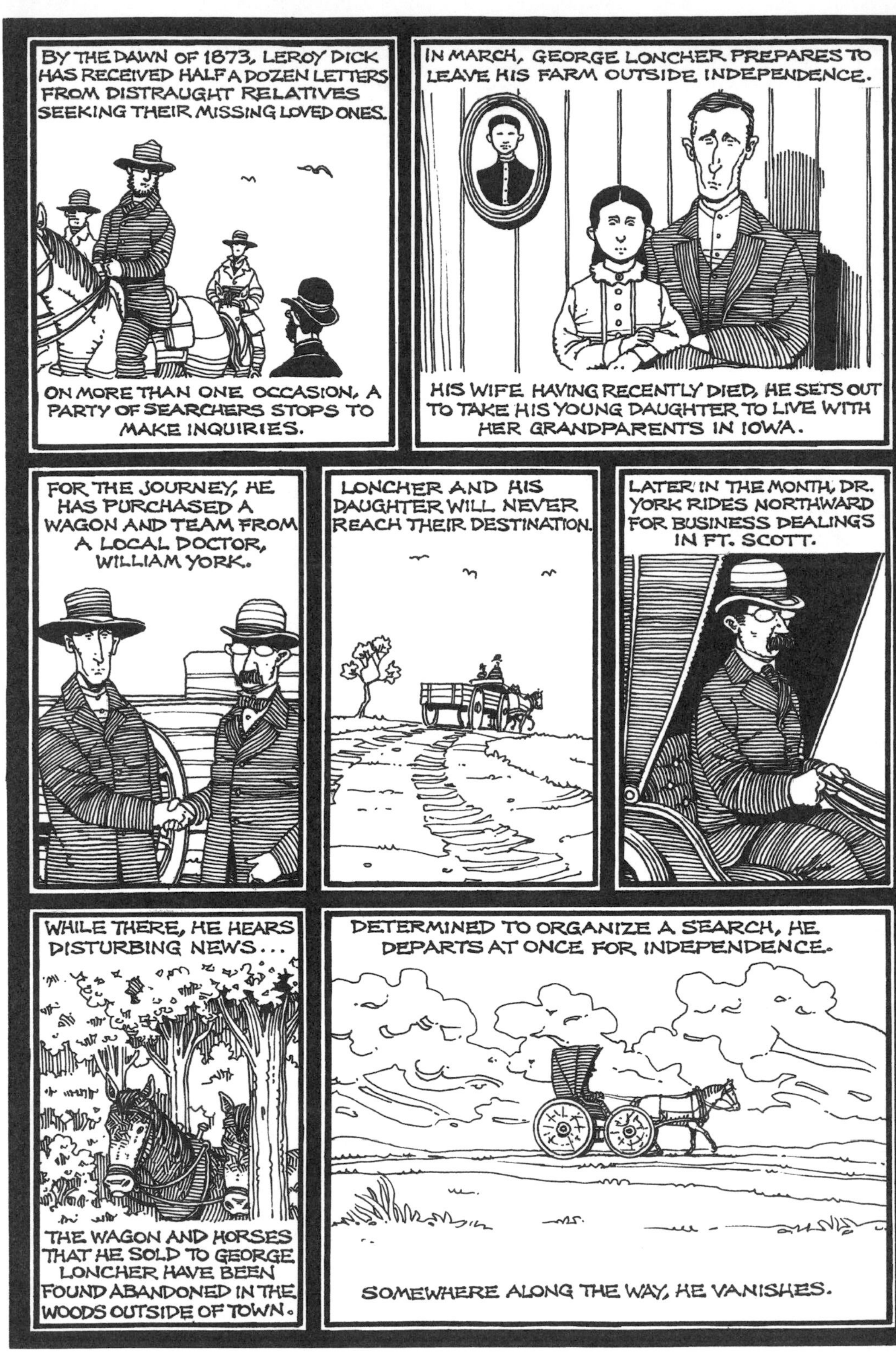
BY THE DAWN OF 1873, LEROY DICK HAS RECEIVED HALF A DOZEN LETTERS FROM DISTRAUGHT RELATIVES SEEKING THEIR MISSING LOVED ONES.
ON MORE THAN ONE OCCASION, A PARTY OF SEARCHERS STOPS TO MAKE INQUIRIES.
IN MARCH, GEORGE LONCHER PREPARES TO LEAVE HIS FARM OUTSIDE INDEPENDENCE.
HIS WIFE HAVING RECENTLY DIED, HE SETS OUT TO TAKE HIS YOUNG DAUGHTER TO LIVE WITH HER GRANDPARENTS IN IOWA.
FOR THE JOURNEY, HE HAS PURCHASED A WAGON AND TEAM FROM A LOCAL DOCTOR, WILLIAM YORK.
LONCHER AND HIS DAUGHTER WILL NEVER REACH THEIR DESTINATION.
LATER IN THE MONTH, DR. YORK RIDES NORTHWARD FOR BUSINESS DEALINGS IN FT. SCOTT.
WHILE THERE, HE HEARS DISTURBING NEWS...
THE WAGON AND HORSES THAT HE SOLD TO GEORGE LONCHER HAVE BEEN FOUND ABANDONED IN THE WOODS OUTSIDE OF TOWN.
DETERMINED TO ORGANIZE A SEARCH, HE DEPARTS AT ONCE FOR INDEPENDENCE.
SOMEWHERE ALONG THE WAY, HE VANISHES.

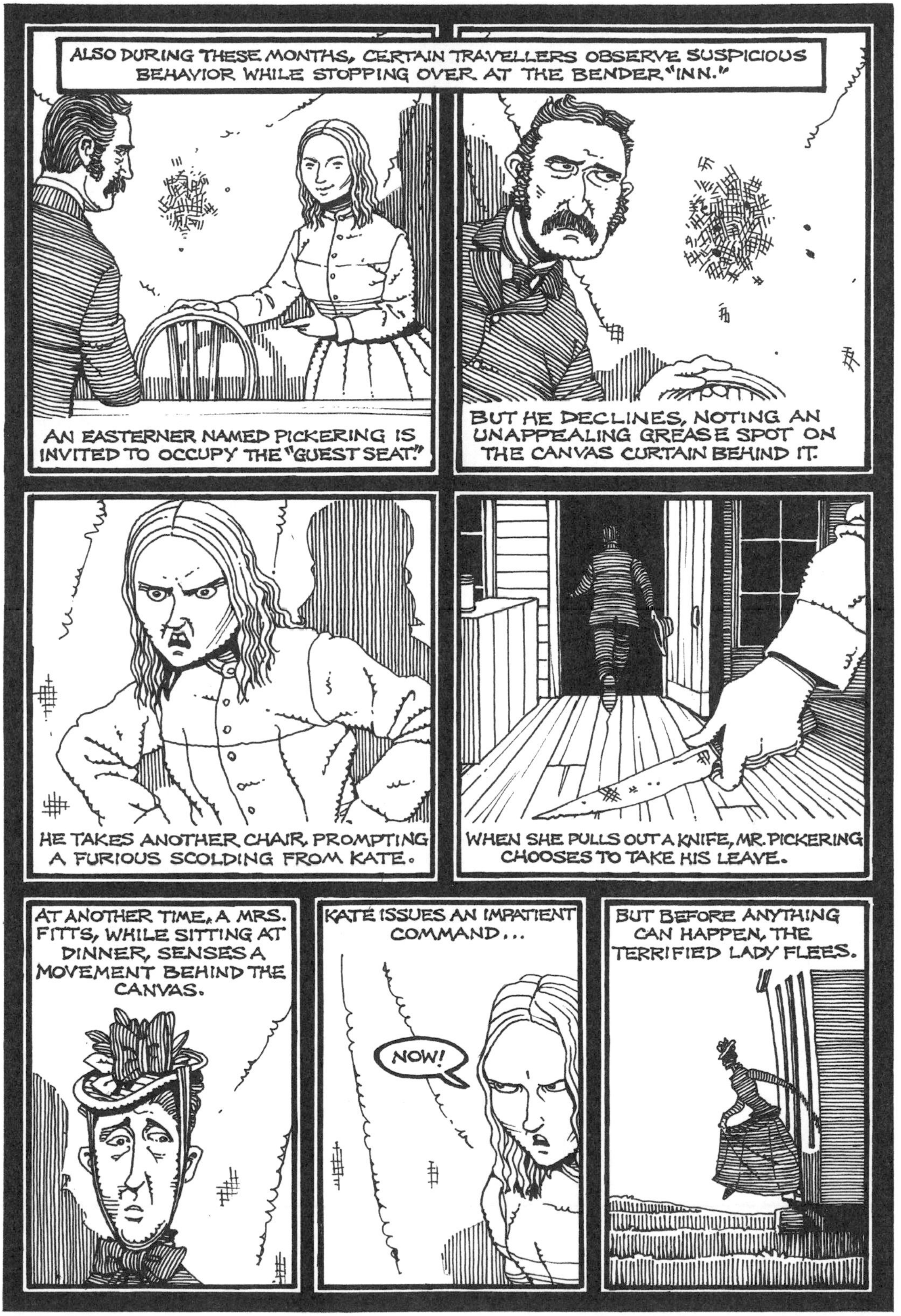
ALSO DURING THESE MONTHS, CERTAIN TRAVELLERS OBSERVE SUSPICIOUS BEHAVIOR WHILE STOPPING OVER AT THE BENDER "INN."
AN EASTERNER NAMED PICKERING IS INVITED TO OCCUPY THE "GUEST SEAT."
BUT HE DECLINES, NOTING AN UNAPPEALING GREASE SPOT ON THE CANVAS CURTAIN BEHIND IT.
HE TAKES ANOTHER CHAIR, PROMPTING A FURIOUS SCOLDING FROM KATE.
WHEN SHE PULLS OUT A KNIFE, MR. PICKERING CHOOSES TO TAKE HIS LEAVE.
AT ANOTHER TIME, A MRS. FITTS, WHILE SITTING AT DINNER, SENSES A MOVEMENT BEHIND THE CANVAS.
KATE ISSUES AN IMPATIENT COMMAND...
NOW!
BUT BEFORE ANYTHING CAN HAPPEN, THE TERRIFIED LADY FLEES.

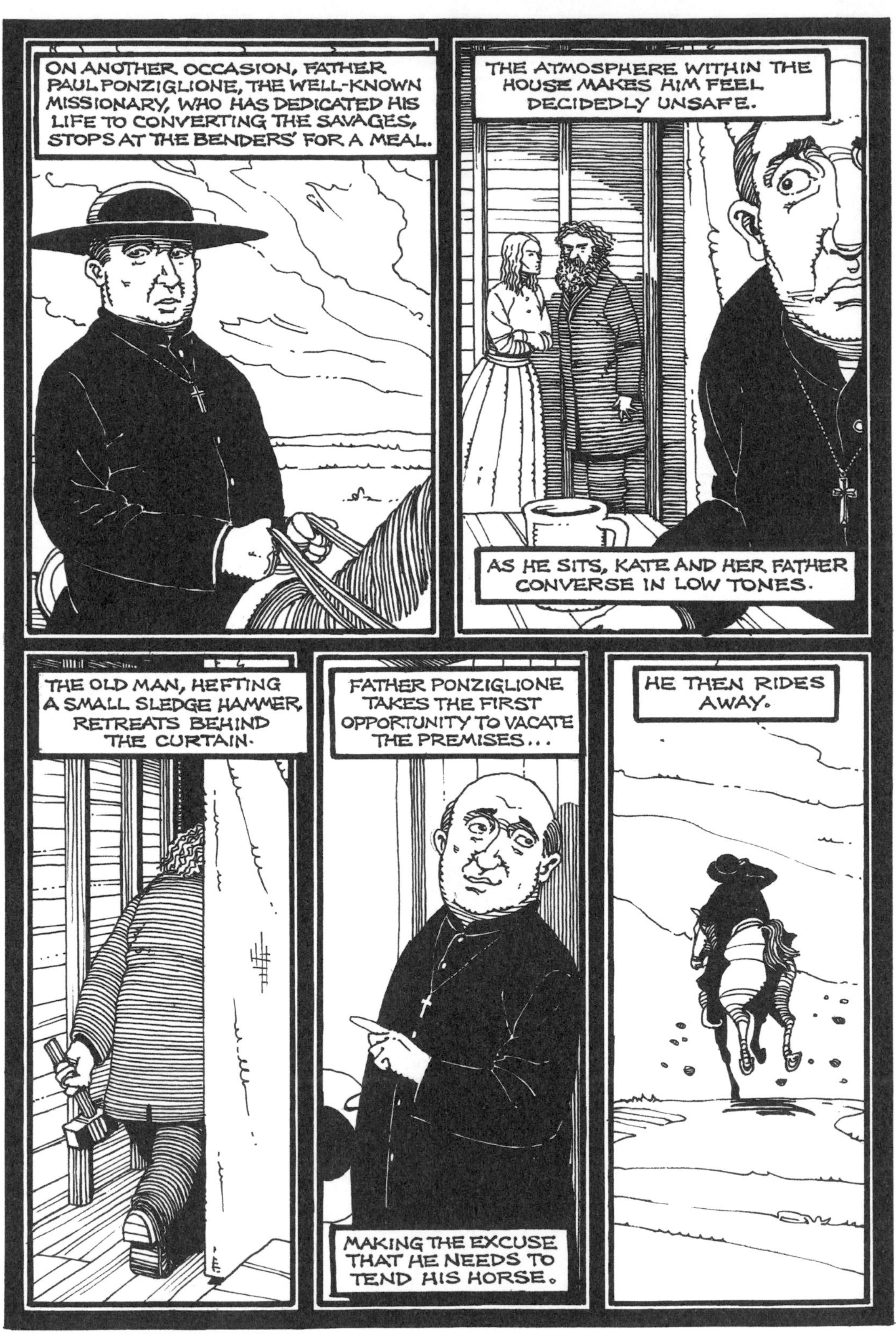
ON ANOTHER OCCASION, FATHER PAUL PONZIGLIONE, THE WELL-KNOWN MISSIONARY, WHO HAS DEDICATED HIS LIFE TO CONVERTING THE SAVAGES, STOPS AT THE BENDERS' FOR A MEAL.
THE ATMOSPHERE WITHIN THE HOUSE MAKES HIM FEEL DECIDEDLY UNSAFE.
AS HE SITS, KATE AND HER FATHER CONVERSE IN LOW TONES.
THE OLD MAN, HEFTING A SMALL SLEDGE HAMMER, RETREATS BEHIND THE CURTAIN.
FATHER PONZIGLIONE TAKES THE FIRST OPPORTUNITY TO VACATE THE PREMISES...
MAKING THE EXCUSE THAT HE NEEDS TO TEND HIS HORSE.
HE THEN RIDES AWAY.

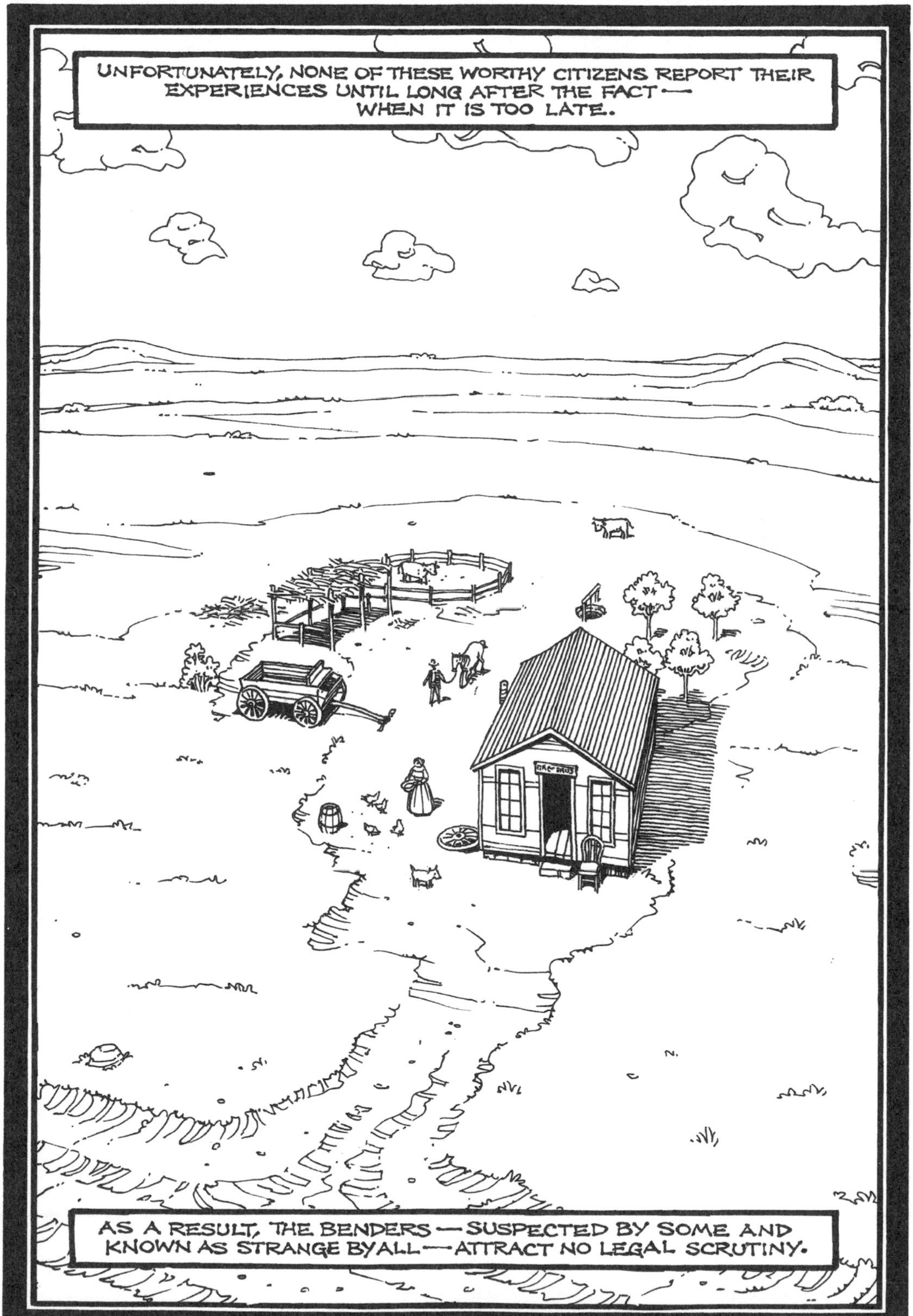
UNFORTUNATELY, NONE OF THESE WORTHY CITIZENS REPORT THEIR EXPERIENCES UNTIL LONG AFTER THE FACT— WHEN IT IS TOO LATE.
AS A RESULT, THE BENDERS—SUSPECTED BY SOME AND KNOWN AS STRANGE BY ALL—ATTRACT NO LEGAL SCRUTINY.

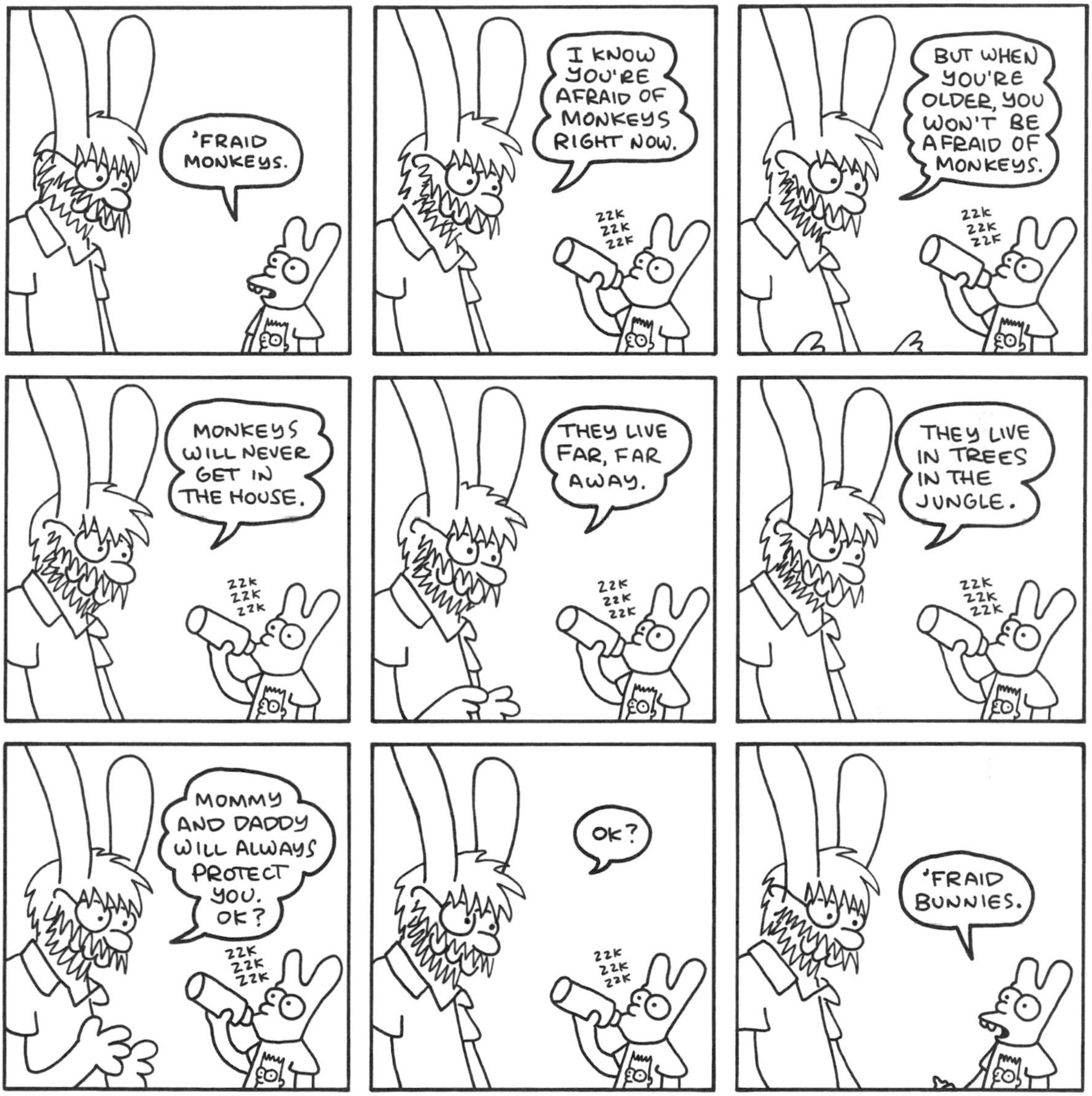
'FRAID MONKEYS.
I KNOW YOU'RE AFRAID OF MONKEYS RIGHT NOW.
ZZK ZZK ZZK
BUT WHEN YOU'RE OLDER, YOU WON'T BE AFRAID OF MONKEYS.
ZZK ZZK ZZK
MONKEYS WILL NEVER GET IN THE HOUSE.
ZZK ZZK ZZK
THEY LIVE FAR, FAR AWAY.
ZZK ZZK ZZK
THEY LIVE IN TREES IN THE JUNGLE.
ZZK ZZK ZZK
MOMMY AND DADDY WILL ALWAYS PROTECT YOU. OK?
ZZK ZZK ZZK
OK?
ZZK ZZK ZZK
'FRAID BUNNIES.

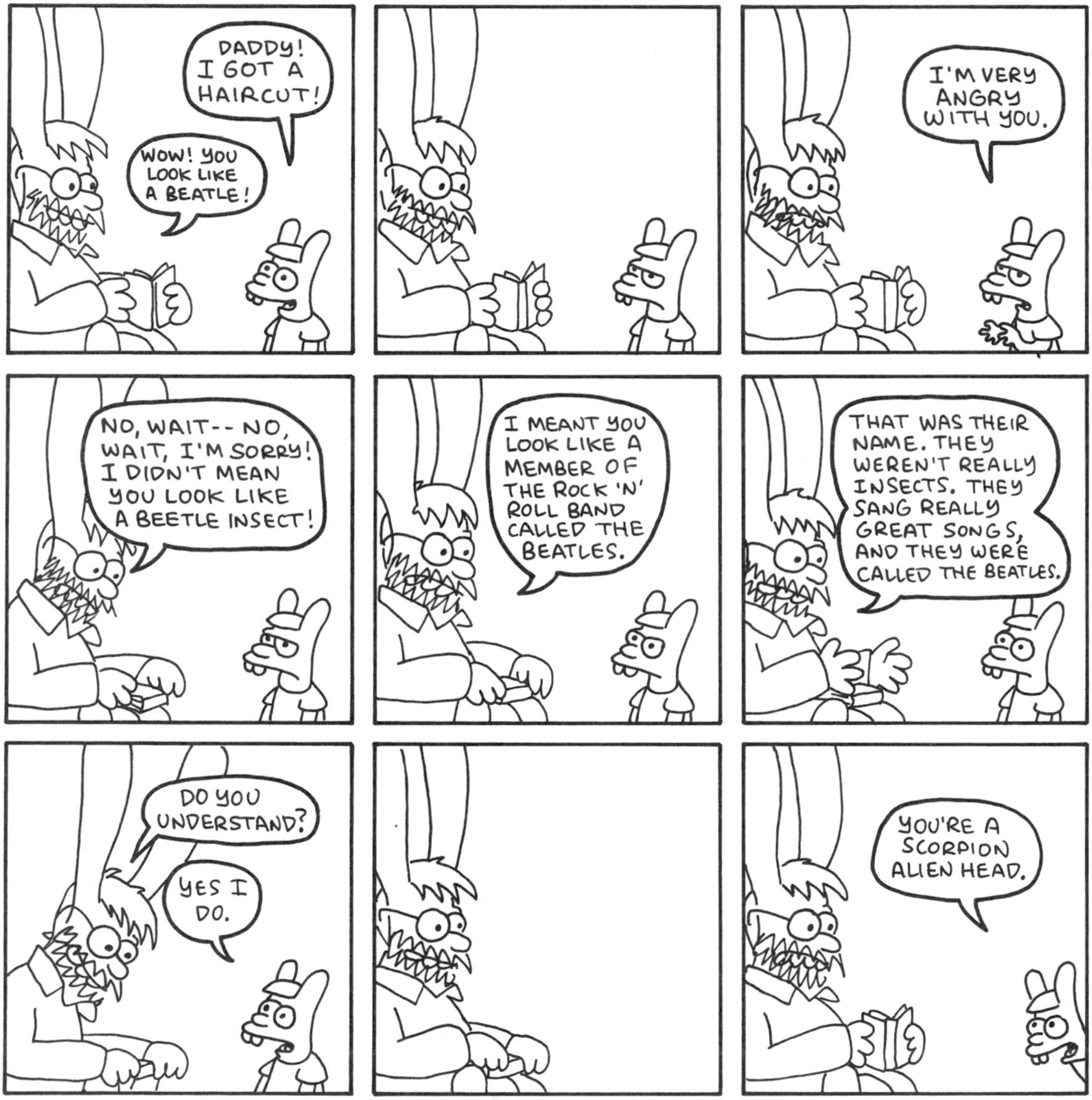
DADDY! I GOT A HAIRCUT!
WOW! YOU LOOK LIKE A BEATLE!
I'M VERY ANGRY WITH YOU.
NO, WAIT-- NO, WAIT, I'M SORRY! I DIDN'T MEAN YOU LOOK LIKE A BEETLE INSECT!
I MEANT YOU LOOK LIKE A MEMBER OF THE ROCK 'N' ROLL BAND CALLED THE BEATLES.
THAT WAS THEIR NAME. THEY WEREN'T REALLY INSECTS. THEY SANG REALLY GREAT SONGS, AND THEY WERE CALLED THE BEATLES.
DO YOU UNDERSTAND?
YES I DO.
YOU'RE A SCORPION ALIEN HEAD.

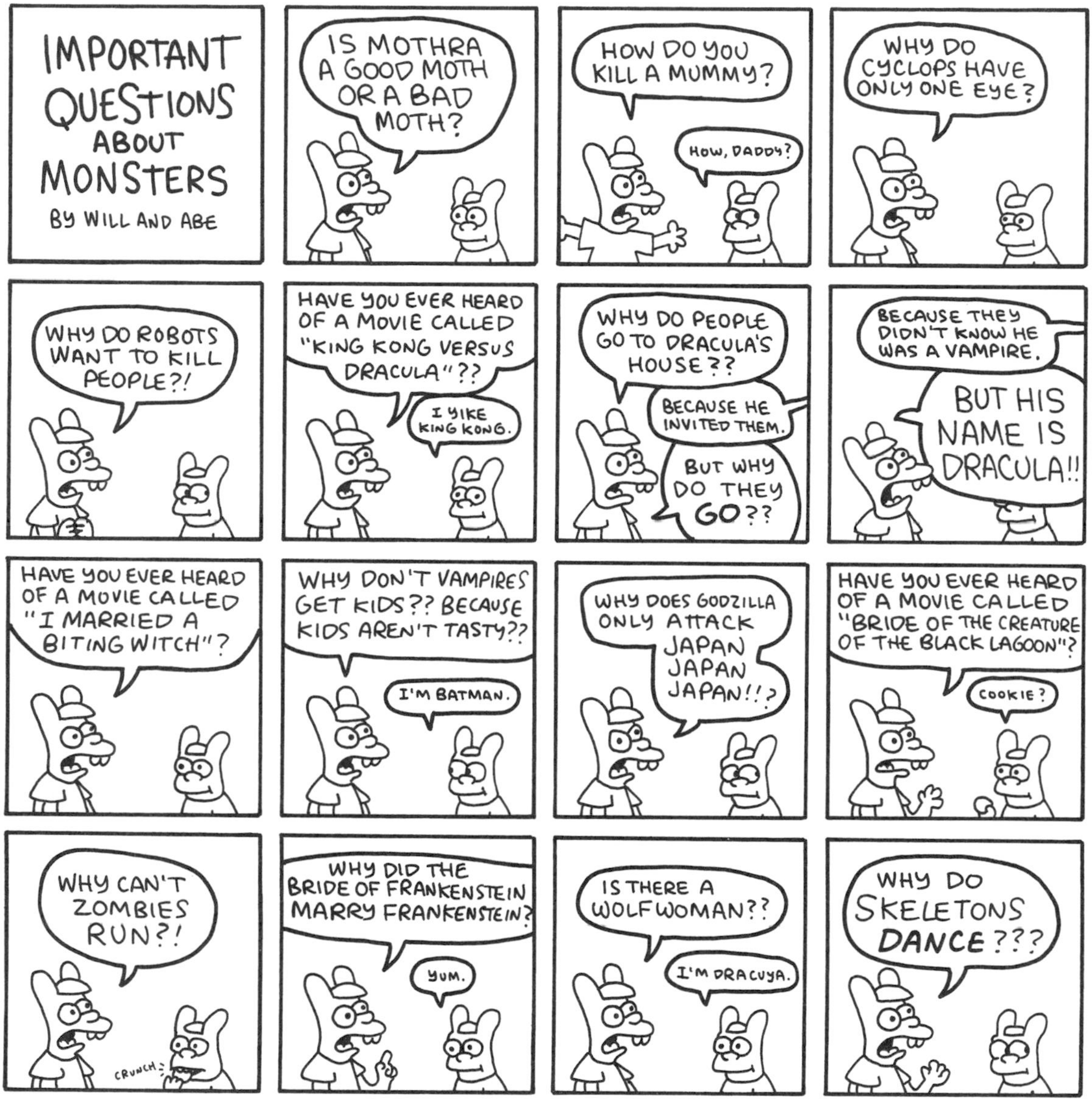
IMPORTANT QUESTIONS ABOUT MONSTERS
BY WILL AND ABE
IS MOTHRA A GOOD MOTH OR A BAD MOTH?
HOW DO YOU KILL A MUMMY?
HOW, DADDY?
WHY DO CYCLOPS HAVE ONLY ONE EYE?
WHY DO ROBOTS WANT TO KILL PEOPLE?!
HAVE YOU EVER HEARD OF A MOVIE CALLED "KING KONG VERSUS DRACULA"??
I YIKE KING KONG.
WHY DO PEOPLE GO TO DRACULA'S HOUSE??
BECAUSE HE INVITED THEM.
BUT WHY DO THEY GO??
BECAUSE THEY DIDN'T KNOW HE WAS A VAMPIRE.
BUT HIS NAME IS DRACULA!!
HAVE YOU EVER HEARD OF A MOVIE CALLED "I MARRIED A BITING WITCH"?
WHY DON'T VAMPIRES GET KIDS?? BECAUSE KIDS AREN'T TASTY??
I'M BATMAN.
WHY DOES GODZILLA ONLY ATTACK JAPAN JAPAN JAPAN!!?
HAVE YOU EVER HEARD OF A MOVIE CALLED "BRIDE OF THE CREATURE OF THE BLACK LAGOON"?
COOKIE?
WHY CAN'T ZOMBIES RUN?!
CRUNCH
WHY DID THE BRIDE OF FRANKENSTEIN MARRY FRANKENSTEIN?
YUM.
IS THERE A WOLFWOMAN??
I'M DRACUYA.
WHY DO SKELETONS DANCE???

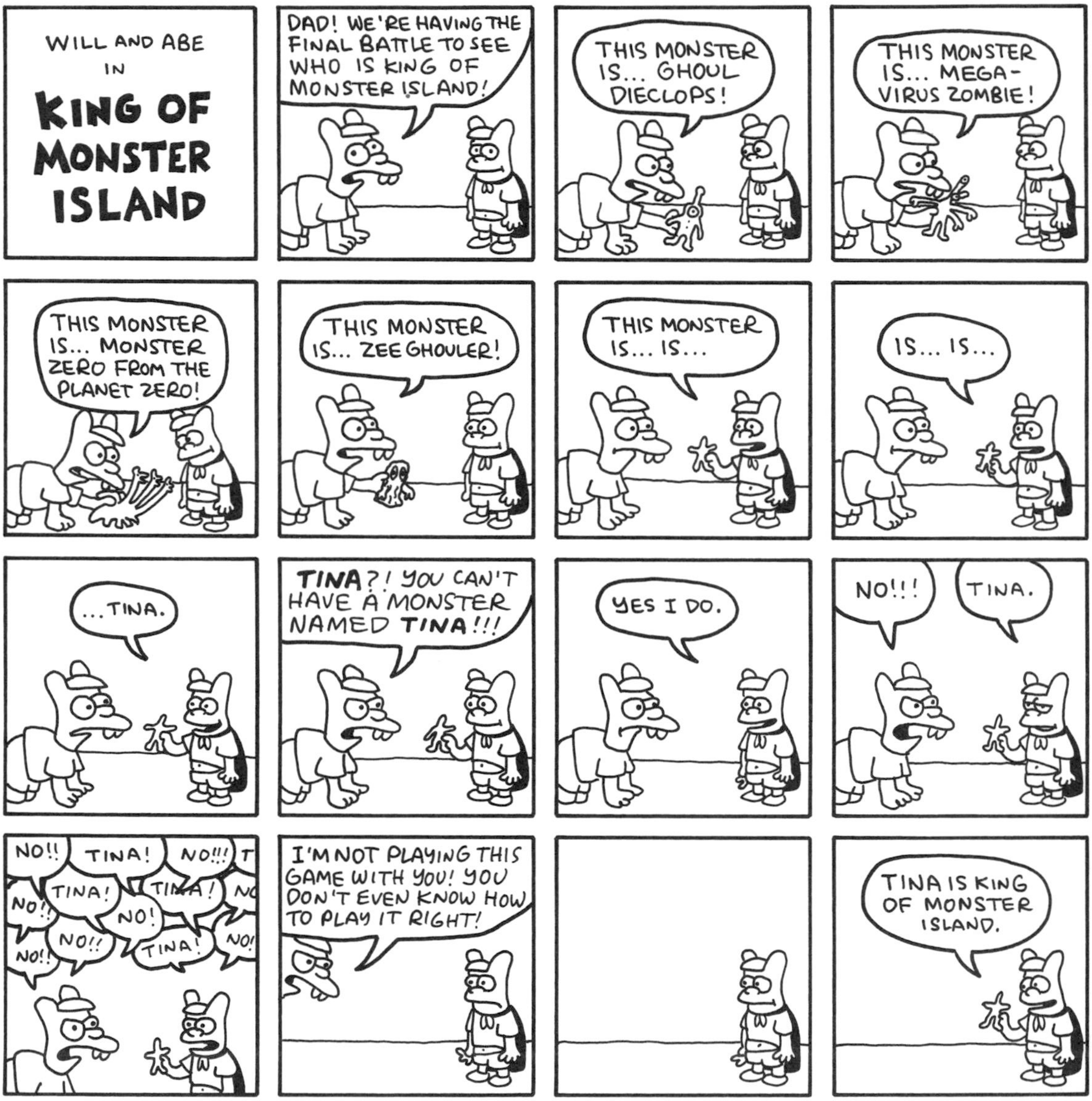
WILL AND ABE
IN
KING OF MONSTER ISLAND
DAD! WE'RE HAVING THE FINAL BATTLE TO SEE WHO IS KING OF MONSTER ISLAND!
THIS MONSTER IS... GHOUL DIECLOPS!
THIS MONSTER IS... MEGA-VIRUS ZOMBIE!
THIS MONSTER IS... MONSTER ZERO FROM THE PLANET ZERO!
THIS MONSTER IS... ZEE GHOULER!
THIS MONSTER IS... IS...
IS... IS...
...TINA.
TINA?! YOU CAN'T HAVE A MONSTER NAMED TINA!!!
YES I DO.
NO!!!
TINA.
NO!!
TINA!
NO!!!
TINA!
NO!!
NO!
NO!!
NO!!
TINA!
NO!
I'M NOT PLAYING THIS GAME WITH YOU! YOU DON'T EVEN KNOW HOW TO PLAY IT RIGHT!
TINA IS KING OF MONSTER ISLAND.

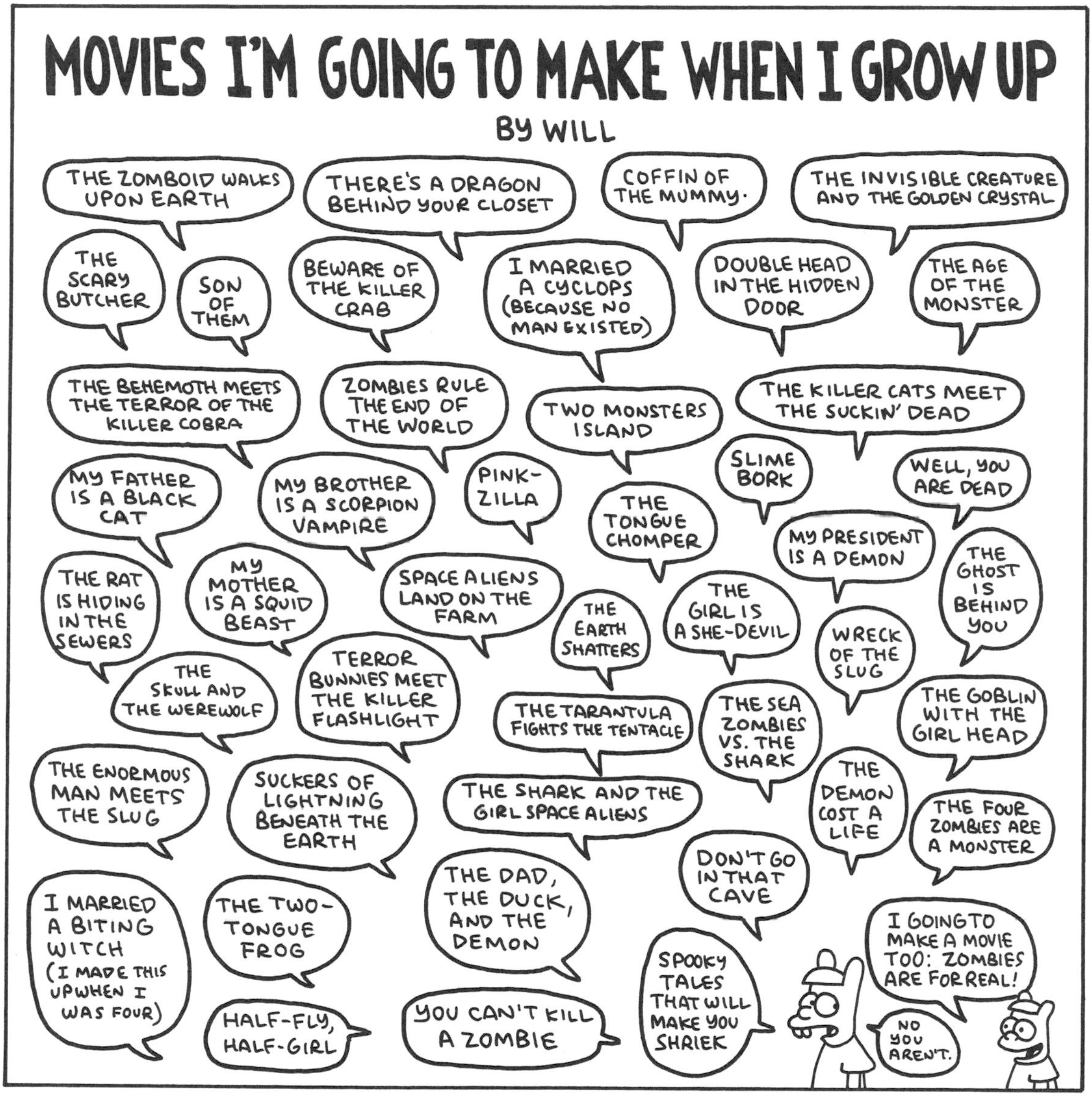
MOVIES I'M GOING TO MAKE WHEN I GROW UP
BY WILL
THE ZOMBOID WALKS UPON EARTH
THERE'S A DRAGON BEHIND YOUR CLOSET
COFFIN OF THE MUMMY.
THE INVISIBLE CREATURE AND THE GOLDEN CRYSTAL
THE SCARY BUTCHER
SON OF THEM
BEWARE OF THE KILLER CRAB
I MARRIED A CYCLOPS (BECAUSE NO MAN EXISTED)
DOUBLE HEAD IN THE HIDDEN DOOR
THE AGE OF THE MONSTER
THE BEHEMOTH MEETS THE TERROR OF THE KILLER COBRA
ZOMBIES RULE THE END OF THE WORLD
TWO MONSTERS ISLAND
THE KILLER CATS MEET THE SUCKIN' DEAD
MY FATHER IS A BLACK CAT
MY BROTHER IS A SCORPION VAMPIRE
PINK-ZILLA
THE TONGUE CHOMPER
SLIME BORK
WELL, YOU ARE DEAD
MY PRESIDENT IS A DEMON
THE RAT IS HIDING IN THE SEWERS
MY MOTHER IS A SQUID BEAST
SPACE ALIENS LAND ON THE FARM
THE EARTH SHATTERS
THE GIRL IS A SHE-DEVIL
WRECK OF THE SLUG
THE GHOST IS BEHIND YOU
THE SKULL AND THE WEREWOLF
TERROR BUNNIES MEET THE KILLER FLASHLIGHT
THE TARANTULA FIGHTS THE TENTACLE
THE SEA ZOMBIES VS. THE SHARK
THE GOBLIN WITH THE GIRL HEAD
THE ENORMOUS MAN MEETS THE SLUG
SUCKERS OF LIGHTNING BENEATH THE EARTH
THE SHARK AND THE GIRL SPACE ALIENS
THE DEMON COST A LIFE
THE FOUR ZOMBIES ARE A MONSTER
DON'T GO IN THAT CAVE
I MARRIED A BITING WITCH (I MADE THIS UP WHEN I WAS FOUR)
THE TWO-TONGUE FROG
THE DAD, THE DUCK, AND THE DEMON
SPOOKY TALES THAT WILL MAKE YOU SHRIEK
I GOING TO MAKE A MOVIE TOO: ZOMBIES ARE FOR REAL!
NO YOU AREN'T.
HALF-FLY, HALF-GIRL
YOU CAN'T KILL A ZOMBIE

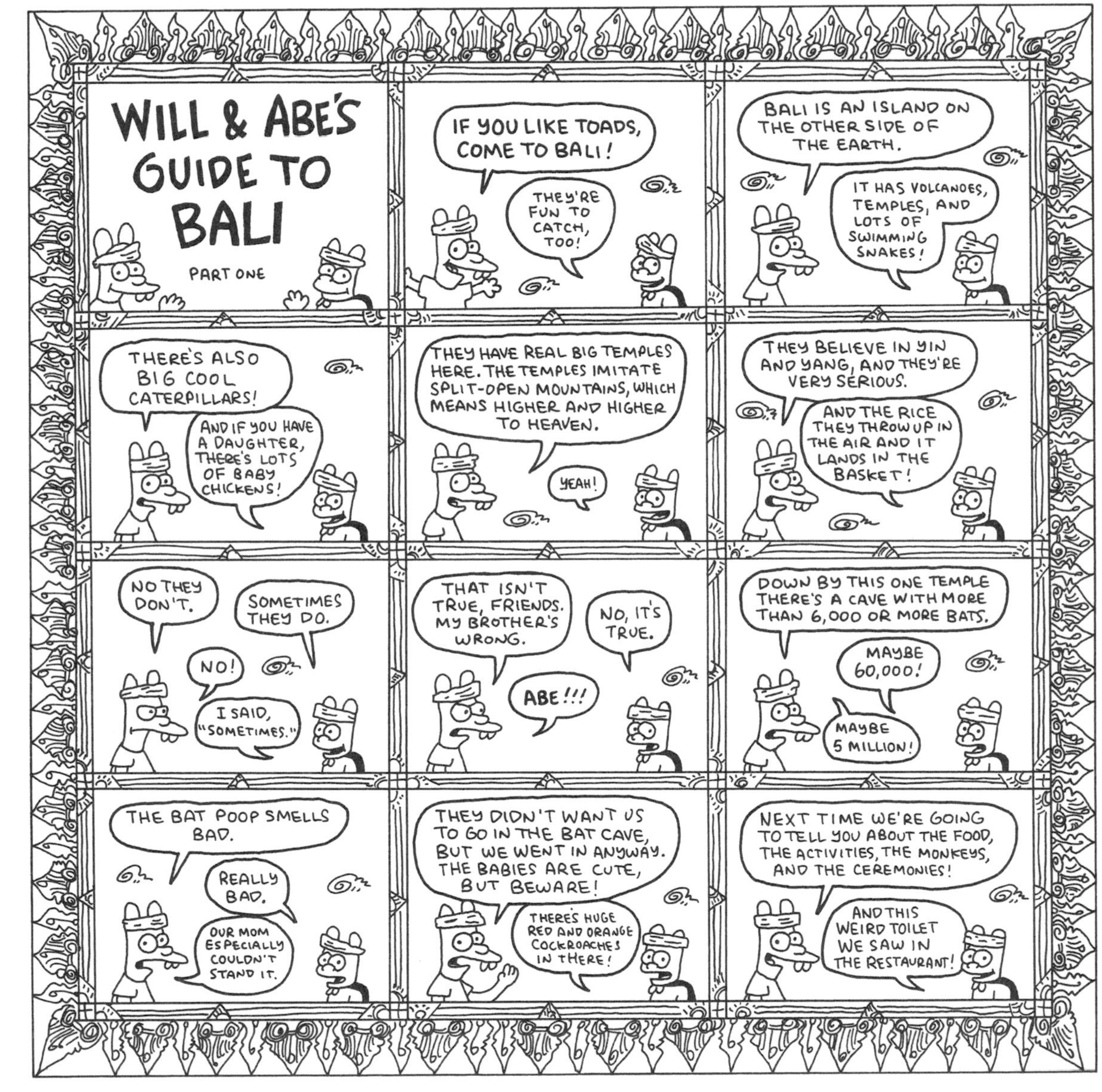
WILL & ABE'S GUIDE TO BALI
PART ONE
IF YOU LIKE TOADS, COME TO BALI!
THEY'RE FUN TO CATCH, TOO!
BALI IS AN ISLAND ON THE OTHER SIDE OF THE EARTH.
IT HAS VOLCANOES, TEMPLES, AND LOTS OF SWIMMING SNAKES!
THERE'S ALSO BIG COOL CATERPILLARS!
AND IF YOU HAVE A DAUGHTER, THERE'S LOTS OF BABY CHICKENS!
THEY HAVE REAL BIG TEMPLES HERE. THE TEMPLES IMITATE SPLIT-OPEN MOUNTAINS, WHICH MEANS HIGHER AND HIGHER TO HEAVEN.
YEAH!
THEY BELIEVE IN YIN AND YANG, AND THEY'RE VERY SERIOUS.
AND THE RICE THEY THROW UP IN THE AIR AND IT LANDS IN THE BASKET!
NO THEY DON'T.
SOMETIMES THEY DO.
NO!
I SAID, "SOMETIMES."
THAT ISN'T TRUE, FRIENDS. MY BROTHER'S WRONG.
NO, IT'S TRUE.
ABE!!!
DOWN BY THIS ONE TEMPLE THERE'S A CAVE WITH MORE THAN 6,000 OR MORE BATS.
MAYBE 60,000!
MAYBE 5 MILLION!
THE BAT POOP SMELLS BAD.
REALLY BAD.
OUR MOM ESPECIALLY COULDN'T STAND IT.
THEY DIDN'T WANT US TO GO IN THE BAT CAVE, BUT WE WENT IN ANYWAY. THE BABIES ARE CUTE, BUT BEWARE!
THERE'S HUGE RED AND ORANGE COCKROACHES IN THERE!
NEXT TIME WE'RE GOING TO TELL YOU ABOUT THE FOOD, THE ACTIVITIES, THE MONKEYS, AND THE CEREMONIES!
AND THIS WEIRD TOILET WE SAW IN THE RESTAURANT!

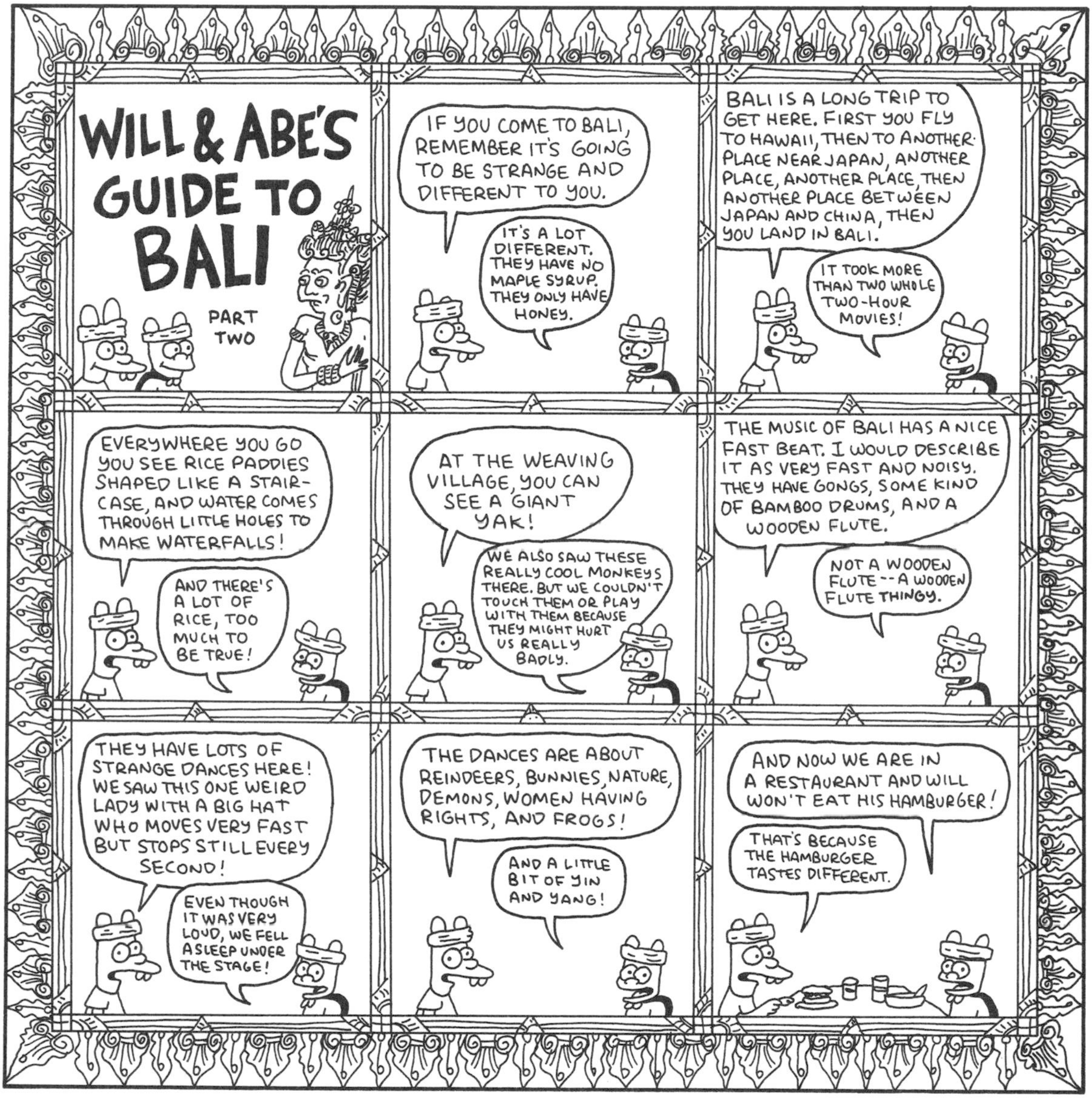
WILL & ABE'S GUIDE TO BALI
PART TWO
IF YOU COME TO BALI, REMEMBER IT'S GOING TO BE STRANGE AND DIFFERENT TO YOU.
IT'S A LOT DIFFERENT. THEY HAVE NO MAPLE SYRUP. THEY ONLY HAVE HONEY.
BALI IS A LONG TRIP TO GET HERE. FIRST YOU FLY TO HAWAII, THEN TO ANOTHER PLACE NEAR JAPAN, ANOTHER PLACE, ANOTHER PLACE, THEN ANOTHER PLACE BETWEEN JAPAN AND CHINA, THEN YOU LAND IN BALI.
IT TOOK MORE THAN TWO WHOLE TWO-HOUR MOVIES!
EVERYWHERE YOU GO YOU SEE RICE PADDIES SHAPED LIKE A STAIR-CASE, AND WATER COMES THROUGH LITTLE HOLES TO MAKE WATERFALLS!
AND THERE'S A LOT OF RICE, TOO MUCH TO BE TRUE!
AT THE WEAVING VILLAGE, YOU CAN SEE A GIANT YAK!
WE ALSO SAW THESE REALLY COOL MONKEYS THERE. BUT WE COULDN'T TOUCH THEM OR PLAY WITH THEM BECAUSE THEY MIGHT HURT US REALLY BADLY.
THE MUSIC OF BALI HAS A NICE FAST BEAT. I WOULD DESCRIBE IT AS VERY FAST AND NOISY. THEY HAVE GONGS, SOME KIND OF BAMBOO DRUMS, AND A WOODEN FLUTE.
NOT A WOODEN FLUTE--A WOODEN FLUTE THINGY.
THEY HAVE LOTS OF STRANGE DANCES HERE! WE SAW THIS ONE WEIRD LADY WITH A BIG HAT WHO MOVES VERY FAST BUT STOPS STILL EVERY SECOND!
EVEN THOUGH IT WAS VERY LOUD, WE FELL ASLEEP UNDER THE STAGE!
THE DANCES ARE ABOUT REINDEERS, BUNNIES, NATURE, DEMONS, WOMEN HAVING RIGHTS, AND FROGS!
AND A LITTLE BIT OF YIN AND YANG!
AND NOW WE ARE IN A RESTAURANT AND WILL WON'T EAT HIS HAMBURGER!
THAT'S BECAUSE THE HAMBURGER TASTES DIFFERENT.

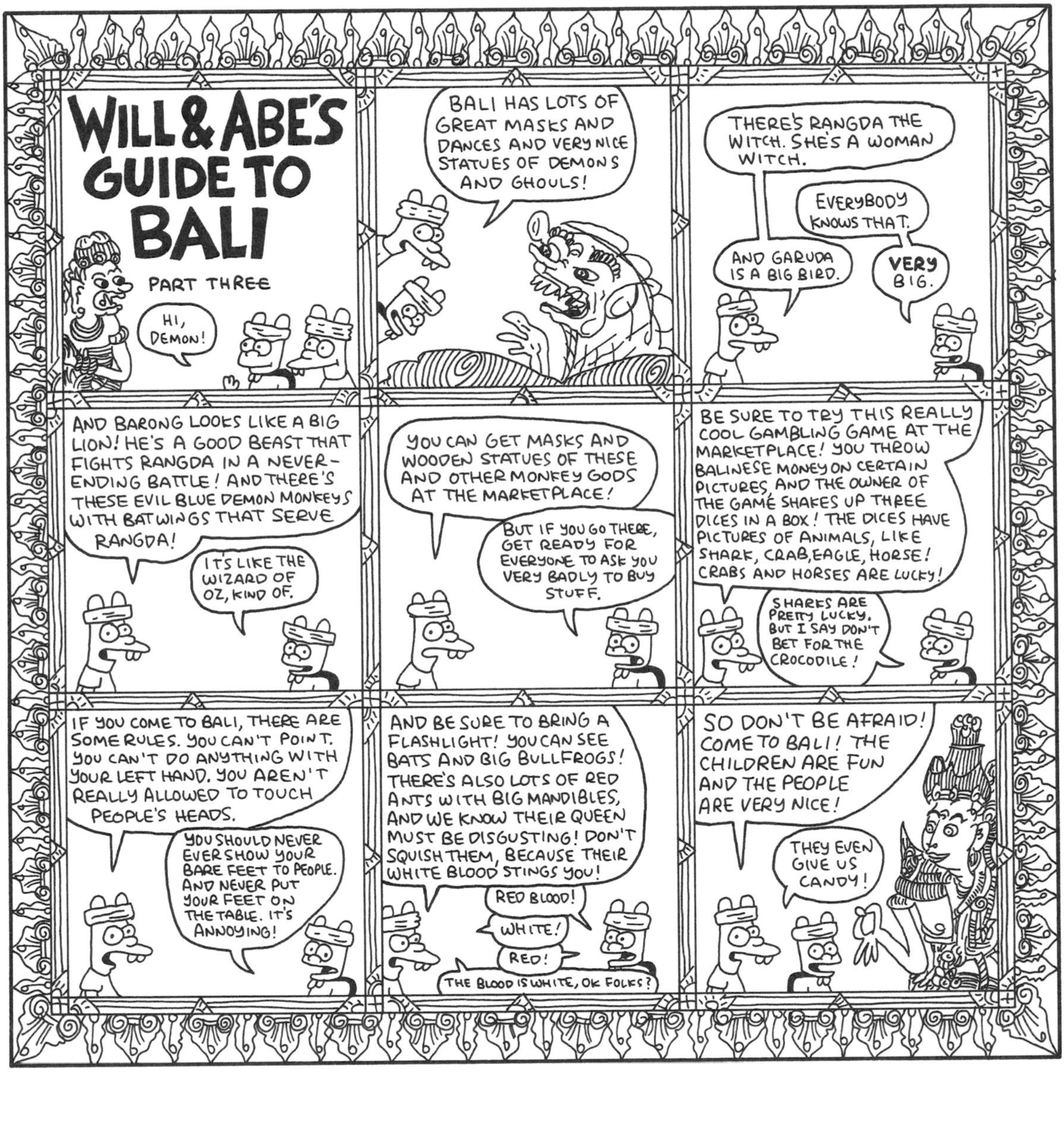
WILL & ABE'S GUIDE TO BALI
PART THREE
HI, DEMON!
BALI HAS LOTS OF GREAT MASKS AND DANCES AND VERY NICE STATUES OF DEMONS AND GHOULS!
THERE'S RANGDA THE WITCH. SHE'S A WOMAN WITCH.
EVERYBODY KNOWS THAT.
AND GARUDA IS A BIG BIRD.
VERY BIG.
AND BARONG LOOKS LIKE A BIG LION! HE'S A GOOD BEAST THAT FIGHTS RANGDA IN A NEVER-ENDING BATTLE! AND THERE'S THESE EVIL BLUE DEMON MONKEYS WITH BATWINGS THAT SERVE RANGDA!
IT'S LIKE THE WIZARD OF OZ, KIND OF.
YOU CAN GET MASKS AND WOODEN STATUES OF THESE AND OTHER MONKEY GODS AT THE MARKETPLACE!
BUT IF YOU GO THERE, GET READY FOR EVERYONE TO ASK YOU VERY BADLY TO BUY STUFF.
BE SURE TO TRY THIS REALLY COOL GAMBLING GAME AT THE MARKETPLACE! YOU THROW BALINESE MONEY ON CERTAIN PICTURES, AND THE OWNER OF THE GAME SHAKES UP THREE DICES IN A BOX! THE DICES HAVE PICTURES OF ANIMALS, LIKE SHARK, CRAB, EAGLE, HORSE! CRABS AND HORSES ARE LUCKY!
SHARKS ARE PRETTY LUCKY. BUT I SAY DON'T BET FOR THE CROCODILE!
IF YOU COME TO BALI, THERE ARE SOME RULES. YOU CAN'T POINT. YOU CAN'T DO ANYTHING WITH YOUR LEFT HAND. YOU AREN'T REALLY ALLOWED TO TOUCH PEOPLE'S HEADS.
YOU SHOULD NEVER EVER SHOW YOUR BARE FEET TO PEOPLE. AND NEVER PUT YOUR FEET ON THE TABLE. IT'S ANNOYING!
AND BE SURE TO BRING A FLASHLIGHT! YOU CAN SEE BATS AND BIG BULLFROGS! THERE'S ALSO LOTS OF RED ANTS WITH BIG MANDIBLES, AND WE KNOW THEIR QUEEN MUST BE DISGUSTING! DON'T SQUISH THEM, BECAUSE THEIR WHITE BLOOD STINGS YOU!
RED BLOOD!
WHITE!
RED!
THE BLOOD IS WHITE, OK FOLKS?
SO DON'T BE AFRAID! COME TO BALI! THE CHILDREN ARE FUN AND THE PEOPLE ARE VERY NICE!
THEY EVEN GIVE US CANDY!

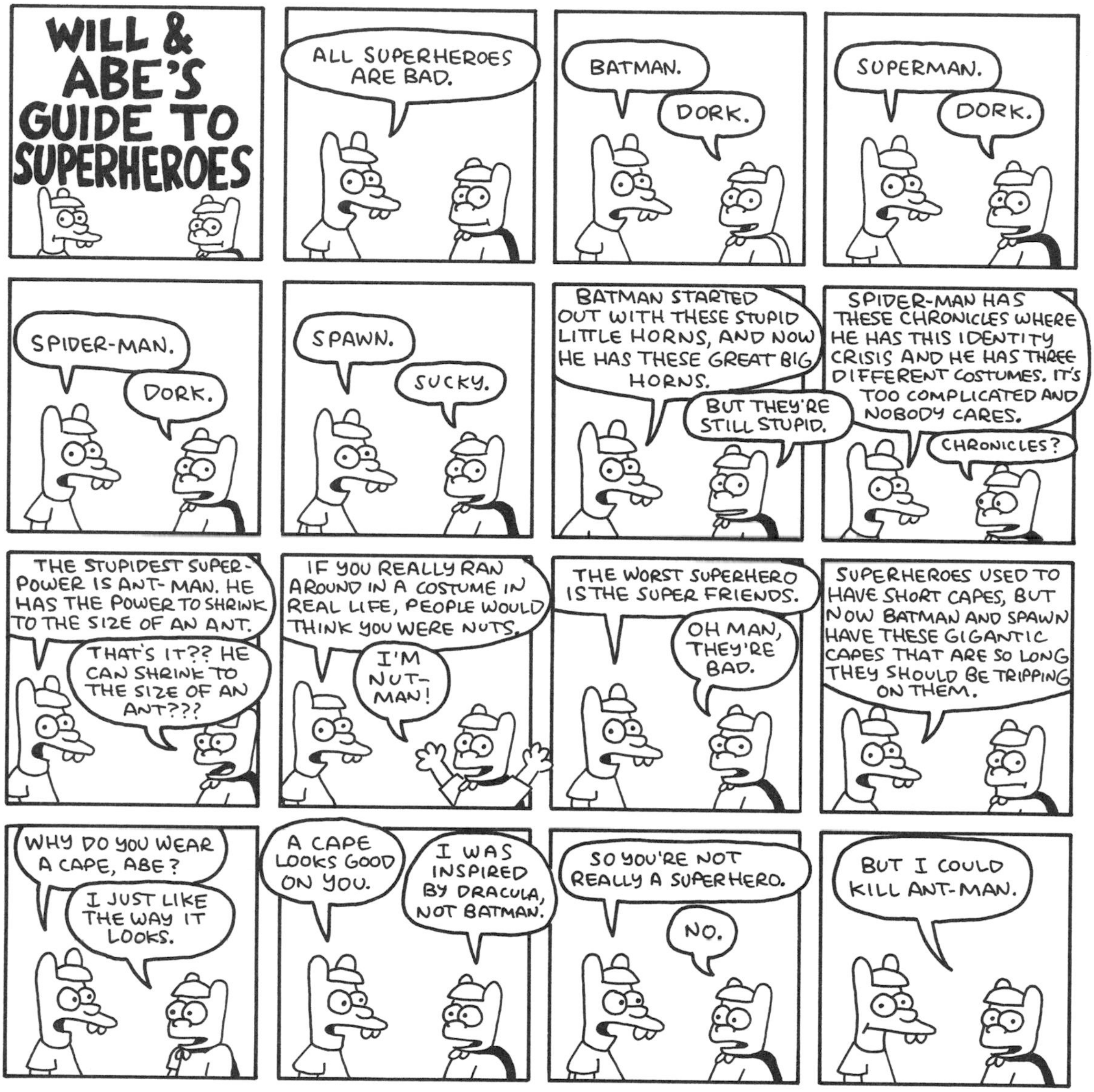
WILL & ABE'S GUIDE TO SUPERHEROES
ALL SUPERHEROES ARE BAD.
BATMAN.
DORK.
SUPERMAN.
DORK.
SPIDER-MAN.
DORK.
SPAWN.
SUCKY.
BATMAN STARTED OUT WITH THESE STUPID LITTLE HORNS, AND NOW HE HAS THESE GREAT BIG HORNS.
BUT THEY'RE STILL STUPID.
SPIDER-MAN HAS THESE CHRONICLES WHERE HE HAS THIS IDENTITY CRISIS AND HE HAS THREE DIFFERENT COSTUMES. IT'S TOO COMPLICATED AND NOBODY CARES.
CHRONICLES?
THE STUPIDEST SUPER-POWER IS ANT-MAN. HE HAS THE POWER TO SHRINK TO THE SIZE OF AN ANT.
THAT'S IT?? HE CAN SHRINK TO THE SIZE OF AN ANT???
IF YOU REALLY RAN AROUND IN A COSTUME IN REAL LIFE, PEOPLE WOULD THINK YOU WERE NUTS.
I'M NUT-MAN!
THE WORST SUPERHERO IS THE SUPER FRIENDS.
OH MAN, THEY'RE BAD.
SUPERHEROES USED TO HAVE SHORT CAPES, BUT NOW BATMAN AND SPAWN HAVE THESE GIGANTIC CAPES THAT ARE SO LONG THEY SHOULD BE TRIPPING ON THEM.
WHY DO YOU WEAR A CAPE, ABE?
I JUST LIKE THE WAY IT LOOKS.
A CAPE LOOKS GOOD ON YOU.
I WAS INSPIRED BY DRACULA, NOT BATMAN.
SO YOU'RE NOT REALLY A SUPERHERO.
NO.
BUT I COULD KILL ANT-MAN.

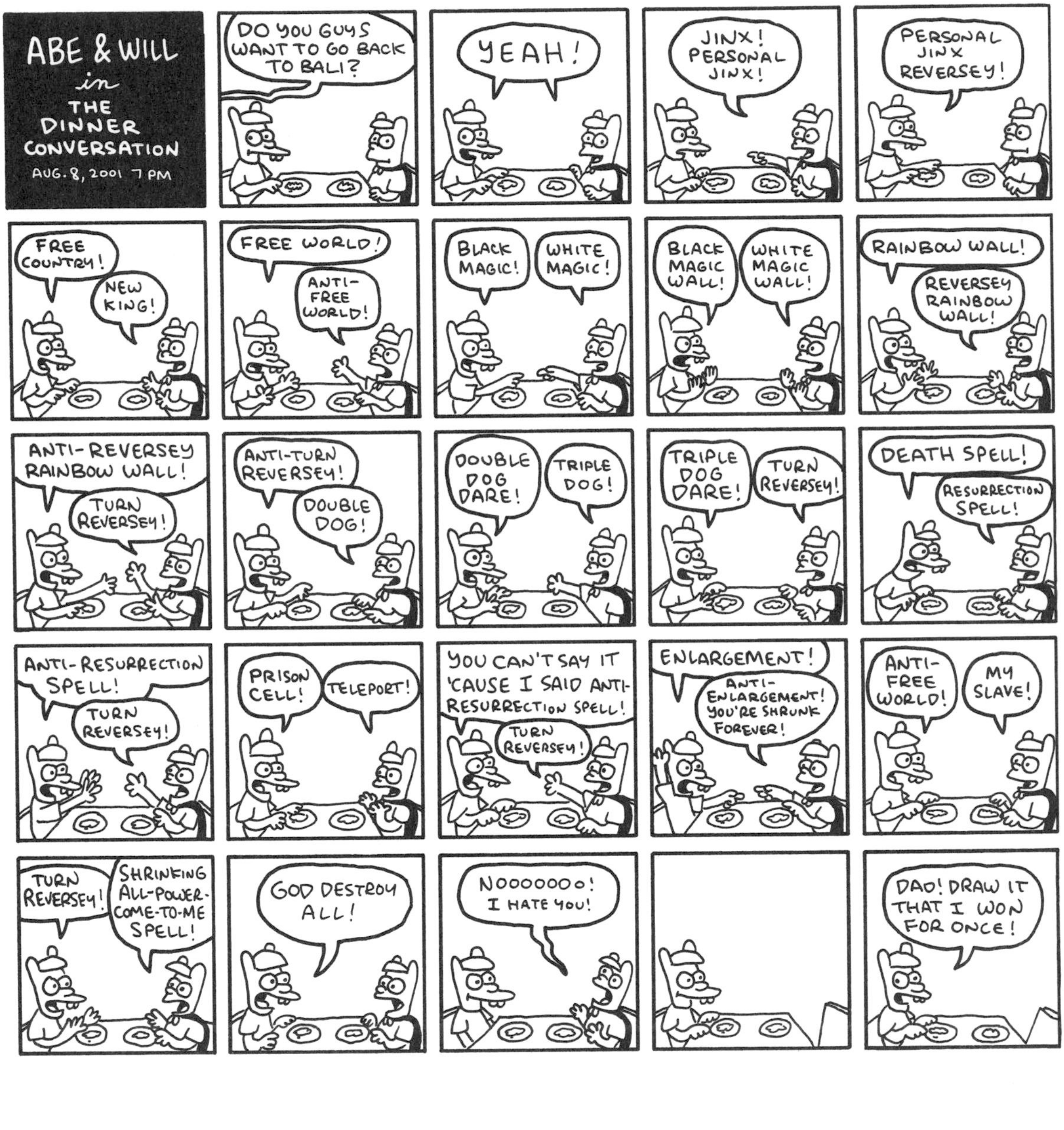
ABE & WILL
in
THE DINNER CONVERSATION
AUG. 8, 2001 7 PM
DO YOU GUYS WANT TO GO BACK TO BALI?
YEAH!
JINX! PERSONAL JINX!
PERSONAL JINX REVERSEY!
FREE COUNTRY!
NEW KING!
FREE WORLD!
ANTI-FREE WORLD!
BLACK MAGIC!
WHITE MAGIC!
BLACK MAGIC WALL!
WHITE MAGIC WALL!
RAINBOW WALL!
REVERSEY RAINBOW WALL!
ANTI-REVERSEY RAINBOW WALL!
TURN REVERSEY!
ANTI-TURN REVERSEY!
DOUBLE DOG!
DOUBLE DOG DARE!
TRIPLE DOG!
TRIPLE DOG DARE!
TURN REVERSEY!
DEATH SPELL!
RESURRECTION SPELL!
ANTI-RESURRECTION SPELL!
TURN REVERSEY!
PRISON CELL!
TELEPORT!
YOU CAN'T SAY IT 'CAUSE I SAID ANTI-RESURRECTION SPELL!
TURN REVERSEY!
ENLARGEMENT!
ANTI-ENLARGEMENT! YOU'RE SHRUNK FOREVER!
ANTI-FREE WORLD!
MY SLAVE!
TURN REVERSEY!
SHRINKING ALL-POWER-COME-TO-ME SPELL!
GOD DESTROY ALL!
NOOOOOOO! I HATE YOU!
DAD! DRAW IT THAT I WON FOR ONCE!

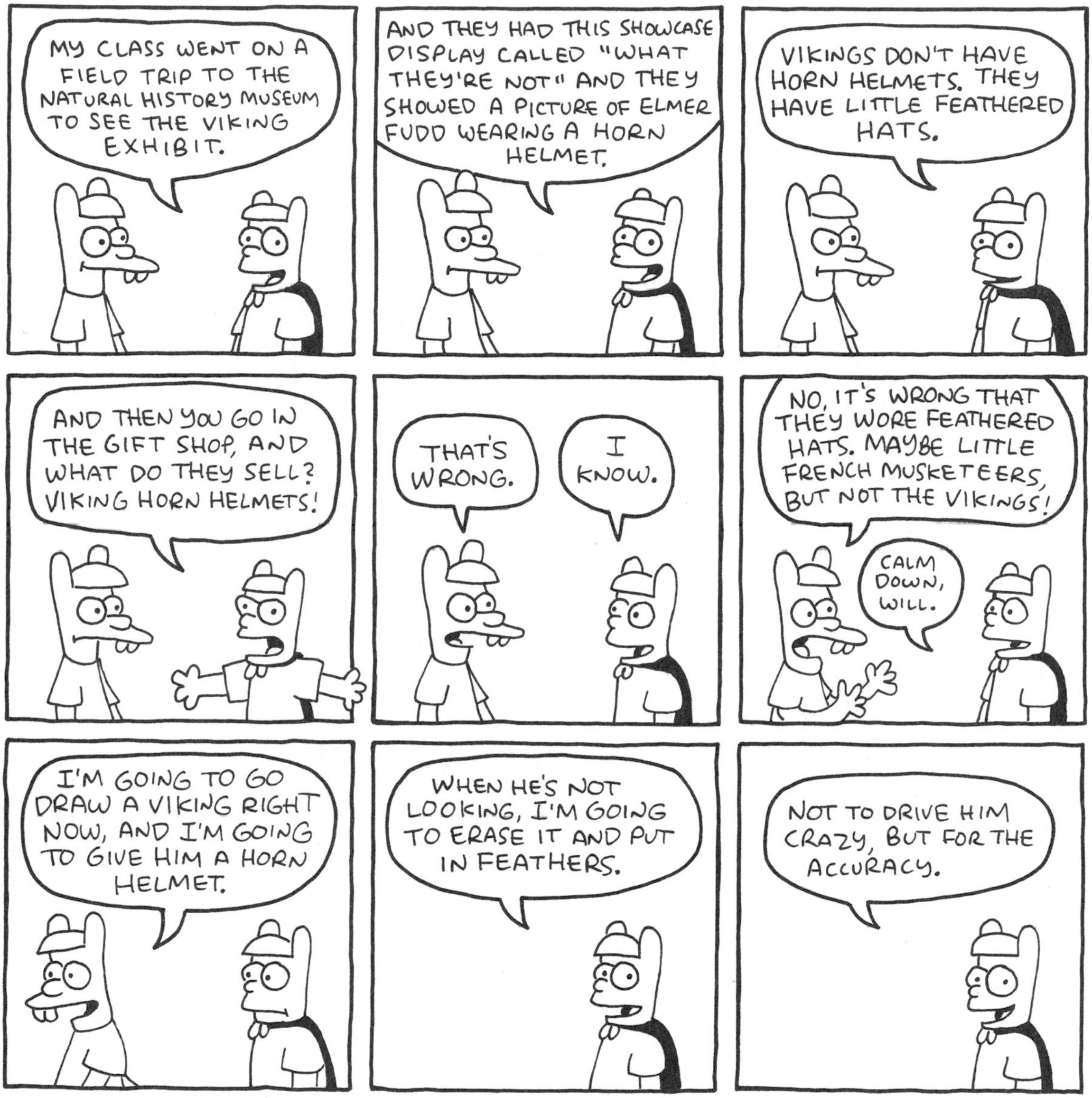
MY CLASS WENT ON A FIELD TRIP TO THE NATURAL HISTORY MUSEUM TO SEE THE VIKING EXHIBIT.
AND THEY HAD THIS SHOWCASE DISPLAY CALLED "WHAT THEY'RE NOT" AND THEY SHOWED A PICTURE OF ELMER FUDD WEARING A HORN HELMET.
VIKINGS DON'T HAVE HORN HELMETS. THEY HAVE LITTLE FEATHERED HATS.
AND THEN YOU GO IN THE GIFT SHOP, AND WHAT DO THEY SELL? VIKING HORN HELMETS!
THAT'S WRONG.
I KNOW.
NO, IT'S WRONG THAT THEY WORE FEATHERED HATS. MAYBE LITTLE FRENCH MUSKETEERS, BUT NOT THE VIKINGS!
CALM DOWN, WILL.
I'M GOING TO GO DRAW A VIKING RIGHT NOW, AND I'M GOING TO GIVE HIM A HORN HELMET.
WHEN HE'S NOT LOOKING, I'M GOING TO ERASE IT AND PUT IN FEATHERS.
NOT TO DRIVE HIM CRAZY, BUT FOR THE ACCURACY.

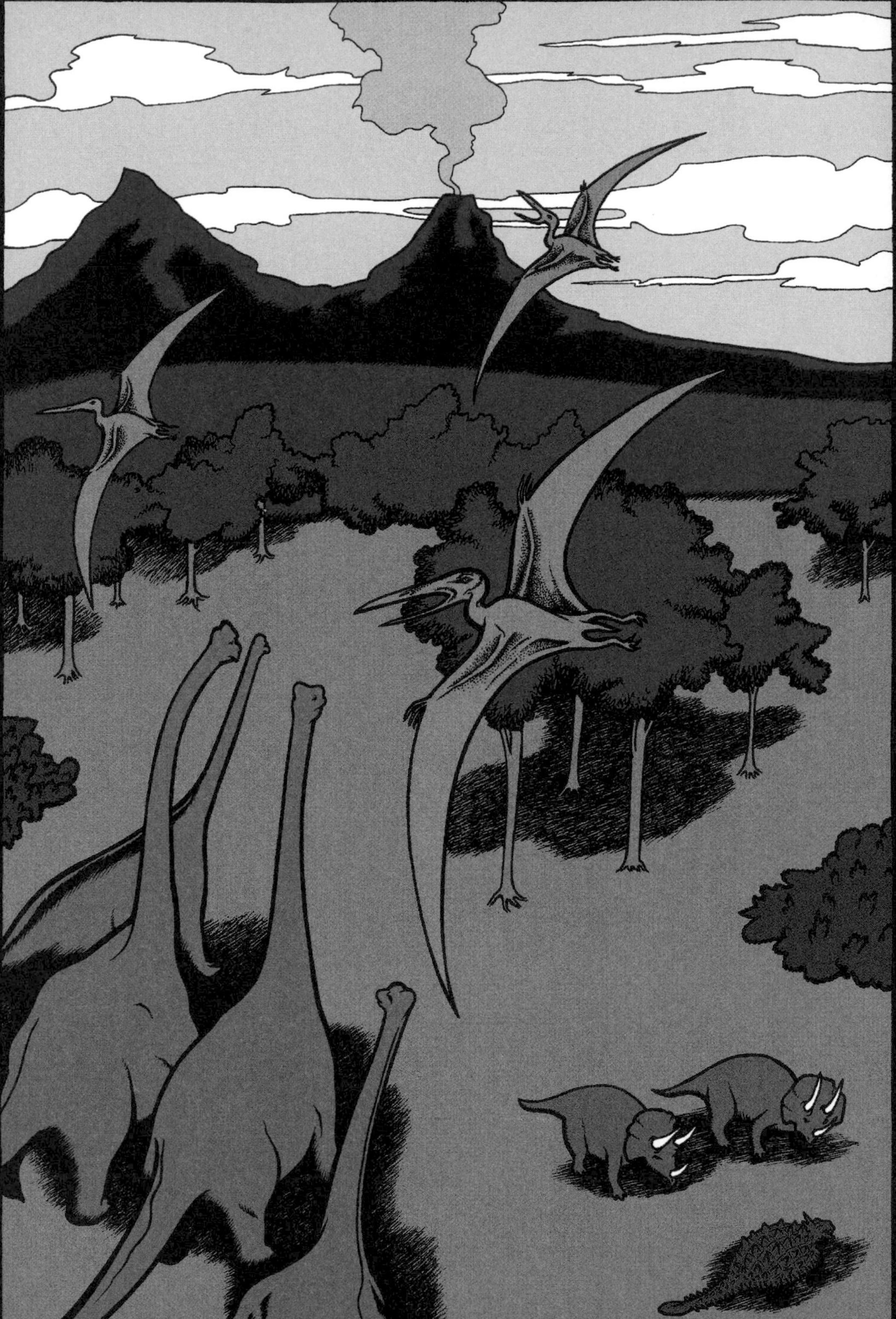

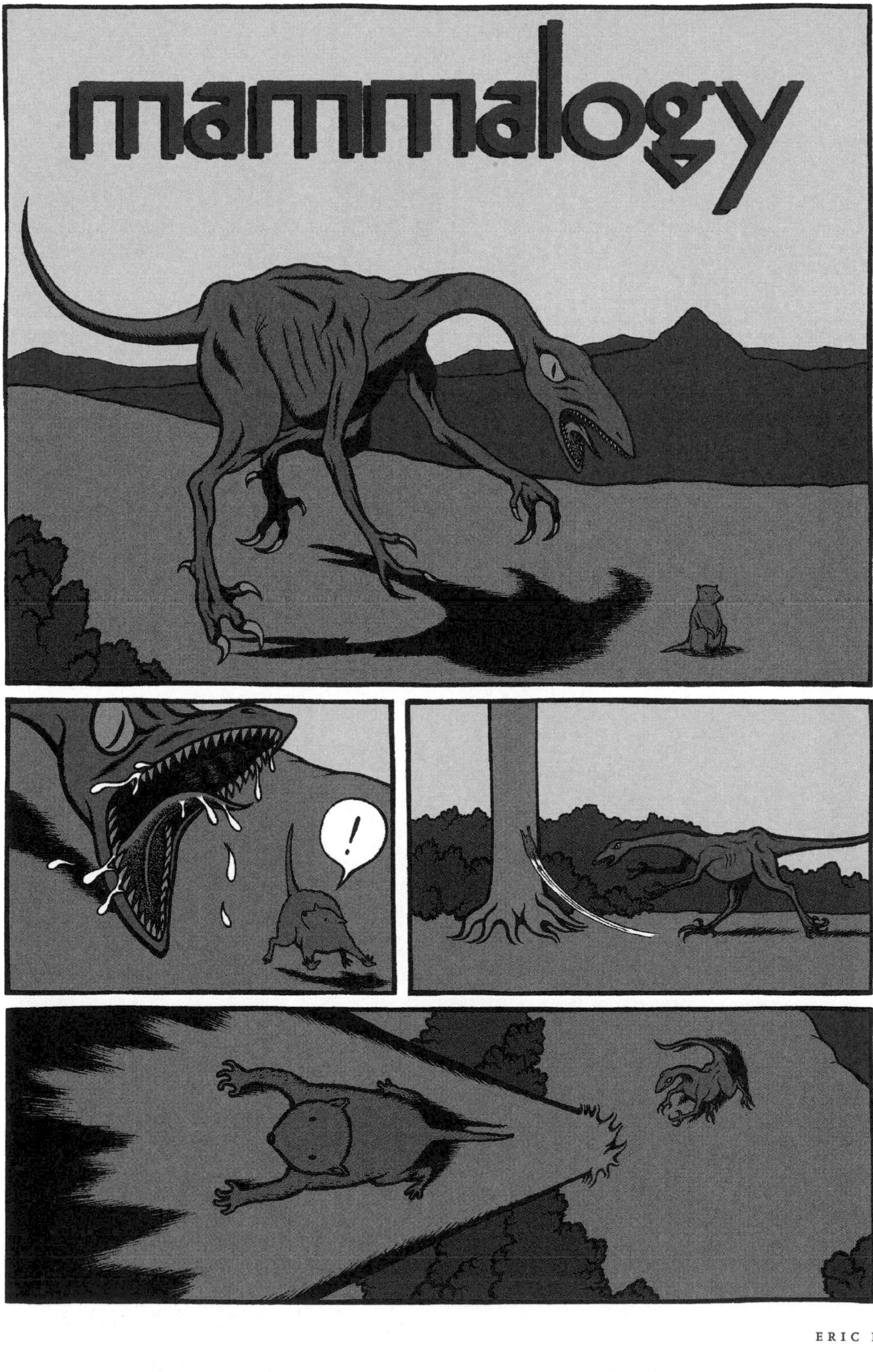
mammalogy
!

ERIC HAVEN

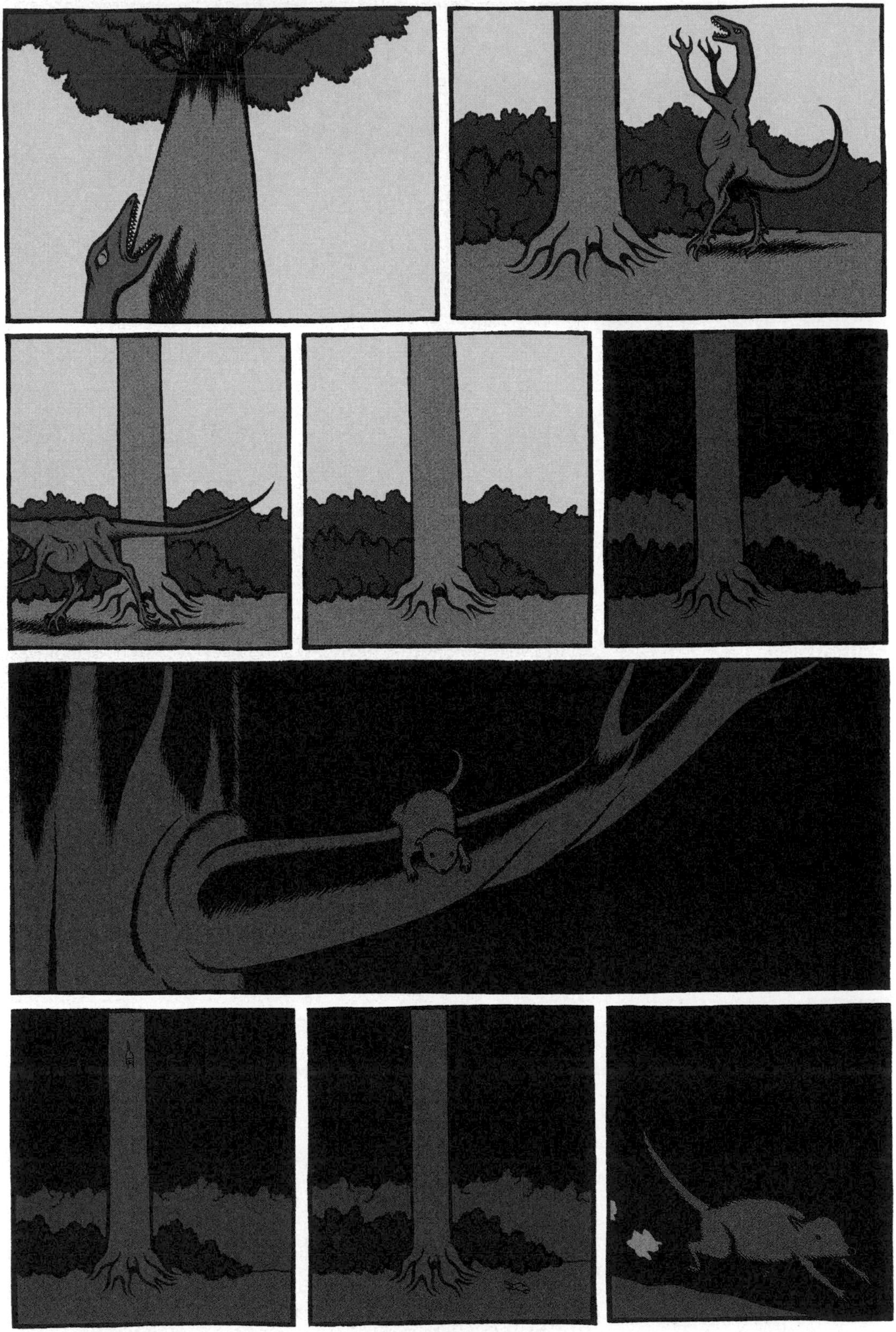

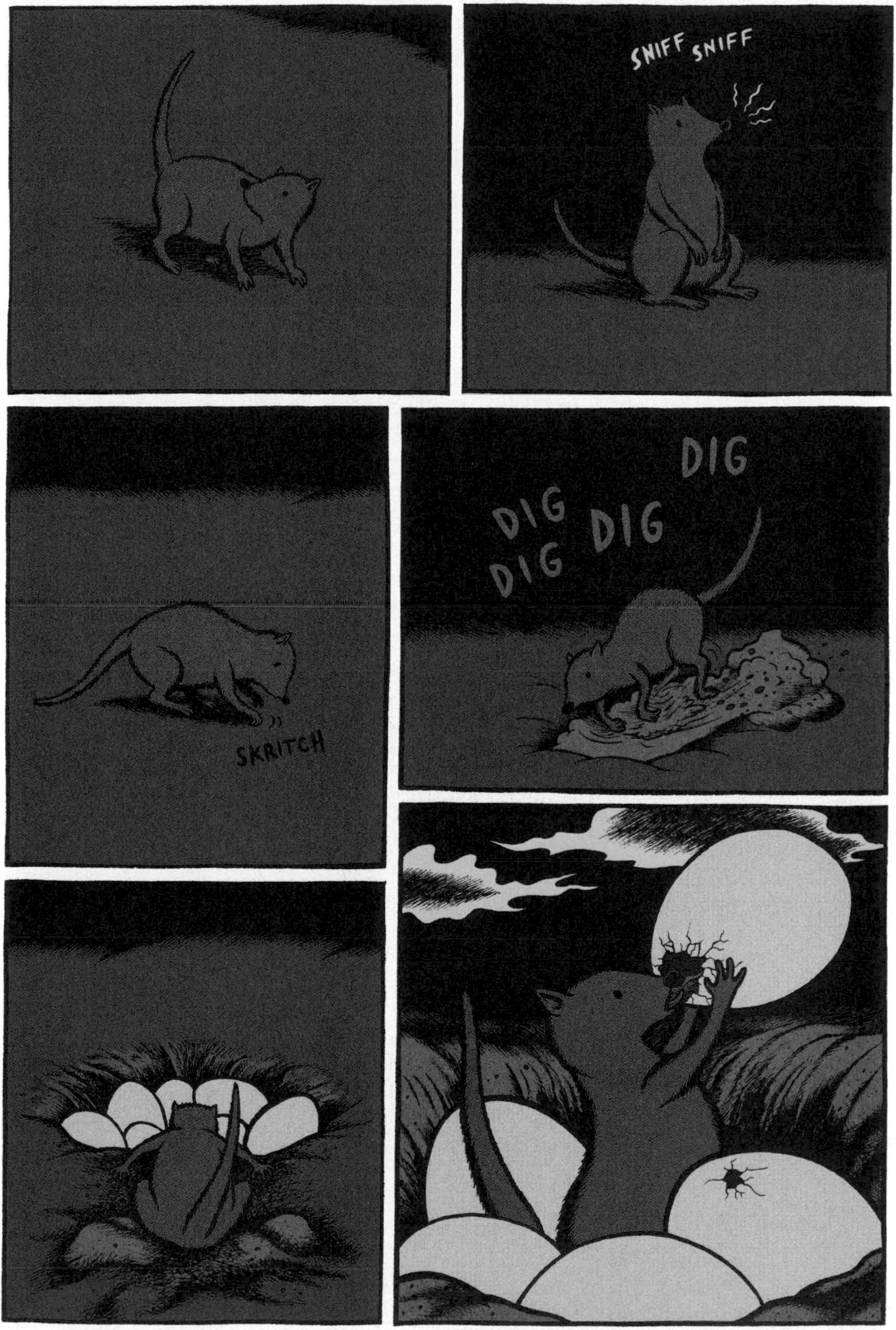
SNIFF SNIFF
SKRITCH
DIG
DIG DIG
DIG

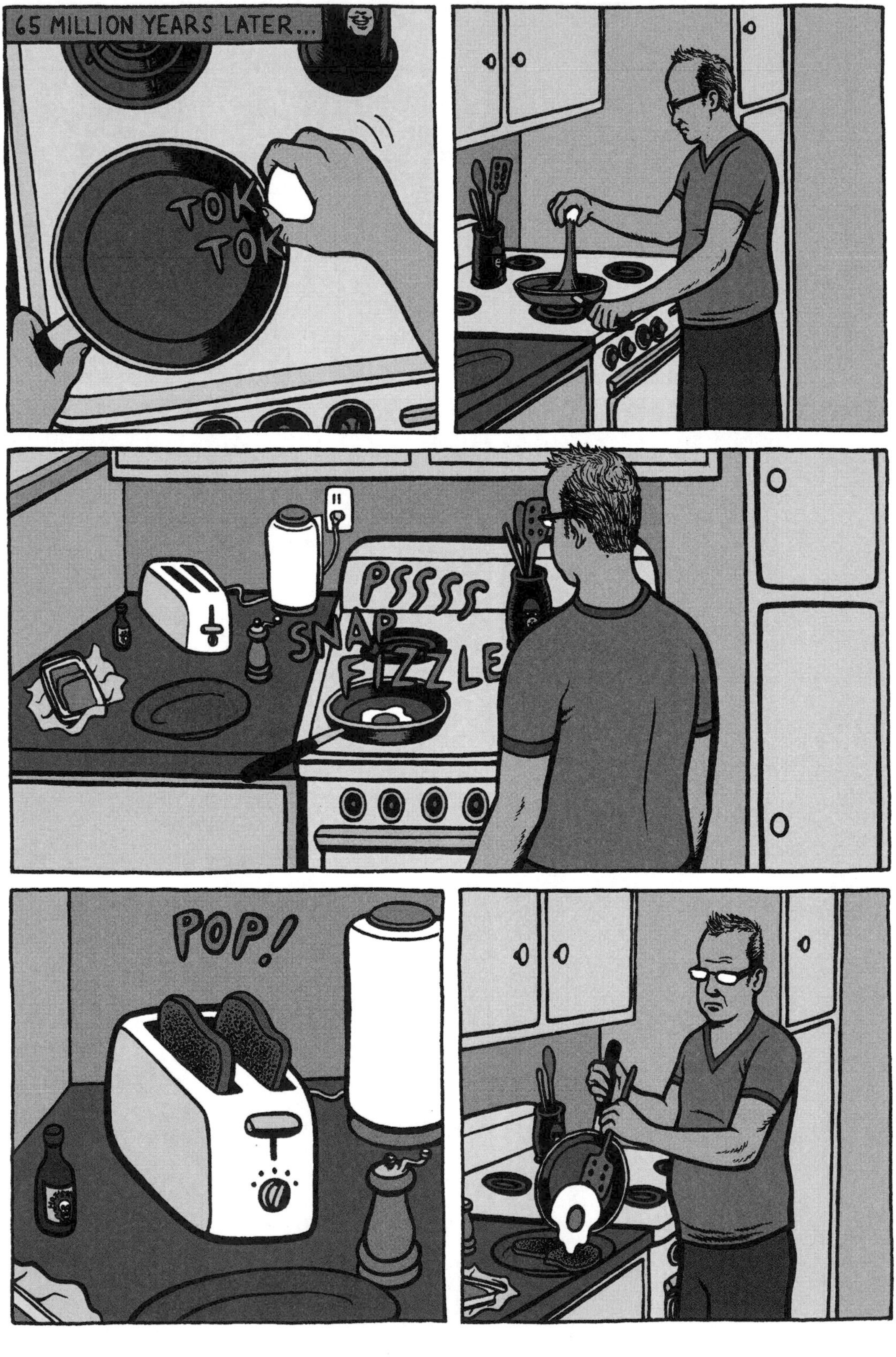
65 MILLION YEARS LATER...
TOK
TOK
PSSSS
SNAP
FIZZLE
POP!

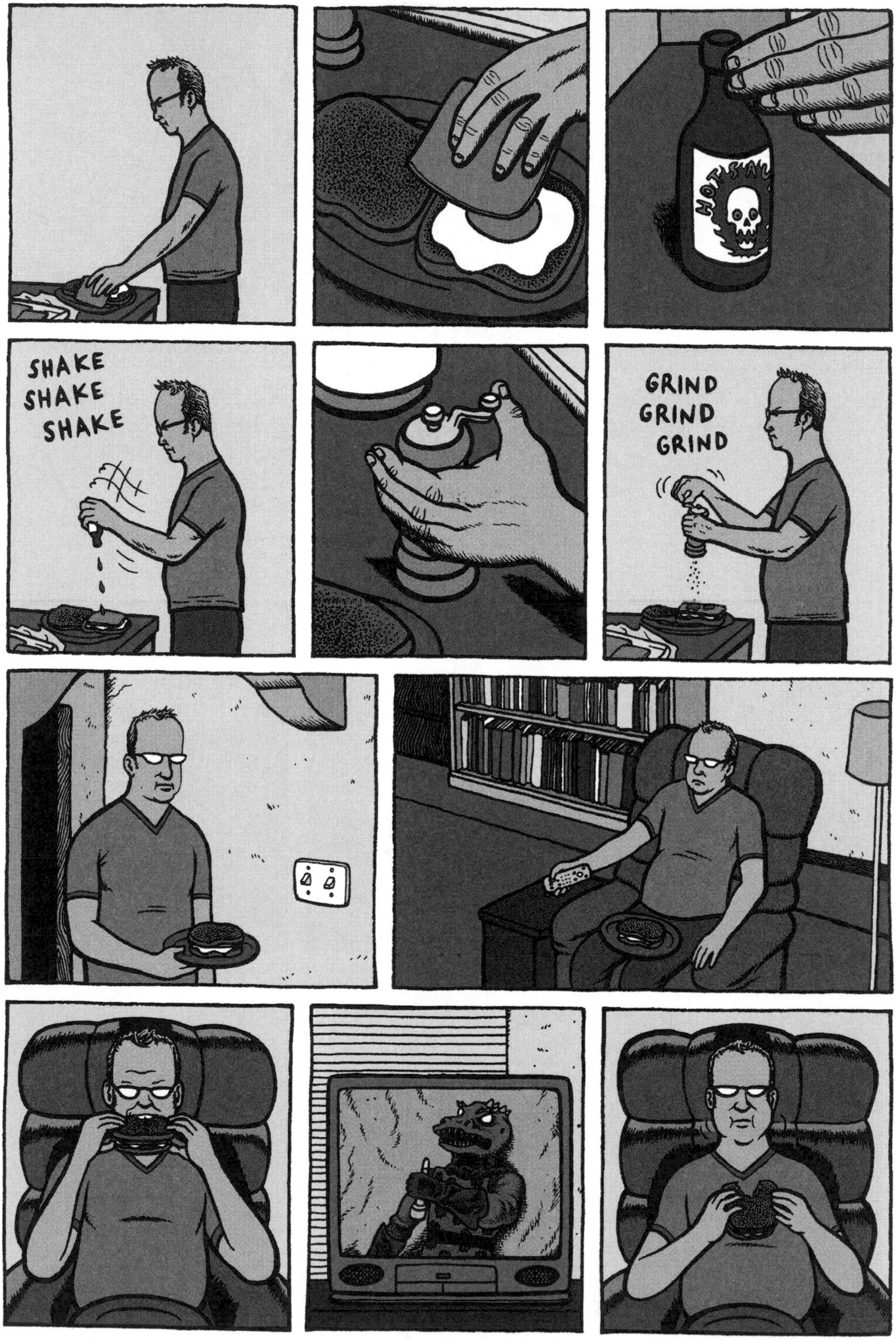
HOT SAU
SHAKE
SHAKE
SHAKE
GRIND
GRIND
GRIND

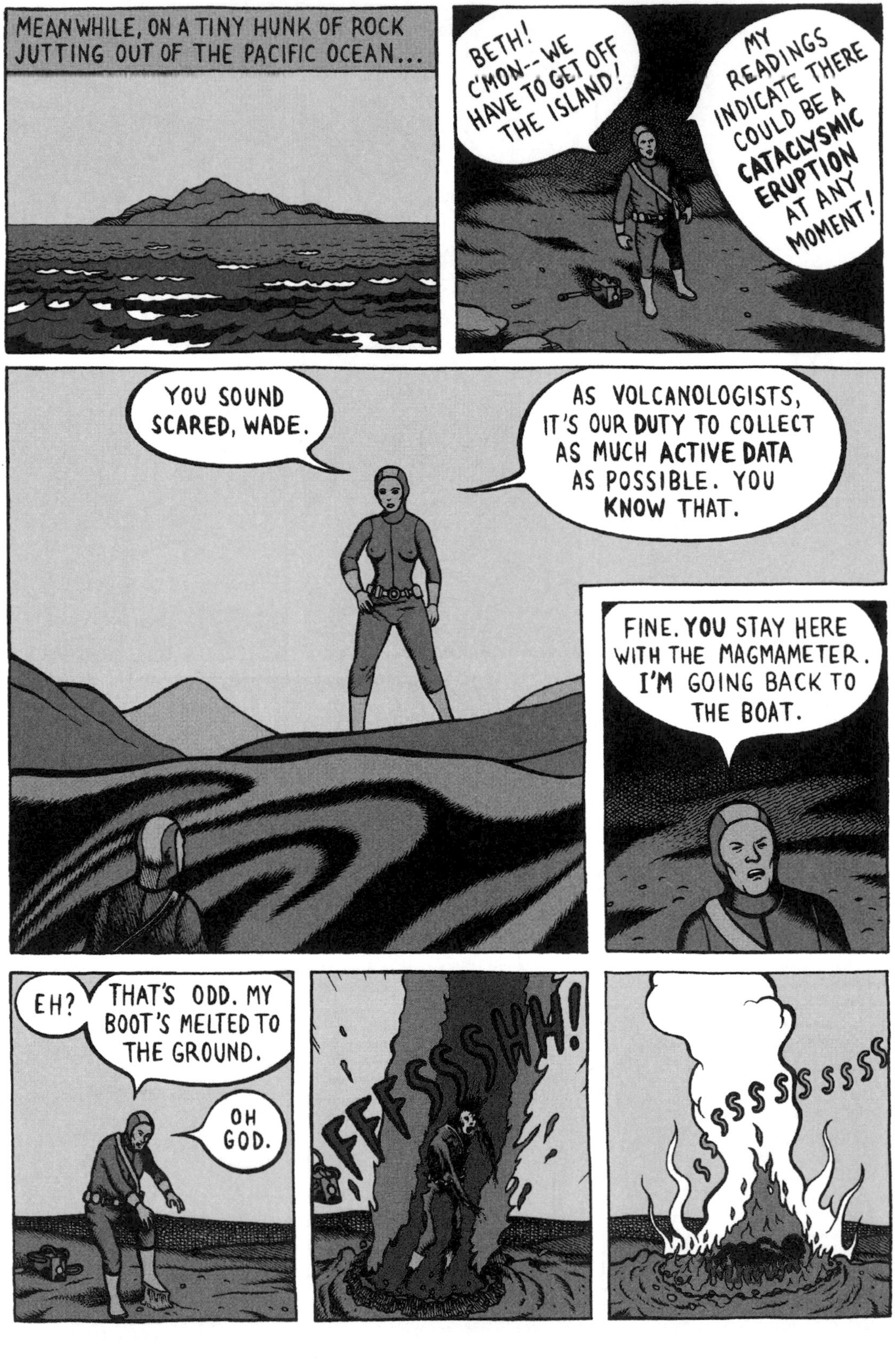

MEANWHILE, ON A TINY HUNK OF ROCK JUTTING OUT OF THE PACIFIC OCEAN...
BETH! C'MON-- WE HAVE TO GET OFF THE ISLAND!
MY READINGS INDICATE THERE COULD BE A CATACLYSMIC ERUPTION AT ANY MOMENT!
YOU SOUND SCARED, WADE.
AS VOLCANOLOGISTS, IT'S OUR DUTY TO COLLECT AS MUCH ACTIVE DATA AS POSSIBLE. YOU KNOW THAT.
FINE. YOU STAY HERE WITH THE MAGMAMETER. I'M GOING BACK TO THE BOAT.
EH?
THAT'S ODD. MY BOOT'S MELTED TO THE GROUND.
OH GOD.
FFFSSSSHH!
SSSSSSSSSS

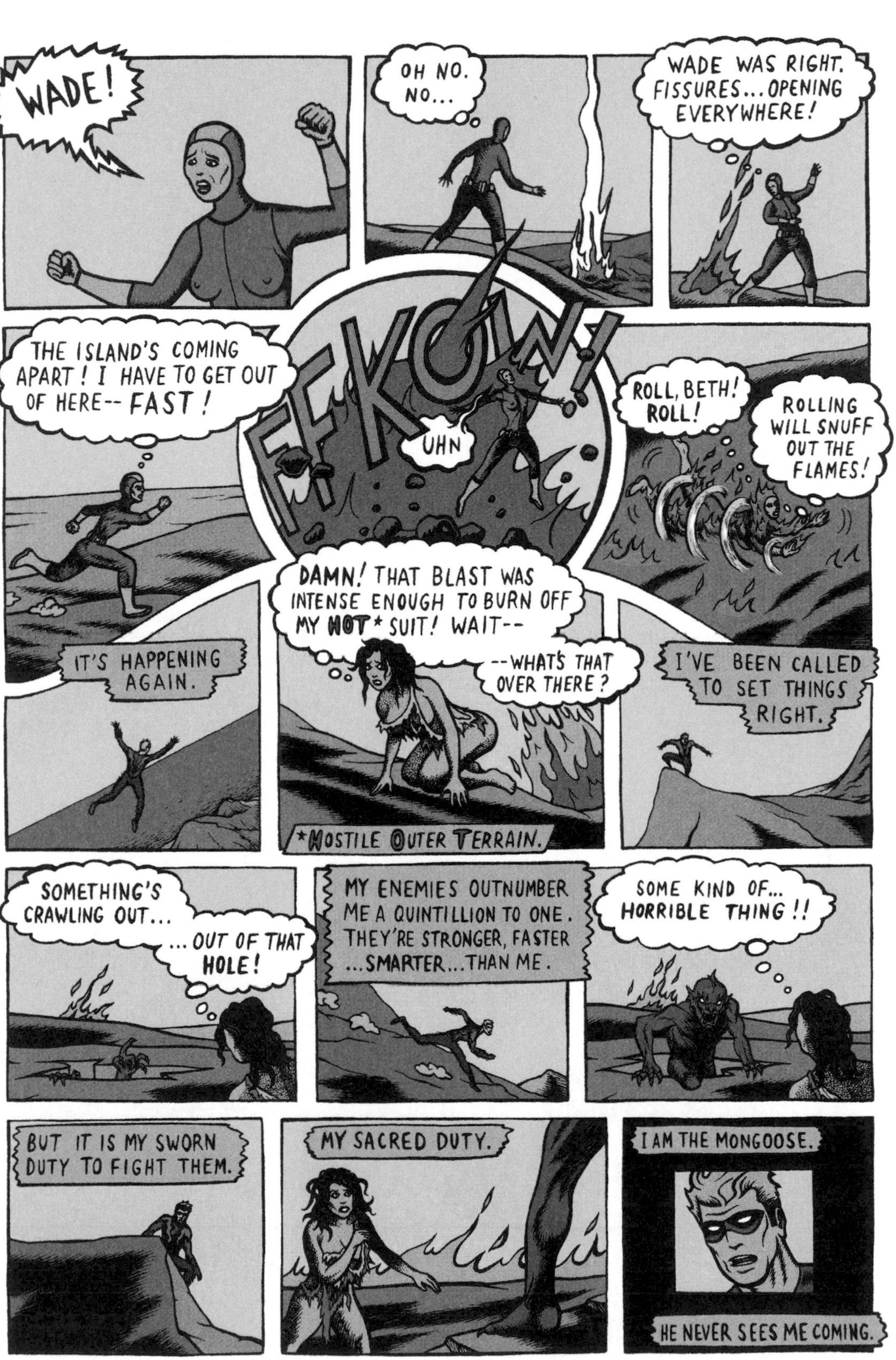
WADE!
OH NO. NO...
WADE WAS RIGHT. FISSURES... OPENING EVERYWHERE!
THE ISLAND'S COMING APART! I HAVE TO GET OUT OF HERE-- FAST!
FFKOW!
UHN
ROLL, BETH! ROLL!
ROLLING WILL SNUFF OUT THE FLAMES!
IT'S HAPPENING AGAIN.
DAMN! THAT BLAST WAS INTENSE ENOUGH TO BURN OFF MY HOT* SUIT! WAIT--
--WHAT'S THAT OVER THERE?
*HOSTILE OUTER TERRAIN.
I'VE BEEN CALLED TO SET THINGS RIGHT.
SOMETHING'S CRAWLING OUT...
...OUT OF THAT HOLE!
MY ENEMIES OUTNUMBER ME A QUINTILLION TO ONE. THEY'RE STRONGER, FASTER ...SMARTER...THAN ME.
SOME KIND OF... HORRIBLE THING!!
BUT IT IS MY SWORN DUTY TO FIGHT THEM.
MY SACRED DUTY.
I AM THE MONGOOSE.
HE NEVER SEES ME COMING.

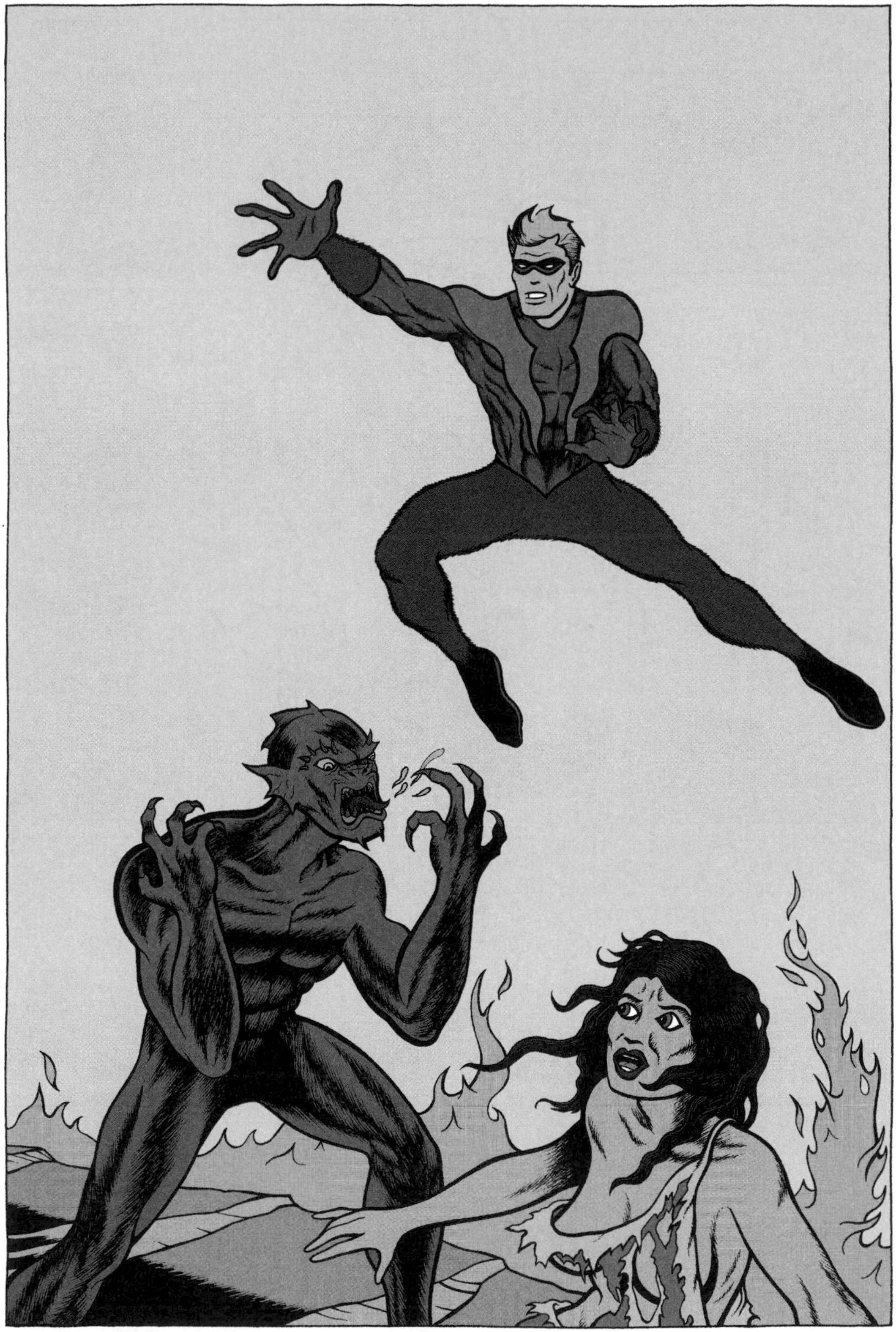

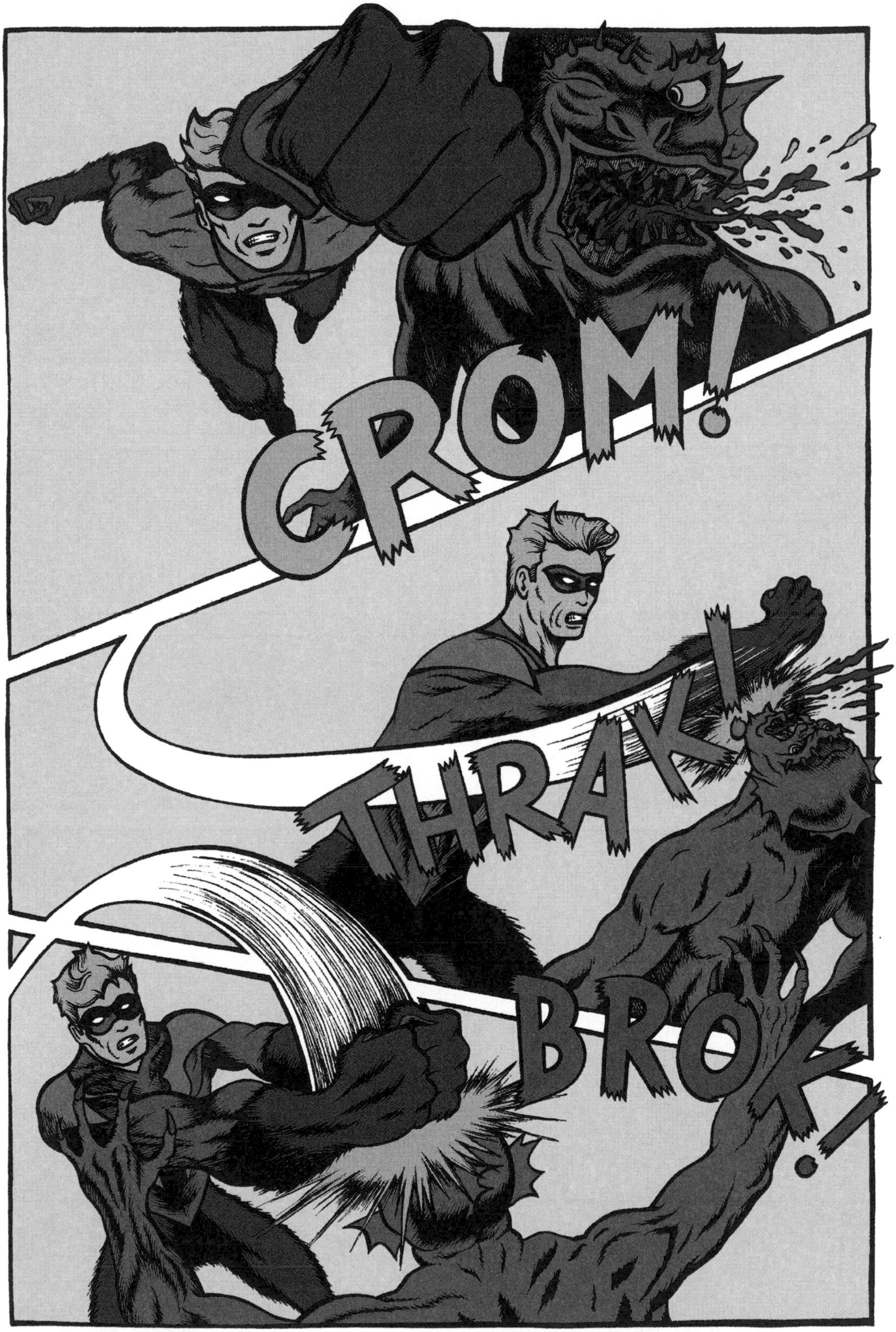
CROM!
THRAK!
BROK!

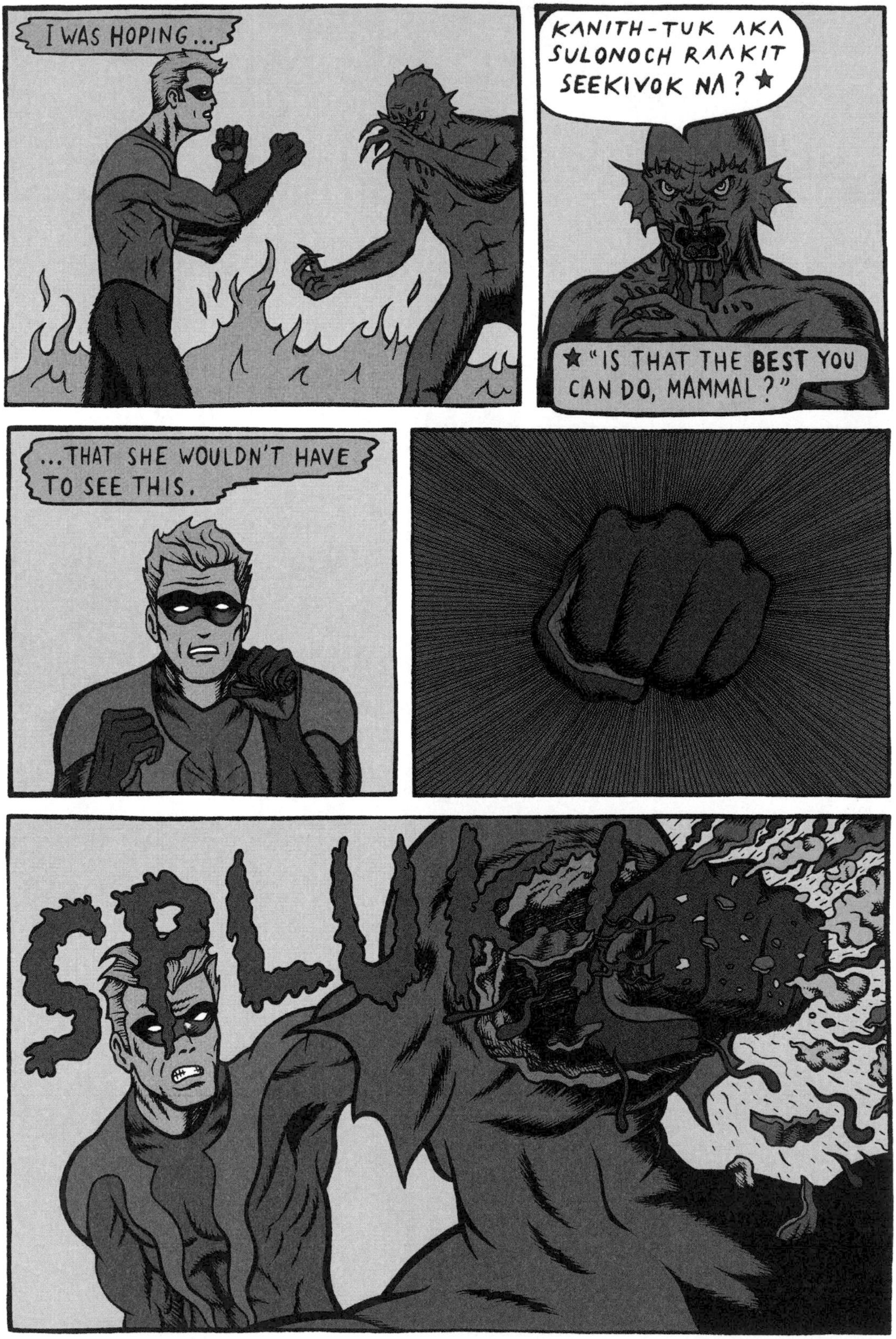
I WAS HOPING...
KANITH-TUK AKA SULONOCH RAAKIT SEEKIVOK NA? ★
★ "IS THAT THE **BEST** YOU CAN DO, MAMMAL?"
...THAT SHE WOULDN'T HAVE TO SEE THIS.
SPLUK

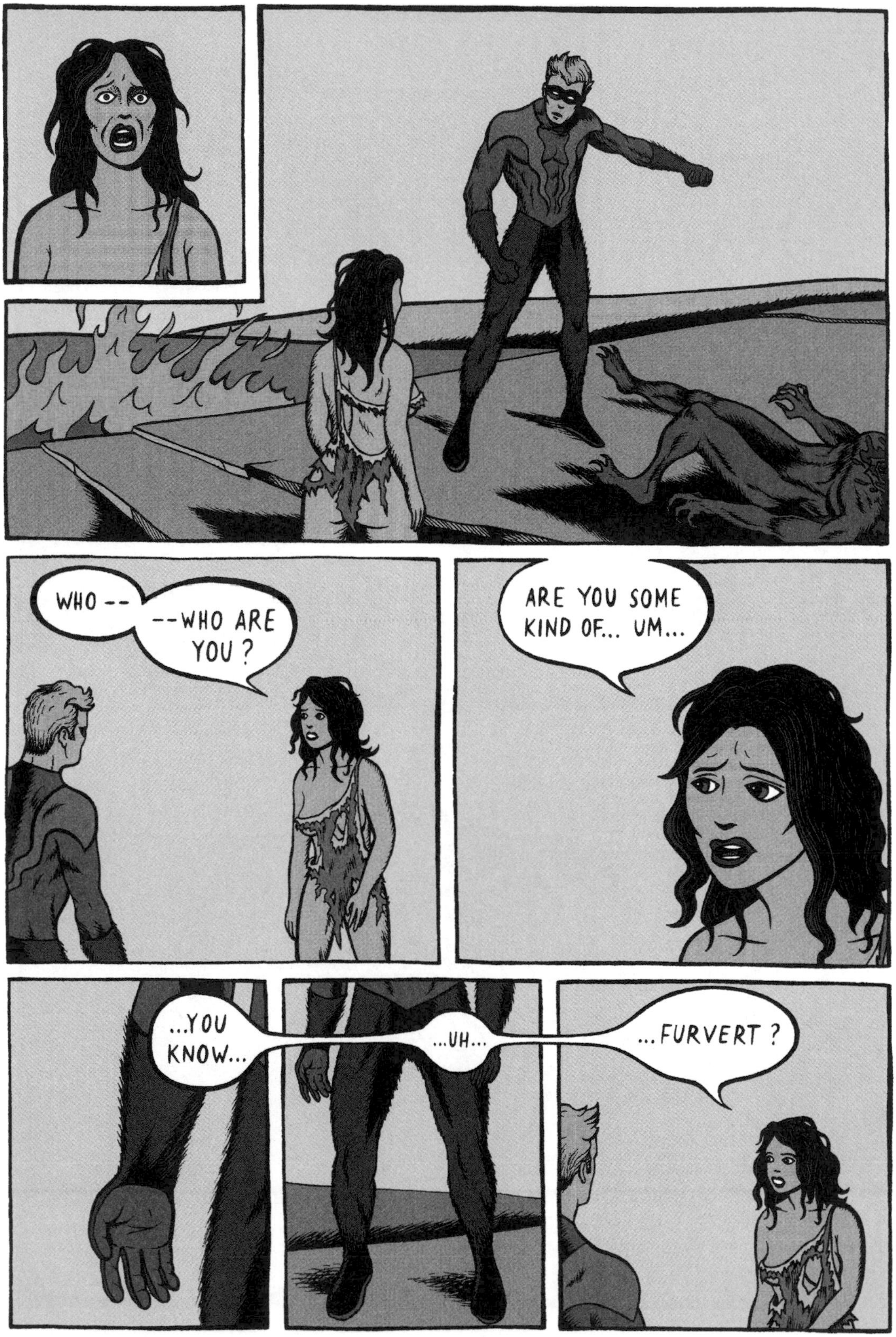
WHO --
--WHO ARE YOU ?
ARE YOU SOME KIND OF... UM...
...YOU KNOW...
...UH...
...FURVERT ?

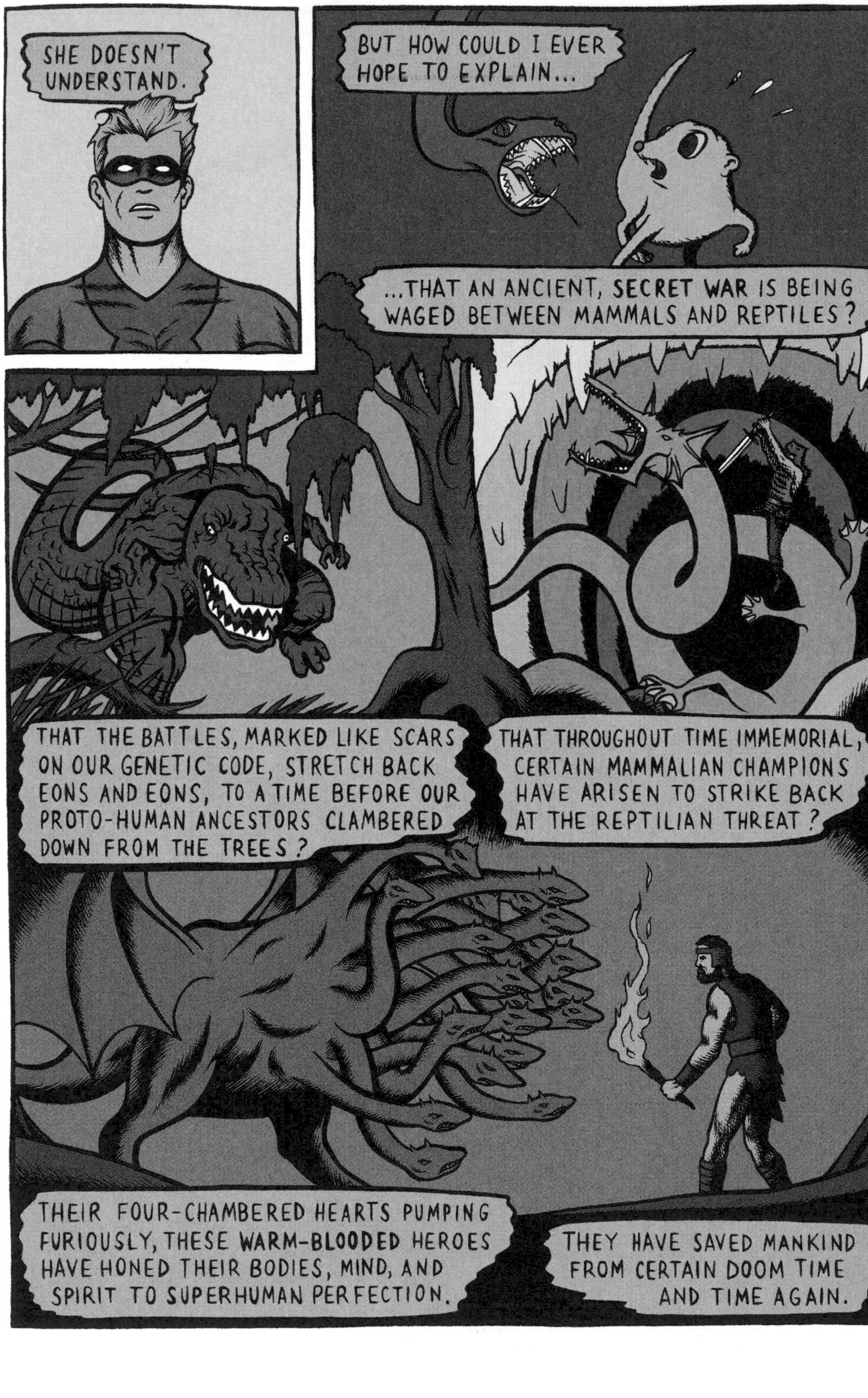
SHE DOESN'T UNDERSTAND.
BUT HOW COULD I EVER HOPE TO EXPLAIN...
...THAT AN ANCIENT, SECRET WAR IS BEING WAGED BETWEEN MAMMALS AND REPTILES?
THAT THE BATTLES, MARKED LIKE SCARS ON OUR GENETIC CODE, STRETCH BACK EONS AND EONS, TO A TIME BEFORE OUR PROTO-HUMAN ANCESTORS CLAMBERED DOWN FROM THE TREES?
THAT THROUGHOUT TIME IMMEMORIAL, CERTAIN MAMMALIAN CHAMPIONS HAVE ARISEN TO STRIKE BACK AT THE REPTILIAN THREAT?
THEIR FOUR-CHAMBERED HEARTS PUMPING FURIOUSLY, THESE WARM-BLOODED HEROES HAVE HONED THEIR BODIES, MIND, AND SPIRIT TO SUPERHUMAN PERFECTION.
THEY HAVE SAVED MANKIND FROM CERTAIN DOOM TIME AND TIME AGAIN.

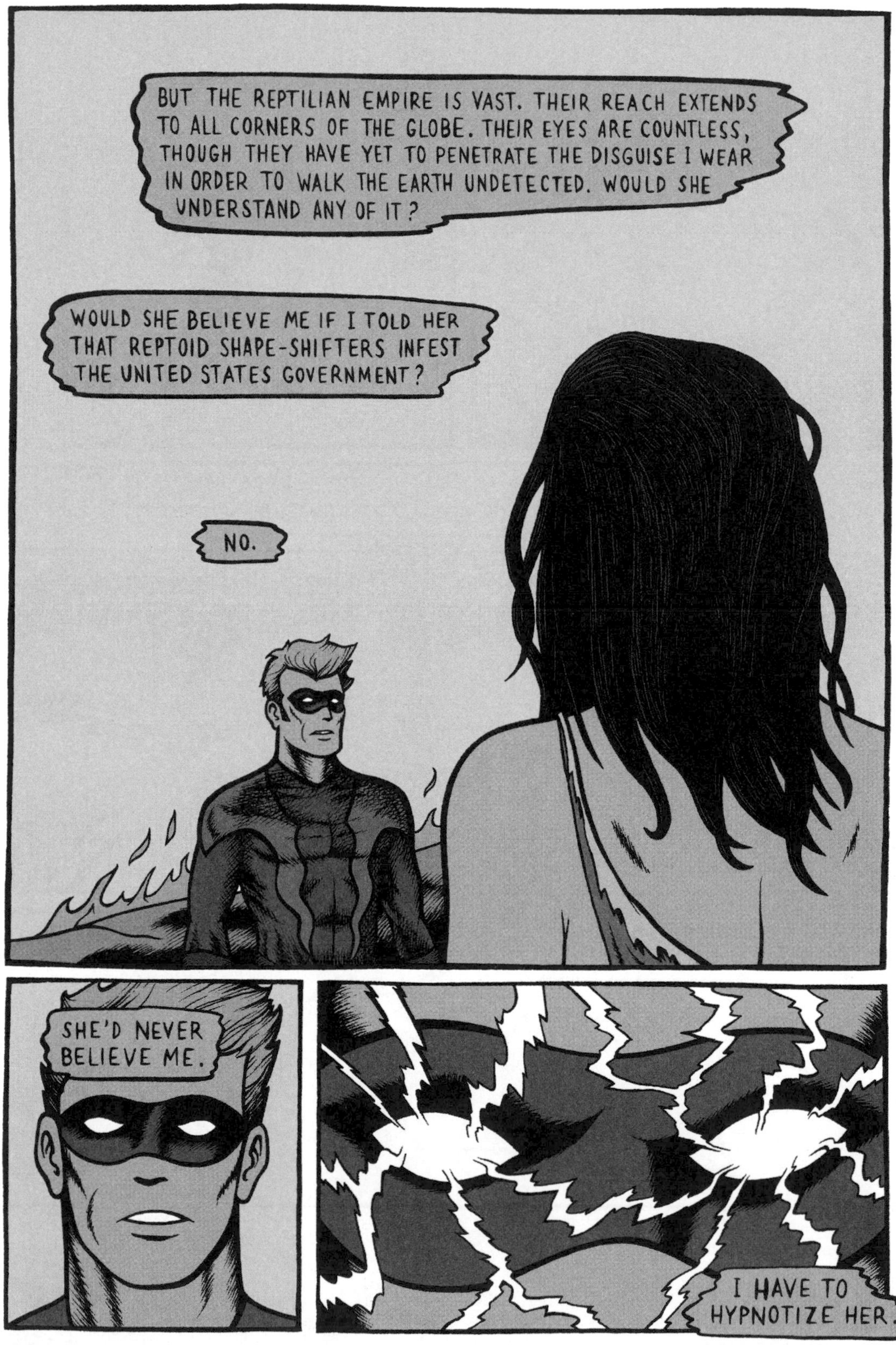
BUT THE REPTILIAN EMPIRE IS VAST. THEIR REACH EXTENDS TO ALL CORNERS OF THE GLOBE. THEIR EYES ARE COUNTLESS, THOUGH THEY HAVE YET TO PENETRATE THE DISGUISE I WEAR IN ORDER TO WALK THE EARTH UNDETECTED. WOULD SHE UNDERSTAND ANY OF IT?
WOULD SHE BELIEVE ME IF I TOLD HER THAT REPTOID SHAPE-SHIFTERS INFEST THE UNITED STATES GOVERNMENT?
NO.
SHE'D NEVER BELIEVE ME.
I HAVE TO HYPNOTIZE HER.

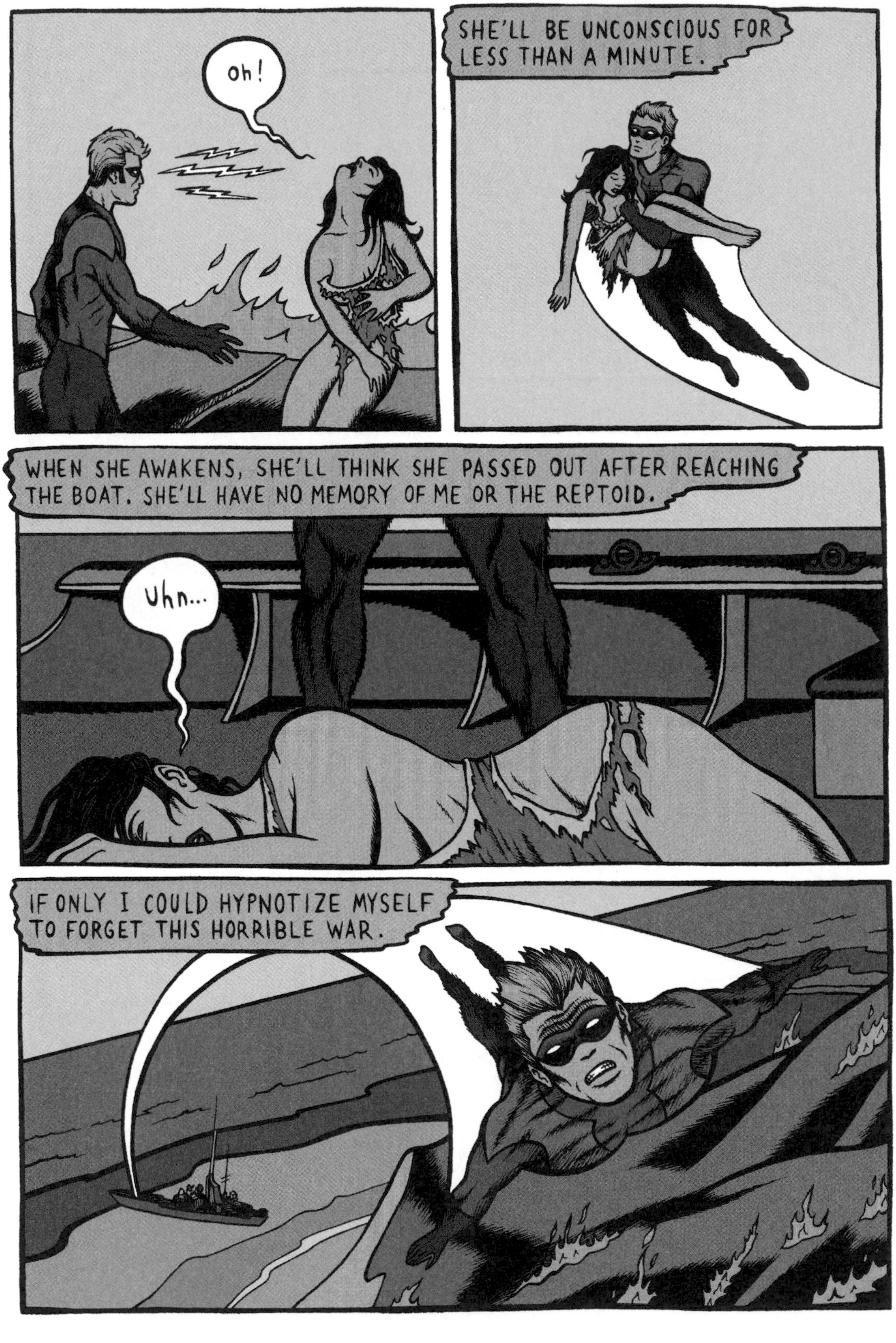

Oh!
SHE'LL BE UNCONSCIOUS FOR LESS THAN A MINUTE.
WHEN SHE AWAKENS, SHE'LL THINK SHE PASSED OUT AFTER REACHING THE BOAT. SHE'LL HAVE NO MEMORY OF ME OR THE REPTOID.
Uhn...
IF ONLY I COULD HYPNOTIZE MYSELF TO FORGET THIS HORRIBLE WAR.

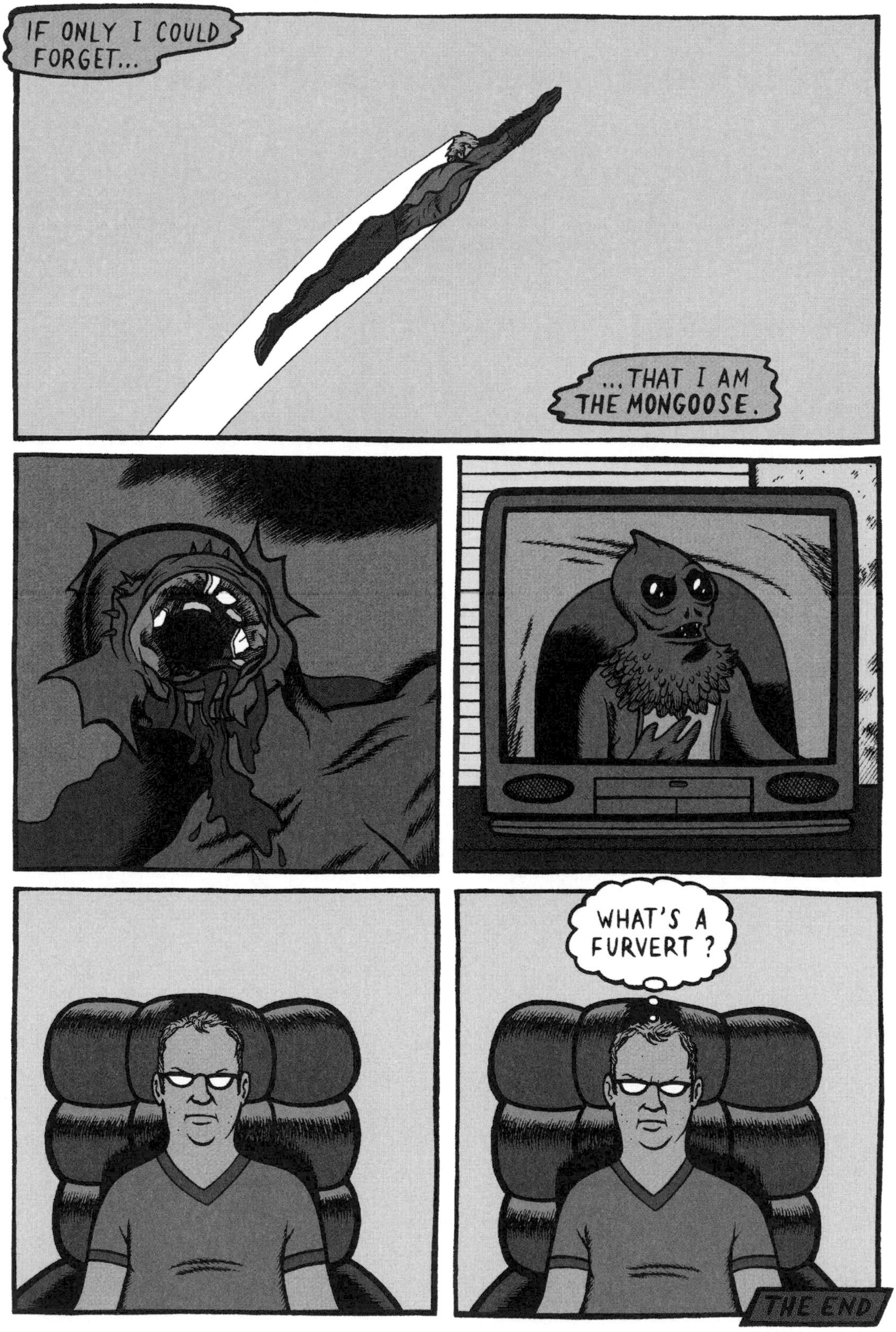
IF ONLY I COULD FORGET...
...THAT I AM THE MONGOOSE.
WHAT'S A FURVERT ?
THE END

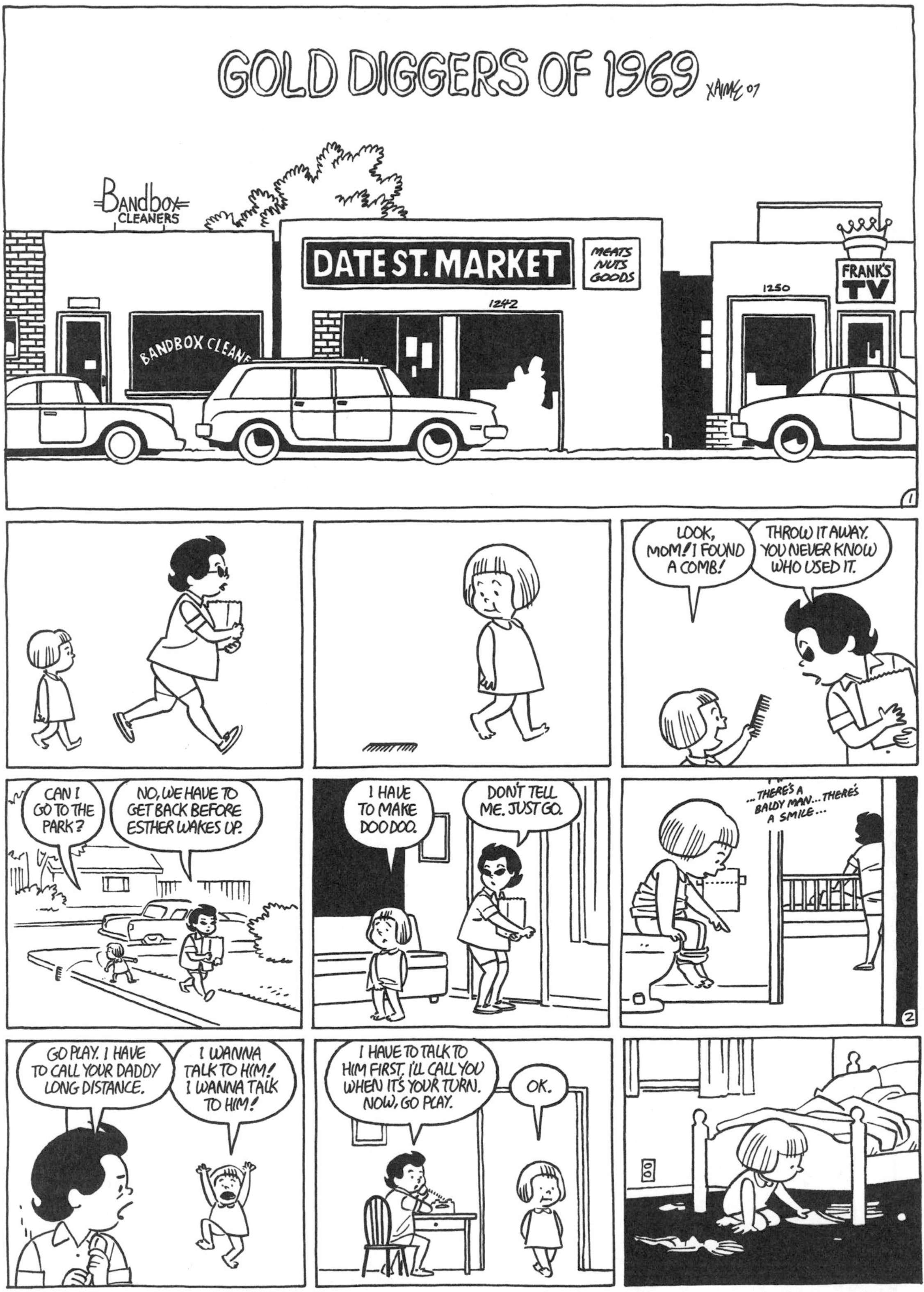
GOLD DIGGERS OF 1969
XAIME 07
Bandbox CLEANERS
DATE ST. MARKET
MEATS NUTS GOODS
FRANK'S TV
1250
1242
BANDBOX CLEANE
1
LOOK, MOM! I FOUND A COMB!
THROW IT AWAY. YOU NEVER KNOW WHO USED IT.
CAN I GO TO THE PARK?
NO, WE HAVE TO GET BACK BEFORE ESTHER WAKES UP.
I HAVE TO MAKE DOO DOO.
DON'T TELL ME. JUST GO.
...THERE'S A BALDY MAN... THERE'S A SMILE...
2
GO PLAY. I HAVE TO CALL YOUR DADDY LONG DISTANCE.
I WANNA TALK TO HIM! I WANNA TALK TO HIM!
I HAVE TO TALK TO HIM FIRST. I'LL CALL YOU WHEN IT'S YOUR TURN. NOW, GO PLAY.
OK.

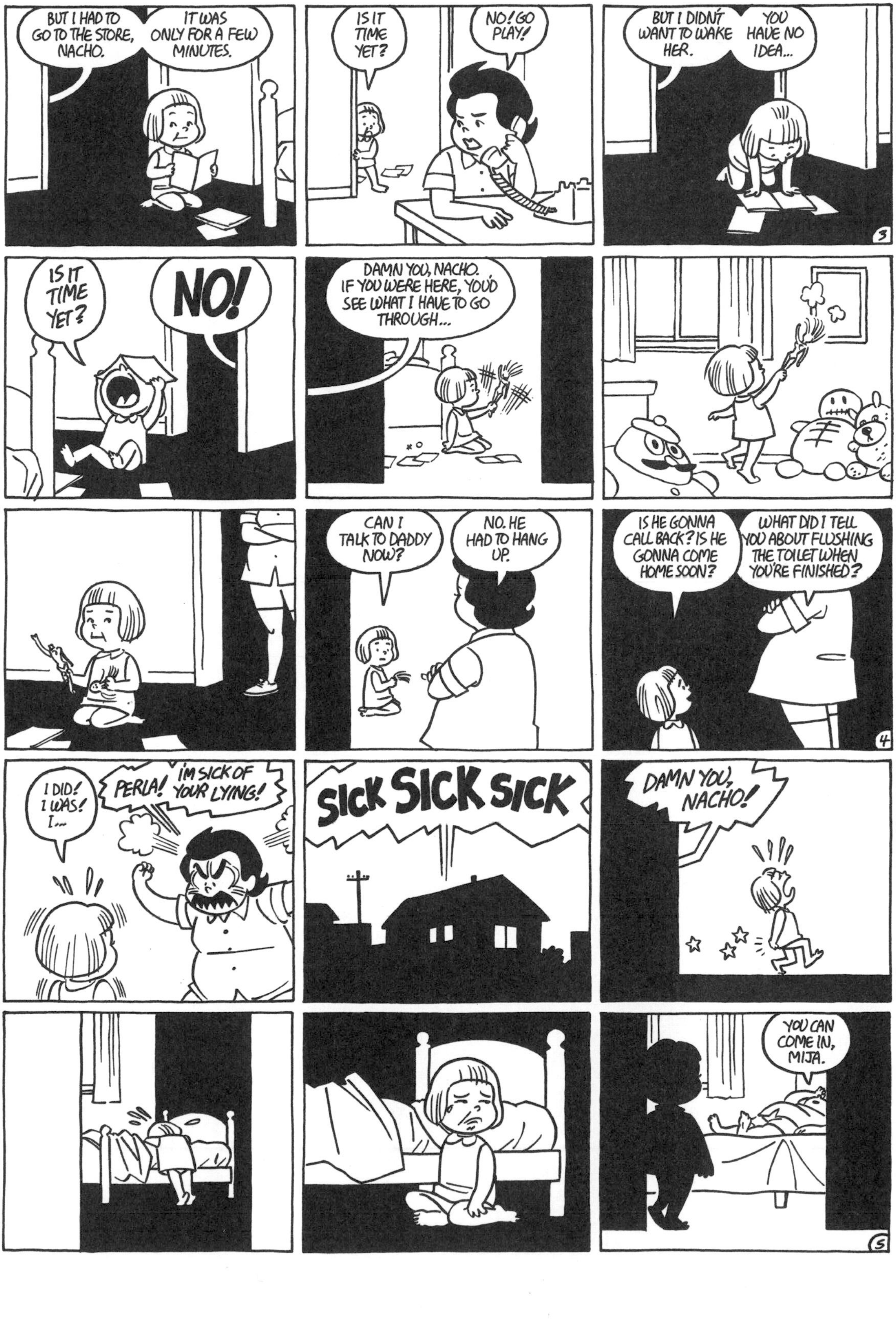
BUT I HAD TO GO TO THE STORE, NACHO.
IT WAS ONLY FOR A FEW MINUTES.
IS IT TIME YET?
NO! GO PLAY!
BUT I DIDN'T WANT TO WAKE HER.
YOU HAVE NO IDEA...
3
IS IT TIME YET?
NO!
DAMN YOU, NACHO. IF YOU WERE HERE, YOU'D SEE WHAT I HAVE TO GO THROUGH...
CAN I TALK TO DADDY NOW?
NO. HE HAD TO HANG UP.
IS HE GONNA CALL BACK? IS HE GONNA COME HOME SOON?
WHAT DID I TELL YOU ABOUT FLUSHING THE TOILET WHEN YOU'RE FINISHED?
4
I DID! I WAS! I...
PERLA!
IM SICK OF YOUR LYING!
SICK SICK SICK
DAMN YOU, NACHO!
YOU CAN COME IN, MIJA.
5

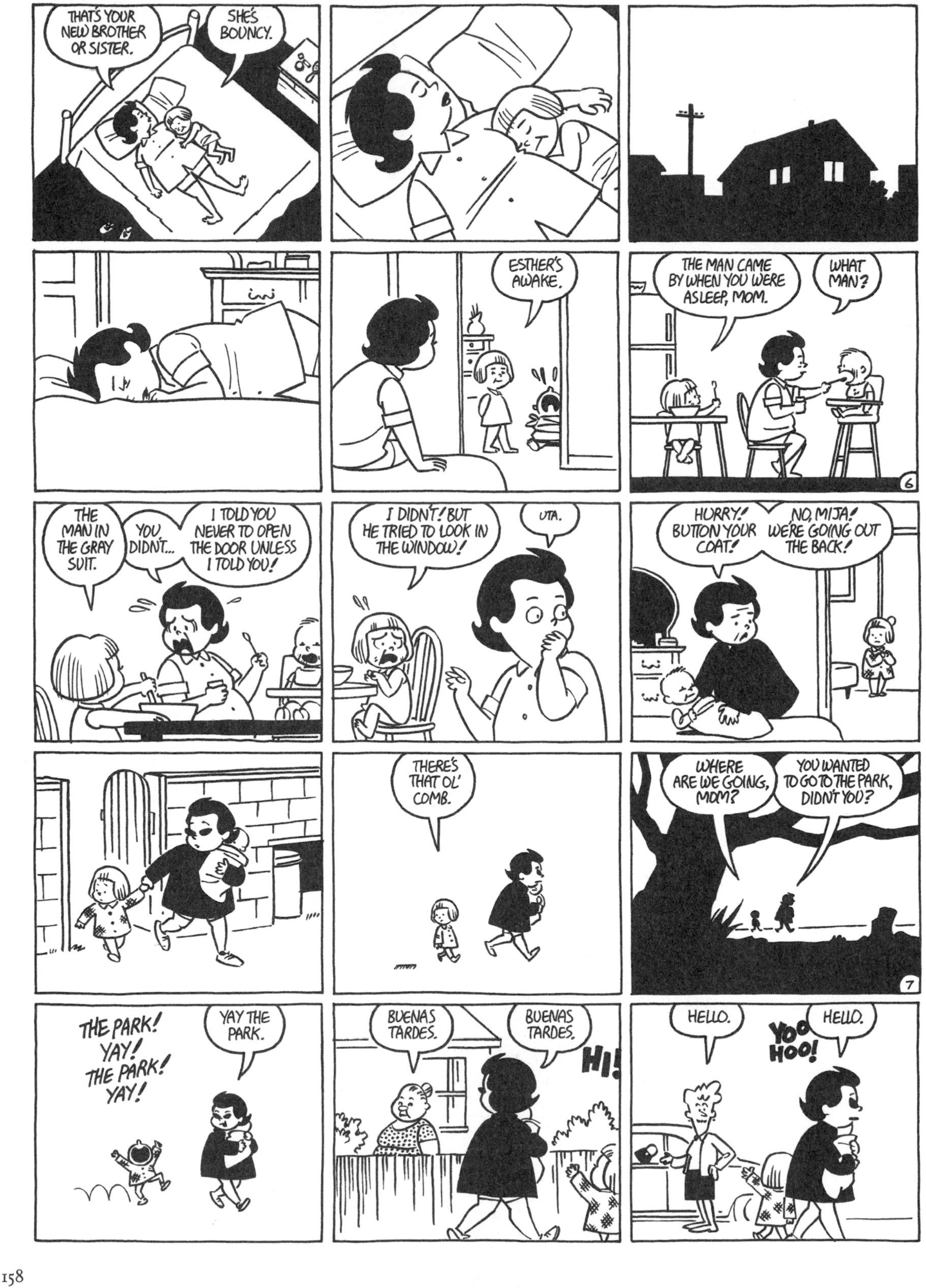
THAT'S YOUR NEW BROTHER OR SISTER.
SHE'S BOUNCY.
ESTHER'S AWAKE.
THE MAN CAME BY WHEN YOU WERE ASLEEP, MOM.
WHAT MAN?
6
THE MAN IN THE GRAY SUIT.
YOU DIDN'T...
I TOLD YOU NEVER TO OPEN THE DOOR UNLESS I TOLD YOU!
I DIDN'T! BUT HE TRIED TO LOOK IN THE WINDOW!
UTA.
HURRY! BUTTON YOUR COAT!
NO, MIJA! WE'RE GOING OUT THE BACK!
THERE'S THAT OL' COMB.
WHERE ARE WE GOING, MOM?
YOU WANTED TO GO TO THE PARK, DIDN'T YOU?
7
THE PARK! YAY! THE PARK! YAY!
YAY THE PARK.
BUENAS TARDES.
BUENAS TARDES.
HI!
HELLO.
YOO HOO!
HELLO.

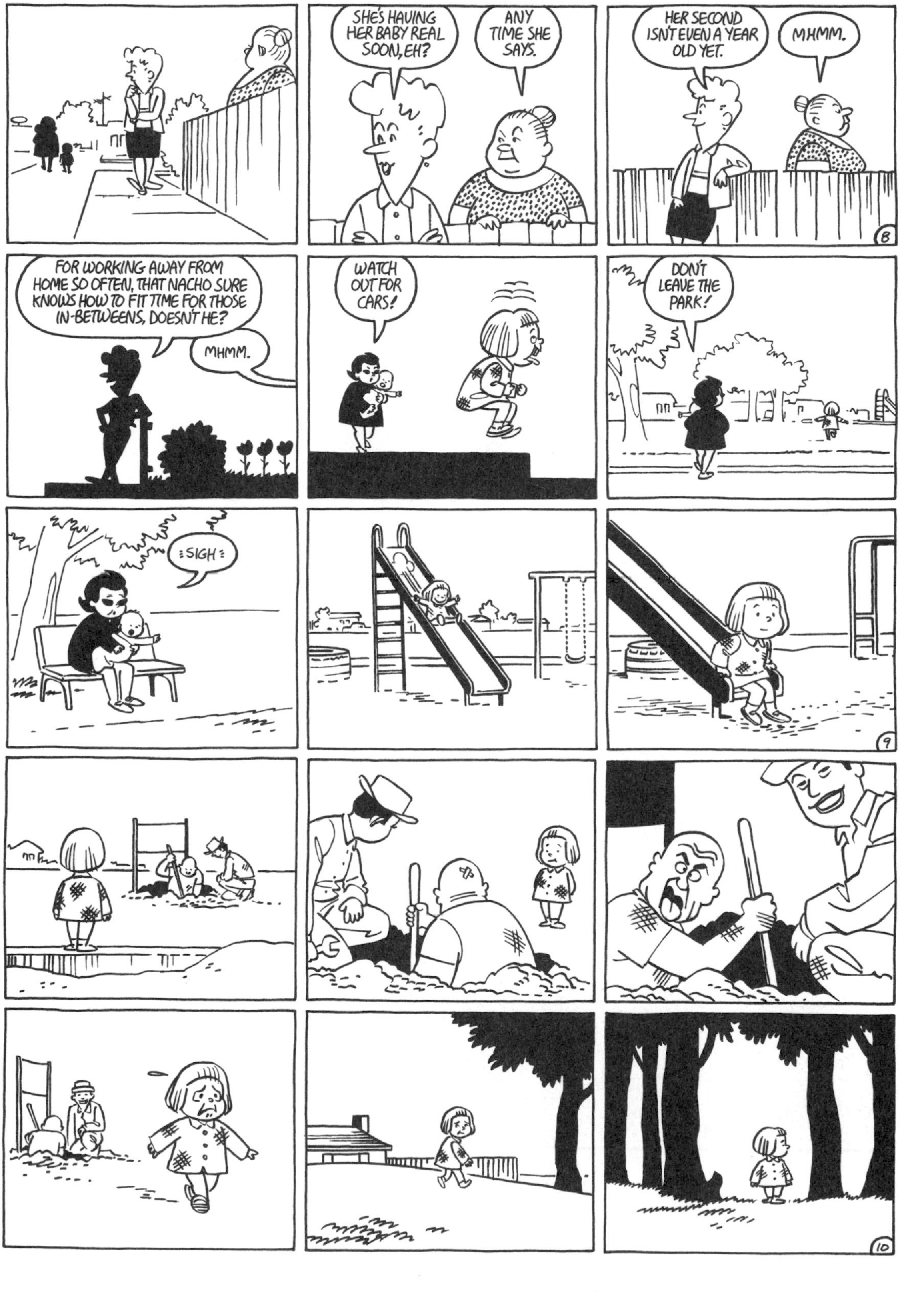
SHE'S HAVING HER BABY REAL SOON, EH?
ANY TIME SHE SAYS.
HER SECOND ISN'T EVEN A YEAR OLD YET.
MHMM.
8
FOR WORKING AWAY FROM HOME SO OFTEN, THAT NACHO SURE KNOWS HOW TO FIT TIME FOR THOSE IN-BETWEENS, DOESN'T HE?
MHMM.
WATCH OUT FOR CARS!
DON'T LEAVE THE PARK!
SIGH
9
10

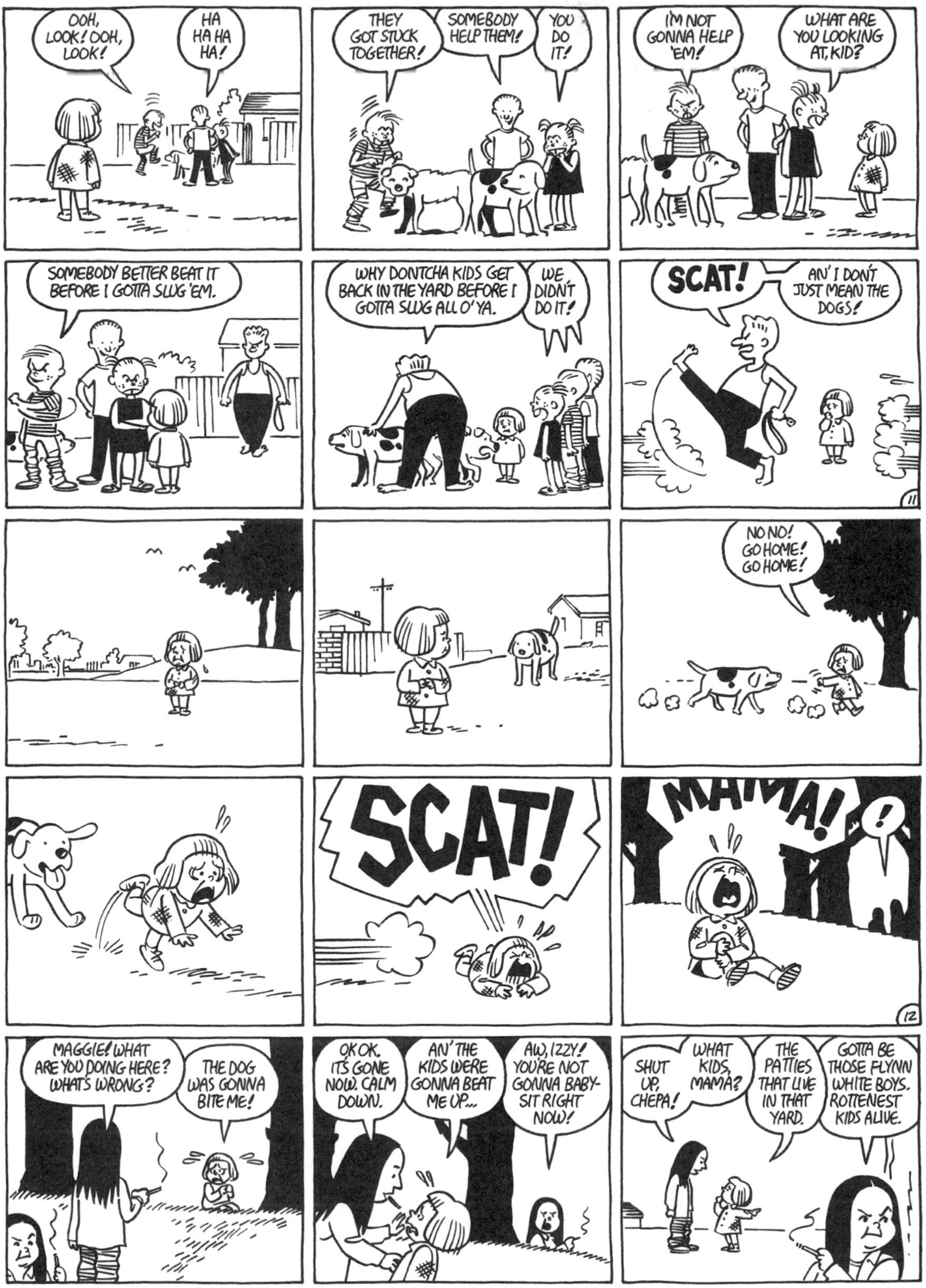
OOH, LOOK! OOH, LOOK!
HA HA HA HA!
THEY GOT STUCK TOGETHER!
SOMEBODY HELP THEM!
YOU DO IT!
I'M NOT GONNA HELP 'EM!
WHAT ARE YOU LOOKING AT, KID?
SOMEBODY BETTER BEAT IT BEFORE I GOTTA SLUG 'EM.
WHY DONTCHA KIDS GET BACK IN THE YARD BEFORE I GOTTA SLUG ALL O' YA.
WE DIDN'T DO IT!
SCAT!
AN' I DON'T JUST MEAN THE DOGS!
11
NO NO! GO HOME! GO HOME!
SCAT!
MAMA!
!
12
MAGGIE! WHAT ARE YOU DOING HERE? WHAT'S WRONG?
THE DOG WAS GONNA BITE ME!
OK OK. IT'S GONE NOW. CALM DOWN.
AN' THE KIDS WERE GONNA BEAT ME UP...
AW, IZZY! YOU'RE NOT GONNA BABY-SIT RIGHT NOW!
SHUT UP, CHEPA!
WHAT KIDS, MAMA?
THE PATTIES THAT LIVE IN THAT YARD.
GOTTA BE THOSE FLYNN WHITE BOYS. ROTTENEST KIDS ALIVE.

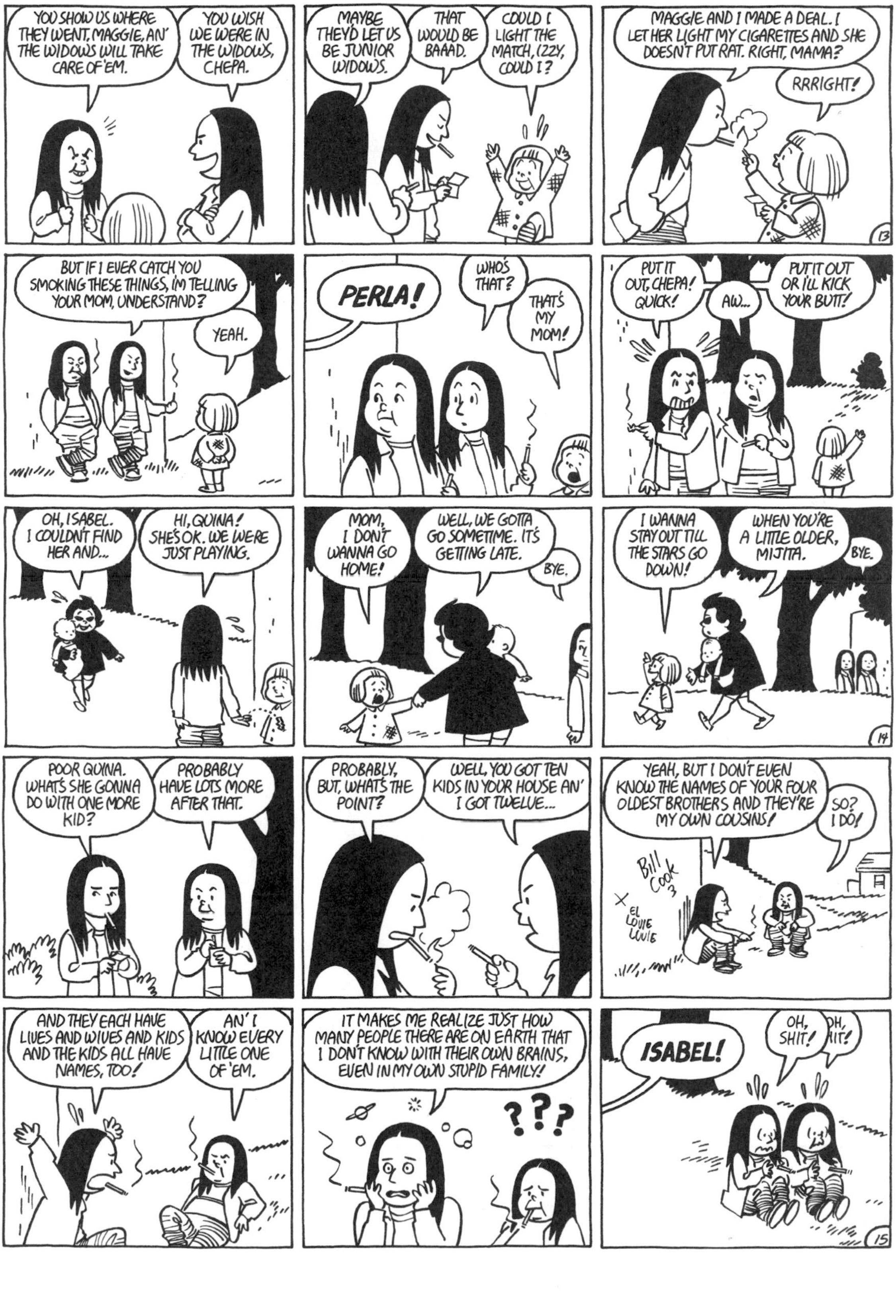

YOU SHOW US WHERE THEY WENT, MAGGIE, AN' THE WIDOWS WILL TAKE CARE OF 'EM.
YOU WISH WE WERE IN THE WIDOWS, CHEPA.
MAYBE THEY'D LET US BE JUNIOR WIDOWS.
THAT WOULD BE BAAAD.
COULD I LIGHT THE MATCH, IZZY, COULD I?
MAGGIE AND I MADE A DEAL. I LET HER LIGHT MY CIGARETTES AND SHE DOESN'T PUT RAT. RIGHT, MAMA?
RRRIGHT!
13
BUT IF I EVER CATCH YOU SMOKING THESE THINGS, I'M TELLING YOUR MOM, UNDERSTAND?
YEAH.
PERLA!
WHO'S THAT?
THAT'S MY MOM!
PUT IT OUT, CHEPA! QUICK!
AW...
PUT IT OUT OR I'LL KICK YOUR BUTT!
OH, ISABEL. I COULDN'T FIND HER AND...
HI, QUINA! SHE'S OK. WE WERE JUST PLAYING.
MOM, I DON'T WANNA GO HOME!
WELL, WE GOTTA GO SOMETIME. IT'S GETTING LATE.
BYE.
I WANNA STAY OUT TILL THE STARS GO DOWN!
WHEN YOU'RE A LITTLE OLDER, MIJITA.
BYE.
14
POOR QUINA. WHAT'S SHE GONNA DO WITH ONE MORE KID?
PROBABLY HAVE LOTS MORE AFTER THAT.
PROBABLY, BUT, WHAT'S THE POINT?
WELL, YOU GOT TEN KIDS IN YOUR HOUSE AN' I GOT TWELVE...
YEAH, BUT I DON'T EVEN KNOW THE NAMES OF YOUR FOUR OLDEST BROTHERS AND THEY'RE MY OWN COUSINS!
SO? I DO!
Bill Cook 3
X EL LOUIE LOUIE
AND THEY EACH HAVE LIVES AND WIVES AND KIDS AND THE KIDS ALL HAVE NAMES, TOO!
AN' I KNOW EVERY LITTLE ONE OF 'EM.
IT MAKES ME REALIZE JUST HOW MANY PEOPLE THERE ARE ON EARTH THAT I DON'T KNOW WITH THEIR OWN BRAINS, EVEN IN MY OWN STUPID FAMILY!
???
ISABEL!
OH, SHIT!
15

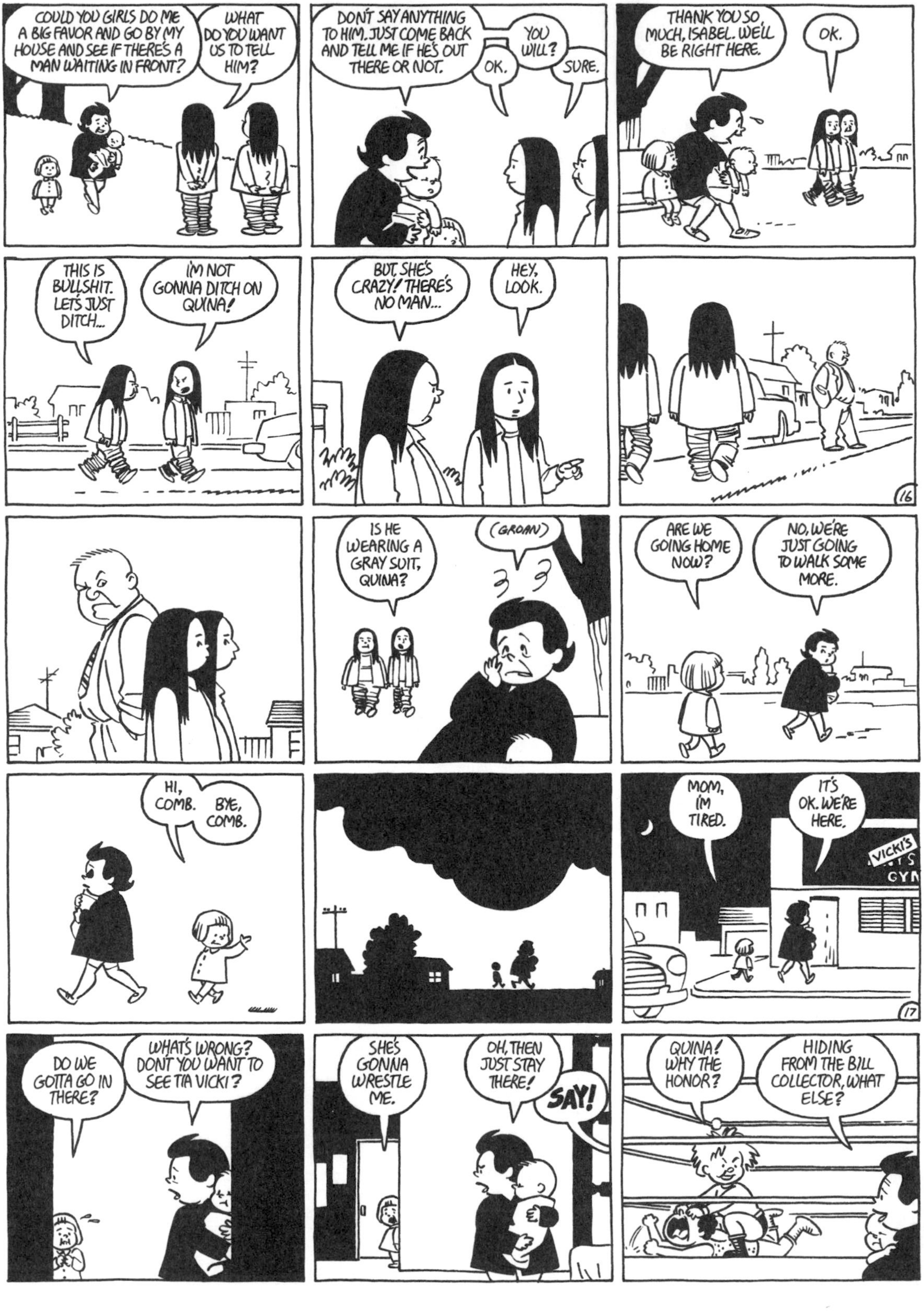

COULD YOU GIRLS DO ME A BIG FAVOR AND GO BY MY HOUSE AND SEE IF THERE'S A MAN WAITING IN FRONT?
WHAT DO YOU WANT US TO TELL HIM?
DON'T SAY ANYTHING TO HIM. JUST COME BACK AND TELL ME IF HE'S OUT THERE OR NOT.
YOU WILL?
OK.
SURE.
THANK YOU SO MUCH, ISABEL. WE'LL BE RIGHT HERE.
OK.
THIS IS BULLSHIT. LET'S JUST DITCH...
I'M NOT GONNA DITCH ON QUINA!
BUT, SHE'S CRAZY! THERE'S NO MAN...
HEY, LOOK.
16
IS HE WEARING A GRAY SUIT, QUINA?
(GROAN)
ARE WE GOING HOME NOW?
NO, WE'RE JUST GOING TO WALK SOME MORE.
HI, COMB.
BYE, COMB.
MOM, I'M TIRED.
IT'S OK. WE'RE HERE.
VICKI'S
GYM
17
DO WE GOTTA GO IN THERE?
WHAT'S WRONG? DON'T YOU WANT TO SEE TIA VICKI?
SHE'S GONNA WRESTLE ME.
OH, THEN JUST STAY THERE!
SAY!
QUINA! WHY THE HONOR?
HIDING FROM THE BILL COLLECTOR, WHAT ELSE?

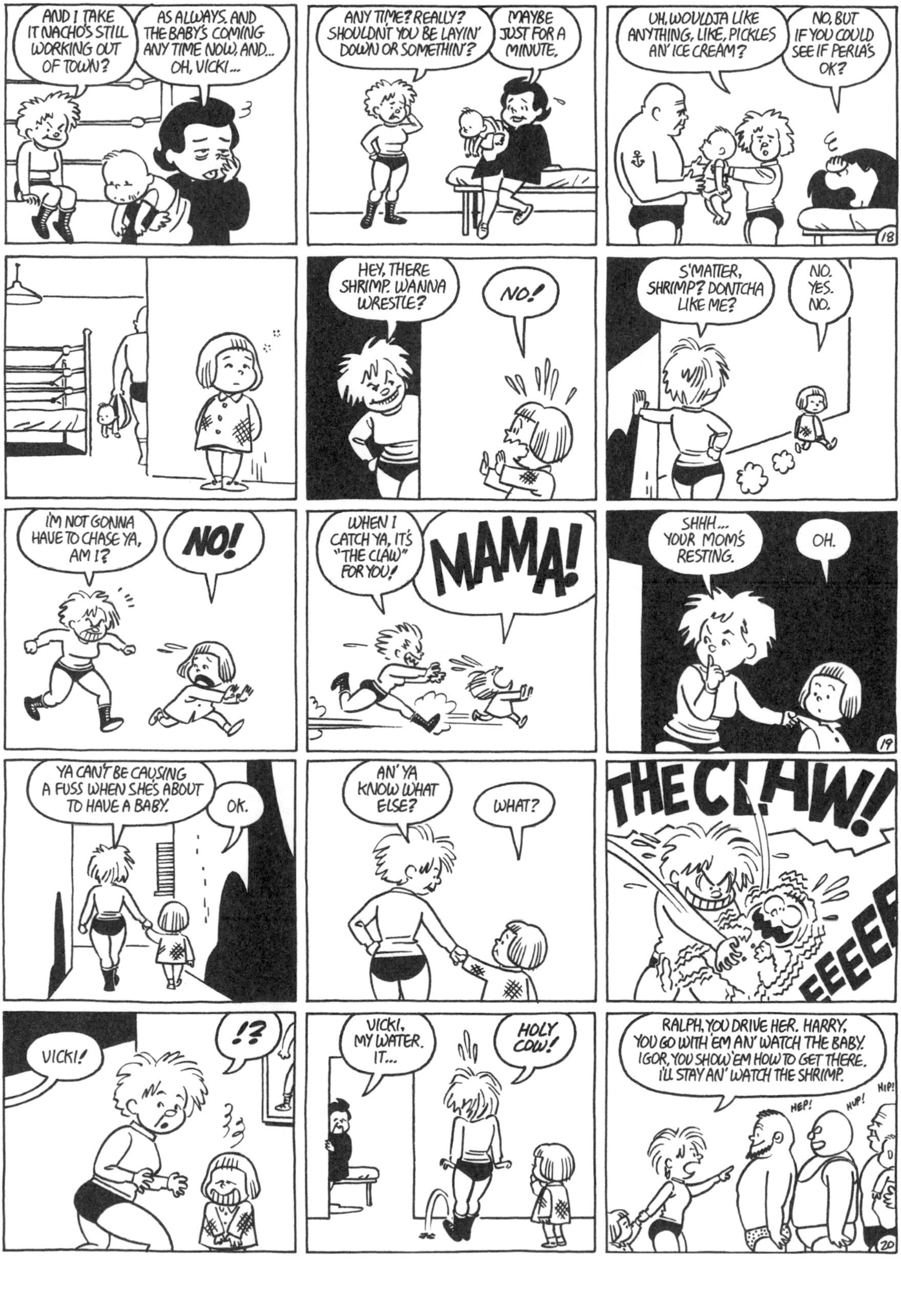
AND I TAKE IT NACHO'S STILL WORKING OUT OF TOWN?
AS ALWAYS. AND THE BABY'S COMING ANY TIME NOW, AND... OH, VICKI...
ANY TIME? REALLY? SHOULDN'T YOU BE LAYIN' DOWN OR SOMETHIN'?
MAYBE JUST FOR A MINUTE.
UH, WOULDJA LIKE ANYTHING, LIKE, PICKLES AN' ICE CREAM?
NO, BUT IF YOU COULD SEE IF PERLA'S OK?
18
HEY, THERE SHRIMP. WANNA WRESTLE?
NO!
S'MATTER, SHRIMP? DONTCHA LIKE ME?
NO. YES. NO.
I'M NOT GONNA HAVE TO CHASE YA, AM I?
NO!
WHEN I CATCH YA, IT'S "THE CLAW" FOR YOU!
MAMA!
SHHH... YOUR MOM'S RESTING.
OH.
19
YA CAN'T BE CAUSING A FUSS WHEN SHE'S ABOUT TO HAVE A BABY.
OK.
AN' YA KNOW WHAT ELSE?
WHAT?
THE CLAW!
EEEEE
VICKI!
!?
VICKI, MY WATER. IT...
HOLY COW!
RALPH, YOU DRIVE HER. HARRY, YOU GO WITH 'EM AN' WATCH THE BABY. IGOR, YOU SHOW 'EM HOW TO GET THERE. I'LL STAY AN' WATCH THE SHRIMP.
HEP!
HUP!
HIP!
20

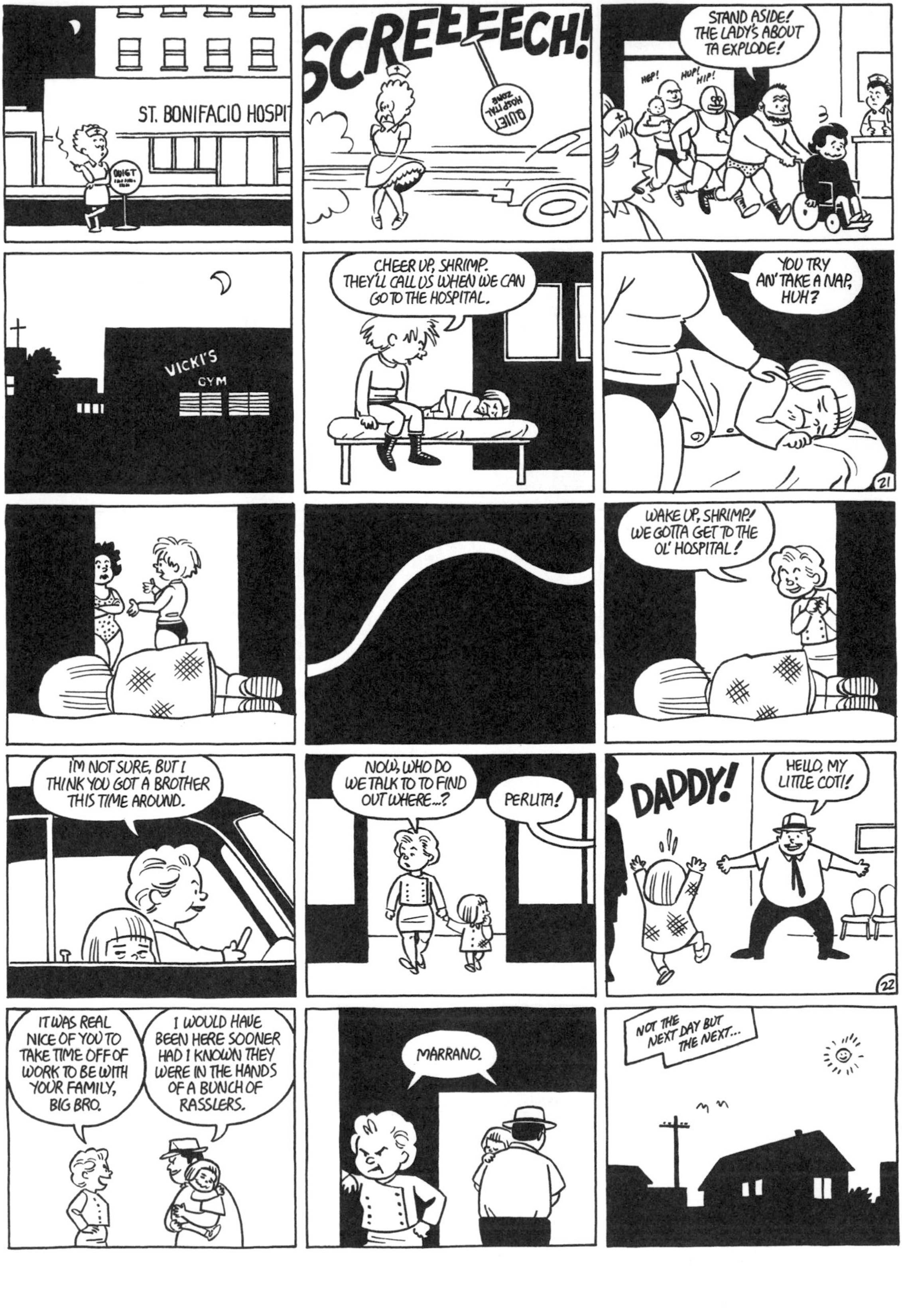

ST. BONIFACIO HOSPIT
SCREEEEECH!
QUIET HOSPITAL ZONE
STAND ASIDE! THE LADY'S ABOUT TA EXPLODE!
HEP!
HUP!
HIP!
VICKI'S GYM
CHEER UP, SHRIMP. THEY'LL CALL US WHEN WE CAN GO TO THE HOSPITAL.
YOU TRY AN' TAKE A NAP, HUH?
21
WAKE UP, SHRIMP! WE GOTTA GET TO THE OL' HOSPITAL!
I'M NOT SURE, BUT I THINK YOU GOT A BROTHER THIS TIME AROUND.
NOW, WHO DO WE TALK TO TO FIND OUT WHERE...?
PERLITA!
DADDY!
HELLO, MY LITTLE COTI!
22
IT WAS REAL NICE OF YOU TO TAKE TIME OFF OF WORK TO BE WITH YOUR FAMILY, BIG BRO.
I WOULD HAVE BEEN HERE SOONER HAD I KNOWN THEY WERE IN THE HANDS OF A BUNCH OF RASSLERS.
MARRANO.
NOT THE NEXT DAY BUT THE NEXT...

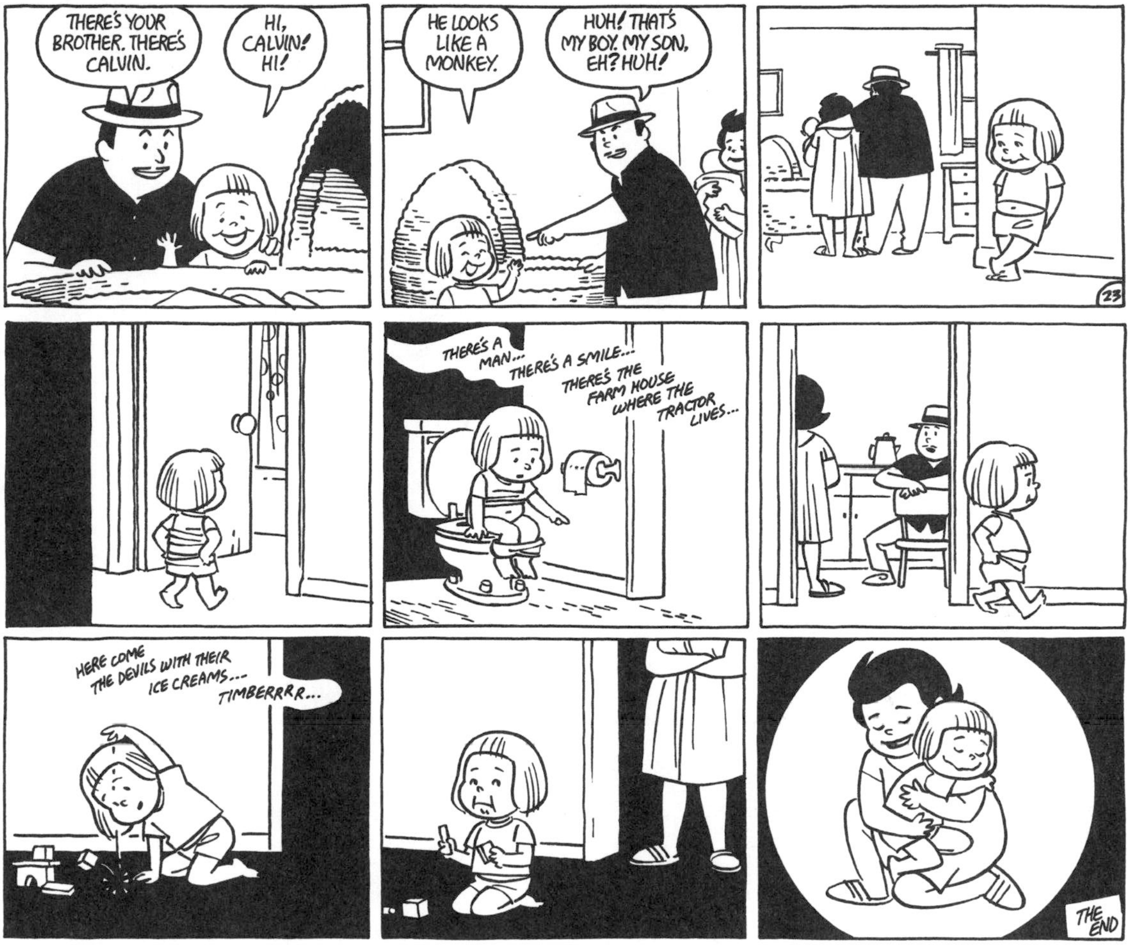

THERE'S YOUR BROTHER. THERE'S CALVIN.
HI, CALVIN! HI!
HE LOOKS LIKE A MONKEY.
HUH! THAT'S MY BOY. MY SON, EH? HUH!
23
THERE'S A MAN... THERE'S A SMILE... THERE'S THE FARM HOUSE WHERE THE TRACTOR LIVES...
HERE COME THE DEVILS WITH THEIR ICE CREAMS... TIMBERRRR...
THE END

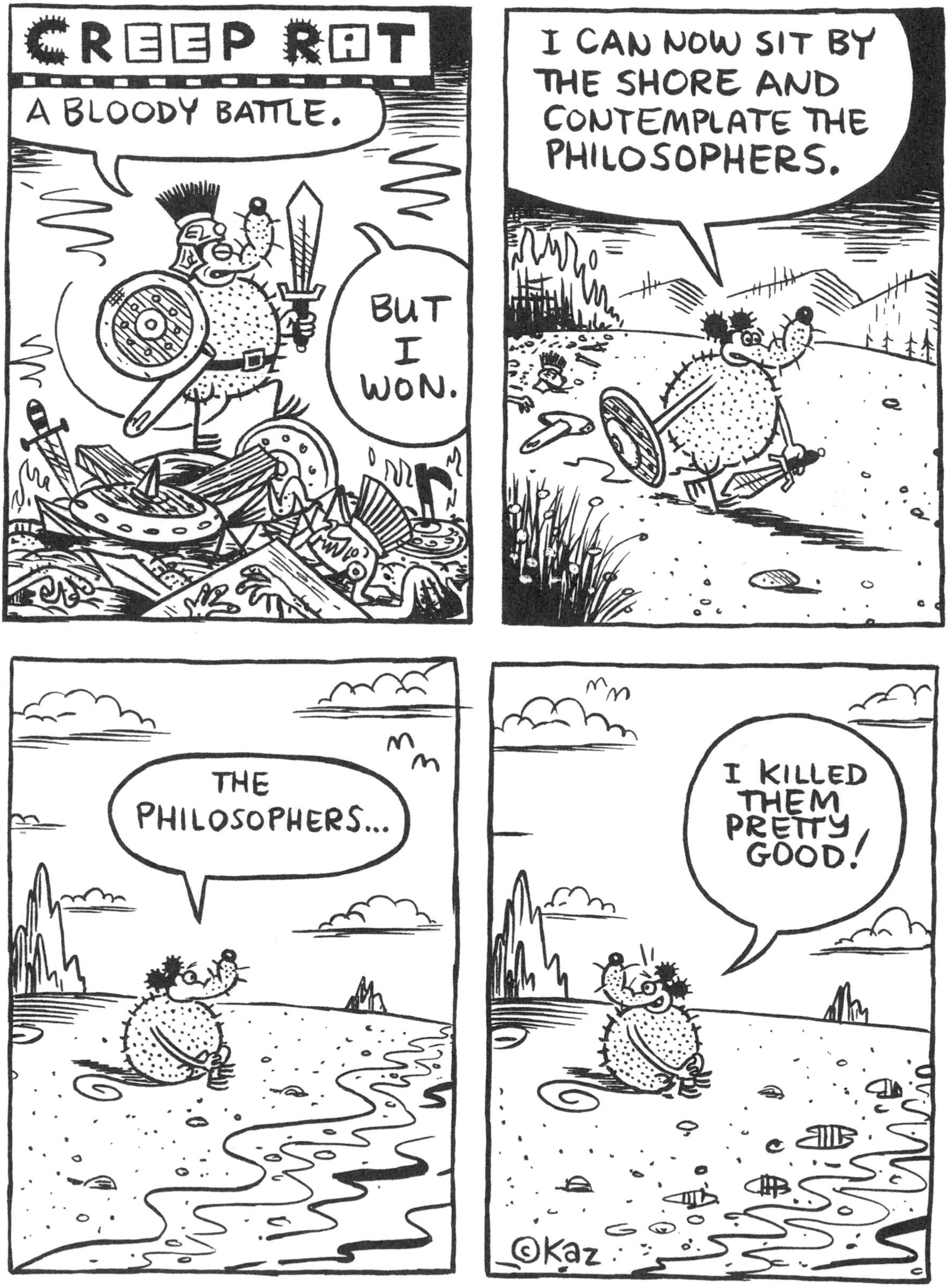
CREEP RAT
A BLOODY BATTLE.
BUT I WON.
I CAN NOW SIT BY THE SHORE AND CONTEMPLATE THE PHILOSOPHERS.
THE PHILOSOPHERS...
I KILLED THEM PRETTY GOOD!
©Kaz

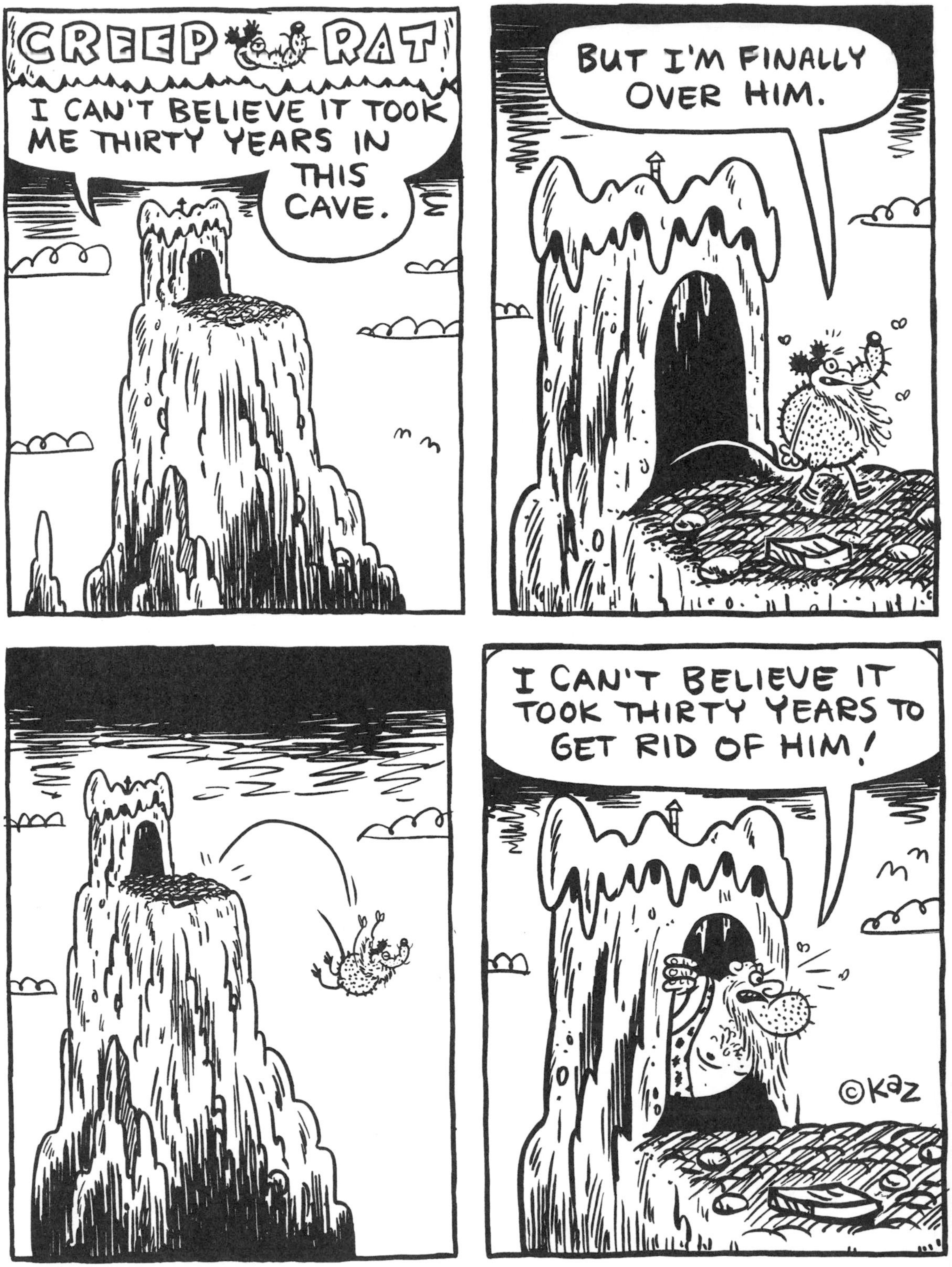
CREEP RAT
I CAN'T BELIEVE IT TOOK ME THIRTY YEARS IN THIS CAVE.
BUT I'M FINALLY OVER HIM.
I CAN'T BELIEVE IT TOOK THIRTY YEARS TO GET RID OF HIM!
©KAZ

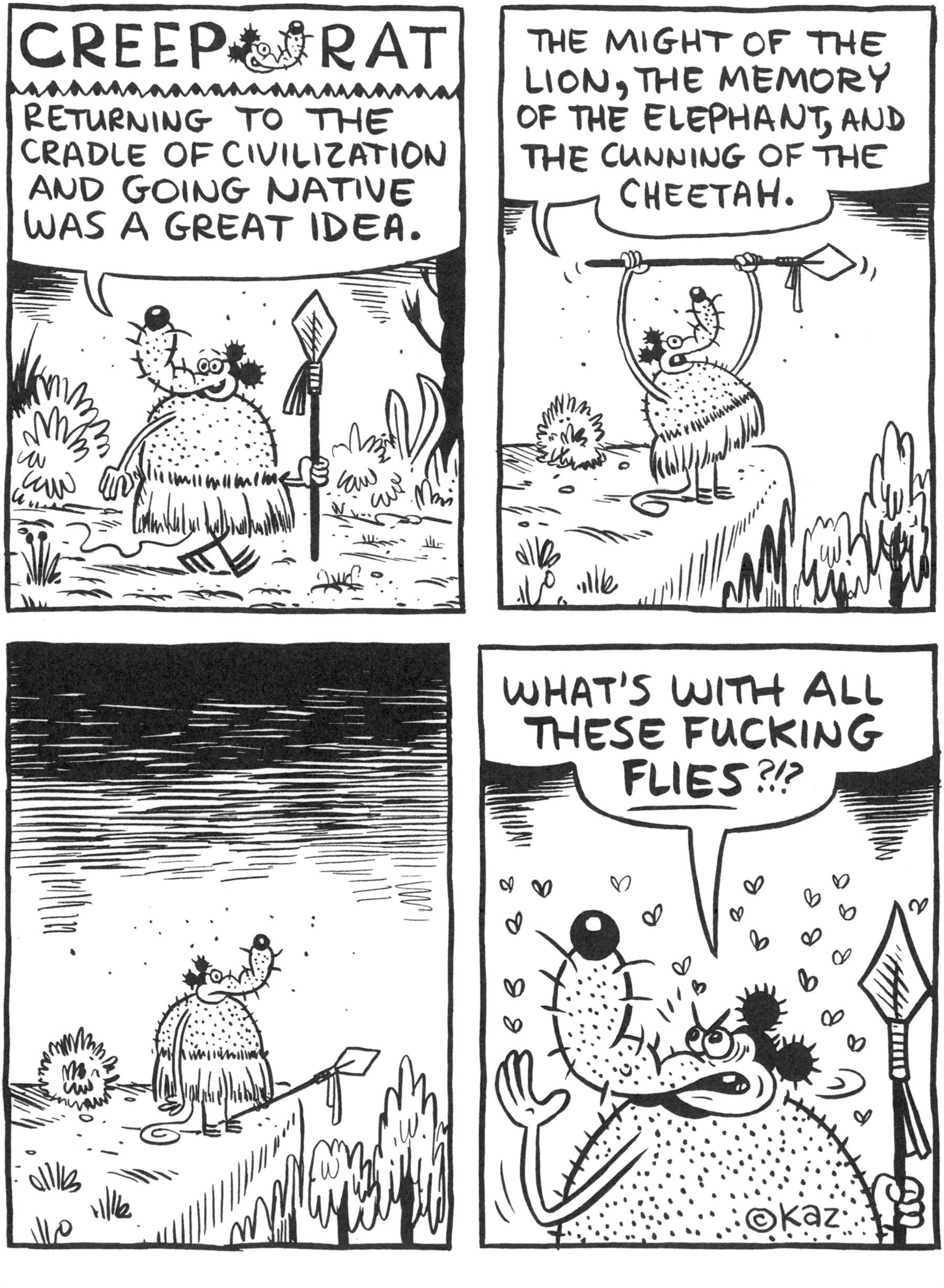
CREEP RAT
RETURNING TO THE CRADLE OF CIVILIZATION AND GOING NATIVE WAS A GREAT IDEA.
THE MIGHT OF THE LION, THE MEMORY OF THE ELEPHANT, AND THE CUNNING OF THE CHEETAH.
WHAT'S WITH ALL THESE FUCKING FLIES?!?
©KAZ

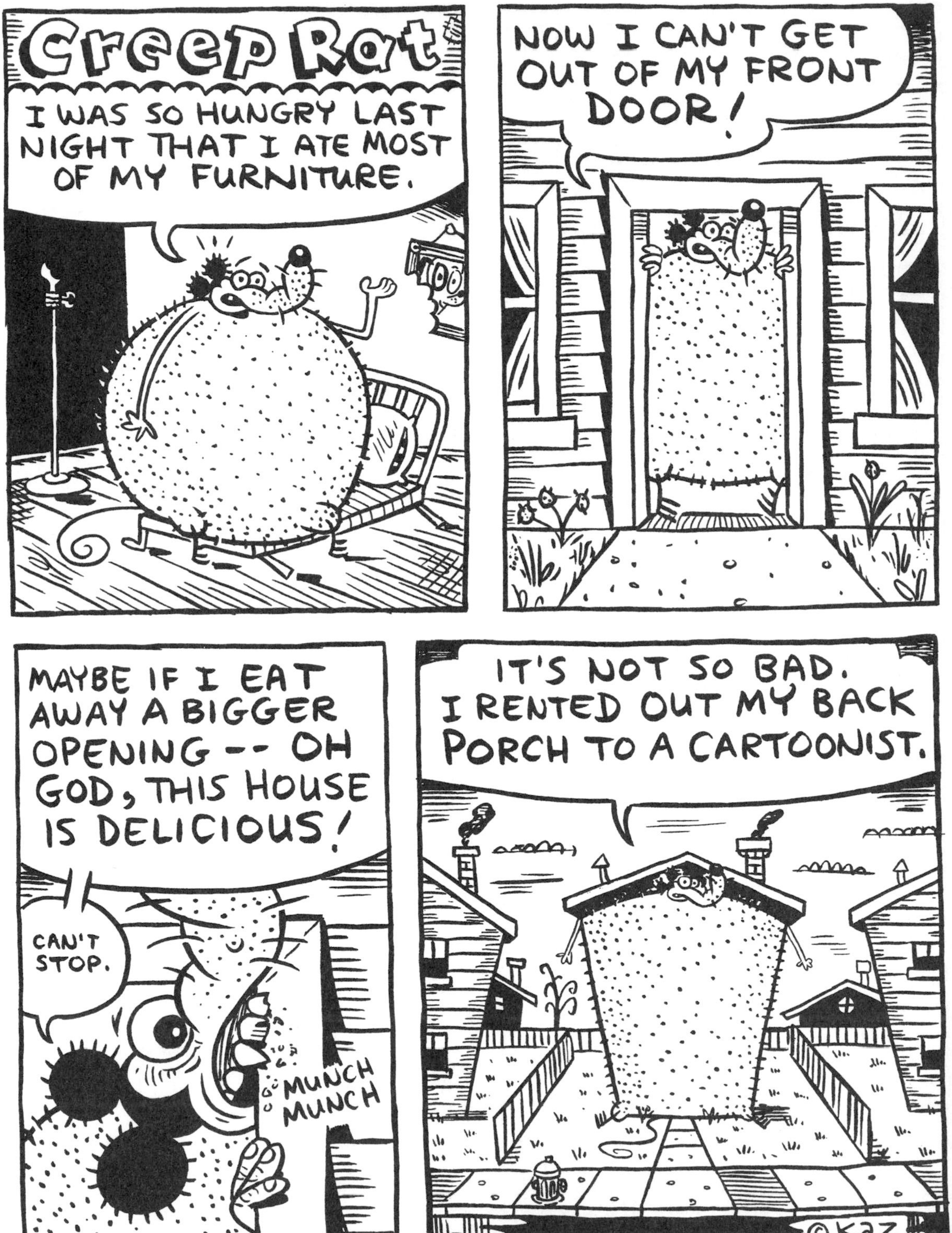
Creep Rat
I WAS SO HUNGRY LAST NIGHT THAT I ATE MOST OF MY FURNITURE.
NOW I CAN'T GET OUT OF MY FRONT DOOR!
MAYBE IF I EAT AWAY A BIGGER OPENING -- OH GOD, THIS HOUSE IS DELICIOUS!
CAN'T STOP.
MUNCH MUNCH
IT'S NOT SO BAD. I RENTED OUT MY BACK PORCH TO A CARTOONIST.
© KAZ

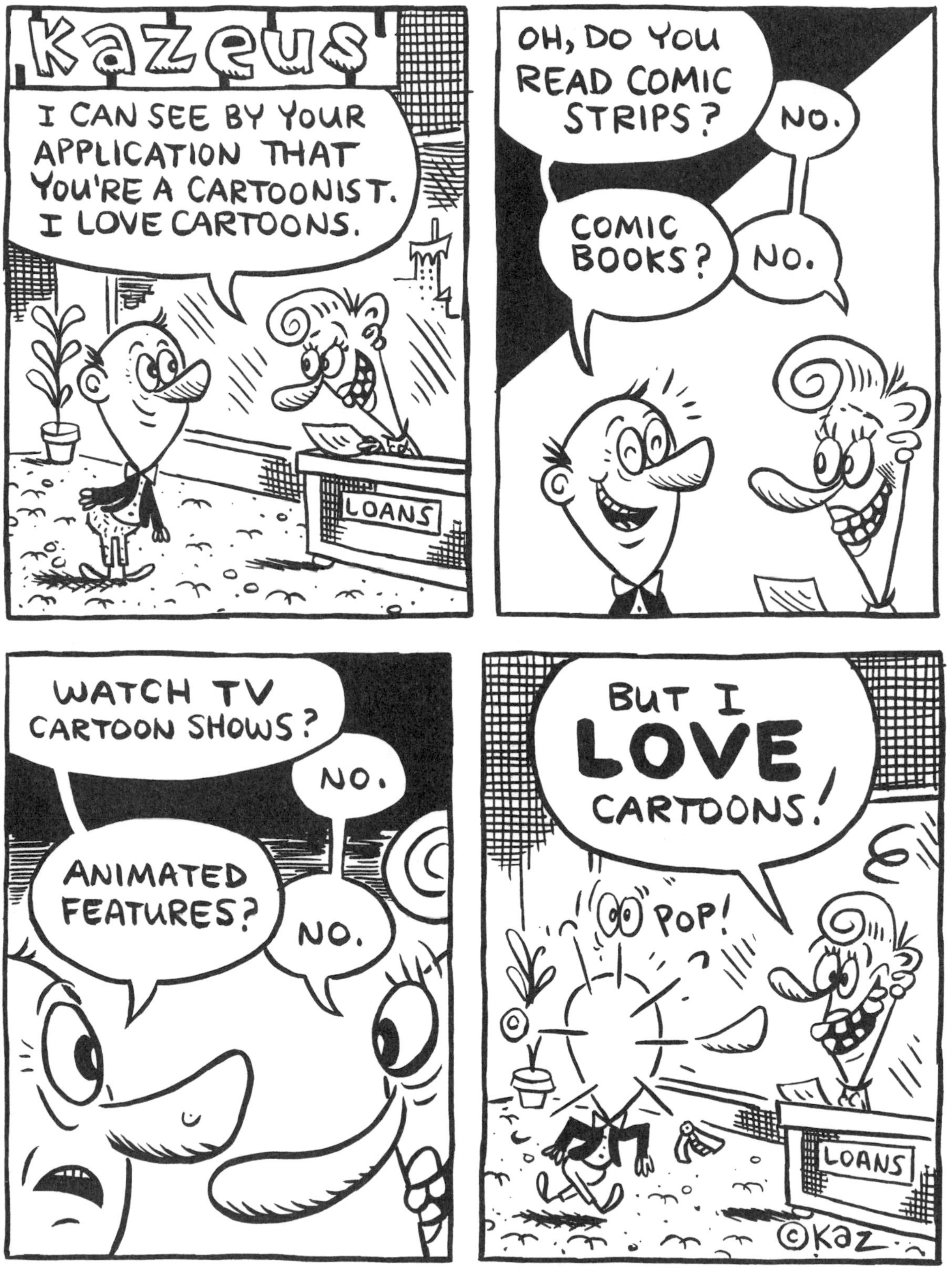
KAZEUS
I CAN SEE BY YOUR APPLICATION THAT YOU'RE A CARTOONIST. I LOVE CARTOONS.
LOANS
OH, DO YOU READ COMIC STRIPS?
NO.
COMIC BOOKS?
NO.
WATCH TV CARTOON SHOWS?
NO.
ANIMATED FEATURES?
NO.
BUT I LOVE CARTOONS!
POP!
LOANS
©KAZ

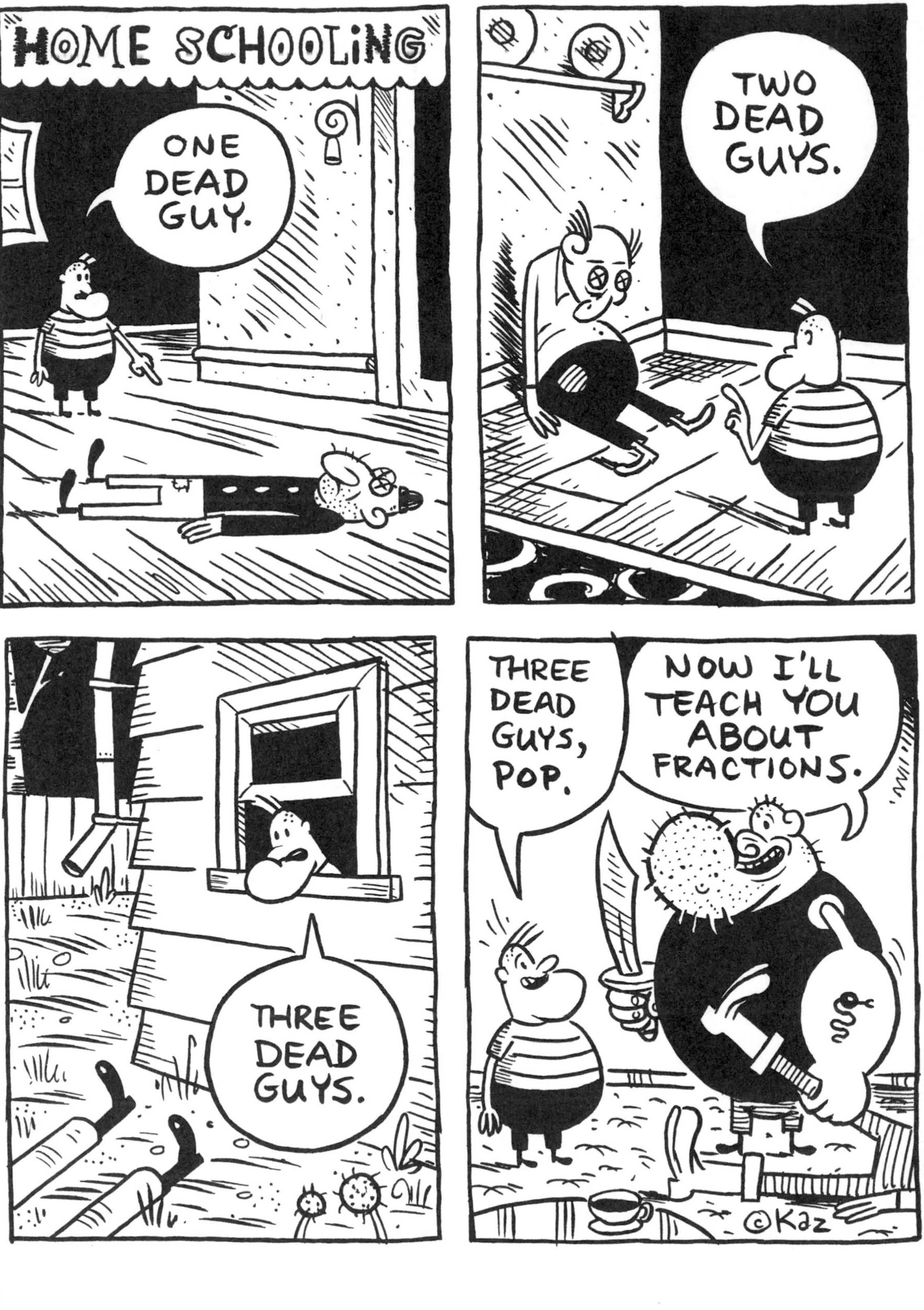
HOME SCHOOLING
ONE DEAD GUY.
TWO DEAD GUYS.
THREE DEAD GUYS.
THREE DEAD GUYS, POP.
NOW I'LL TEACH YOU ABOUT FRACTIONS.
©Kaz

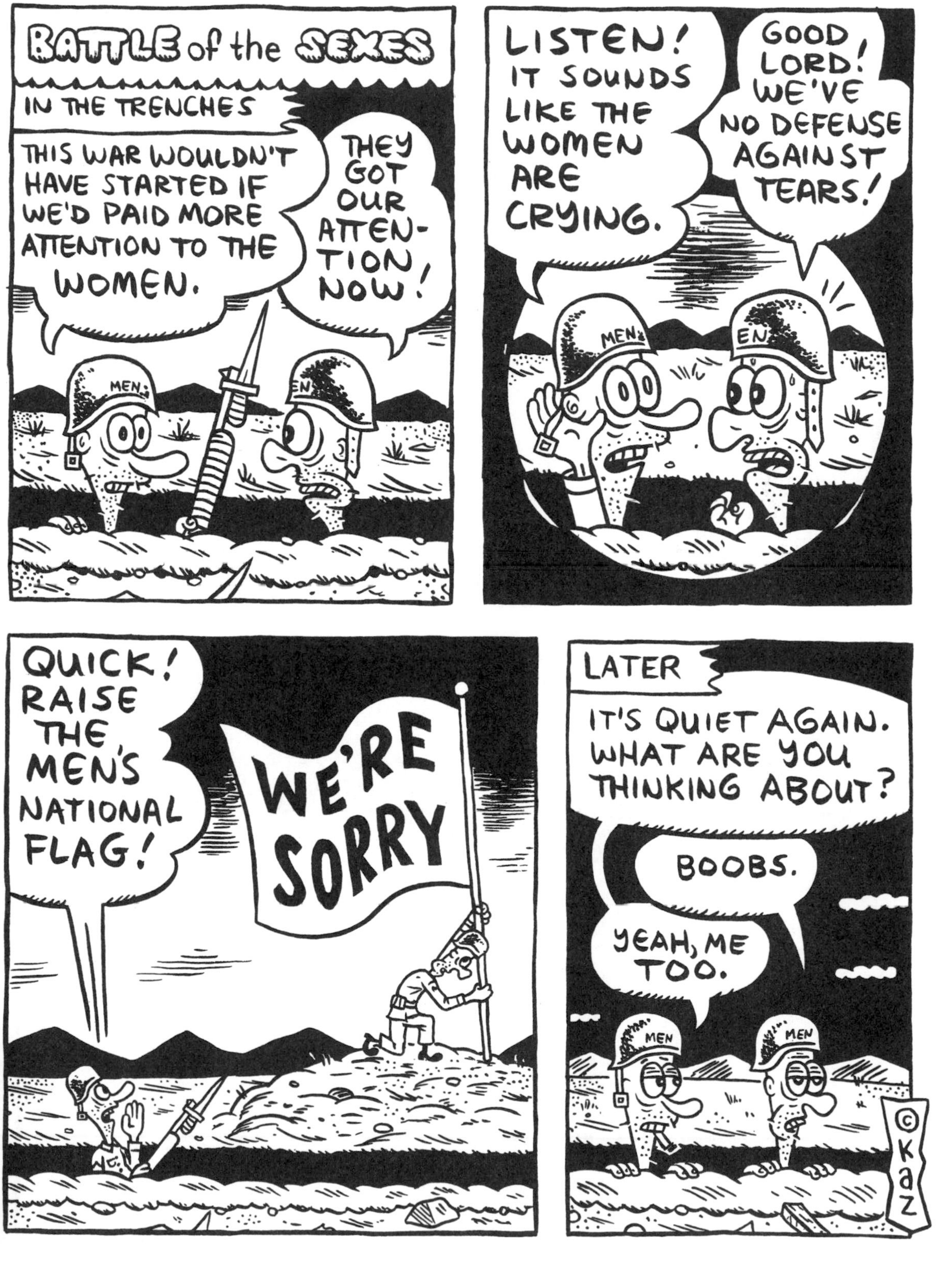
BATTLE of the SEXES
IN THE TRENCHES
THIS WAR WOULDN'T HAVE STARTED IF WE'D PAID MORE ATTENTION TO THE WOMEN.
THEY GOT OUR ATTEN-TION NOW!
MEN
EN
LISTEN! IT SOUNDS LIKE THE WOMEN ARE CRYING.
GOOD LORD! WE'VE NO DEFENSE AGAINST TEARS!
QUICK! RAISE THE MEN'S NATIONAL FLAG!
WE'RE SORRY
LATER
IT'S QUIET AGAIN. WHAT ARE YOU THINKING ABOUT?
BOOBS.
YEAH, ME TOO.
© KAZ

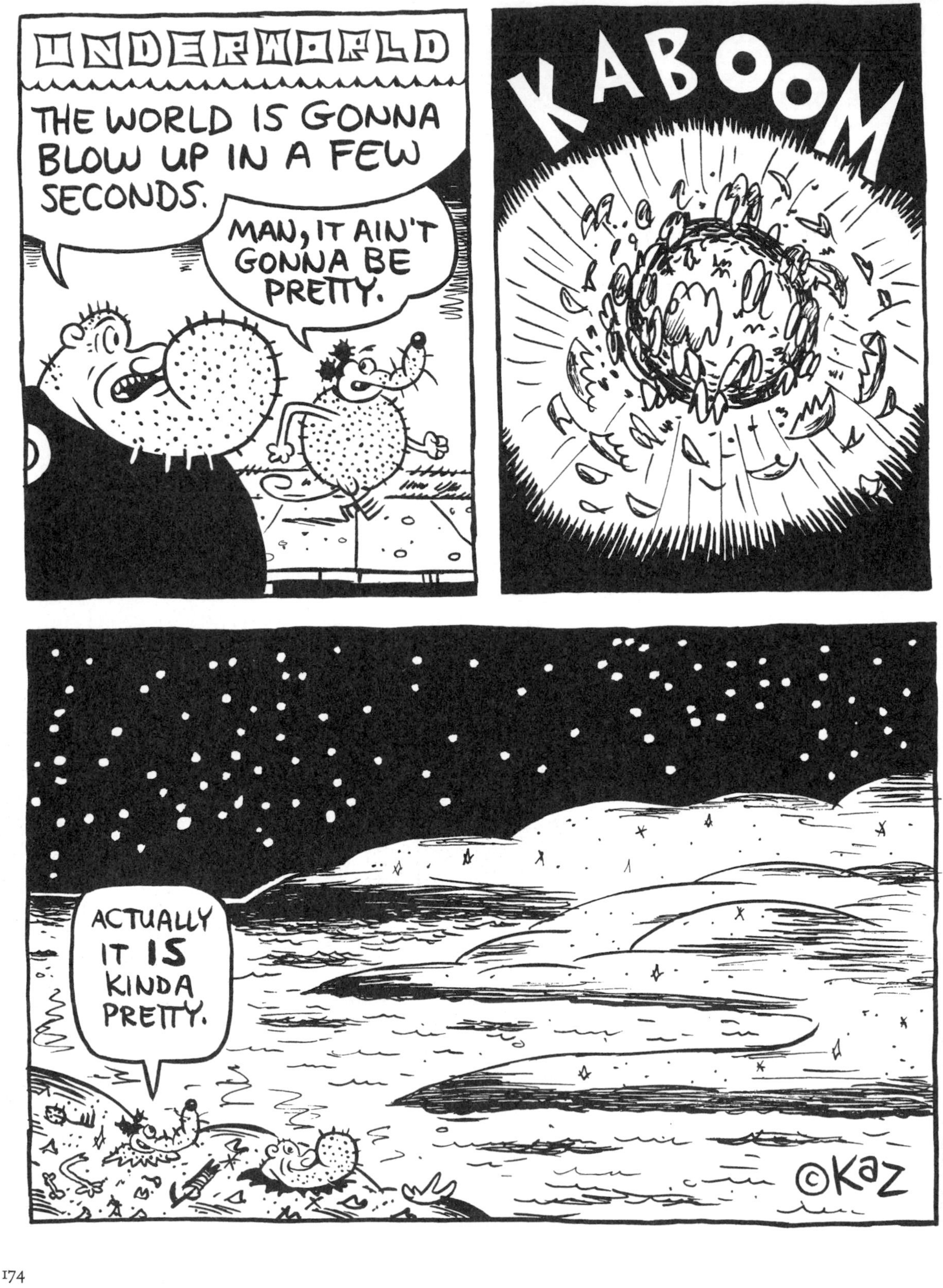
UNDERWORLD
THE WORLD IS GONNA BLOW UP IN A FEW SECONDS.
MAN, IT AIN'T GONNA BE PRETTY.
KABOOM
ACTUALLY IT IS KINDA PRETTY.
©KAZ

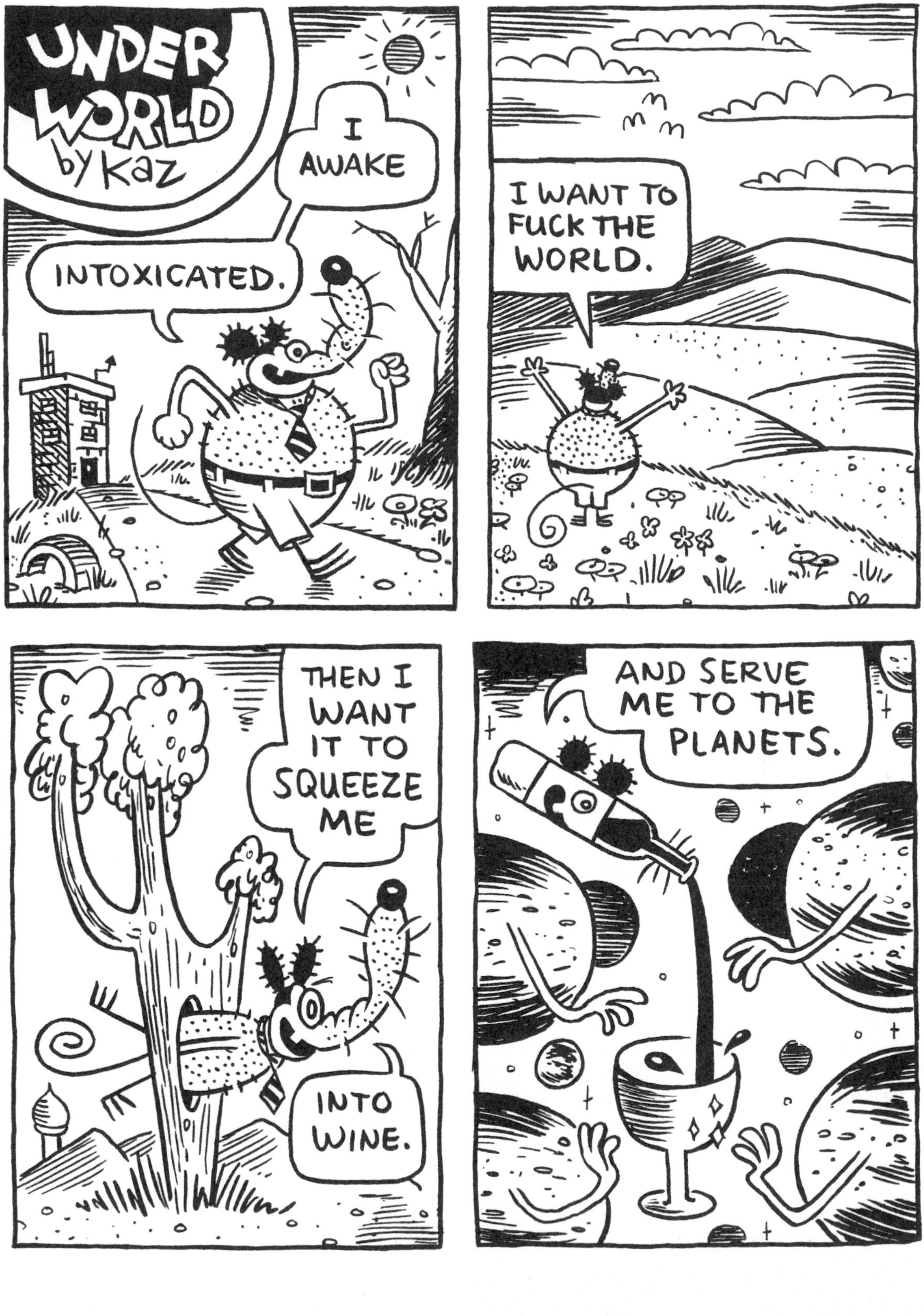
UNDER WORLD
by Kaz
I AWAKE
INTOXICATED.
I WANT TO FUCK THE WORLD.
THEN I WANT IT TO SQUEEZE ME
INTO WINE.
AND SERVE ME TO THE PLANETS.

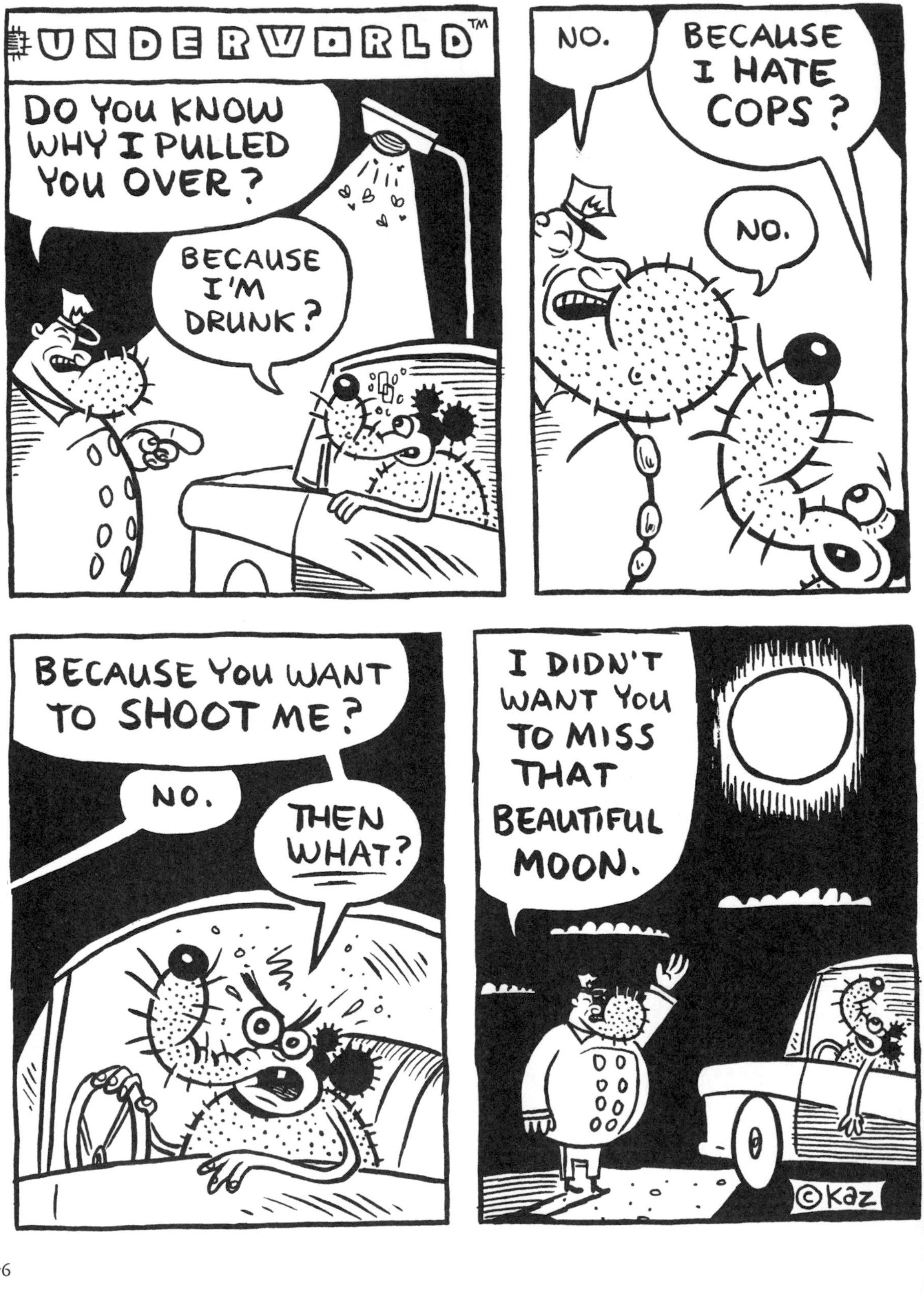
UNDERWORLD™
DO YOU KNOW WHY I PULLED YOU OVER?
BECAUSE I'M DRUNK?
NO.
BECAUSE I HATE COPS?
NO.
BECAUSE YOU WANT TO SHOOT ME?
NO.
THEN WHAT?
I DIDN'T WANT YOU TO MISS THAT BEAUTIFUL MOON.
©KAZ

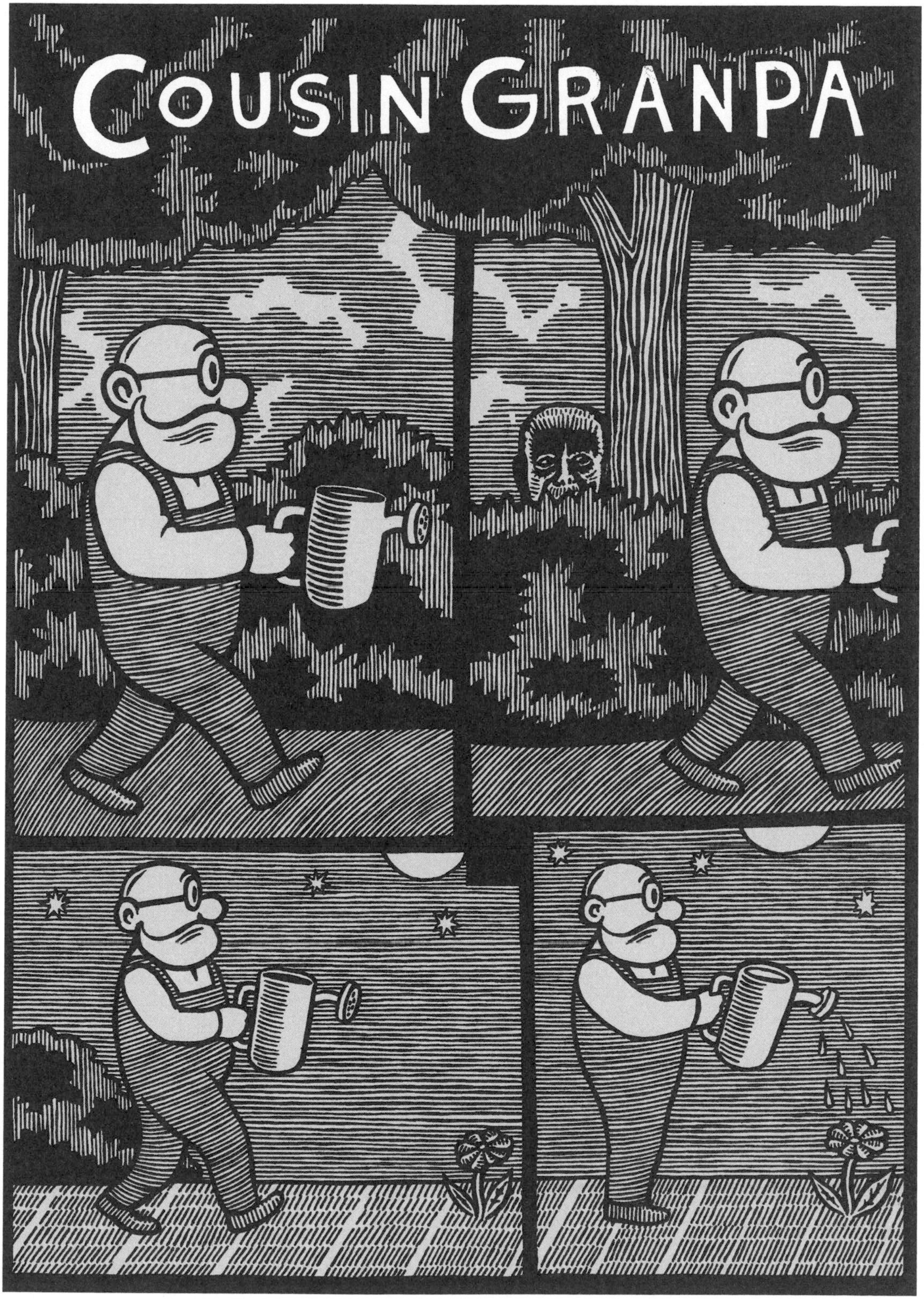
COUSIN GRANPA

MICHAEL KUPPERMAN

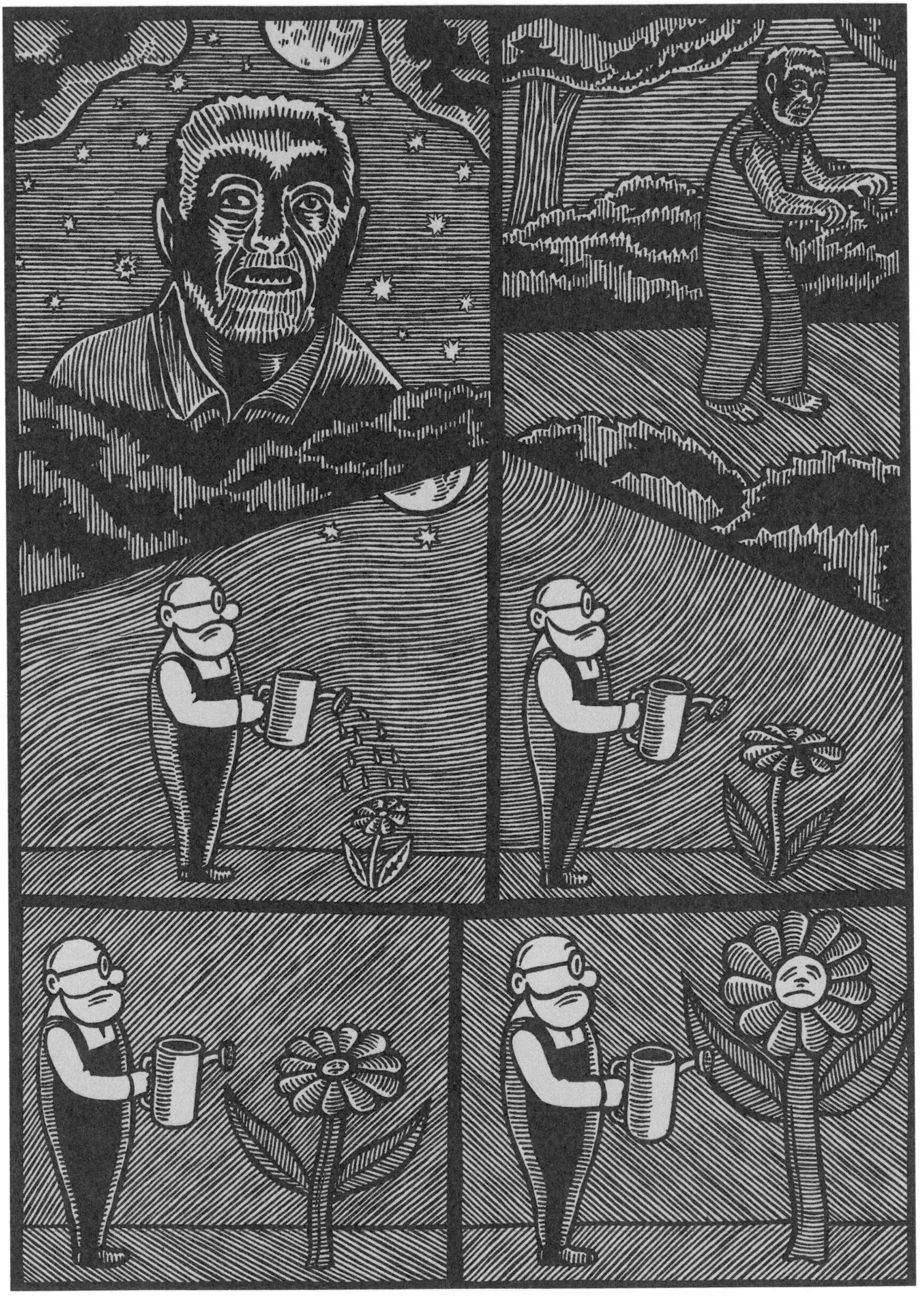

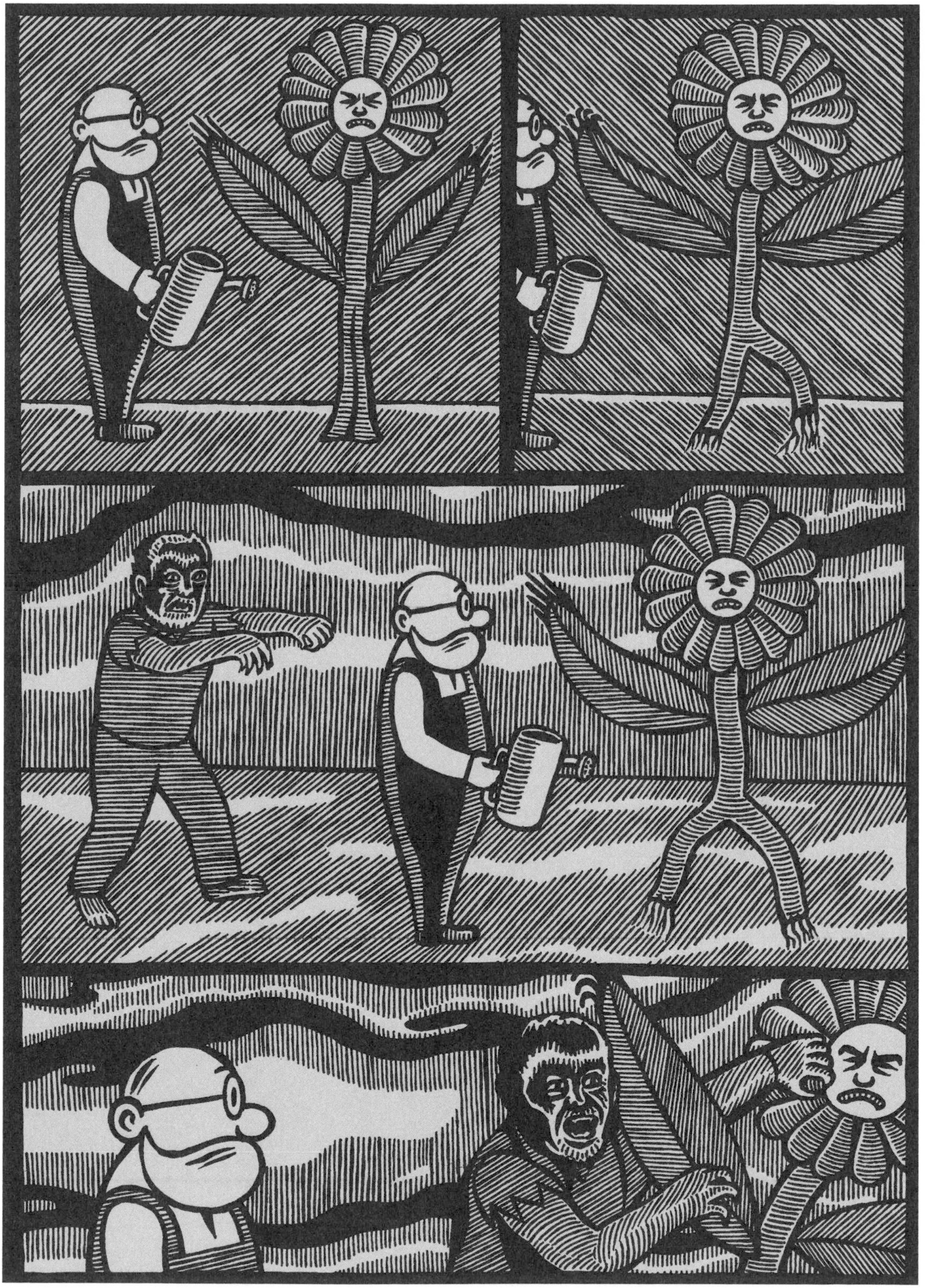

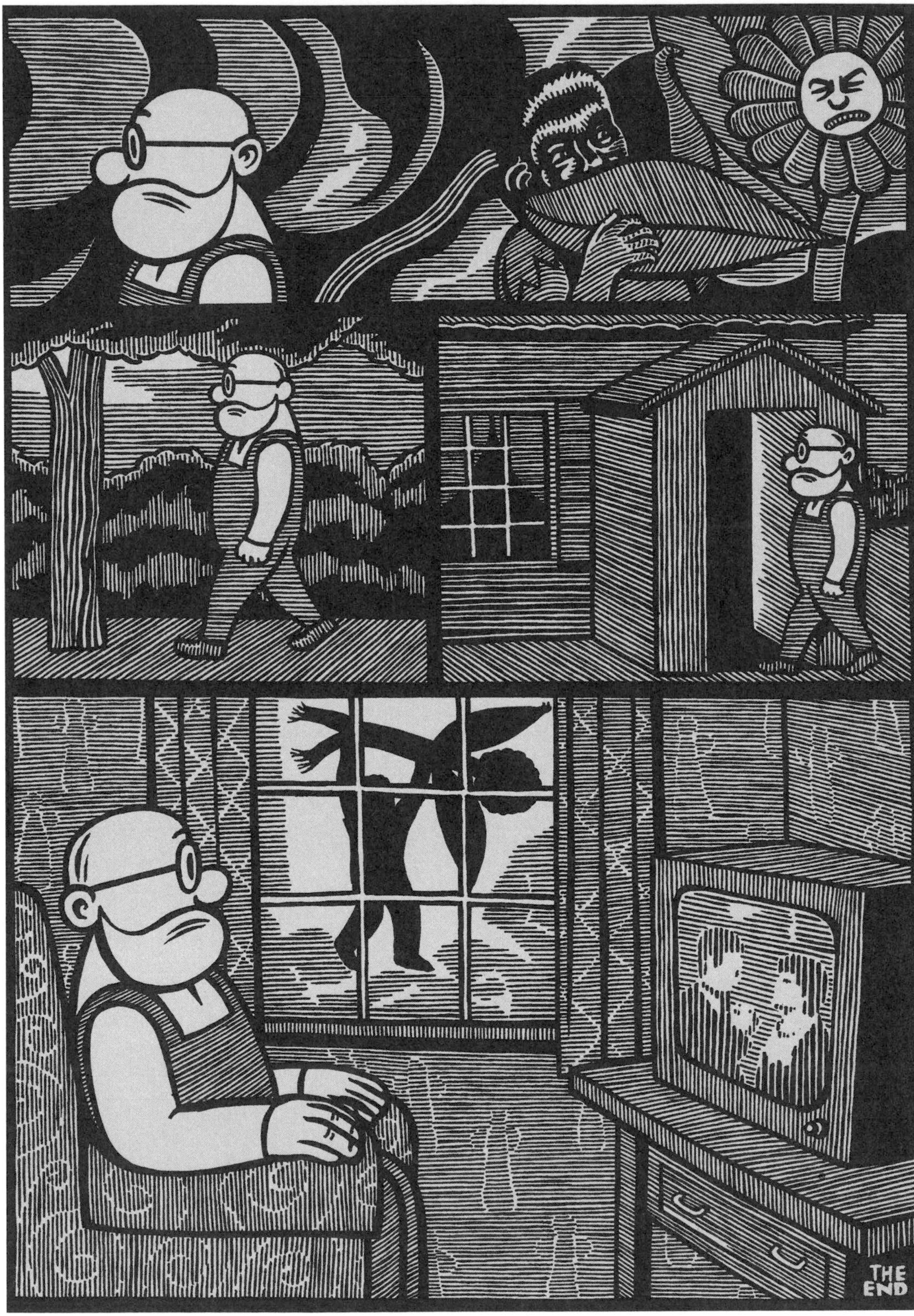
THE END

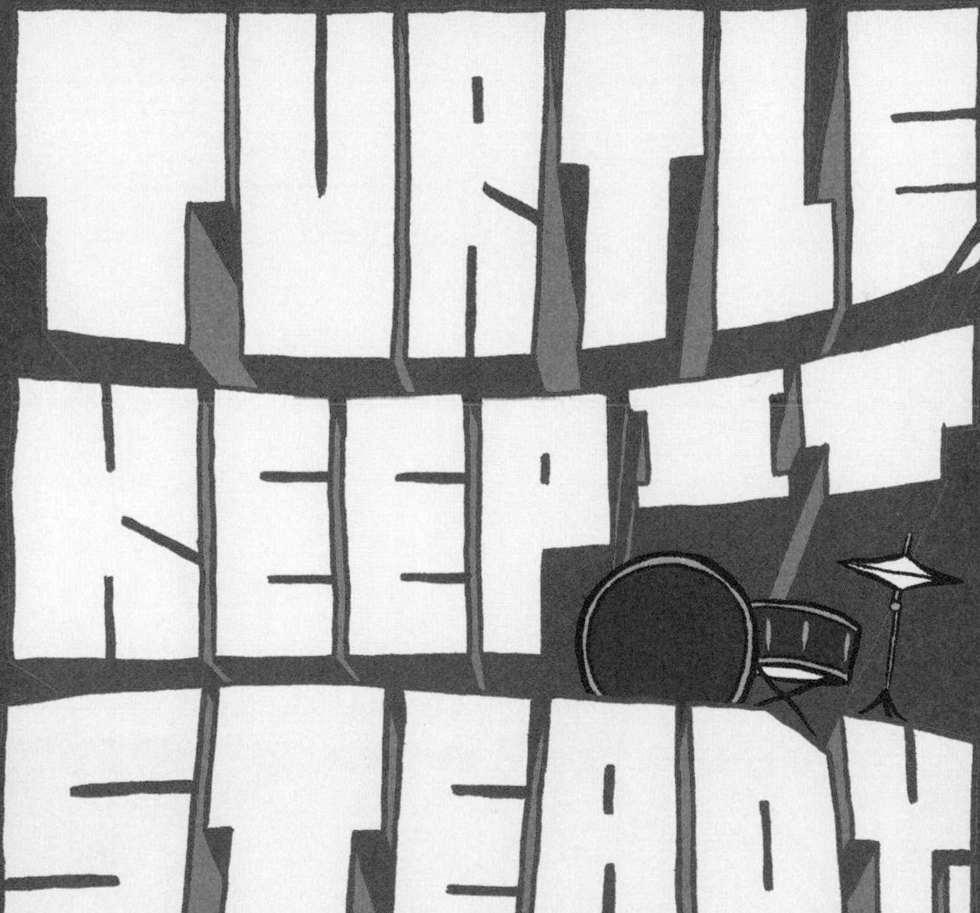
TURTLE
KEEP IT
STEADY!

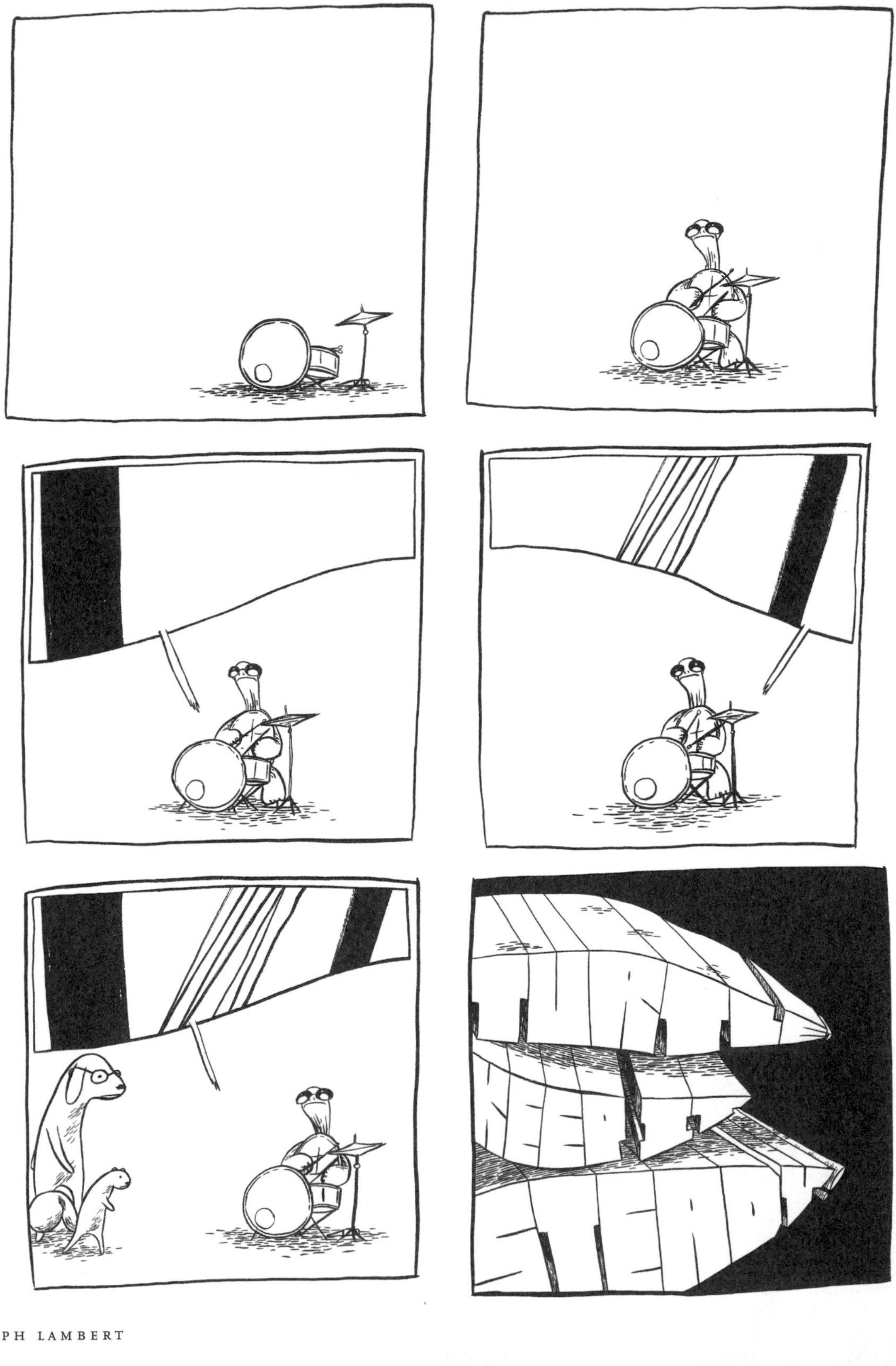

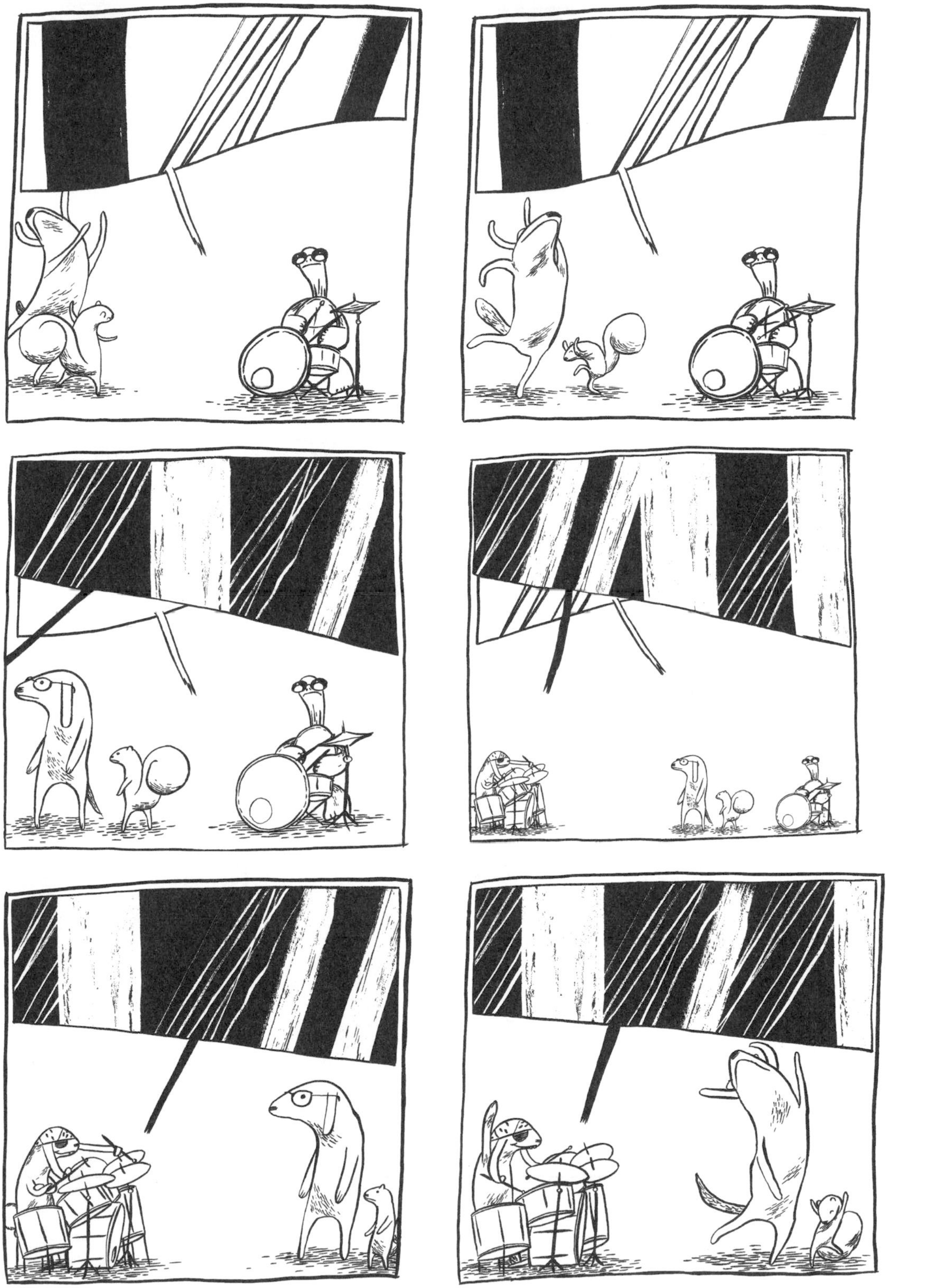

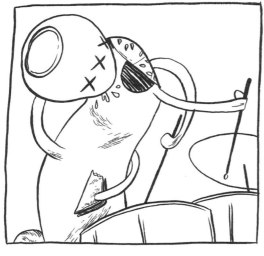

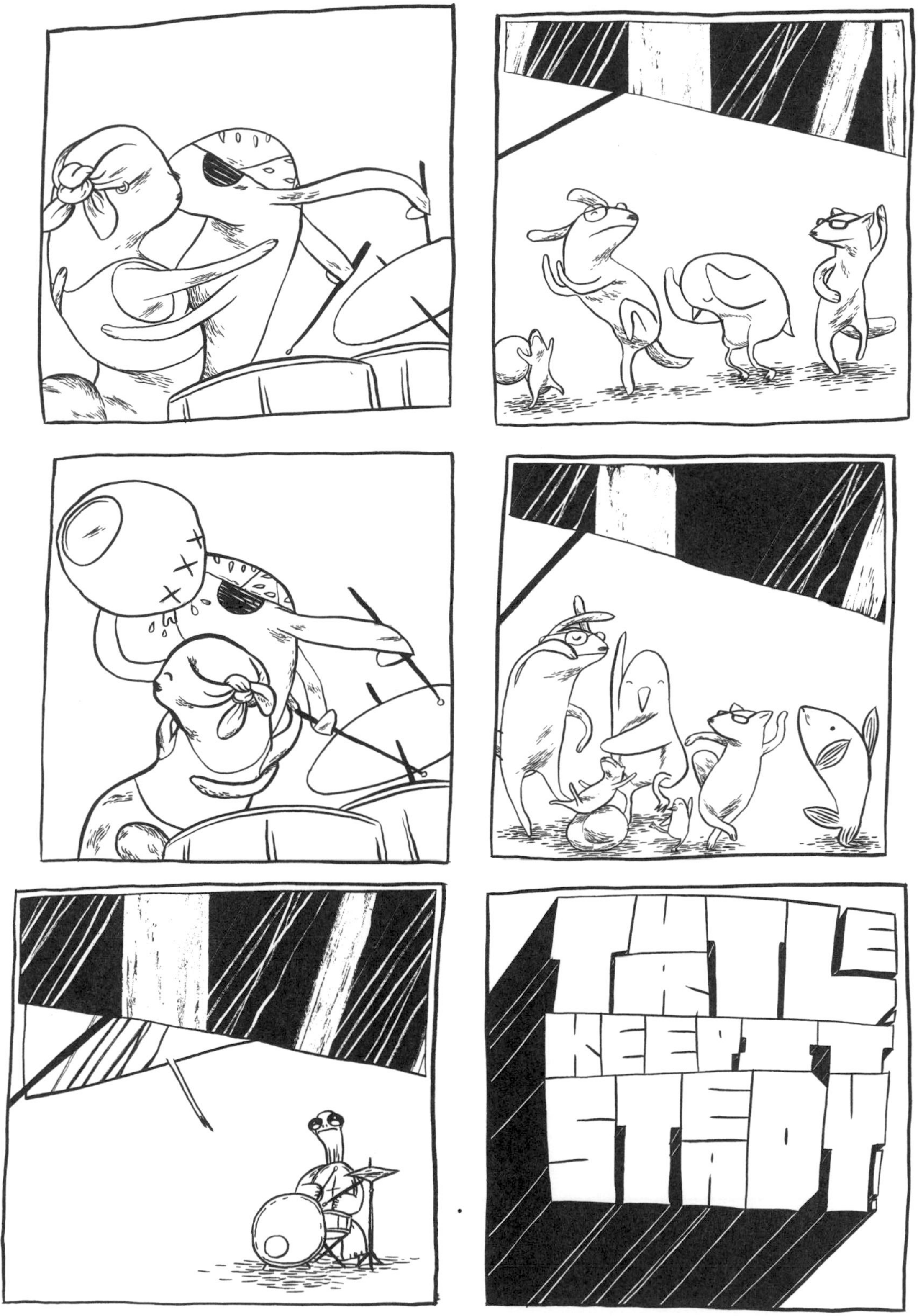
TURTLE
KEEP IT
STEADY!

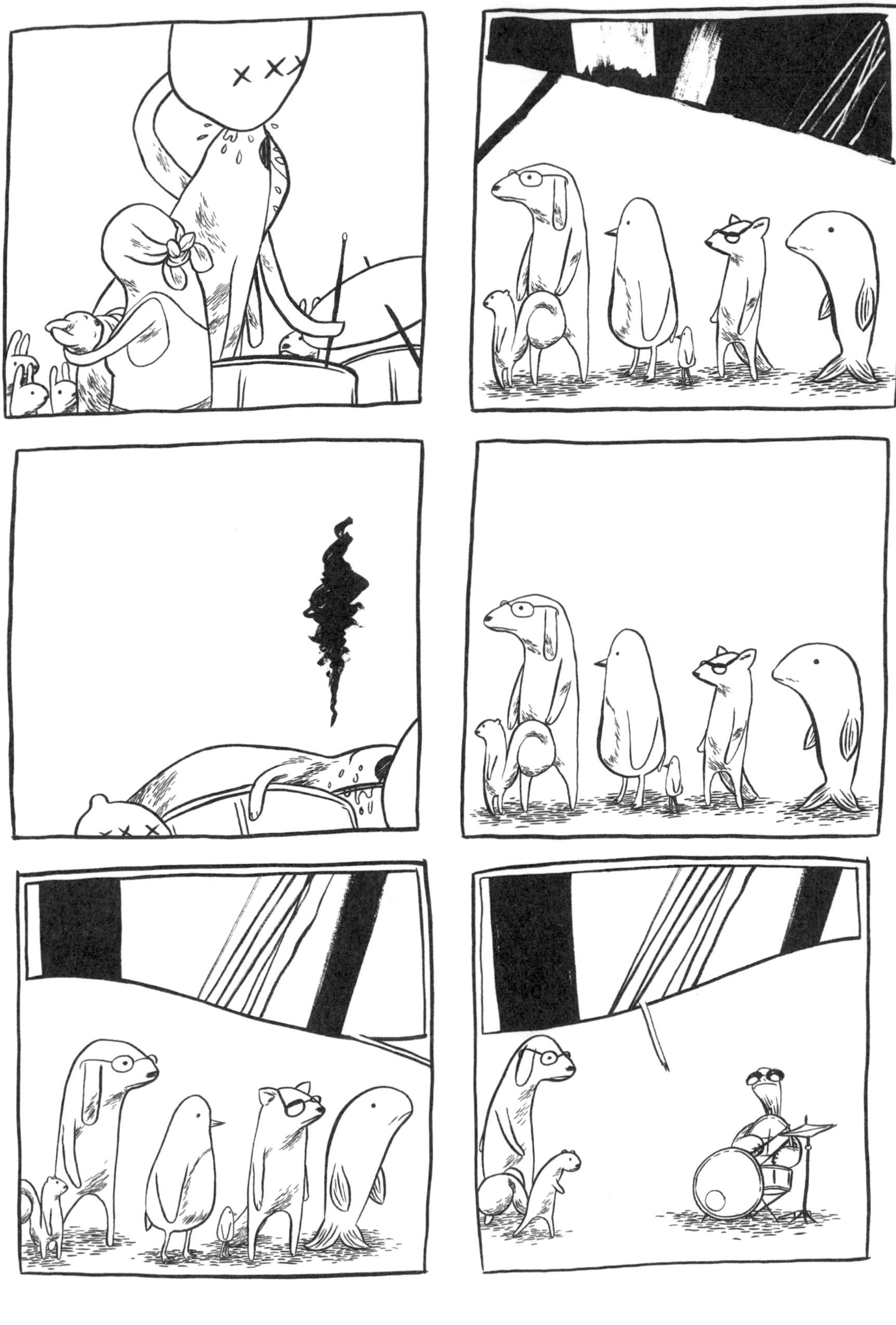

TURTLE
IT
STEADY!

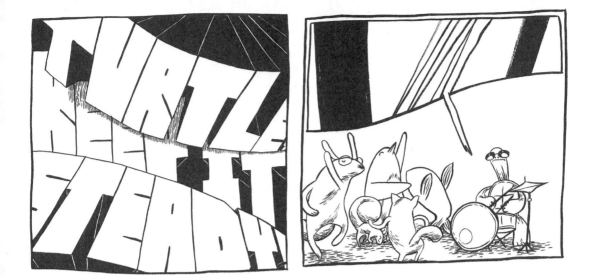

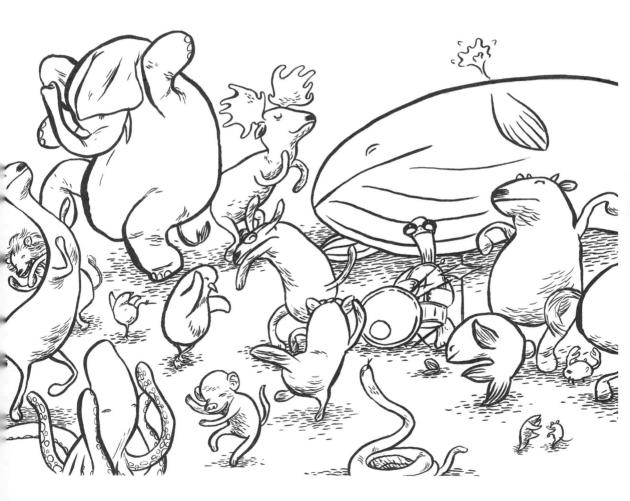

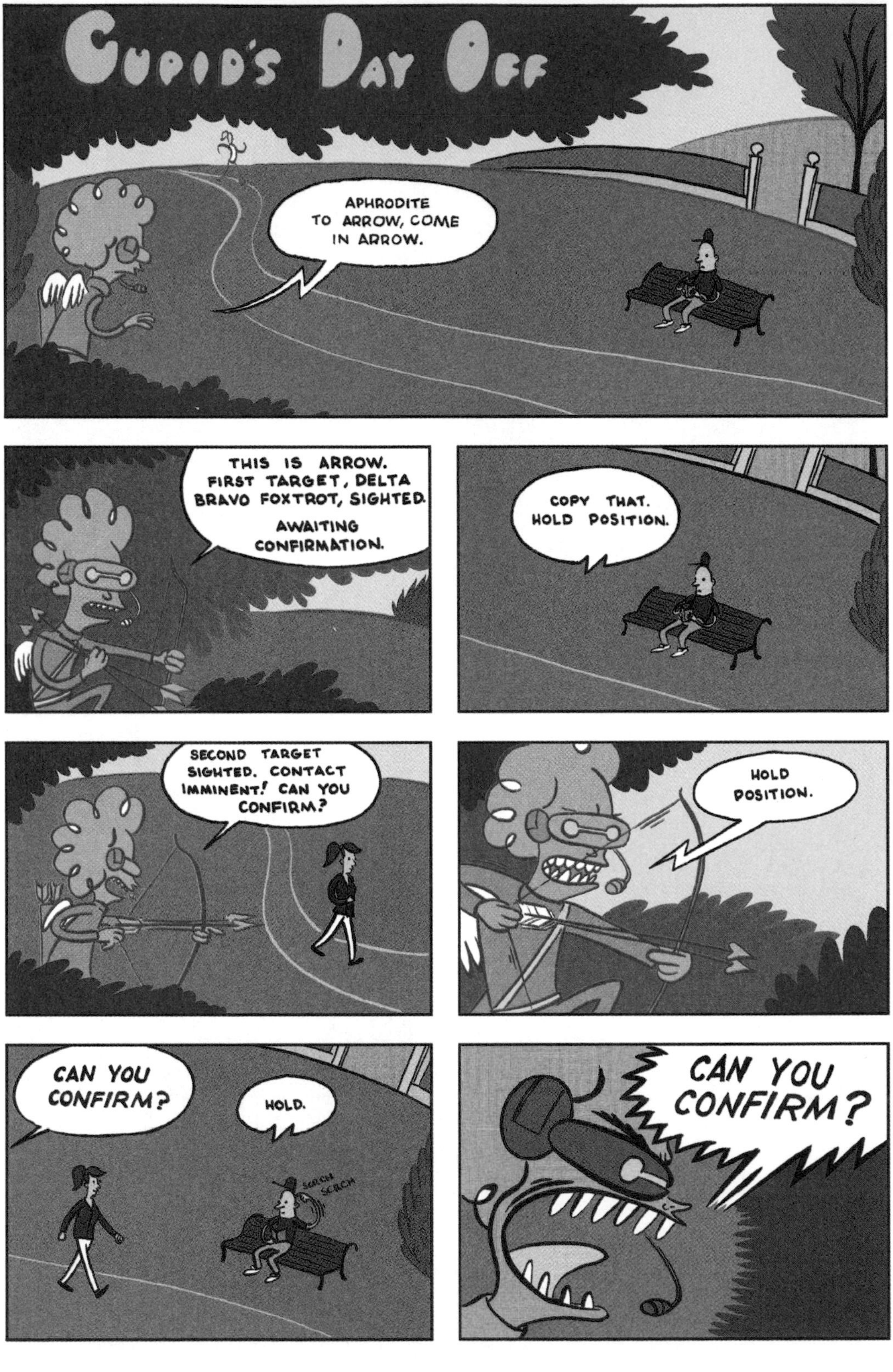
Cupid's Day Off
APHRODITE TO ARROW, COME IN ARROW.
THIS IS ARROW. FIRST TARGET, DELTA BRAVO FOXTROT, SIGHTED.
AWAITING CONFIRMATION.
COPY THAT. HOLD POSITION.
SECOND TARGET SIGHTED. CONTACT IMMINENT! CAN YOU CONFIRM?
HOLD POSITION.
CAN YOU CONFIRM?
HOLD.
CAN YOU CONFIRM?

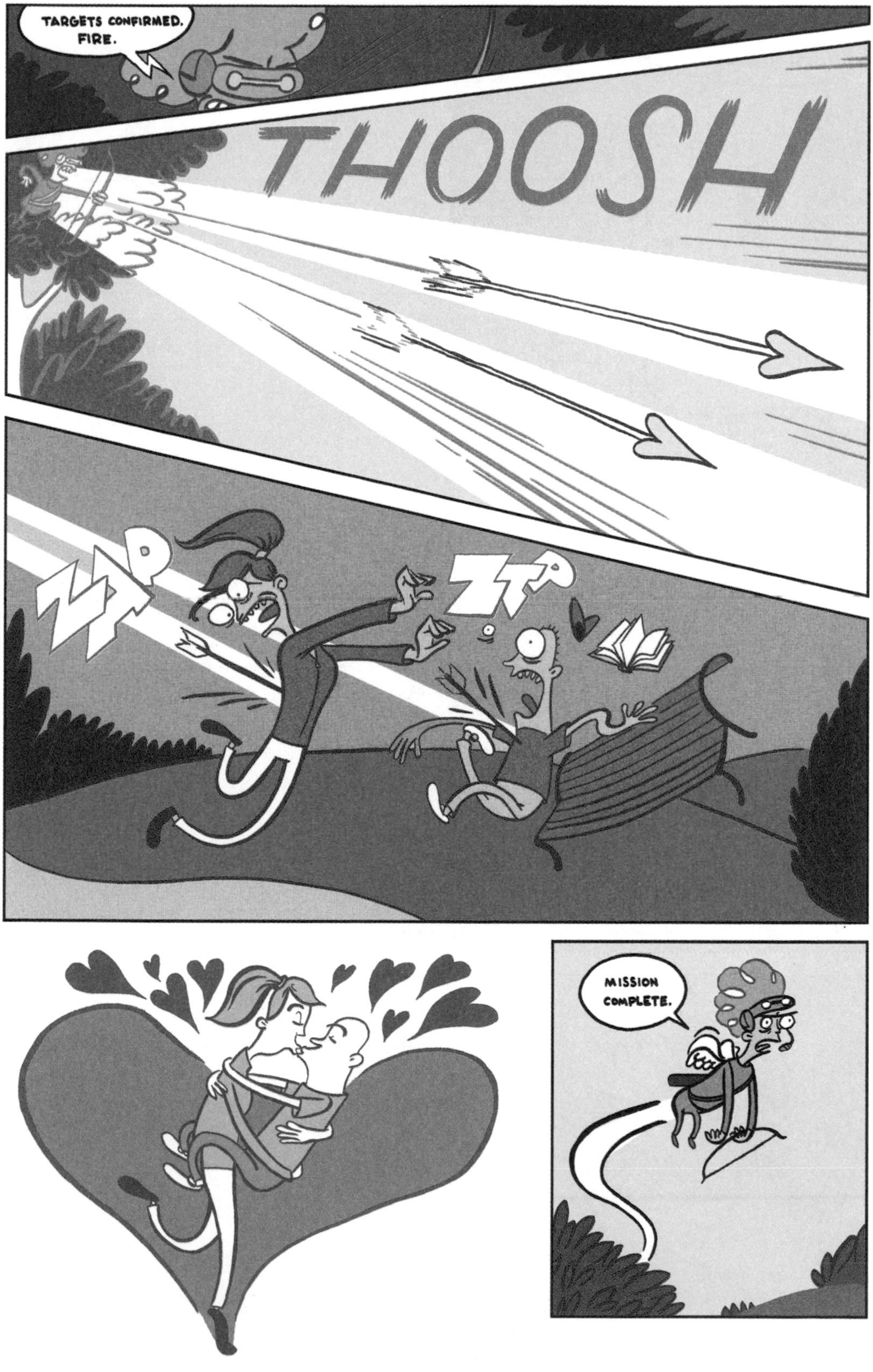
TARGETS CONFIRMED. FIRE.
THOOSH
ZAP
ZIP
MISSION COMPLETE.

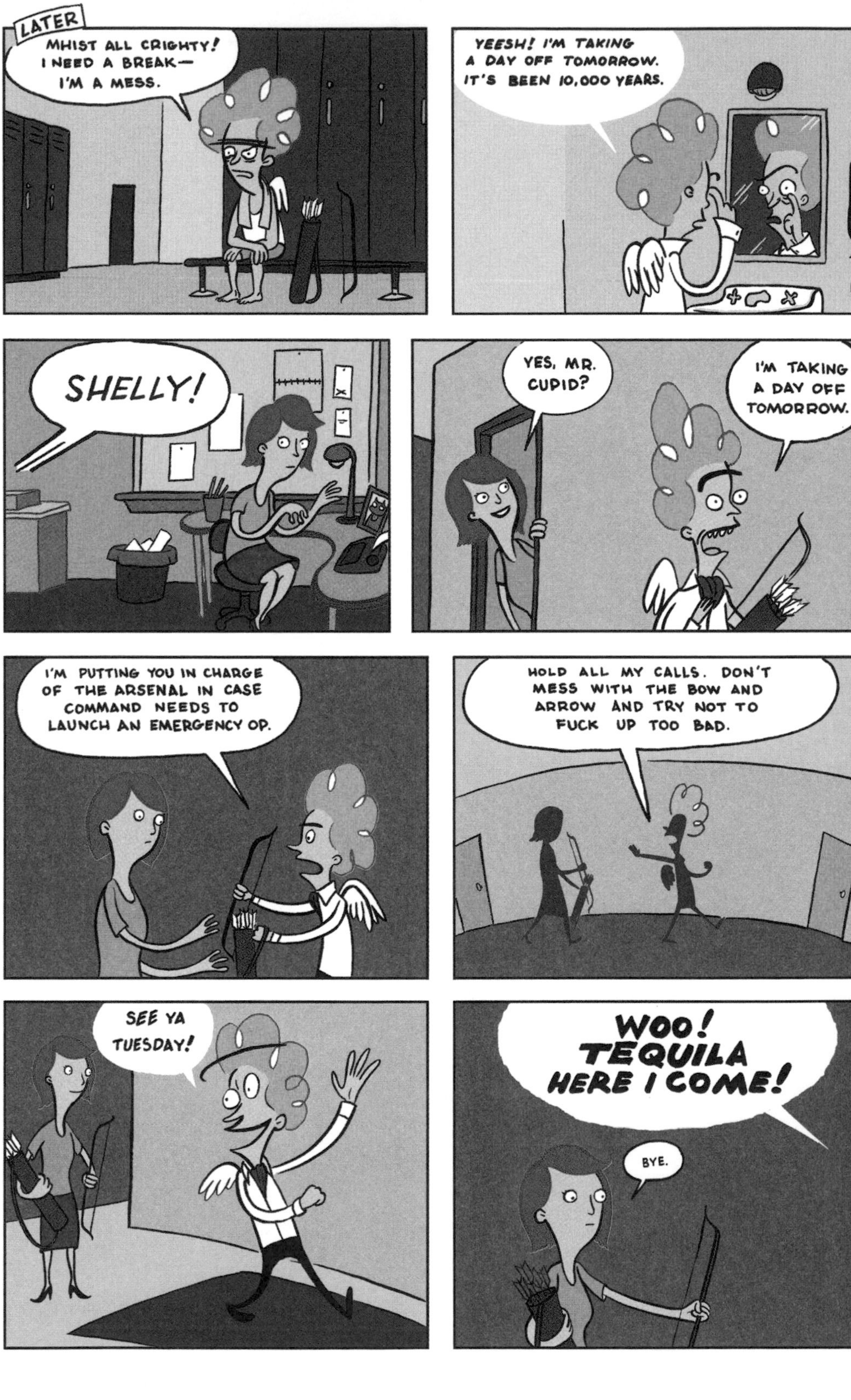
LATER
MHIST ALL CRIGHTY! I NEED A BREAK— I'M A MESS.
YEESH! I'M TAKING A DAY OFF TOMORROW. IT'S BEEN 10,000 YEARS.
SHELLY!
YES, MR. CUPID?
I'M TAKING A DAY OFF TOMORROW.
I'M PUTTING YOU IN CHARGE OF THE ARSENAL IN CASE COMMAND NEEDS TO LAUNCH AN EMERGENCY OP.
HOLD ALL MY CALLS. DON'T MESS WITH THE BOW AND ARROW AND TRY NOT TO FUCK UP TOO BAD.
SEE YA TUESDAY!
WOO! TEQUILA HERE I COME!
BYE.

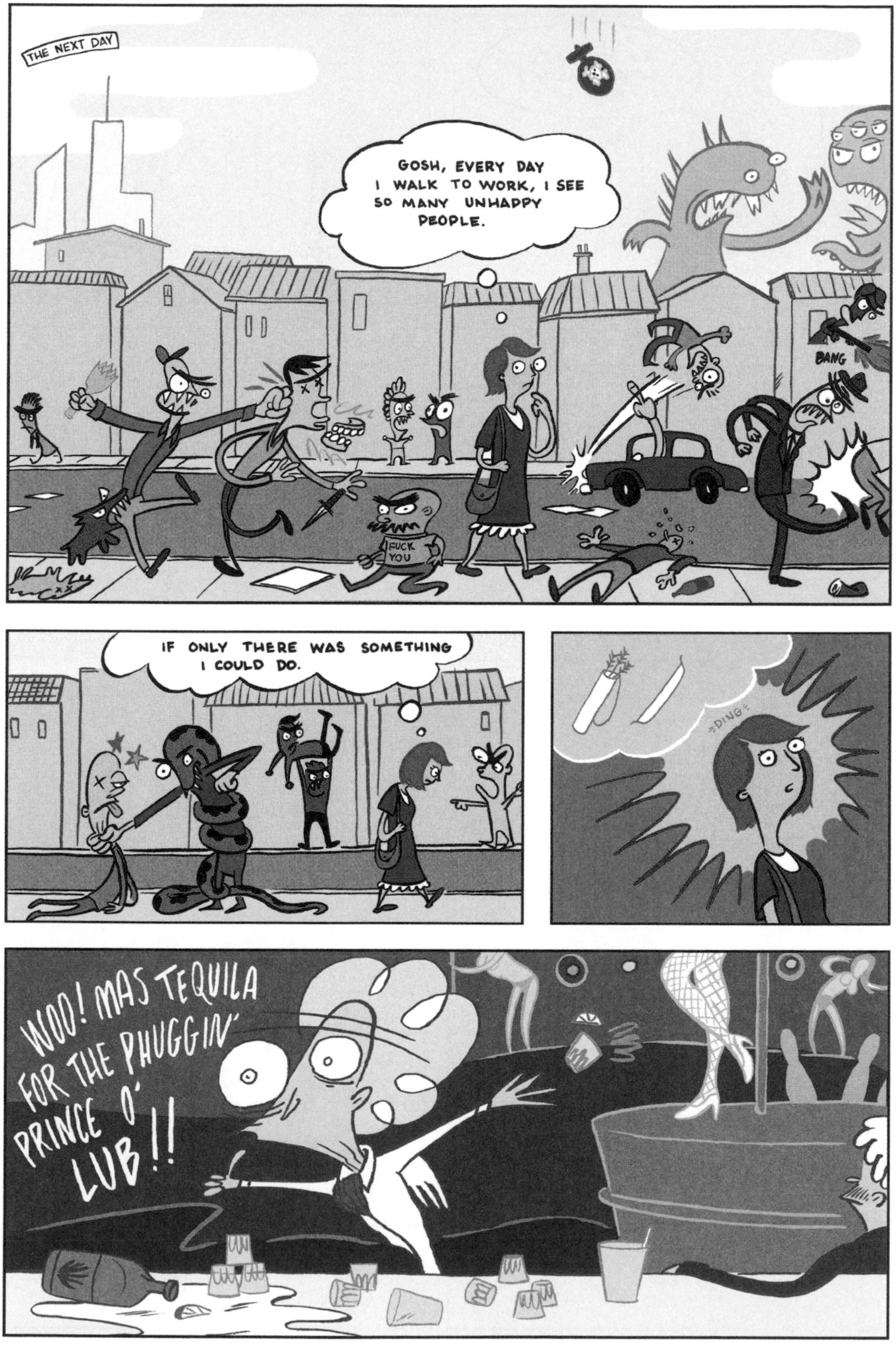
THE NEXT DAY
GOSH, EVERY DAY I WALK TO WORK, I SEE SO MANY UNHAPPY PEOPLE.
BANG
FUCK YOU
IF ONLY THERE WAS SOMETHING I COULD DO.
DING
WOO! MAS TEQUILA FOR THE PHUGGIN' PRINCE O' LUB!!

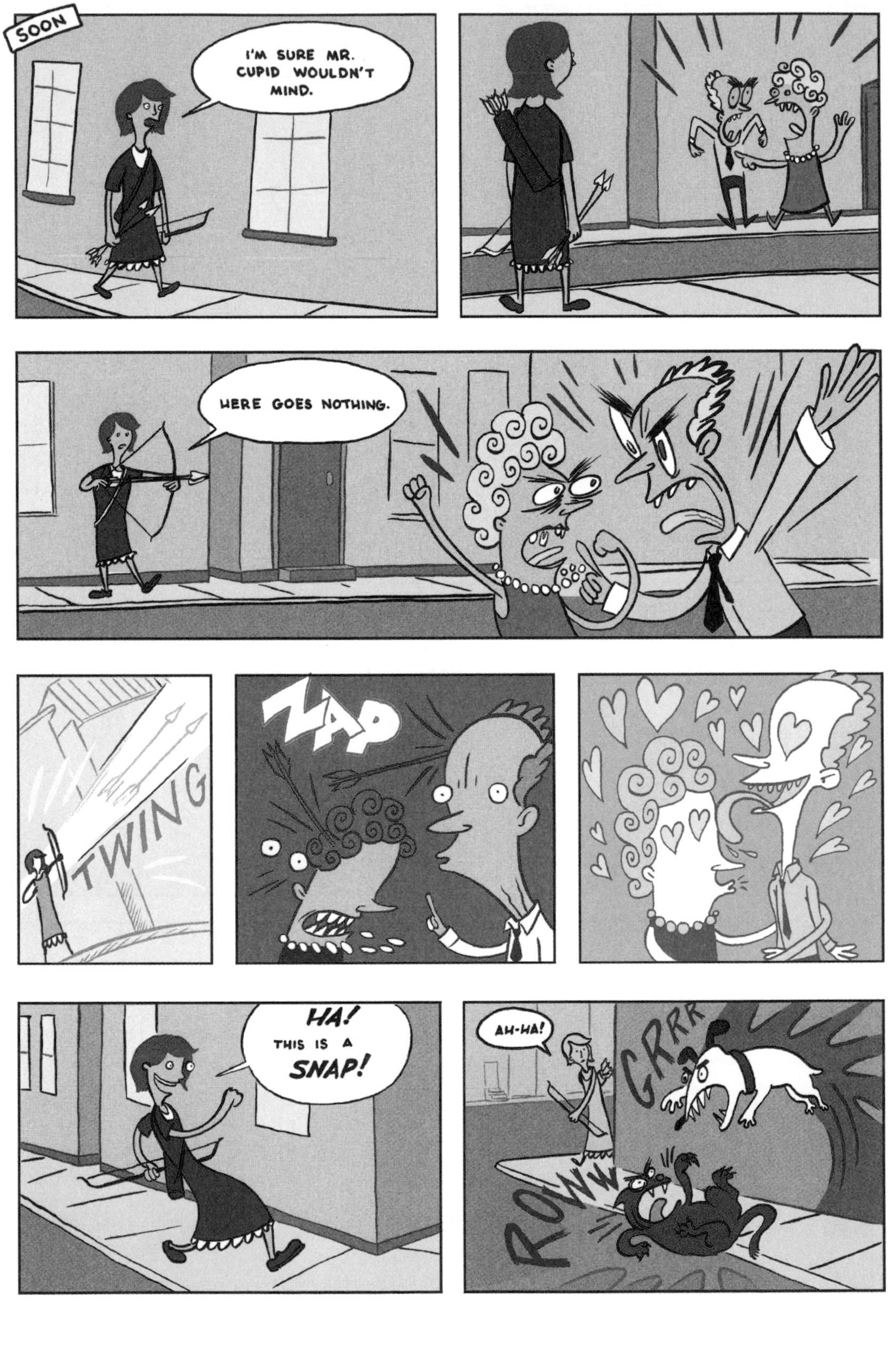
SOON
I'M SURE MR. CUPID WOULDN'T MIND.
HERE GOES NOTHING.
TWING
ZAP
HA! THIS IS A SNAP!
AH-HA!
GRRR
ROWW

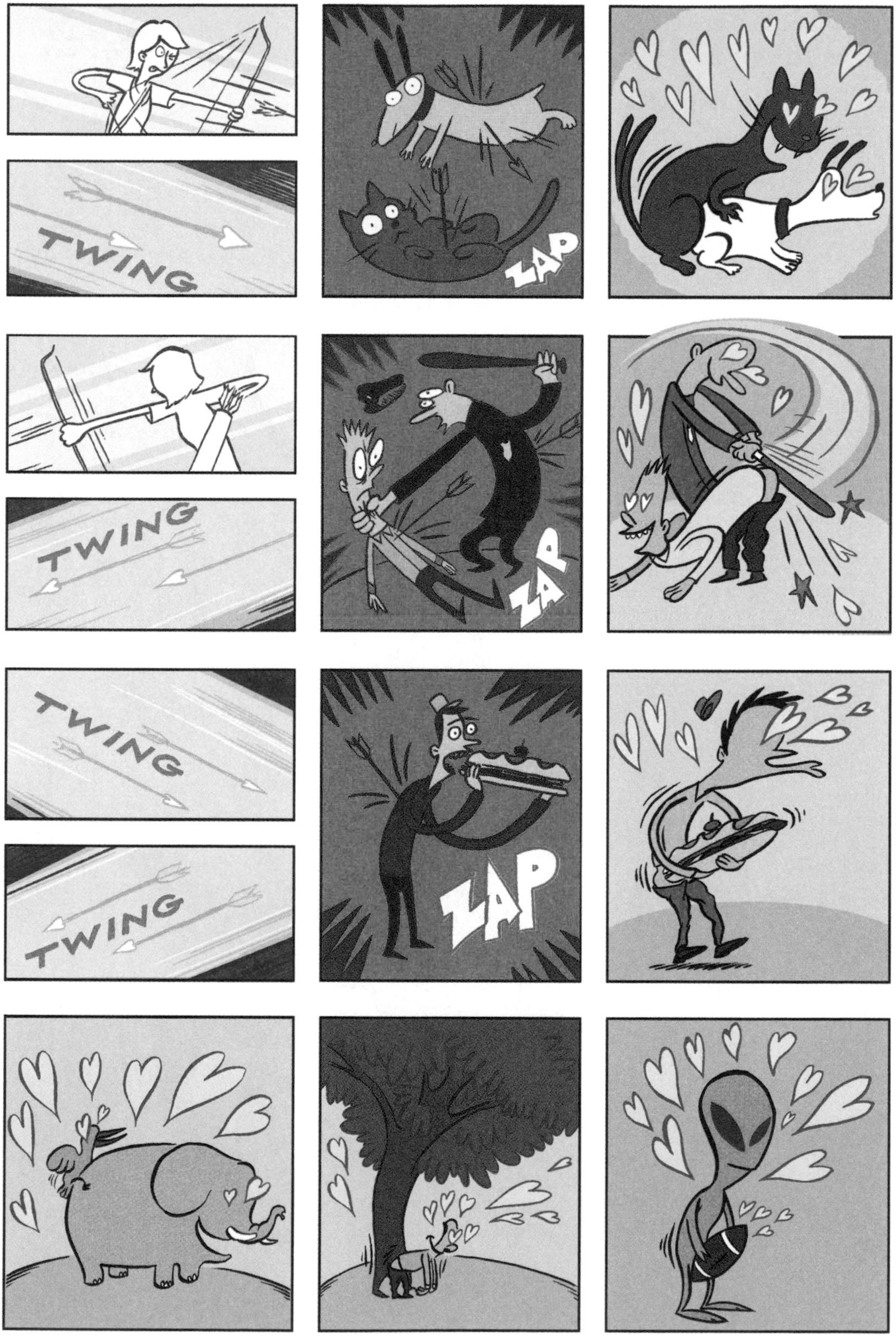
TWING
ZAP
TWING
ZAP
TWING
ZAP
TWING

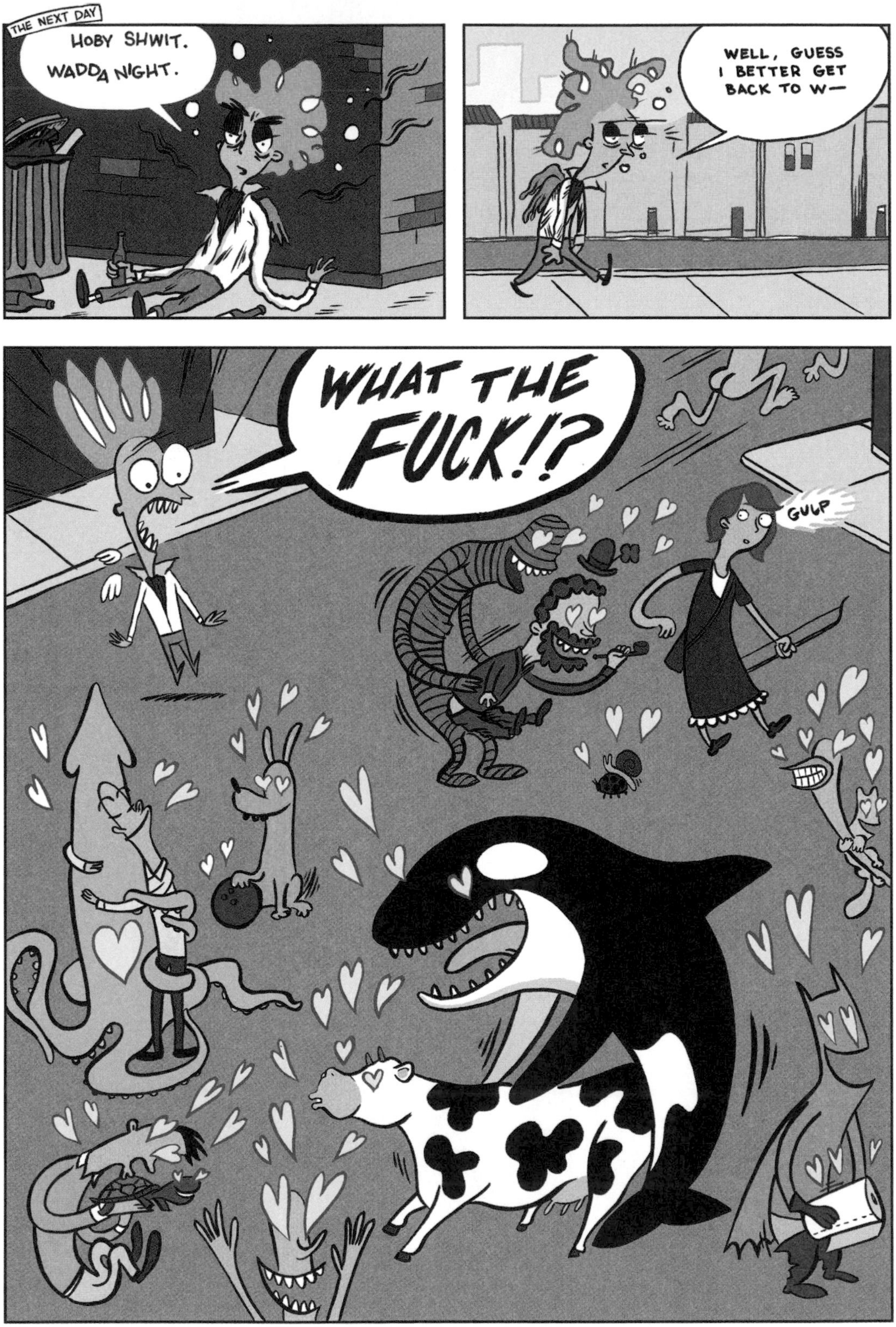
THE NEXT DAY
HOBY SHWIT. WADDA NIGHT.
WELL, GUESS I BETTER GET BACK TO W—
WHAT THE FUCK!?
GULP

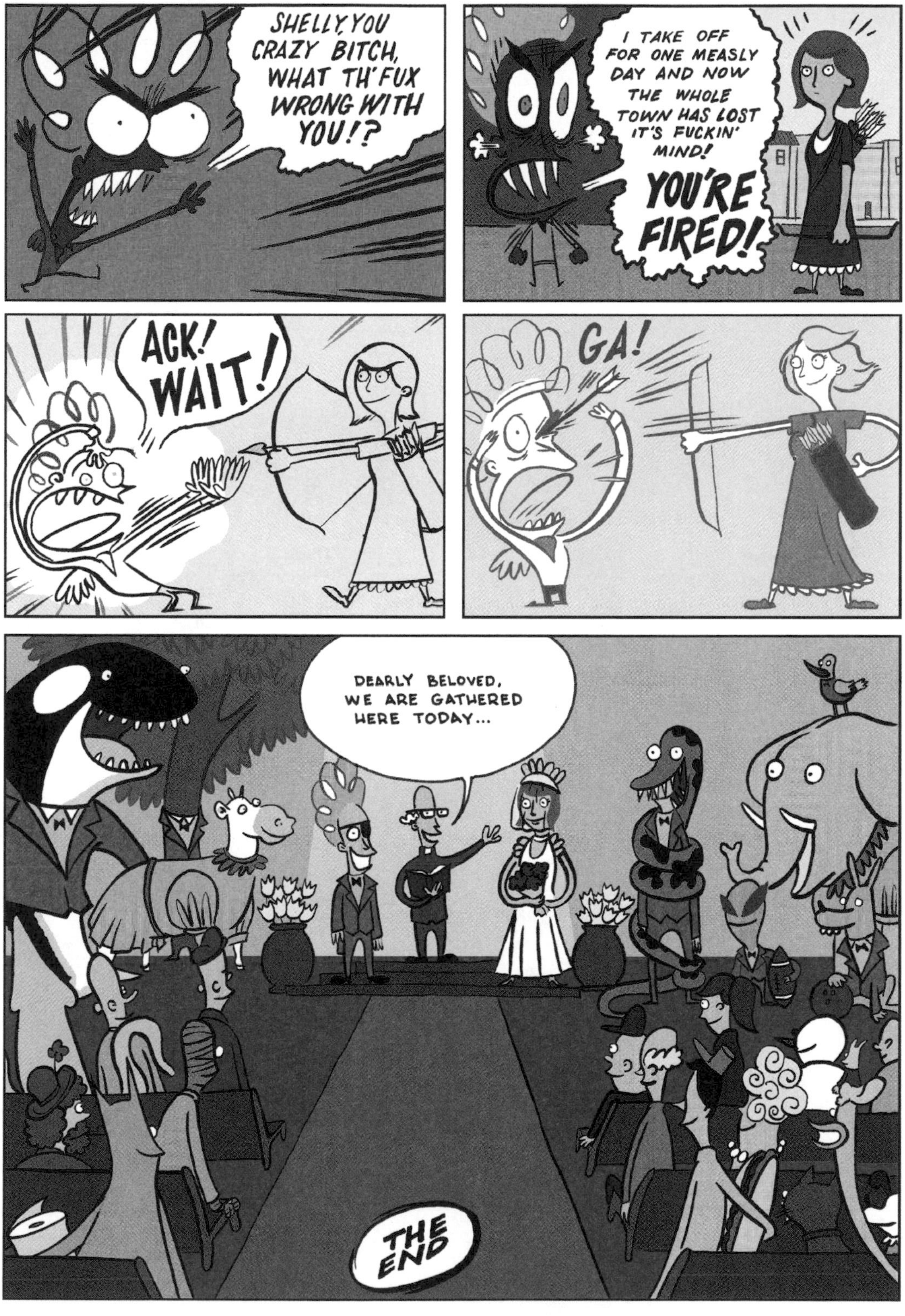
SHELLY, YOU CRAZY BITCH, WHAT TH' FUX WRONG WITH YOU!?
I TAKE OFF FOR ONE MEASLY DAY AND NOW THE WHOLE TOWN HAS LOST IT'S FUCKIN' MIND!
YOU'RE FIRED!
ACK! WAIT!
GA!
DEARLY BELOVED, WE ARE GATHERED HERE TODAY...
THE END

berlin

jason lutes

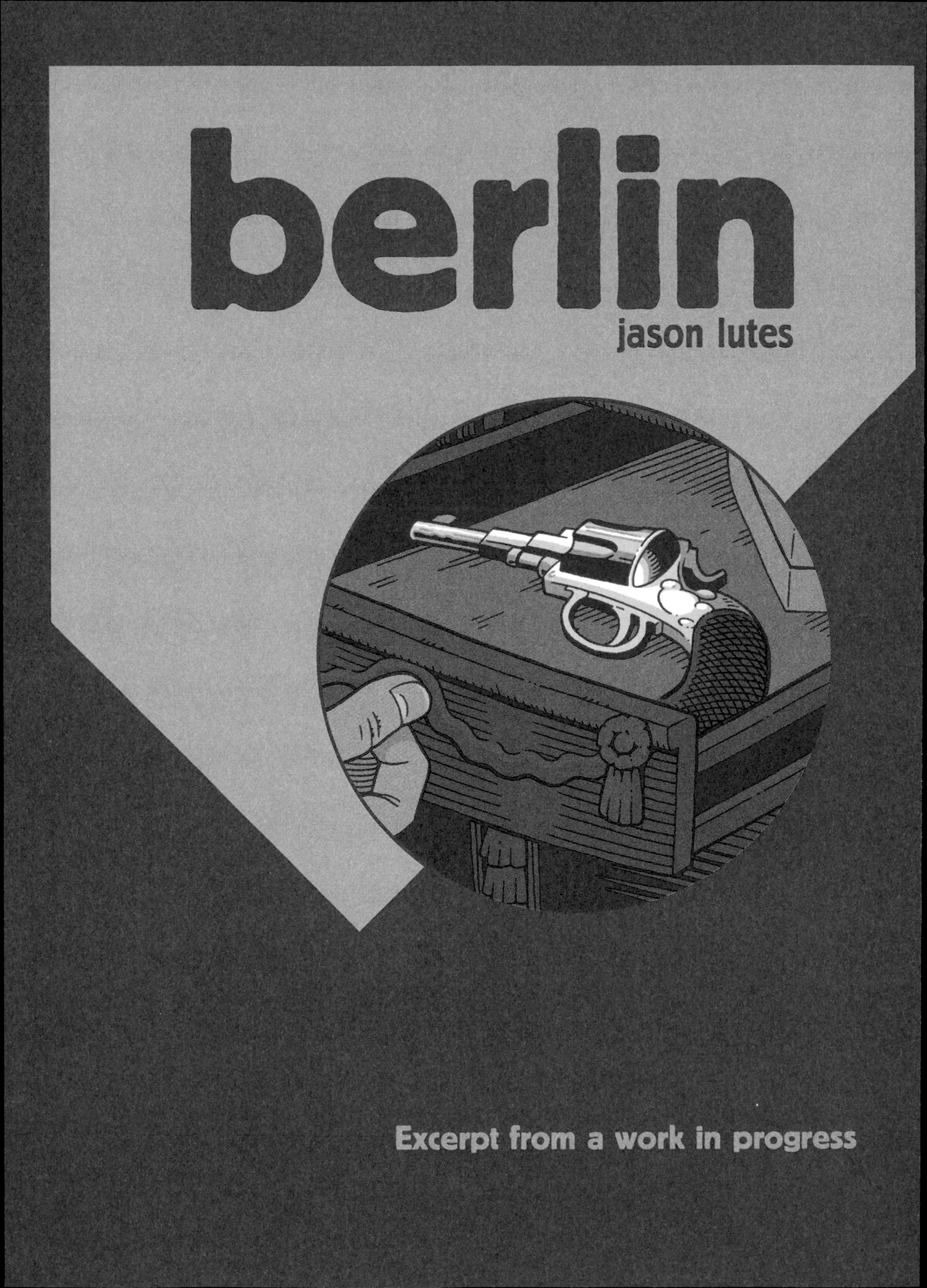

Excerpt from a work in progress

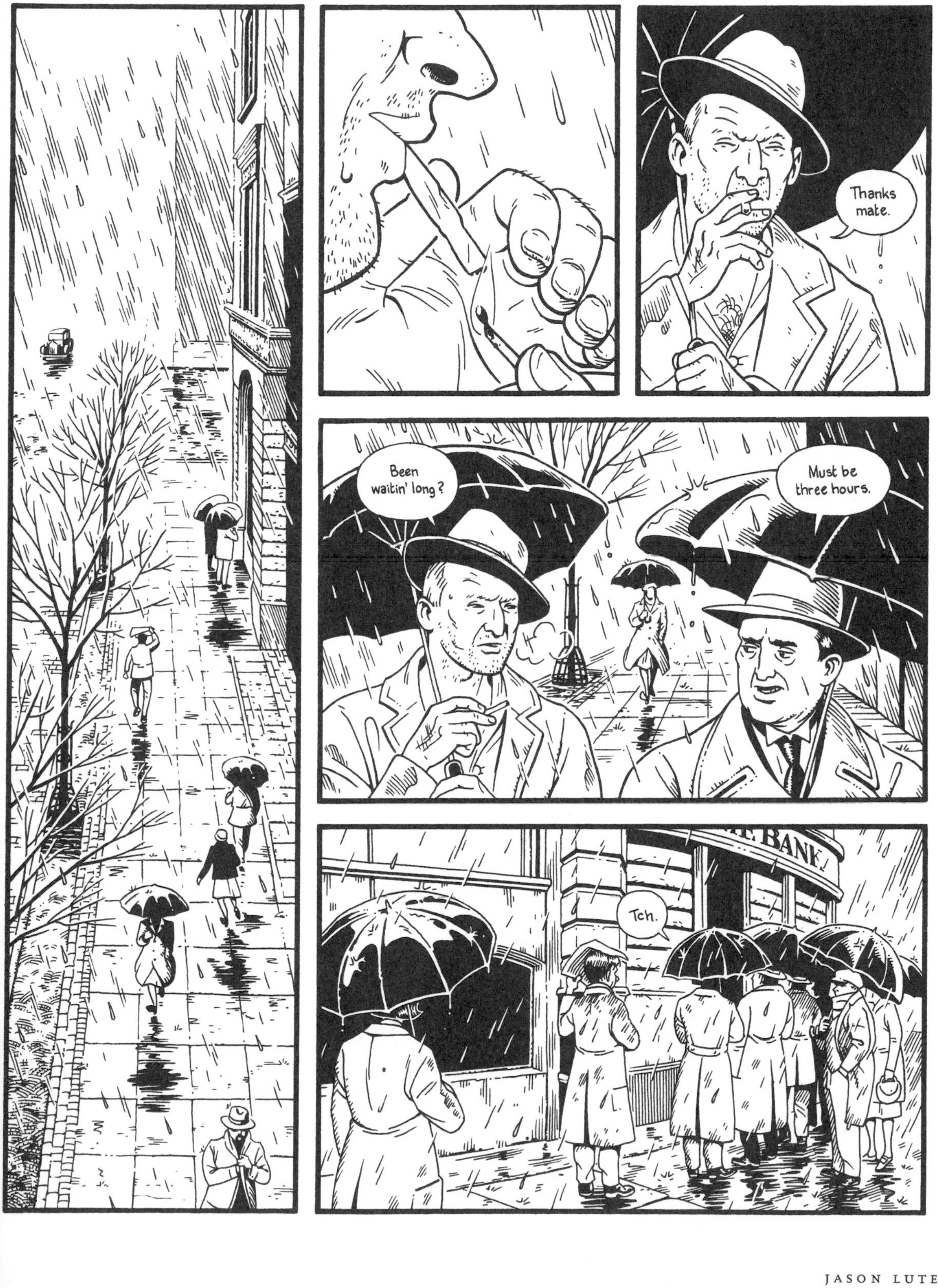
Thanks mate.
Been waitin' long?
Must be three hours.
BANK
Tch.

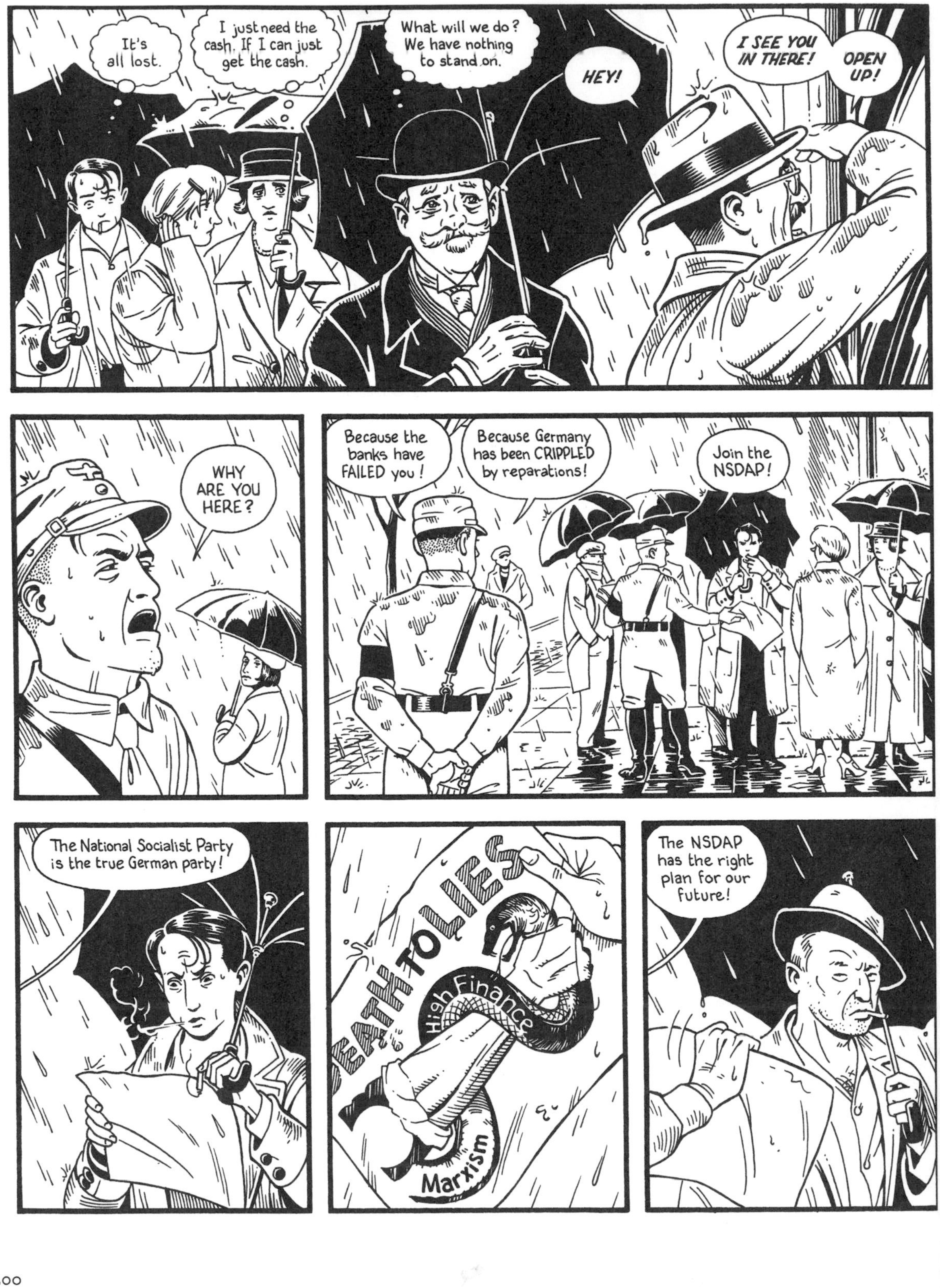
It's all lost.
I just need the cash. If I can just get the cash.
What will we do? We have nothing to stand on.
HEY!
I SEE YOU IN THERE!
OPEN UP!
WHY ARE YOU HERE?
Because the banks have FAILED you!
Because Germany has been CRIPPLED by reparations!
Join the NSDAP!
The National Socialist Party is the true German party!
DEATH TO LIES
High Finance
Marxism
The NSDAP has the right plan for our future!

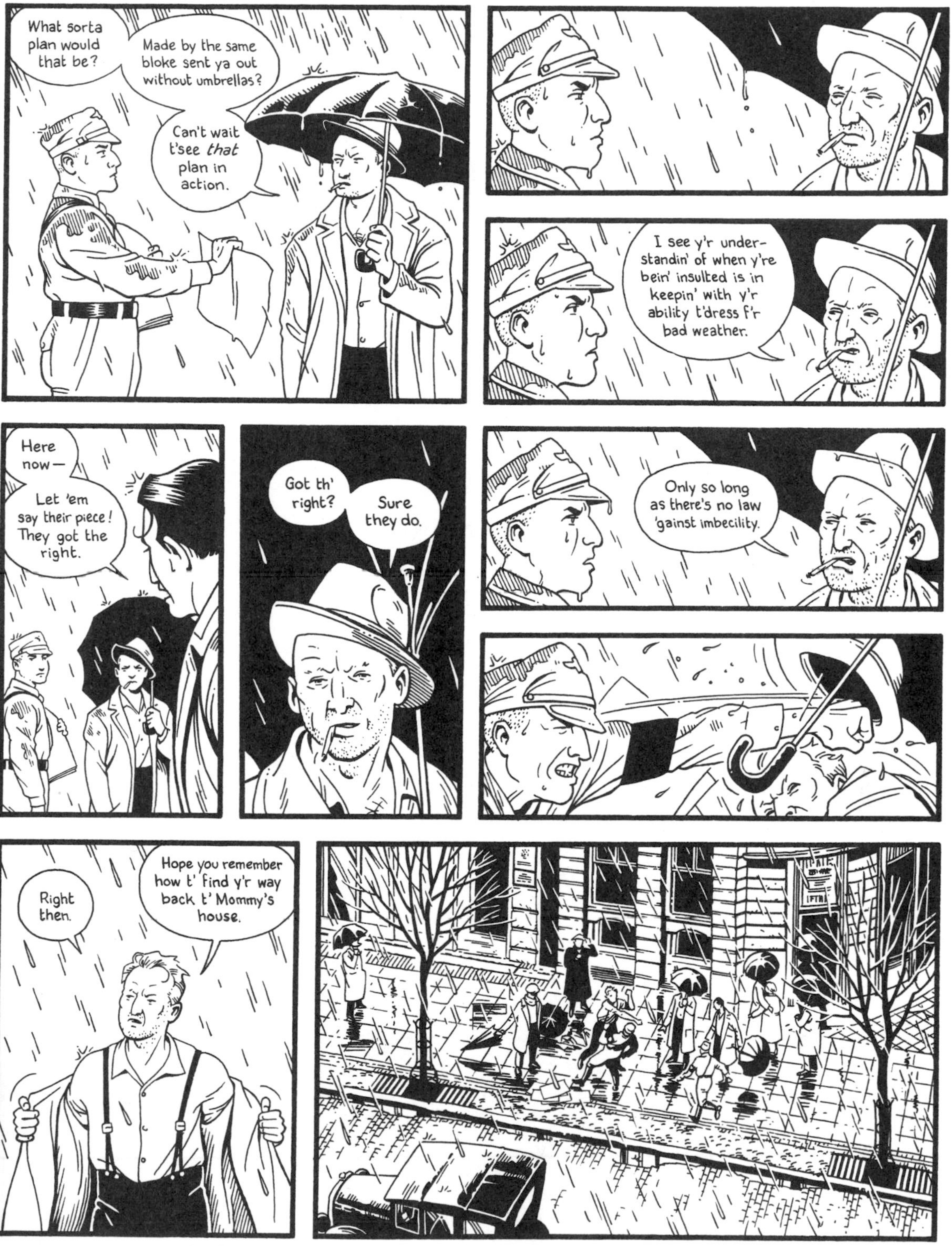
What sorta plan would that be?
Made by the same bloke sent ya out without umbrellas?
Can't wait t'see *that* plan in action.
I see y'r under-standin' of when y're bein' insulted is in keepin' with y'r ability t'dress f'r bad weather.
Here now—
Let 'em say their piece! They got the right.
Got th' right?
Sure they do.
Only so long as there's no law 'gainst imbecility.
Right then.
Hope you remember how t' find y'r way back t' Mommy's house.

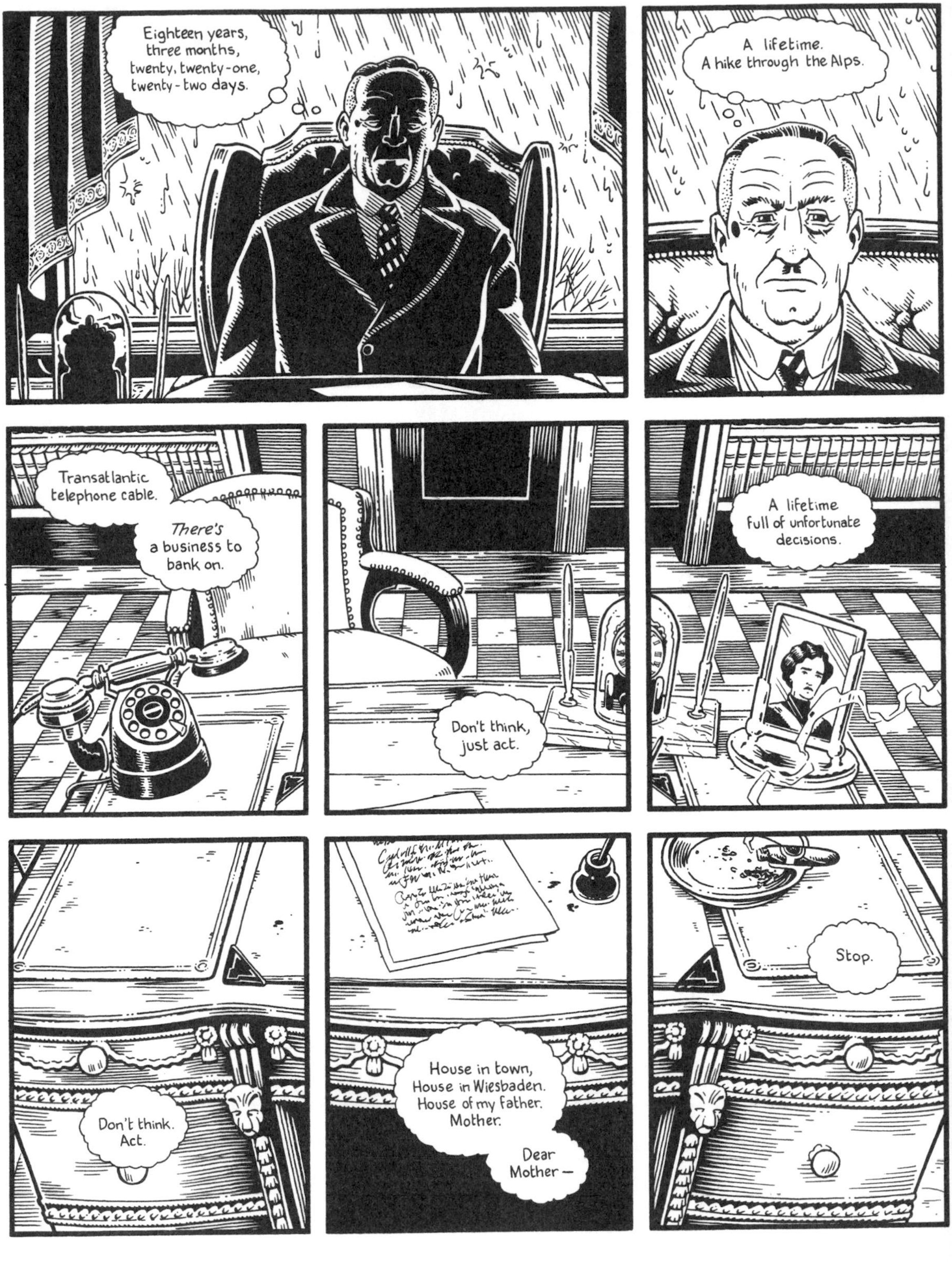
Eighteen years, three months, twenty, twenty-one, twenty-two days.
A lifetime. A hike through the Alps.
Transatlantic telephone cable.
There's a business to bank on.
Don't think, just act.
A lifetime full of unfortunate decisions.
Don't think. Act.
House in town, House in Wiesbaden. House of my father. Mother.
Dear Mother —
Stop.

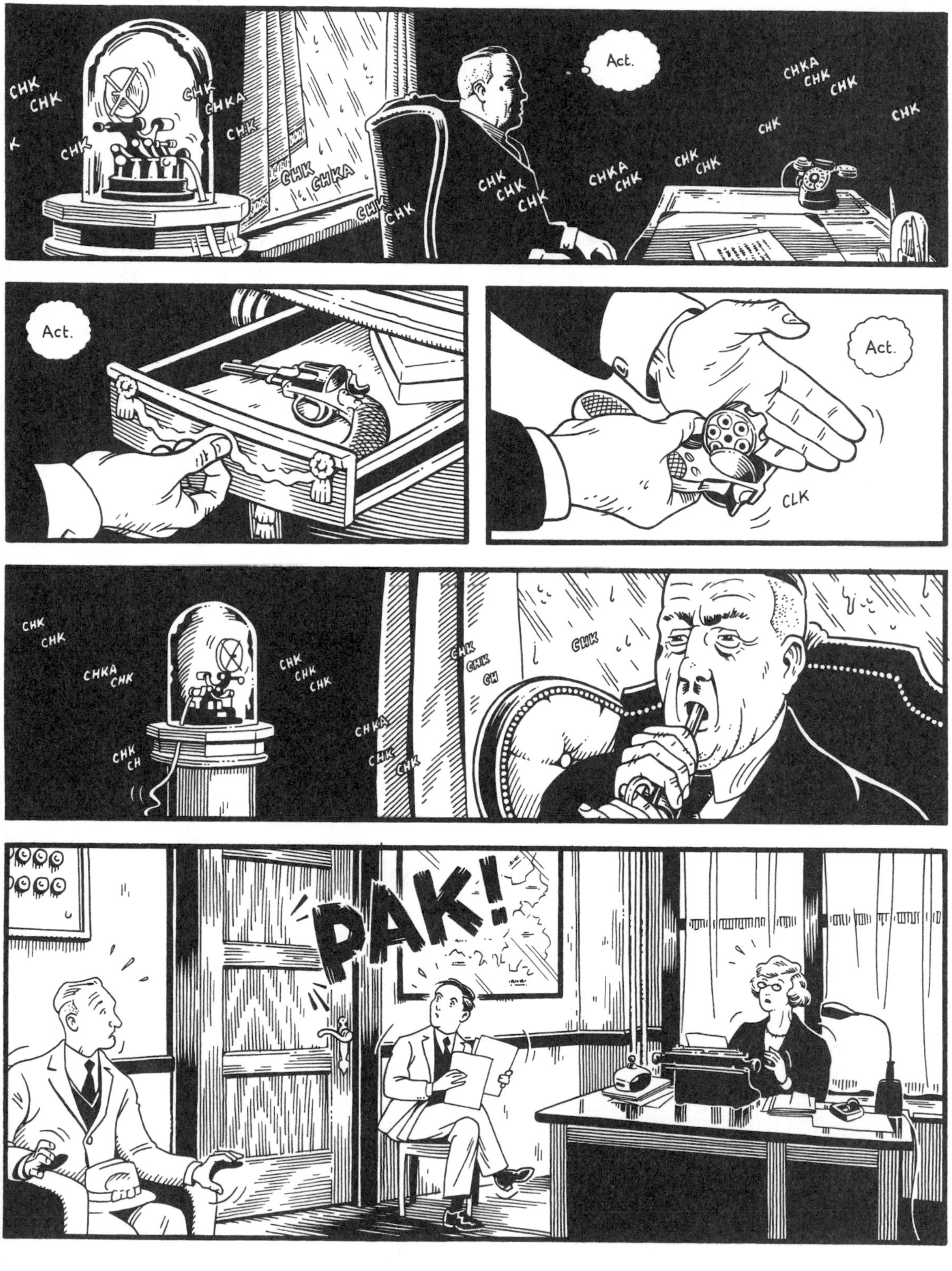
CHK
CHK
CHK
CHKA
CHK
CHK
CHK
CHKA
CHK
CHK
Act.
CHK
CHK
CHK
CHKA
CHK
CHK
CHK
CHKA
CHK
CHK
CHK
CHK
Act.
Act.
CLK
CHK
CHK
CHKA
CHK
CHK
CHK
CHK
CHK
CH
CHK
CH
CHKA
CHK
CHK
CHK
PAK!

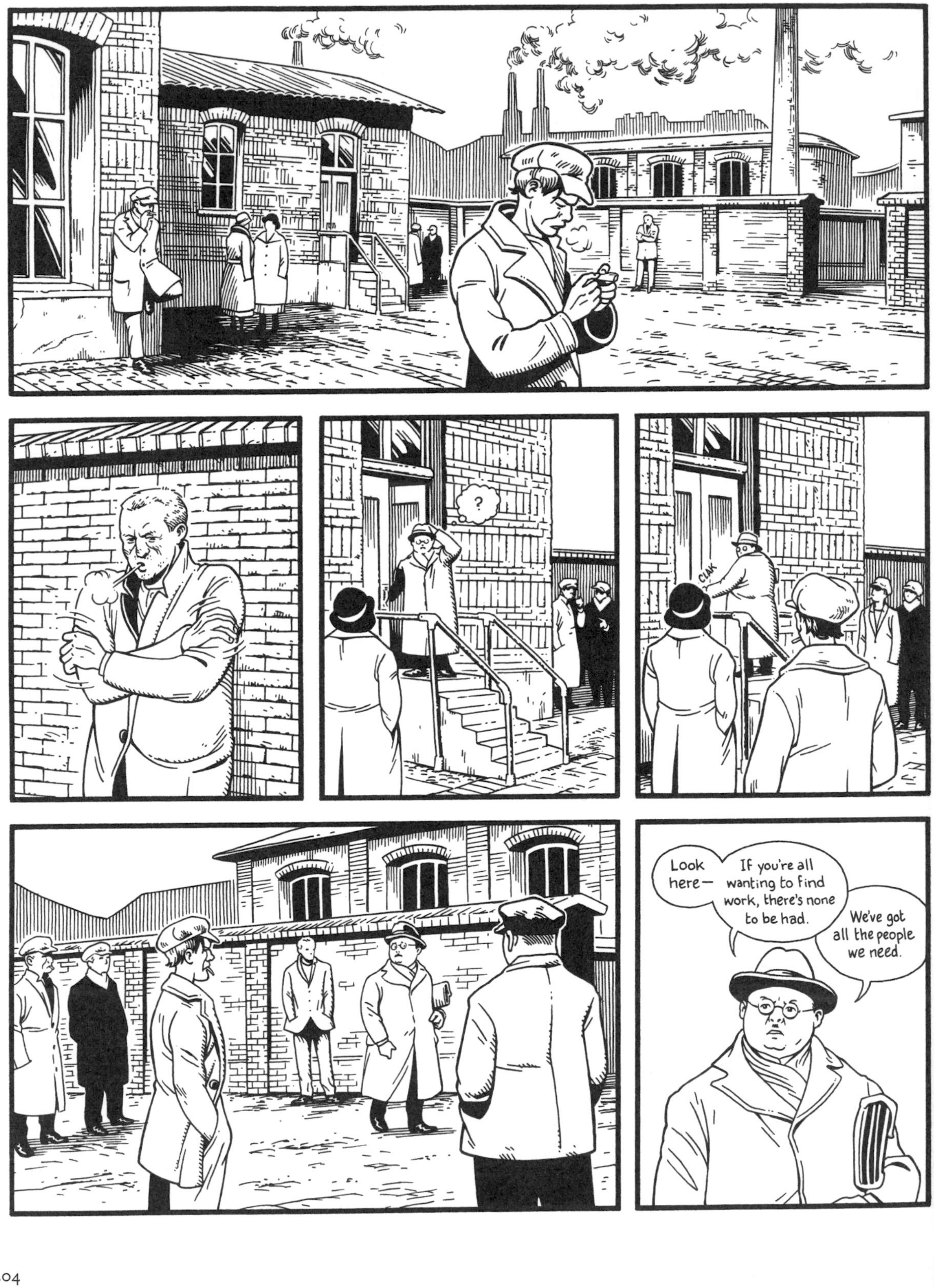
?
CLAK
Look here—
If you're all wanting to find work, there's none to be had.
We've got all the people we need.

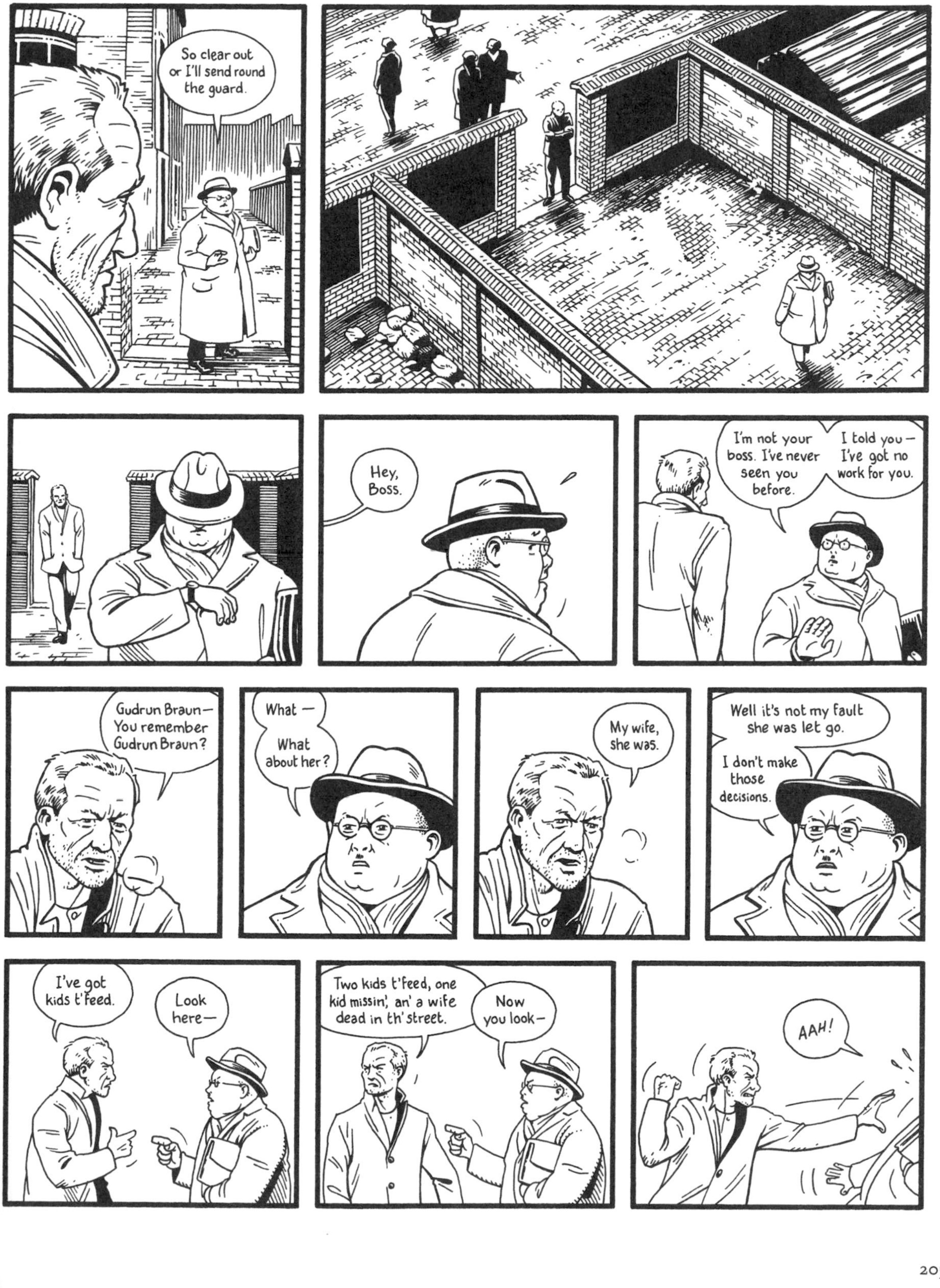
So clear out or I'll send round the guard.
Hey, Boss.
I'm not your boss. I've never seen you before.
I told you — I've got no work for you.
Gudrun Braun — You remember Gudrun Braun?
What —
What about her?
My wife, she was.
Well it's not my fault she was let go.
I don't make those decisions.
I've got kids t'feed.
Look here —
Two kids t'feed, one kid missin', an' a wife dead in th' street.
Now you look —
AAH!

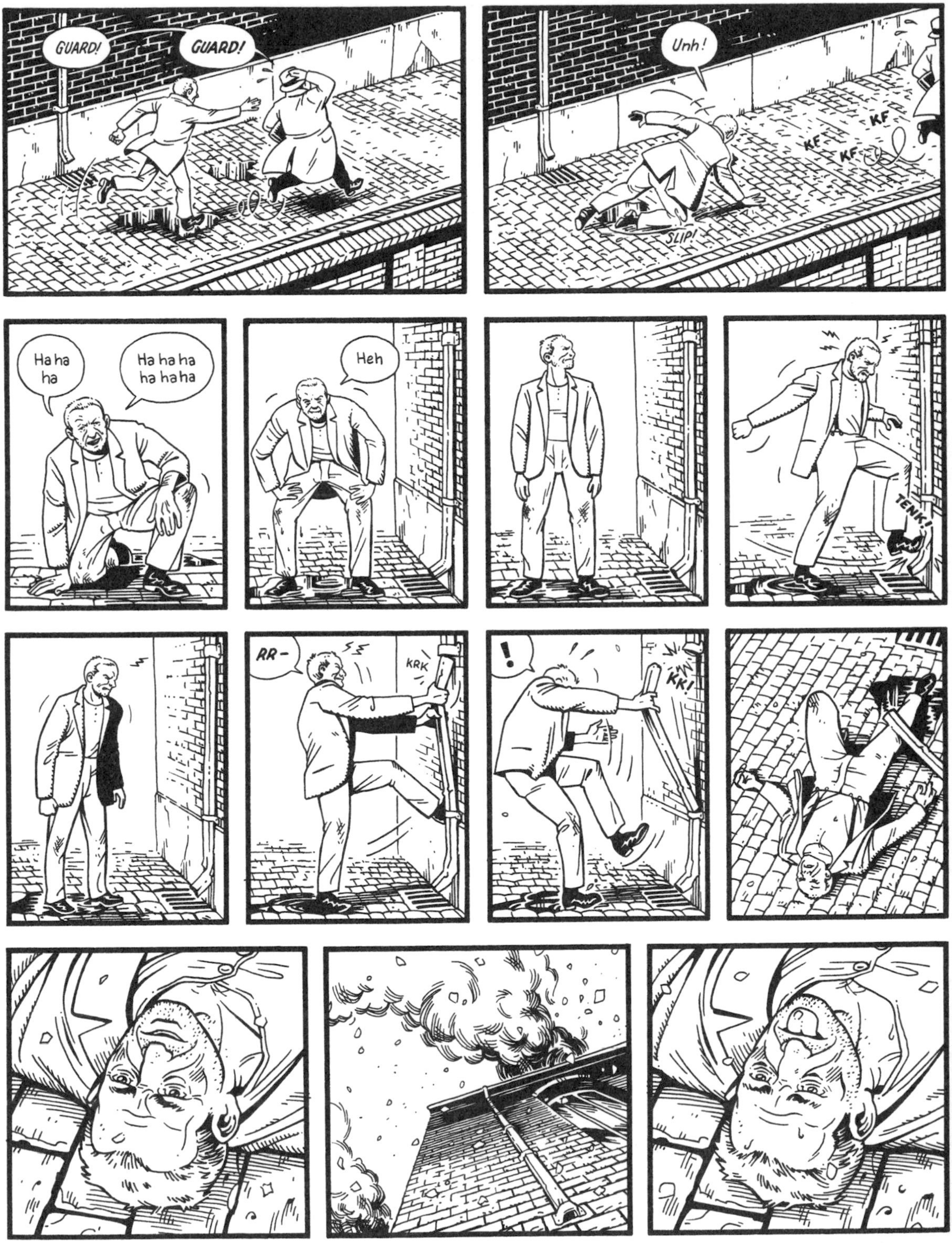
GUARD!
GUARD!
Unh!
KF
KF
KF
SLIP!
Ha ha ha
Ha ha ha ha ha ha
Heh
TENK!
RR-
KRK
!
KK!

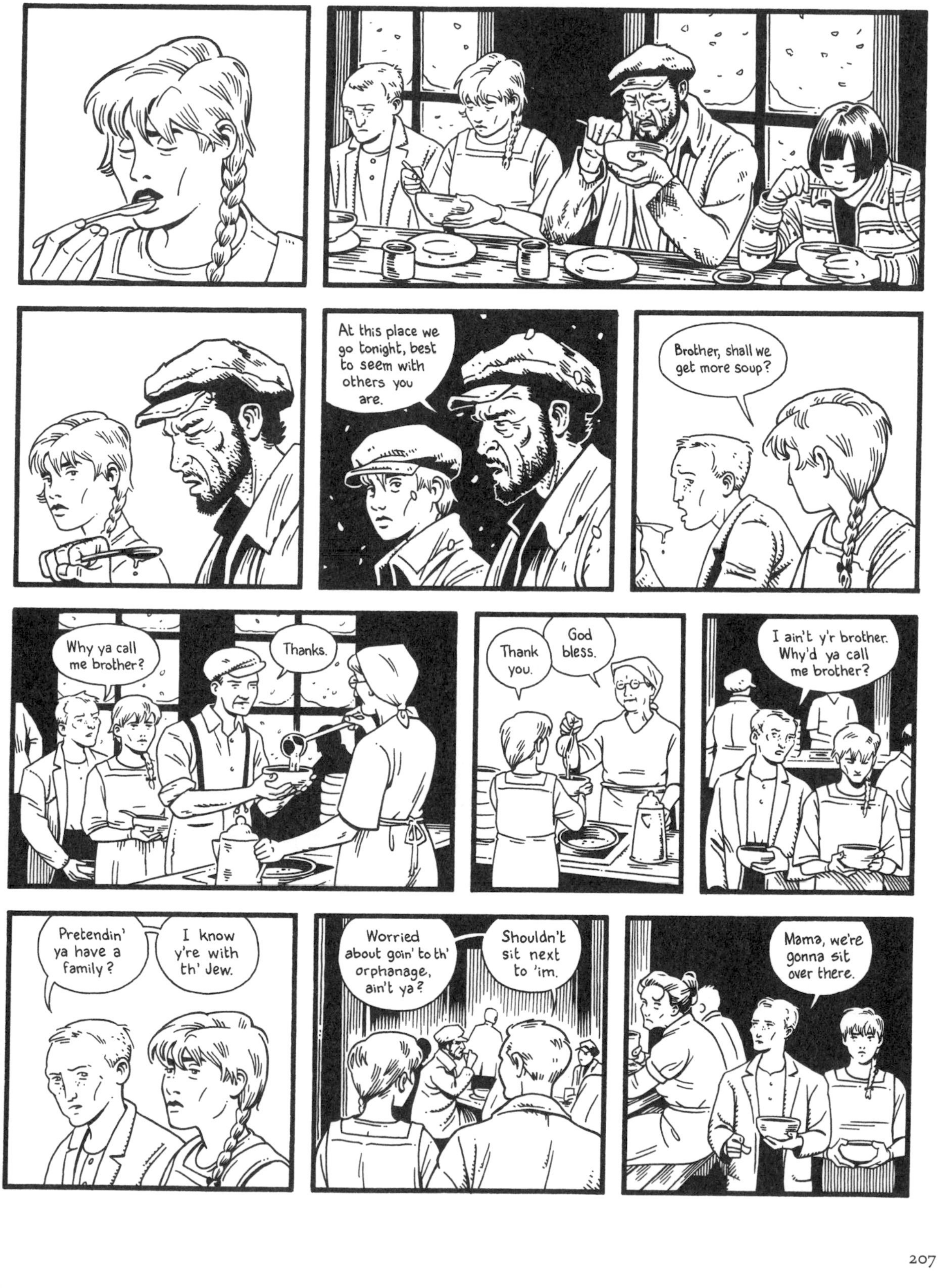
At this place we go tonight, best to seem with others you are.
Brother, shall we get more soup?
Why ya call me brother?
Thanks.
Thank you.
God bless.
I ain't y'r brother. Why'd ya call me brother?
Pretendin' ya have a family?
I know y're with th' Jew.
Worried about goin' to th' orphanage, ain't ya?
Shouldn't sit next to 'im.
Mama, we're gonna sit over there.

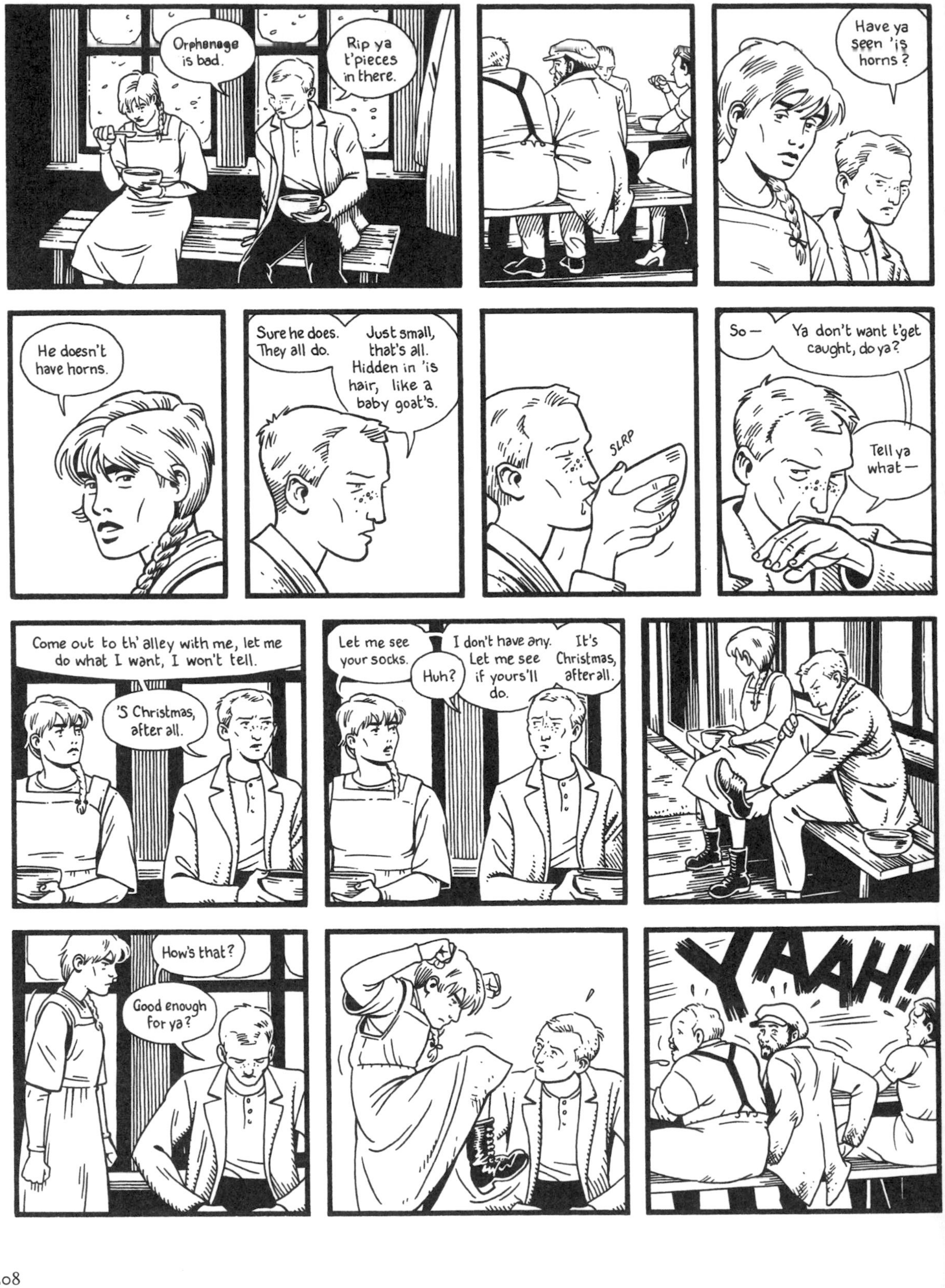
Orphanage is bad.
Rip ya t'pieces in there.
Have ya seen 'is horns?
He doesn't have horns.
Sure he does. They all do.
Just small, that's all. Hidden in 'is hair, like a baby goat's.
SLRP
So—
Ya don't want t'get caught, do ya?
Tell ya what—
Come out to th' alley with me, let me do what I want, I won't tell.
'S Christmas, after all.
Let me see your socks.
Huh?
I don't have any. Let me see if yours'll do.
It's Christmas, after all.
How's that?
Good enough for ya?
YAAH!!

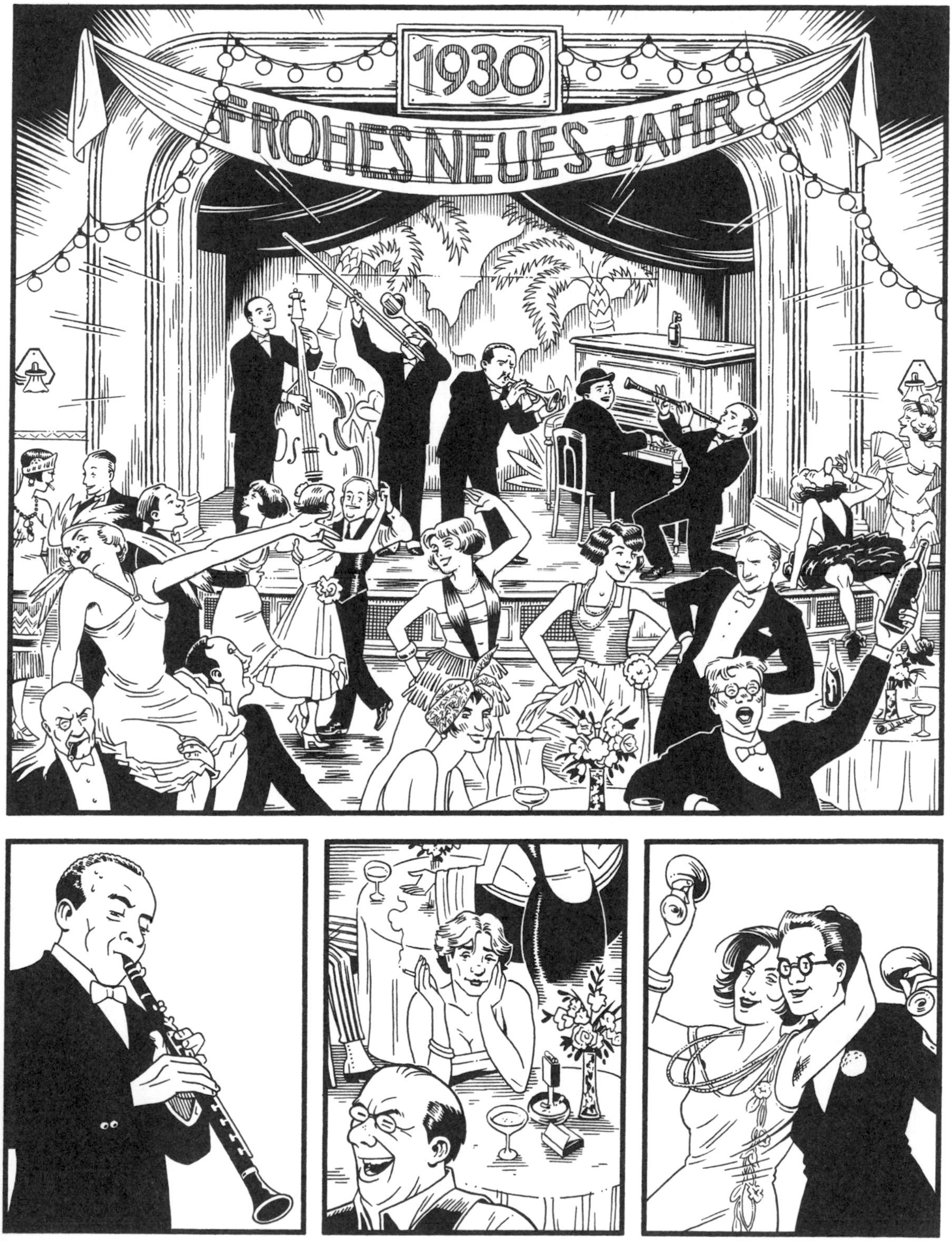
1930
FROHES NEUES JAHR

CRASH!

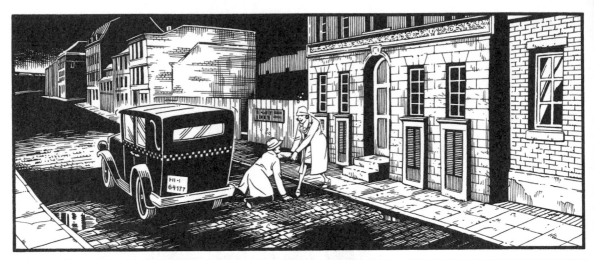

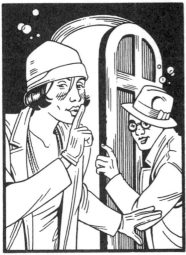

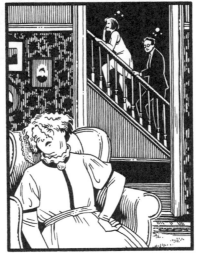

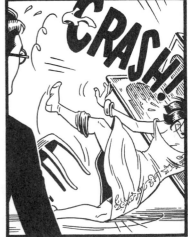

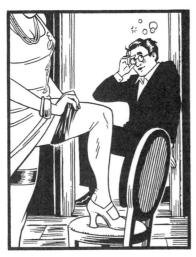

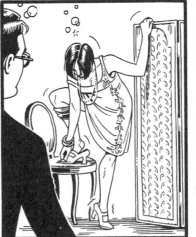

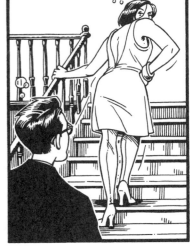

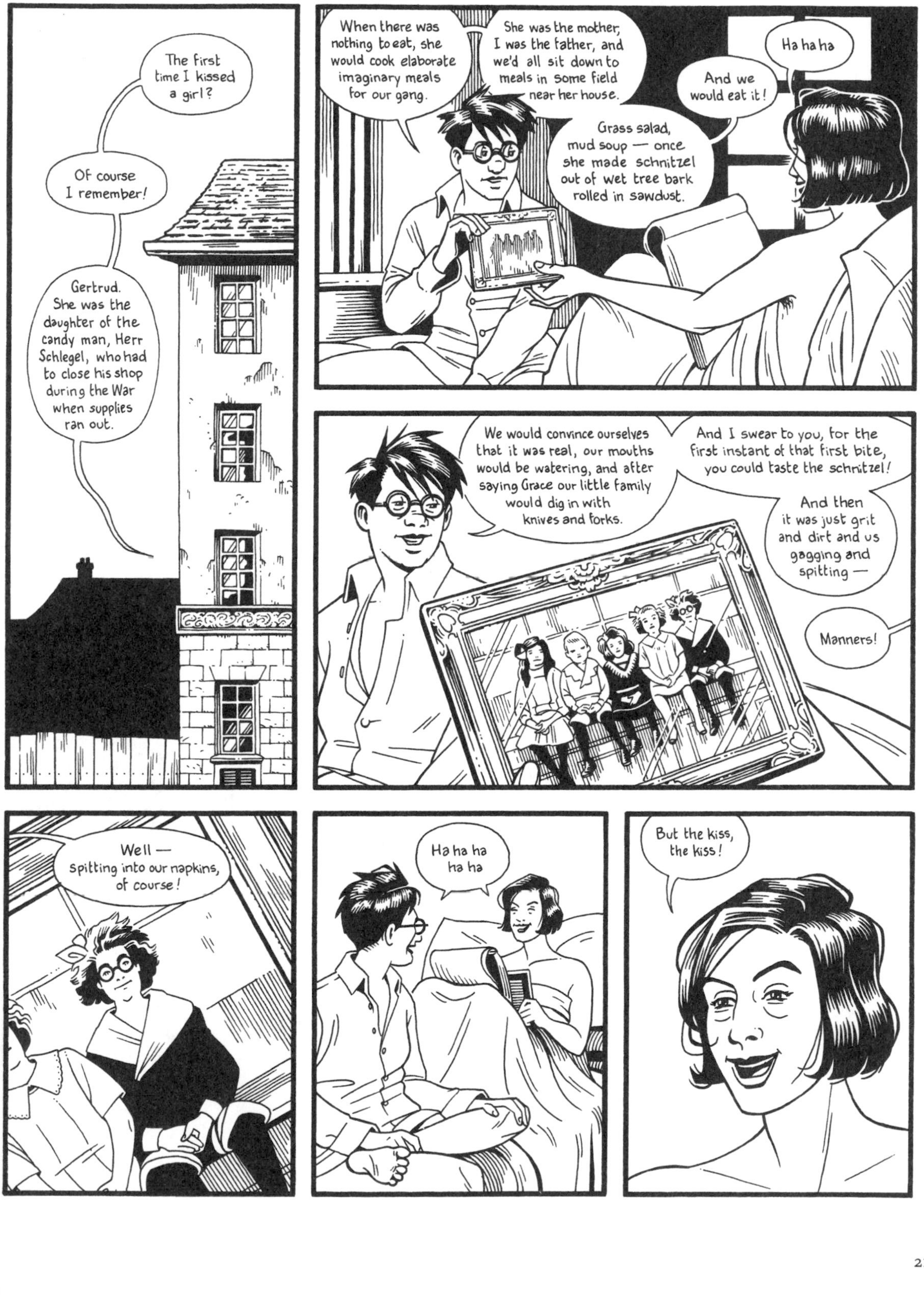

The first time I kissed a girl?
Of course I remember!
Gertrud. She was the daughter of the candy man, Herr Schlegel, who had to close his shop during the War when supplies ran out.
When there was nothing to eat, she would cook elaborate imaginary meals for our gang.
She was the mother, I was the father, and we'd all sit down to meals in some field near her house.
Grass salad, mud soup — once she made schnitzel out of wet tree bark rolled in sawdust.
And we would eat it!
Ha ha ha
We would convince ourselves that it was real, our mouths would be watering, and after saying Grace our little family would dig in with knives and forks.
And I swear to you, for the first instant of that first bite, you could taste the schnitzel!
And then it was just grit and dirt and us gagging and spitting —
Manners!
Well — spitting into our napkins, of course!
Ha ha ha ha ha
But the kiss, the kiss!

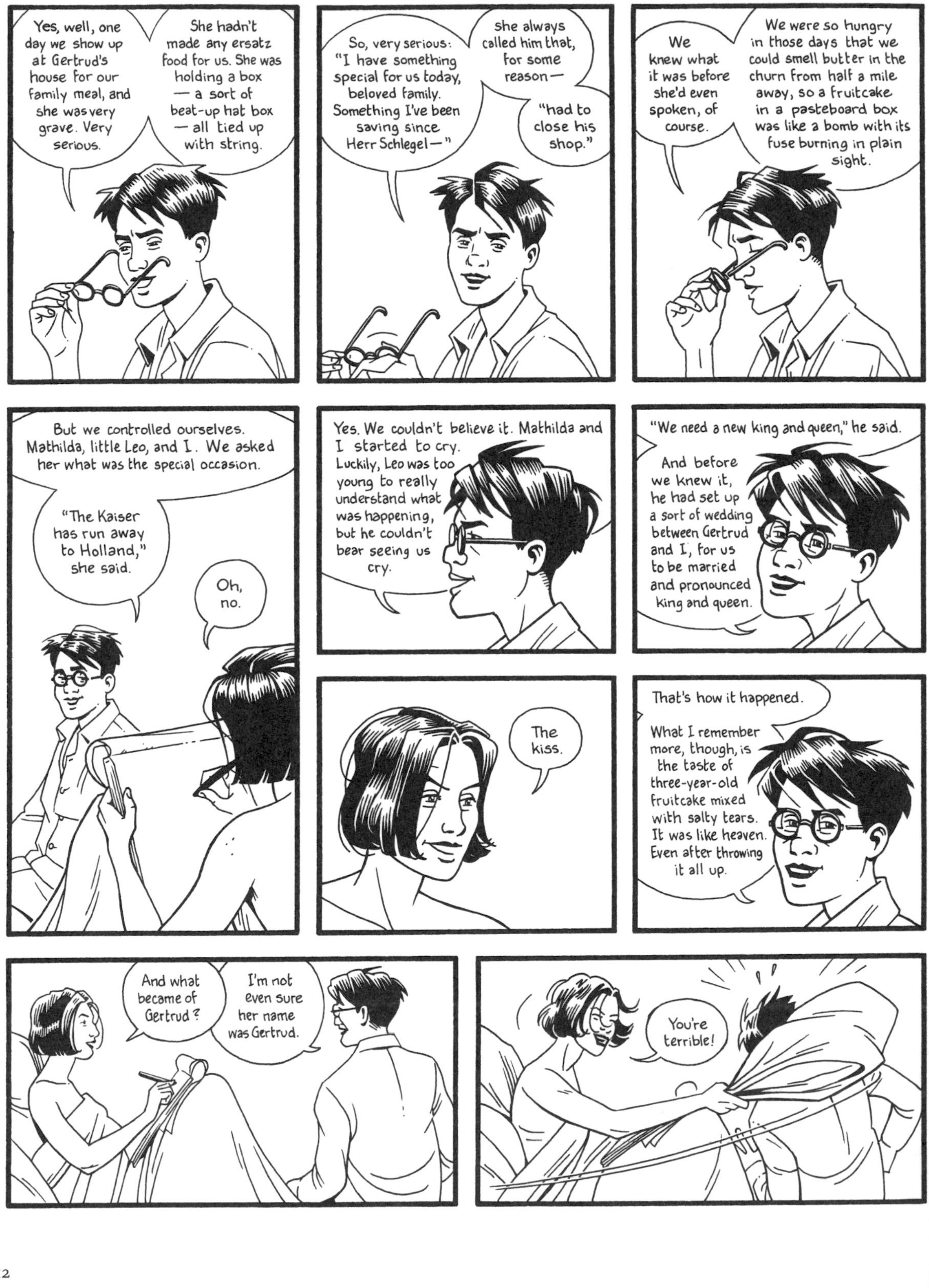
Yes, well, one day we show up at Gertrud's house for our family meal, and she was very grave. Very serious.
She hadn't made any ersatz food for us. She was holding a box — a sort of beat-up hat box — all tied up with string.
So, very serious: "I have something special for us today, beloved family. Something I've been saving since Herr Schlegel—"
she always called him that, for some reason—
"had to close his shop."
We knew what it was before she'd even spoken, of course.
We were so hungry in those days that we could smell butter in the churn from half a mile away, so a fruitcake in a pasteboard box was like a bomb with its fuse burning in plain sight.
But we controlled ourselves. Mathilda, little Leo, and I. We asked her what was the special occasion.
"The Kaiser has run away to Holland," she said.
Oh, no.
Yes. We couldn't believe it. Mathilda and I started to cry. Luckily, Leo was too young to really understand what was happening, but he couldn't bear seeing us cry.
"We need a new king and queen," he said.
And before we knew it, he had set up a sort of wedding between Gertrud and I, for us to be married and pronounced king and queen.
The kiss.
That's how it happened.
What I remember more, though, is the taste of three-year-old fruitcake mixed with salty tears. It was like heaven. Even after throwing it all up.
And what became of Gertrud?
I'm not even sure her name was Gertrud.
You're terrible!

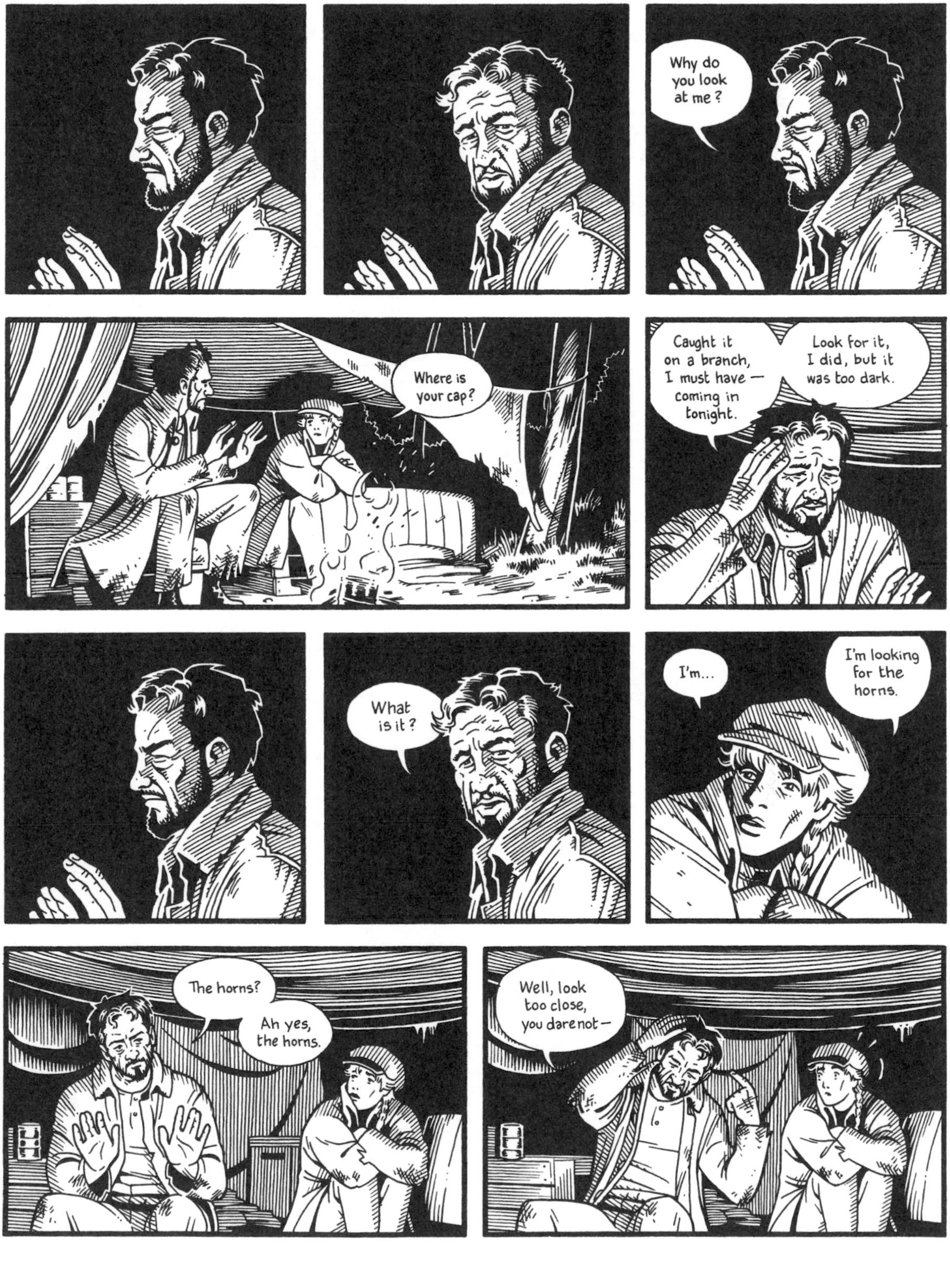
Why do you look at me?
Where is your cap?
Caught it on a branch, I must have — coming in tonight.
Look for it, I did, but it was too dark.
What is it?
I'm...
I'm looking for the horns.
The horns?
Ah yes, the horns.
Well, look too close, you darenot —

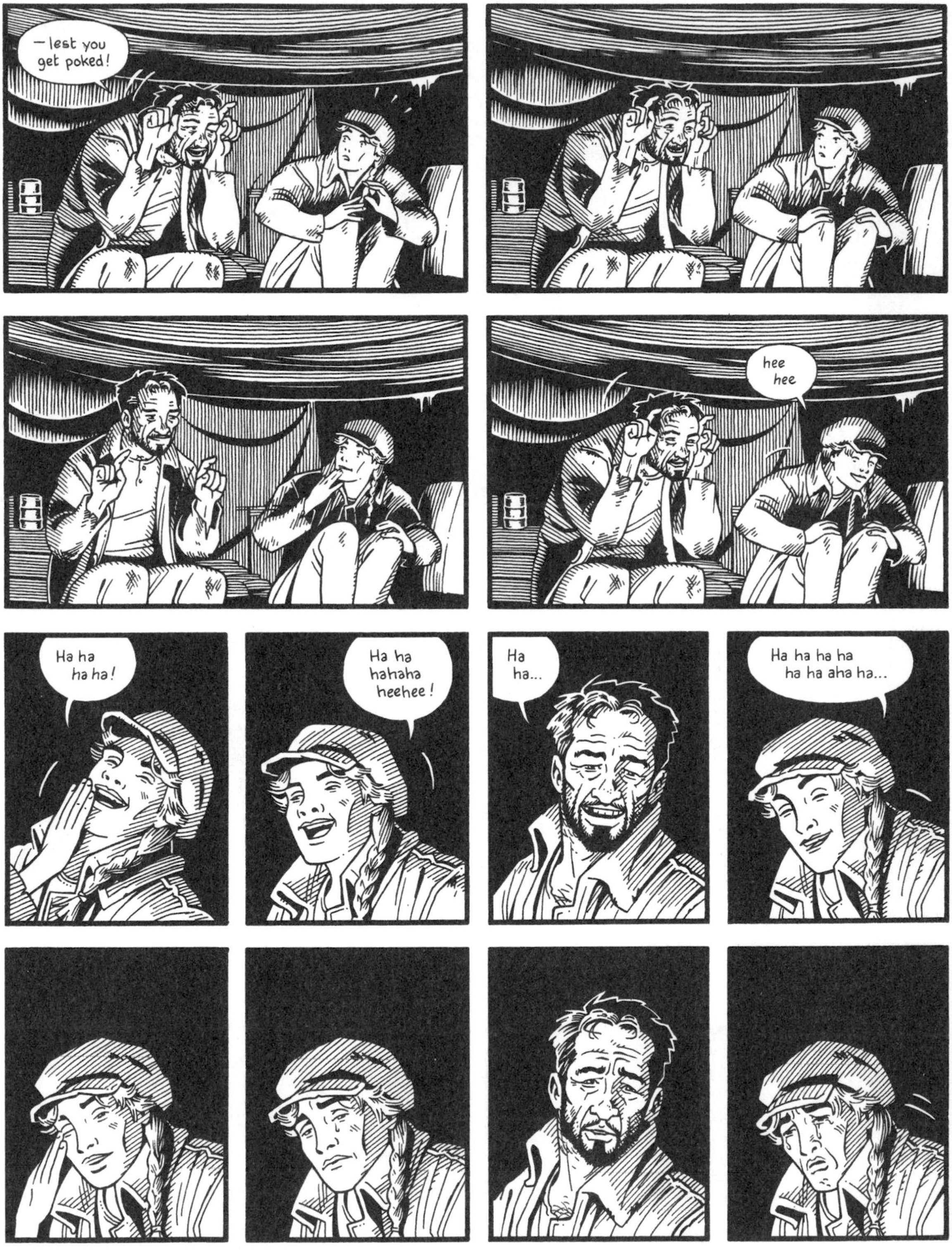
—lest you get poked!
hee hee
Ha ha ha ha!
Ha ha hahaha heehee!
Ha ha...
Ha ha ha ha ha ha aha ha...

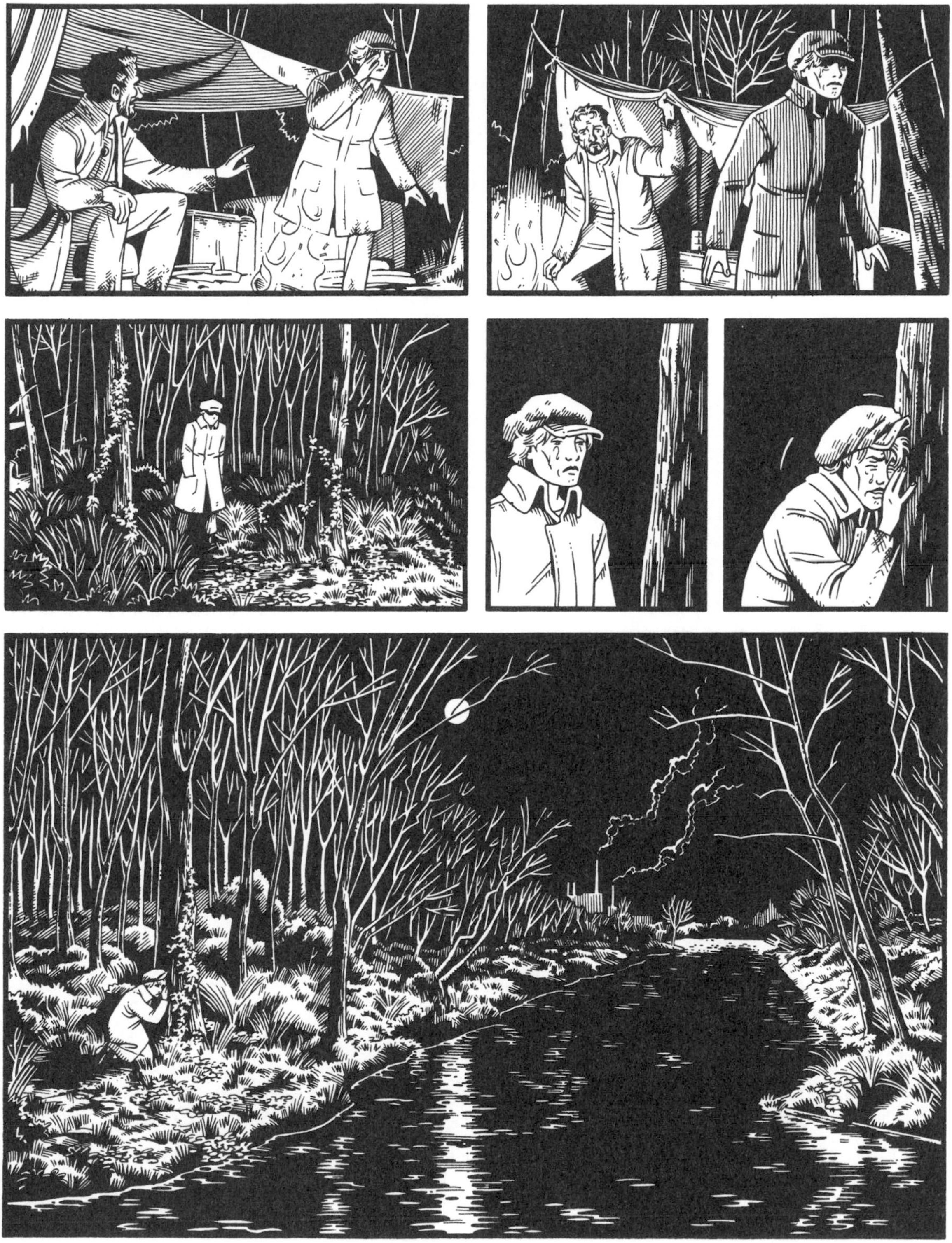

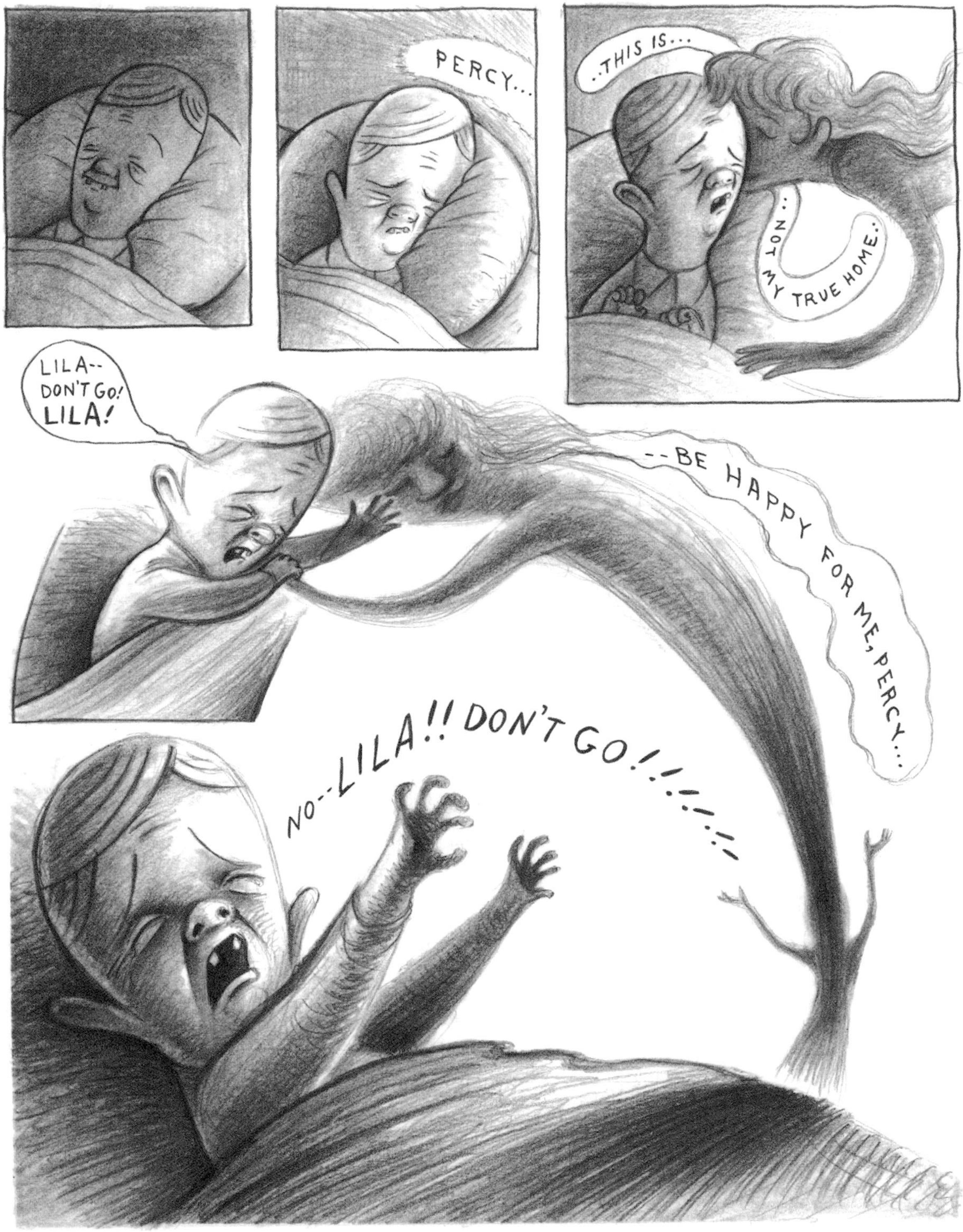
PERCY...
..THIS IS...
..NOT MY TRUE HOME..
LILA-- DON'T GO! LILA!
--BE HAPPY FOR ME, PERCY...
NO--LILA!! DON'T GO!!!!!!!

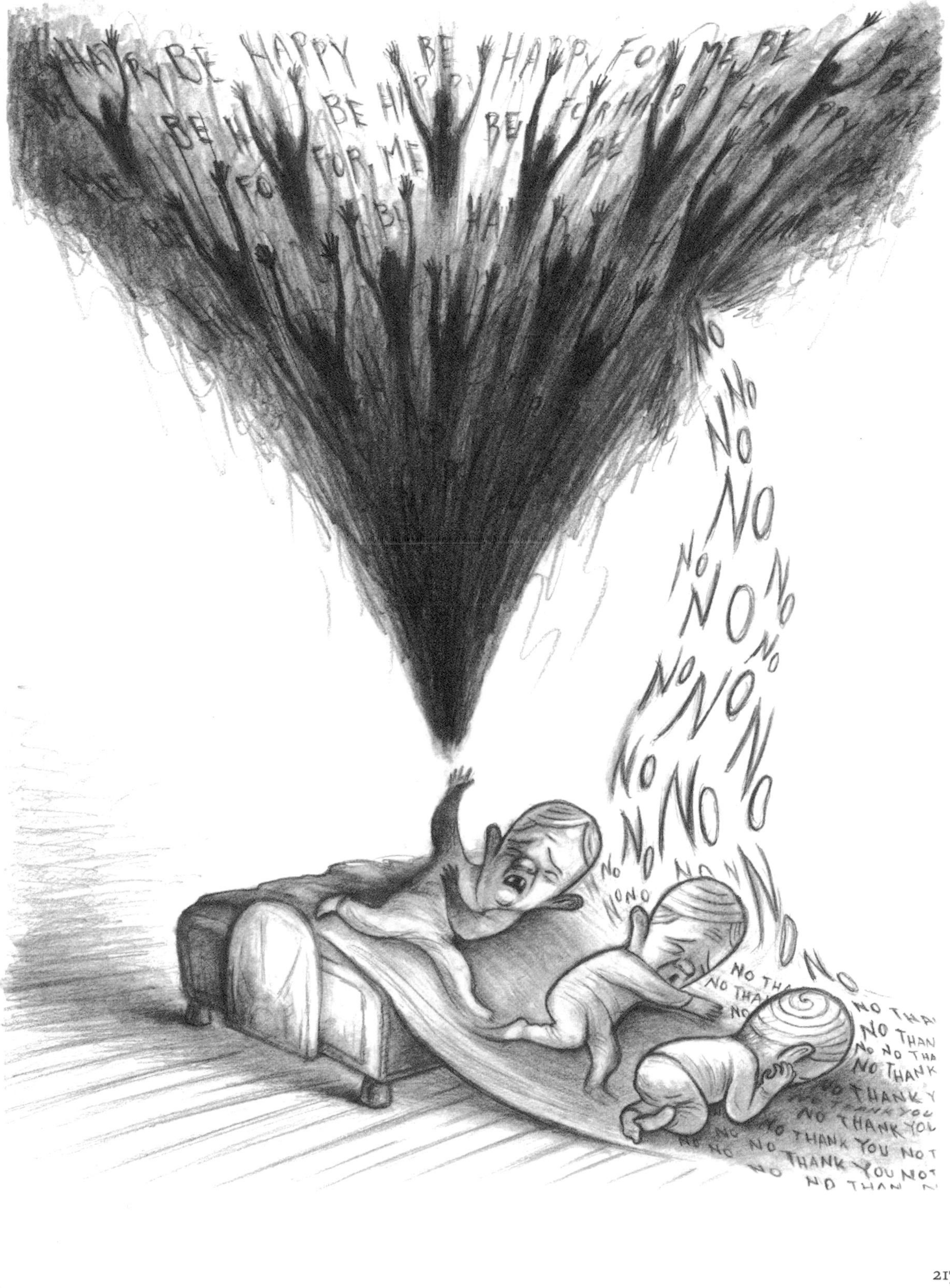
BE HAPPY
BE HAPPY FOR ME
NO
NO THANK YOU

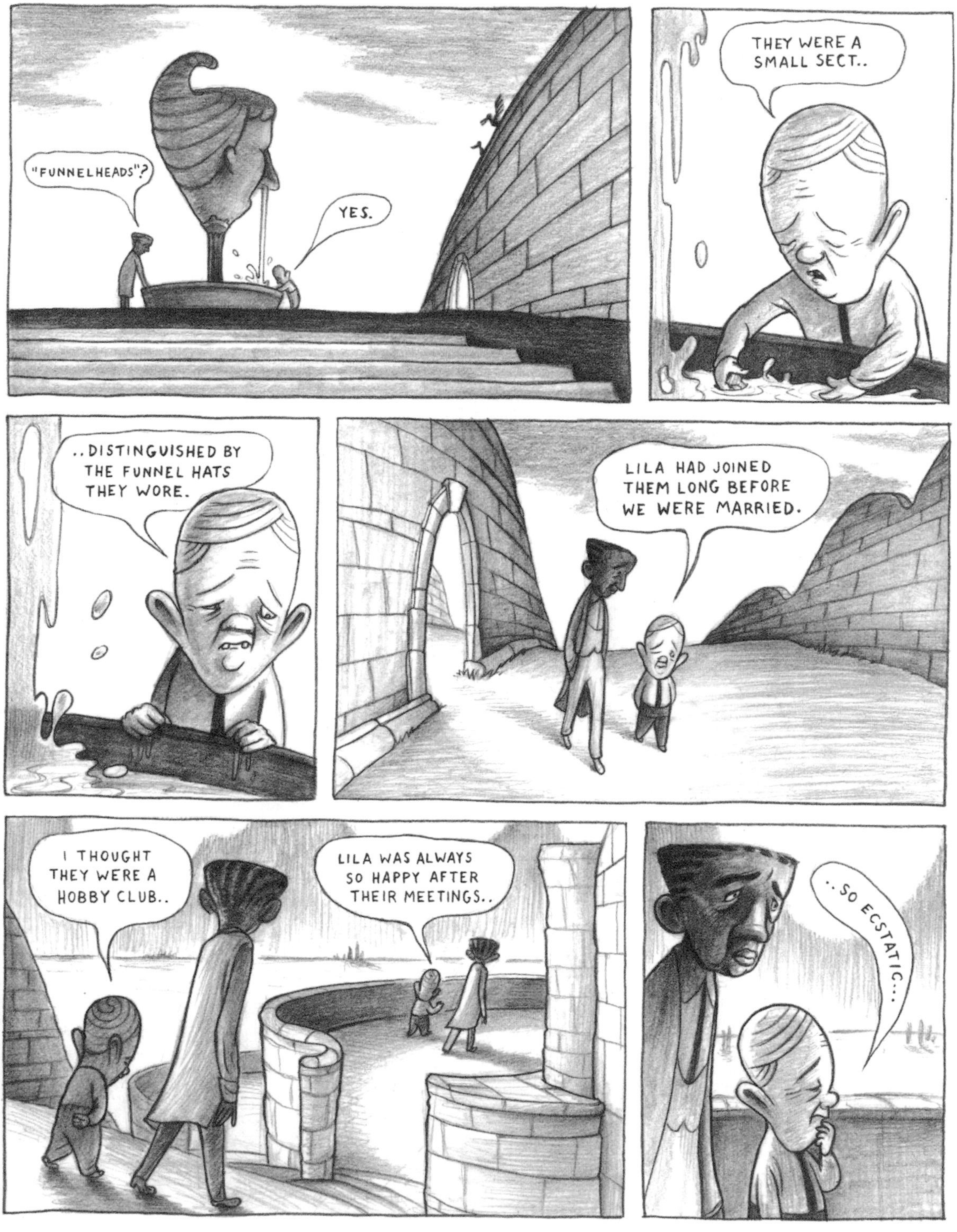
"FUNNELHEADS"?
YES.
THEY WERE A SMALL SECT..
..DISTINGUISHED BY THE FUNNEL HATS THEY WORE.
LILA HAD JOINED THEM LONG BEFORE WE WERE MARRIED.
I THOUGHT THEY WERE A HOBBY CLUB..
LILA WAS ALWAYS SO HAPPY AFTER THEIR MEETINGS..
..SO ECSTATIC...

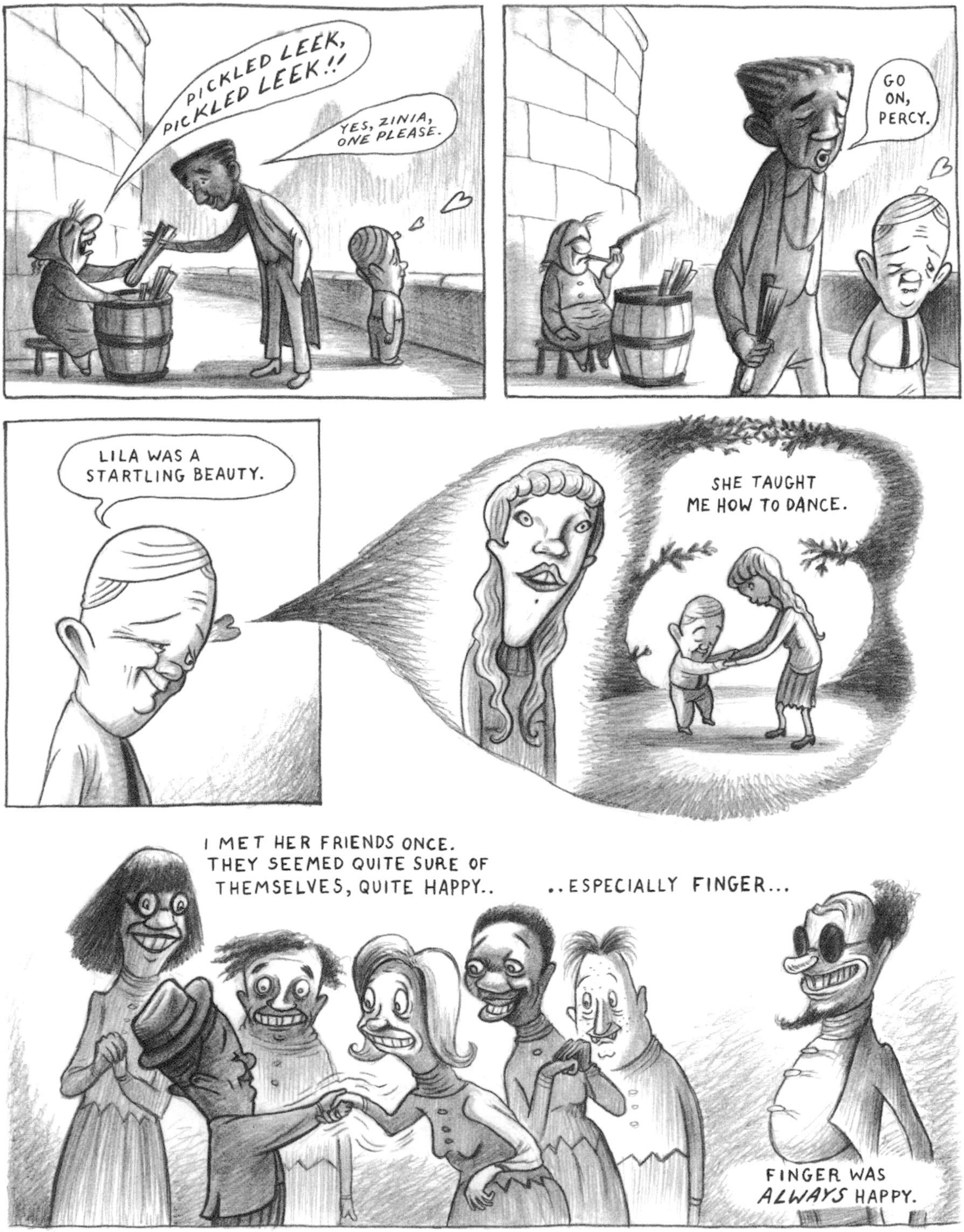
PICKLED LEEK, PICKLED LEEK.!!
YES, ZINIA, ONE PLEASE.
GO ON, PERCY.
LILA WAS A STARTLING BEAUTY.
SHE TAUGHT ME HOW TO DANCE.
I MET HER FRIENDS ONCE. THEY SEEMED QUITE SURE OF THEMSELVES, QUITE HAPPY..
..ESPECIALLY FINGER...
FINGER WAS ALWAYS HAPPY.

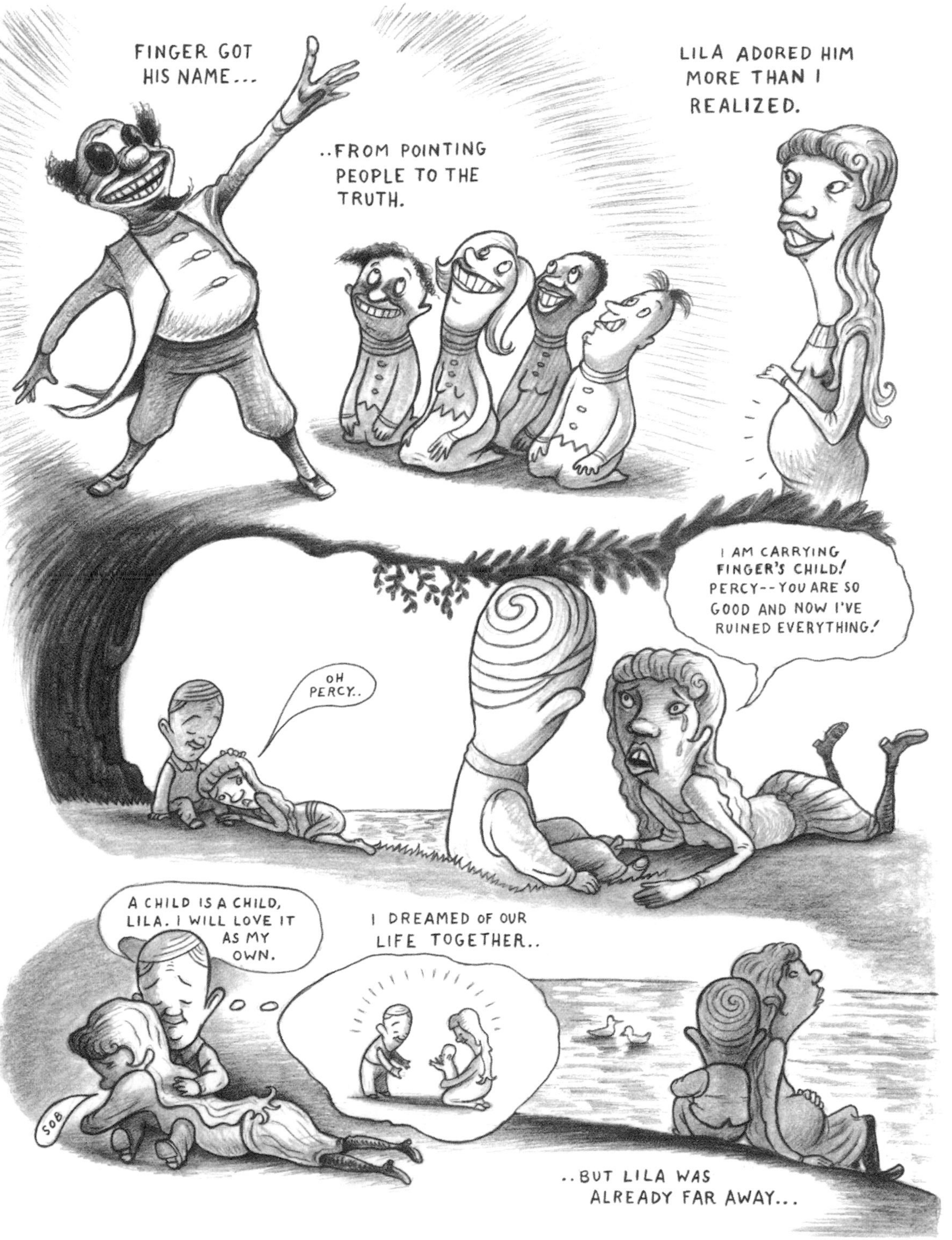
FINGER GOT HIS NAME...
..FROM POINTING PEOPLE TO THE TRUTH.
LILA ADORED HIM MORE THAN I REALIZED.
I AM CARRYING FINGER'S CHILD! PERCY--YOU ARE SO GOOD AND NOW I'VE RUINED EVERYTHING!
OH PERCY..
A CHILD IS A CHILD, LILA. I WILL LOVE IT AS MY OWN.
SOB
I DREAMED OF OUR LIFE TOGETHER..
..BUT LILA WAS ALREADY FAR AWAY...

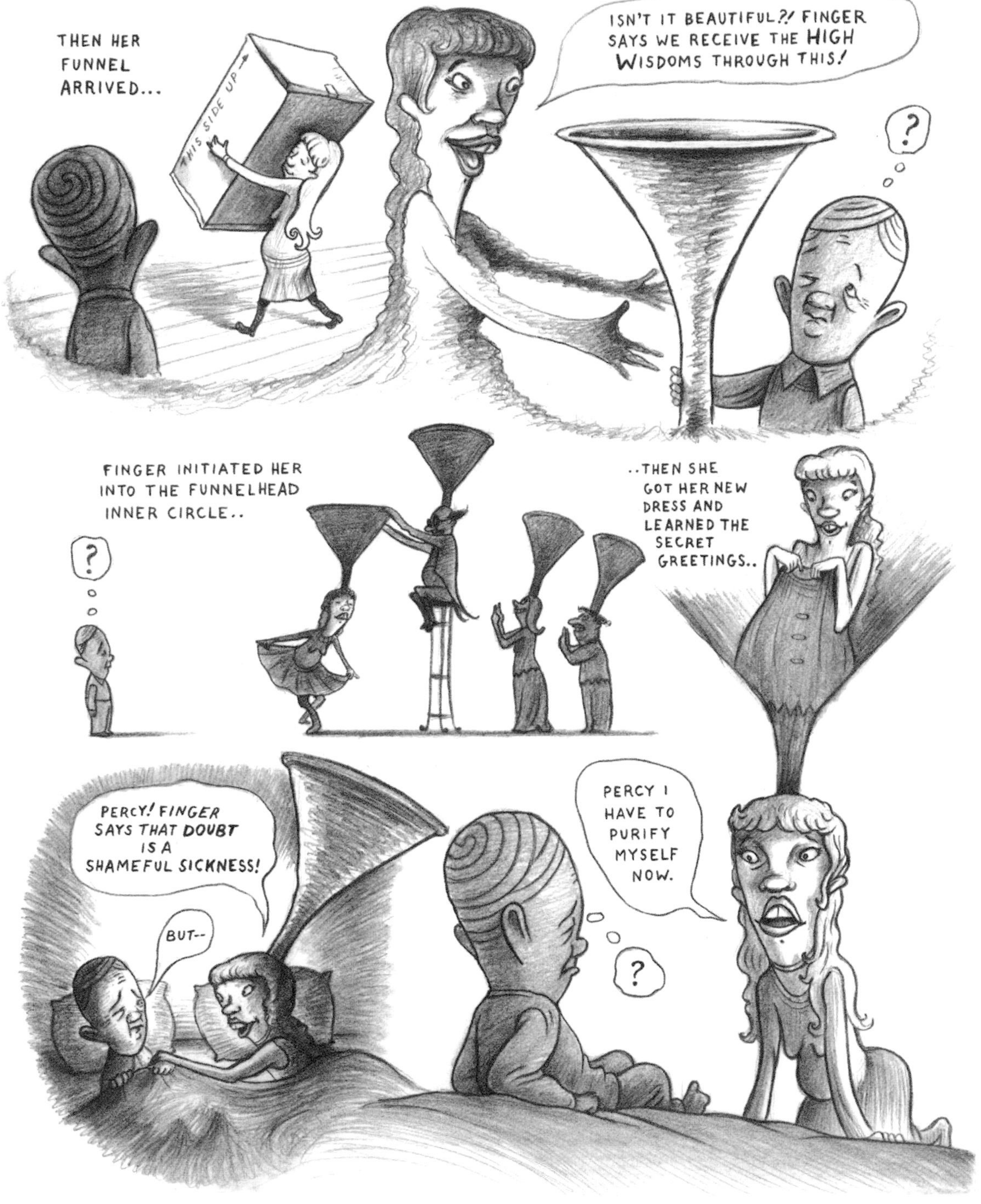
THEN HER FUNNEL ARRIVED...
THIS SIDE UP
ISN'T IT BEAUTIFUL?! FINGER SAYS WE RECEIVE THE HIGH WISDOMS THROUGH THIS!
?
FINGER INITIATED HER INTO THE FUNNELHEAD INNER CIRCLE..
?
..THEN SHE GOT HER NEW DRESS AND LEARNED THE SECRET GREETINGS..
PERCY! FINGER SAYS THAT DOUBT IS A SHAMEFUL SICKNESS!
BUT--
?
PERCY I HAVE TO PURIFY MYSELF NOW.

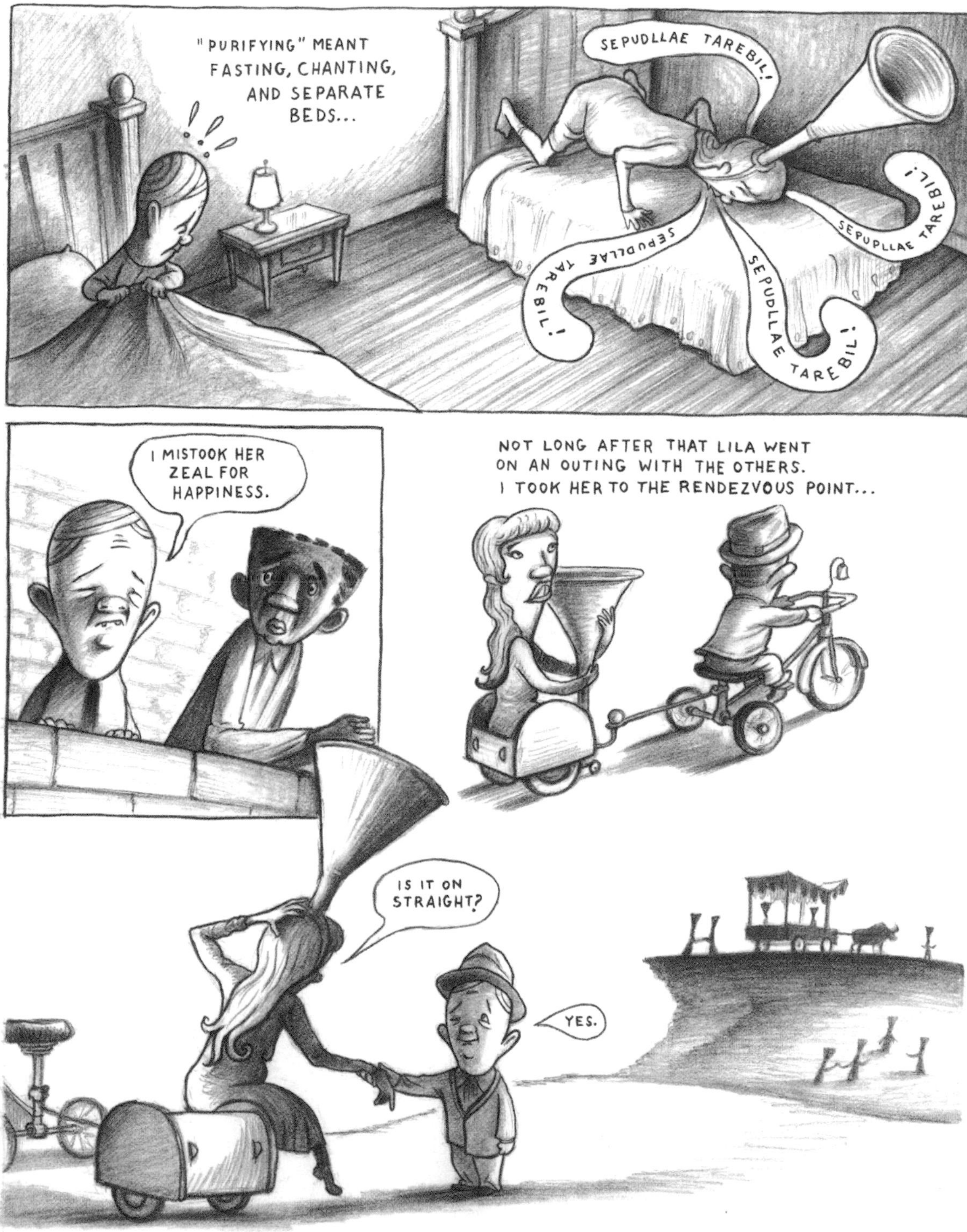

"PURIFYING" MEANT FASTING, CHANTING, AND SEPARATE BEDS...
! !
SEPUDLLAE TAREBIL!
SEPUPLLAE TAREBIL!
SEPUDLLAE TAREBIL!
SEPUDLLAE TAREBIL!
I MISTOOK HER ZEAL FOR HAPPINESS.
NOT LONG AFTER THAT LILA WENT ON AN OUTING WITH THE OTHERS. I TOOK HER TO THE RENDEZVOUS POINT...
IS IT ON STRAIGHT?
YES.

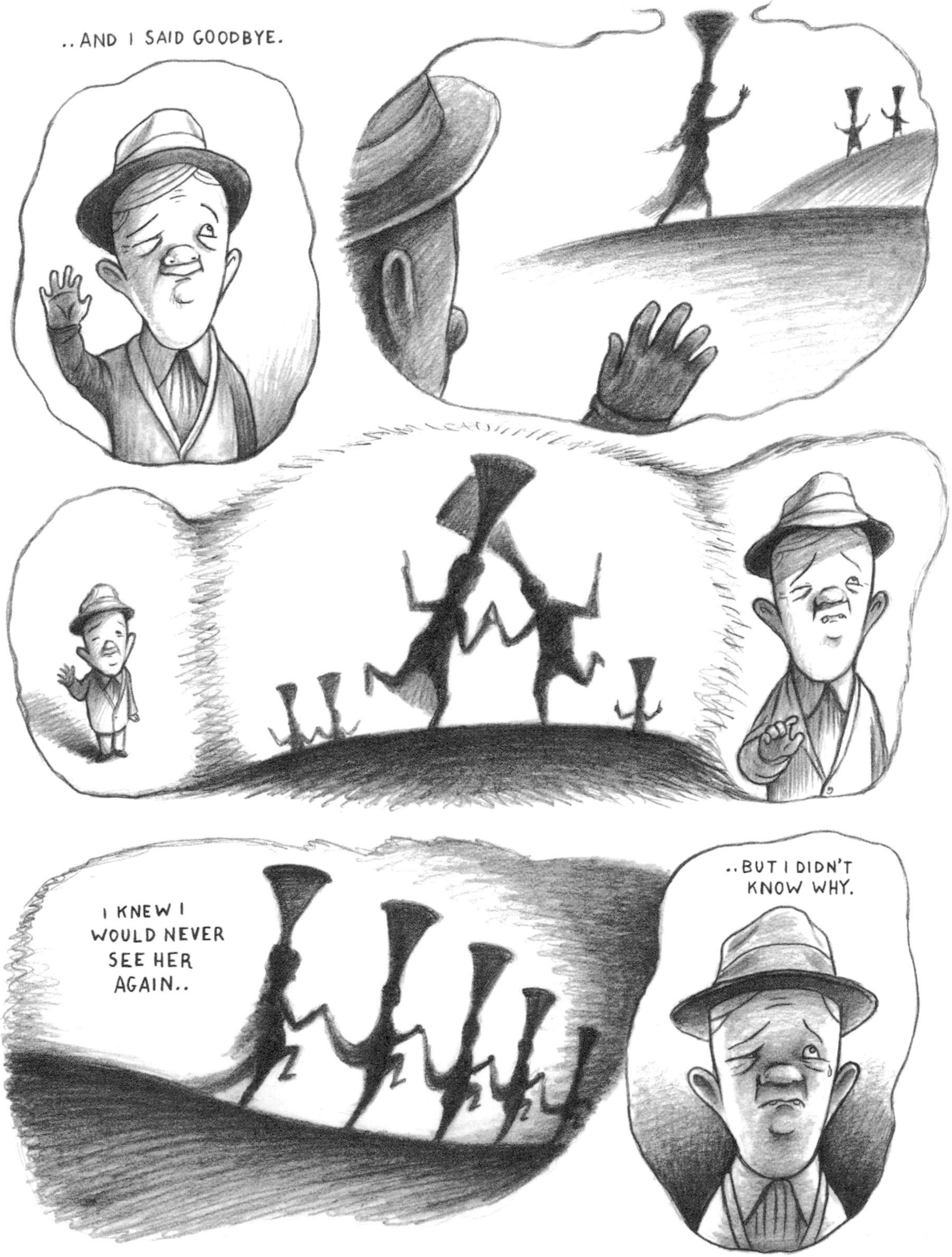
..AND I SAID GOODBYE.
I KNEW I WOULD NEVER SEE HER AGAIN..
..BUT I DIDN'T KNOW WHY.

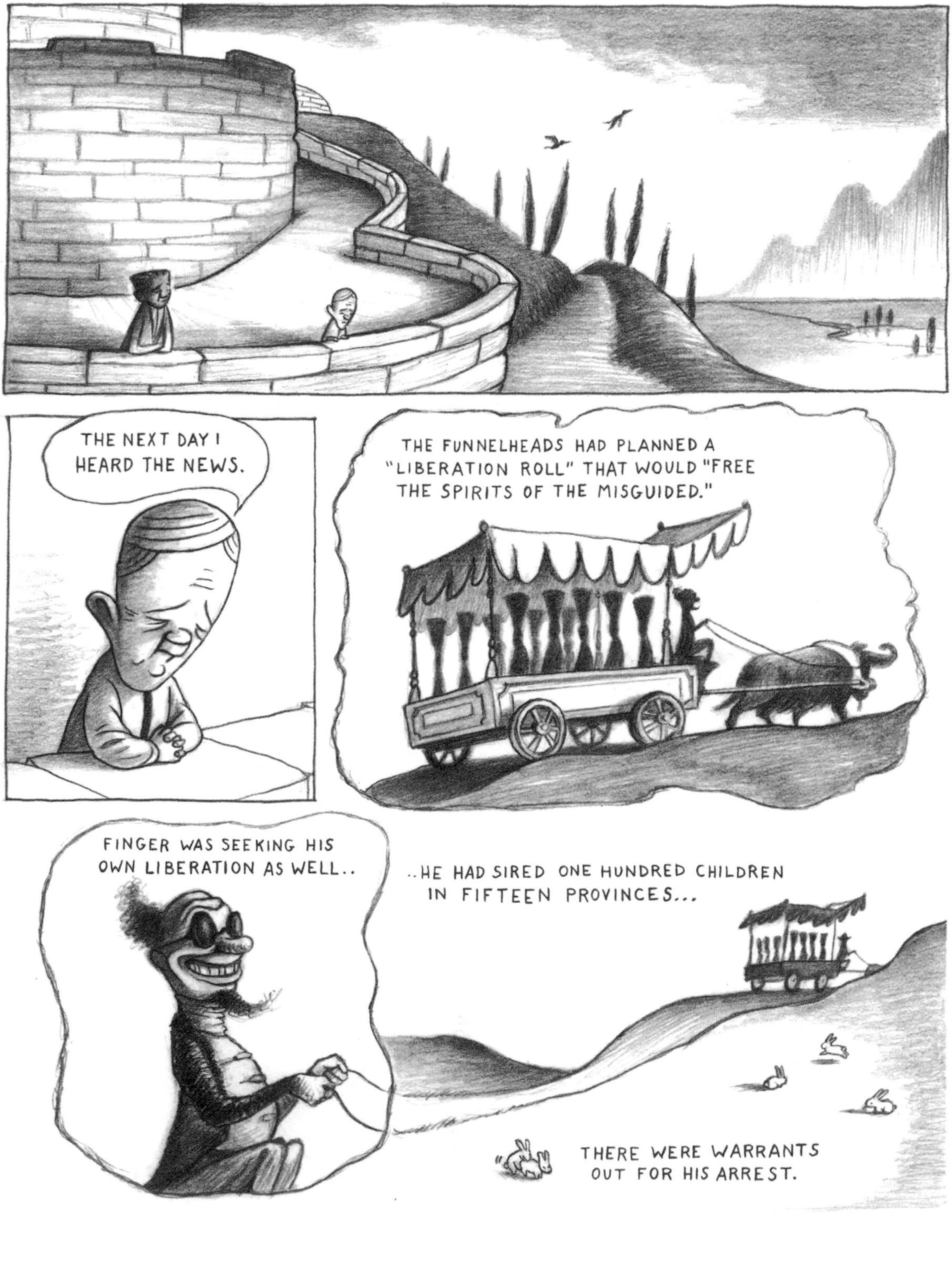
THE NEXT DAY I HEARD THE NEWS.
THE FUNNELHEADS HAD PLANNED A "LIBERATION ROLL" THAT WOULD "FREE THE SPIRITS OF THE MISGUIDED."
FINGER WAS SEEKING HIS OWN LIBERATION AS WELL..
..HE HAD SIRED ONE HUNDRED CHILDREN IN FIFTEEN PROVINCES...
THERE WERE WARRANTS OUT FOR HIS ARREST.

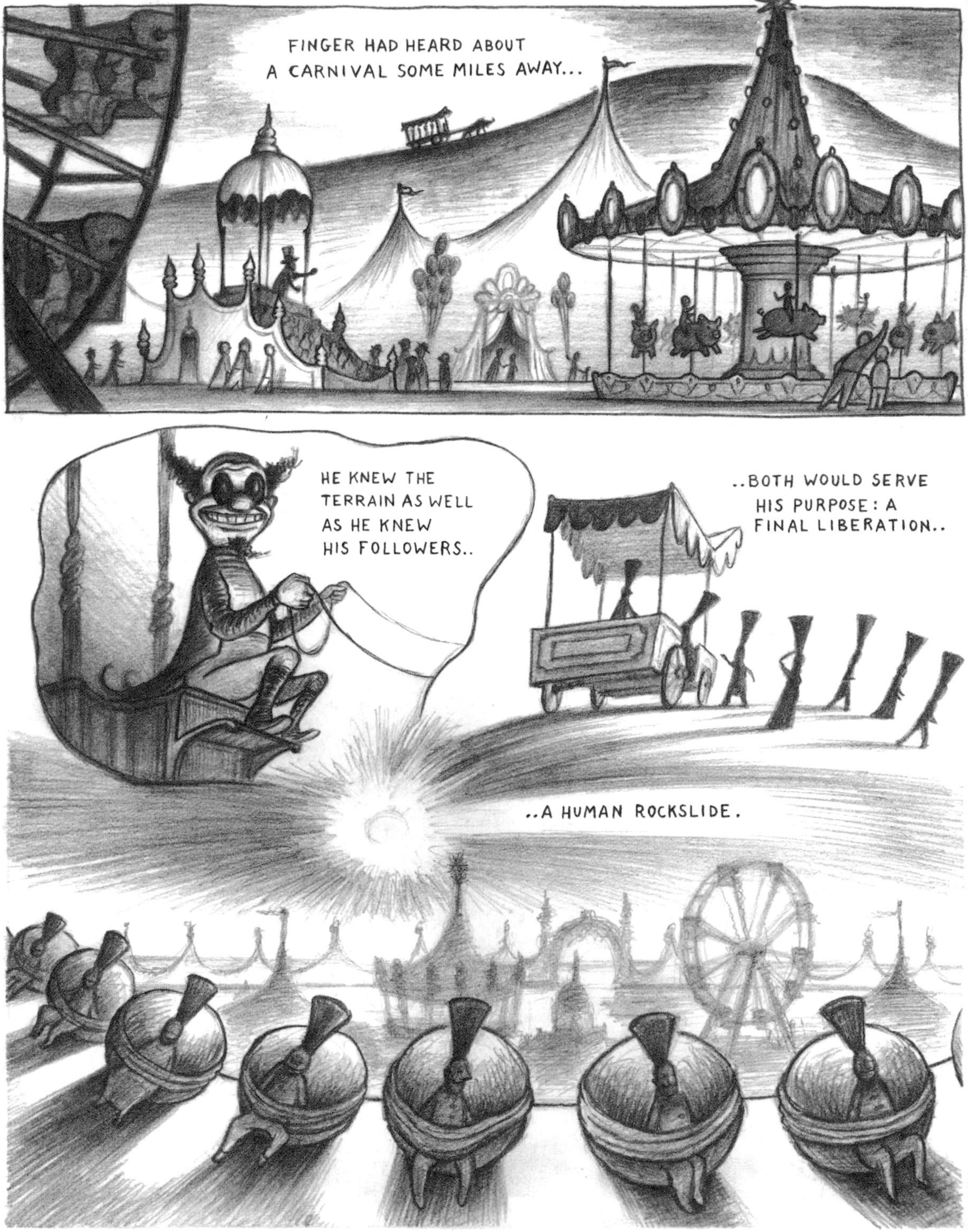
FINGER HAD HEARD ABOUT A CARNIVAL SOME MILES AWAY...
HE KNEW THE TERRAIN AS WELL AS HE KNEW HIS FOLLOWERS..
..BOTH WOULD SERVE HIS PURPOSE: A FINAL LIBERATION..
..A HUMAN ROCKSLIDE.

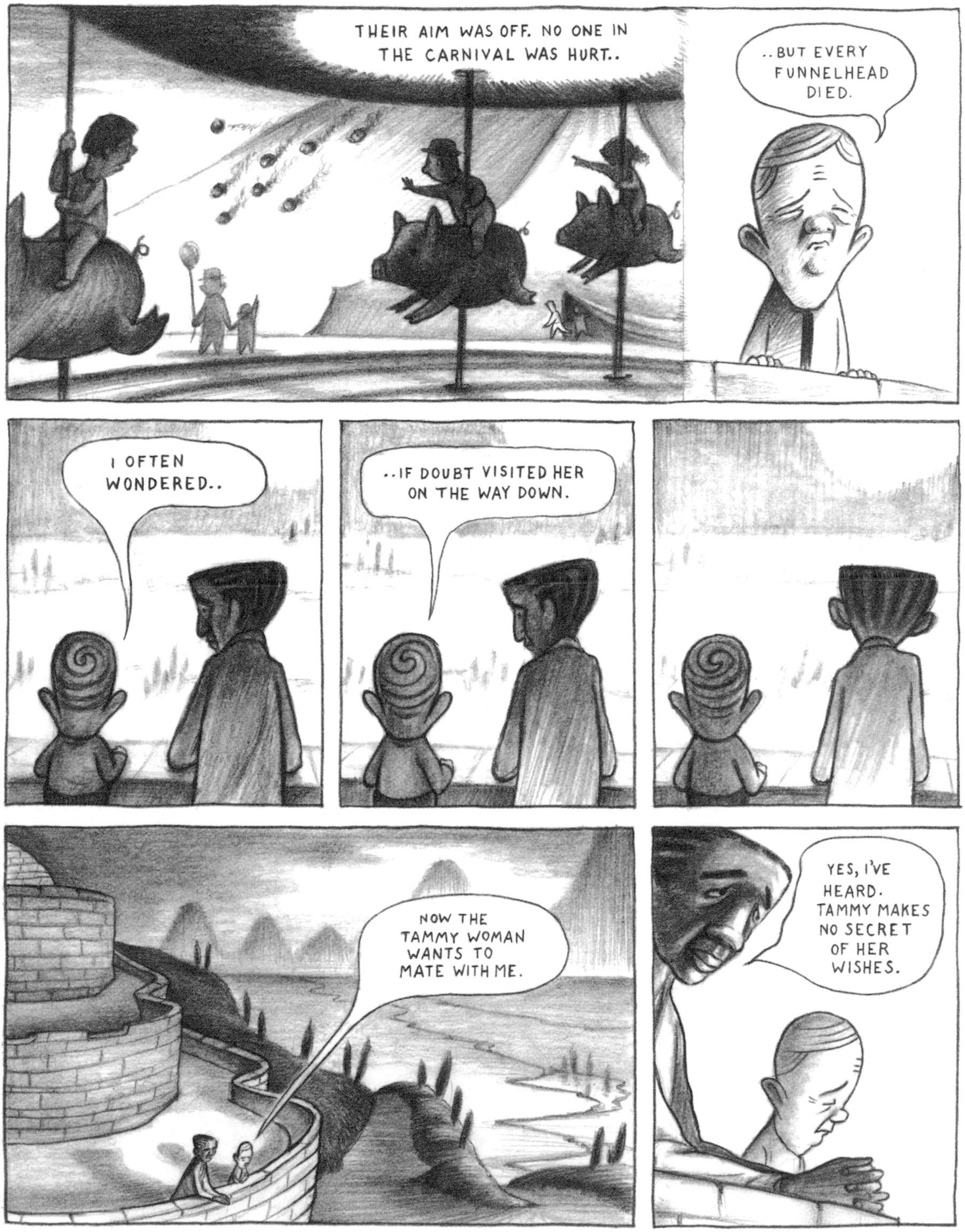
THEIR AIM WAS OFF. NO ONE IN THE CARNIVAL WAS HURT..
..BUT EVERY FUNNELHEAD DIED.
I OFTEN WONDERED..
..IF DOUBT VISITED HER ON THE WAY DOWN.
NOW THE TAMMY WOMAN WANTS TO MATE WITH ME.
YES, I'VE HEARD. TAMMY MAKES NO SECRET OF HER WISHES.

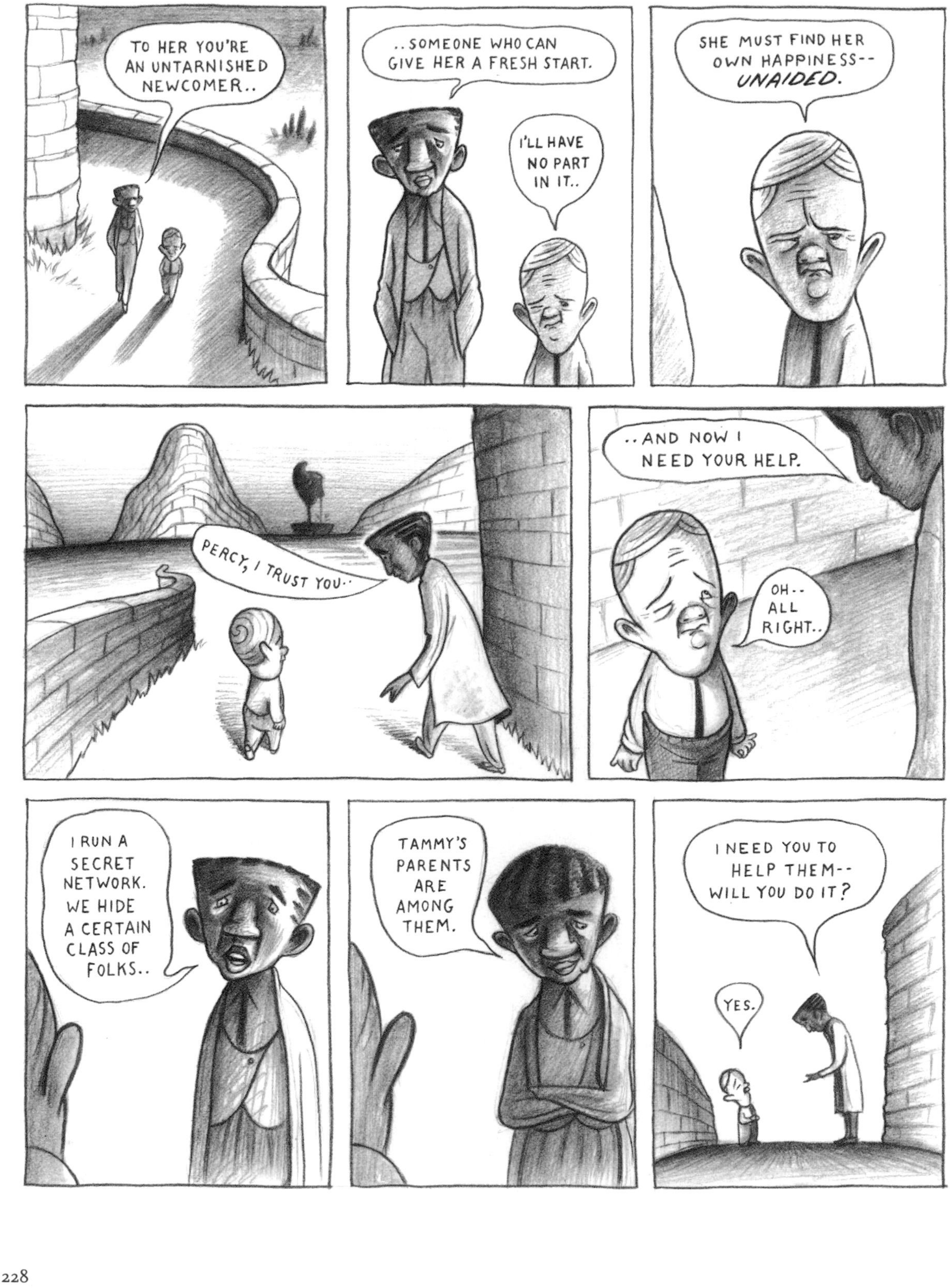
TO HER YOU'RE AN UNTARNISHED NEWCOMER..
..SOMEONE WHO CAN GIVE HER A FRESH START.
I'LL HAVE NO PART IN IT..
SHE MUST FIND HER OWN HAPPINESS-- UNAIDED.
PERCY, I TRUST YOU..
..AND NOW I NEED YOUR HELP.
OH.. ALL RIGHT..
I RUN A SECRET NETWORK. WE HIDE A CERTAIN CLASS OF FOLKS..
TAMMY'S PARENTS ARE AMONG THEM.
I NEED YOU TO HELP THEM-- WILL YOU DO IT?
YES.

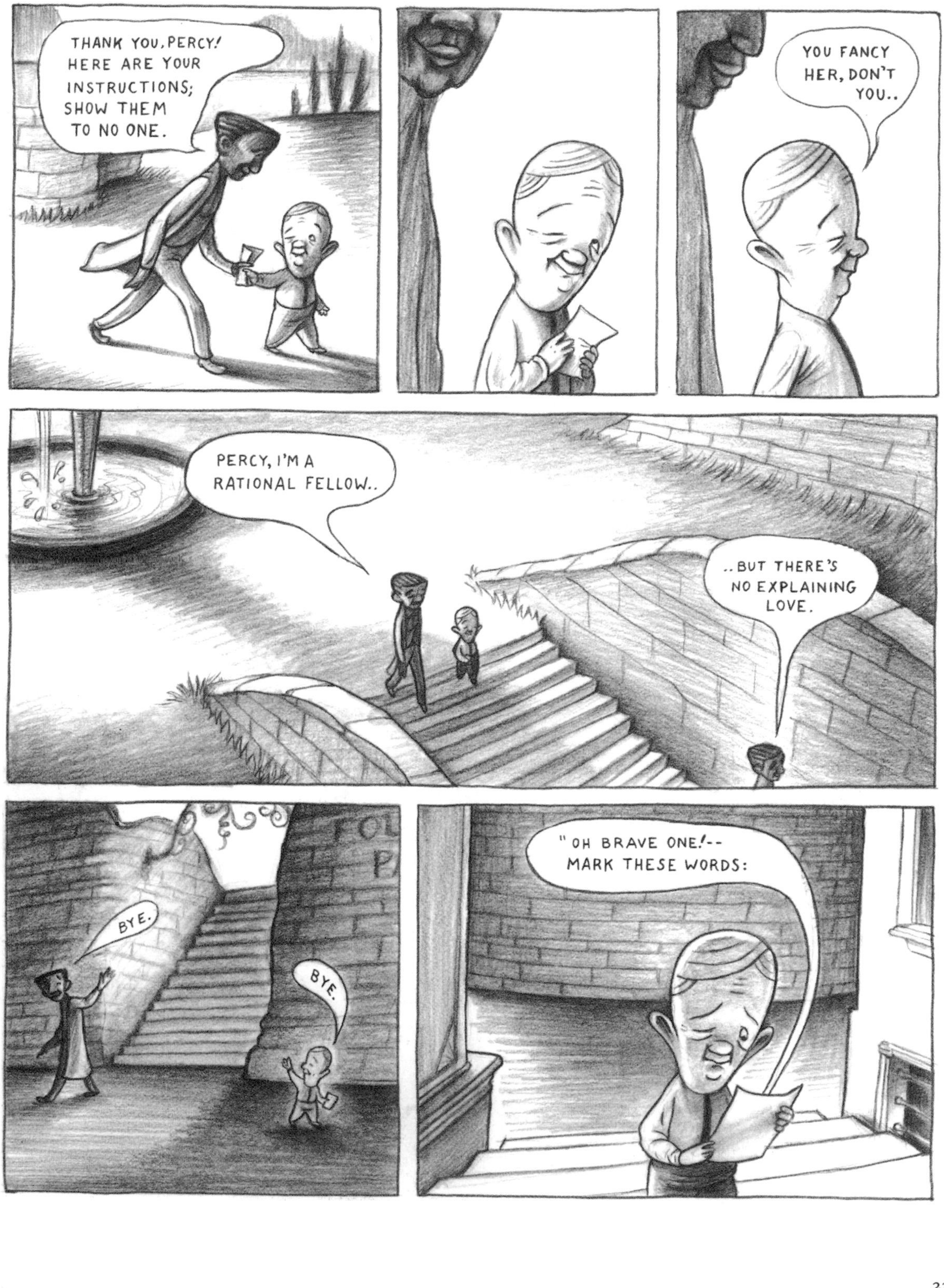
THANK YOU, PERCY! HERE ARE YOUR INSTRUCTIONS; SHOW THEM TO NO ONE.
YOU FANCY HER, DON'T YOU..
PERCY, I'M A RATIONAL FELLOW..
..BUT THERE'S NO EXPLAINING LOVE.
BYE.
BYE.
"OH BRAVE ONE!-- MARK THESE WORDS:

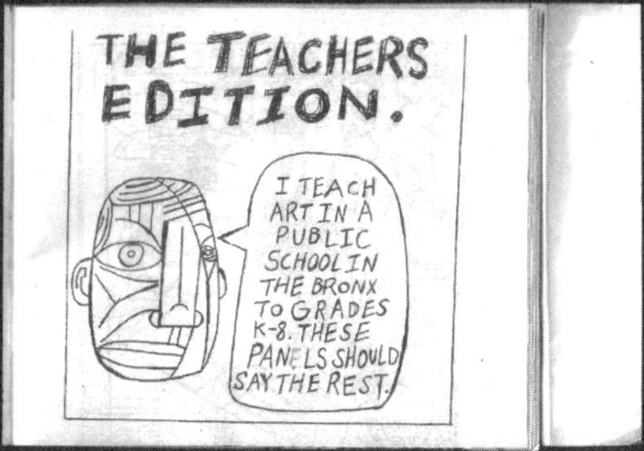
THE TEACHERS EDITION.
I TEACH ART IN A PUBLIC SCHOOL IN THE BRONX TO GRADES K-8. THESE PANELS SHOULD SAY THE REST.

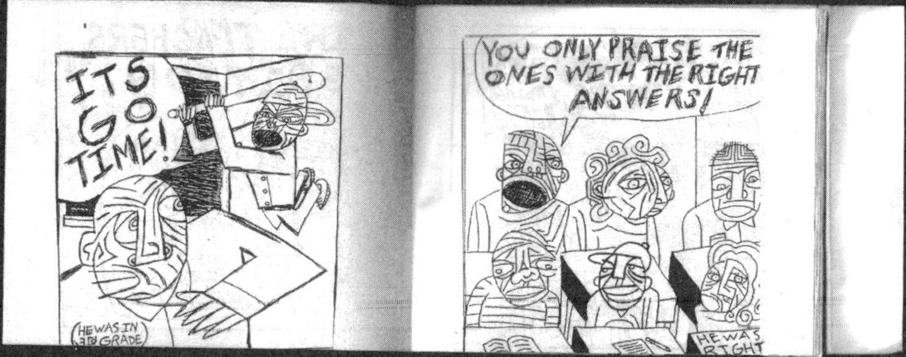
ITS GO TIME!
(HE WAS IN 3RD GRADE)
YOU ONLY PRAISE THE ONES WITH THE RIGHT ANSWERS!
HE WAS RIGHT

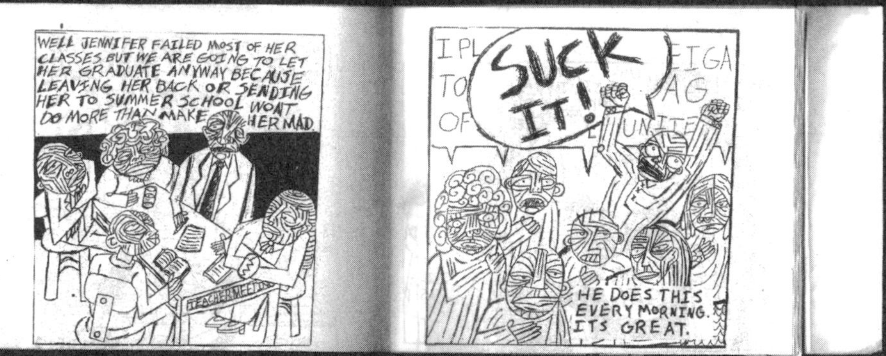
WELL JENNIFER FAILED MOST OF HER CLASSES BUT WE ARE GOING TO LET HER GRADUATE ANYWAY BECAUSE LEAVING HER BACK OR SENDING HER TO SUMMER SCHOOL WONT DO MORE THAN MAKE HER MAD
SUCK IT!
HE DOES THIS EVERY MORNING. ITS GREAT.

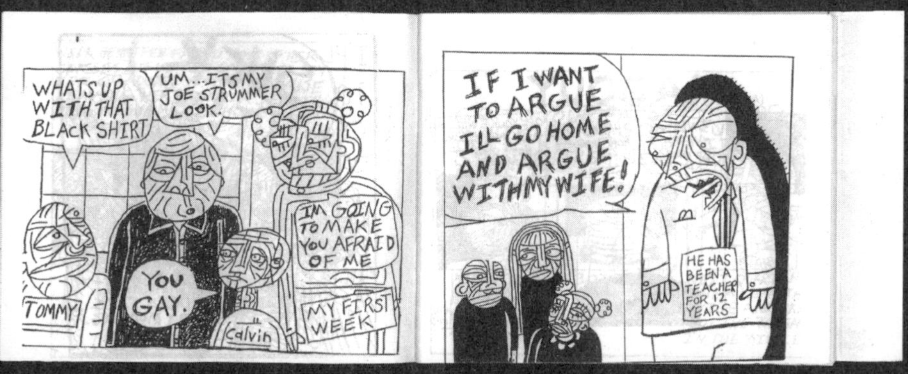
WHATS UP WITH THAT BLACK SHIRT
UM...ITS MY JOE STRUMMER LOOK.
IM GOING TO MAKE YOU AFRAID OF ME
YOU GAY.
TOMMY
Calvin
MY FIRST WEEK
IF I WANT TO ARGUE ILL GO HOME AND ARGUE WITH MY WIFE!
HE HAS BEEN A TEACHER FOR 12 YEARS

JOHN MEJIAS

JAZMINE SIT DOWN
OH...THAT KID
SHE'S SILLY
ISNT IT DISGUSTING ?
I SAW HER EAT GRASS
SHE CRAZY.
JAZMINE! LISTEN!
POOR THING WHAT TO DO?
SHE NEVER SITS STILL
ONE DAY I SPOTTED HER IN CHORUS PRACTICE.
HEY MR. BRENNER, I SEE YOU HAVE JAZMINE PLAYING MARACAS
WELL SHE REALLY COULDNT KEEP UP WITH THE SONG SO...
OK GOOD JOB GUYS! TAKE FIVE
....
HEY MR. BRENNER JAZMIES STILL PLAYING BUT I DONT HEAR ANY SOUND.
NO. I TOOK THE BEANS OUT OF HER MARACAS WEEKS AGO.
ANOTHER TIME, A FEW TEACHER'S PUT ON A PLAY FOR SPANISH HERITAGE MONTH. CAPARUCITA ROJA (LITTLE RED RIDING HOOD) THE WHOL PLAY WAS IN SPANISH. WE WOULD PRACTICE EVERYDAY DURING LUNCH.
¡QUE OJOS TAN GRADE!
AT THE END OF THE PLAY, SOME KIDS WERE SUPPOSED TO SING "ITS A SMALL WORLD".
?
JAZMINE WAS HAVING A BIT OF TROUBLE
JODI (A THIRD GRADE TEACHER) TRIED TO HELP
IF YOU DONT KNOW THE WORDS, JUST SING "PEA'S AND CARROTS"
SO SHE DID
ITS A SMALL WORLD AFTER ALL
PEA'S AND CARROTS

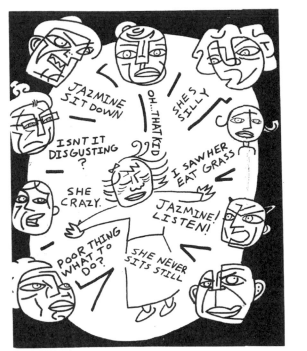

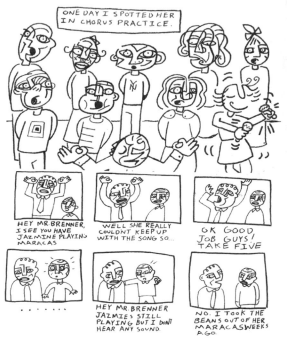

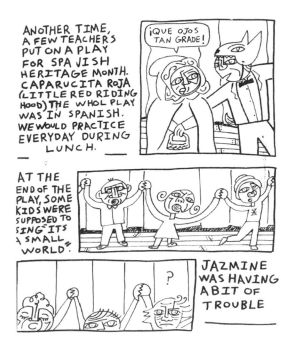

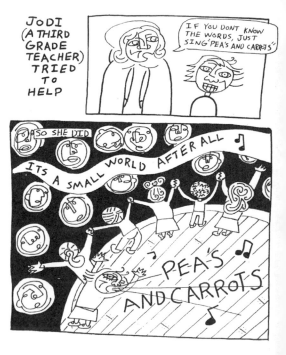

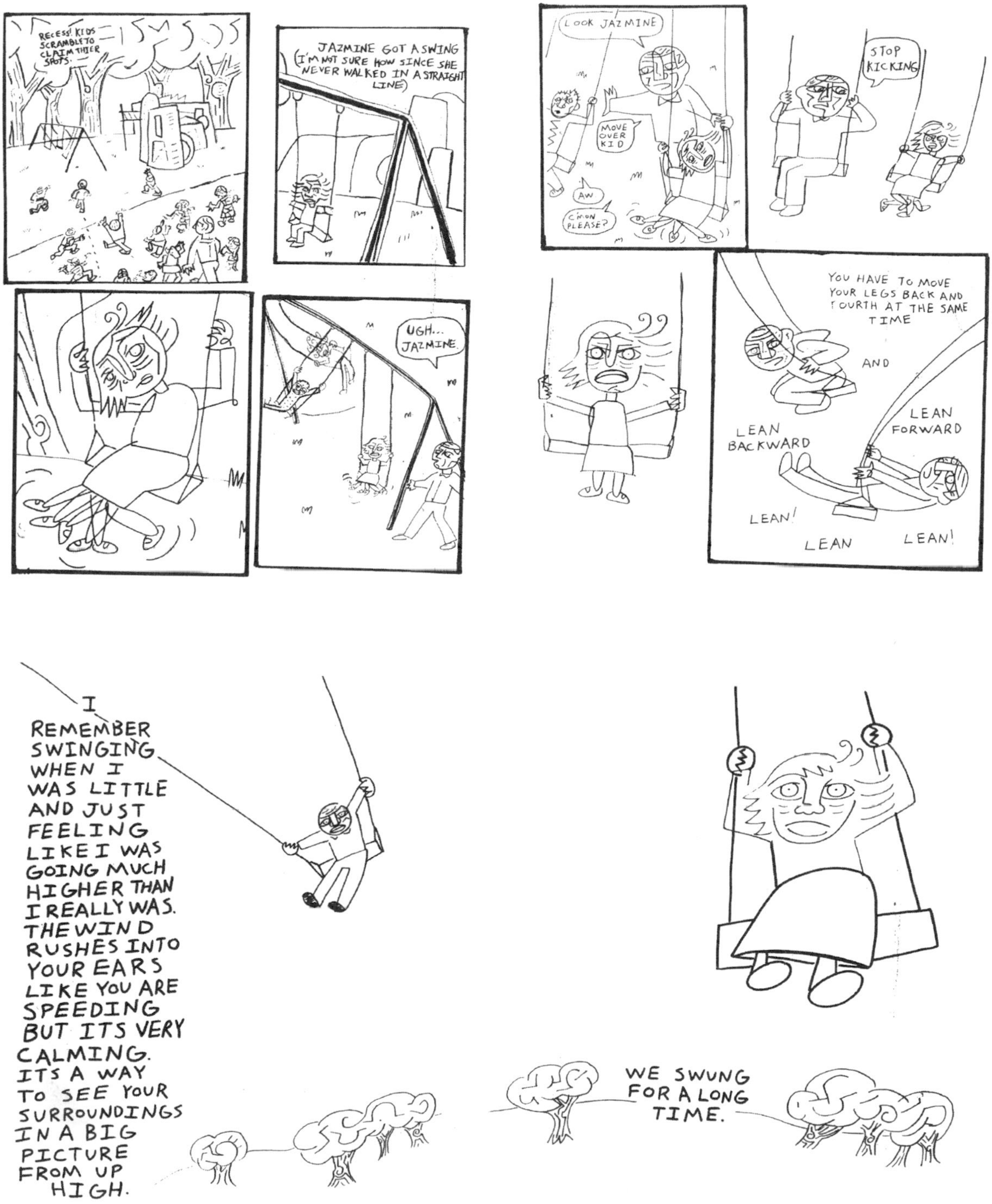
RECESS! KIDS SCRAMBLE TO CLAIM THIER SPOTS.
JAZMINE GOT A SWING (I'M NOT SURE HOW SINCE SHE NEVER WALKED IN A STRAIGHT LINE)
UGH... JAZMINE
LOOK JAZMINE
MOVE OVER KID
AW
C'MON PLEASE?
STOP KICKING
YOU HAVE TO MOVE YOUR LEGS BACK AND FOURTH AT THE SAME TIME
AND
LEAN BACKWARD
LEAN FORWARD
LEAN!
LEAN
LEAN!
I REMEMBER SWINGING WHEN I WAS LITTLE AND JUST FEELING LIKE I WAS GOING MUCH HIGHER THAN I REALLY WAS. THE WIND RUSHES INTO YOUR EARS LIKE YOU ARE SPEEDING BUT ITS VERY CALMING. ITS A WAY TO SEE YOUR SURROUNDINGS IN A BIG PICTURE FROM UP HIGH.
WE SWUNG FOR A LONG TIME.

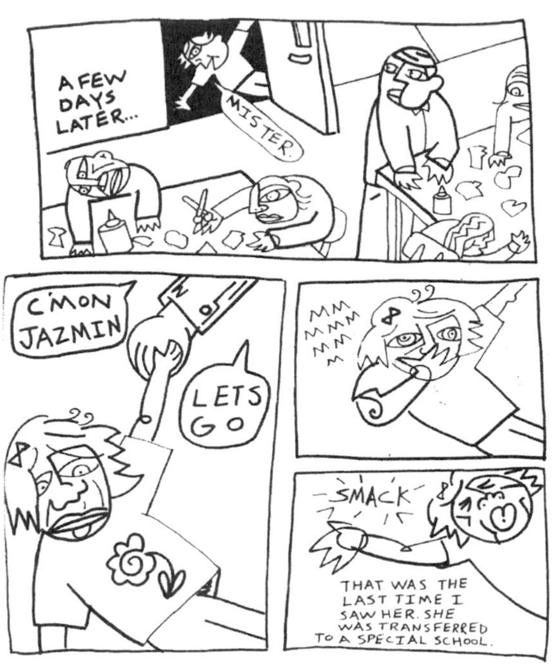
A FEW DAYS LATER...
MISTER
C'MON JAZMIN
LETS GO
MM MMM MM M
SMACK
THAT WAS THE LAST TIME I SAW HER. SHE WAS TRANSFERRED TO A SPECIAL SCHOOL.

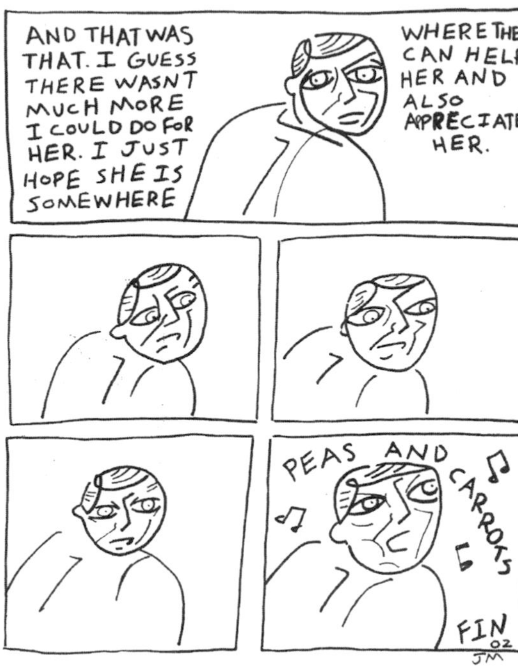
AND THAT WAS THAT. I GUESS THERE WASNT MUCH MORE I COULD DO FOR HER. I JUST HOPE SHE IS SOMEWHERE
WHERE THEY CAN HELP HER AND ALSO APPRECIATE HER.
PEAS AND CARROTS
FIN 02
JM

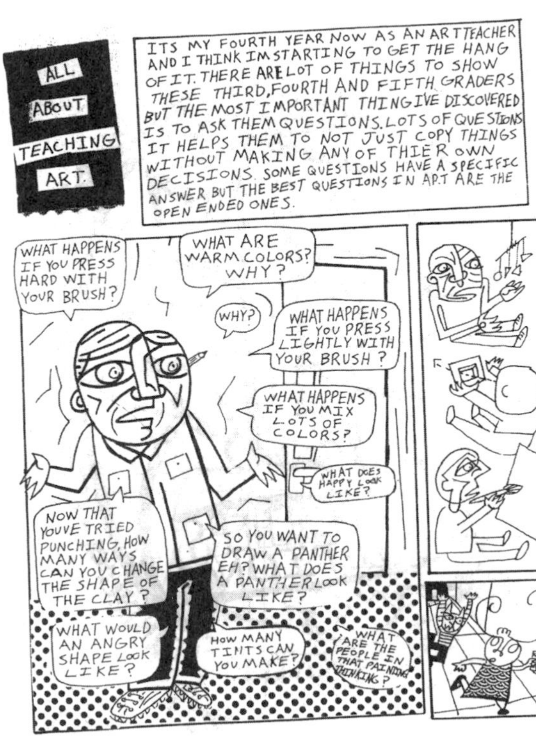
ALL ABOUT TEACHING ART.
ITS MY FOURTH YEAR NOW AS AN ART TEACHER AND I THINK IM STARTING TO GET THE HANG OF IT. THERE ARE LOT OF THINGS TO SHOW THESE THIRD, FOURTH AND FIFTH GRADERS BUT THE MOST IMPORTANT THING IVE DISCOVERED IS TO ASK THEM QUESTIONS. LOTS OF QUESTIONS IT HELPS THEM TO NOT JUST COPY THINGS WITHOUT MAKING ANY OF THIER OWN DECISIONS. SOME QUESTIONS HAVE A SPECIFIC ANSWER BUT THE BEST QUESTIONS IN ART ARE THE OPEN ENDED ONES.
WHAT HAPPENS IF YOU PRESS HARD WITH YOUR BRUSH?
WHAT ARE WARM COLORS? WHY?
WHY?
WHAT HAPPENS IF YOU PRESS LIGHTLY WITH YOUR BRUSH?
WHAT HAPPENS IF YOU MIX LOTS OF COLORS?
WHAT DOES HAPPY LOOK LIKE?
NOW THAT YOUVE TRIED PUNCHING, HOW MANY WAYS CAN YOU CHANGE THE SHAPE OF THE CLAY?
SO YOU WANT TO DRAW A PANTHER EH? WHAT DOES A PANTHER LOOK LIKE?
WHAT WOULD AN ANGRY SHAPE LOOK LIKE?
HOW MANY TINTS CAN YOU MAKE?
WHAT ARE THE PEOPLE IN THAT PAINTING THINKING?

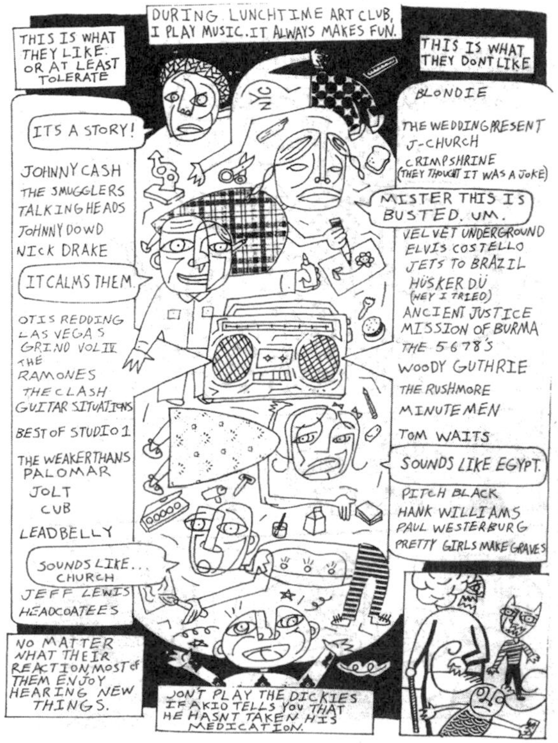
DURING LUNCHTIME ART CLUB, I PLAY MUSIC. IT ALWAYS MAKES FUN.
THIS IS WHAT THEY LIKE. OR AT LEAST TOLERATE
THIS IS WHAT THEY DONT LIKE
NYC
ITS A STORY!
JOHNNY CASH
THE SMUGGLERS
TALKING HEADS
JOHNNY DOWD
NICK DRAKE
IT CALMS THEM.
OTIS REDDING
LAS VEGAS GRIND VOL II
THE RAMONES
THE CLASH
GUITAR SITUATIONS
BEST OF STUDIO 1
THE WEAKERTHANS
PALOMAR
JOLT
CUB
LEADBELLY
SOUNDS LIKE... CHURCH
JEFF LEWIS
HEADCOATEES
BLONDIE
THE WEDDING PRESENT
J-CHURCH
CRIMPSHRINE (THEY THOUGHT IT WAS A JOKE)
MISTER THIS IS BUSTED. UM.
VELVET UNDERGROUND
ELVIS COSTELLO
JETS TO BRAZIL
HÜSKER DÜ (HEY I TRIED)
ANCIENT JUSTICE
MISSION OF BURMA
THE 5678'S
WOODY GUTHRIE
THE RUSHMORE
MINUTEMEN
TOM WAITS
SOUNDS LIKE EGYPT.
PITCH BLACK
HANK WILLIAMS
PAUL WESTERBURG
PRETTY GIRLS MAKE GRAVES
NO MATTER WHAT THEIR REACTION, MOST OF THEM ENJOY HEARING NEW THINGS.
DON'T PLAY THE DICKIES IF AKIO TELLS YOU THAT HE HASNT TAKEN HIS MEDICATION.

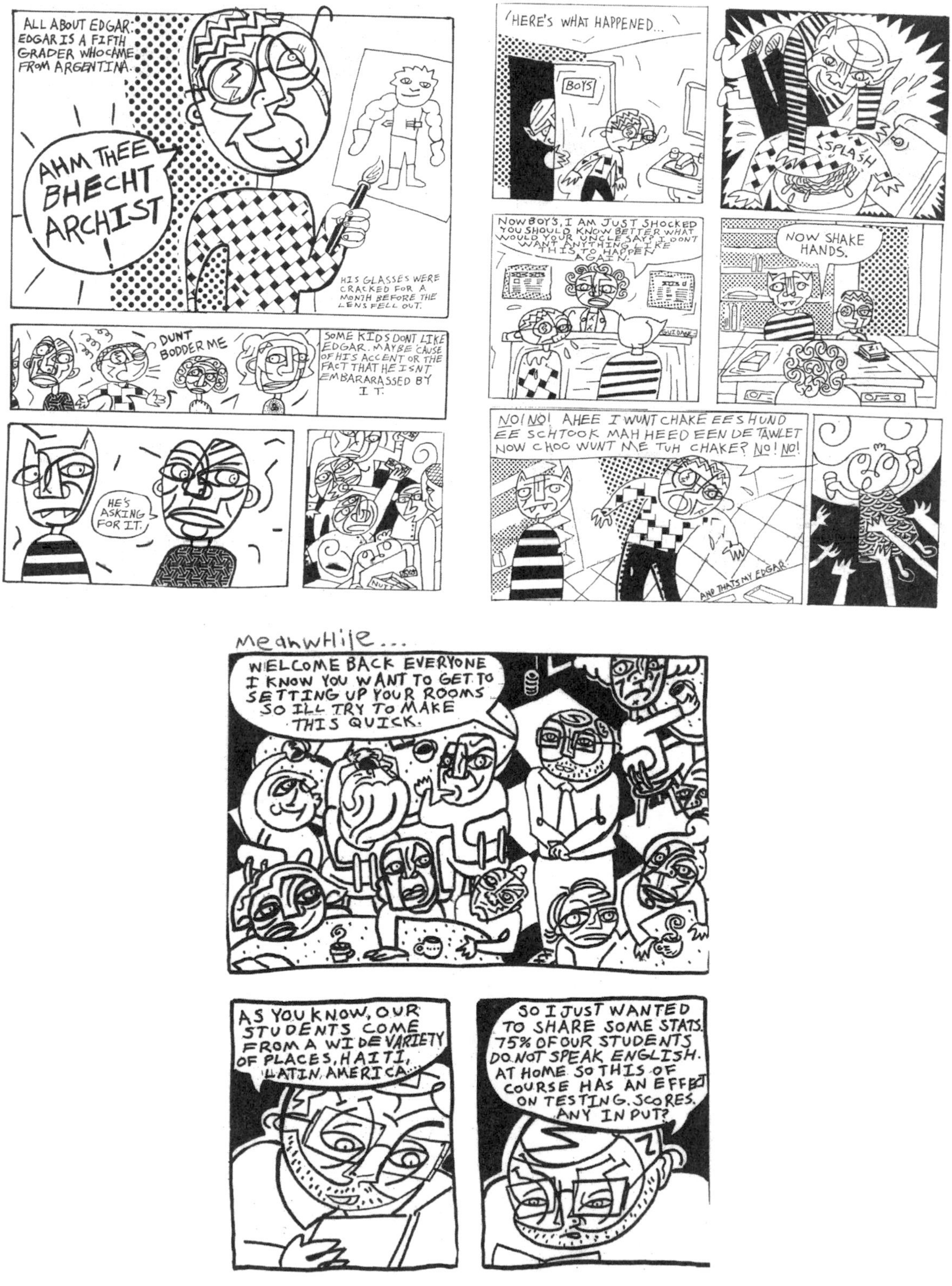
ALL ABOUT EDGAR: EDGAR IS A FIFTH GRADER WHO CAME FROM ARGENTINA.
AHM THEE BHECHT ARCHIST!
HIS GLASSES WERE CRACKED FOR A MONTH BEFORE THE LENS FELL OUT.
DUNT BODDER ME
SOME KIDS DONT LIKE EDGAR. MAYBE CAUSE OF HIS ACCENT OR THE FACT THAT HE ISNT EMBARARASSED BY IT.
HE'S ASKING FOR IT.
HERE'S WHAT HAPPENED...
BOYS
SPLASH
NOW BOY'S, I AM JUST SHOCKED YOU SHOULD KNOW BETTER WHAT WOULD YOUR UNCLE SAY? I DONT WANT ANYTHING LIKE THIS TO HAPPEN AGAIN.
GUIDANCE
NOW SHAKE HANDS.
NO! NO! AHEE I WUNT CHAKE EES HUND EE SCHTOOK MAH HEED EEN DE TAWLET NOW CHOO WUNT ME TUH CHAKE? NO! NO!
AND THAT'S MY EDGAR
MeanwHile...
WELCOME BACK EVERYONE I KNOW YOU WANT TO GET TO SETTING UP YOUR ROOMS SO ILL TRY TO MAKE THIS QUICK.
AS YOU KNOW, OUR STUDENTS COME FROM A WIDE VARIETY OF PLACES, HAITI, LATIN AMERICA...
SO I JUST WANTED TO SHARE SOME STATS. 75% OF OUR STUDENTS DO NOT SPEAK ENGLISH AT HOME SO THIS OF COURSE HAS AN EFFECT ON TESTING SCORES. ANY INPUT?

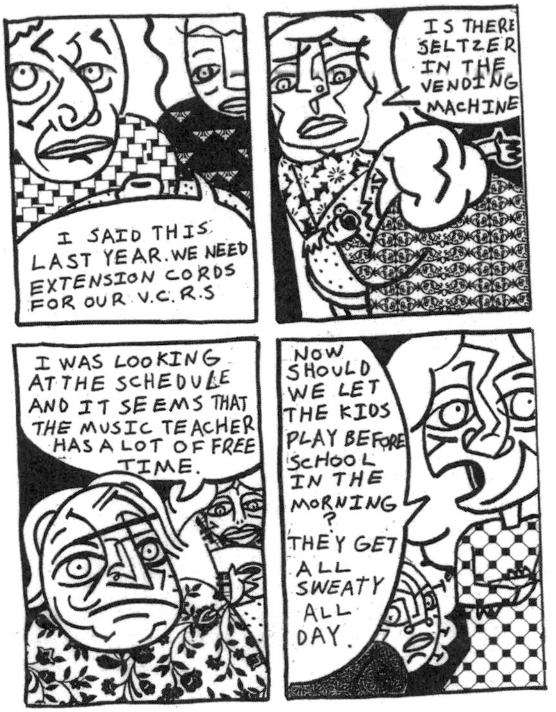
I SAID THIS LAST YEAR. WE NEED EXTENSION CORDS FOR OUR V.C.R.S
IS THERE SELTZER IN THE VENDING MACHINE
I WAS LOOKING AT THE SCHEDULE AND IT SEEMS THAT THE MUSIC TEACHER HAS A LOT OF FREE TIME.
NOW SHOULD WE LET THE KIDS PLAY BEFORE SCHOOL IN THE MORNING ? THEY GET ALL SWEATY ALL DAY.

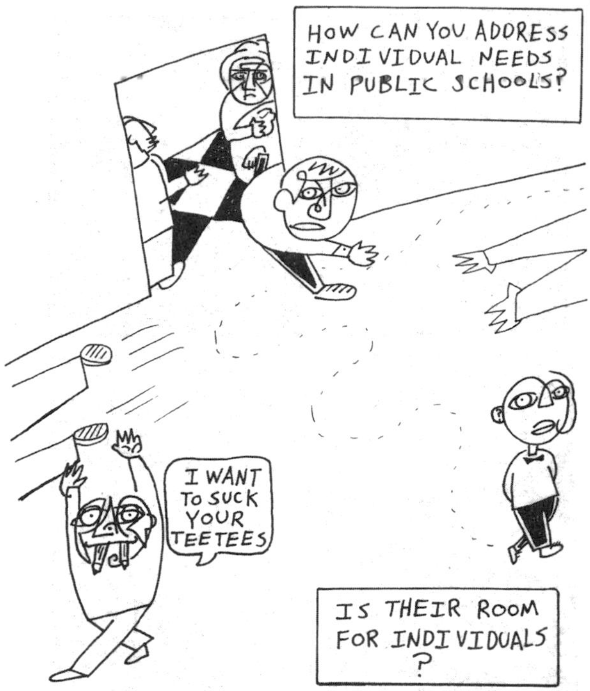
HOW CAN YOU ADDRESS INDIVIDUAL NEEDS IN PUBLIC SCHOOLS?
I WANT TO SUCK YOUR TEETEES
IS THEIR ROOM FOR INDIVIDUALS ?

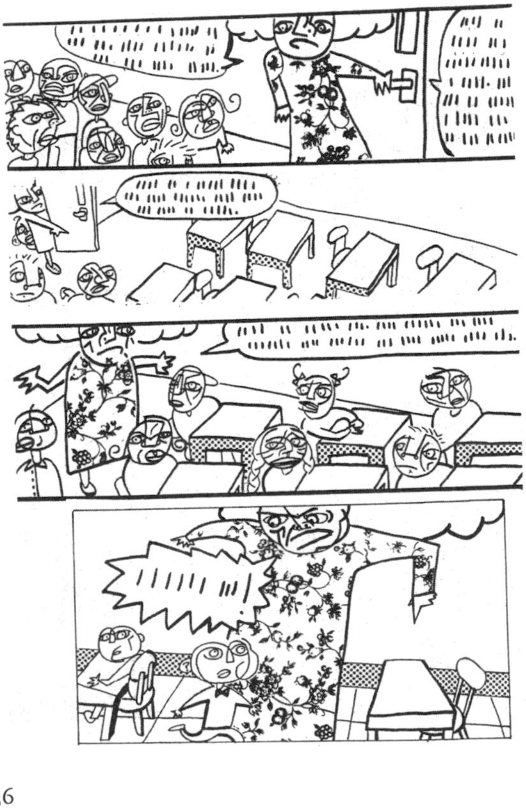

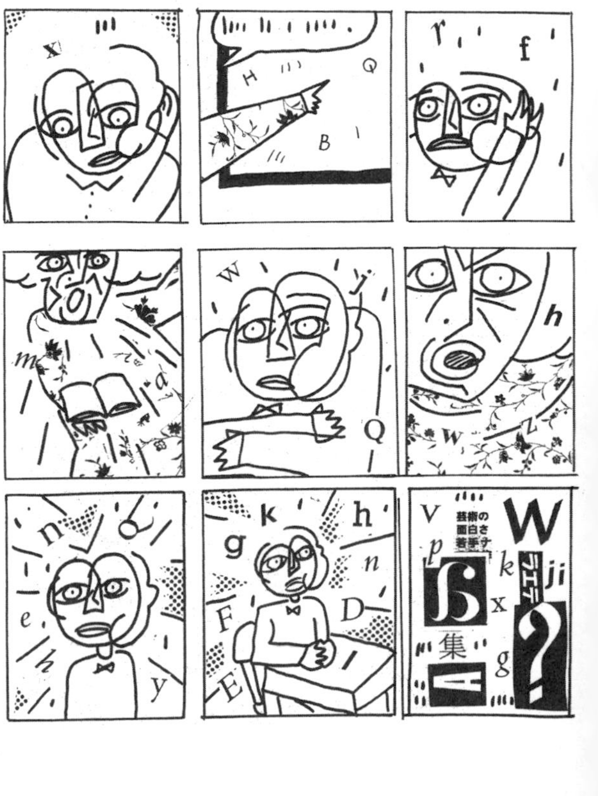

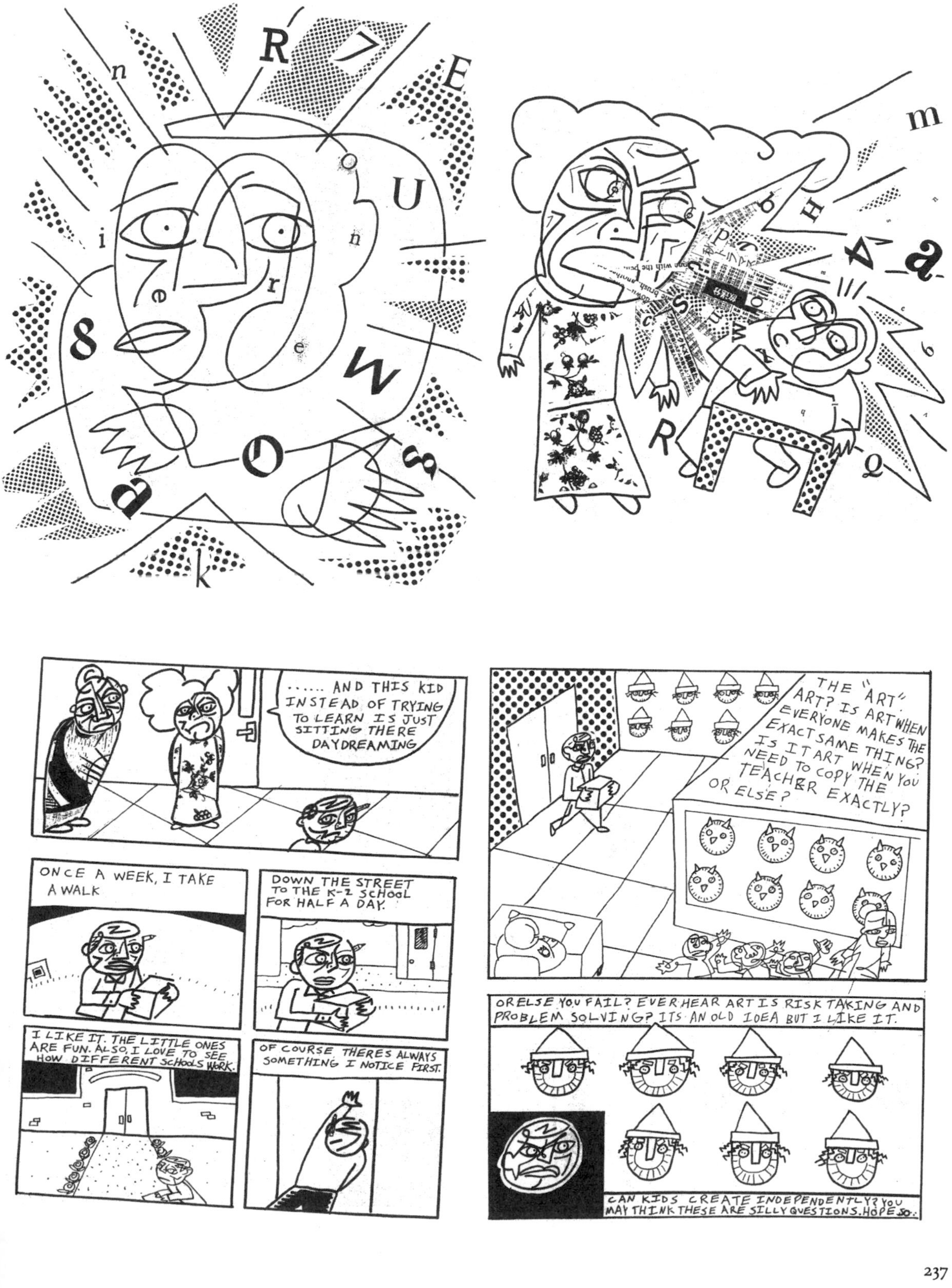

...... AND THIS KID INSTEAD OF TRYING TO LEARN IS JUST SITTING THERE DAYDREAMING
ONCE A WEEK, I TAKE A WALK
DOWN THE STREET TO THE K-2 SCHOOL FOR HALF A DAY.
I LIKE IT. THE LITTLE ONES ARE FUN. ALSO, I LOVE TO SEE HOW DIFFERENT SCHOOLS WORK.
OF COURSE THERES ALWAYS SOMETHING I NOTICE FIRST.
THE "ART" ART? IS ART WHEN EVERYONE MAKES THE EXACT SAME THING? IS IT ART WHEN YOU NEED TO COPY THE TEACHER EXACTLY? OR ELSE?
OR ELSE YOU FAIL? EVER HEAR ART IS RISK TAKING AND PROBLEM SOLVING? ITS AN OLD IDEA BUT I LIKE IT.
CAN KIDS CREATE INDEPENDENTLY? YOU MAY THINK THESE ARE SILLY QUESTIONS. HOPE SO.

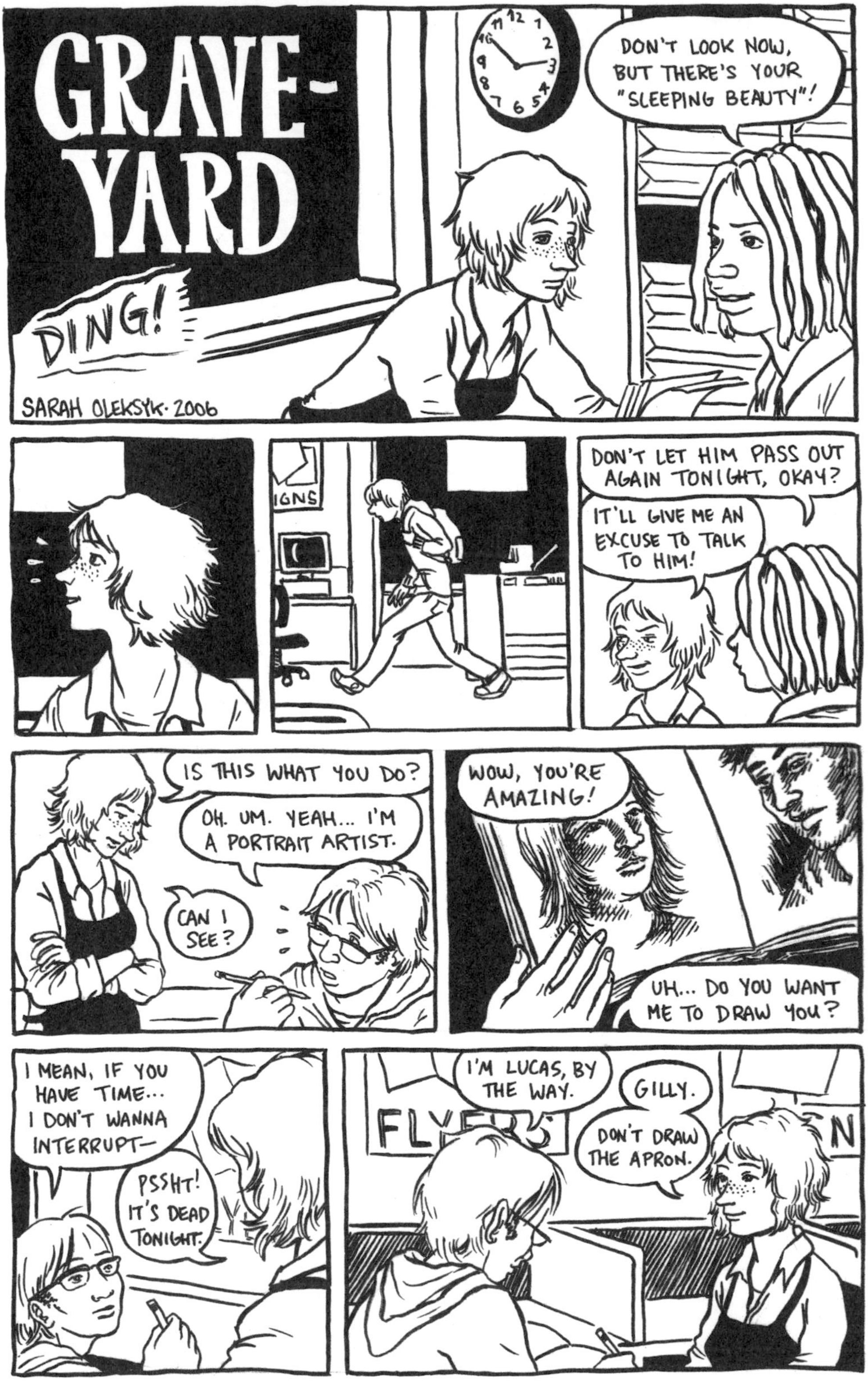
GRAVE-YARD
DING!
SARAH OLEKSYK · 2006
DON'T LOOK NOW, BUT THERE'S YOUR "SLEEPING BEAUTY"!
IGNS
DON'T LET HIM PASS OUT AGAIN TONIGHT, OKAY?
IT'LL GIVE ME AN EXCUSE TO TALK TO HIM!
IS THIS WHAT YOU DO?
OH. UM. YEAH... I'M A PORTRAIT ARTIST.
CAN I SEE?
WOW, YOU'RE AMAZING!
UH... DO YOU WANT ME TO DRAW YOU?
I MEAN, IF YOU HAVE TIME... I DON'T WANNA INTERRUPT—
PSSHT! IT'S DEAD TONIGHT.
I'M LUCAS, BY THE WAY.
GILLY.
DON'T DRAW THE APRON.

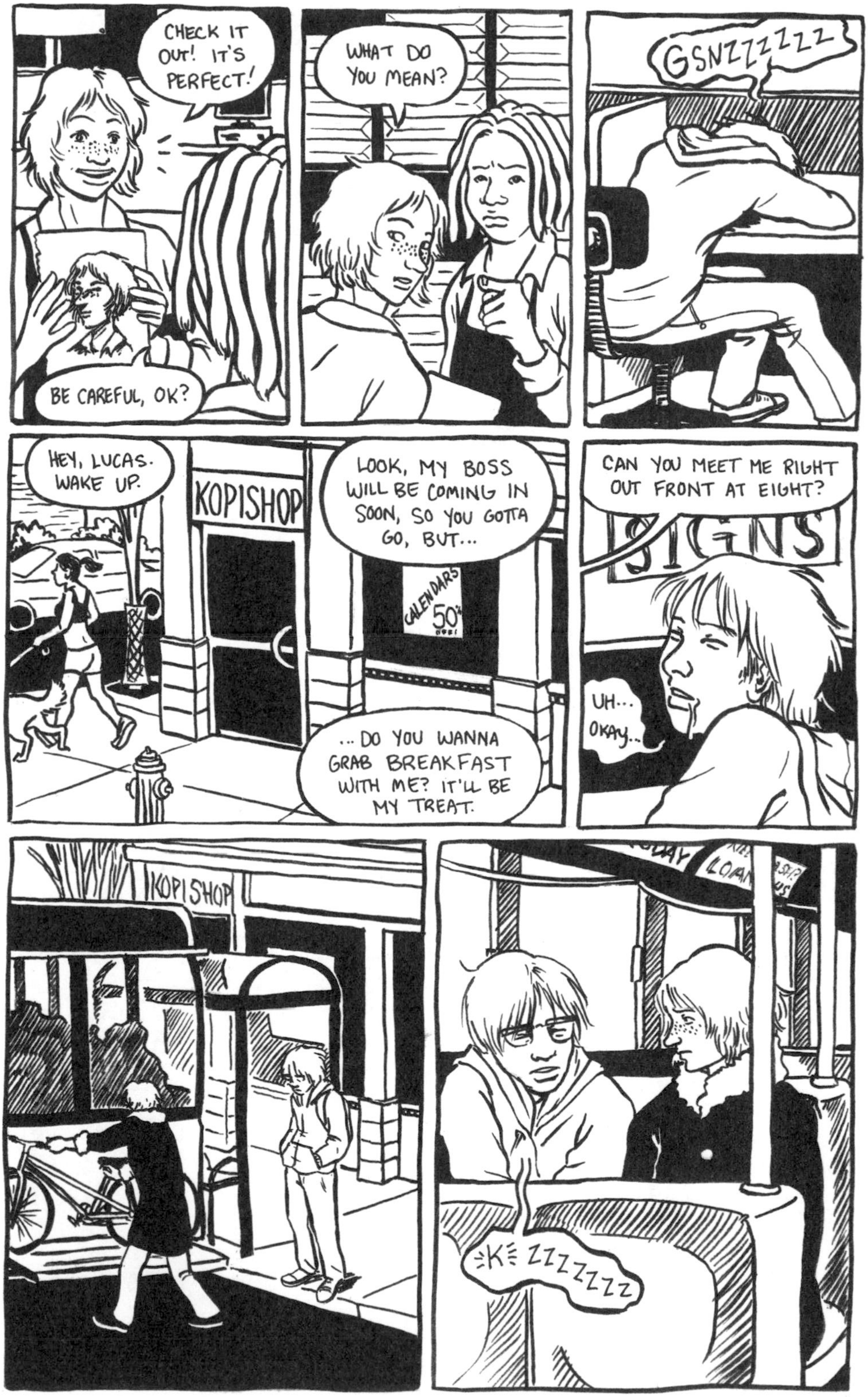
CHECK IT OUT! IT'S PERFECT!
BE CAREFUL, OK?
WHAT DO YOU MEAN?
GSNZZZZZZ
HEY, LUCAS. WAKE UP.
KOPISHOP
LOOK, MY BOSS WILL BE COMING IN SOON, SO YOU GOTTA GO, BUT...
CALENDARS 50%
...DO YOU WANNA GRAB BREAKFAST WITH ME? IT'LL BE MY TREAT.
CAN YOU MEET ME RIGHT OUT FRONT AT EIGHT?
SIGNS
UH... OKAY...
KOPISHOP
KZZZZZZZ

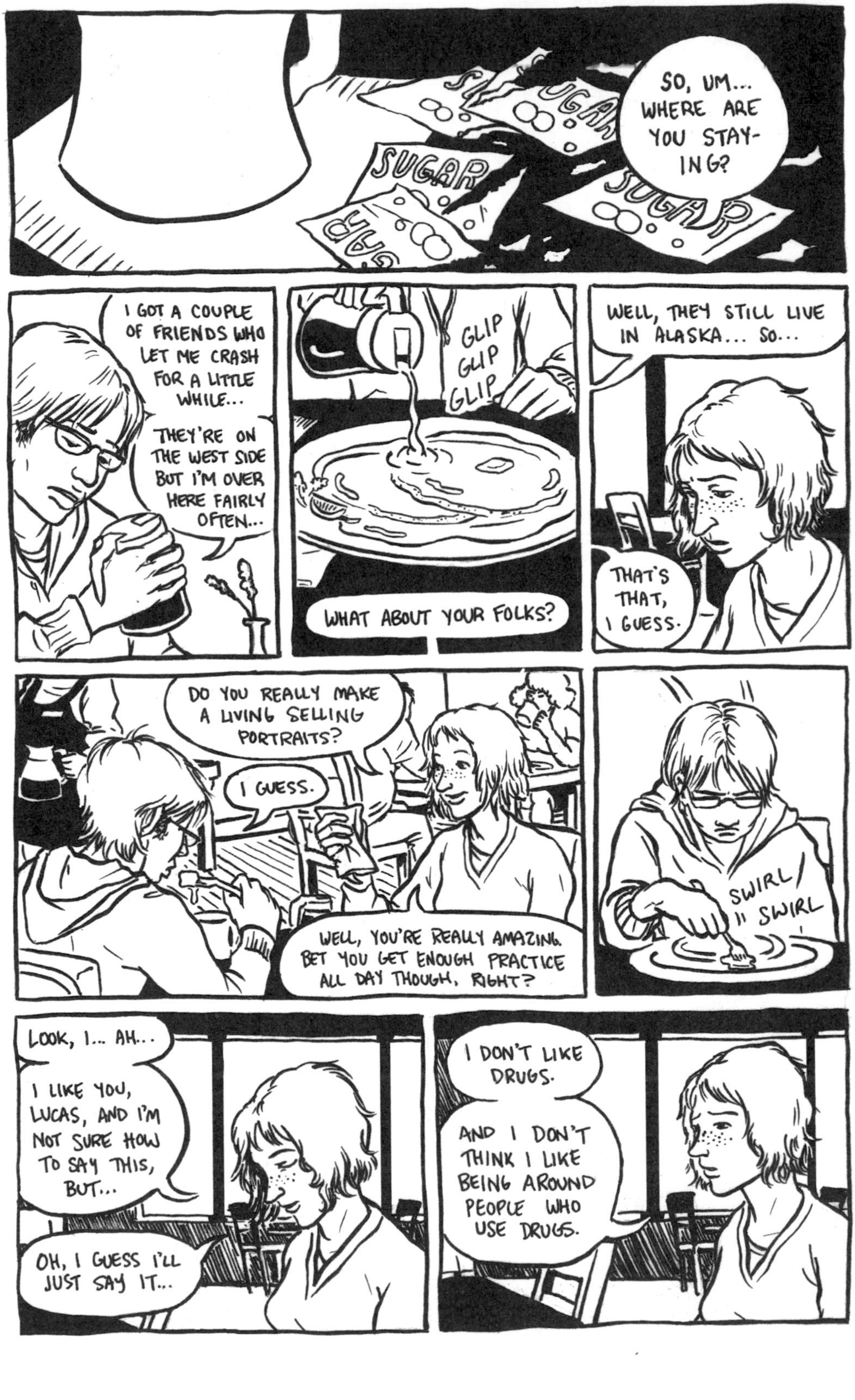
SO, UM... WHERE ARE YOU STAYING?
SUGAR
I GOT A COUPLE OF FRIENDS WHO LET ME CRASH FOR A LITTLE WHILE...
THEY'RE ON THE WEST SIDE BUT I'M OVER HERE FAIRLY OFTEN...
GLIP GLIP GLIP
WHAT ABOUT YOUR FOLKS?
WELL, THEY STILL LIVE IN ALASKA... SO...
THAT'S THAT, I GUESS.
DO YOU REALLY MAKE A LIVING SELLING PORTRAITS?
I GUESS.
WELL, YOU'RE REALLY AMAZING. BET YOU GET ENOUGH PRACTICE ALL DAY THOUGH, RIGHT?
SWIRL SWIRL
LOOK, I... AH...
I LIKE YOU, LUCAS, AND I'M NOT SURE HOW TO SAY THIS, BUT...
OH, I GUESS I'LL JUST SAY IT...
I DON'T LIKE DRUGS.
AND I DON'T THINK I LIKE BEING AROUND PEOPLE WHO USE DRUGS.

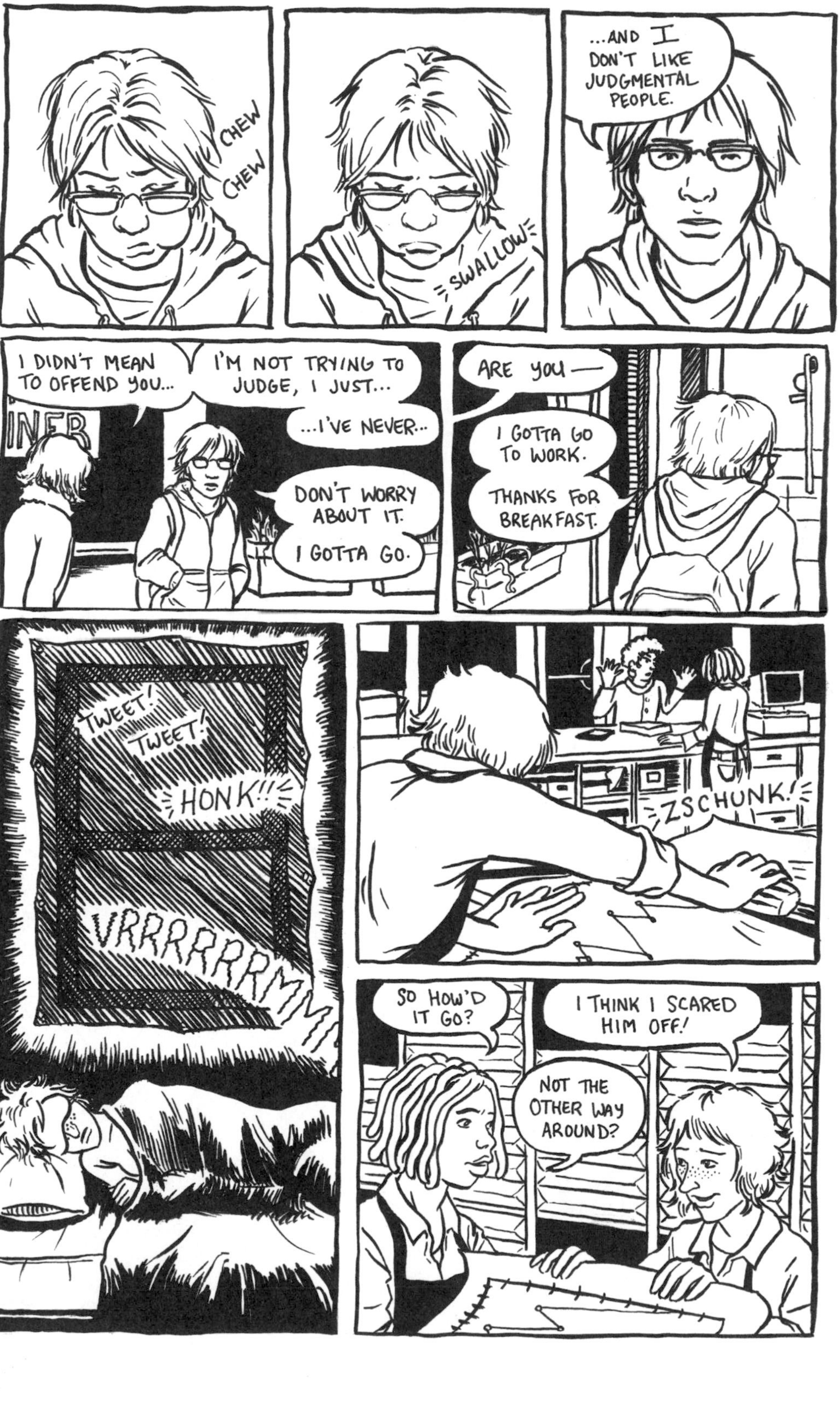
CHEW
CHEW
SWALLOW
...AND I DON'T LIKE JUDGMENTAL PEOPLE.
I DIDN'T MEAN TO OFFEND YOU...
I'M NOT TRYING TO JUDGE, I JUST...
...I'VE NEVER...
DON'T WORRY ABOUT IT.
I GOTTA GO.
ARE YOU—
I GOTTA GO TO WORK.
THANKS FOR BREAKFAST.
TWEET! TWEET!
HONK!!
VRRRRRRRRMMM
ZSCHUNK!
SO HOW'D IT GO?
I THINK I SCARED HIM OFF!
NOT THE OTHER WAY AROUND?

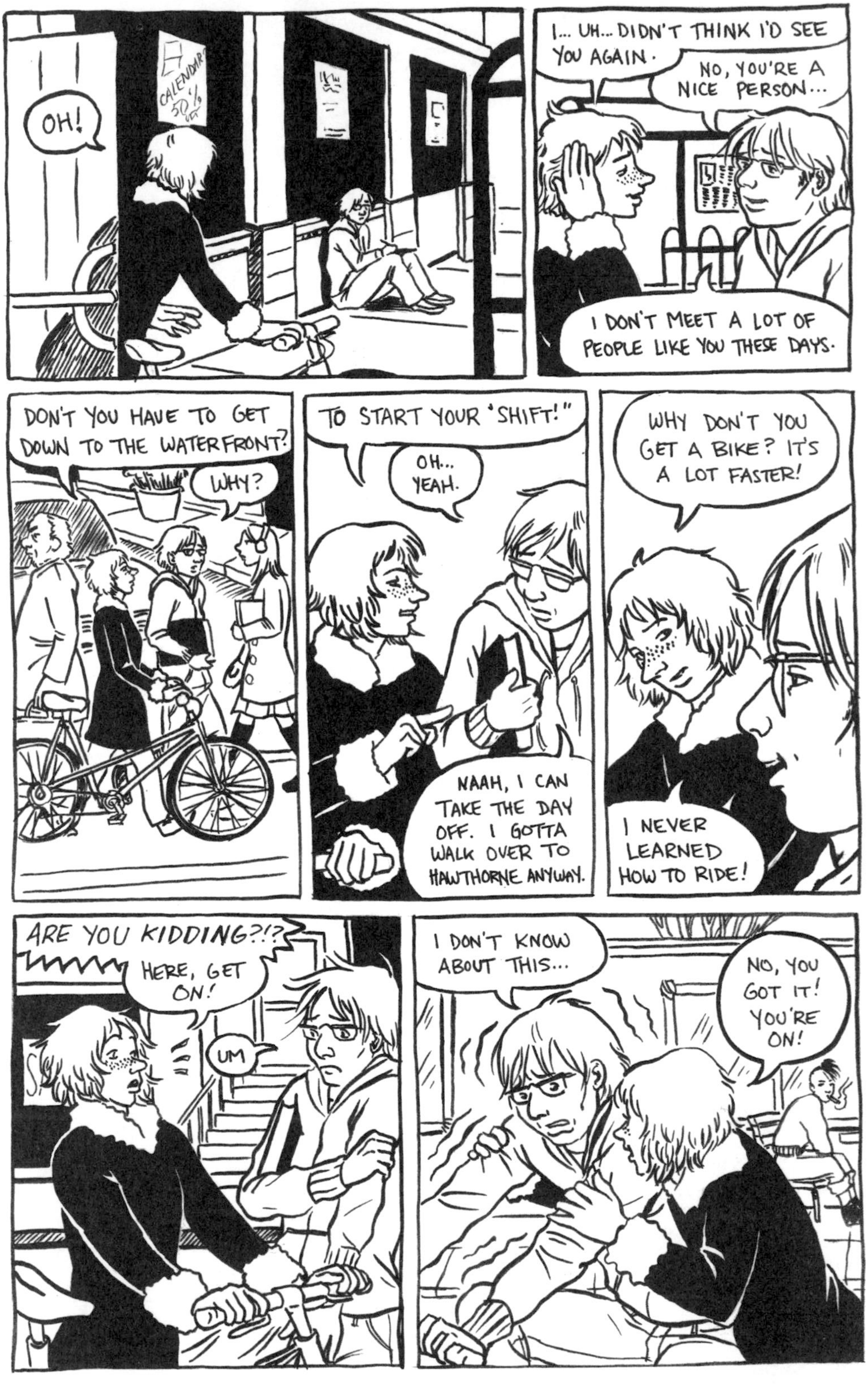
OH!
I... UH... DIDN'T THINK I'D SEE YOU AGAIN.
NO, YOU'RE A NICE PERSON...
I DON'T MEET A LOT OF PEOPLE LIKE YOU THESE DAYS.
DON'T YOU HAVE TO GET DOWN TO THE WATERFRONT?
WHY?
TO START YOUR "SHIFT!"
OH... YEAH.
NAAH, I CAN TAKE THE DAY OFF. I GOTTA WALK OVER TO HAWTHORNE ANYWAY.
WHY DON'T YOU GET A BIKE? IT'S A LOT FASTER!
I NEVER LEARNED HOW TO RIDE!
ARE YOU KIDDING?!?
HERE, GET ON!
UM
I DON'T KNOW ABOUT THIS...
NO, YOU GOT IT! YOU'RE ON!

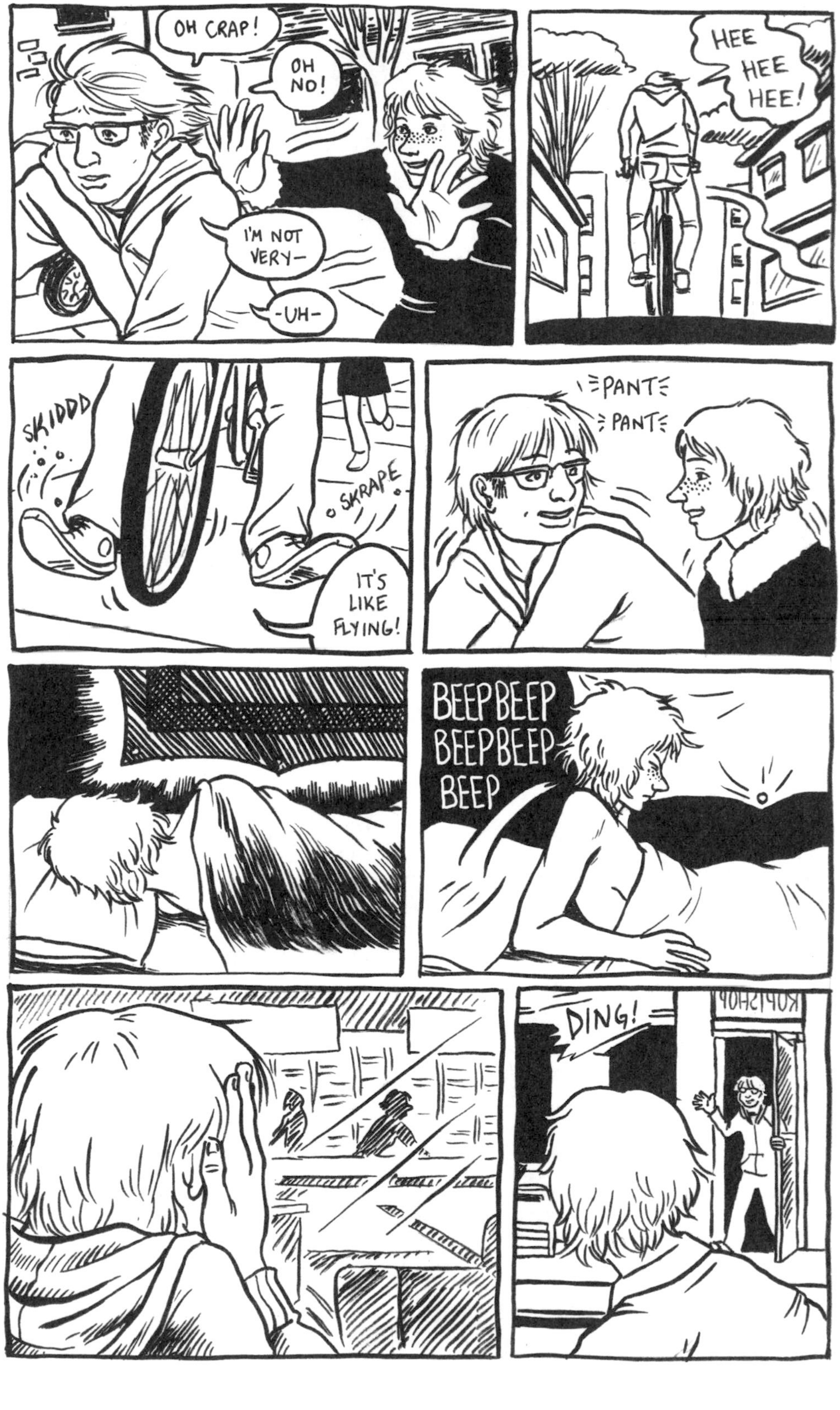

OH CRAP!
OH NO!
I'M NOT VERY—
-UH-
HEE HEE HEE!
SKIDDD
SKRAPE
IT'S LIKE FLYING!
PANT
PANT
BEEPBEEP BEEPBEEP-BEEP
DING!

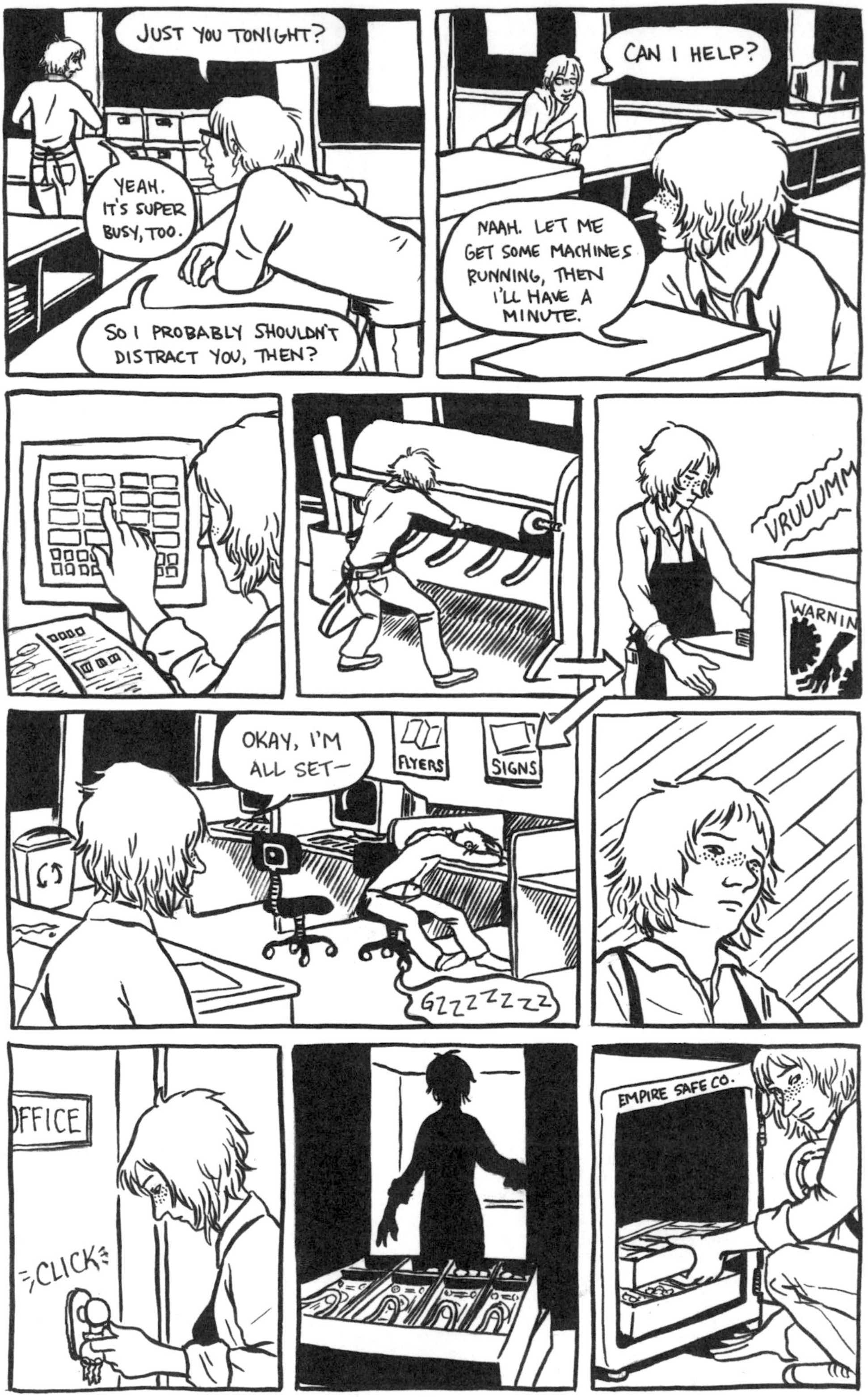
JUST YOU TONIGHT?
YEAH. IT'S SUPER BUSY, TOO.
SO I PROBABLY SHOULDN'T DISTRACT YOU, THEN?
CAN I HELP?
NAAH. LET ME GET SOME MACHINES RUNNING, THEN I'LL HAVE A MINUTE.
VRUUUMM
WARNIN
OKAY, I'M ALL SET—
FLYERS
SIGNS
GZZZZZZZ
OFFICE
CLICK
EMPIRE SAFE CO.

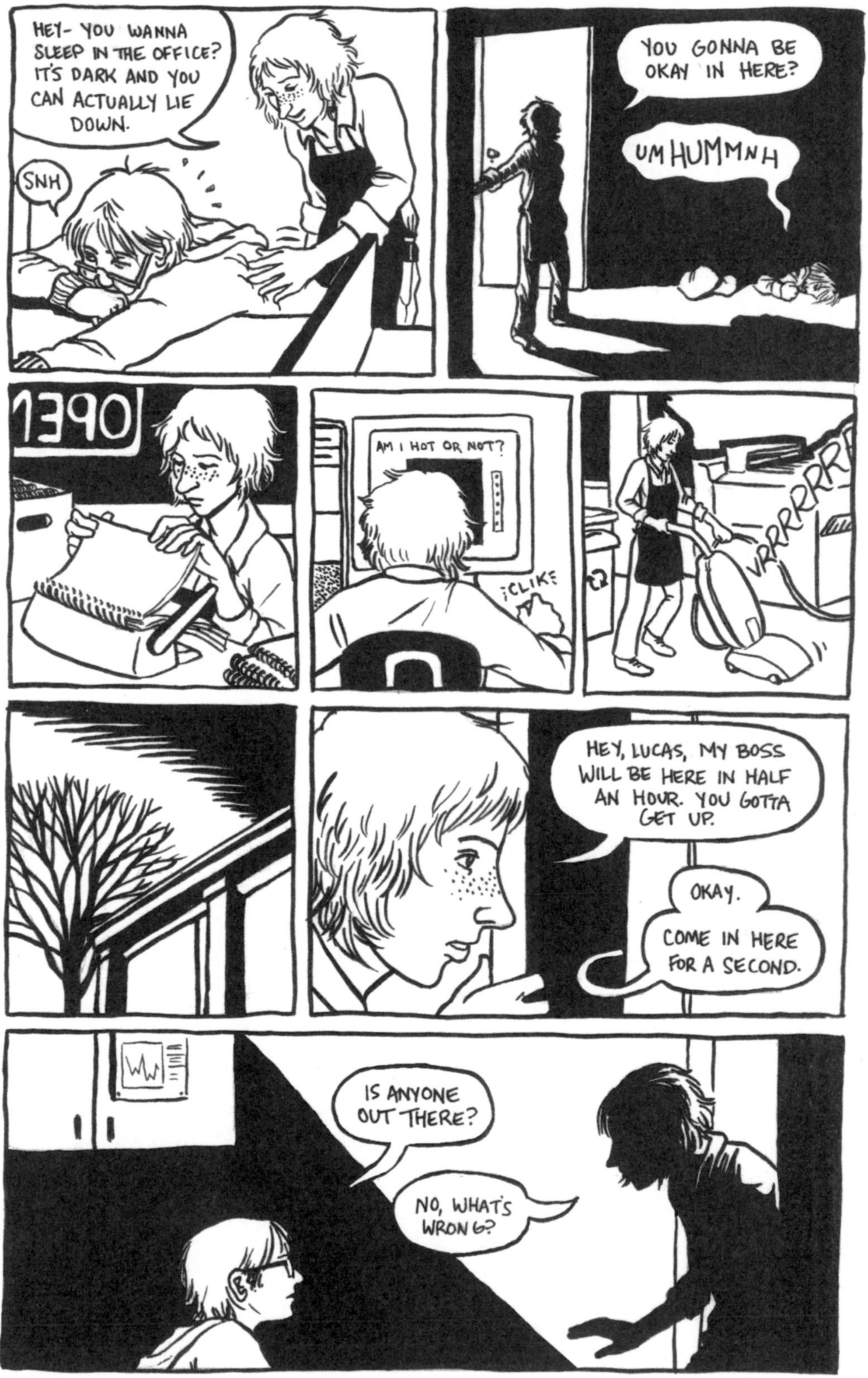
HEY- YOU WANNA SLEEP IN THE OFFICE? IT'S DARK AND YOU CAN ACTUALLY LIE DOWN.
SNH
YOU GONNA BE OKAY IN HERE?
UM HUMMNH
OPEN
AM I HOT OR NOT?
CLIK
VRRRRRRRR
HEY, LUCAS, MY BOSS WILL BE HERE IN HALF AN HOUR. YOU GOTTA GET UP.
OKAY.
COME IN HERE FOR A SECOND.
IS ANYONE OUT THERE?
NO, WHAT'S WRONG?

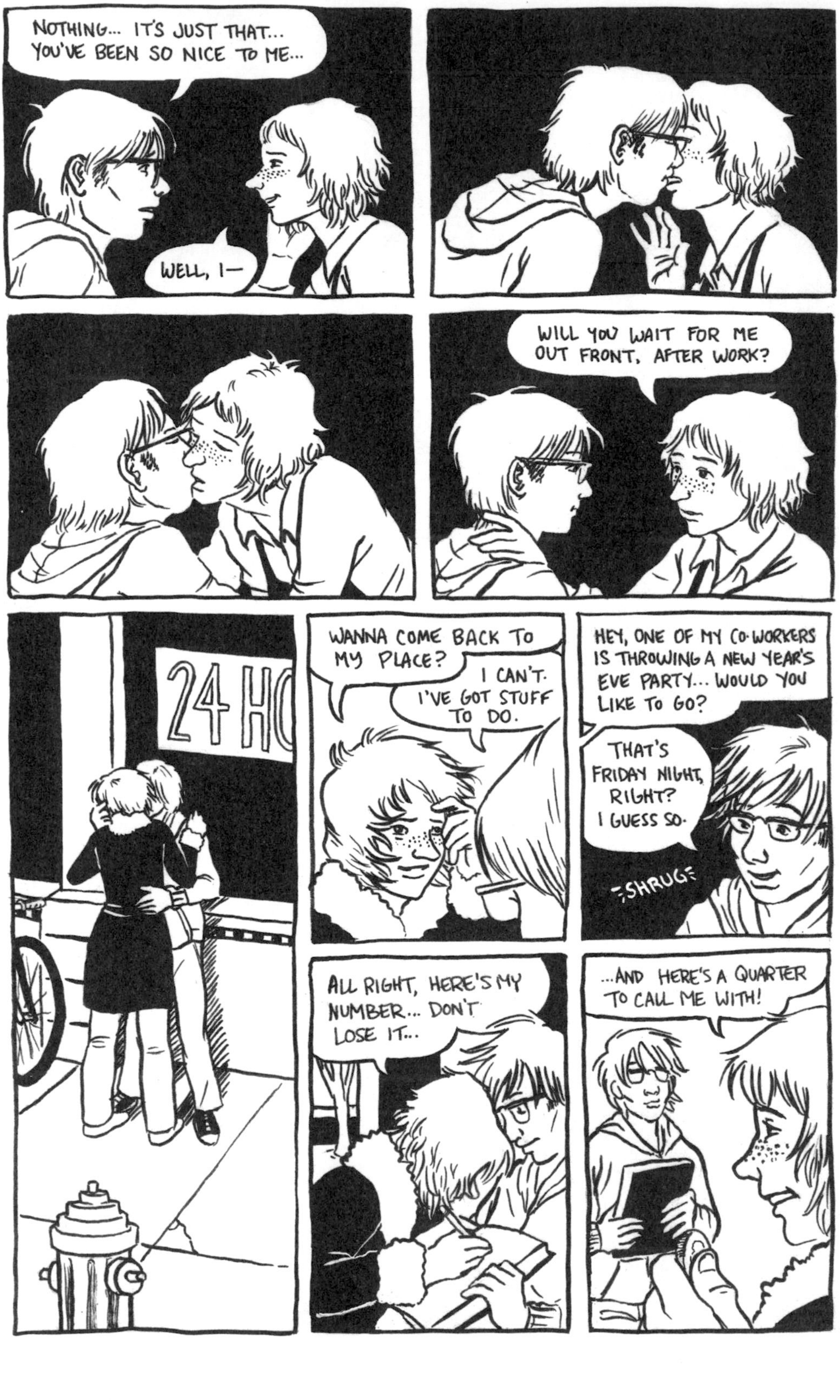

NOTHING... IT'S JUST THAT... YOU'VE BEEN SO NICE TO ME...
WELL, I—
WILL YOU WAIT FOR ME OUT FRONT, AFTER WORK?
24 HO
WANNA COME BACK TO MY PLACE?
I CAN'T. I'VE GOT STUFF TO DO.
HEY, ONE OF MY CO-WORKERS IS THROWING A NEW YEAR'S EVE PARTY... WOULD YOU LIKE TO GO?
THAT'S FRIDAY NIGHT, RIGHT? I GUESS SO.
SHRUG
ALL RIGHT, HERE'S MY NUMBER... DON'T LOSE IT...
...AND HERE'S A QUARTER TO CALL ME WITH!

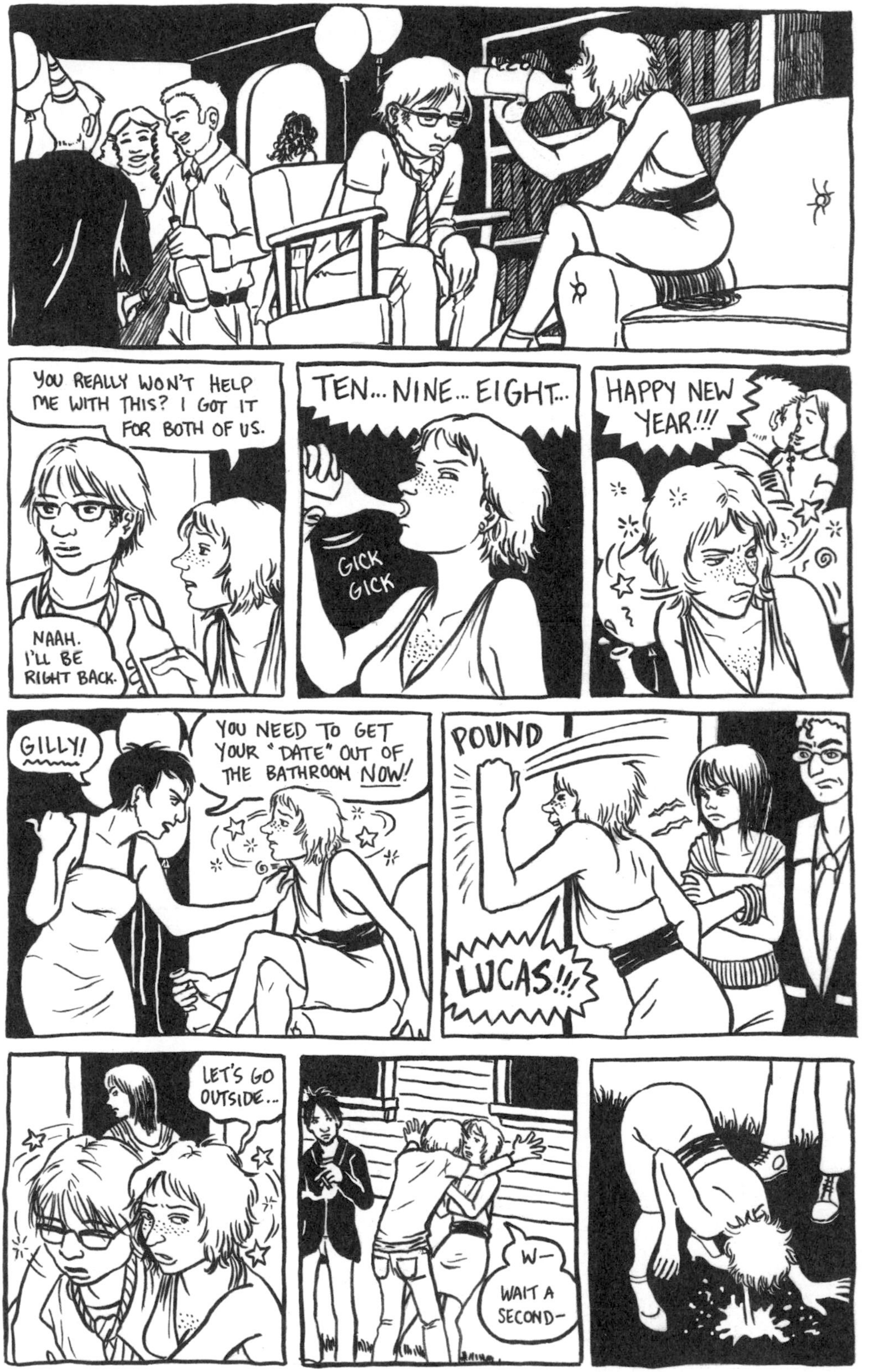
YOU REALLY WON'T HELP ME WITH THIS? I GOT IT FOR BOTH OF US.
NAAH. I'LL BE RIGHT BACK.
TEN... NINE... EIGHT...
GICK GICK
HAPPY NEW YEAR!!!
GILLY!
YOU NEED TO GET YOUR "DATE" OUT OF THE BATHROOM NOW!
POUND
LUCAS!!!
LET'S GO OUTSIDE...
W—
WAIT A SECOND—

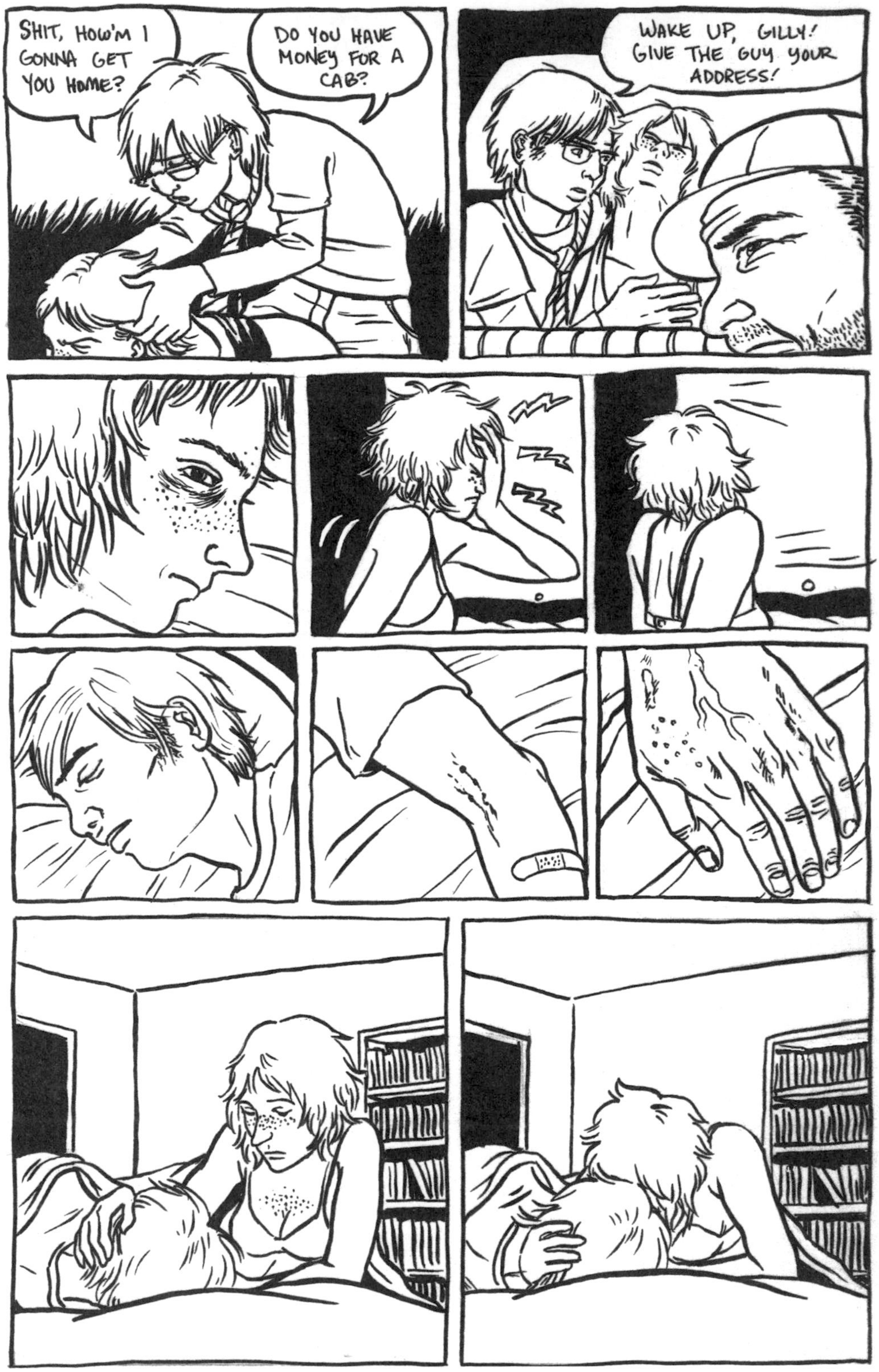
SHIT, HOW'M I GONNA GET YOU HOME?
DO YOU HAVE MONEY FOR A CAB?
WAKE UP, GILLY! GIVE THE GUY YOUR ADDRESS!

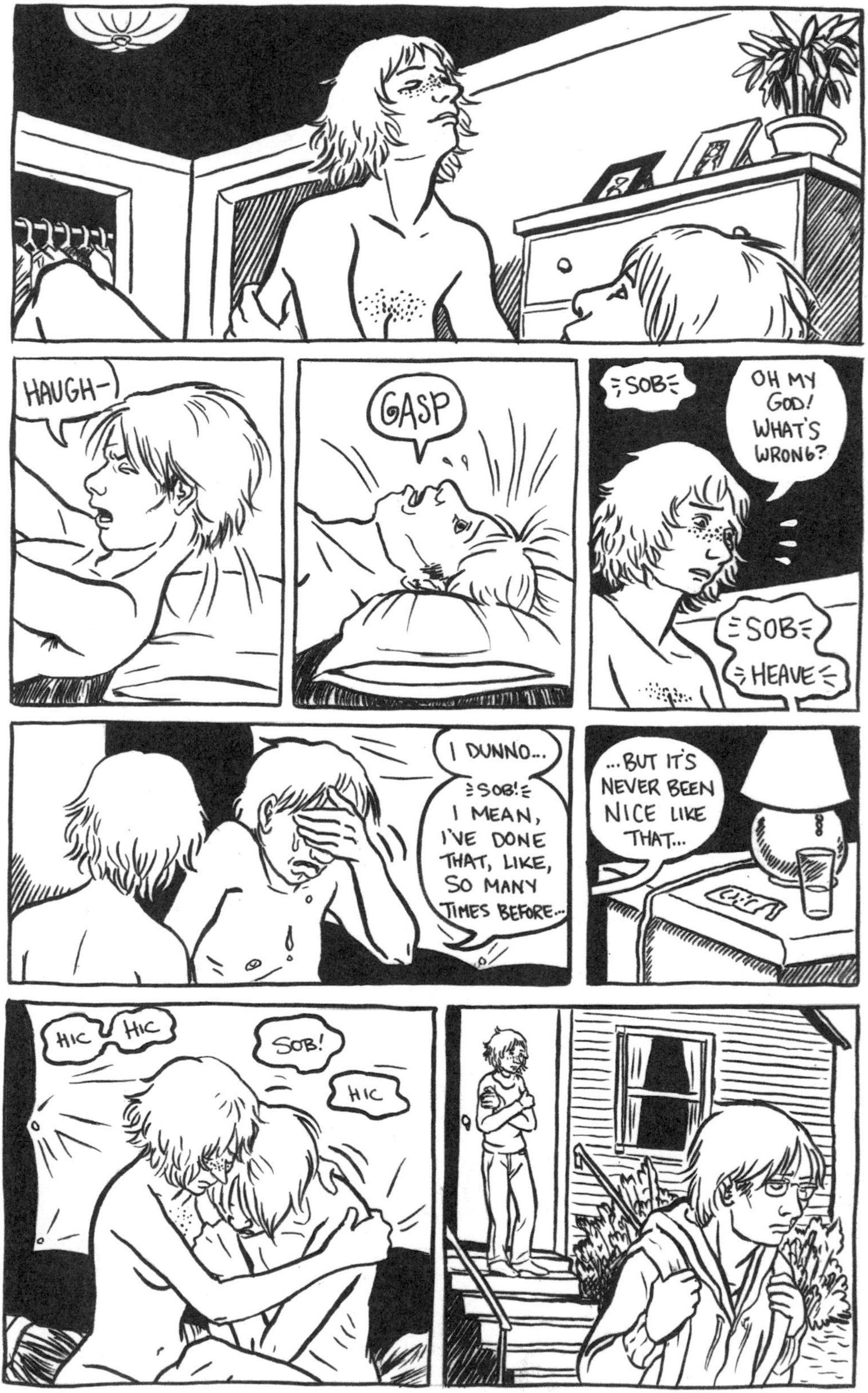
HAUGH-
GASP
SOB
OH MY GOD! WHAT'S WRONG?
SOB
HEAVE
I DUNNO...
SOB!
I MEAN, I'VE DONE THAT, LIKE, SO MANY TIMES BEFORE...
...BUT IT'S NEVER BEEN NICE LIKE THAT...
HIC
HIC
SOB!
HIC

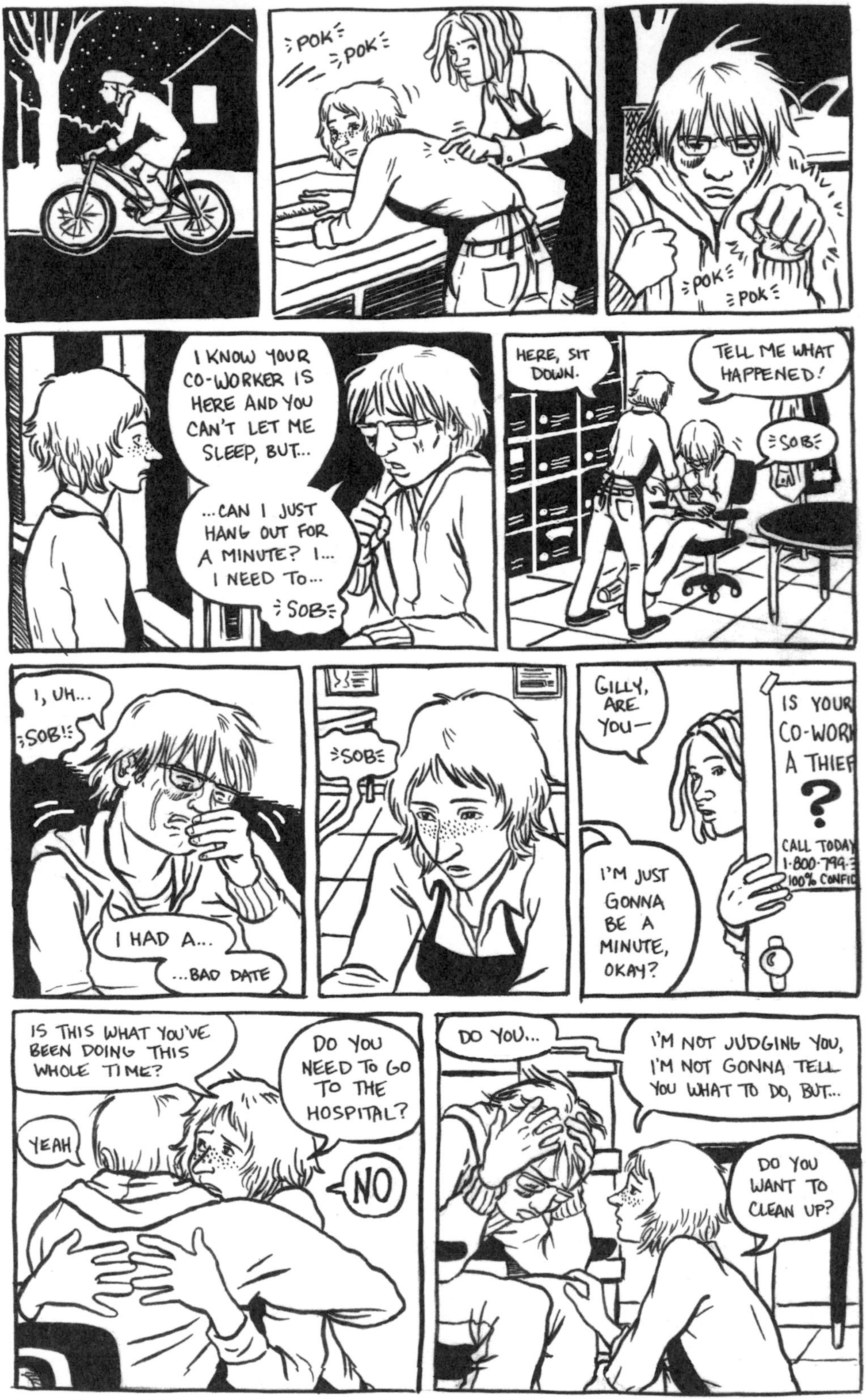
POK
POK
POK
POK
I KNOW YOUR CO-WORKER IS HERE AND YOU CAN'T LET ME SLEEP, BUT...
...CAN I JUST HANG OUT FOR A MINUTE? I... I NEED TO...
SOB
HERE, SIT DOWN.
TELL ME WHAT HAPPENED!
SOB
I, UH...
SOB!
I HAD A...
...BAD DATE
SOB
GILLY, ARE YOU—
I'M JUST GONNA BE A MINUTE, OKAY?
IS YOUR CO-WORK A THIEF ?
CALL TODAY 1-800-799-
100% CONFID
IS THIS WHAT YOU'VE BEEN DOING THIS WHOLE TIME?
YEAH
DO YOU NEED TO GO TO THE HOSPITAL?
NO
DO YOU...
I'M NOT JUDGING YOU, I'M NOT GONNA TELL YOU WHAT TO DO, BUT...
DO YOU WANT TO CLEAN UP?

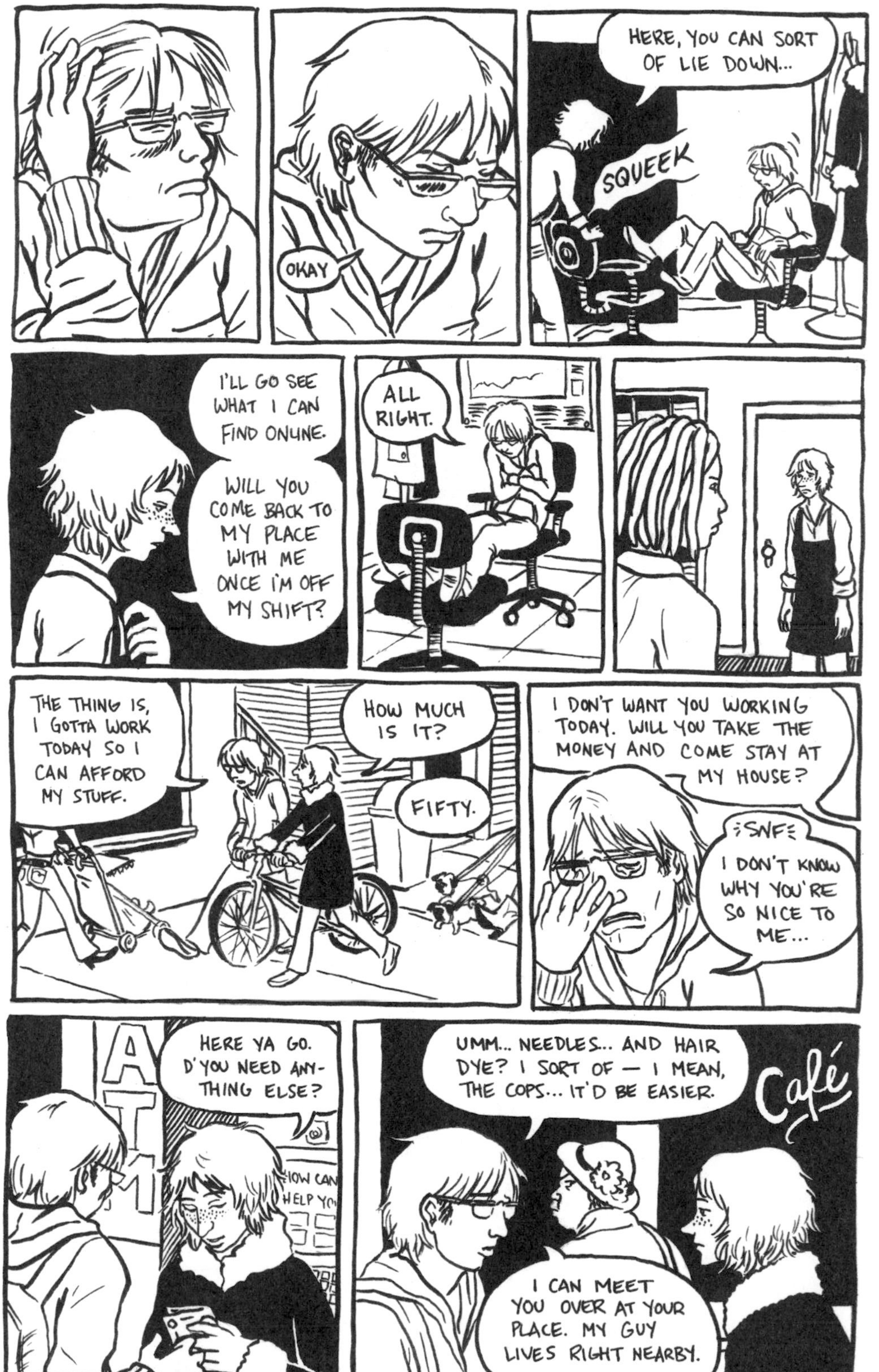

OKAY
HERE, YOU CAN SORT OF LIE DOWN...
SQUEEK
I'LL GO SEE WHAT I CAN FIND ONLINE.
WILL YOU COME BACK TO MY PLACE WITH ME ONCE I'M OFF MY SHIFT?
ALL RIGHT.
THE THING IS, I GOTTA WORK TODAY SO I CAN AFFORD MY STUFF.
HOW MUCH IS IT?
FIFTY.
I DON'T WANT YOU WORKING TODAY. WILL YOU TAKE THE MONEY AND COME STAY AT MY HOUSE?
SNF
I DON'T KNOW WHY YOU'RE SO NICE TO ME...
ATM
HERE YA GO. D'YOU NEED ANYTHING ELSE?
HOW CAN HELP YOU
UMM... NEEDLES... AND HAIR DYE? I SORT OF — I MEAN, THE COPS... IT'D BE EASIER.
Café
I CAN MEET YOU OVER AT YOUR PLACE. MY GUY LIVES RIGHT NEARBY.

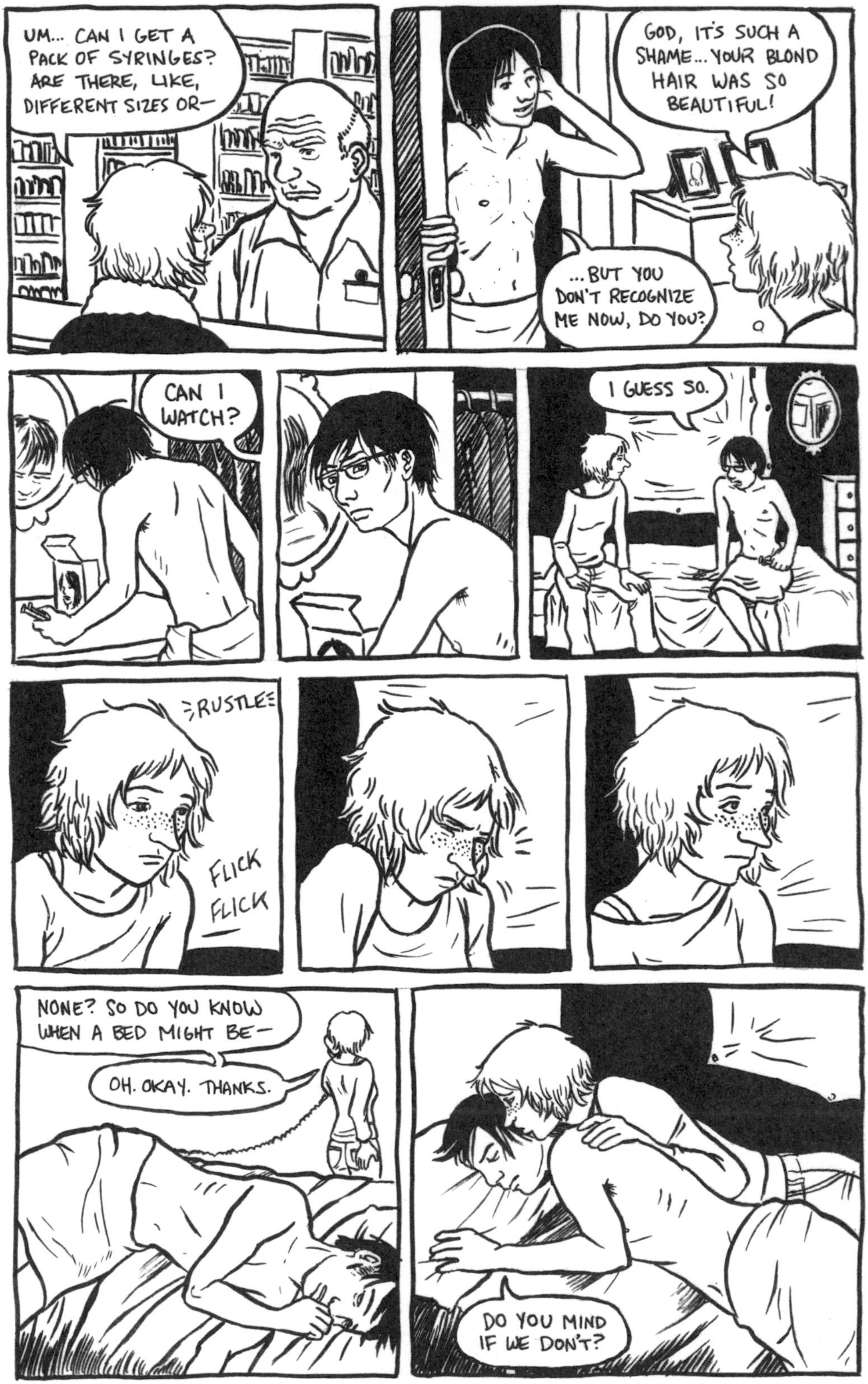
UM... CAN I GET A PACK OF SYRINGES? ARE THERE, LIKE, DIFFERENT SIZES OR—
GOD, IT'S SUCH A SHAME... YOUR BLOND HAIR WAS SO BEAUTIFUL!
...BUT YOU DON'T RECOGNIZE ME NOW, DO YOU?
CAN I WATCH?
I GUESS SO.
RUSTLE
FLICK FLICK
NONE? SO DO YOU KNOW WHEN A BED MIGHT BE—
OH. OKAY. THANKS.
DO YOU MIND IF WE DON'T?

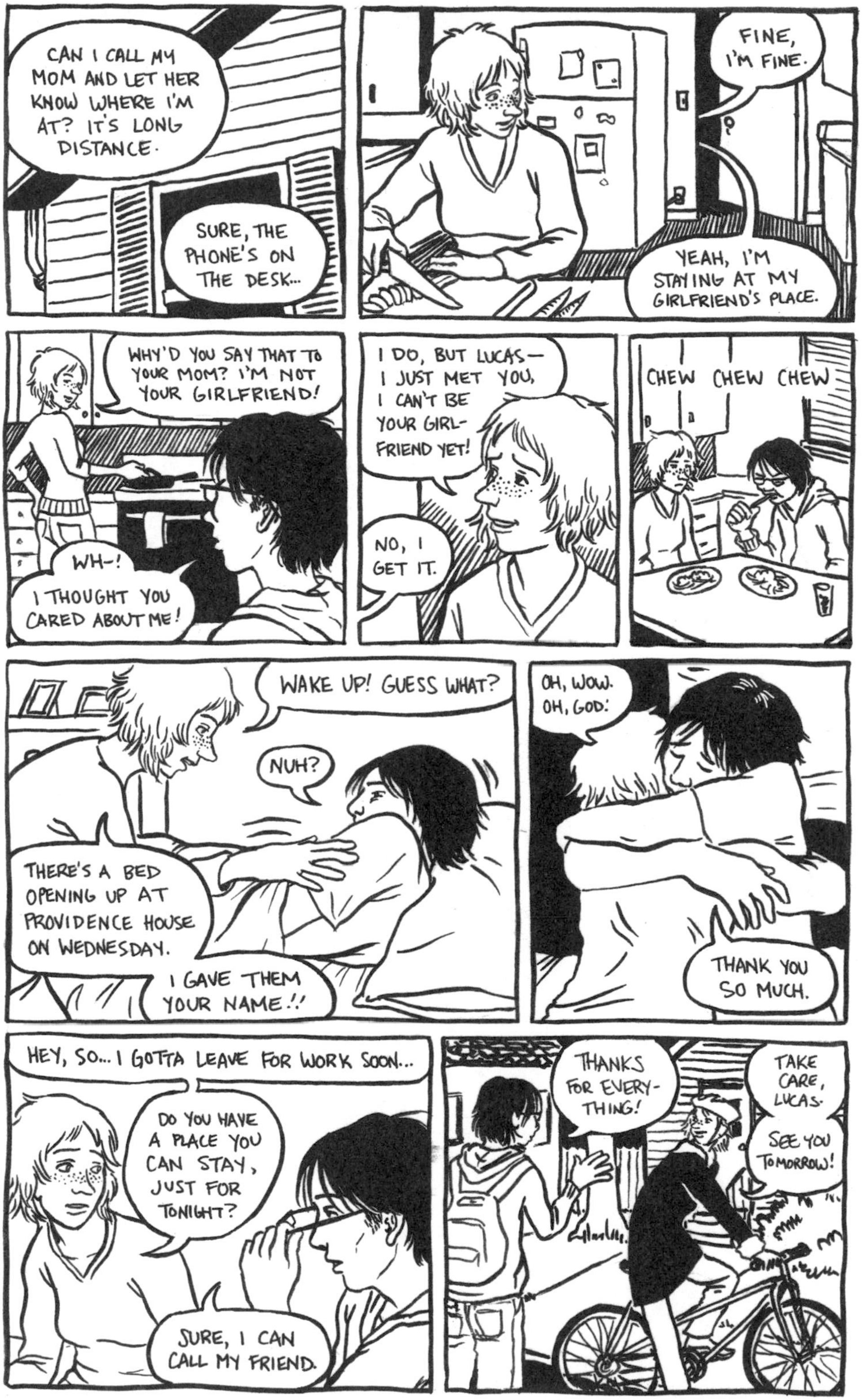
CAN I CALL MY MOM AND LET HER KNOW WHERE I'M AT? IT'S LONG DISTANCE.
SURE, THE PHONE'S ON THE DESK...
FINE, I'M FINE.
YEAH, I'M STAYING AT MY GIRLFRIEND'S PLACE.
WHY'D YOU SAY THAT TO YOUR MOM? I'M NOT YOUR GIRLFRIEND!
WH-! I THOUGHT YOU CARED ABOUT ME!
I DO, BUT LUCAS— I JUST MET YOU, I CAN'T BE YOUR GIRL-FRIEND YET!
NO, I GET IT.
CHEW CHEW CHEW
WAKE UP! GUESS WHAT?
NUH?
THERE'S A BED OPENING UP AT PROVIDENCE HOUSE ON WEDNESDAY.
I GAVE THEM YOUR NAME!!
OH, WOW. OH, GOD!
THANK YOU SO MUCH.
HEY, SO... I GOTTA LEAVE FOR WORK SOON...
DO YOU HAVE A PLACE YOU CAN STAY, JUST FOR TONIGHT?
SURE, I CAN CALL MY FRIEND.
THANKS FOR EVERY-THING!
TAKE CARE, LUCAS.
SEE YOU TOMORROW!

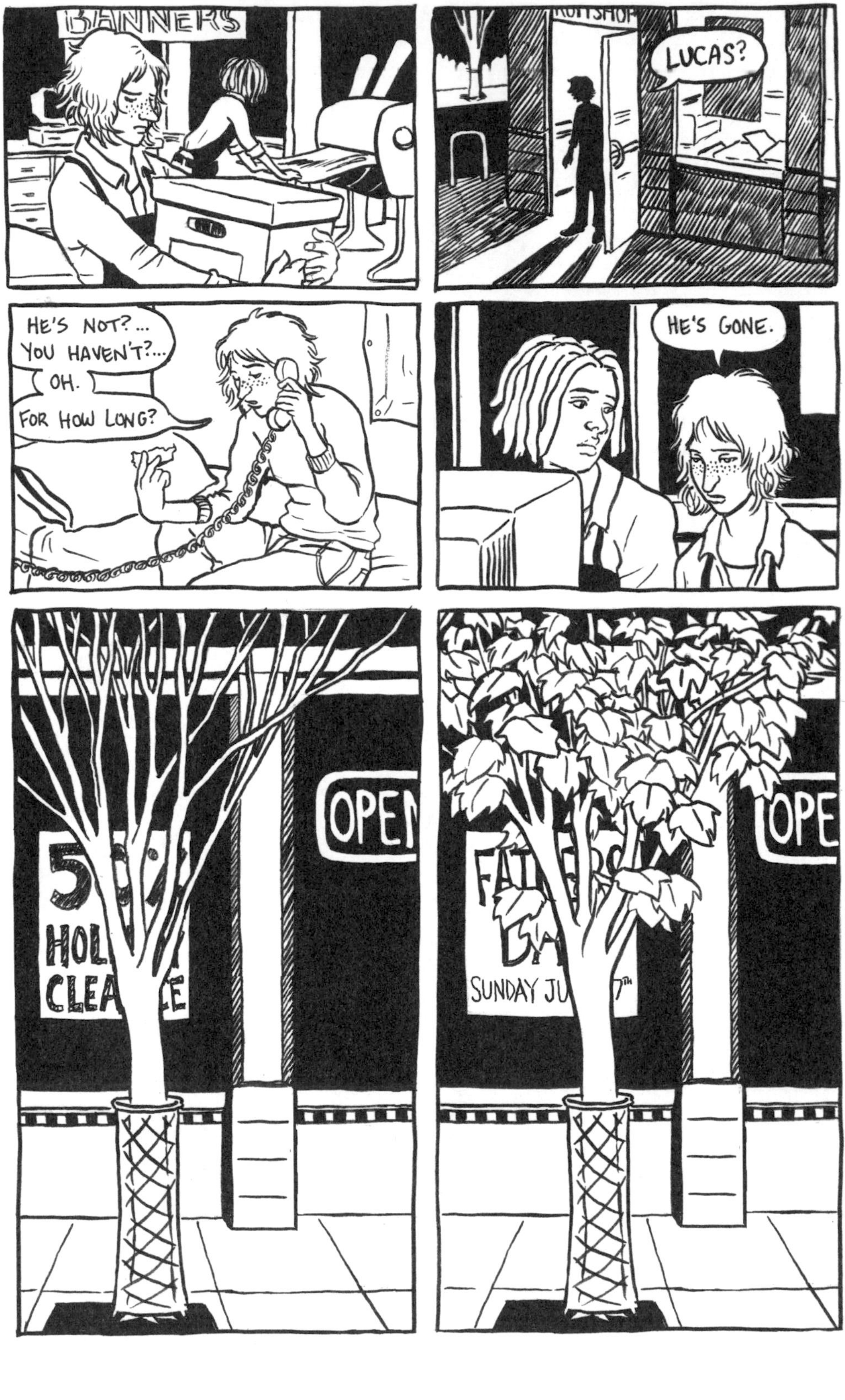
BANNERS
LUCAS?
HE'S NOT?...
YOU HAVEN'T?...
OH.
FOR HOW LONG?
HE'S GONE.

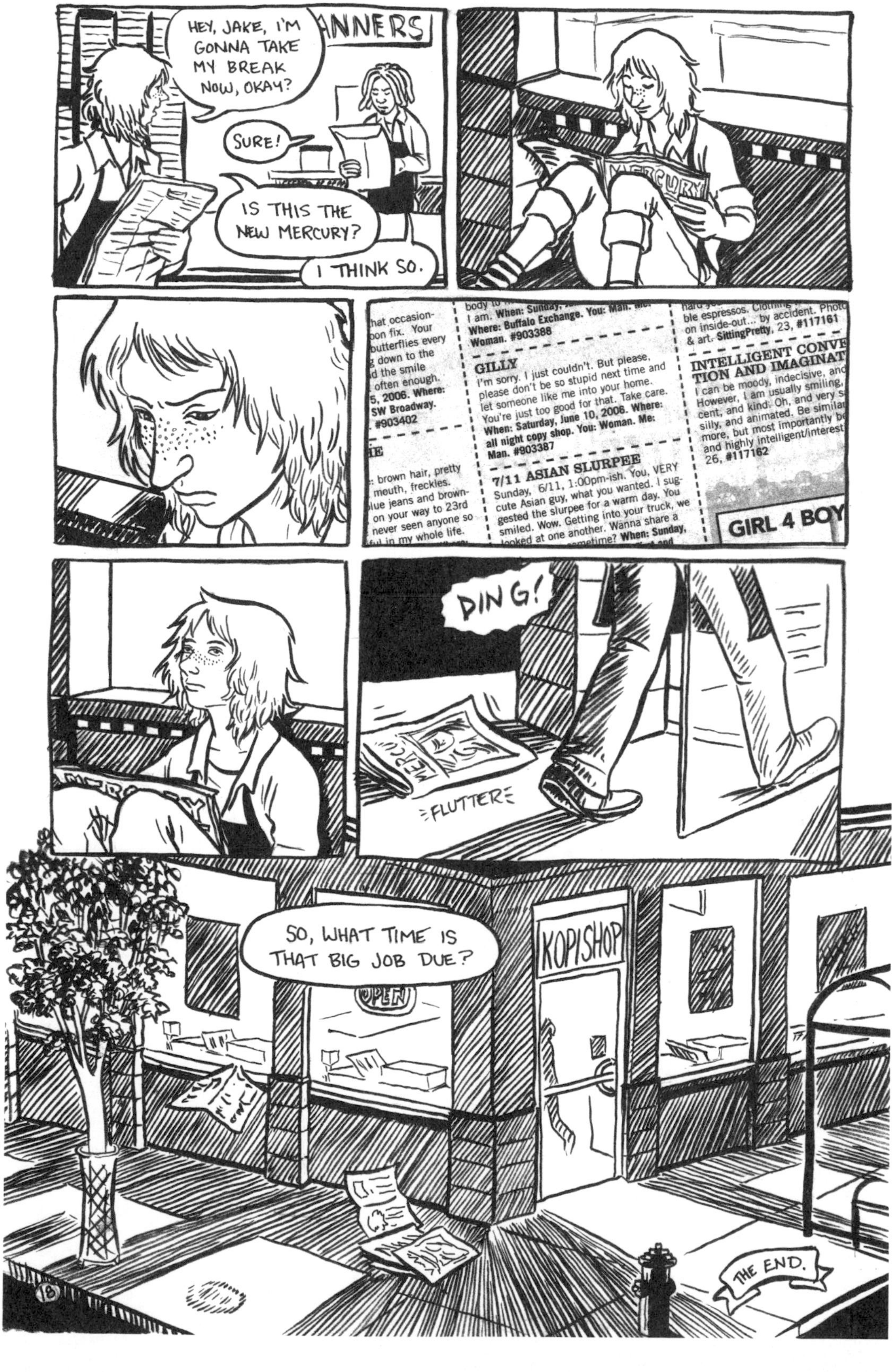
ANNERS
HEY, JAKE, I'M GONNA TAKE MY BREAK NOW, OKAY?
SURE!
IS THIS THE NEW MERCURY?
I THINK SO.
MERCURY
GILLY
I'm sorry. I just couldn't. But please, please don't be so stupid next time and let someone like me into your home. You're just too good for that. Take care. When: Saturday, June 10, 2006. Where: all night copy shop. You: Woman. Me: Man. #903387
7/11 ASIAN SLURPEE
Sunday, 6/11, 1:00pm-ish. You, VERY cute Asian guy, what you wanted. I suggested the slurpee for a warm day. You smiled. Wow. Getting into your truck, we looked at one another. Wanna share a
Where: Buffalo Exchange. You: Man. Me: Woman. #903388
on inside-out... by accident.
& art. SittingPretty, 23, #117161
GIRL 4 BOY
DING!
FLUTTER
SO, WHAT TIME IS THAT BIG JOB DUE?
KOPISHOP
OPEN
THE END.
18

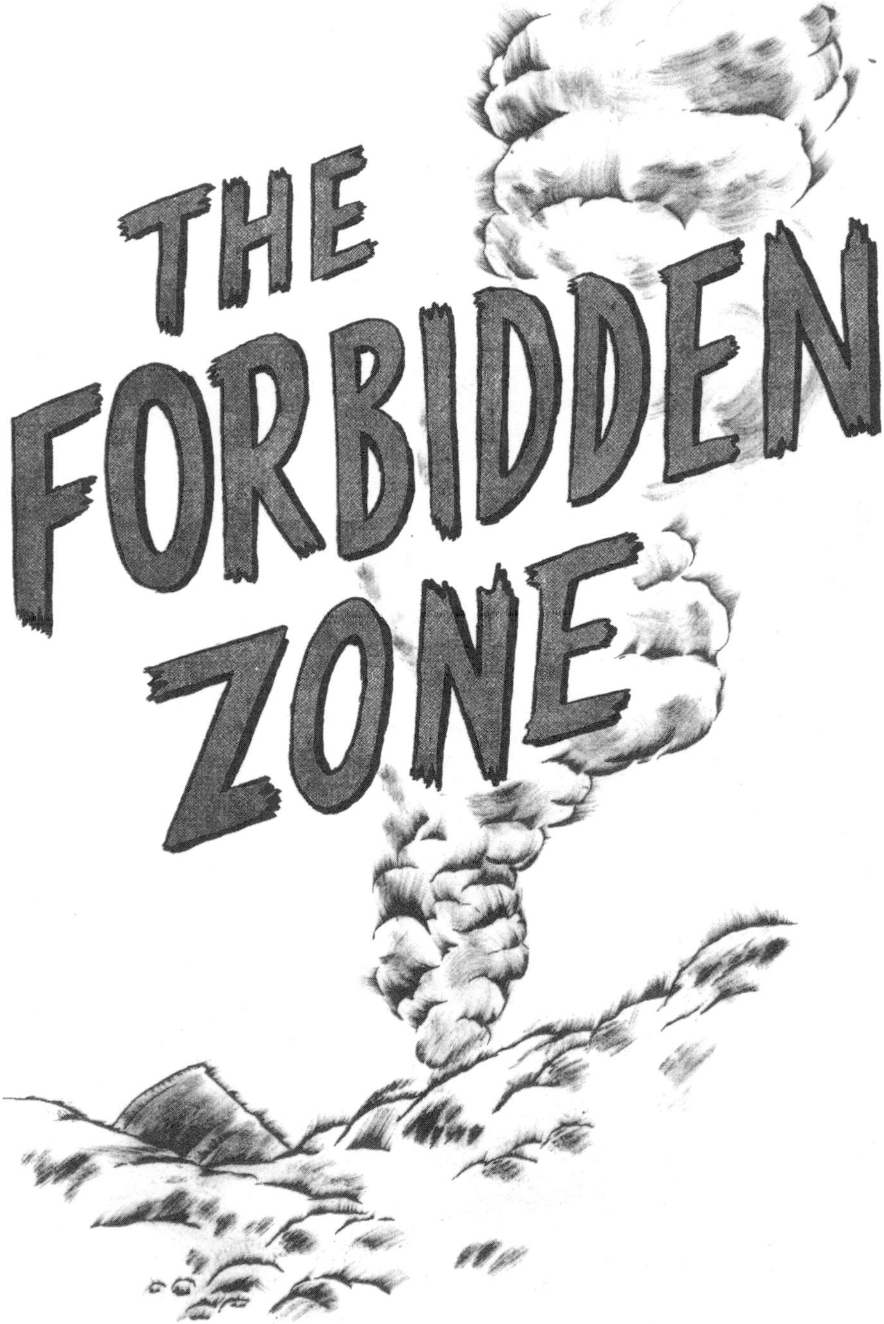
THE
FORBIDDEN
ZONE

KEVIN PYLE

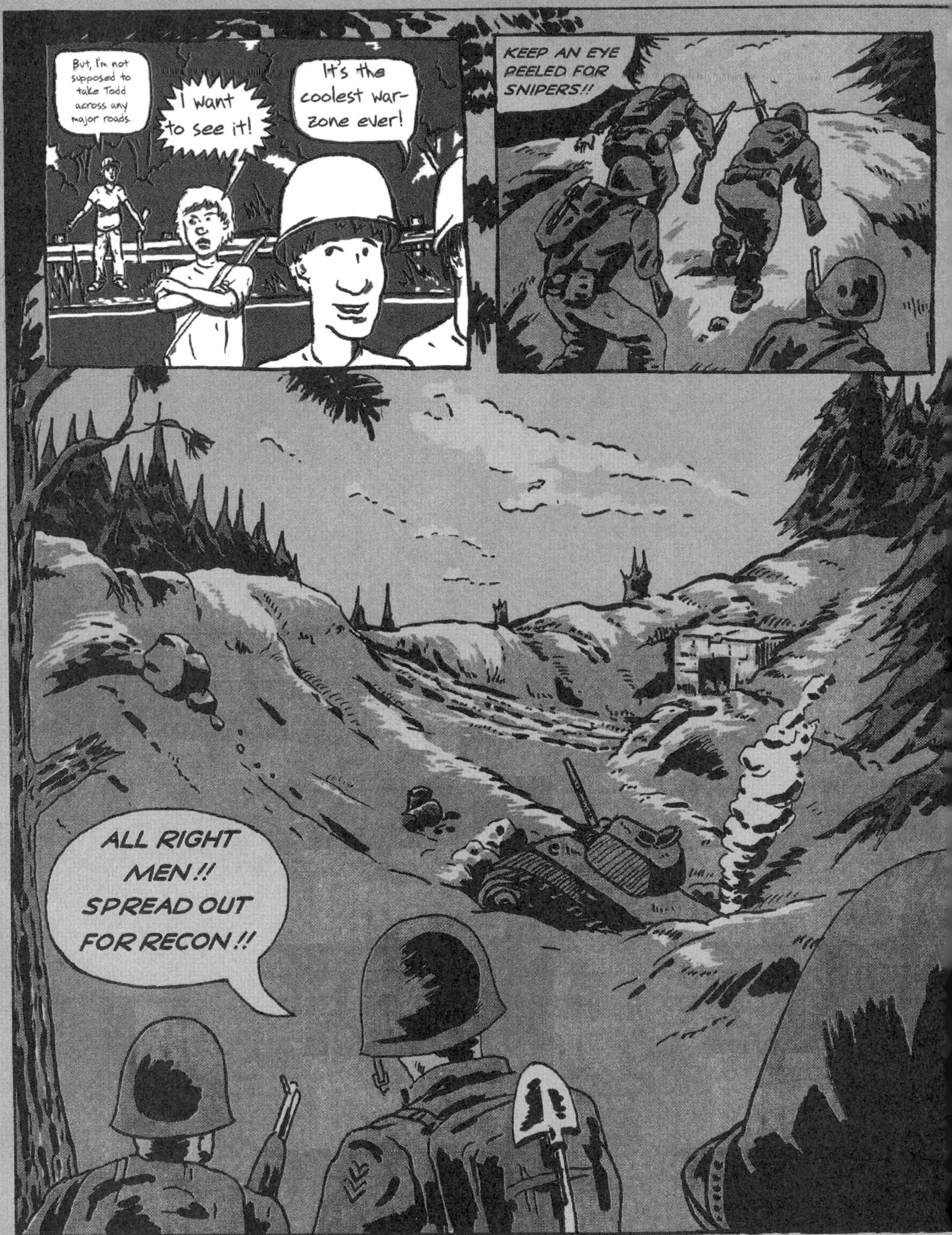
But, I'm not supposed to take Todd across any major roads.
I want to see it!
It's the coolest war-zone ever!
KEEP AN EYE PEELED FOR SNIPERS!!
ALL RIGHT MEN!! SPREAD OUT FOR RECON!!

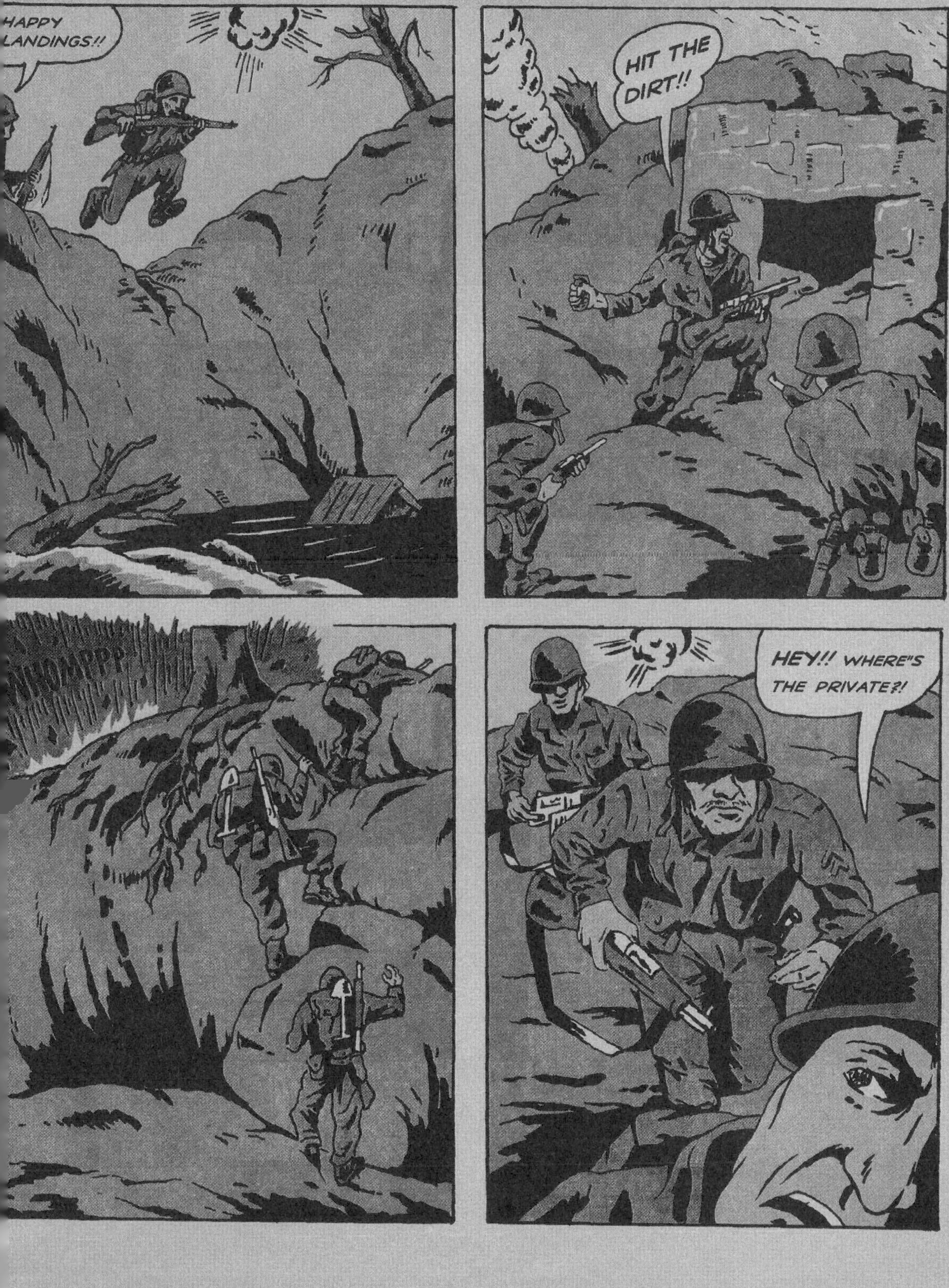
HAPPY LANDINGS!!
HIT THE DIRT!!
HEY!! WHERE"S THE PRIVATE?!

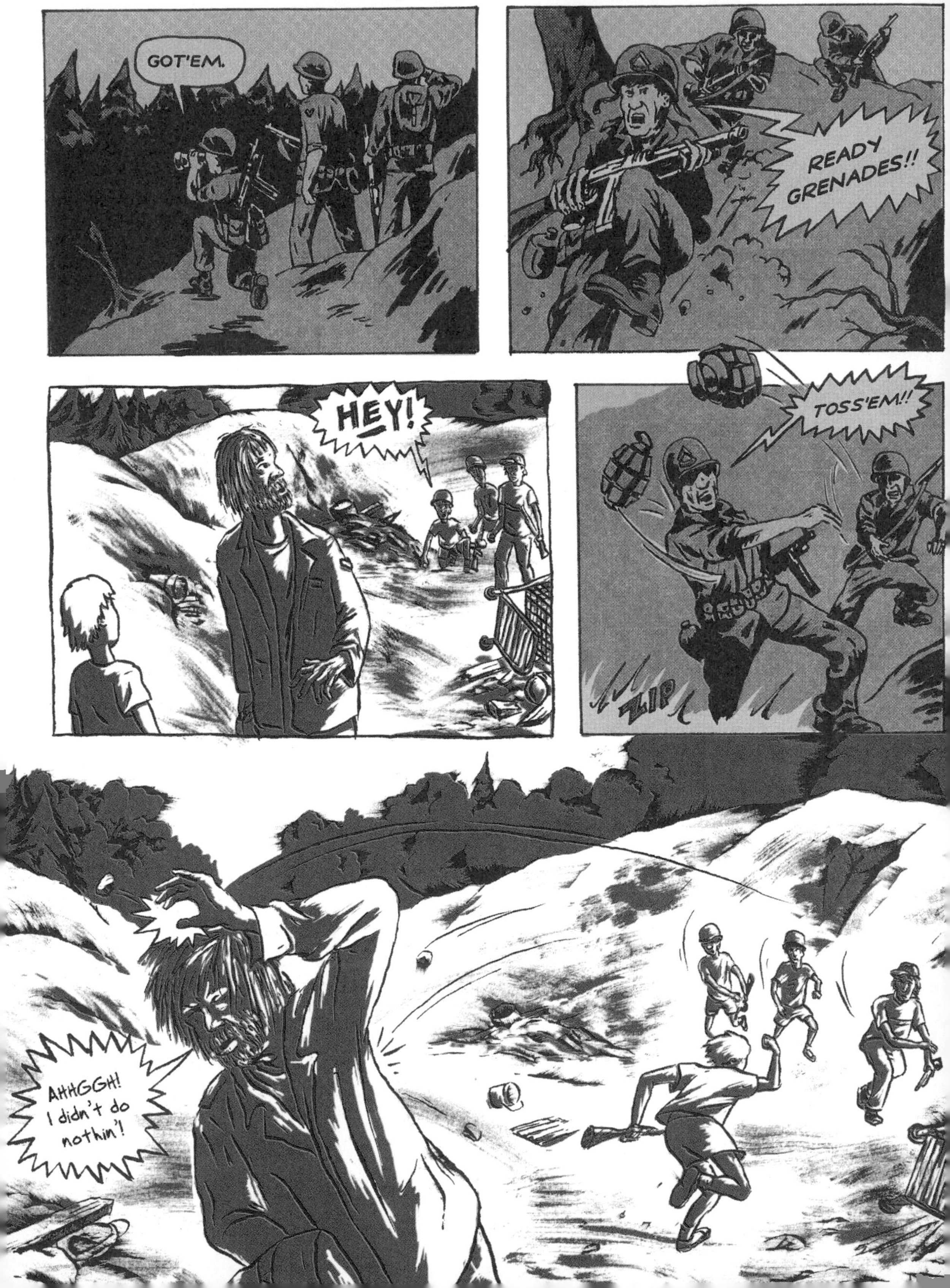
GOT'EM.
READY GRENADES!!
HEY!
TOSS'EM!!
ZIP
AHHGGH! I didn't do nothin'!

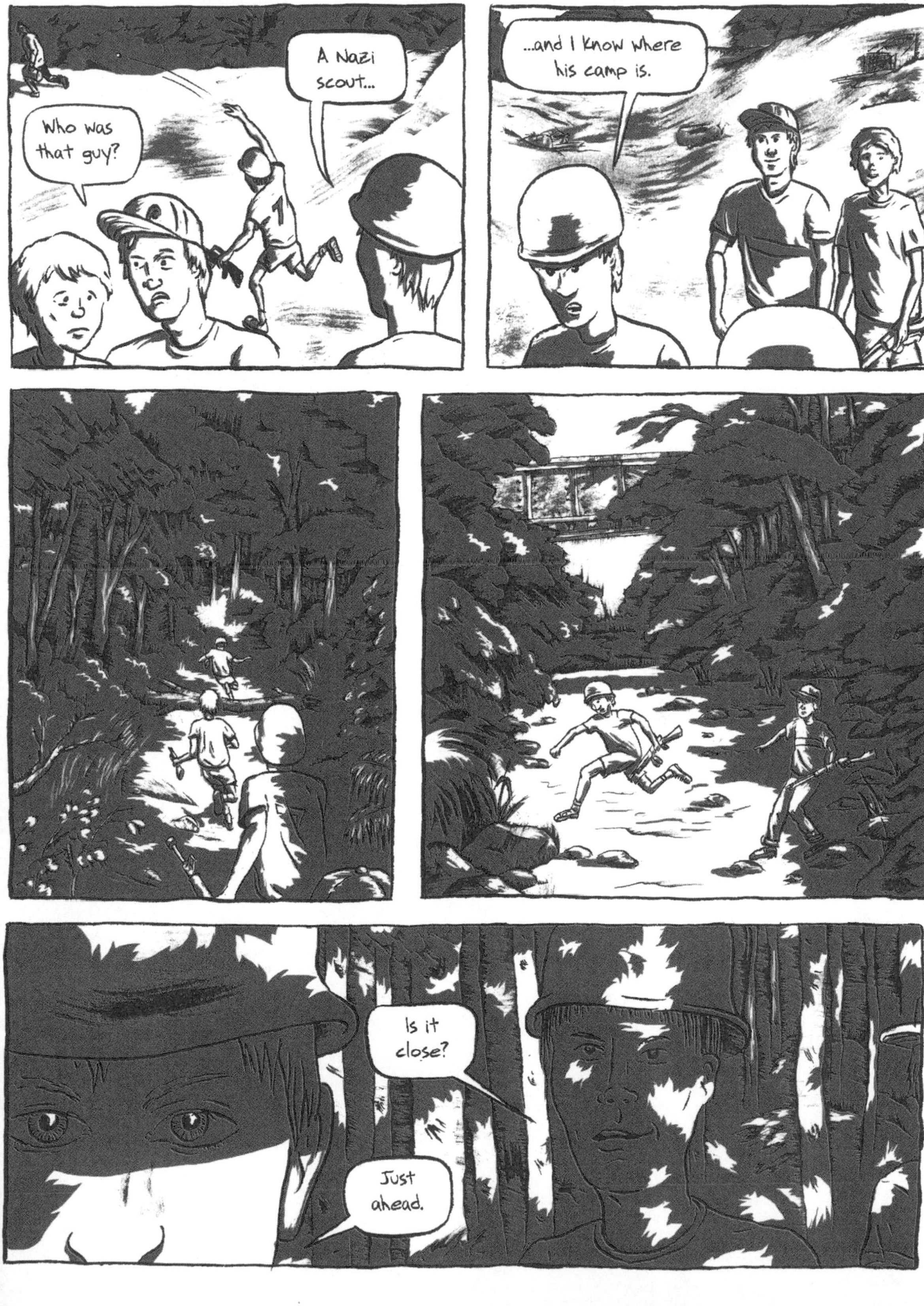
Who was that guy?
A Nazi scout...
...and I know where his camp is.
Is it close?
Just ahead.

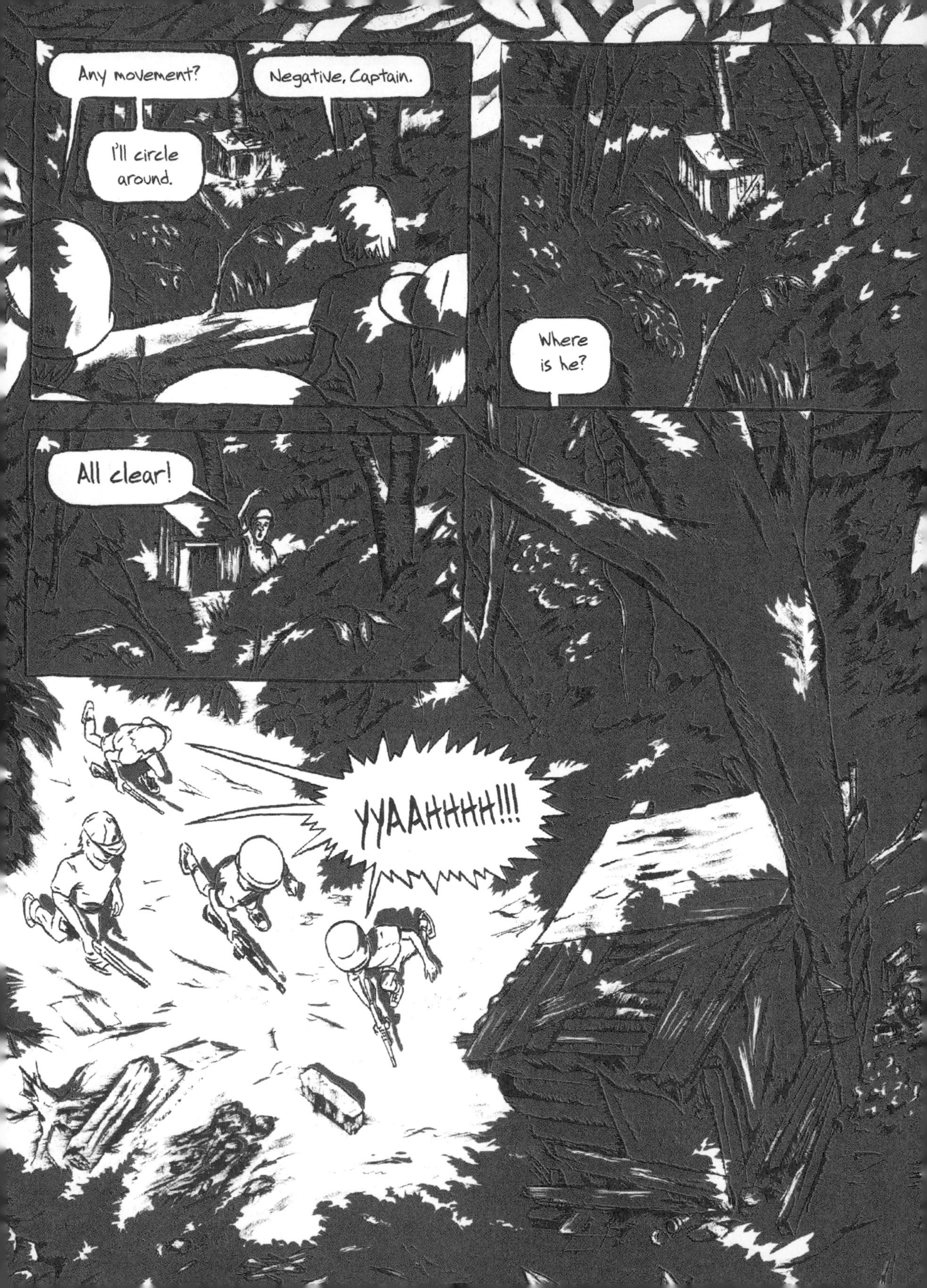
Any movement?
Negative, Captain.
I'll circle around.
Where is he?
All clear!
YYAAHHHH!!!

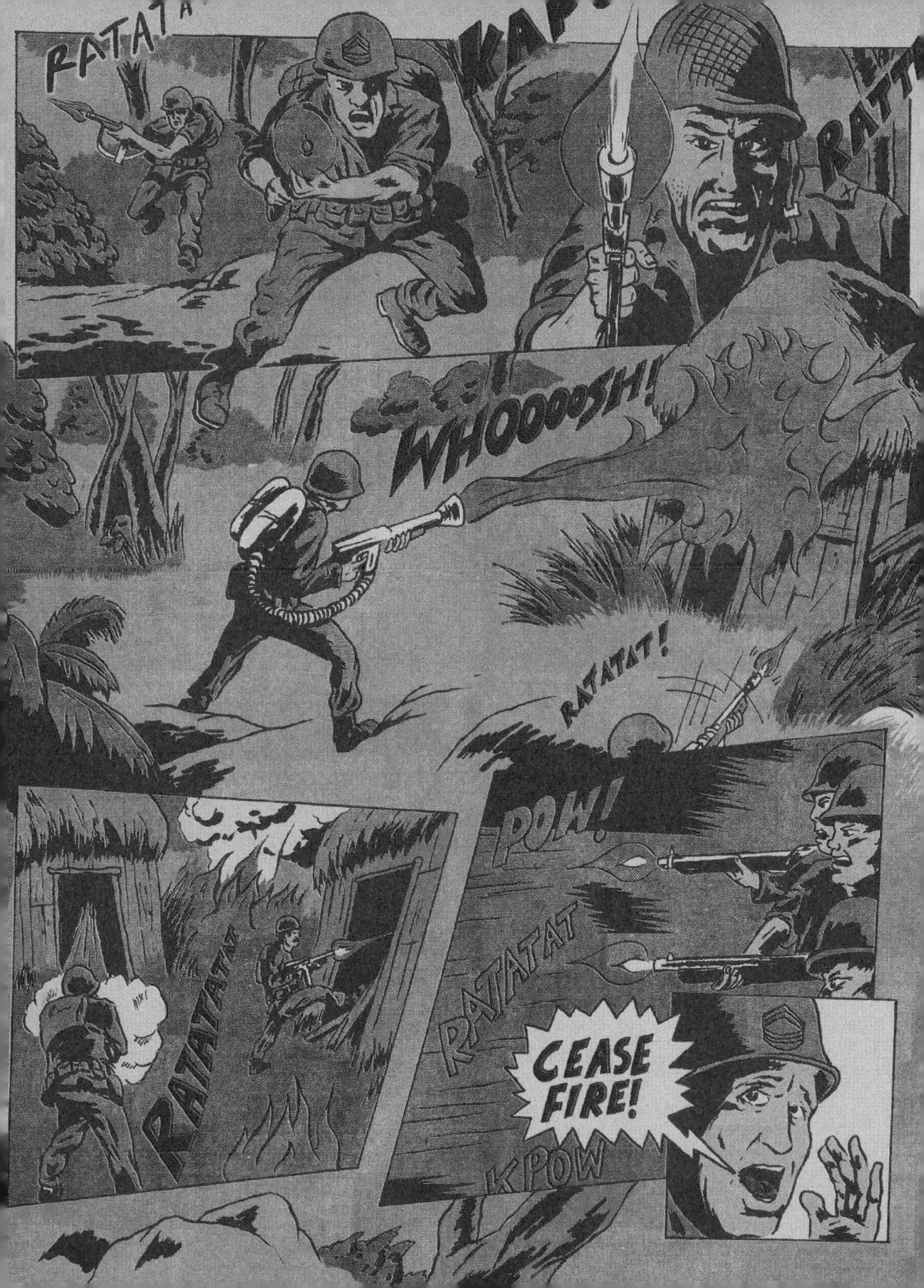
RATATA
KAP
RATT
WHOOOOOSH!
RATATAT!
POW!
RATATAT
RATATATAT
CEASE FIRE!
KPOW

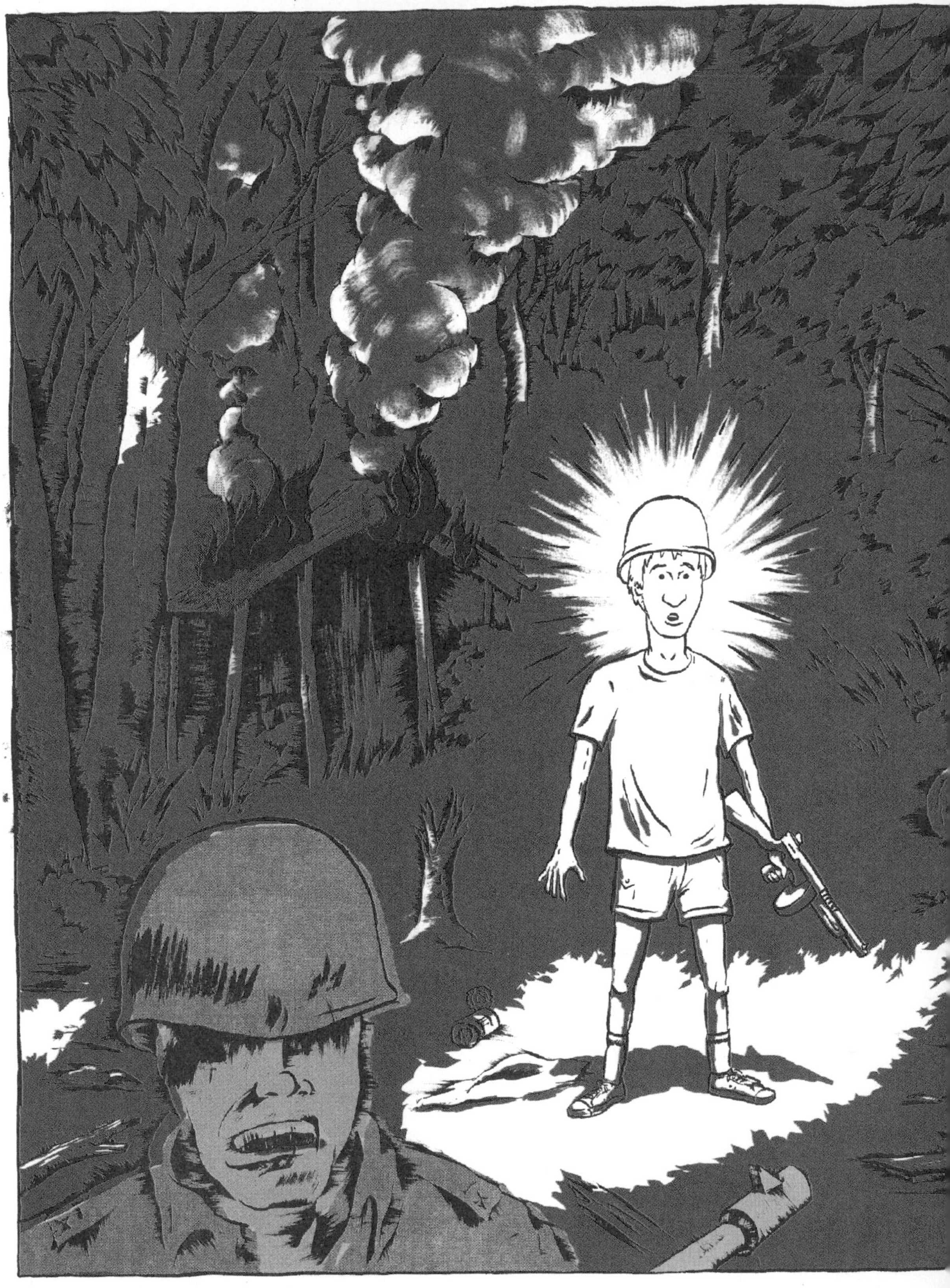

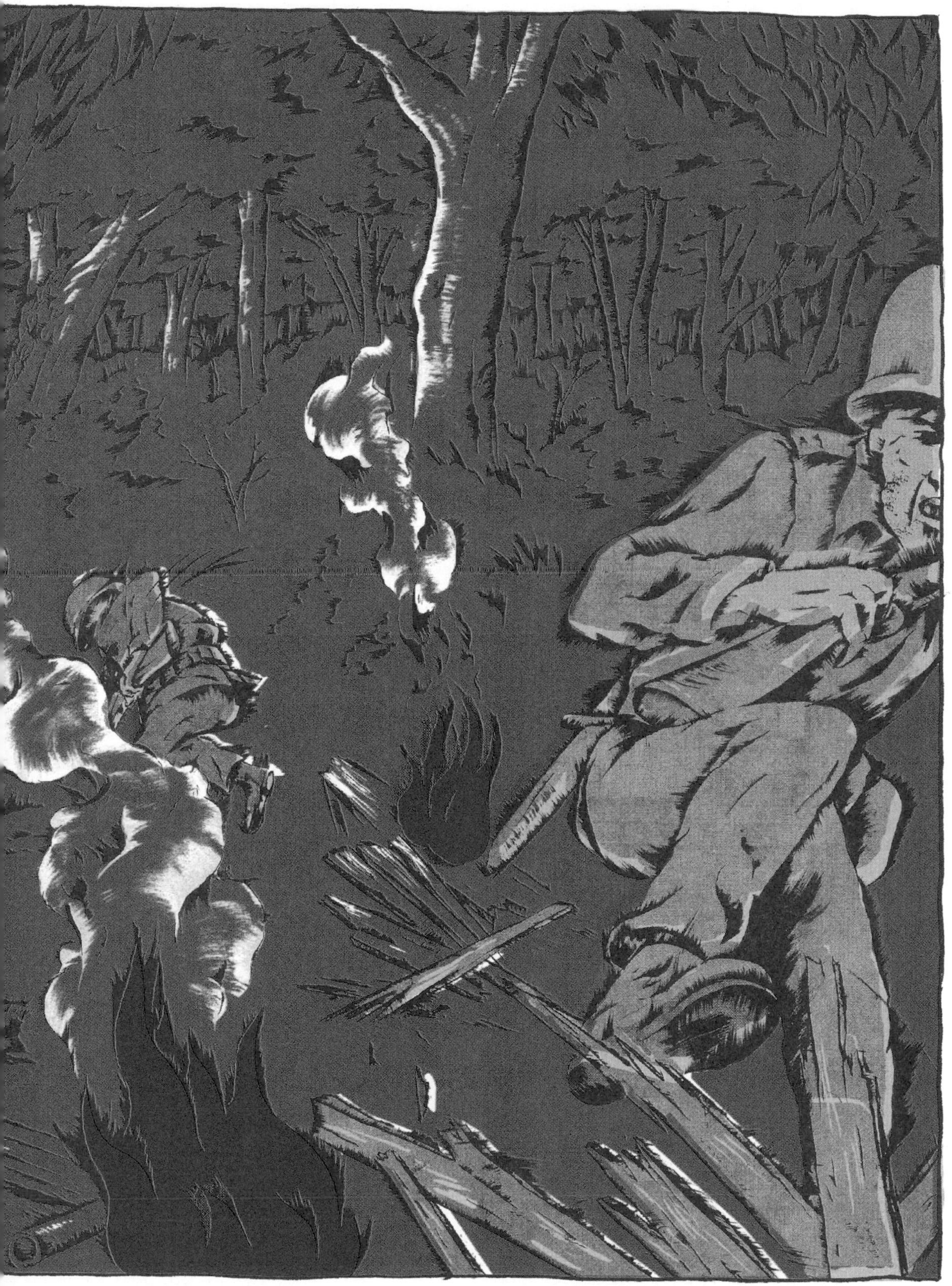

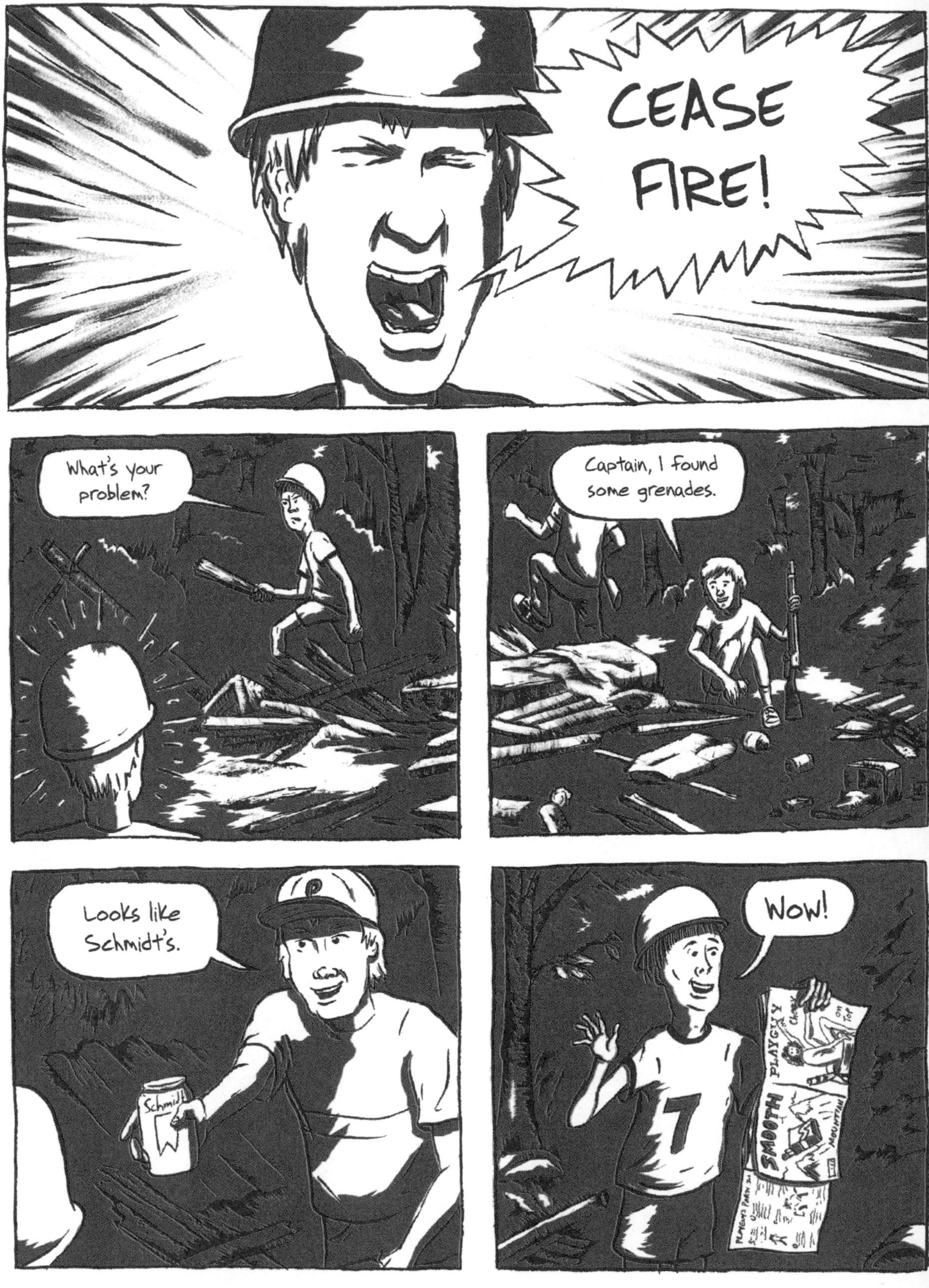
CEASE FIRE!
What's your problem?
Captain, I found some grenades.
Looks like Schmidt's.
Schmidt
Wow!
PLAYGUY
SMOOTH
MOUNTAIN

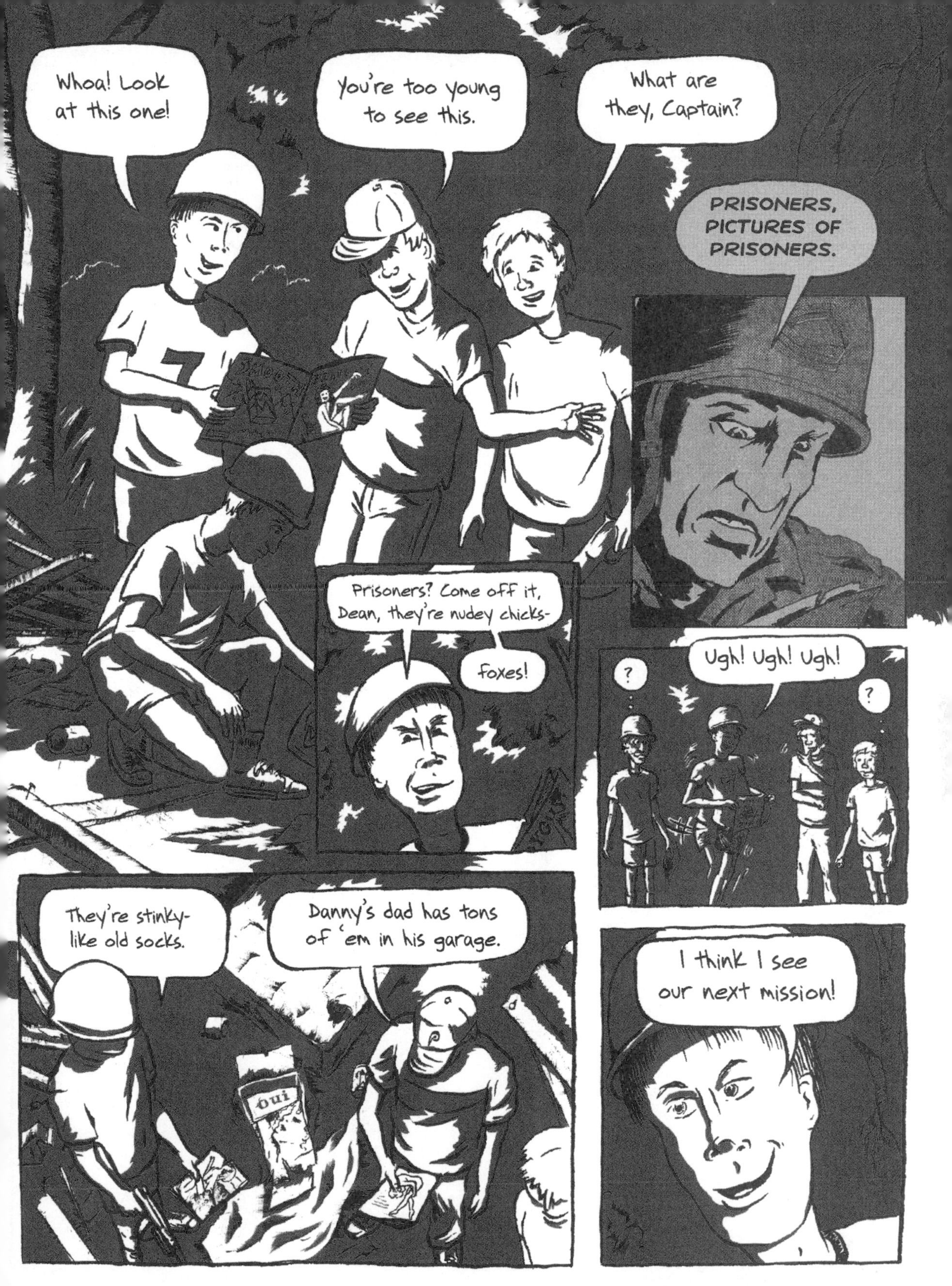
Whoa! Look at this one!
You're too young to see this.
What are they, Captain?
PRISONERS, PICTURES OF PRISONERS.
Prisoners? Come off it, Dean, they're nudey chicks-
foxes!
?
Ugh! Ugh! Ugh!
?
They're stinky- like old socks.
Danny's dad has tons of 'em in his garage.
oui
I think I see our next mission!

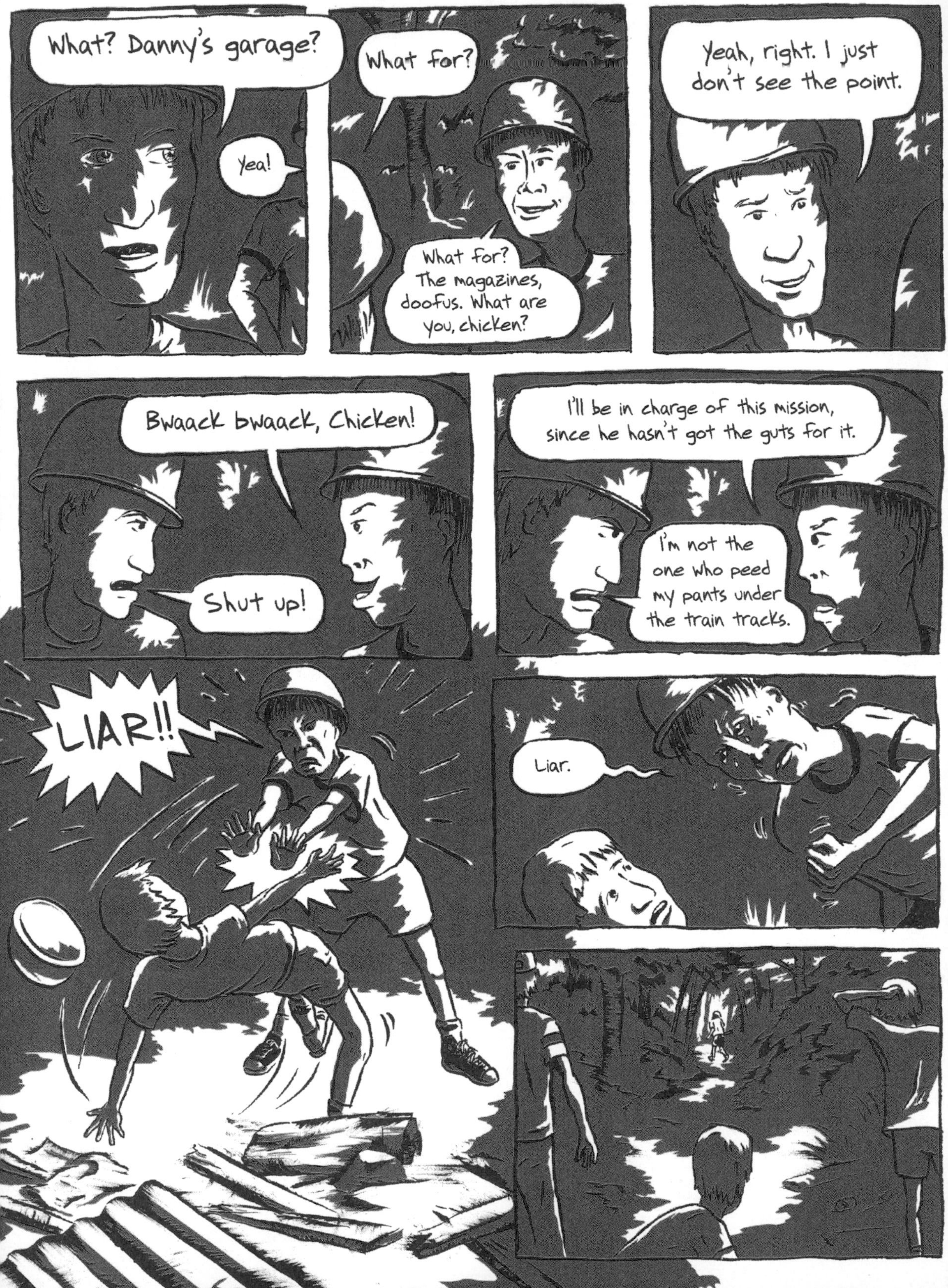
What? Danny's garage?
Yea!
What for?
What for? The magazines, doofus. What are you, chicken?
Yeah, right. I just don't see the point.
Bwaack bwaack, Chicken!
Shut up!
I'll be in charge of this mission, since he hasn't got the guts for it.
I'm not the one who peed my pants under the train tracks.
LIAR!!
Liar.

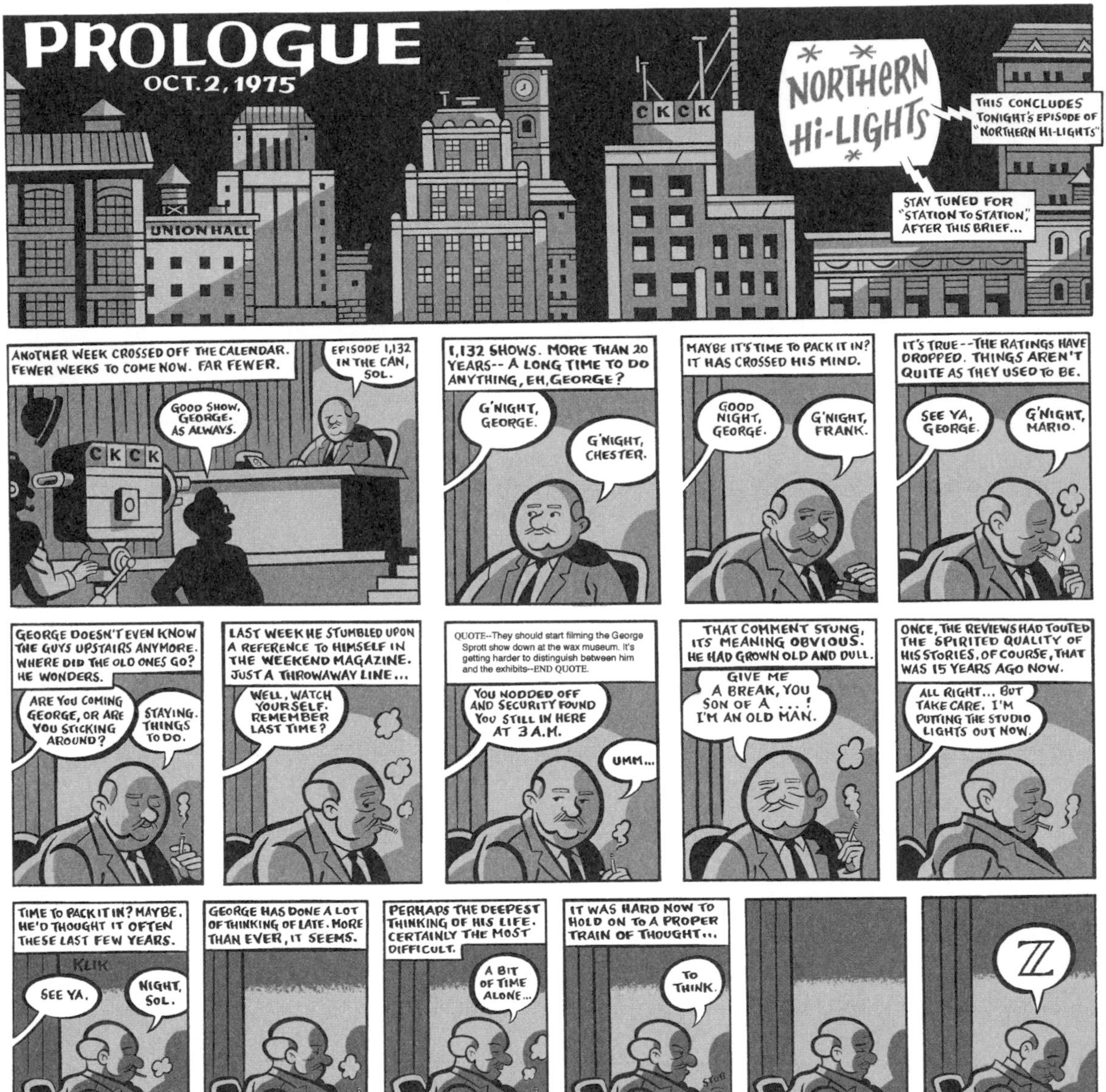
PROLOGUE
OCT. 2, 1975
UNION HALL
CKCK
NORTHERN HI-LIGHTS
THIS CONCLUDES TONIGHT'S EPISODE OF "NORTHERN HI-LIGHTS"
STAY TUNED FOR "STATION TO STATION," AFTER THIS BRIEF...
ANOTHER WEEK CROSSED OFF THE CALENDAR. FEWER WEEKS TO COME NOW. FAR FEWER.
EPISODE 1,132 IN THE CAN, SOL.
GOOD SHOW, GEORGE. AS ALWAYS.
CKCK
1,132 SHOWS. MORE THAN 20 YEARS-- A LONG TIME TO DO ANYTHING, EH, GEORGE?
G'NIGHT, GEORGE.
G'NIGHT, CHESTER.
MAYBE IT'S TIME TO PACK IT IN? IT HAS CROSSED HIS MIND.
GOOD NIGHT, GEORGE.
G'NIGHT, FRANK.
IT'S TRUE--THE RATINGS HAVE DROPPED. THINGS AREN'T QUITE AS THEY USED TO BE.
SEE YA, GEORGE.
G'NIGHT, MARIO.
GEORGE DOESN'T EVEN KNOW THE GUYS UPSTAIRS ANYMORE. WHERE DID THE OLD ONES GO? HE WONDERS.
ARE YOU COMING GEORGE, OR ARE YOU STICKING AROUND?
STAYING. THINGS TO DO.
LAST WEEK HE STUMBLED UPON A REFERENCE TO HIMSELF IN THE WEEKEND MAGAZINE. JUST A THROWAWAY LINE...
WELL, WATCH YOURSELF. REMEMBER LAST TIME?
QUOTE--They should start filming the George Sprott show down at the wax museum. It's getting harder to distinguish between him and the exhibits--END QUOTE.
YOU NODDED OFF AND SECURITY FOUND YOU STILL IN HERE AT 3 A.M.
UMM...
THAT COMMENT STUNG, ITS MEANING OBVIOUS. HE HAD GROWN OLD AND DULL.
GIVE ME A BREAK, YOU SON OF A ...! I'M AN OLD MAN.
ONCE, THE REVIEWS HAD TOUTED THE SPIRITED QUALITY OF HIS STORIES, OF COURSE, THAT WAS 15 YEARS AGO NOW.
ALL RIGHT... BUT TAKE CARE. I'M PUTTING THE STUDIO LIGHTS OUT NOW.
TIME TO PACK IT IN? MAYBE. HE'D THOUGHT IT OFTEN THESE LAST FEW YEARS.
KLIK
SEE YA.
NIGHT, SOL.
GEORGE HAS DONE A LOT OF THINKING OF LATE. MORE THAN EVER, IT SEEMS.
PERHAPS THE DEEPEST THINKING OF HIS LIFE. CERTAINLY THE MOST DIFFICULT.
A BIT OF TIME ALONE...
IT WAS HARD NOW TO HOLD ON TO A PROPER TRAIN OF THOUGHT...
TO THINK.
Z

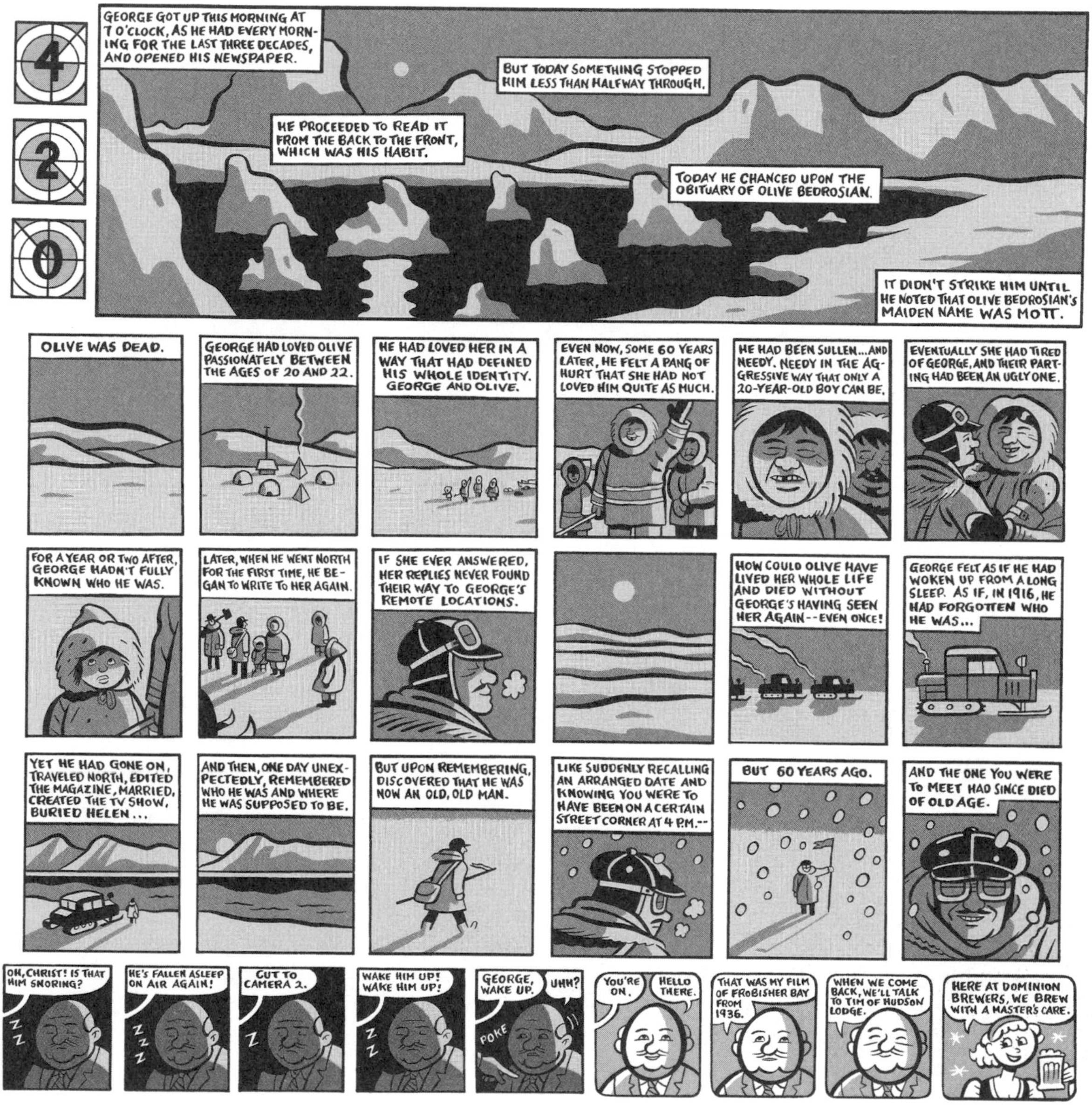
4
2
0
GEORGE GOT UP THIS MORNING AT 7 O'CLOCK, AS HE HAD EVERY MORNING FOR THE LAST THREE DECADES, AND OPENED HIS NEWSPAPER.
HE PROCEEDED TO READ IT FROM THE BACK TO THE FRONT, WHICH WAS HIS HABIT.
BUT TODAY SOMETHING STOPPED HIM LESS THAN HALFWAY THROUGH.
TODAY HE CHANCED UPON THE OBITUARY OF OLIVE BEDROSIAN.
IT DIDN'T STRIKE HIM UNTIL HE NOTED THAT OLIVE BEDROSIAN'S MAIDEN NAME WAS MOTT.
OLIVE WAS DEAD.
GEORGE HAD LOVED OLIVE PASSIONATELY BETWEEN THE AGES OF 20 AND 22.
HE HAD LOVED HER IN A WAY THAT HAD DEFINED HIS WHOLE IDENTITY. GEORGE AND OLIVE.
EVEN NOW, SOME 60 YEARS LATER, HE FELT A PANG OF HURT THAT SHE HAD NOT LOVED HIM QUITE AS MUCH.
HE HAD BEEN SULLEN...AND NEEDY. NEEDY IN THE AGGRESSIVE WAY THAT ONLY A 20-YEAR-OLD BOY CAN BE.
EVENTUALLY SHE HAD TIRED OF GEORGE, AND THEIR PARTING HAD BEEN AN UGLY ONE.
FOR A YEAR OR TWO AFTER, GEORGE HADN'T FULLY KNOWN WHO HE WAS.
LATER, WHEN HE WENT NORTH FOR THE FIRST TIME, HE BEGAN TO WRITE TO HER AGAIN.
IF SHE EVER ANSWERED, HER REPLIES NEVER FOUND THEIR WAY TO GEORGE'S REMOTE LOCATIONS.
HOW COULD OLIVE HAVE LIVED HER WHOLE LIFE AND DIED WITHOUT GEORGE'S HAVING SEEN HER AGAIN--EVEN ONCE!
GEORGE FELT AS IF HE HAD WOKEN UP FROM A LONG SLEEP. AS IF, IN 1916, HE HAD FORGOTTEN WHO HE WAS...
YET HE HAD GONE ON, TRAVELED NORTH, EDITED THE MAGAZINE, MARRIED, CREATED THE TV SHOW, BURIED HELEN...
AND THEN, ONE DAY UNEXPECTEDLY, REMEMBERED WHO HE WAS AND WHERE HE WAS SUPPOSED TO BE.
BUT UPON REMEMBERING, DISCOVERED THAT HE WAS NOW AN OLD, OLD MAN.
LIKE SUDDENLY RECALLING AN ARRANGED DATE AND KNOWING YOU WERE TO HAVE BEEN ON A CERTAIN STREET CORNER AT 4 P.M.--
BUT 60 YEARS AGO.
AND THE ONE YOU WERE TO MEET HAD SINCE DIED OF OLD AGE.
OH, CHRIST! IS THAT HIM SNORING?
Z Z
HE'S FALLEN ASLEEP ON AIR AGAIN!
Z Z Z
CUT TO CAMERA 2.
Z
WAKE HIM UP! WAKE HIM UP!
Z Z
GEORGE, WAKE UP.
UHH?
POKE
YOU'RE ON.
HELLO THERE.
THAT WAS MY FILM OF FROBISHER BAY FROM 1936.
WHEN WE COME BACK, WE'LL TALK TO TIM OF HUDSON LODGE.
HERE AT DOMINION BREWERS, WE BREW WITH A MASTER'S CARE.

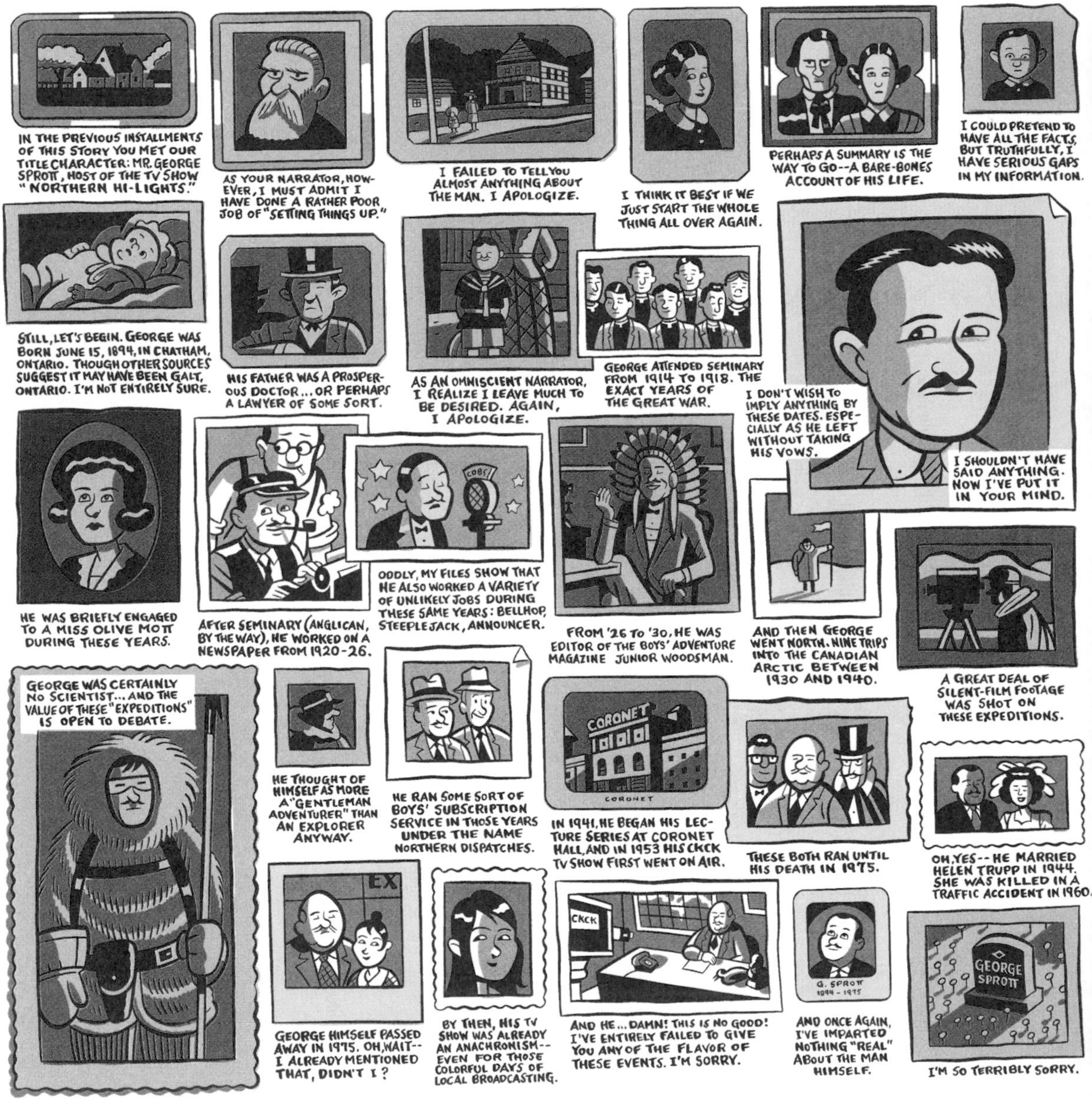
IN THE PREVIOUS INSTALLMENTS OF THIS STORY YOU MET OUR TITLE CHARACTER: MR. GEORGE SPROTT, HOST OF THE TV SHOW "NORTHERN HI-LIGHTS."
AS YOUR NARRATOR, HOWEVER, I MUST ADMIT I HAVE DONE A RATHER POOR JOB OF "SETTING THINGS UP."
I FAILED TO TELL YOU ALMOST ANYTHING ABOUT THE MAN. I APOLOGIZE.
I THINK IT BEST IF WE JUST START THE WHOLE THING ALL OVER AGAIN.
PERHAPS A SUMMARY IS THE WAY TO GO--A BARE-BONES ACCOUNT OF HIS LIFE.
I COULD PRETEND TO HAVE ALL THE FACTS, BUT TRUTHFULLY, I HAVE SERIOUS GAPS IN MY INFORMATION.
STILL, LET'S BEGIN. GEORGE WAS BORN JUNE 15, 1894, IN CHATHAM, ONTARIO. THOUGH OTHER SOURCES SUGGEST IT MAY HAVE BEEN GALT, ONTARIO. I'M NOT ENTIRELY SURE.
HIS FATHER WAS A PROSPEROUS DOCTOR... OR PERHAPS A LAWYER OF SOME SORT.
AS AN OMNISCIENT NARRATOR, I REALIZE I LEAVE MUCH TO BE DESIRED. AGAIN, I APOLOGIZE.
GEORGE ATTENDED SEMINARY FROM 1914 TO 1918. THE EXACT YEARS OF THE GREAT WAR.
I DON'T WISH TO IMPLY ANYTHING BY THESE DATES. ESPECIALLY AS HE LEFT WITHOUT TAKING HIS VOWS.
I SHOULDN'T HAVE SAID ANYTHING. NOW I'VE PUT IT IN YOUR MIND.
HE WAS BRIEFLY ENGAGED TO A MISS OLIVE MOTT DURING THESE YEARS.
AFTER SEMINARY (ANGLICAN, BY THE WAY), HE WORKED ON A NEWSPAPER FROM 1920-26.
ODDLY, MY FILES SHOW THAT HE ALSO WORKED A VARIETY OF UNLIKELY JOBS DURING THESE SAME YEARS: BELLHOP, STEEPLEJACK, ANNOUNCER.
FROM '26 TO '30, HE WAS EDITOR OF THE BOYS' ADVENTURE MAGAZINE JUNIOR WOODSMAN.
AND THEN GEORGE WENT NORTH. NINE TRIPS INTO THE CANADIAN ARCTIC BETWEEN 1930 AND 1940.
A GREAT DEAL OF SILENT-FILM FOOTAGE WAS SHOT ON THESE EXPEDITIONS.
GEORGE WAS CERTAINLY NO SCIENTIST... AND THE VALUE OF THESE "EXPEDITIONS" IS OPEN TO DEBATE.
HE THOUGHT OF HIMSELF AS MORE A "GENTLEMAN ADVENTURER" THAN AN EXPLORER ANYWAY.
HE RAN SOME SORT OF BOYS' SUBSCRIPTION SERVICE IN THOSE YEARS UNDER THE NAME NORTHERN DISPATCHES.
CORONET
CORONET
IN 1941, HE BEGAN HIS LECTURE SERIES AT CORONET HALL, AND IN 1953 HIS CKCK TV SHOW FIRST WENT ON AIR.
THESE BOTH RAN UNTIL HIS DEATH IN 1975.
OH, YES--HE MARRIED HELEN TRUPP IN 1944. SHE WAS KILLED IN A TRAFFIC ACCIDENT IN 1960.
EX
GEORGE HIMSELF PASSED AWAY IN 1975. OH, WAIT--I ALREADY MENTIONED THAT, DIDN'T I?
BY THEN, HIS TV SHOW WAS ALREADY AN ANACHRONISM--EVEN FOR THOSE COLORFUL DAYS OF LOCAL BROADCASTING.
CKCK
AND HE... DAMN! THIS IS NO GOOD! I'VE ENTIRELY FAILED TO GIVE YOU ANY OF THE FLAVOR OF THESE EVENTS. I'M SORRY.
G. SPROTT 1894-1975
AND ONCE AGAIN, I'VE IMPARTED NOTHING "REAL" ABOUT THE MAN HIMSELF.
GEORGE SPROTT
I'M SO TERRIBLY SORRY.

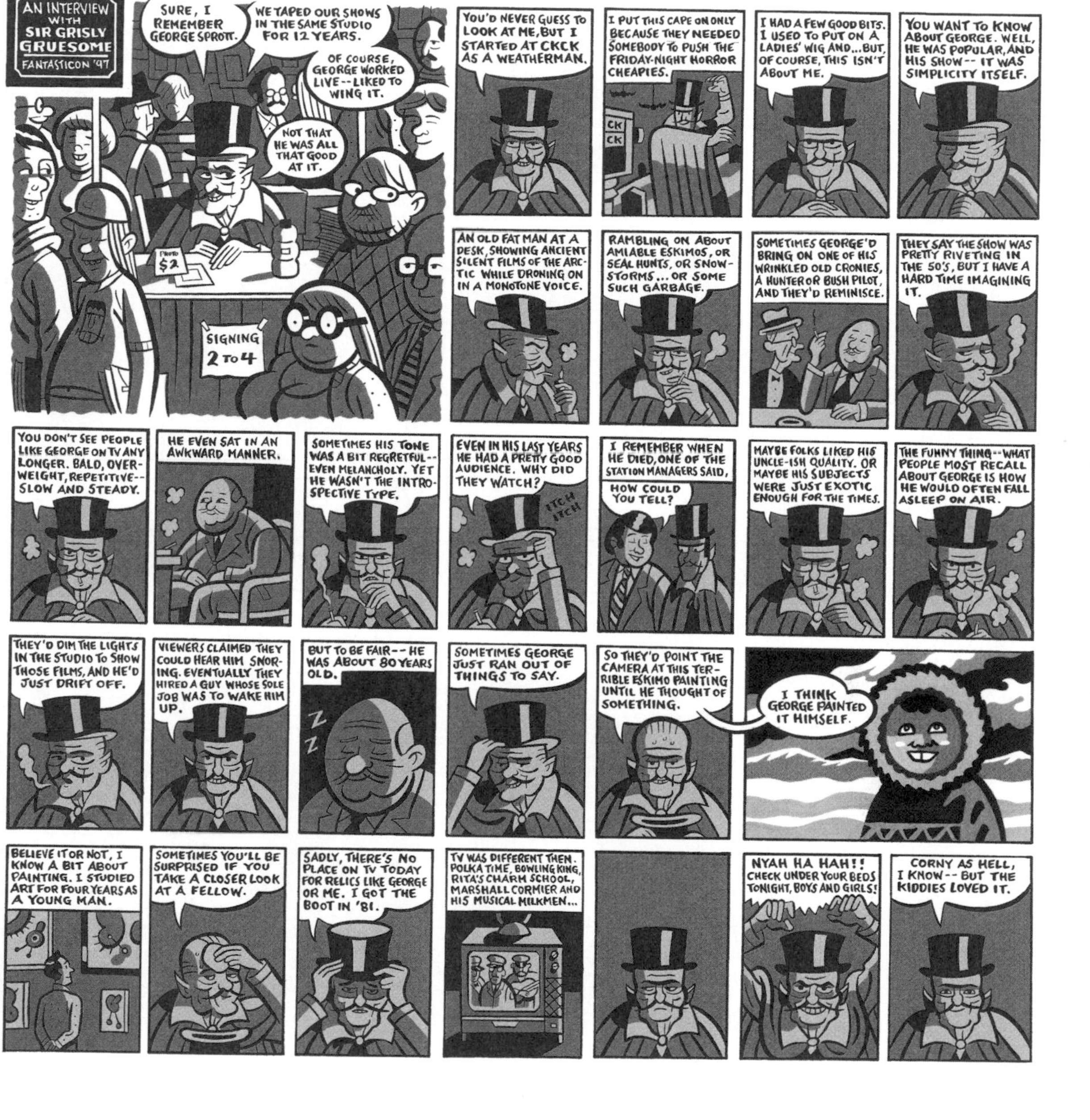

AN INTERVIEW WITH SIR GRISLY GRUESOME
FANTASTICON '97
SURE, I REMEMBER GEORGE SPROTT.
WE TAPED OUR SHOWS IN THE SAME STUDIO FOR 12 YEARS.
OF COURSE, GEORGE WORKED LIVE -- LIKED TO WING IT.
NOT THAT HE WAS ALL THAT GOOD AT IT.
PHOTO $2
SIGNING 2 TO 4
YOU'D NEVER GUESS TO LOOK AT ME, BUT I STARTED AT CKCK AS A WEATHERMAN.
I PUT THIS CAPE ON ONLY BECAUSE THEY NEEDED SOMEBODY TO PUSH THE FRIDAY-NIGHT HORROR CHEAPIES.
CK
CK
I HAD A FEW GOOD BITS. I USED TO PUT ON A LADIES' WIG AND... BUT, OF COURSE, THIS ISN'T ABOUT ME.
YOU WANT TO KNOW ABOUT GEORGE. WELL, HE WAS POPULAR, AND HIS SHOW -- IT WAS SIMPLICITY ITSELF.
AN OLD FAT MAN AT A DESK, SHOWING ANCIENT SILENT FILMS OF THE ARCTIC WHILE DRONING ON IN A MONOTONE VOICE.
RAMBLING ON ABOUT AMIABLE ESKIMOS, OR SEAL HUNTS, OR SNOWSTORMS... OR SOME SUCH GARBAGE.
SOMETIMES GEORGE'D BRING ON ONE OF HIS WRINKLED OLD CRONIES, A HUNTER OR BUSH PILOT, AND THEY'D REMINISCE.
THEY SAY THE SHOW WAS PRETTY RIVETING IN THE 50'S, BUT I HAVE A HARD TIME IMAGINING IT.
YOU DON'T SEE PEOPLE LIKE GEORGE ON TV ANY LONGER. BALD, OVERWEIGHT, REPETITIVE -- SLOW AND STEADY.
HE EVEN SAT IN AN AWKWARD MANNER.
SOMETIMES HIS TONE WAS A BIT REGRETFUL -- EVEN MELANCHOLY. YET HE WASN'T THE INTROSPECTIVE TYPE.
EVEN IN HIS LAST YEARS HE HAD A PRETTY GOOD AUDIENCE. WHY DID THEY WATCH?
ITCH ITCH
I REMEMBER WHEN HE DIED, ONE OF THE STATION MANAGERS SAID,
HOW COULD YOU TELL?
MAYBE FOLKS LIKED HIS UNCLE-ISH QUALITY. OR MAYBE HIS SUBJECTS WERE JUST EXOTIC ENOUGH FOR THE TIMES.
THE FUNNY THING -- WHAT PEOPLE MOST RECALL ABOUT GEORGE IS HOW HE WOULD OFTEN FALL ASLEEP ON AIR.
THEY'D DIM THE LIGHTS IN THE STUDIO TO SHOW THOSE FILMS, AND HE'D JUST DRIFT OFF.
VIEWERS CLAIMED THEY COULD HEAR HIM SNORING. EVENTUALLY THEY HIRED A GUY WHOSE SOLE JOB WAS TO WAKE HIM UP.
BUT TO BE FAIR -- HE WAS ABOUT 80 YEARS OLD.
Z Z
SOMETIMES GEORGE JUST RAN OUT OF THINGS TO SAY.
SO THEY'D POINT THE CAMERA AT THIS TERRIBLE ESKIMO PAINTING UNTIL HE THOUGHT OF SOMETHING.
I THINK GEORGE PAINTED IT HIMSELF.
BELIEVE IT OR NOT, I KNOW A BIT ABOUT PAINTING. I STUDIED ART FOR FOUR YEARS AS A YOUNG MAN.
SOMETIMES YOU'LL BE SURPRISED IF YOU TAKE A CLOSER LOOK AT A FELLOW.
SADLY, THERE'S NO PLACE ON TV TODAY FOR RELICS LIKE GEORGE OR ME. I GOT THE BOOT IN '81.
TV WAS DIFFERENT THEN. POLKA TIME, BOWLING KING, RITA'S CHARM SCHOOL, MARSHALL CORMIER AND HIS MUSICAL MILKMEN...
NYAH HA HAH!! CHECK UNDER YOUR BEDS TONIGHT, BOYS AND GIRLS!
CORNY AS HELL, I KNOW -- BUT THE KIDDIES LOVED IT.

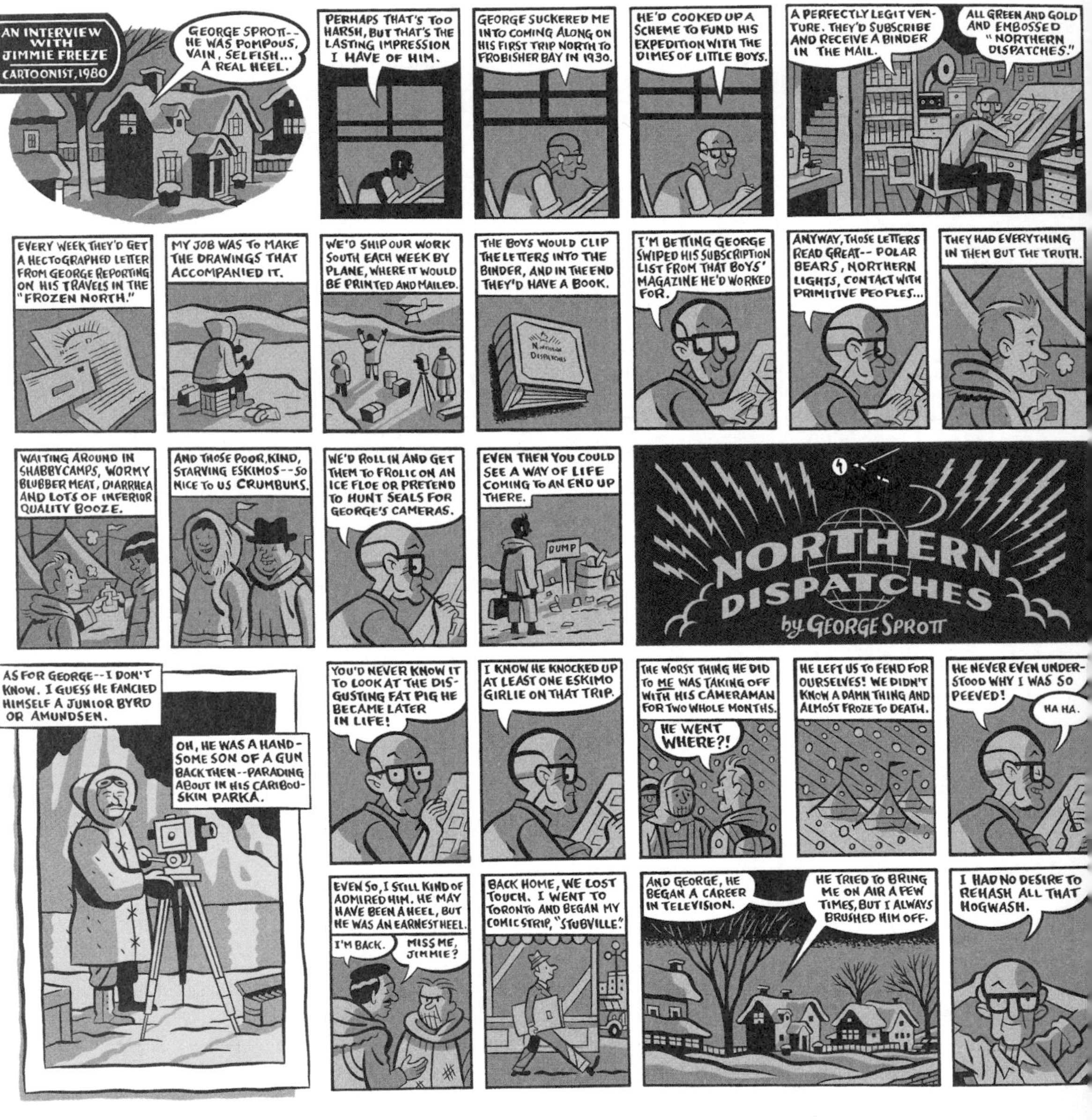
AN INTERVIEW WITH JIMMIE FREEZE
CARTOONIST, 1980
GEORGE SPROTT--HE WAS POMPOUS, VAIN, SELFISH... A REAL HEEL.
PERHAPS THAT'S TOO HARSH, BUT THAT'S THE LASTING IMPRESSION I HAVE OF HIM.
GEORGE SUCKERED ME INTO COMING ALONG ON HIS FIRST TRIP NORTH TO FROBISHER BAY IN 1930.
HE'D COOKED UP A SCHEME TO FUND HIS EXPEDITION WITH THE DIMES OF LITTLE BOYS.
A PERFECTLY LEGIT VENTURE. THEY'D SUBSCRIBE AND RECEIVE A BINDER IN THE MAIL.
ALL GREEN AND GOLD AND EMBOSSED "NORTHERN DISPATCHES."
EVERY WEEK THEY'D GET A HECTOGRAPHED LETTER FROM GEORGE REPORTING ON HIS TRAVELS IN THE "FROZEN NORTH."
MY JOB WAS TO MAKE THE DRAWINGS THAT ACCOMPANIED IT.
WE'D SHIP OUR WORK SOUTH EACH WEEK BY PLANE, WHERE IT WOULD BE PRINTED AND MAILED.
THE BOYS WOULD CLIP THE LETTERS INTO THE BINDER, AND IN THE END THEY'D HAVE A BOOK.
I'M BETTING GEORGE SWIPED HIS SUBSCRIPTION LIST FROM THAT BOYS' MAGAZINE HE'D WORKED FOR.
ANYWAY, THOSE LETTERS READ GREAT-- POLAR BEARS, NORTHERN LIGHTS, CONTACT WITH PRIMITIVE PEOPLES...
THEY HAD EVERYTHING IN THEM BUT THE TRUTH.
WAITING AROUND IN SHABBY CAMPS, WORMY BLUBBER MEAT, DIARRHEA AND LOTS OF INFERIOR QUALITY BOOZE.
AND THOSE POOR, KIND, STARVING ESKIMOS--SO NICE TO US CRUMBUMS.
WE'D ROLL IN AND GET THEM TO FROLIC ON AN ICE FLOE OR PRETEND TO HUNT SEALS FOR GEORGE'S CAMERAS.
EVEN THEN YOU COULD SEE A WAY OF LIFE COMING TO AN END UP THERE.
DUMP
NORTHERN DISPATCHES
by GEORGE SPROTT
AS FOR GEORGE--I DON'T KNOW. I GUESS HE FANCIED HIMSELF A JUNIOR BYRD OR AMUNDSEN.
OH, HE WAS A HANDSOME SON OF A GUN BACK THEN--PARADING ABOUT IN HIS CARIBOU-SKIN PARKA.
YOU'D NEVER KNOW IT TO LOOK AT THE DISGUSTING FAT PIG HE BECAME LATER IN LIFE!
I KNOW HE KNOCKED UP AT LEAST ONE ESKIMO GIRLIE ON THAT TRIP.
THE WORST THING HE DID TO ME WAS TAKING OFF WITH HIS CAMERAMAN FOR TWO WHOLE MONTHS.
HE WENT WHERE?!
HE LEFT US TO FEND FOR OURSELVES! WE DIDN'T KNOW A DAMN THING AND ALMOST FROZE TO DEATH.
HE NEVER EVEN UNDERSTOOD WHY I WAS SO PEEVED!
HA HA.
EVEN SO, I STILL KIND OF ADMIRED HIM. HE MAY HAVE BEEN A HEEL, BUT HE WAS AN EARNEST HEEL.
I'M BACK.
MISS ME, JIMMIE?
BACK HOME, WE LOST TOUCH. I WENT TO TORONTO AND BEGAN MY COMIC STRIP, "STUBVILLE."
AND GEORGE, HE BEGAN A CAREER IN TELEVISION.
HE TRIED TO BRING ME ON AIR A FEW TIMES, BUT I ALWAYS BRUSHED HIM OFF.
I HAD NO DESIRE TO REHASH ALL THAT HOGWASH.

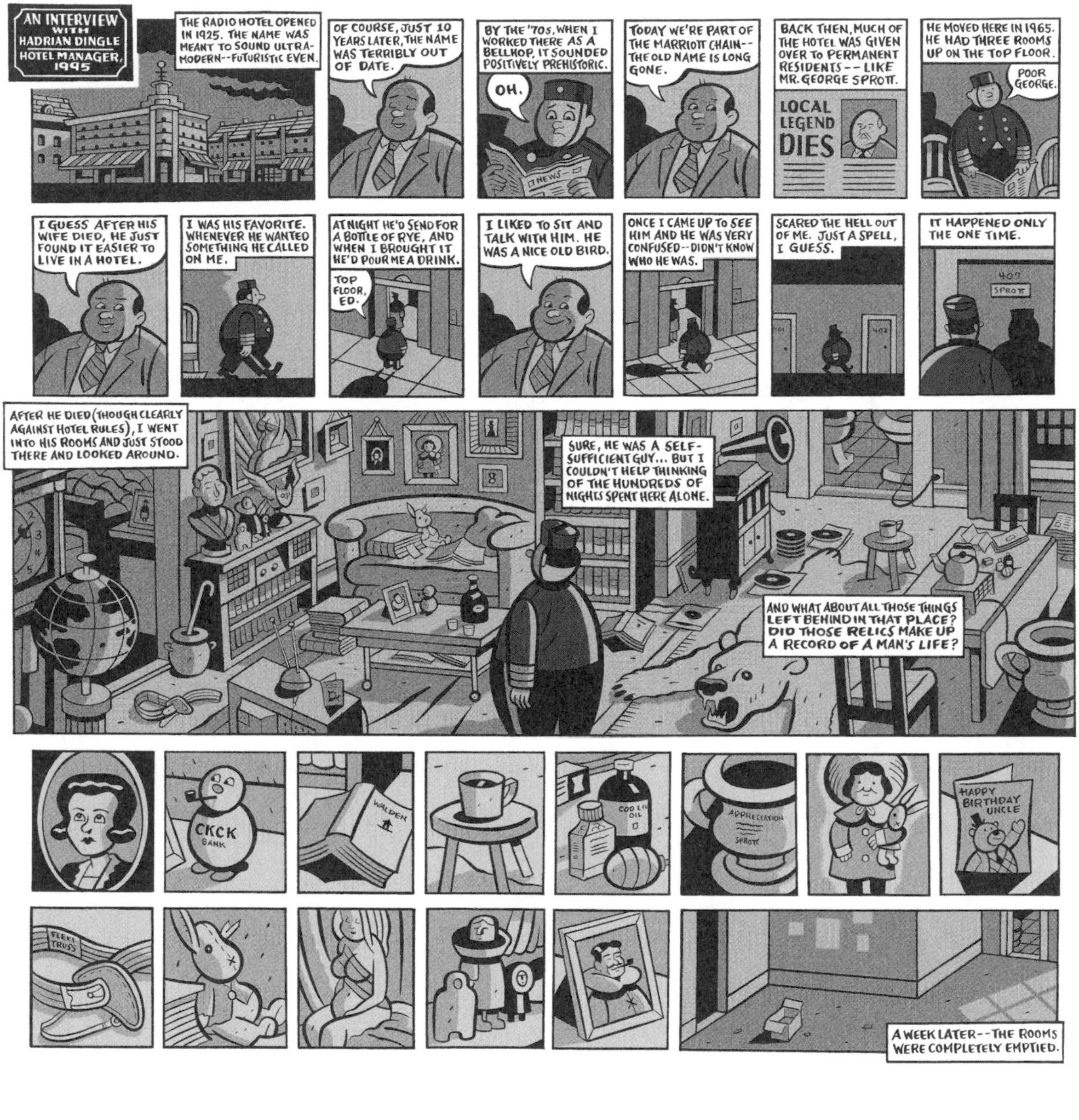
AN INTERVIEW WITH HADRIAN DINGLE
HOTEL MANAGER, 1995
THE RADIO HOTEL OPENED IN 1925. THE NAME WAS MEANT TO SOUND ULTRA-MODERN--FUTURISTIC EVEN.
OF COURSE, JUST 10 YEARS LATER, THE NAME WAS TERRIBLY OUT OF DATE.
BY THE '70S, WHEN I WORKED THERE AS A BELLHOP, IT SOUNDED POSITIVELY PREHISTORIC.
OH.
NEWS
TODAY WE'RE PART OF THE MARRIOTT CHAIN--THE OLD NAME IS LONG GONE.
BACK THEN, MUCH OF THE HOTEL WAS GIVEN OVER TO PERMANENT RESIDENTS--LIKE MR. GEORGE SPROTT.
LOCAL LEGEND DIES
HE MOVED HERE IN 1965. HE HAD THREE ROOMS UP ON THE TOP FLOOR.
POOR GEORGE.
I GUESS AFTER HIS WIFE DIED, HE JUST FOUND IT EASIER TO LIVE IN A HOTEL.
I WAS HIS FAVORITE. WHENEVER HE WANTED SOMETHING HE CALLED ON ME.
AT NIGHT HE'D SEND FOR A BOTTLE OF RYE, AND WHEN I BROUGHT IT HE'D POUR ME A DRINK.
TOP FLOOR, ED.
I LIKED TO SIT AND TALK WITH HIM. HE WAS A NICE OLD BIRD.
ONCE I CAME UP TO SEE HIM AND HE WAS VERY CONFUSED--DIDN'T KNOW WHO HE WAS.
SCARED THE HELL OUT OF ME. JUST A SPELL, I GUESS.
IT HAPPENED ONLY THE ONE TIME.
407
SPROTT
AFTER HE DIED (THOUGH CLEARLY AGAINST HOTEL RULES), I WENT INTO HIS ROOMS AND JUST STOOD THERE AND LOOKED AROUND.
SURE, HE WAS A SELF-SUFFICIENT GUY... BUT I COULDN'T HELP THINKING OF THE HUNDREDS OF NIGHTS SPENT HERE ALONE.
AND WHAT ABOUT ALL THOSE THINGS LEFT BEHIND IN THAT PLACE? DID THOSE RELICS MAKE UP A RECORD OF A MAN'S LIFE?
CKCK BANK
WALDEN
COD LIV OIL
APPRECIATION SPROTT
HAPPY BIRTHDAY UNCLE
FLEXI TRUSS
A WEEK LATER--THE ROOMS WERE COMPLETELY EMPTIED.

AN INTERVIEW WITH DAISY SPROTT 2007
NARWHAL BOOKS
UNCLE GEORGE LEFT A DEEP AND LASTING IMPRESSION ON MY LIFE.
FOR 15 YEARS I'VE PUBLISHED THIS SMALL MAGAZINE.
WE PRINT POETRY, FICTION, ESSAYS, DRAWINGS, OLD PHOTOS... HISTORIC MAPS--ANYTHING RELATED TO THE CANADIAN ARCTIC.
NO. 40
The NORTHWINDS JOURNAL
IT EXISTS BECAUSE OF UNCLE GEORGE.
Y'KNOW, I MARRIED TWICE, AND BOTH MARRIAGES FAILED.
NARWHAL BOOKS
IT MAY SOUND SILLY-- BUT NEITHER OF THEM COULD LIVE UP TO HIM.
UNCLE GEORGE WAS JUST SO VITAL. HE MADE EVERYTHING INTERESTING.
IT WASN'T THEIR FAULT IF THEY WERE JUST REGULAR HUMDRUM GUYS.
UNCLE GEORGE SHOWED SUCH A GENUINE CONCERN FOR ME. I LOVED HIM.
EVEN AT THE END WHEN HE WAS SO DIFFICULT... HE WAS KIND TO ME.
KLIK
AFTER UNCLE GEORGE DIED, I HAD TO WRAP UP HIS AFFAIRS.
I WAS SHELL SHOCKED AT THE TIME. I MADE SOME VERY POOR DECISIONS.
I FOOLISHLY SOLD OFF A LOT OF THE STUFF LEFT BEHIND IN HIS HOTEL ROOMS.
I DID KEEP THE MOST IMPORTANT ITEMS... PHOTO ALBUMS AND SUCH.
IT DIDN'T OCCUR TO ME FOR A LONG TIME TO APPROACH CKCK TV ABOUT HIS FILMS AND TAPED EPISODES.
I'D WAITED TOO LONG. THEY'D DISPOSED OF IT ALL-- DUMPED THEIR ENTIRE PRE-1980 VIDEO LIBRARY.
GEORGE SPROTT
THAT WAS A REAL BLOW.
I'D SOLD HIS BOUND LECTURES TO A NICE LADY WHO ATTENDED CORONET HALL FOR YEARS.
I REGRET THAT NOW. I COULD HAVE PUBLISHED THEM.
THOUGH WHO'D HAVE BOUGHT THAT BOOK?! I'M ON MY LAST LEGS AS IT IS.
I'M CEASING PRODUCTION ON NORTHWINDS AFTER THE NEXT ISSUE.
THERE'S NO AUDIENCE FOR IT. I'M BARELY MAKING LUNCH MONEY.
I WON'T BE OUT OF BUSINESS. I STILL HAVE THE NARWHAL PRESS.
WE PUBLISH BOOKS ON LOCAL HISTORY, CANADIANA... THAT SORT OF THING.
KLIK
WITH A BIT OF GOVERNMENT HELP, WE SHOULD SQUEAK BY.
ARCAD
BUT I WAS TALKING ABOUT UNCLE GEORGE, WASN'T I...?
THE OTHER DAY I SAW A MAN WHO LOOKED LIKE UNCLE GEORGE.
IT WAS IN THE STREET, AND ONLY FROM THE BACK.
BUT I WAS SURPRISED AT THE INTENSITY OF MY REACTION.
TEARS ALMOST POPPED RIGHT OUT OF MY EYES.

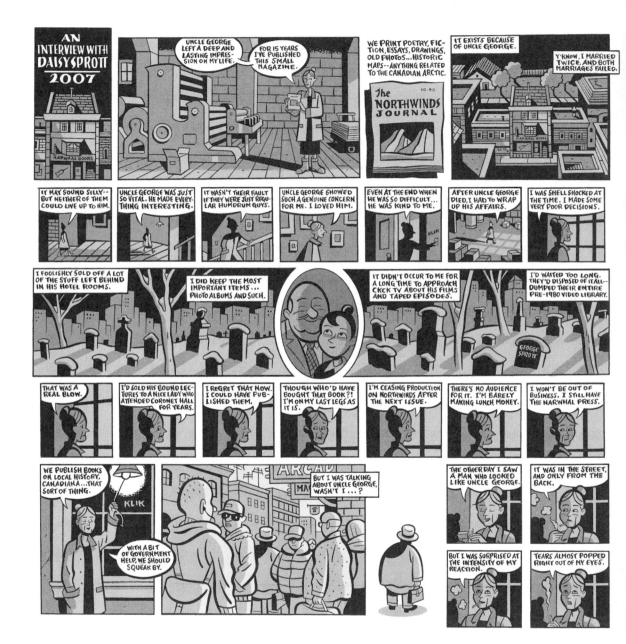

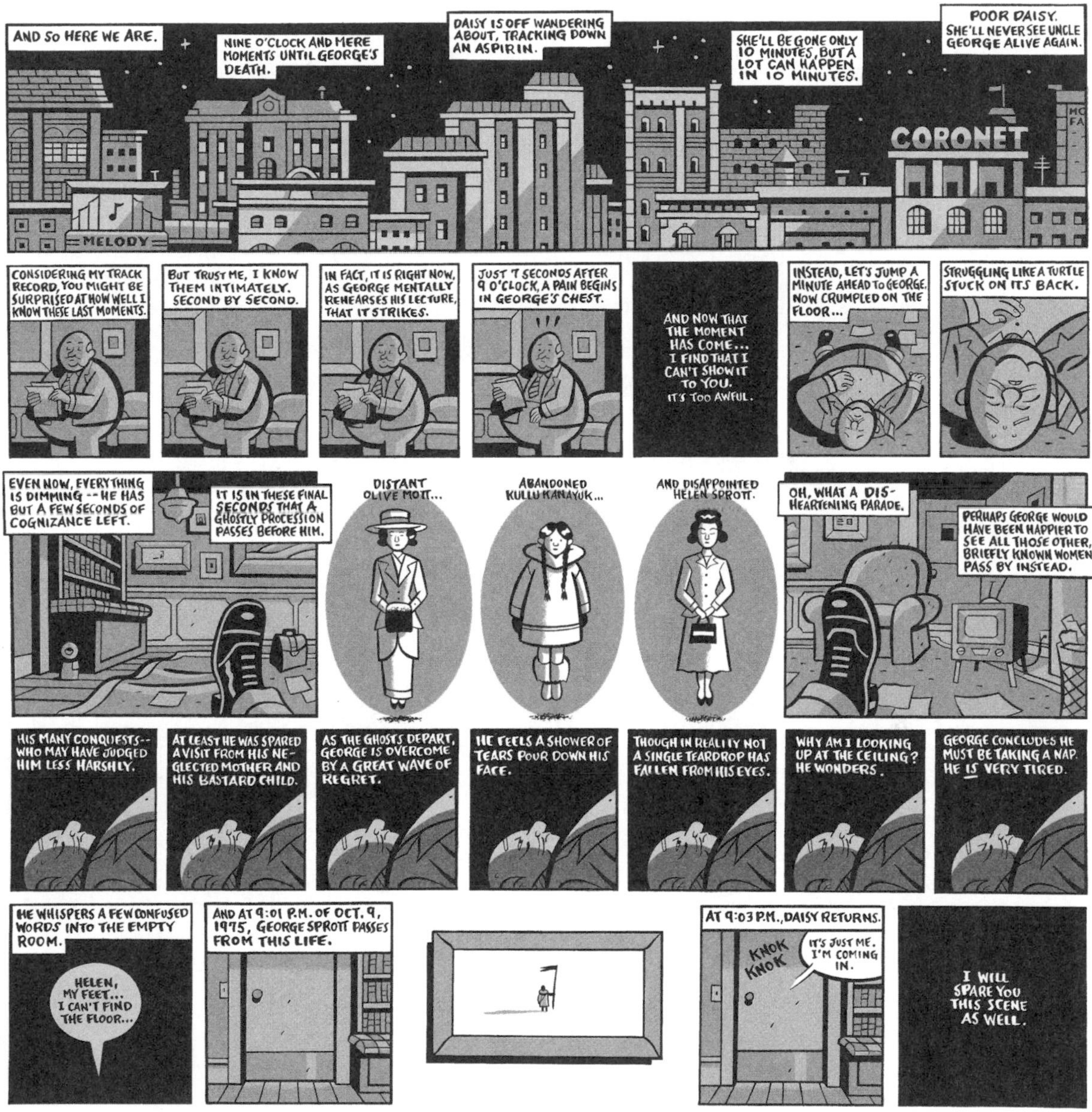

AND SO HERE WE ARE.
NINE O'CLOCK AND MERE MOMENTS UNTIL GEORGE'S DEATH.
DAISY IS OFF WANDERING ABOUT, TRACKING DOWN AN ASPIRIN.
SHE'LL BE GONE ONLY 10 MINUTES, BUT A LOT CAN HAPPEN IN 10 MINUTES.
POOR DAISY. SHE'LL NEVER SEE UNCLE GEORGE ALIVE AGAIN.
MELODY
CORONET
CONSIDERING MY TRACK RECORD, YOU MIGHT BE SURPRISED AT HOW WELL I KNOW THESE LAST MOMENTS.
BUT TRUST ME, I KNOW THEM INTIMATELY. SECOND BY SECOND.
IN FACT, IT IS RIGHT NOW, AS GEORGE MENTALLY REHEARSES HIS LECTURE, THAT IT STRIKES.
JUST 7 SECONDS AFTER 9 O'CLOCK, A PAIN BEGINS IN GEORGE'S CHEST.
AND NOW THAT THE MOMENT HAS COME... I FIND THAT I CAN'T SHOW IT TO YOU. IT'S TOO AWFUL.
INSTEAD, LET'S JUMP A MINUTE AHEAD TO GEORGE, NOW CRUMPLED ON THE FLOOR...
STRUGGLING LIKE A TURTLE STUCK ON ITS BACK.
EVEN NOW, EVERYTHING IS DIMMING -- HE HAS BUT A FEW SECONDS OF COGNIZANCE LEFT.
IT IS IN THESE FINAL SECONDS THAT A GHOSTLY PROCESSION PASSES BEFORE HIM.
DISTANT OLIVE MOTT...
ABANDONED KULLU KANAYUK...
AND DISAPPOINTED HELEN SPROTT.
OH, WHAT A DISHEARTENING PARADE.
PERHAPS GEORGE WOULD HAVE BEEN HAPPIER TO SEE ALL THOSE OTHER, BRIEFLY KNOWN WOMEN PASS BY INSTEAD.
HIS MANY CONQUESTS-- WHO MAY HAVE JUDGED HIM LESS HARSHLY.
AT LEAST HE WAS SPARED A VISIT FROM HIS NEGLECTED MOTHER AND HIS BASTARD CHILD.
AS THE GHOSTS DEPART, GEORGE IS OVERCOME BY A GREAT WAVE OF REGRET.
HE FEELS A SHOWER OF TEARS POUR DOWN HIS FACE.
THOUGH IN REALITY NOT A SINGLE TEARDROP HAS FALLEN FROM HIS EYES.
WHY AM I LOOKING UP AT THE CEILING? HE WONDERS.
GEORGE CONCLUDES HE MUST BE TAKING A NAP. HE IS VERY TIRED.
HE WHISPERS A FEW CONFUSED WORDS INTO THE EMPTY ROOM.
HELEN, MY FEET... I CAN'T FIND THE FLOOR...
AND AT 9:01 P.M. OF OCT. 9, 1975, GEORGE SPROTT PASSES FROM THIS LIFE.
AT 9:03 P.M., DAISY RETURNS.
KNOK KNOK
IT'S JUST ME. I'M COMING IN.
I WILL SPARE YOU THIS SCENE AS WELL.

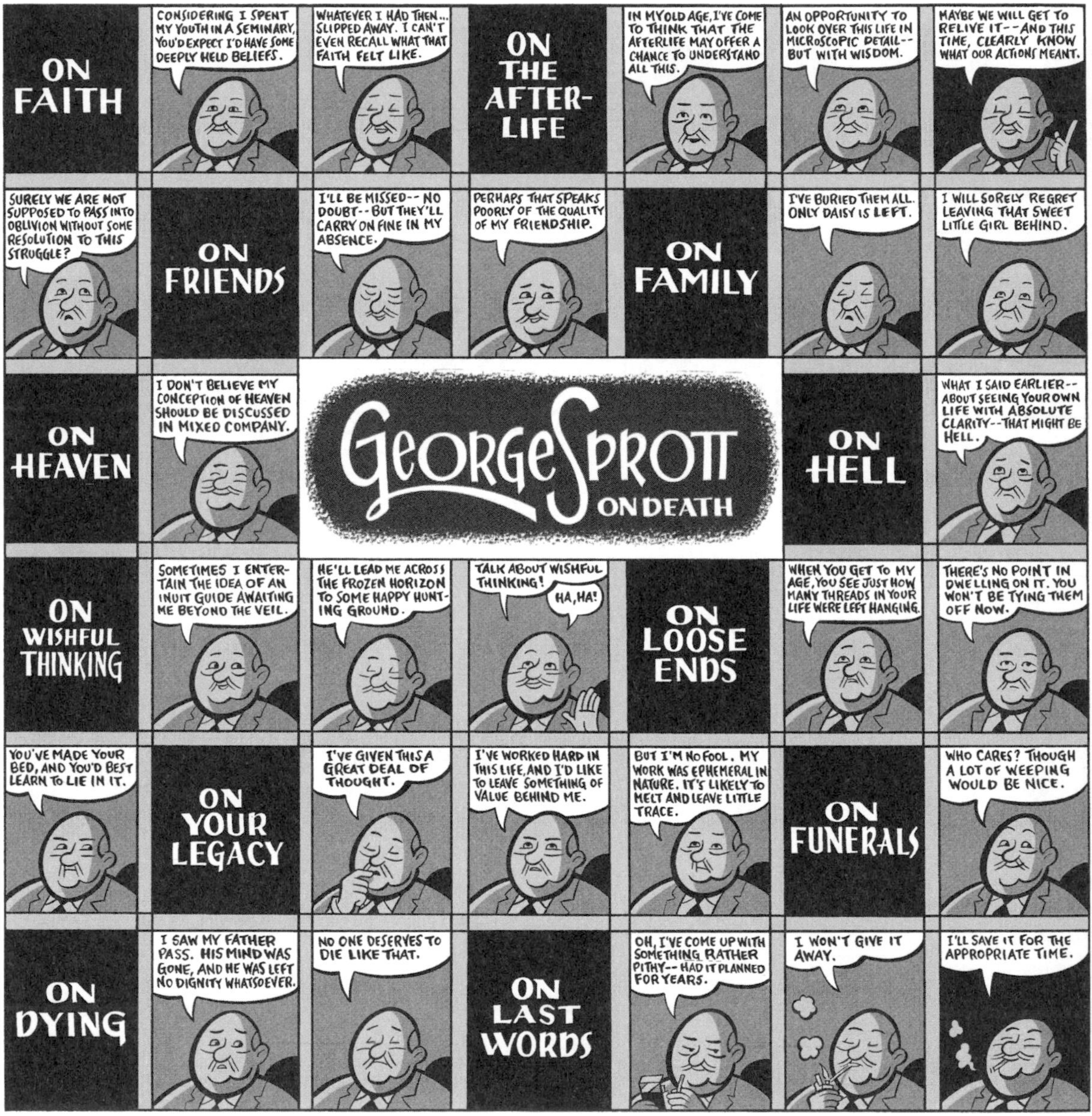
ON FAITH
CONSIDERING I SPENT MY YOUTH IN A SEMINARY, YOU'D EXPECT I'D HAVE SOME DEEPLY HELD BELIEFS.
WHATEVER I HAD THEN... SLIPPED AWAY. I CAN'T EVEN RECALL WHAT THAT FAITH FELT LIKE.
ON THE AFTER-LIFE
IN MY OLD AGE, I'VE COME TO THINK THAT THE AFTERLIFE MAY OFFER A CHANCE TO UNDERSTAND ALL THIS.
AN OPPORTUNITY TO LOOK OVER THIS LIFE IN MICROSCOPIC DETAIL-- BUT WITH WISDOM.
MAYBE WE WILL GET TO RELIVE IT--AND THIS TIME, CLEARLY KNOW WHAT OUR ACTIONS MEANT.
SURELY WE ARE NOT SUPPOSED TO PASS INTO OBLIVION WITHOUT SOME RESOLUTION TO THIS STRUGGLE?
ON FRIENDS
I'LL BE MISSED-- NO DOUBT--BUT THEY'LL CARRY ON FINE IN MY ABSENCE.
PERHAPS THAT SPEAKS POORLY OF THE QUALITY OF MY FRIENDSHIP.
ON FAMILY
I'VE BURIED THEM ALL. ONLY DAISY IS LEFT.
I WILL SORELY REGRET LEAVING THAT SWEET LITTLE GIRL BEHIND.
ON HEAVEN
I DON'T BELIEVE MY CONCEPTION OF HEAVEN SHOULD BE DISCUSSED IN MIXED COMPANY.
GEORGE SPROTT ON DEATH
ON HELL
WHAT I SAID EARLIER-- ABOUT SEEING YOUR OWN LIFE WITH ABSOLUTE CLARITY--THAT MIGHT BE HELL.
ON WISHFUL THINKING
SOMETIMES I ENTERTAIN THE IDEA OF AN INUIT GUIDE AWAITING ME BEYOND THE VEIL.
HE'LL LEAD ME ACROSS THE FROZEN HORIZON TO SOME HAPPY HUNTING GROUND.
TALK ABOUT WISHFUL THINKING!
HA, HA!
ON LOOSE ENDS
WHEN YOU GET TO MY AGE, YOU SEE JUST HOW MANY THREADS IN YOUR LIFE WERE LEFT HANGING.
THERE'S NO POINT IN DWELLING ON IT. YOU WON'T BE TYING THEM OFF NOW.
YOU'VE MADE YOUR BED, AND YOU'D BEST LEARN TO LIE IN IT.
ON YOUR LEGACY
I'VE GIVEN THIS A GREAT DEAL OF THOUGHT.
I'VE WORKED HARD IN THIS LIFE, AND I'D LIKE TO LEAVE SOMETHING OF VALUE BEHIND ME.
BUT I'M NO FOOL. MY WORK WAS EPHEMERAL IN NATURE. IT'S LIKELY TO MELT AND LEAVE LITTLE TRACE.
ON FUNERALS
WHO CARES? THOUGH A LOT OF WEEPING WOULD BE NICE.
ON DYING
I SAW MY FATHER PASS. HIS MIND WAS GONE, AND HE WAS LEFT NO DIGNITY WHATSOEVER.
NO ONE DESERVES TO DIE LIKE THAT.
ON LAST WORDS
OH, I'VE COME UP WITH SOMETHING RATHER PITHY-- HAD IT PLANNED FOR YEARS.
I WON'T GIVE IT AWAY.
I'LL SAVE IT FOR THE APPROPRIATE TIME.

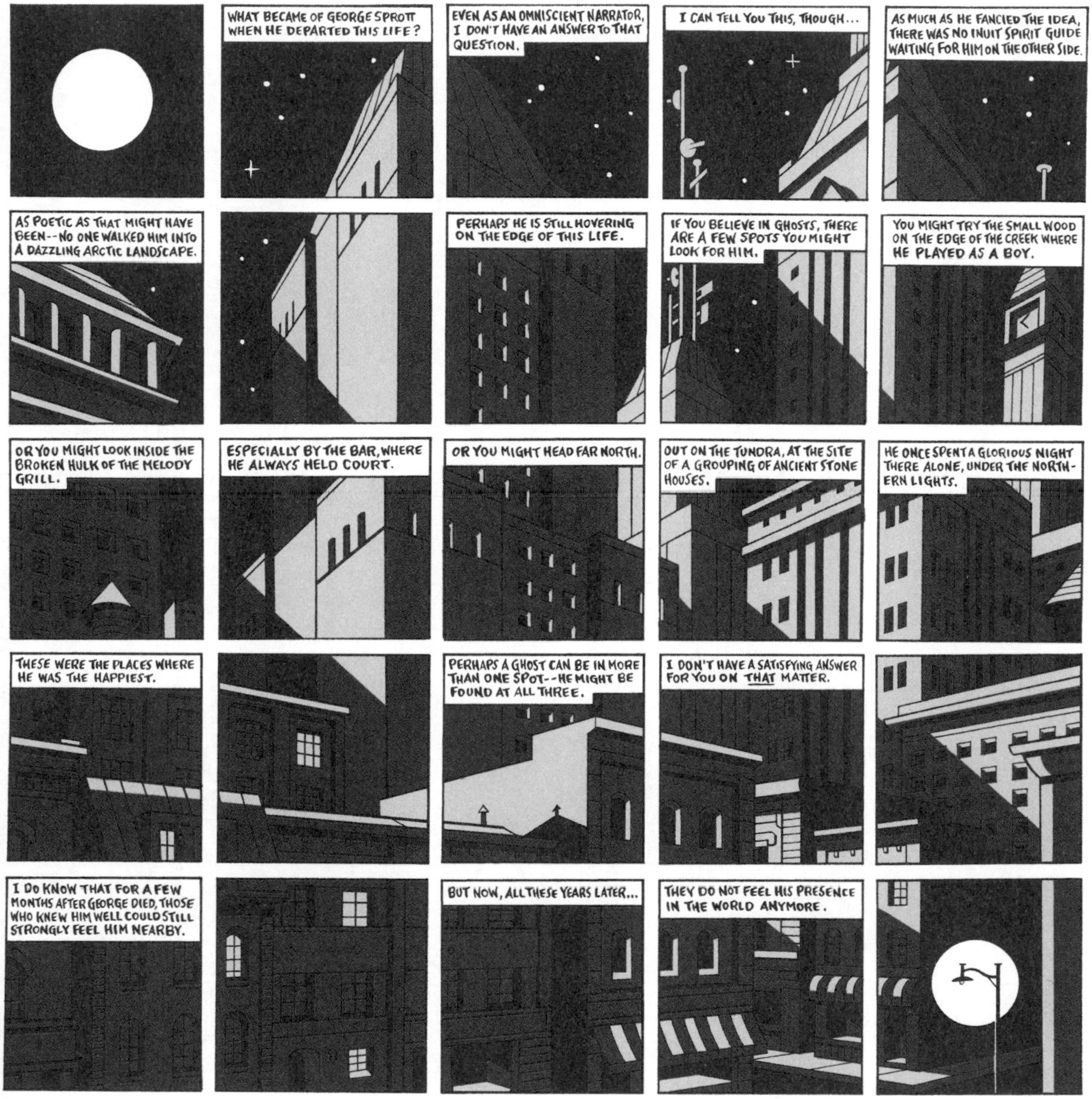
WHAT BECAME OF GEORGE SPROTT WHEN HE DEPARTED THIS LIFE?
EVEN AS AN OMNISCIENT NARRATOR, I DON'T HAVE AN ANSWER TO THAT QUESTION.
I CAN TELL YOU THIS, THOUGH...
AS MUCH AS HE FANCIED THE IDEA, THERE WAS NO INUIT SPIRIT GUIDE WAITING FOR HIM ON THE OTHER SIDE.
AS POETIC AS THAT MIGHT HAVE BEEN--NO ONE WALKED HIM INTO A DAZZLING ARCTIC LANDSCAPE.
PERHAPS HE IS STILL HOVERING ON THE EDGE OF THIS LIFE.
IF YOU BELIEVE IN GHOSTS, THERE ARE A FEW SPOTS YOU MIGHT LOOK FOR HIM.
YOU MIGHT TRY THE SMALL WOOD ON THE EDGE OF THE CREEK WHERE HE PLAYED AS A BOY.
OR YOU MIGHT LOOK INSIDE THE BROKEN HULK OF THE MELODY GRILL.
ESPECIALLY BY THE BAR, WHERE HE ALWAYS HELD COURT.
OR YOU MIGHT HEAD FAR NORTH.
OUT ON THE TUNDRA, AT THE SITE OF A GROUPING OF ANCIENT STONE HOUSES.
HE ONCE SPENT A GLORIOUS NIGHT THERE ALONE, UNDER THE NORTHERN LIGHTS.
THESE WERE THE PLACES WHERE HE WAS THE HAPPIEST.
PERHAPS A GHOST CAN BE IN MORE THAN ONE SPOT--HE MIGHT BE FOUND AT ALL THREE.
I DON'T HAVE A SATISFYING ANSWER FOR YOU ON THAT MATTER.
I DO KNOW THAT FOR A FEW MONTHS AFTER GEORGE DIED, THOSE WHO KNEW HIM WELL COULD STILL STRONGLY FEEL HIM NEARBY.
BUT NOW, ALL THESE YEARS LATER...
THEY DO NOT FEEL HIS PRESENCE IN THE WORLD ANYMORE.

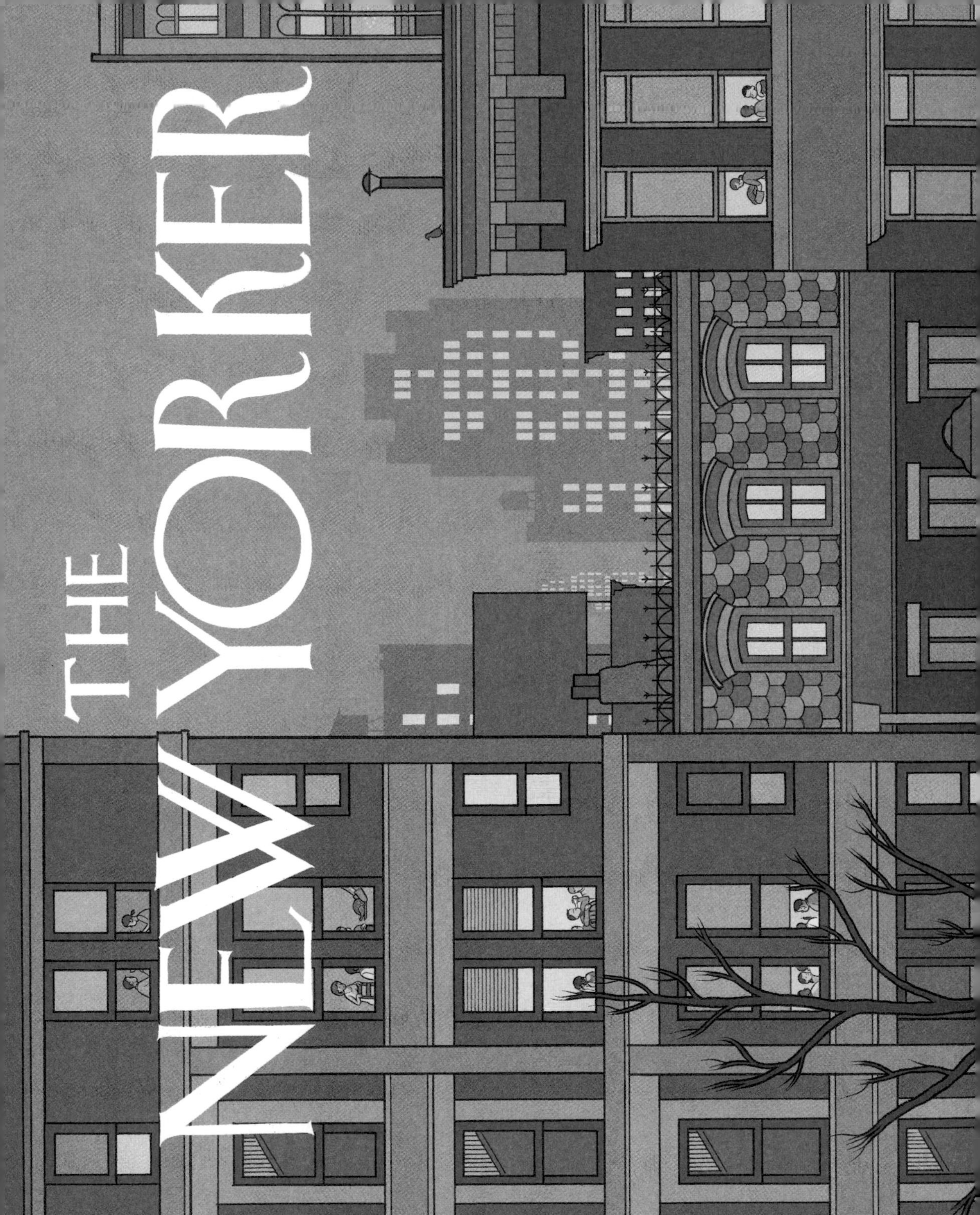
THE NEW YORKER

CHRIS WARE

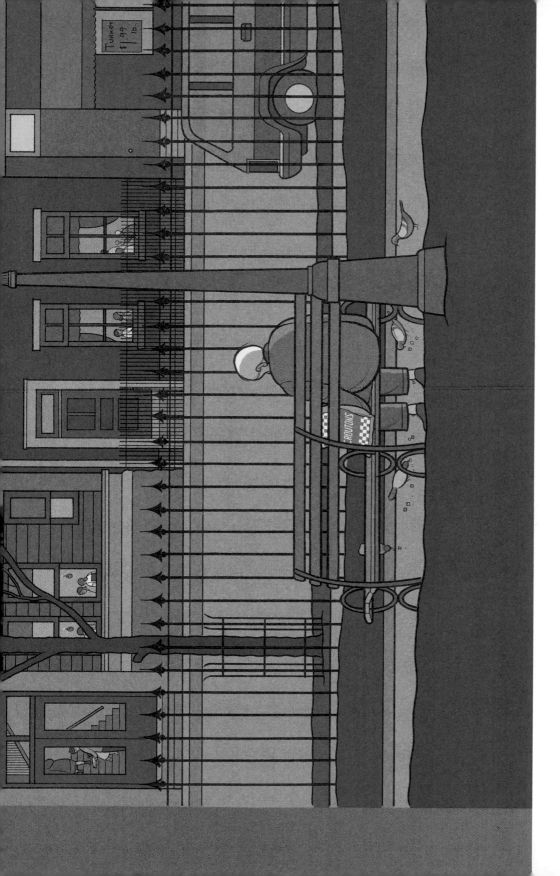

Thanksgiving. — *I. Stuffing.*

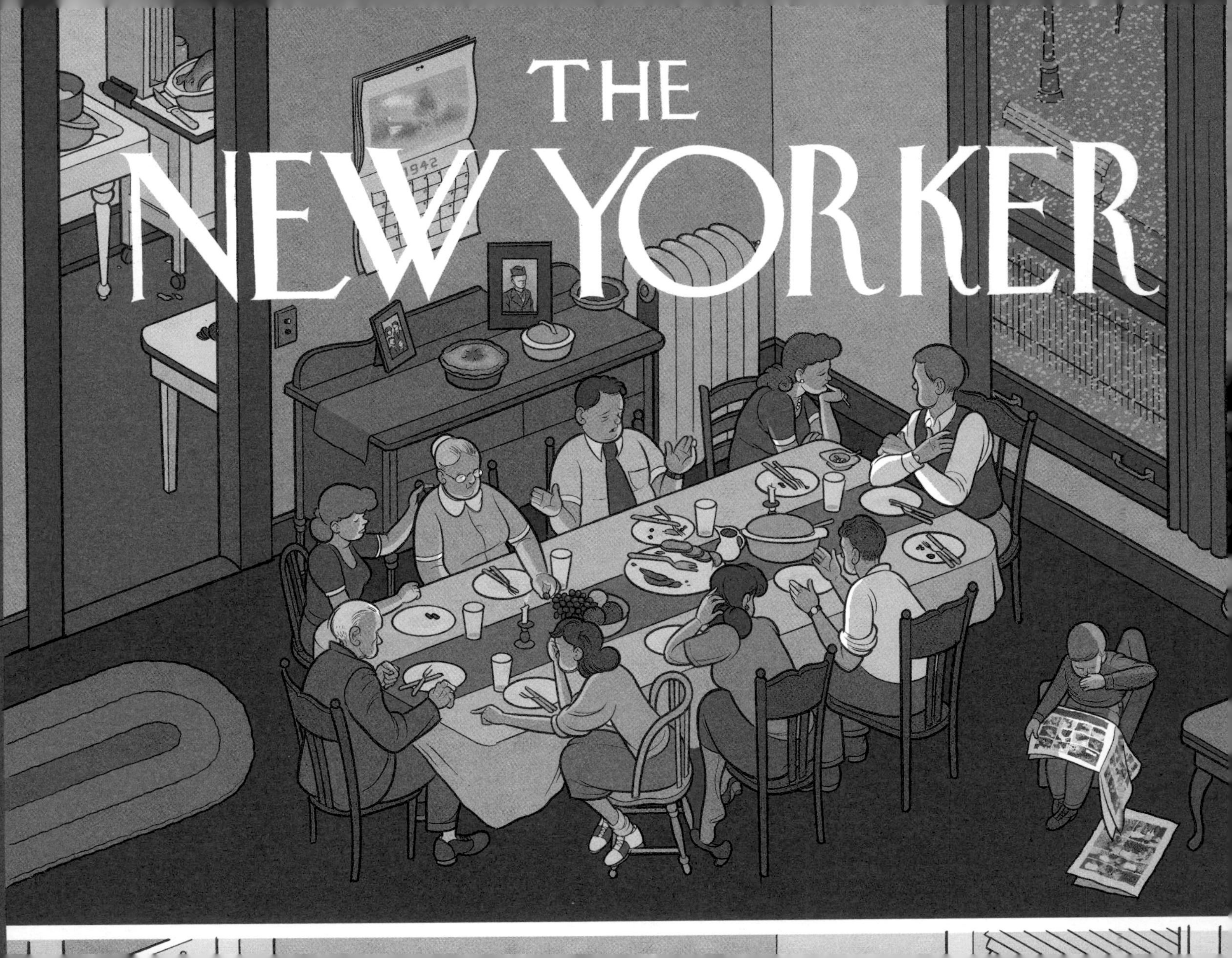
THE NEW YORKER
1942

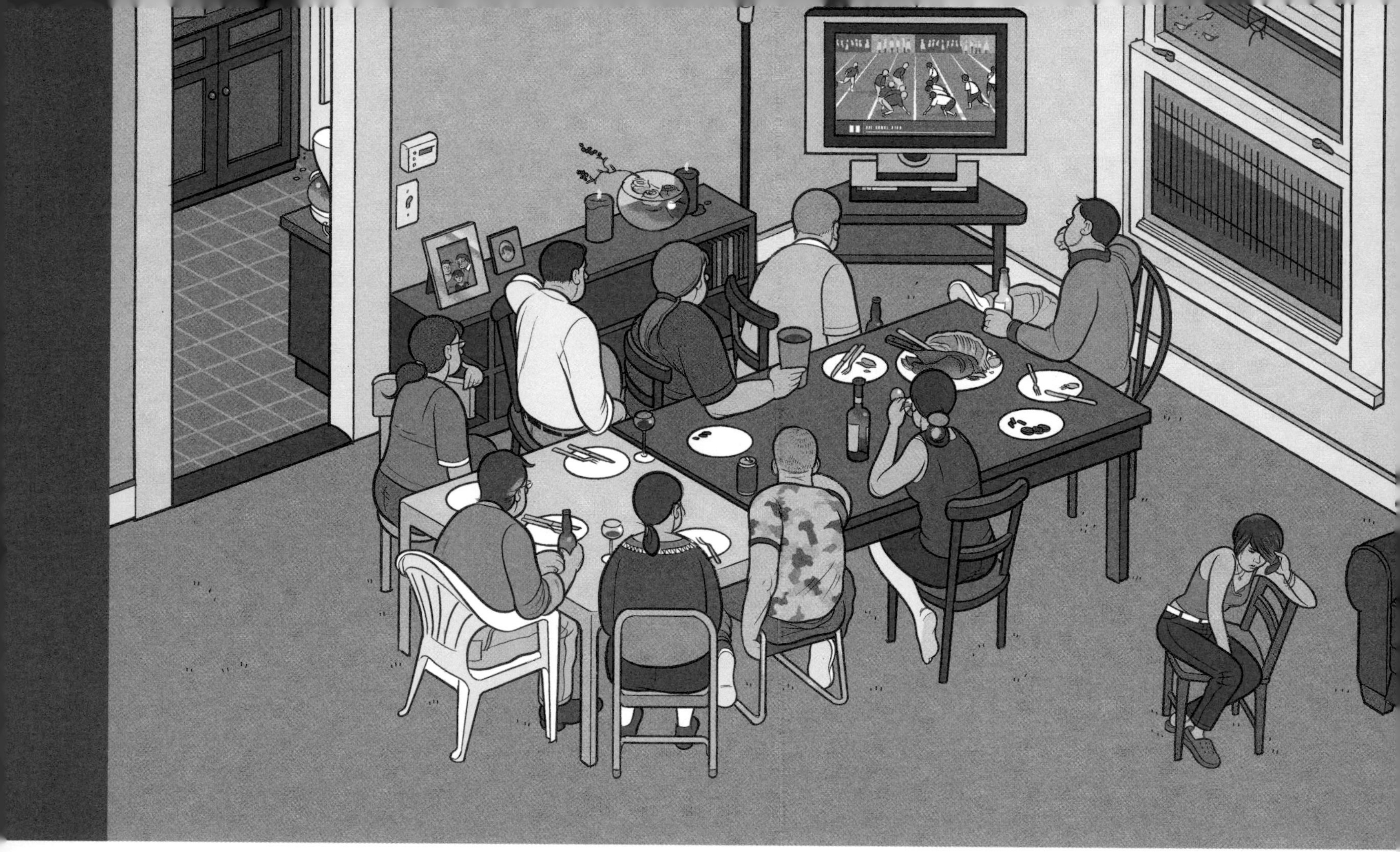

Thanksgiving. — II. Conversation.

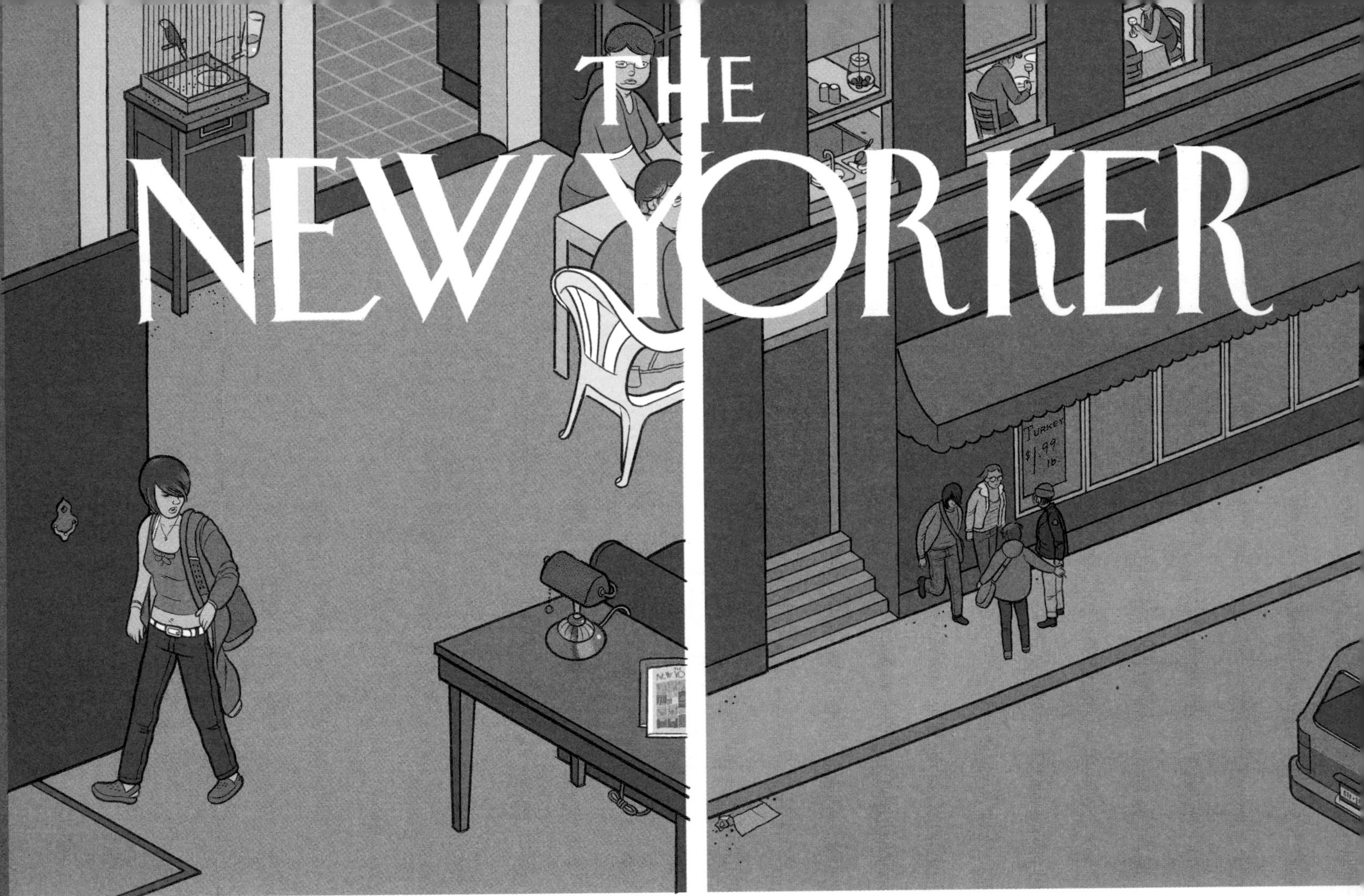
THE NEW YORKER
TURKEY $1.99 lb.

"O.K., Mom and Dad, I'm going!
Happy #*$@*# Thanksgiving!"

"I mean, I TOLD her not to use butter in the stuffing
because I wouldn't eat it … She has absolutely no respect for me
or my political beliefs!"

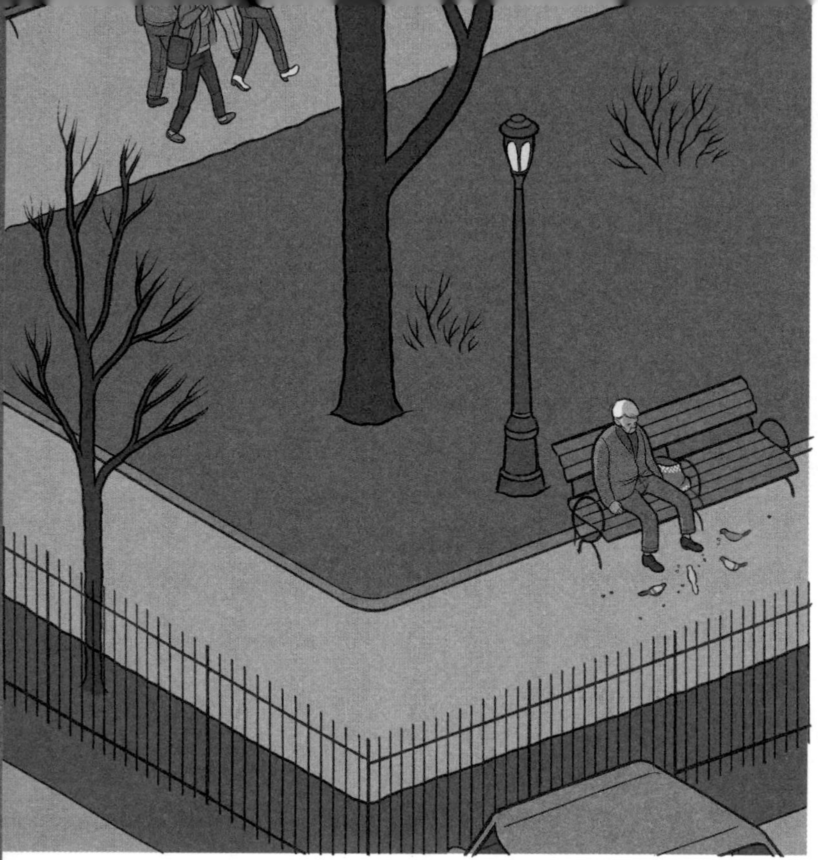

*"No, seriously—you have to check that guy out! He is so EMO …
DUDE! YOU ARE SO EMO!"*

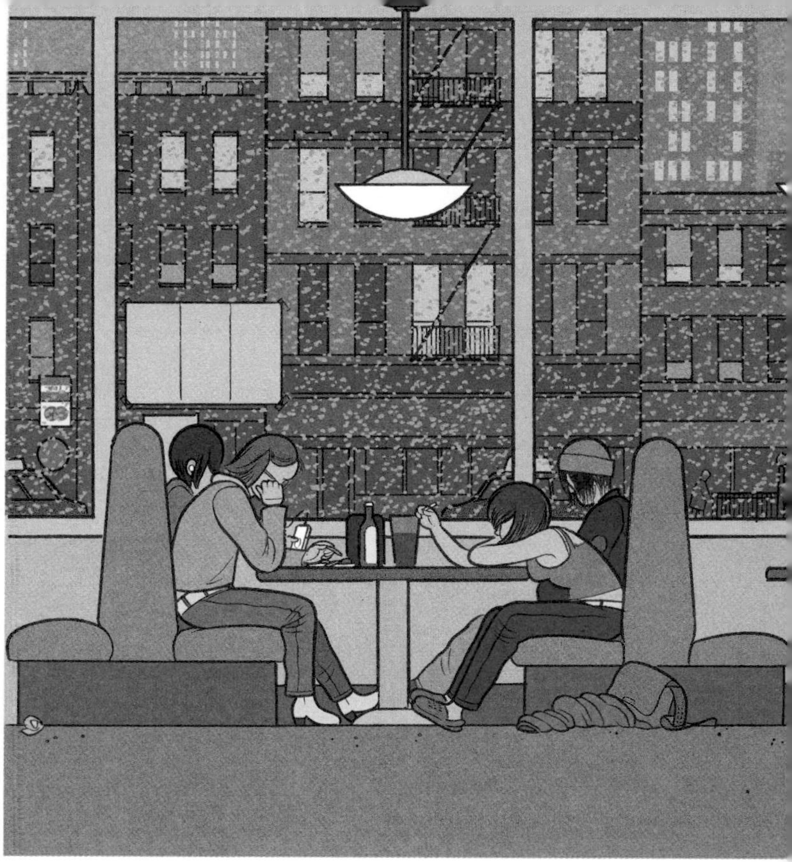

*"Well, at least we can be thankful there's no slavery anymore, right?
I mean, that, like, totally sucked."*

THE NEW YORKER

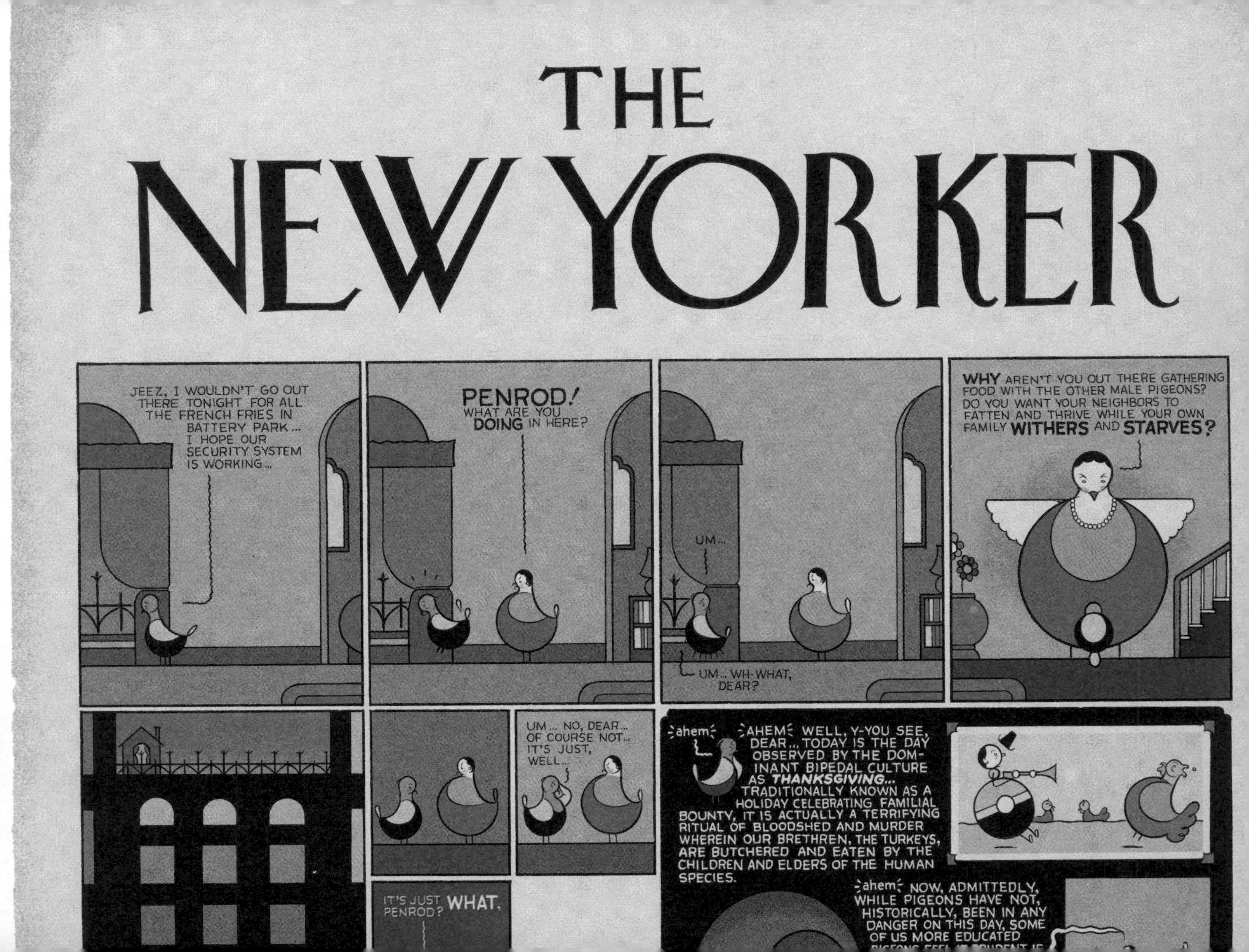
JEEZ, I WOULDN'T GO OUT THERE TONIGHT FOR ALL THE FRENCH FRIES IN BATTERY PARK... I HOPE OUR SECURITY SYSTEM IS WORKING...
PENROD! WHAT ARE YOU DOING IN HERE?
UM...
UM... WH-WHAT, DEAR?
WHY AREN'T YOU OUT THERE GATHERING FOOD WITH THE OTHER MALE PIGEONS? DO YOU WANT YOUR NEIGHBORS TO FATTEN AND THRIVE WHILE YOUR OWN FAMILY WITHERS AND STARVES?
UM... NO, DEAR... OF COURSE NOT... IT'S JUST, WELL...
IT'S JUST PENROD? WHAT.
ahem
AHEM WELL, Y-YOU SEE, DEAR... TODAY IS THE DAY OBSERVED BY THE DOMINANT BIPEDAL CULTURE AS THANKSGIVING... TRADITIONALLY KNOWN AS A HOLIDAY CELEBRATING FAMILIAL BOUNTY, IT IS ACTUALLY A TERRIFYING RITUAL OF BLOODSHED AND MURDER WHEREIN OUR BRETHREN, THE TURKEYS, ARE BUTCHERED AND EATEN BY THE CHILDREN AND ELDERS OF THE HUMAN SPECIES.
ahem NOW, ADMITTEDLY, WHILE PIGEONS HAVE NOT, HISTORICALLY, BEEN IN ANY DANGER ON THIS DAY, SOME OF US MORE EDUCATED

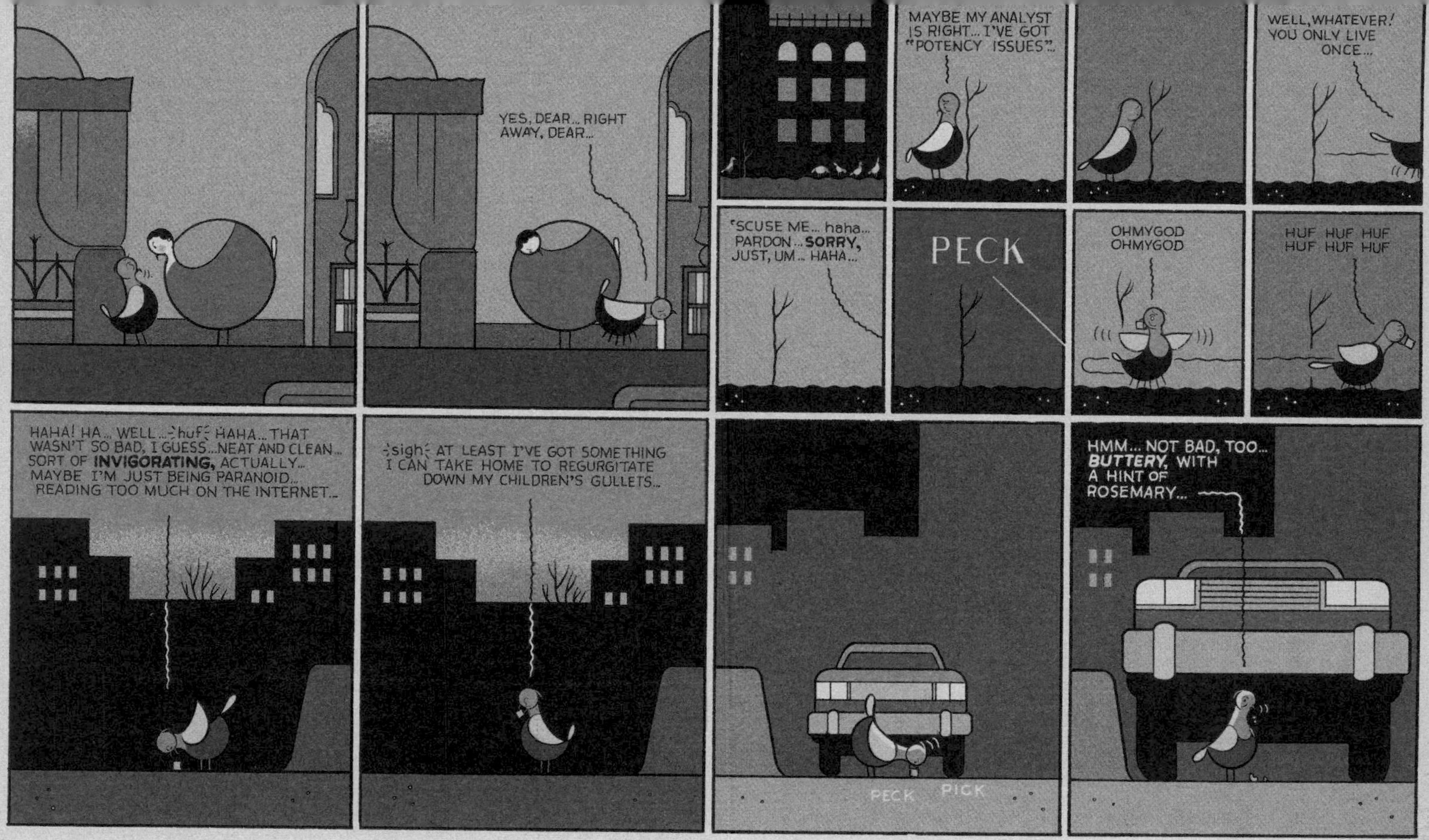
YES, DEAR... RIGHT AWAY, DEAR...
MAYBE MY ANALYST IS RIGHT... I'VE GOT "POTENCY ISSUES"...
WELL, WHATEVER! YOU ONLY LIVE ONCE...
'SCUSE ME... haha... PARDON... SORRY, JUST, UM... HAHA...
PECK
OHMYGOD OHMYGOD
HUF HUF HUF HUF HUF HUF
HAHA! HA... WELL... huf HAHA... THAT WASN'T SO BAD, I GUESS... NEAT AND CLEAN... SORT OF INVIGORATING, ACTUALLY... MAYBE I'M JUST BEING PARANOID... READING TOO MUCH ON THE INTERNET...
sigh AT LEAST I'VE GOT SOMETHING I CAN TAKE HOME TO REGURGITATE DOWN MY CHILDREN'S GULLETS...
PECK PICK
HMM... NOT BAD, TOO... BUTTERY, WITH A HINT OF ROSEMARY...

Thanksgiving. — *IV. Main Course.*

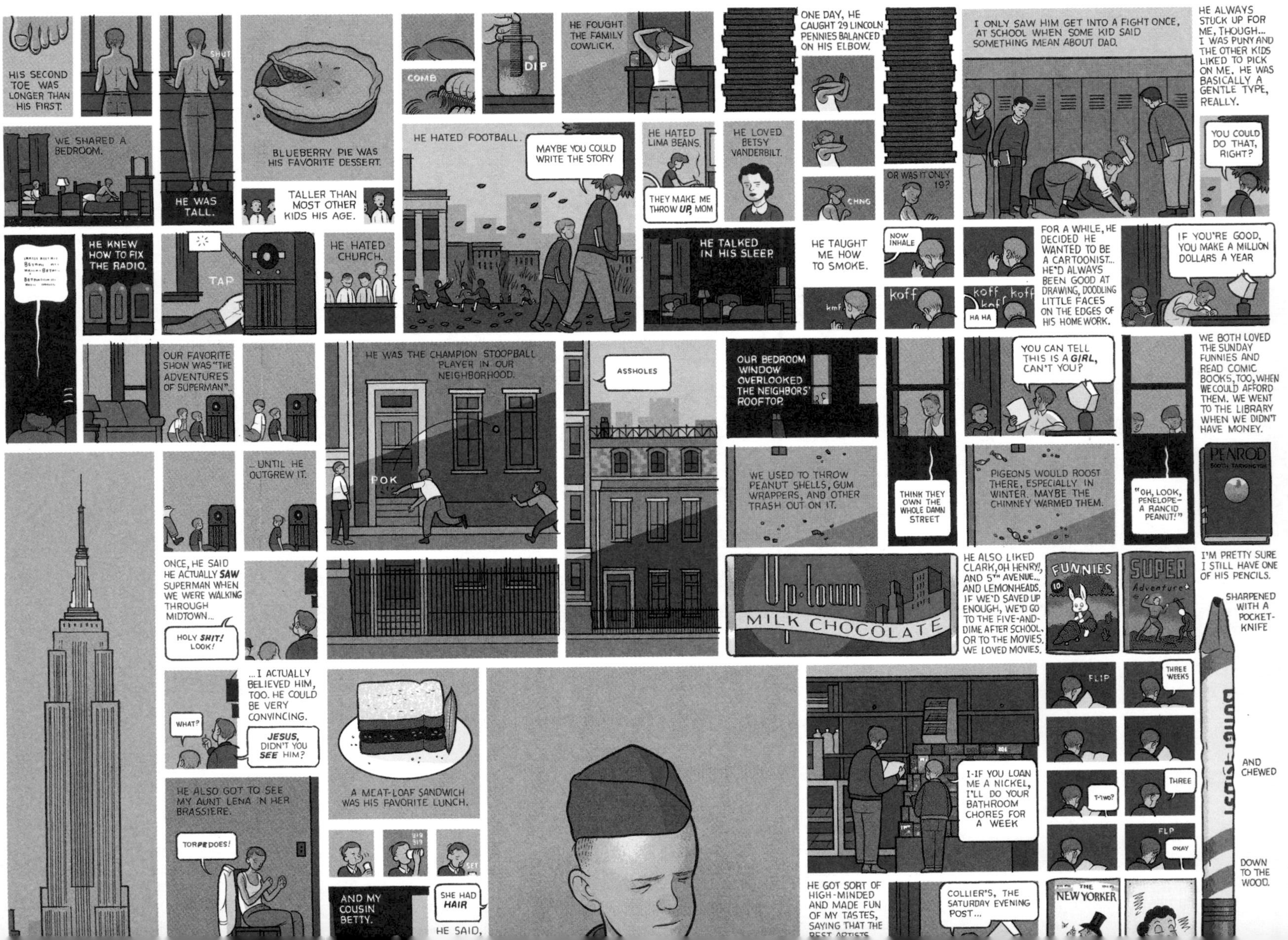
HIS SECOND TOE WAS LONGER THAN HIS FIRST.
SHUT
BLUEBERRY PIE WAS HIS FAVORITE DESSERT.
COMB
DIP
HE FOUGHT THE FAMILY COWLICK.
ONE DAY, HE CAUGHT 29 LINCOLN PENNIES BALANCED ON HIS ELBOW.
I ONLY SAW HIM GET INTO A FIGHT ONCE, AT SCHOOL WHEN SOME KID SAID SOMETHING MEAN ABOUT DAD.
HE ALWAYS STUCK UP FOR ME, THOUGH... I WAS PUNY AND THE OTHER KIDS LIKED TO PICK ON ME. HE WAS BASICALLY A GENTLE TYPE, REALLY.
WE SHARED A BEDROOM.
HE WAS TALL.
TALLER THAN MOST OTHER KIDS HIS AGE.
HE HATED FOOTBALL.
MAYBE YOU COULD WRITE THE STORY
HE HATED LIMA BEANS.
THEY MAKE ME THROW UP, MOM
HE LOVED BETSY VANDERBILT.
CHNG
OR WAS IT ONLY 19?
YOU COULD DO THAT, RIGHT?
HE KNEW HOW TO FIX THE RADIO.
TAP
HE HATED CHURCH.
HE TALKED IN HIS SLEEP.
HE TAUGHT ME HOW TO SMOKE.
NOW INHALE
kmf
koff
koff koff koff
HA HA
FOR A WHILE, HE DECIDED HE WANTED TO BE A CARTOONIST... HE'D ALWAYS BEEN GOOD AT DRAWING, DOODLING LITTLE FACES ON THE EDGES OF HIS HOMEWORK.
IF YOU'RE GOOD, YOU MAKE A MILLION DOLLARS A YEAR
OUR FAVORITE SHOW WAS "THE ADVENTURES OF SUPERMAN"...
HE WAS THE CHAMPION STOOPBALL PLAYER IN OUR NEIGHBORHOOD.
POK
ASSHOLES
OUR BEDROOM WINDOW OVERLOOKED THE NEIGHBORS' ROOFTOP.
YOU CAN TELL THIS IS A GIRL, CAN'T YOU?
WE BOTH LOVED THE SUNDAY FUNNIES AND READ COMIC BOOKS, TOO, WHEN WE COULD AFFORD THEM. WE WENT TO THE LIBRARY WHEN WE DIDN'T HAVE MONEY.
...UNTIL HE OUTGREW IT.
WE USED TO THROW PEANUT SHELLS, GUM WRAPPERS, AND OTHER TRASH OUT ON IT.
THINK THEY OWN THE WHOLE DAMN STREET
PIGEONS WOULD ROOST THERE, ESPECIALLY IN WINTER. MAYBE THE CHIMNEY WARMED THEM.
"OH, LOOK, PENELOPE—A RANCID PEANUT!"
PENROD
BOOTH TARKINGTON
ONCE, HE SAID HE ACTUALLY SAW SUPERMAN WHEN WE WERE WALKING THROUGH MIDTOWN...
HOLY SHIT! LOOK!
Up-town
MILK CHOCOLATE
HE ALSO LIKED CLARK, OH HENRY!, AND 5TH AVENUE... AND LEMONHEADS. IF WE'D SAVED UP ENOUGH, WE'D GO TO THE FIVE-AND-DIME AFTER SCHOOL, OR TO THE MOVIES. WE LOVED MOVIES.
FUNNIES
10¢
SUPER
Adventure
I'M PRETTY SURE I STILL HAVE ONE OF HIS PENCILS.
SHARPENED WITH A POCKET-KNIFE
AND CHEWED
DOWN TO THE WOOD.
WHAT?
...I ACTUALLY BELIEVED HIM, TOO. HE COULD BE VERY CONVINCING.
JESUS, DIDN'T YOU SEE HIM?
A MEAT-LOAF SANDWICH WAS HIS FAVORITE LUNCH.
HE ALSO GOT TO SEE MY AUNT LENA IN HER BRASSIERE.
TORPEDOES!
AND MY COUSIN BETTY.
SHE HAD HAIR
HE SAID,
I-IF YOU LOAN ME A NICKEL, I'LL DO YOUR BATHROOM CHORES FOR A WEEK
FLIP
THREE WEEKS
T-TWO?
THREE
FLP
OKAY
HE GOT SORT OF HIGH-MINDED AND MADE FUN OF MY TASTES, SAYING THAT THE
COLLIER'S, THE SATURDAY EVENING POST...
THE NEW YORKER

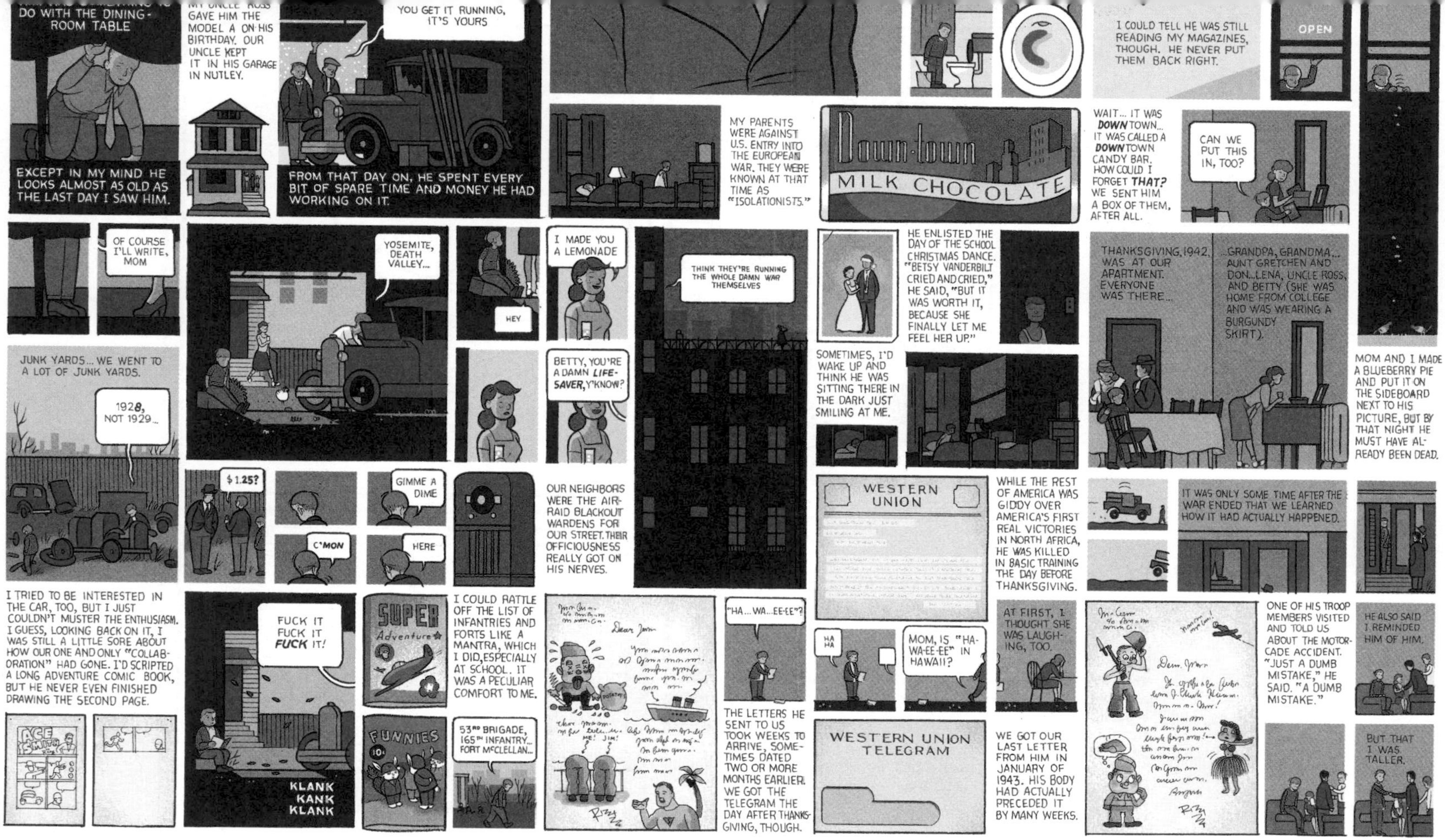
DO WITH THE DINING-ROOM TABLE
EXCEPT IN MY MIND HE LOOKS ALMOST AS OLD AS THE LAST DAY I SAW HIM.
GAVE HIM THE MODEL A ON HIS BIRTHDAY. OUR UNCLE KEPT IT IN HIS GARAGE IN NUTLEY.
YOU GET IT RUNNING, IT'S YOURS
FROM THAT DAY ON, HE SPENT EVERY BIT OF SPARE TIME AND MONEY HE HAD WORKING ON IT.
OF COURSE I'LL WRITE, MOM
YOSEMITE, DEATH VALLEY...
HEY
JUNK YARDS... WE WENT TO A LOT OF JUNK YARDS.
1928, NOT 1929...
$1.25?
GIMME A DIME
C'MON
HERE
I TRIED TO BE INTERESTED IN THE CAR, TOO, BUT I JUST COULDN'T MUSTER THE ENTHUSIASM. I GUESS, LOOKING BACK ON IT, I WAS STILL A LITTLE SORE ABOUT HOW OUR ONE AND ONLY "COLLABORATION" HAD GONE. I'D SCRIPTED A LONG ADVENTURE COMIC BOOK, BUT HE NEVER EVEN FINISHED DRAWING THE SECOND PAGE.
ACE SMITH
FUCK IT FUCK IT FUCK IT!
KLANK KANK KLANK
SUPER Adventure
FUNNIES 10¢
I COULD RATTLE OFF THE LIST OF INFANTRIES AND FORTS LIKE A MANTRA, WHICH I DID, ESPECIALLY AT SCHOOL. IT WAS A PECULIAR COMFORT TO ME.
53RD BRIGADE, 165TH INFANTRY... FORT McCLELLAN...
MY PARENTS WERE AGAINST U.S. ENTRY INTO THE EUROPEAN WAR. THEY WERE KNOWN AT THAT TIME AS "ISOLATIONISTS."
I MADE YOU A LEMONADE
BETTY, YOU'RE A DAMN LIFE-SAVER, Y'KNOW?
THINK THEY'RE RUNNING THE WHOLE DAMN WAR THEMSELVES
OUR NEIGHBORS WERE THE AIR-RAID BLACKOUT WARDENS FOR OUR STREET. THEIR OFFICIOUSNESS REALLY GOT ON HIS NERVES.
Dear Jim
"HA... WA... EE-EE"?
THE LETTERS HE SENT TO US TOOK WEEKS TO ARRIVE, SOMETIMES DATED TWO OR MORE MONTHS EARLIER. WE GOT THE TELEGRAM THE DAY AFTER THANKSGIVING, THOUGH.
Down-town MILK CHOCOLATE
HE ENLISTED THE DAY OF THE SCHOOL CHRISTMAS DANCE. "BETSY VANDERBILT CRIED AND CRIED," HE SAID, "BUT IT WAS WORTH IT, BECAUSE SHE FINALLY LET ME FEEL HER UP."
SOMETIMES, I'D WAKE UP AND THINK HE WAS SITTING THERE IN THE DARK JUST SMILING AT ME.
WESTERN UNION
HA HA
MOM, IS "HA-WA-EE-EE" IN HAWAII?
WESTERN UNION TELEGRAM
WHILE THE REST OF AMERICA WAS GIDDY OVER AMERICA'S FIRST REAL VICTORIES IN NORTH AFRICA, HE WAS KILLED IN BASIC TRAINING THE DAY BEFORE THANKSGIVING.
AT FIRST, I THOUGHT SHE WAS LAUGHING, TOO.
WE GOT OUR LAST LETTER FROM HIM IN JANUARY OF 1943. HIS BODY HAD ACTUALLY PRECEDED IT BY MANY WEEKS.
I COULD TELL HE WAS STILL READING MY MAGAZINES, THOUGH. HE NEVER PUT THEM BACK RIGHT.
WAIT... IT WAS DOWNTOWN... IT WAS CALLED A DOWNTOWN CANDY BAR. HOW COULD I FORGET THAT? WE SENT HIM A BOX OF THEM, AFTER ALL.
CAN WE PUT THIS IN, TOO?
OPEN
THANKSGIVING, 1942, WAS AT OUR APARTMENT. EVERYONE WAS THERE...
...GRANDPA, GRANDMA... AUNT GRETCHEN AND DON...LENA, UNCLE ROSS, AND BETTY (SHE WAS HOME FROM COLLEGE AND WAS WEARING A BURGUNDY SKIRT).
MOM AND I MADE A BLUEBERRY PIE AND PUT IT ON THE SIDEBOARD NEXT TO HIS PICTURE, BUT BY THAT NIGHT HE MUST HAVE ALREADY BEEN DEAD.
IT WAS ONLY SOME TIME AFTER THE WAR ENDED THAT WE LEARNED HOW IT HAD ACTUALLY HAPPENED.
Dear Jim
ONE OF HIS TROOP MEMBERS VISITED AND TOLD US ABOUT THE MOTORCADE ACCIDENT. "JUST A DUMB MISTAKE," HE SAID. "A DUMB MISTAKE."
HE ALSO SAID I REMINDED HIM OF HIM.
BUT THAT I WAS TALLER.

Thanksgiving. — *V. Leftovers.*

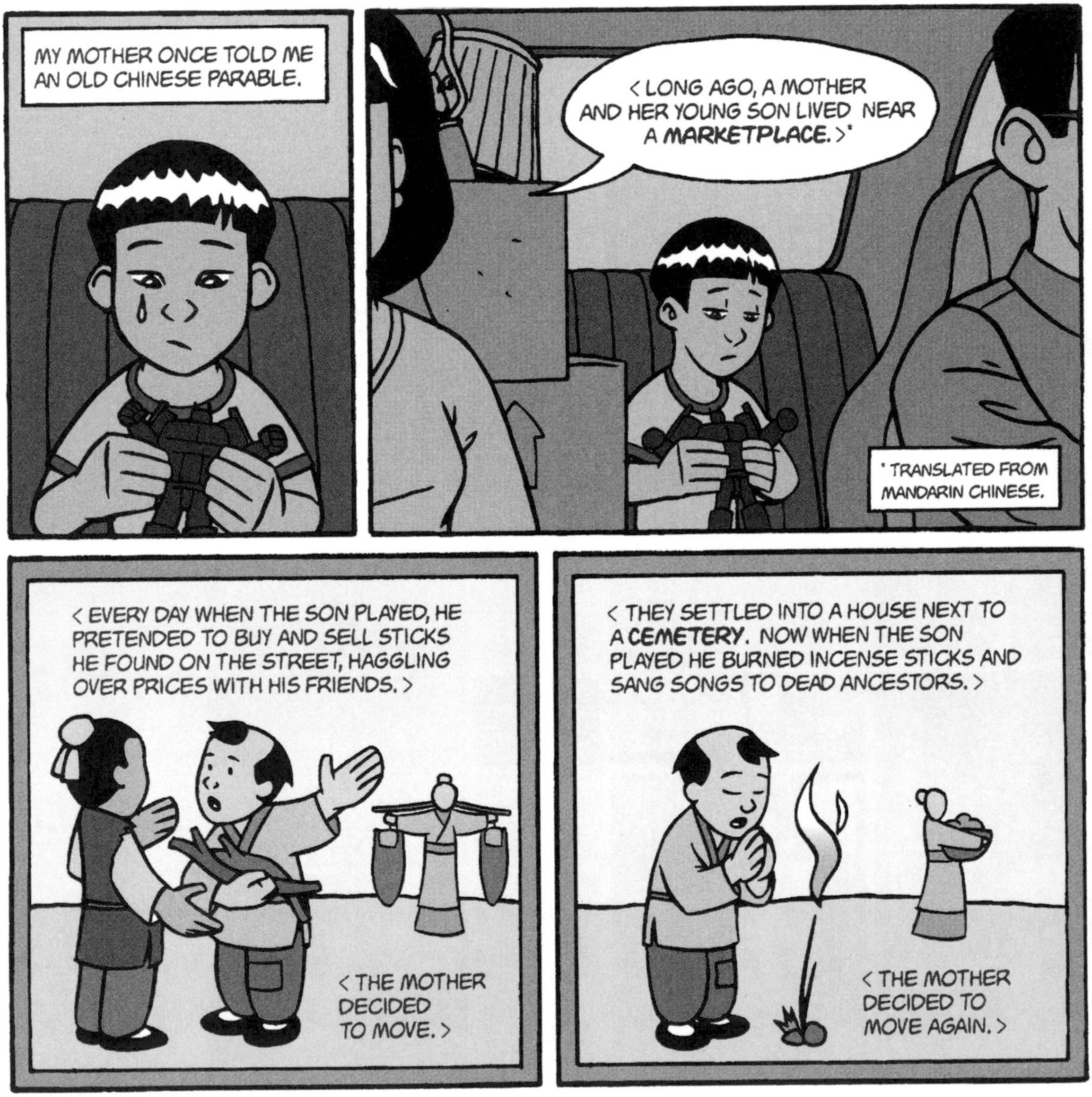
MY MOTHER ONCE TOLD ME AN OLD CHINESE PARABLE.
< LONG AGO, A MOTHER AND HER YOUNG SON LIVED NEAR A **MARKETPLACE**. >*
* TRANSLATED FROM MANDARIN CHINESE.
< EVERY DAY WHEN THE SON PLAYED, HE PRETENDED TO BUY AND SELL STICKS HE FOUND ON THE STREET, HAGGLING OVER PRICES WITH HIS FRIENDS. >
< THE MOTHER DECIDED TO MOVE. >
< THEY SETTLED INTO A HOUSE NEXT TO A **CEMETERY**. NOW WHEN THE SON PLAYED HE BURNED INCENSE STICKS AND SANG SONGS TO DEAD ANCESTORS. >
< THE MOTHER DECIDED TO MOVE AGAIN. >

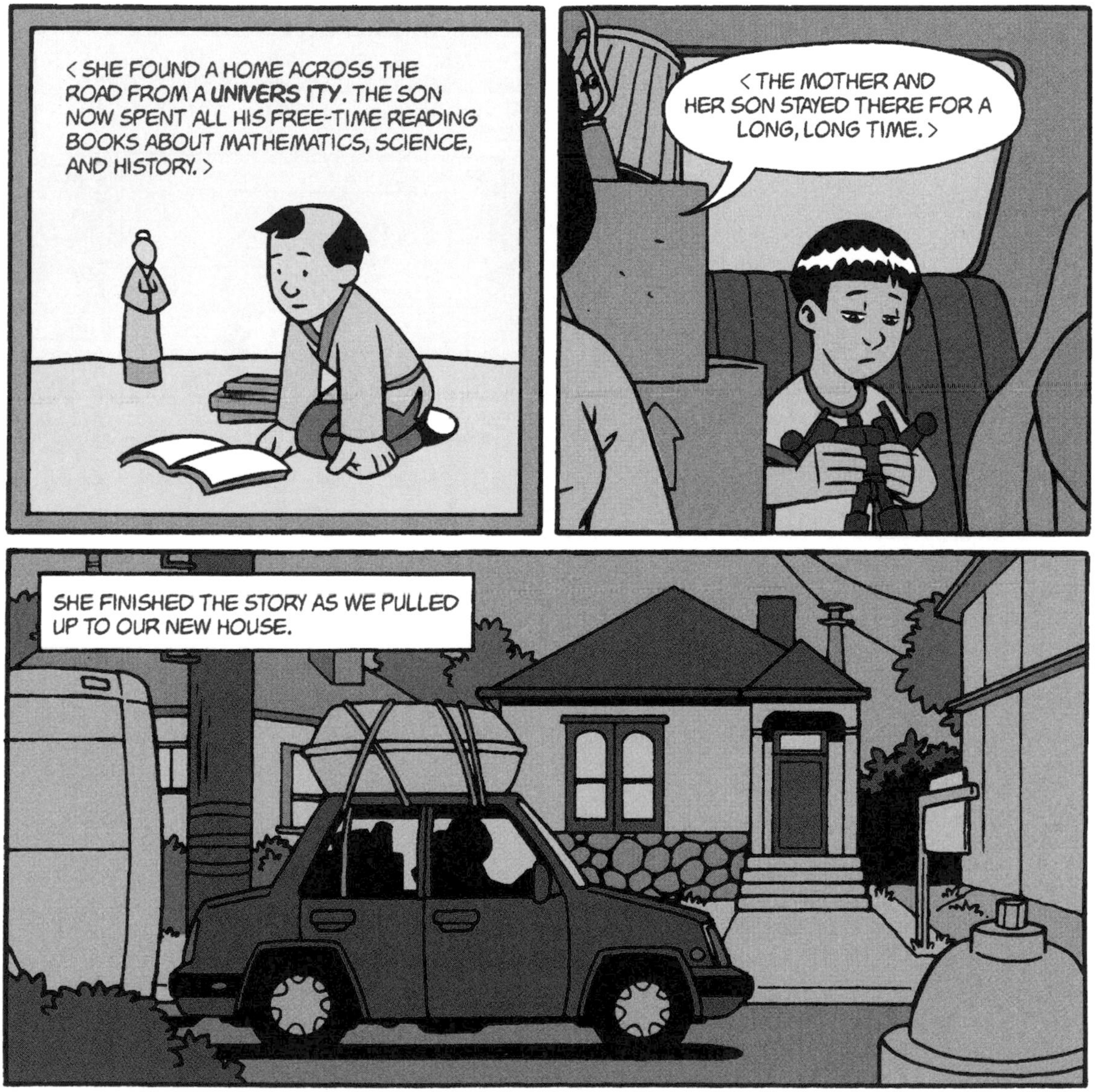
< SHE FOUND A HOME ACROSS THE ROAD FROM A UNIVERS ITY. THE SON NOW SPENT ALL HIS FREE-TIME READING BOOKS ABOUT MATHEMATICS, SCIENCE, AND HISTORY. >
< THE MOTHER AND HER SON STAYED THERE FOR A LONG, LONG TIME. >
SHE FINISHED THE STORY AS WE PULLED UP TO OUR NEW HOUSE.

MY PARENTS ARRIVED IN **AMERICA** AT THE SAME AIRPORT WITHIN A WEEK OF EACH OTHER.

IRONICALLY, THEY DIDN'T MEET UNTIL A YEAR AND A HALF LATER, IN THE LIBRARY OF SAN FRANCISCO STATE UNIVERSITY. THEY WERE BOTH GRADUATE STUDENTS.

FOR TUITION MONEY, MY MOTHER WORKED AT A CANNERY.

MY FATHER SOLD WIGS DOOR-TO-DOOR.

SUAVE!

EVENTUALLY, MY FATHER BECAME AN ENGINEER AND MY MOTHER A LIBRARIAN. JUST BEFORE I WAS BORN, THEY MOVED INTO AN APARTMENT NEAR SAN FRANCISCO **CHINATOWN**. WE STAYED THERE FOR NINE YEARS.

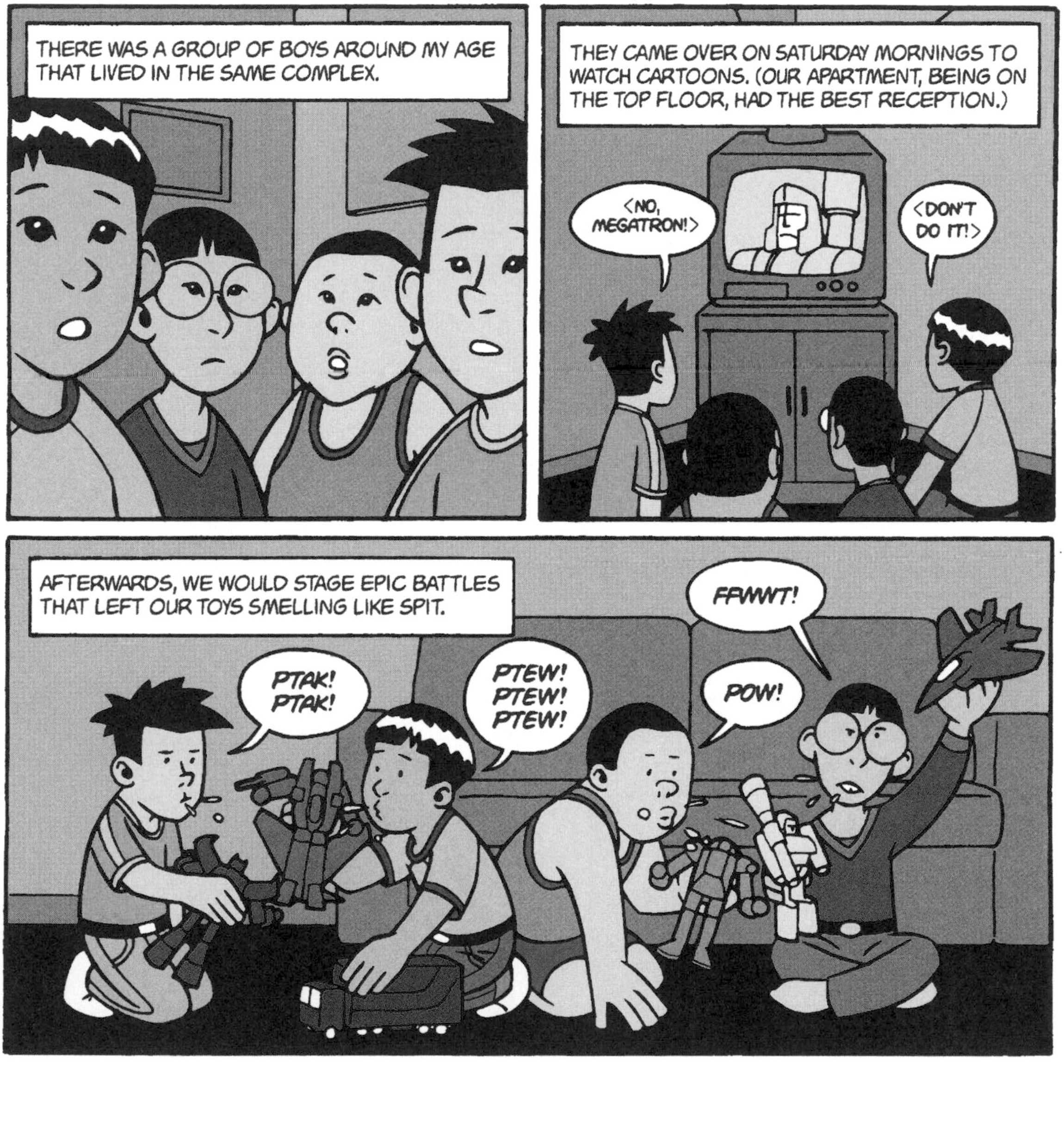
THERE WAS A GROUP OF BOYS AROUND MY AGE THAT LIVED IN THE SAME COMPLEX.
THEY CAME OVER ON SATURDAY MORNINGS TO WATCH CARTOONS. (OUR APARTMENT, BEING ON THE TOP FLOOR, HAD THE BEST RECEPTION.)
<NO, MEGATRON!>
<DON'T DO IT!>
AFTERWARDS, WE WOULD STAGE EPIC BATTLES THAT LEFT OUR TOYS SMELLING LIKE SPIT.
FFWWT!
PTAK! PTAK!
PTEW! PTEW! PTEW!
POW!

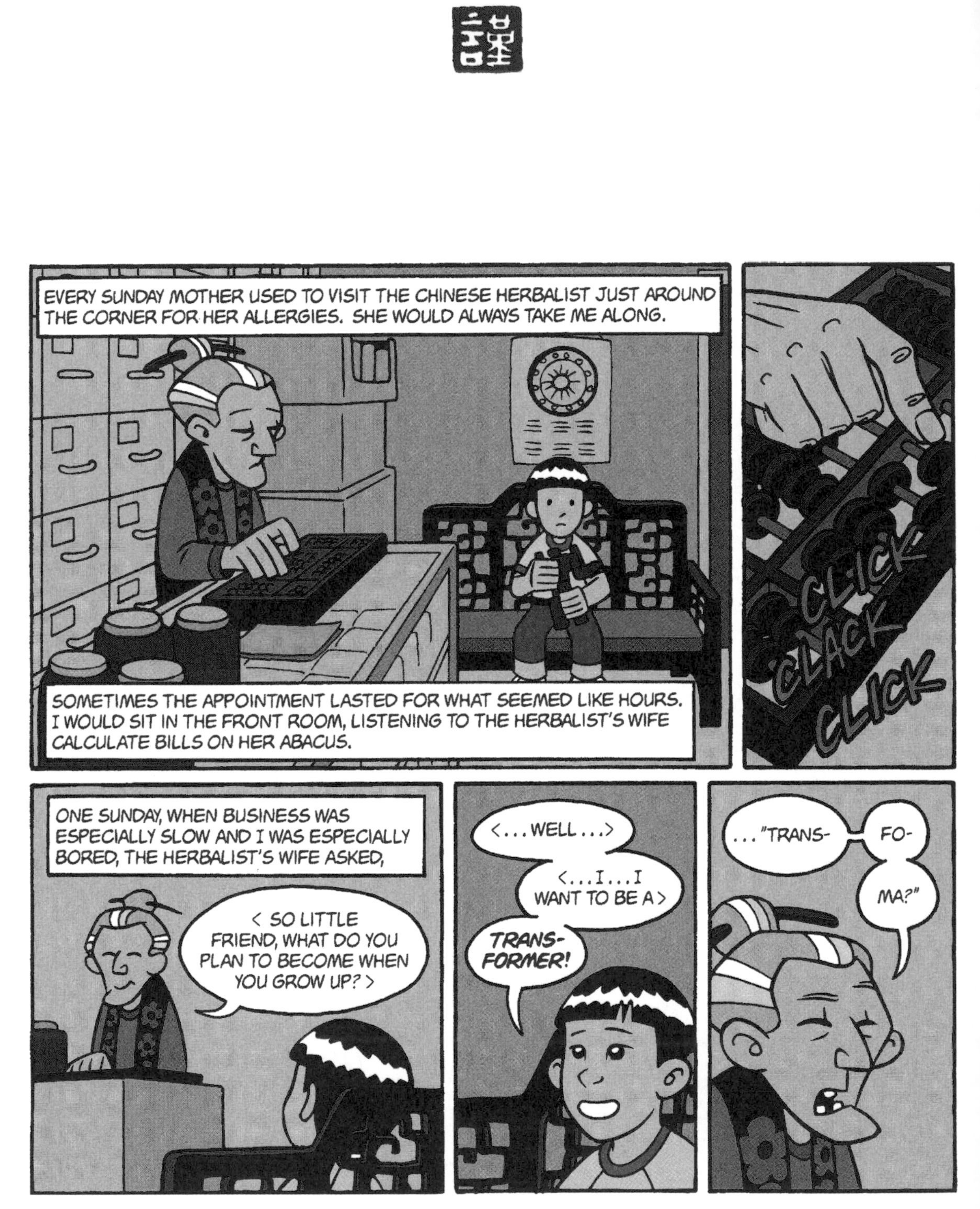
EVERY SUNDAY MOTHER USED TO VISIT THE CHINESE HERBALIST JUST AROUND THE CORNER FOR HER ALLERGIES. SHE WOULD ALWAYS TAKE ME ALONG.
SOMETIMES THE APPOINTMENT LASTED FOR WHAT SEEMED LIKE HOURS. I WOULD SIT IN THE FRONT ROOM, LISTENING TO THE HERBALIST'S WIFE CALCULATE BILLS ON HER ABACUS.
CLICK CLACK CLICK
ONE SUNDAY, WHEN BUSINESS WAS ESPECIALLY SLOW AND I WAS ESPECIALLY BORED, THE HERBALIST'S WIFE ASKED,
< SO LITTLE FRIEND, WHAT DO YOU PLAN TO BECOME WHEN YOU GROW UP? >
<. . . WELL . . .>
<. . . I . . . I WANT TO BE A >
TRANS-FORMER!
. . . "TRANS-
FO-
MA?"

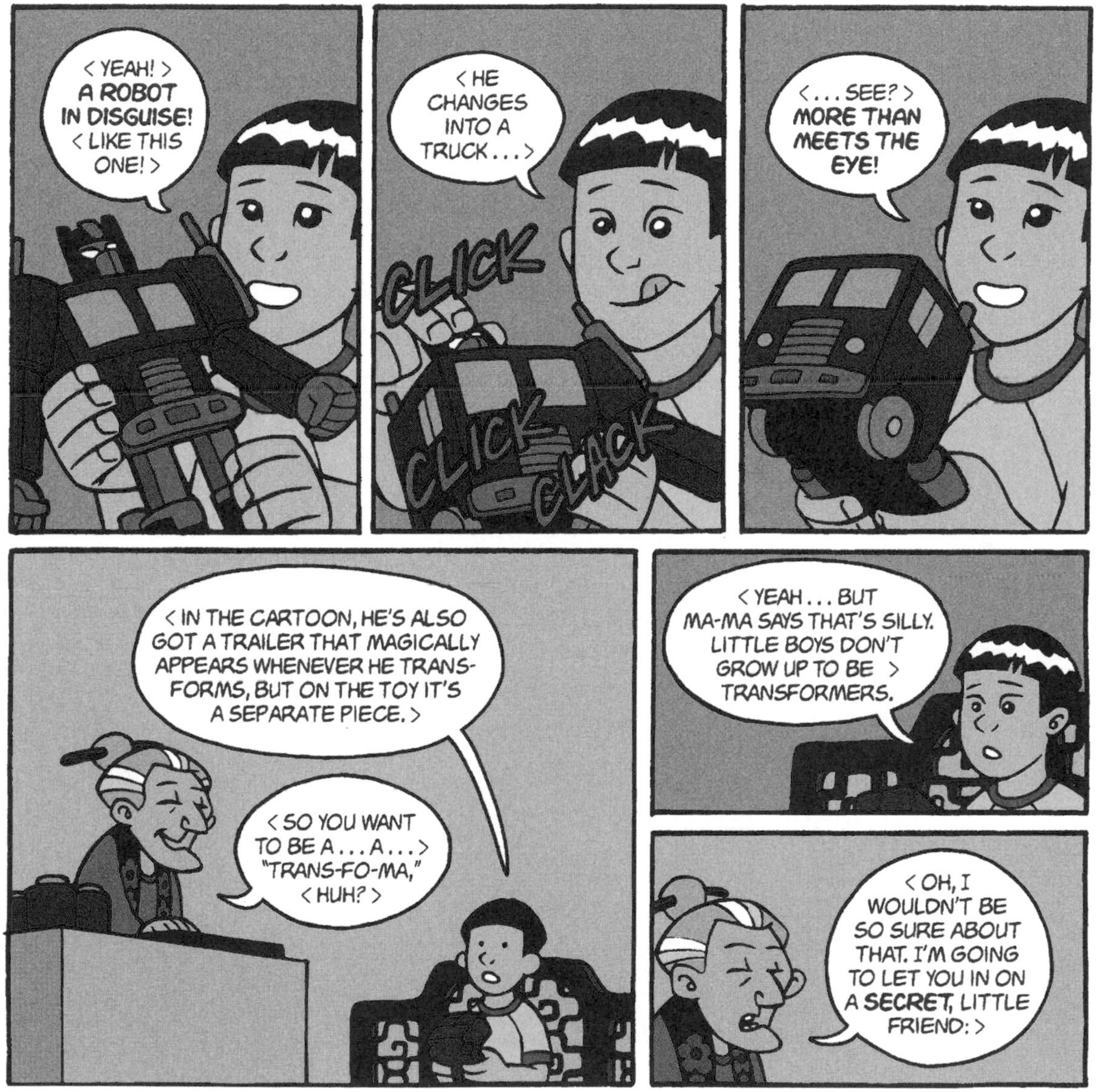
< YEAH! > A ROBOT IN DISGUISE! < LIKE THIS ONE! >
< HE CHANGES INTO A TRUCK . . . >
CLICK
CLICK
CLACK
< . . . SEE? > MORE THAN MEETS THE EYE!
< IN THE CARTOON, HE'S ALSO GOT A TRAILER THAT MAGICALLY APPEARS WHENEVER HE TRANS-FORMS, BUT ON THE TOY IT'S A SEPARATE PIECE. >
< SO YOU WANT TO BE A . . . A . . . > "TRANS-FO-MA," < HUH? >
< YEAH . . . BUT MA-MA SAYS THAT'S SILLY. LITTLE BOYS DON'T GROW UP TO BE > TRANSFORMERS.
< OH, I WOULDN'T BE SO SURE ABOUT THAT. I'M GOING TO LET YOU IN ON A SECRET, LITTLE FRIEND: >

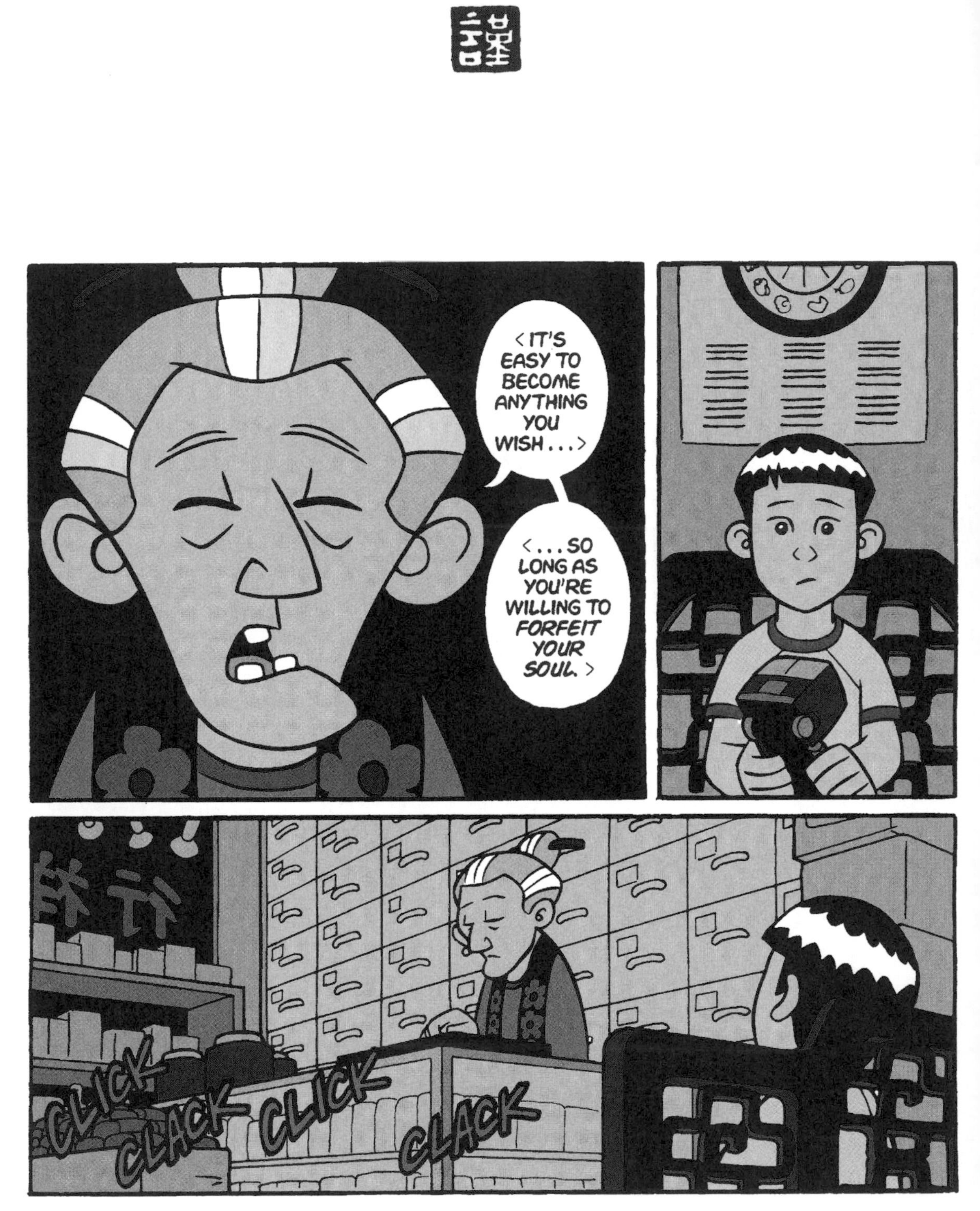
<IT'S EASY TO BECOME ANYTHING YOU WISH . . .>
<. . . SO LONG AS YOU'RE WILLING TO FORFEIT YOUR SOUL.>
CLICK
CLACK
CLICK
CLACK

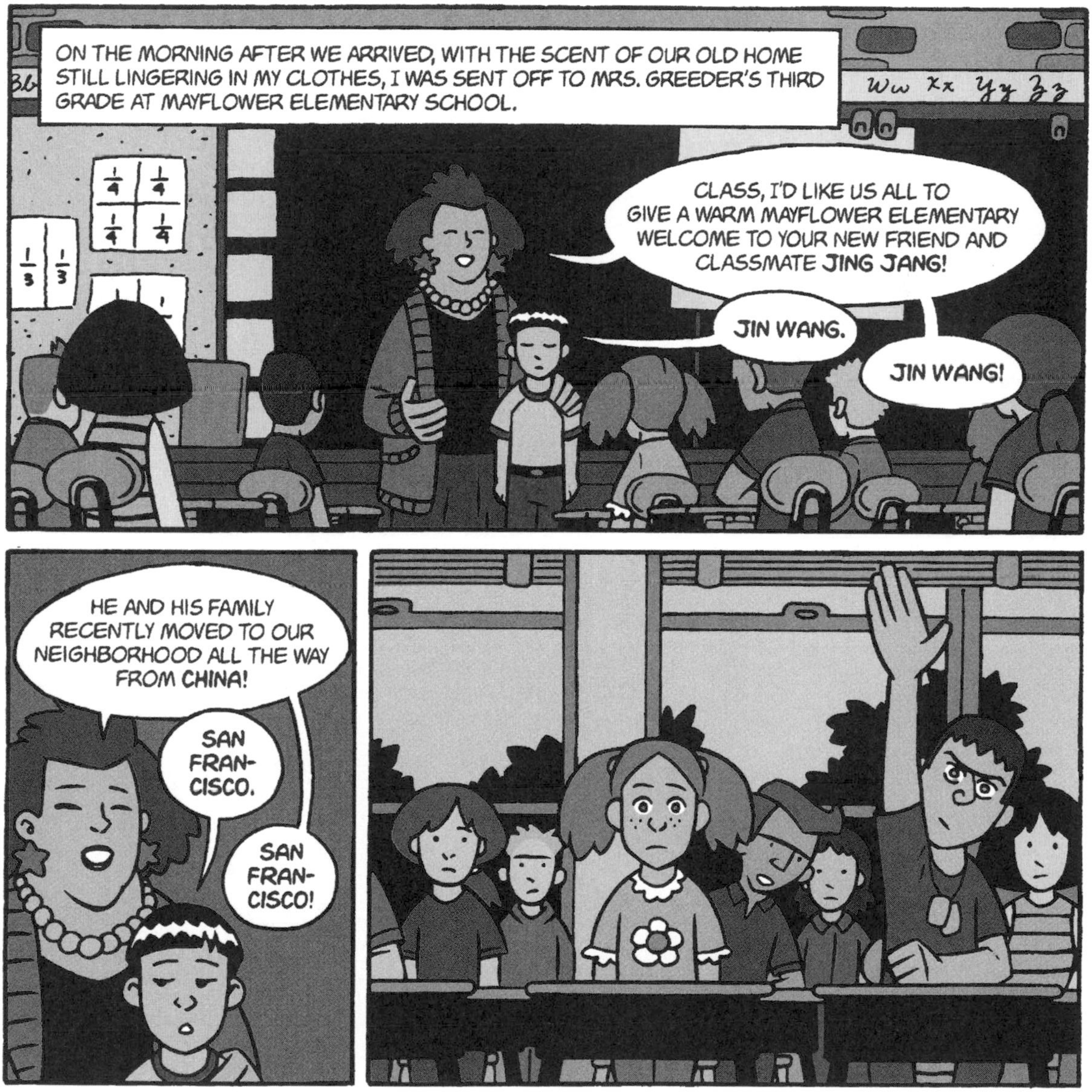
ON THE MORNING AFTER WE ARRIVED, WITH THE SCENT OF OUR OLD HOME STILL LINGERING IN MY CLOTHES, I WAS SENT OFF TO MRS. GREEDER'S THIRD GRADE AT MAYFLOWER ELEMENTARY SCHOOL.
CLASS, I'D LIKE US ALL TO GIVE A WARM MAYFLOWER ELEMENTARY WELCOME TO YOUR NEW FRIEND AND CLASSMATE **JING JANG!**
JIN WANG.
JIN WANG!
HE AND HIS FAMILY RECENTLY MOVED TO OUR NEIGHBORHOOD ALL THE WAY FROM **CHINA!**
SAN FRAN-CISCO.
SAN FRAN-CISCO!

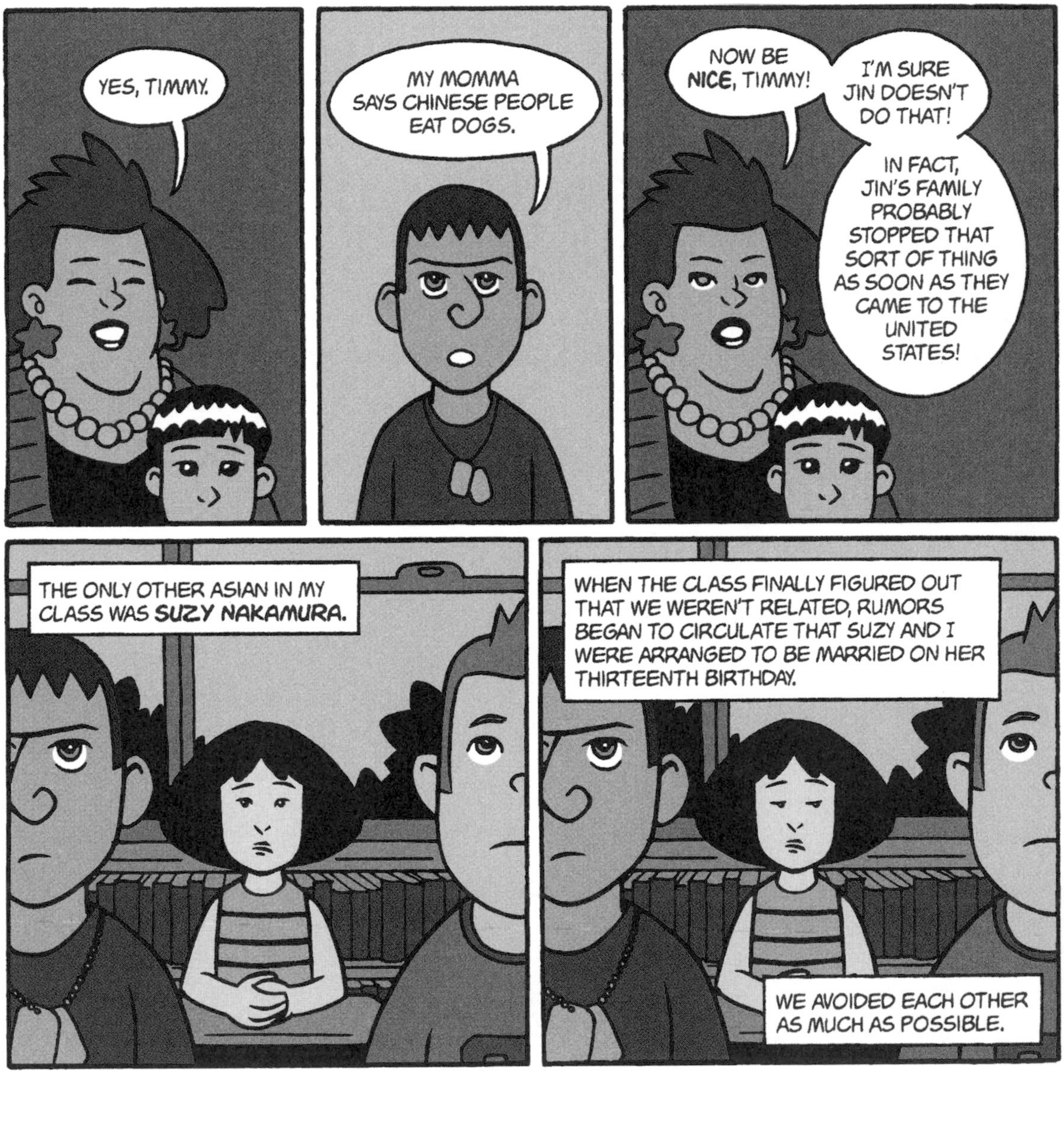
YES, TIMMY.
MY MOMMA SAYS CHINESE PEOPLE EAT DOGS.
NOW BE NICE, TIMMY!
I'M SURE JIN DOESN'T DO THAT!
IN FACT, JIN'S FAMILY PROBABLY STOPPED THAT SORT OF THING AS SOON AS THEY CAME TO THE UNITED STATES!
THE ONLY OTHER ASIAN IN MY CLASS WAS SUZY NAKAMURA.
WHEN THE CLASS FINALLY FIGURED OUT THAT WE WEREN'T RELATED, RUMORS BEGAN TO CIRCULATE THAT SUZY AND I WERE ARRANGED TO BE MARRIED ON HER THIRTEENTH BIRTHDAY.
WE AVOIDED EACH OTHER AS MUCH AS POSSIBLE.

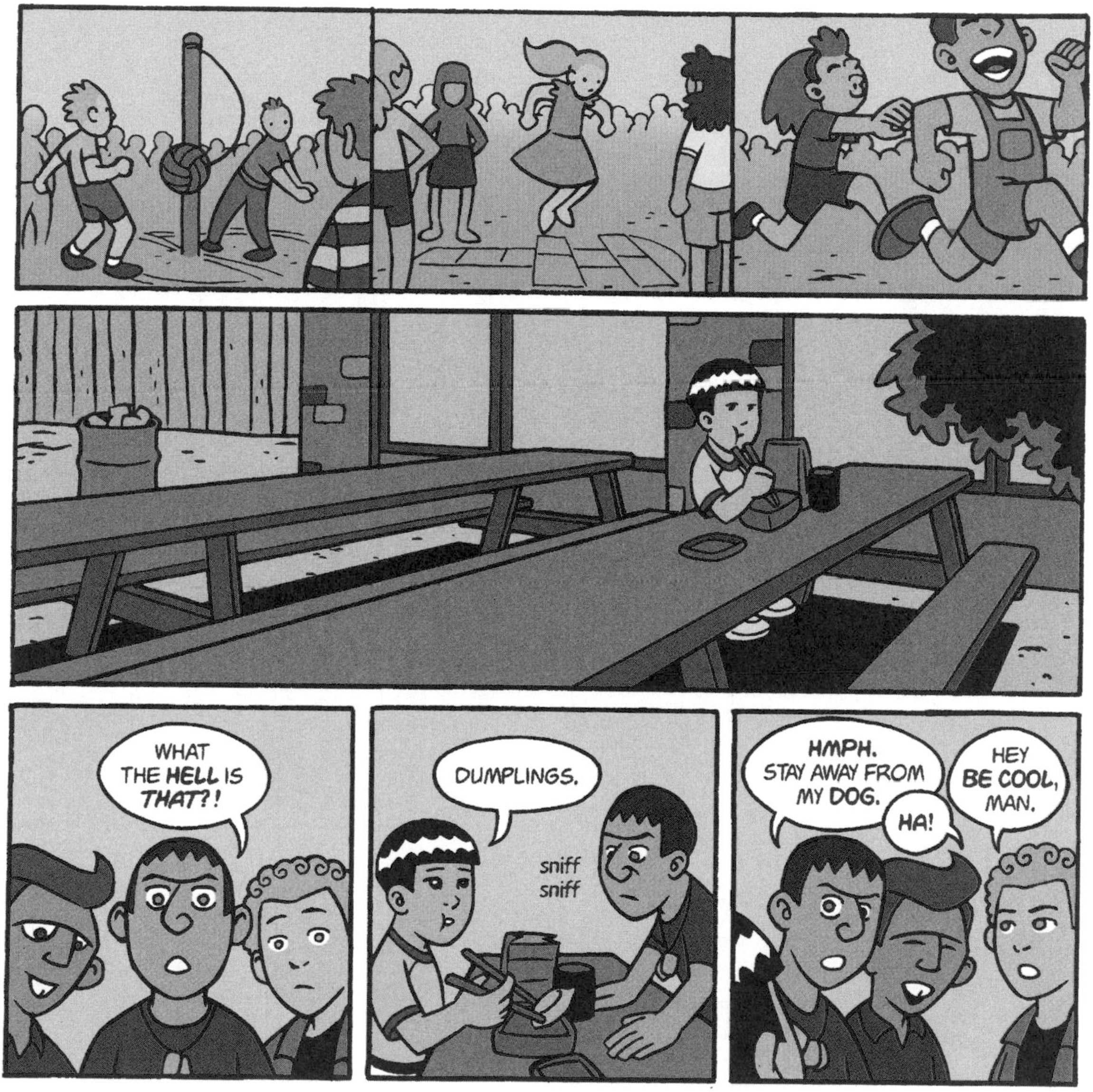
WHAT THE HELL IS THAT?!
DUMPLINGS.
sniff sniff
HMPH. STAY AWAY FROM MY DOG.
HA!
HEY BE COOL, MAN.

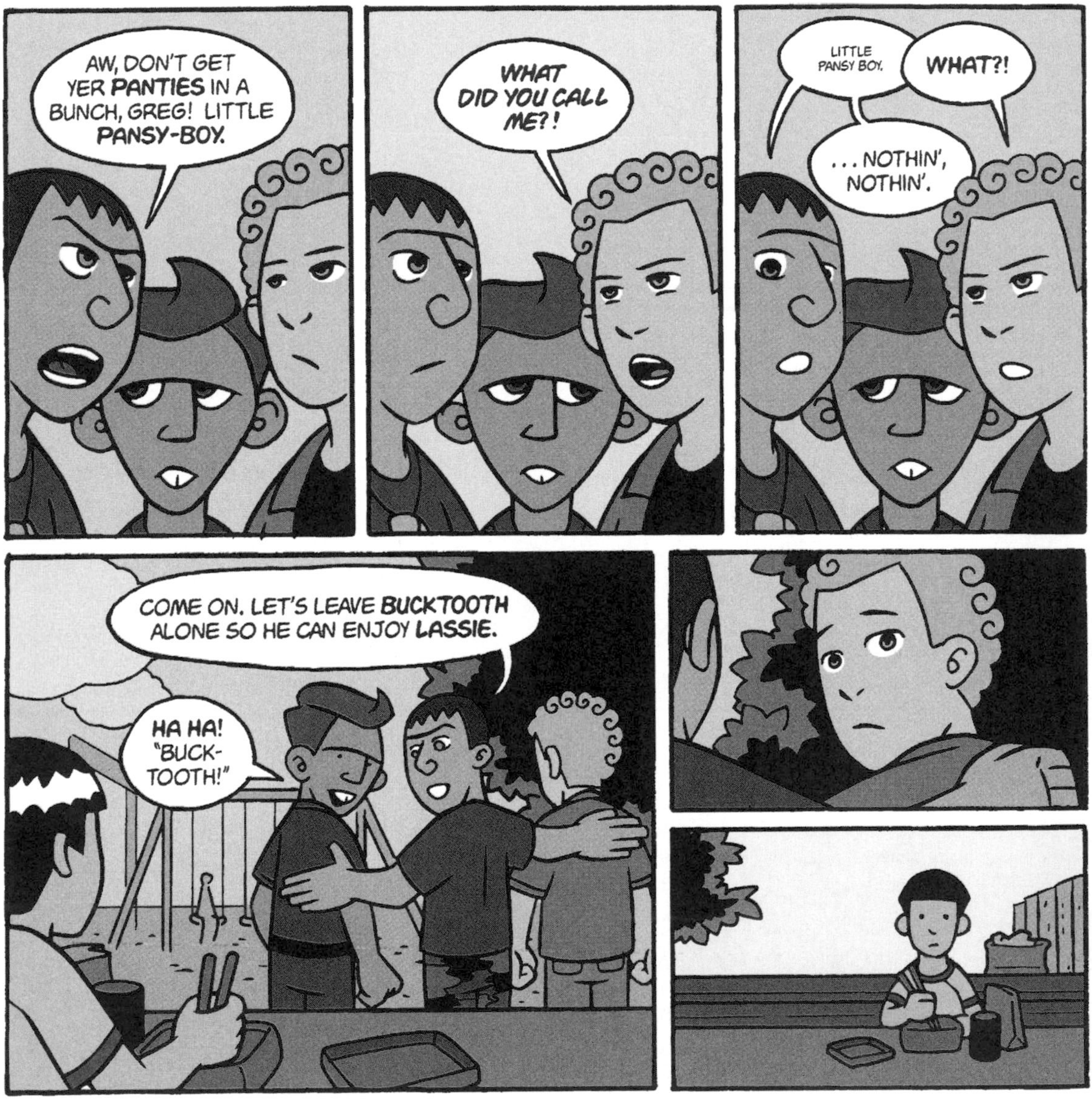
AW, DON'T GET YER PANTIES IN A BUNCH, GREG! LITTLE PANSY-BOY.
WHAT DID YOU CALL ME?!
LITTLE PANSY BOY.
WHAT?!
. . . NOTHIN', NOTHIN'.
COME ON. LET'S LEAVE BUCKTOOTH ALONE SO HE CAN ENJOY LASSIE.
HA HA! "BUCK-TOOTH!"

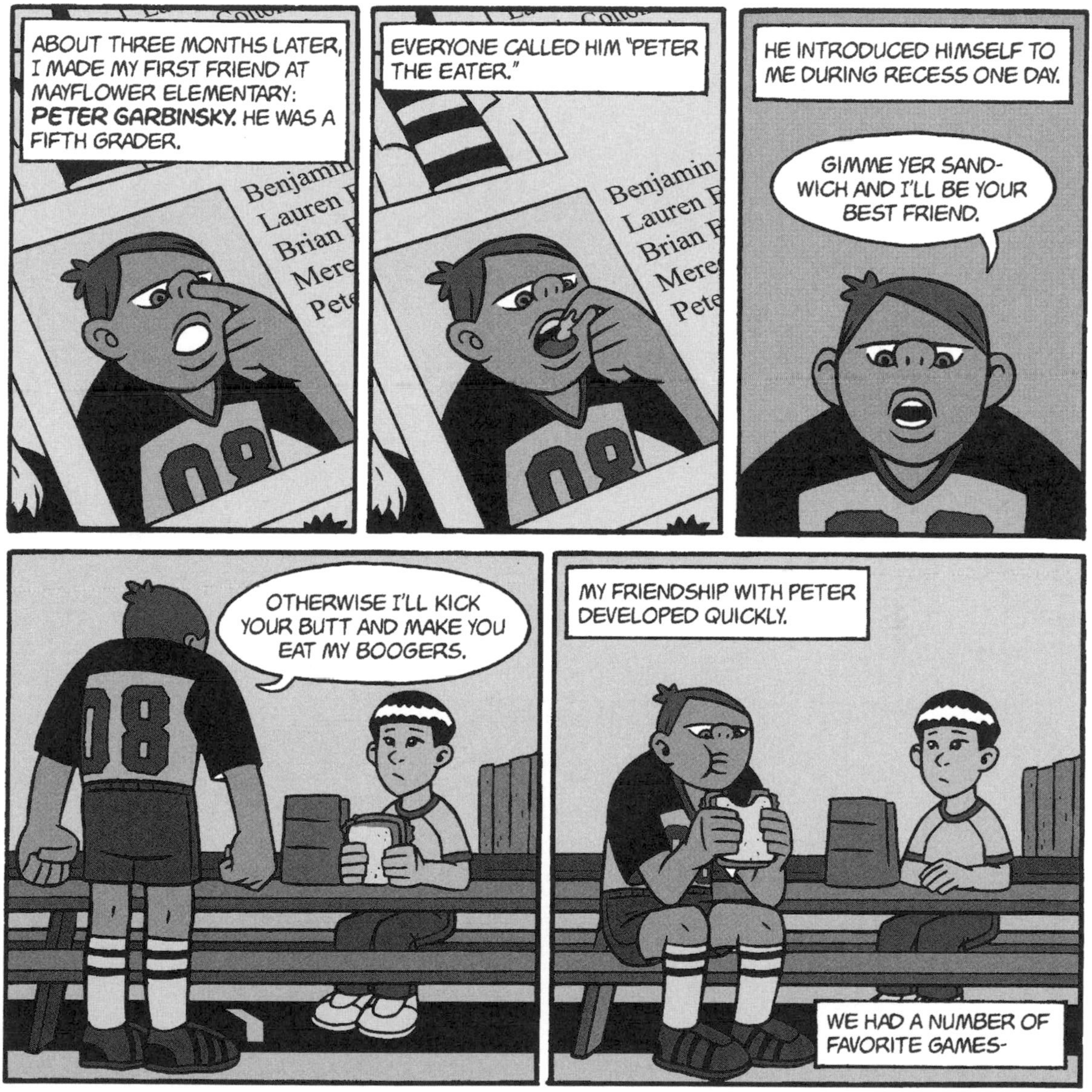
ABOUT THREE MONTHS LATER, I MADE MY FIRST FRIEND AT MAYFLOWER ELEMENTARY: **PETER GARBINSKY.** HE WAS A FIFTH GRADER.
EVERYONE CALLED HIM "PETER THE EATER."
HE INTRODUCED HIMSELF TO ME DURING RECESS ONE DAY.
GIMME YER SAND-WICH AND I'LL BE YOUR BEST FRIEND.
OTHERWISE I'LL KICK YOUR BUTT AND MAKE YOU EAT MY BOOGERS.
MY FRIENDSHIP WITH PETER DEVELOPED QUICKLY.
WE HAD A NUMBER OF FAVORITE GAMES-

- "KILL THE PILL" -

- "CRACK THE WHIP" -

- AND "LET'S BE JEWS." WE USUALLY HAD TO STEAL AN ITEM OR TWO FROM MRS. GARBINSKY'S DRESSER DRAWER FOR THIS GAME.

HAR! JIN, YOU'RE SUCH A FRIGGIN' RIOT!

JUST BEFORE WINTER BREAK DURING MY FIFTH GRADE YEAR (PETER WAS IN SIXTH), PETER TOLD ME HE WAS GOING TO VISIT HIS FATHER IN PENNSYLVANIA. "THE FRIGGIN' GOVERNMENT FINALLY CAME TO ITS FRIGGIN' SENSES," HE SAID.

WHEN WINTER BREAK WAS OVER, PETER NEVER CAME BACK.

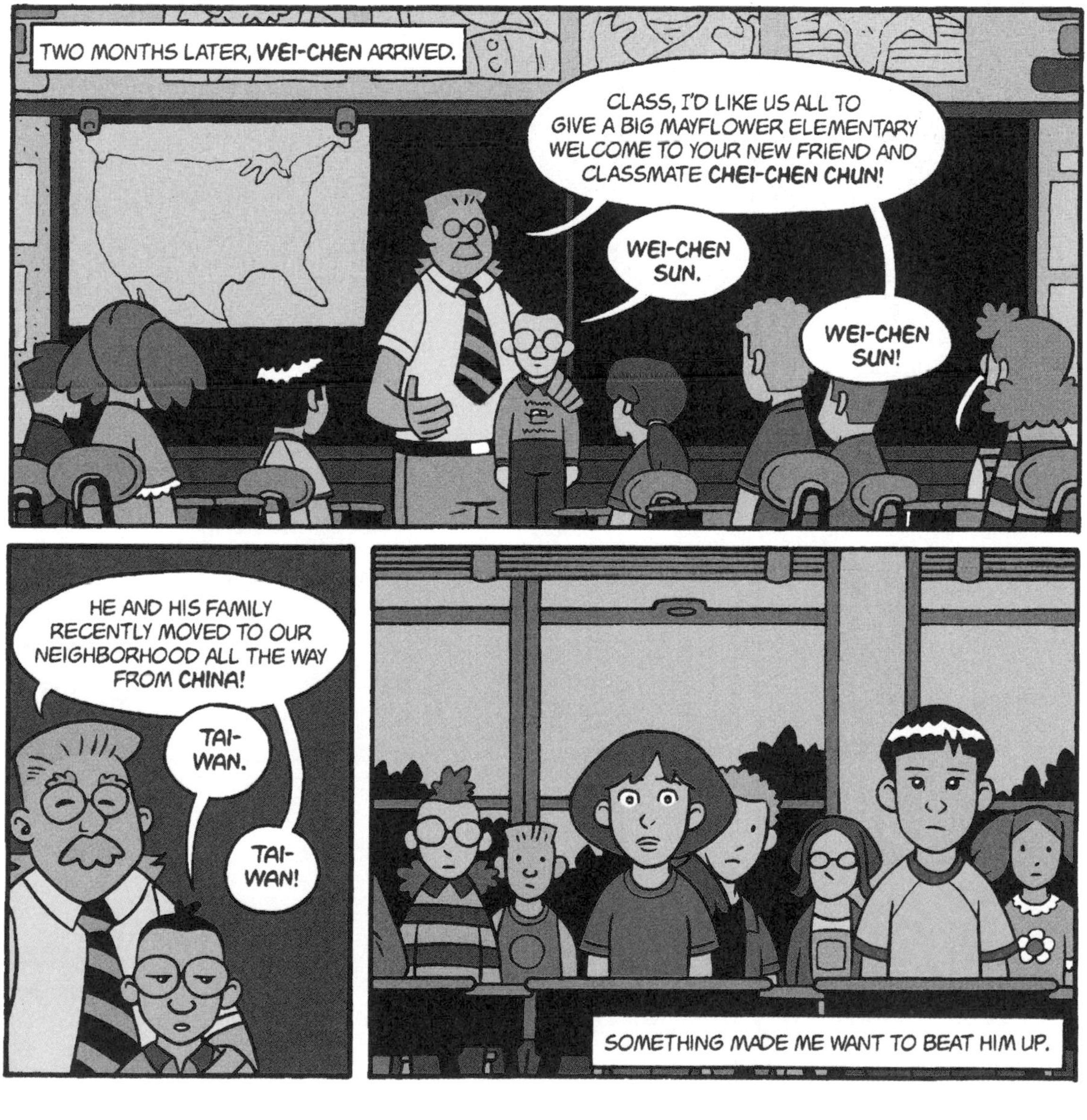
TWO MONTHS LATER, WEI-CHEN ARRIVED.
CLASS, I'D LIKE US ALL TO GIVE A BIG MAYFLOWER ELEMENTARY WELCOME TO YOUR NEW FRIEND AND CLASSMATE CHEI-CHEN CHUN!
WEI-CHEN SUN.
WEI-CHEN SUN!
HE AND HIS FAMILY RECENTLY MOVED TO OUR NEIGHBORHOOD ALL THE WAY FROM CHINA!
TAI-WAN.
TAI-WAN!
SOMETHING MADE ME WANT TO BEAT HIM UP.

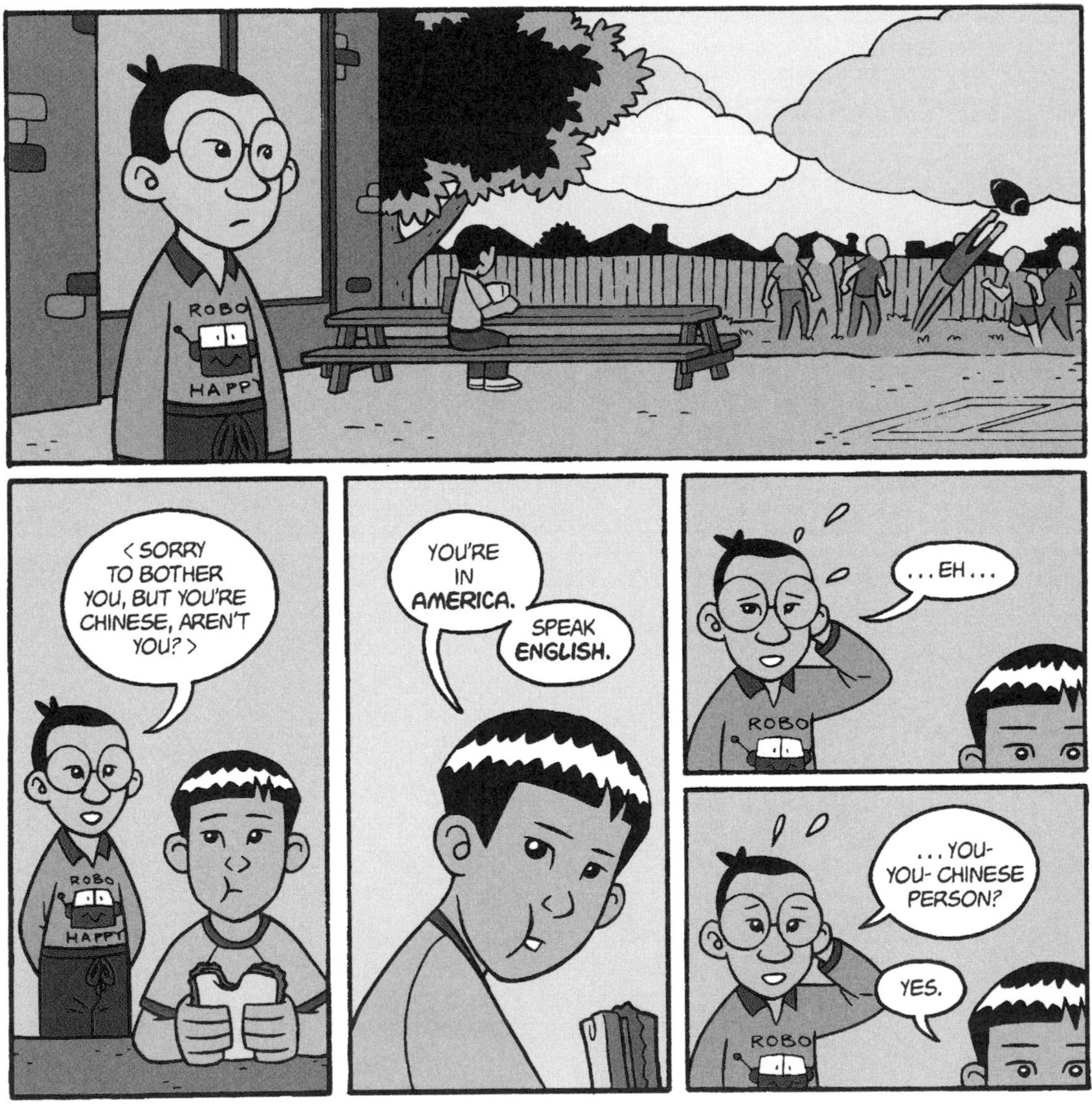
ROBO HAPPY
< SORRY TO BOTHER YOU, BUT YOU'RE CHINESE, AREN'T YOU? >
YOU'RE IN AMERICA.
SPEAK ENGLISH.
...EH...
...YOU- YOU- CHINESE PERSON?
YES.

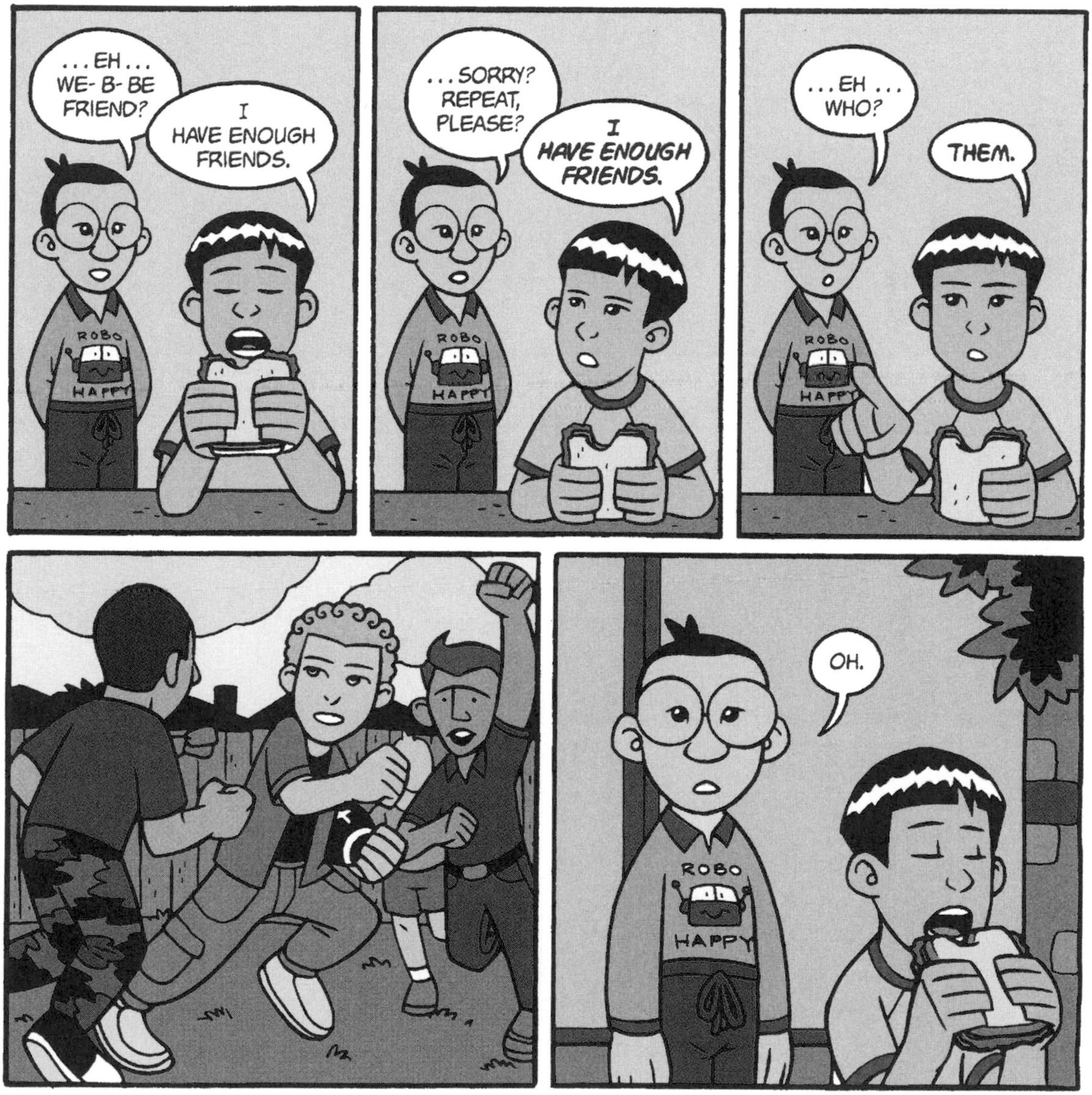
...EH... WE- B- BE FRIEND?
I HAVE ENOUGH FRIENDS.
...SORRY? REPEAT, PLEASE?
I HAVE ENOUGH FRIENDS.
...EH ... WHO?
THEM.
OH.

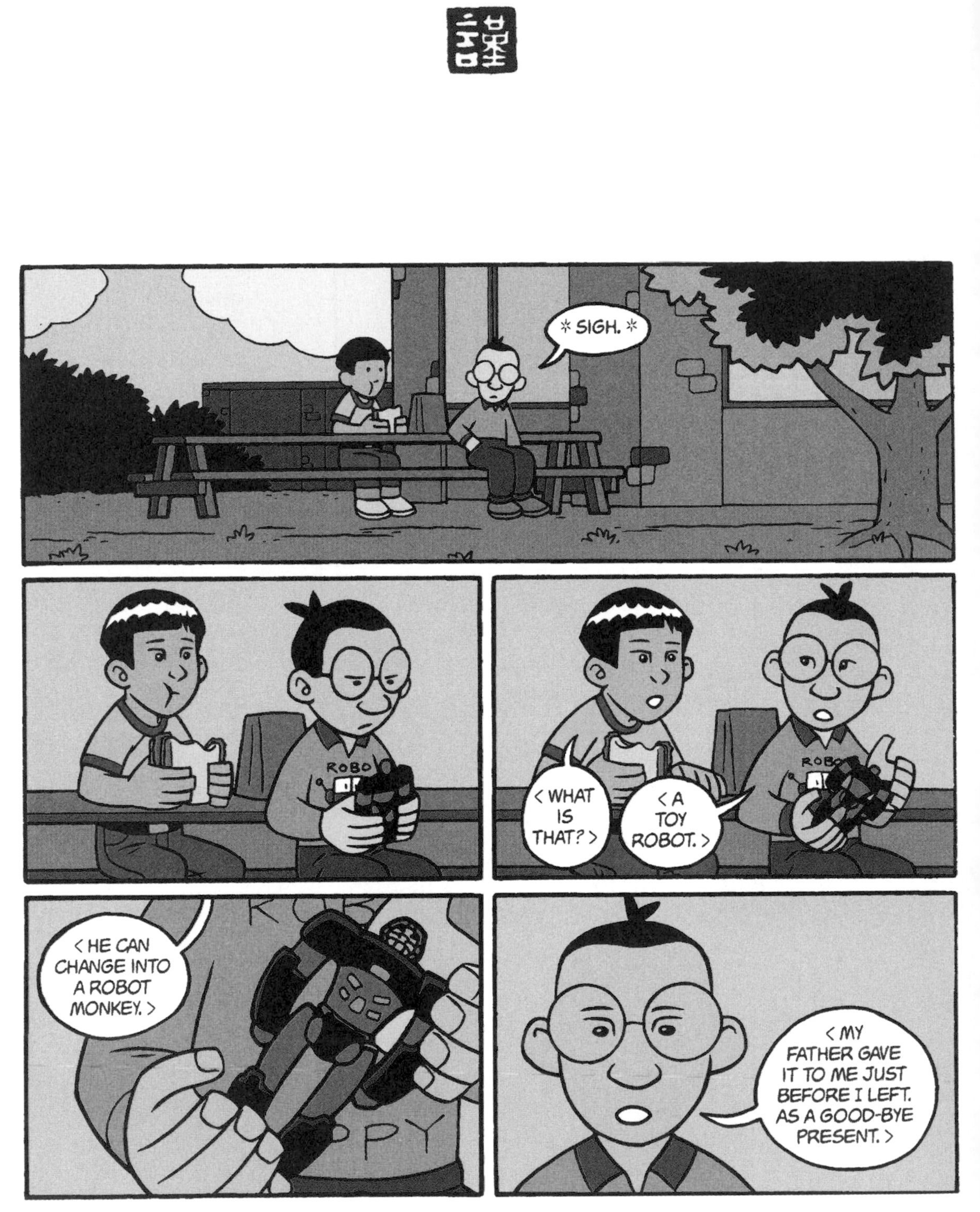
* SIGH. *
< WHAT IS THAT? >
< A TOY ROBOT. >
< HE CAN CHANGE INTO A ROBOT MONKEY. >
< MY FATHER GAVE IT TO ME JUST BEFORE I LEFT. AS A GOOD-BYE PRESENT. >

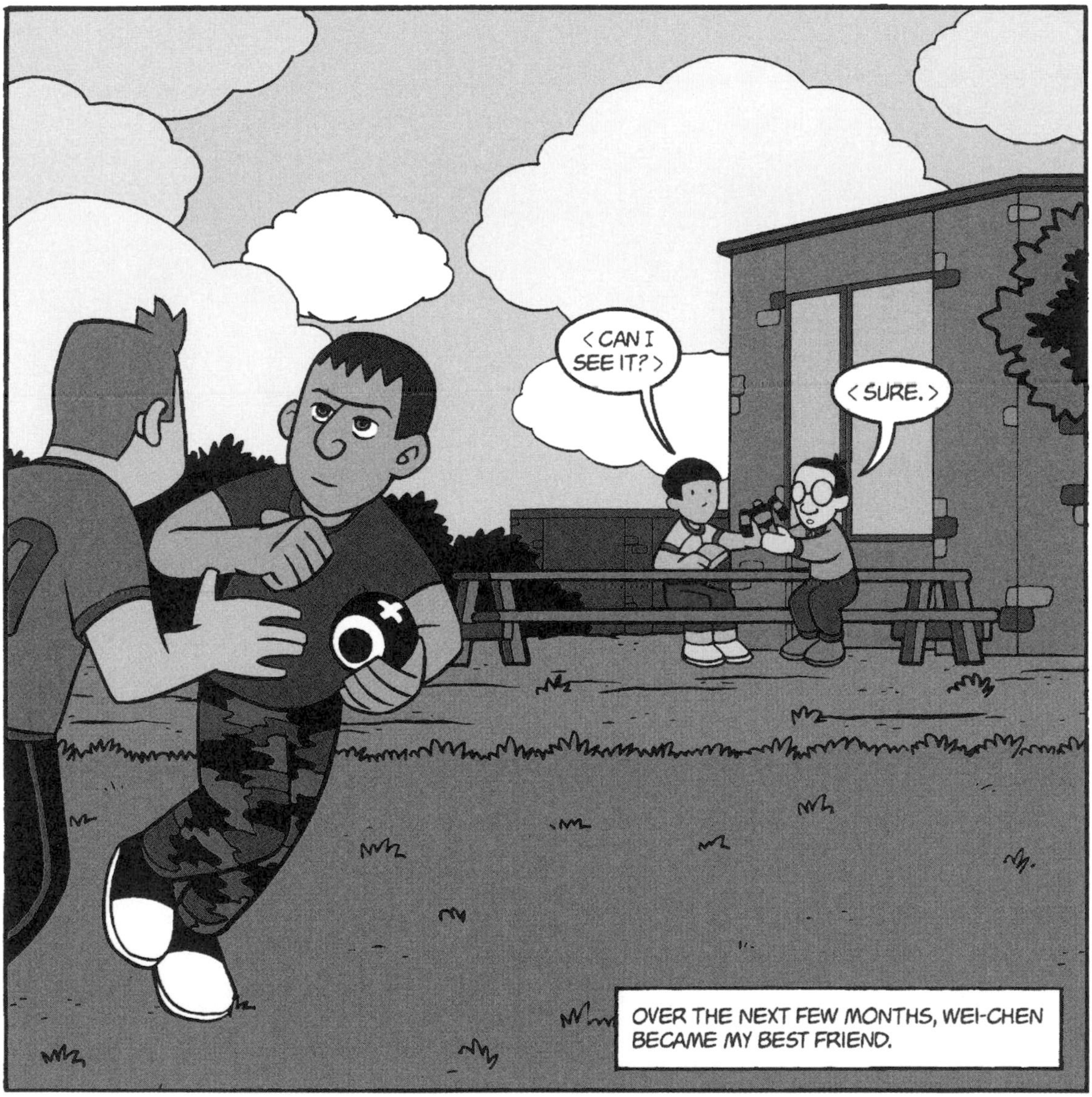
< CAN I SEE IT? >
< SURE. >
OVER THE NEXT FEW MONTHS, WEI-CHEN BECAME MY BEST FRIEND.

Contributors' Notes

Graham Annable was born in Sault Ste. Marie, Ontario, Canada. As a child, his collection of *Peanuts* and *Archie* digests was unrivaled in the neighborhood. He spent a good portion of his career animating in the games industry for such companies as LucasArts and Telltale Games. Annable's first published comic effort, *Grickle*, was nominated for a Best New Talent Harvey in 2002. He was also named the Bay Area's best unknown local cartoonist by *San Francisco Weekly* in 2004. His other comic works have appeared in such publications as *Nickelodeon*, *Too Much Coffee Man*, and *Flight*. Annable now resides in Portland, Oregon, where he works by day as a film story artist and by night as a comic creator.

▪ My wife had gotten me reading a bunch of Raymond Chandler novels at the time and I'd also been watching and listening to a lot of David Lynch. The combination of those sources formed the inspiration for "Burden." I was very interested in portraying a character who had done something horrendous but believes it's rationally the right thing. I liked the notion of this very thin veneer covering over a truly horrific course of logic.

David Axe is a Washington, D.C.-based freelance journalist and, since 2005, part-time war correspondent for the *Village Voice*, the *Washington Times*, C-SPAN, BBC Radio, PBS, *Wired*, and many others. He has covered conflicts in Iraq, Afghanistan, East Timor, Lebanon, and Somalia. *War-Fix*, the first in a trilogy of war memoirs, was named best graphic novel of 2006 by *Foreword* magazine and the same year made Amazon.com's list of top ten graphic novels. David collaborates with cartoonist Matt Bors on the war-correspondence comic strip *War Is Boring*, published on his blog at www.warisboring.com.

T. Edward Bak was born and brought up in Denver, Colorado. He was drawing at an early age, encouraged by his mother's watercolor work. Charles Schulz's *Peanuts* and Russ Manning's daily *Star Wars* newspaper strips, as well as children's book illustrations by Maurice Sendak, Jean Charlot, and Syd Hoff, eventually distracted him, too.

Bak spent several years working at various jobs in Athens, Georgia, developing material that would become his first comic strip. The autobiographical *Service Industry* appeared in the local arts newsweekly *Flagpole* from 2002 to 2005.

In early 2002, Bak founded a regional comics event in Athens, and his comics have since appeared in various North American anthologies and publications. In 2007, he was awarded the Fellowship at the Center for Cartoon Studies in White River Junction, Vermont. "Trouble" originally appeared in *Project: Romantic* from AdHouse Books.

▪ Through travels, dreams, failures, heartbreak, and lunacy, I've been inquiring about the process of life and human liberty. Beyond that, I've witnessed comics transform and transcend communication in a manner that is impotent in language, symbols, or images alone.

The human condition is itself a state of perpetual transition — moving from one place to the next, from slavery to freedom, from dreams to reality, from nonexistence into life, into death and returning to nonexistence—I am interested in the medium as a conduit to the automatic narrative process, beyond the chaotic music of memory. To me, comics are a way of figuring out time.

"Trouble" was a static template with which I was able to examine youthful ideas and dynamic characterization through the intimacies of a juvenile dialogue.

Alison Bechdel was born in 1960 in central Pennsylvania to eccentric schoolteachers whose deep, dark secrets she grew up to expose in her graphic memoir, *Fun Home* (2006). She has also been cranking out regular biweekly episodes of the comic strip *Dykes to Watch Out For* her entire adult life. Indeed, Alison is utterly bereft of employable skills and hasn't had a real job since the 1980s, when she pasted up a weekly newspaper using an X-Acto knife and rubber cement. She is thus very fortunate that her comic strip has garnered a select but pervervid readership, and that a bulky compendium of her work, *The Essential Dykes to Watch Out For*, has just been published by Houghton Mifflin.

▪ I produce an episode of *Dykes to Watch Out For* every two weeks, which is rather a long interval for a serial comic strip. I have at least a dozen main characters whose stories I try to keep up with. And I also feel compelled to shoehorn information about what's going on in the world into each episode, as if it's a historical chronicle. Given all these constraints, keeping a coherent narrative going often feels impossible. In particular, the mix of fiction and nonfiction perplexes me to no end. But I'm fascinated with the interplay between our domestic lives and the political context we live in, so each strip is kind of an experiment, an effort to get a little more data about how this works. Can our personal lives have an impact? Or are we all just getting buffeted around by systems that are out of our control? Often my individual experiments fail, and I end up with a strip that's overly didactic or just a dorky sitcom. But if I look at the big picture, the whole decades-long arc of the story, I seem to be making progress.

Nick Bertozzi: I was born in New York City in 1970, the son of a lawyer and an art teacher. I have three younger sisters. I'm married to a beautiful science teacher and I have two daughters. My favorite comic is a post-apocalyptic *Planet of the Apes* rip-off called *Kamandi* by Jack Kirby.

▪ I drew *The Salon* having missed the basic idea behind Cubism during art history class due to being hung-over or stoned. I knew there WAS this thing called a "picture plane," but I wanted to know WHAT it DID and drawing a comic for a couple of years trying to figure this out seemed like the right way to solve the problem. Also, I really hate the way that the story of art movements are told in our culture; you almost get the idea that Van Gogh and Picasso were hit with bolts of lightning on a Friday and on Saturday had their manifestoes written in stone. I think it's much more human and inspiring to believe that Picasso and a few of his buddies were simultaneously painting and fooling around, and that their discovery of a new way to depict reality came from hard work, happy coincidence, generous patronage, playing music, and a good sense of humor. If you get that from *The Salon* I'll be very happy—if you don't, I hope you don't mind a slice of life in the raw.

Lilli Carré was born in 1983 and grew up in Los Angeles. She left California to attend the School of the Art Institute of Chicago, where she drifted from department to department but mostly hovered around the Experimental Animation, Printmaking, and Writing departments. She became especially enamored of the Heidelberg offset press at the school, taking the offset class four times and self-publishing her stories. She has since stayed in the city and works on making comics and animations, and otherwise works as an illustrator and at a movie place. Her animations have shown in various festivals in the United States and abroad, including the Aurora Film Festival and the Sundance Film Festival. Her first published collection of originally self-published comics is *Tales of Woodsman Pete,* which came out in 2006 and was nominated for Ignatz, Eisner, and Harvey awards. Her newest story, *The Lagoon,* is to be published by Fantagraphics in late 2008. Bits of her work can be seen at www.lillicarre.com.

- The seed of this comic was planted in my head when a friend was telling me about an ostensibly true story that he's remembered since he was a kid—a little "spooky but true" kind of story he had read in the goofy part of the newspaper. I don't recall much of the actual events or details, but I remember that in his recollection a man came home and found himself sleeping in his own bed. I liked the idea of that moment, so I started with that and formed my own story around it, centering it instead around a woman who lives like a broken record until she has that moment of seeing herself in her own bed. It took off on its own legs and I ended up with the story included here.

Martin Cendreda was born and raised in Los Angeles, California. A lifelong fan of comics, cartoons, and other junk media, he was inspired to draw his own comics after reading three books: *Slow Jams, Good-bye, Chunky Rice,* and *Cave-In.* His comics and drawings have been published in *Mome, Drawn & Quarterly: Showcase, Dang!, Dazed & Confused,* and *Giant Robot.* He works in animation to help pay the bills and has worked on various shows including *South Park* and *Making Fiends* (debuting in 2008). He lives in Los Angeles with his wife, Jenny, and daughter, Margot, and their two feline overlords, Monkey and Snuggins.

- I've found that most of the stories I've done have started out as idle doodles that I kept mindlessly drawing over and over. The characters of the Lil' Orphans started out this way. They looked really interesting to me, so I put them in my first comic, *Dang!,* published by Top Shelf. They seem very vivid to me, almost real in fact. While driving around, I'll see an alley or an abandoned building and wonder if they're in there rooting around in a dumpster, turning other people's trash into something fun, and turning the city into a playground while the rest of the world sleeps. At times, it almost feels like I'm documenting their stories as opposed to creating them.

Shawn Cheng was born in 1980 and split his childhood between Yuanlin, Taiwan, and Long Island, U.S.A. He started drawing comics in earnest in college, where he contributed a weekly strip for the *Yale Herald.* He is a member of the comics collective Partyka (www.PartykaUSA .com) and the author of handmade, self-published mini-comics like *The Would-Be Bridegrooms, Vengeance at Cackling Mountain,* and *The Good Samaritan.* His work has also appeared in collections such as the *SPX Anthology, Paping,* and *Fluke.* Shawn lives in Brooklyn with his wife and cats.

- *The Monkey and the Crab,* done with Sara Edward-Corbett, is an adaptation of the Japanese folktale "Sarukani Gassen" ("The Monkey and the Crab War"). We were on the lookout for a project to collaborate on, and it seemed perfect because it was a two-part story featuring many of our favorite plot elements—trickery, betrayal, and murder; followed by sleuthing, the laying of a trap, and vengeance.

We worked together to figure out the overall plotline and rough character designs, then split the narrative down the middle and worked separately. Shawn wrote and drew the first half, and Sara wrote and drew the second half. We met about once a week to compare notes and commiserate. We also threw together a website where we would post panels in various states of completion. It turned out to be a very helpful way of seeing our progress and keeping ourselves motivated.

Eleanor Davis was born in Tucson, Arizona, and now lives in Athens, Georgia. Her parents read a lot of comics, so she and her sister did, too. She's been drawing her own comics for about eighteen years, and after a life-changing introduction to *King-Cat Comics and Stories*, printing her own minis for ten years. She's a regular contributor to the comics anthology *Mome*. She's hard at work on a rip-roaring kid's adventure graphic novel called *The Secret Science Alliance*, coming out soon from Bloomsbury Children's. And she works on just about everything hand-in-hand with her boyfriend, fellow cartoonist Drew Weing.

 ▪ My mom is a teacher and recently used my "Seven Sacks" story in one of her classes to talk about personal ethics (which made me really happy). She asked the kids, "What did the ferryman think was in the sacks? What were those monsters up to? What was the ferryman's responsibility?" Some of them said the ferryman had no obligation to even consider what was in the sacks. Some of them said the monsters were hiding something awful. And some of them said, "There are rabbits in the sacks?! The ferryman has to go rescue the rabbits!"

I liked that, because it made me remember being a kid, when absolute altruism was more than just possible, it was imperative. Right and Wrong weren't all muddled up like they seem to me now. And even rabbits ought to be rescued.

Derf sold his first cartoon, a nude portrait of his sixth-grade teacher, for two dollars to a classmate who used it for unspeakable purposes. Today his comic strip, *The City*, is one of the most widely read alternative cartoons, appearing regularly in weekly papers nationwide, including the *Village Voice, Dallas Observer, Denver Westword, St. Louis Riverfront Times, Pittsburgh City Paper,* and *Cleveland Scene.*

The cartoonist, who works out of an attic studio in his Cleveland home, grew up in a rural small town in Ohio and went to high school with the serial killer Jeffrey Dahmer. *My Friend Dahmer,* a comic book about his friendship with Dahmer, has, according to the *Boston Globe*, "the compactness and revelation of a nightmare; Derf packs enormous depth into a very short work."

An art school dropout, Derf worked on a garbage truck before deciding to give cartooning a try. But he was fired from his first cartooning gig at a Florida paper for, as the editor put it, "general tastelessness." He moved to Cleveland and *The City* debuted in the now-defunct *Cleveland Edition* in 1990.

His work has been displayed in museums and galleries worldwide. He has been nominated for two Eisner Awards, was named best cartoonist by the Alternative Newsweekly Awards in 2005, and was the recipient of a Robert F. Kennedy Award for political cartooning in 2006.

 ▪ When I write a strip, it all starts with the punch line. These things can pop into my head at any time of the day. Once I have the punch line, I write the strip backwards from there, slogging it out a panel at a time. That's how I did "The Bunker." The idea of George W as Adolf came to me in a flash. And then I drew it up several different ways (actually I set it aside for a month or so) until I worked out the one I liked, slowly panning around the bunker until the strip finishes on the delusional Führer urging his tattered troops to "Fight on." My frequent *True Stories,* on the other hand, are just manna from heaven. There have been times when I let out a bellow of joy when one of them unfolded before me. That's what happened with "The Man." I was practically dancing around the sidewalk. I was on vacation up in Canada and the locals must have thought I was one of those deranged Americans they'd heard about. Weeks where I have a *True Story* scheduled—and I do only one a month—are like mini-vacations. They're fun, they're easy. And I consider them the cornerstone of the strip. It's become more and more political satire over the years, but *True Stories* keep it grounded as a cartoon portrayal of urban life, which was the original concept. That's why it's called . . . *The City.*

When **Sara Edward-Corbett** was a child in Rhode Island, she and her sister kept thick sketchbooks filled with stories about their stuffed animals, Michael Jackson, and the devil. She studied art at Yale University and began drawing comics for the weekly student newspaper. Later, her weekly comic strip, *See-Saw,* was published by the *New York Press.* She works as a designer and illustrator and makes mini-comics by night; her website is www.greenfog.com. She lives in Brooklyn with her pet lizards.

Rick Geary was born in Kansas City, Missouri, and grew up in Wichita, Kansas. His work has appeared in *National Lampoon, MAD,* the *New York Times, Heavy Metal, Disney Adventures,* and many other publications. As artist for the new series of Gumby comics, he received the 2007 Eisner Award for Best Publication for a Younger Audience. He has produced nine volumes in his "Treasury of Victorian Murder" series and has initiated "A Treasury of XXth Century Murder" with *The Lindbergh Child.* He wrote and illustrated *J. Edgar Hoover: A Graphic Biography,* which was released in 2008 by Hill and Wang. He lives with his wife, Deborah, in Carrizozo, New Mexico.

- *The Saga of the Bloody Benders* is the ninth volume in "A Treasury of Victorian Murder," and the excerpt published here covers the years between the family's arrival on the Kansas prairie and their mysterious disappearance three years later, just prior to the discovery of their grisly deeds. As a former Kansan, I'd heard about the Benders for years, but their story had become so encrusted by legend and misinformation that it cried out to be told in an authentic way. In my historical pieces, I strive for clarity and accuracy above all, and this subject gave me the chance to seek out primary sources and use maps and overhead views to fix the characters in time and space.

Matt Groening was born and raised in Portland, Oregon. Since 1980 he has drawn the weekly comic strip *Life in Hell.* He is the publisher of Bongo Comics, and the creator of *The Simpsons* and *Futurama.* He lives in Los Angeles and fantasizes about moving to a tropical island or maybe back to Portland.

- I've always loved comics, children's folklore, unreliable narrators, and the way kids actually talk, so when I had sons of my own, I knew I was going to figure out a way to sneak 'em into my comic strip. And, man, Will and Abe really delivered, with fairy tales, arguments, jingles, rants, and theories about everything from Godzilla to girls, all of which I transcribed and illustrated. I highly recommend you do this with your own kids. Over the years I've cranked out a ton of stuff, but the Abe and Will strips remain my favorites. Thanks, dudes.

Eric Haven was born in Syracuse, New York, in 1967. His first comic book, *Angryman,* was published by Caliber's Iconografix imprint from 1992 to 1993. Somewhat alarmed by the experience, he decided to hone his craft by creating numerous mini-comics until 2003, when Sparkplug Comic Books started publishing his "Tales to Demolish." He's also had comics published in the *San Francisco Bay Guardian,* the *Los Angeles Weekly,* the Dark Horse anthology *Strip Search,* and the mammoth *Kramer's Ergot 7.* In addition, his hand can be seen on television drawing blueprint sketches for the Discovery Channel show *MythBusters,* where he works as an associate producer. He lives in Oakland, California, and is currently working on a new comic book series for Buenaventura Press.

- I got the idea for "Mammalogy" after reading Carl Sagan's *The Dragons of Eden* and David E. Jones's *An Instinct for Dragons.* Both books dealt with, among other things, the innate mammalian fear of reptiles. I thought that this base, instinctual dread would be an interesting platform upon which to build a superhero story. However, I couldn't resist adding an autobiographical layer to suggest these musings were the result of watching too much television, or eating an egg sandwich too late at night.

Jaime Hernandez, along with his brother Gilbert and another brother Mario, self-published the first issue of *Love and Rockets* in 1981. It was picked up by Fantagraphics Books in 1982 and ran for fifty issues before the brothers took a break to pursue solo projects. Jaime's titles include *Whoa, Nellie!, Maggie and Hopey Color Fun,* and *Penny Century. Love and Rockets* was revived in 2000 and continues today. Jaime lives in Pasadena with his wife and daughter.

  ▪ I basically did this strip to show a closer, possibly healthier relationship between my character Maggie and her mother, as I've never really shown it much in the past.

Born in Hoboken, the famous New Jersey punch line, it was inevitable that **Kaz** would wind up writing jokes. His Lithuanian immigrant father christened him Kazimieras Gediminus Prapuolenis—a name that most people give up on halfway. He grew up a working-class brat who loved comics, animated cartoons, monster movies, rock 'n' roll, and fine arts. Kaz has lived in and around New York City for all of his life. He studied cartooning at the School of Visual Arts under Art Spiegelman and Harvey Kurtzman. After art school, Kaz drew and published alternative comics while maintaining a career as a commercial illustrator. In 1991, he created a weekly newspaper comic strip called *Underworld* that continues to be published in alternative papers across the United States. In 2001, he was hired as a writer and director on Nickelodeon's *Spongebob Squarepants* TV show. This has evolved into a parallel career in the Los Angeles animation industry. He has written and directed storyboards for feature films and Cartoon Network shows, and he has just finished his own animated short, *Zoot Rumpus.*

  ▪ The *Underworld* pages in this collection were all drawn while I was working on Cartoon Network's *Camp Lazlo* show. Typically, I would drive to my office in Burbank on a Sunday, rule out four panels on Xerox paper, and take stock of my emotions. Then I'd project how I was feeling into my cartoon characters. The inspiration might be an overheard conversation, watching a cartoon, or digging through one of my old sketchbooks for some half-chewed idea I'd abandoned. The goal for me is always to put on a cartoon show in the limited space a newspaper allots my comic strip. When I'm writing for children, I try to tap into the playful and confusing things I thought about as a child. It's fun and liberating. But when I'm writing for adults, my comics tend to be dark, dirty, and painful because that's what makes a grown man from Punch Line City, New Jersey, laugh like a freaking idiot.

Michael Kupperman was born in Connecticut, unfortunately, and has since escaped to the relative safety and culture of New York City. His illustrations and comics have littered the pages of such publications as *The New Yorker, Fortune,* and *Rural Telecommunications* magazine. His comics have been collected in his book *Snake 'N' Bacon's Cartoon Cabaret* and the ongoing series *Tales Designed to Thrizzle,* and have been animated for *TV Funhouse;* current projects continue to develop, probably.

  ▪ Is it satire? Allegory? A prophecy of things to come? Frankly, I'm mystified. I'm not sure what I was trying to say with this story or why I thought it was a good idea to do it. Any reasonably intelligent person could look at it and come up with at least as good an analysis as I could. Certainly I do enjoy drawing, and there is a lot of it in this, so that's something. The theme I guess I would describe as "Nature vs. Nature," which memory tells me was *not* one of the themes allowed to us by English class. Werewolves are natural, aren't they? Or supernatural, which is just a souped-up version of the same thing. Cousin Granpa himself obviously is a reflection on how I think old people are really ridiculous a lot of the time. Except for you, of course, if you're reading this and you're an old person. Congratulations on staying "with it."

Joseph Lambert grew up in Newton, Kansas. After spending time in New York and Denver, he attended the Center for Cartoon Studies in Vermont, where he now lives with his wife.

■ "Turtle, Keep It Steady!" came out of an assignment from the first-year cartooning studio class at CCS. The assignment was to retell the story of the tortoise and the hare. The original mini-comic, put together for my classmates as part of the assignment, was roughly 8 inches square and had one to four panels per page. A few months later, I redrew a few pages and put together a smaller (about 4.5 inches square) mini that debuted at 2008's MoCCA. The original art was drawn on typing paper with a #3 nylon brush; for subsequent corrections and redrawn panels I used a Pentel Pocket Brush.

The idea for the story came from sketchbook doodles and a love for the drums. I should also say that the abstract shapes on the top half of most of the panels are meant to be drum sounds. Sometimes people think they look like bad drawings of trees.

Evan Larson grew up in Chantilly, Virginia, just outside of Washington, D.C., and started drawing seriously around age thirteen after reading his first comic book, *Fantastic Four #298*. He graduated from the Rhode Island School of Design with a BFA in illustration in 1999. His work has appeared in *Nickelodeon* magazine, *American Illustration 26*, and *Project: Romantic*, as well as several self-published mini-comics including *Bixarre* and *The Flying Bear*. He has taught comics and cartooning through RISD's Continuing Education department. He is an avid fan of comedy, comics, animation, and rock music. He resides in Providence, Rhode Island, where he and his girlfriend, the sculptor Ann Smith, share an apartment and studio. He is currently writing and developing an animated series. His ongoing work can be seen at www.postmodernfrog .blogspot.com.

■ I have always enjoyed characters that you can identify with, who also happen to be arrogant jerks (because, perhaps, *I* am an arrogant jerk). My stories typically center around someone like this — a character who has you on their side but has you gleefully rooting for their undoing at the same time. Two instincts drive this: the desire to see the villain get his just desserts and an inclination to find villains more interesting than other characters. I also try to find stories that take characters to their extremes. I love to draw characters in extreme states of joy, panic, sadness, and so forth because, for an instant, you can change the rules about what that character looks like. For example, when a character panics in a cartoon, eyes no longer need to be attached to their heads, tongues can swell to gargantuan proportions, bodies shrink, foreheads balloon, and the character becomes a reflection of that condition rather than a representation of a person or thing. It also handily alleviates the tedium that is intrinsic in making comics — having to draw the same character over and over again. After that, I just try to put in as many naked people running around as possible — because sex sells.

"Cupid's Day Off" was made for *Project: Romantic* by AdHouse Books, a collection of short stories devoted to love and romance. At first I was developing a more dramatic piece, but eventually I gave up and went back to more familiar, goofball territory. The publisher and editor, Chris Pitzer, had asked everyone, if at all possible, to try and keep the stories clean so the book might make it into some school libraries and such; I definitely missed that memo. He also asked that the stories be kept to eight pages or less. This was a challenge when I tried to balance out the pacing of the story. Though the events certainly aren't complex, there was a lot to establish before the story could move forward. The beginning still feels a bit rushed to me, but perhaps that's for the best since it quickly moves on to the meat of the story where the funny stuff starts happening. The punch line has always reminded me of a Wes Anderson movie (*Rushmore* in particular), where all the characters get together in the end.

Following graduation from the Rhode Island School of Design in 1991, inspired by the likes of Art Spiegelman, Ben Katchor, and David Mazzuchelli, **Jason Lutes** moved to Seattle with high hopes for the future of comics. After a year's worth of dispiriting encounters with the industry, he chose instead to pursue a career in dishwashing. This came to an abrupt end when he was offered a low-level production job at *The Stranger*, a free weekly paper. In 1993, he was given the opportunity to draw a serialized comics story for the paper, which was published in 1996 as the graphic novella *Jar of Fools*. Some time after climbing the single rung necessary to become art director of the paper, Jason decided to quit and try his hand at being a full-time cartoonist. In the intervening years, he has published a handful of comics short stories, but his main and on-going project has been *Berlin*, a fictional account of the German city during the twilight years of the Weimar Republic. *Berlin: City of Stones*, the first part of this intended trilogy, was first published in 2001; the second part, *Berlin: City of Smoke*, will be available by the end of 2008. The last, *Berlin: City of Light*, is still some four to six years off. At the time of this writing, Jason lives with his partner and daughter in rural Vermont, where he teaches at the Center for Cartoon Studies.

▪ I undertake storytelling as an exploration, with the hope that readers will join me in it. In *Berlin*, this investigation is a sustained attempt to understand, or at least to *see*, a specific time and place from the varying points of view of its inhabitants. After absorbing as much information as I can about the subject, I try to create characters that are both different from me and true to their world. In the end, they will all still contain some part of me, but the overriding goal is one of empathy: how does this person feel, what will that feeling make her do next? Everything, especially the dialogue, starts out highly improvisational, with no clear narrative goal, since that's how I see life. The story is hung on the pegs of actual historical events — the May Day Massacre of 1928, the Reichstag elections of 1930 — but how the threads of my characters' lives are strung from peg to peg is something that I discover as I go along.

Cathy Malkasian has spent years following characters around in her head. Since the early 1990s, she's worked as a director and storyboard artist for animation, gathering influences from film, comics, and colleagues. In 1996, she drew her first short-form comic for Robert Goodin's Robot Publishing. More followed, and, intrigued with the possibility of a long-form work, she dedicated a year to doing *Percy Gloom* in 2004. Her first graphic novel does not appear to fit into any traditional categories. Like most of her work, it takes an introspective and absurd approach to existential anxieties, offering more questions than answers. This seems to be the only strain of realism running through her work. She is currently working on another graphic novel and a short comic.

▪ Doing comics is my way of turning a senseless world into something coherent that I can contain and reflect upon. I make stories with the intent of sharing, helping, and connecting to other people on a deep level. *Percy Gloom* was created as a reaction to all the unkindness and extremism I was observing in the world. Percy has been through the hell of what extreme views can do. In the end, he realizes he has to choose to be happy and kind, in spite of the fanatical social structures that seem to impede him.

As we all know, most fears stem from a fear of death. Embedded in this is the fear of ostracism, isolation, and being removed from contexts that define us. *Any* loss or change will chip away at one's identity while at the same time restructuring it. Still, we fight to maintain our static comforts, fighting time, fighting change, sometimes isolating ourselves from the very life we cling to. This paradox seems to be one of the conditions of being alive, and it is explored throughout the story. It's absurdly funny to me, because we keep making the same silly mistakes based on the same fears and assumptions, often with great pomp and bravado! Yet there is a timelessness in each of us, too. Subatomic particles don't really care about time, and we are made up of these. We live on many levels at any moment. And so a character like Percy, who is conscious of his timeless aspect, will undergo many losses and changes. He will travel through many contexts, yet stay who he is. This coexistence of the perennial with the mutable is very interesting to me; reassuring and unsettling at the same time.

John Mejias was born in 1972 to a police sergeant and a school teacher. He is the publisher of the comic/zine *Paping* (his father's nickname), which features his own work and artists he believes in. Handmade elements such as screenprinting are an integral part of his publications.

- I had never seen or read anything that I felt adequately explained the experience of being a public school teacher. My ongoing comic, *The Teachers Edition,* hopes to document my dealings with board of education bureaucracies as I try to make human connections in an inhuman atmosphere.

Sarah Oleksyk spent her early years on a farm in rural New England before moving to Portland, Maine, where she decided at the age of eleven to pursue a career as a cartoonist. It was during her time studying illustration at the Parsons School of Design that she self-published the first of six issues of her mini-comic, *Roadside.* Since then she has contributed to numerous comics anthologies as well as producing several short animations. She currently lives in Portland, Oregon, with four cats and her boyfriend, with whom she creates limited-edition silkscreens of her illustrations. She has almost completed her first full-length graphic novel, *Ivy,* which she is serializing chapter by chapter in mini-comics form. Her comics, prints, and a sneak preview of *Ivy* are available at www.saraholeksyk.com.

- Occasionally people enter your life who you might never have expected to meet. They might not be good for you; they might be destructive, but for a little while they bring to you a new experience and perspective that you couldn't have foreseen. This story describes the way in which an unlikely liaison develops between two opposing personalities, and how a tenuous bridge forms to connect two radically differing lives.

Steve Olexa is an illustrator, graphic designer, and sometime cartoonist (time permitting) residing in Columbia, South Carolina. He attended the University of Tennessee, where his comic strips and editorial cartoons received numerous distinctions, including the Charles Schulz Cartooning Award and an Associated Collegiate Press award. *War-Fix* marks his first step into the realm of graphic novels.

Currently, he lives in a basement downtown, where in his free time he is easily distracted by vintage manga and comic strips, a variety of cheap electric guitars, and an arcade machine. He is at work on a new comic strip and his second graphic novel — at least insofar as the fast-paced worlds of graphic design and commercial art allow.

- I really appreciate the idea of comics as a language, particularly in the way that language can grow and evolve. From a creator's perspective, I think there are micro- and macroscopic approaches to this concept — working creatively within traditional structure, and trying to expand on that traditional structure.

War-Fix struck me as the kind of story more suited for the macroscopic approach, so I pursued directions in its layout that were new for me — using the meta panel to show simultaneous action, deletion of facial detail for emotional effect, and point-of-view shifts to allow the reader to both observe as the protagonist and to judge him.

I realize now that this macroscopic approach often pushes people out of the reading experience instead of communicating a greater range of ideas. But I've also come away with a greater sense of the learning that's going on in the process of comics — for cartoonists, it means determining the boundaries of the audience and weighing those against the necessity or utility of a new storytelling idea; for the audience, it means becoming comfortable (to the point of being unaware) with new ways to read and understand. And I think it's from these two points that the medium really does grow.

I take a lot of consolation in the fact that even a word balloon must have been confusing to someone back along the lines of history. Although, I have to admit—every time someone tells me that they find a layout confusing, the designer in me cries a little.

Kevin Pyle was born in 1964 and has lived in California, New Jersey, Illinois, Kansas, Brooklyn, Philadelphia, and again, New Jersey. From 1990 to 1991 he ran Minor Injury, a nonprofit alternative space in Williamsburg, Brooklyn. Around this time he cofounded the willfully obscure and unwieldy comic compendium, *Hodags and Hodaddies.* Shortly thereafter Kevin began coediting and contributing to *World War 3 Illustrated,* America's longest-running radical comics anthology. Much of the work done for *WW3 Illustrated* was collected in his 2001 docu-comic, *Lab U.S.A.: Illuminated Documents,* a nonfiction investigation of clandestine racist and authoritarian science. *Lab U.S.A.* won the Silver Medal for Sequential Art from the Society of Illustrators. Pyle has done performance and installations based on the book at the Brooklyn Museum of Art, Mass MOCA, and numerous gallery settings. He produced another nonfiction comic, *Prison Town,* before drawing *Blindspot,* his first graphic novel. He is currently working on *Katman,* to be published by Henry Holt in the spring of 2009. He resides with his wife and son in a creaky old house somewhere just past the swamps of Jersey.

▪ The spark for *Blindspot* came on a bus coming back from visiting a friend who lives twenty miles down dirt roads among the primeval Northern Californian redwoods. I made a map in order to remember the territory we had explored, and that led to making a map of the woods I played in as a preteen. Years later, when I was trying to figure out what to do after *Lab U.S.A.,* I came across this map in a sketchbook. Early in the process of pulling together a story, I remembered how much reading Sgt. Rock comics was part of that whole experience of playing army in the woods. This provided a visual hook for the story that really fueled the fire. Despite its origin, it would be inaccurate to call *Blindspot* a memoir. While the characters, setting, and some incidents are based on real events, the story really became shaped by the demands of plot and the story I wanted to tell. Still, in the end, I was surprised by how many of the themes of my previous nonfiction work seeped into the story.

Seth was born Gregory Gallant on September 16, 1962, in Clinton, a small town in southern Ontario. Since childhood, he has had a great love of cartooning and comic books. While attending the Ontario College of Art in the 1980s he discovered the work of R. Crumb, the Hernandez bros., John Stanley, and the cool, wry wit of the early *New Yorker* cartoonists. Drawing deeply from this disparate group of inspirations, Seth has distilled one of the most distinctive and recognizable cartooning styles of the past decade. Drawn & Quarterly published *Palooka-Ville #1* in 1991 and publishes new issues of this series as frequently as Seth's busy schedule will permit him to produce them. His books include: *It's a Good Life, If You Don't Weaken; Clyde Fans Book One; Wimbledon Green;* and *Bannock, Beans and Black Tea.*

As an illustrator and designer, he has worked on a wide range of publications, notably the best-selling *Complete Peanuts* and the upcoming *Collected Doug Wright.*

The *New York Times* ran his story, *George Sprott,* in their funny pages from 2006 until its conclusion in mid 2007.

Seth lives in Guelph, Ontario, with his cats, his books, and his patient wife.

▪ When I was asked to do a strip for the *New York Times,* I gave them three ideas. The first was to finish an aborted story I had begun in another magazine, the second was a meditative piece about an empty street, and the third was a very vague idea I had about an old television host. Of course, they chose the one I was least excited about—the TV host. Ultimately though, I was grateful for this decision because it forced me to bring to fruition an idea that would have most likely died on the vine if it had not been chosen. It also forced me to reexamine how I tell a story. I knew, for a newspaper readership, that I wanted each installment to be self-contained. The year previously I had experimented with using short, interconnected strips in my book *Wimbledon Green*. However, in that case I was in control of the format and space—each strip could be as long as I needed. Here I had a very rigid weekly space in which to work—at best twenty or thirty panels tops to tell each installment. This was a good education in brevity and hard editing. The first draft of each segment was always twice as long as the space allowed. I learned to cut to the bone. An educational exercise. Now, working on the book version of *George Sprott,* I am getting the opportunity to fill in some of the spaces I had to prune out for serialization. I've actually learned a lot doing this story.

Chris Ware is the author of *Jimmy Corrigan—The Smartest Kid on Earth* and the annual amateur periodical *The ACME Novelty Library*. A contributor to *The New Yorker* and the *Virginia Quarterly Review,* Mr. Ware was the first cartoonist chosen to regularly serialize an ongoing story in the *New York Times Magazine* in 2005 and 2006. He edited the thirteenth issue of *McSweeney's Quarterly Concern* in 2004, as well as Houghton Mifflin's *Best American Comics 2007,* and his work was the focus of an exhibit at the Museum of Contemporary Art Chicago in 2006 and the Sheldon Memorial Art Gallery in Lincoln, Nebraska, in 2007. Mr. Ware lives in Oak Park, Illinois, with his wife, Marnie, a high school science teacher, and their daughter, Clara.

▪ The idea of running a number of concurrent covers grew out of an experiment I tried many years before as a cartoonist at the University of Texas at Austin: occasionally, in order to accommodate an odd number of pages, I discovered that the printers would publish two identical editions of the student newspaper simultaneously, making duplicate plates for every page. So, I figured—why not print two different comic strips? Françoise Mouly, the art editor for covers at *The New Yorker,* suggested my idea to editor David Remnick, who graciously okayed it, and then, after much exhaustive research into the circulation processes at Condé Nast, she sorted out actually how to make it work.

I was given the Thanksgiving issue as the subject and drew four covers (or five, depending on how one counts them) to suit. Beginning with a single street corner and the Tolstoy quote "As long as there are slaughterhouses, there will be battlefields," the covers chew over how unquestioning generational respect for tradition and ritual can lead to some genuinely awful and inhumane things. They also make gentle fun of Tolstoy's (and my own) vegetarianism. I ran into some difficulties of visual continuity, like how to make it clear that an old man on two of the covers is also a child on two of the other ones, but by resorting to primary colors for such coding, I think the end result is more or less readable. Having always wanted to put a comic strip on the cover of *The New Yorker* (just as one of the characters in the story wants to become a cartoonist/cover artist), I tried to allude to the natural growth of comics, fiction (and memory) as a function of subdivision by beginning with the single image of the typical *New Yorker* cover, dividing it in two, and then squaring the "grid" on which the subsequent covers' panel structures are based (4, 16, 256) as the story drops farther and farther into the mind and imagination of one of its characters. The final, fifth image appeared only on the Internet concurrently with the covers' runs, though here it appears printed as part of the whole. The comic strip on which the fourth cover, "Penrod the Pigeon," is based—*The Smythes* by Rea Irvin—is obscure today, though Irvin's fame is secure for designing not only the very first cover of *The New Yorker,* but also the magazine's distinctive hand-lettered logo. A portfolio of all five prints appeared in late 2007.

Gene Luen Yang began drawing comic books in the fifth grade. In 1997, he received the Xeric Grant for *Gordon Yamamoto and the King of the Geeks*, his first comics work as an adult. He has since written and drawn a number of titles, including *Duncan's Kingdom* (with art by Derek Kirk Kim) and *The Rosary Comic Book*. His latest book *American Born Chinese* was the first graphic novel to be nominated for a National Book Award and winner of the American Library Association's 2007 Michael L. Printz Award.

Gene lives in the San Francisco Bay Area with his lovely wife and children and teaches computer science at a Roman Catholic high school.

▪ When I was in third or fourth grade, a Chinese boy a year younger than me immigrated to my neighborhood from Taiwan and began attending my school. He spoke Mandarin Chinese and very little English. Because I too spoke Mandarin Chinese, the teachers on yard duty were intensely interested in us becoming friends. "You can really help him out," they told me.

I didn't want to be friends with him. I didn't want to from the deepest parts of me, for reasons I didn't understand at the time. He followed me around for several days, wearing his annoying fobby clothes and talking his annoying fobby talk. He finally left me alone after my white best friend and I threw tanbark at him.

In many ways, *American Born Chinese* is my apology to him, this boy whose name I don't remember, who could have been a friend.

Notable Comics

from August 31, 2006, to September 1, 2007

Selected by Jessica Abel and Matt Madden

JOSH BAYER
Bike Rider, 2007.

GABRIELLE BELL
Hit Me. *Stuck in the Middle,* 2007.

JONATHAN BENNETT
Meditation on the Grid. *Mome,* Summer 2007.

GREGORY BENTON
Warum, 2007.

NICK BERTOZZI
The Voyage of the James Caird. *Syncopated* vol. 3.

JEFFREY BROWN
Construction. *Feeble Attempts,* 2007.
Crossing the Street. *Feeble Attempts,* 2007.
Can You Feel Jesus In Your Heart. *Feeble Attempts,* 2007.

CULLEN BUNN AND BRIAN HURTT
The Damned, 2007.

BEN CATMULL
Civilization Studies Illustrated. *Monster Parade* no. 1.

ROBYN CHAPMAN
Sourpuss no. 1.

BRIAN CHIPPENDALE
Ninja, 2006.

GREG COOK
My Dorchester Neighbors. *Syncopated* vol. 3.

WARREN CRAGHEAD
How to Be Everywhere, 2007.

JORDAN CRANE
Take Me Home. *Uptight* no. 2.
Before They Got Better. *Uptight* no 2.

KIM DEITCH
Alias the Cat, 2007.
Shadowland, 2006.

CAROL AND MATT DEMBICKI
Mr. Big, 2007.

EVAN DORKIN
Dork no. 11.

RAY FENWICK
The King and the Beast. *Ballyhoo Stories,* 2007.

ELLEN FORNEY
I Love Led Zeppelin, 2007.

CHUCK FORSMAN
Drunks #1: Sea Colony, 2007.

LINE GAMACHE
Hello, Me Pretty, 2007.

MOLLIE GOLDSTROM
Abscond, 2007.

RICHARD HAHN
Wordlessness (on Steinberg?). *Windy Corner Magazine* vol. 1, no. 1.

JOHN HANKIEWICZ
Asthma, 2007.

TOM HART
Hutch Owen comic strip. New York and Boston *Metro,* 2006–2007.

TIM HENSLEY
Wally Gropius, Teen Millionaire. *Mome,* Fall 2006.

JAIME HERNANDEZ
Trampas Pero No Trampan. *Love and Rockets* vol. II, no. 18.

KEVIN HUIZENGA
The Curse. *Curses,* 2006.

DAMIEN JAY
The Tinderbox, 2007.

TOM KACZYNSKI
10,000 Years. *Mome,* Summer 2007.

JAMES KOCHALKA
American Elf, Volume 2, 2007.

PETER KUPER
Stop Forgetting to Remember, 2007.

DAVID LAPHAM
Silverfish, 2007.

MISS LASKO-GROSS
Giving In. *Escape from "Special,"* 2006.
Cartoonists. *Escape from "Special,"* 2006.
Freakout. *Escape from "Special,"* 2006.

JEFF LEMIRE
Tales from the Farm. *Essex County* vol. 1.

JON LEWIS
Local Stations, 2007.

ANDREW LIN
Andrew Lin's Mountain of Sadness, 2007.

VASILIS LOLOS
The Last Call, Volume 1, 2007.

TONY MILLIONAIRE
Sock Monkey: The "Inches" Incident, 2007.

JIM MUNROE AND SALGOOD SAM
Therefore Repent!, 2007.

KEVIN MUTCH
Uncertainty Principle. *Blurred Vision* no. 3.

LELAND MYRICK
The Fire Cracker Tree. *Missouri Boy*, 2006.

TOM NEELY
The Blot, 2007.

JOSH NEUFELD
A.D., New Orleans after the Flood, 2007.

MARK NEWGARDEN AND MEGAN
MONTAGUE CASH
Bow-Wow Bugs a Bug, 2007.

ANDERS NILSEN
The End no. 1.

GEORGE O'CONNOR (from the writings of
H. M. Van den Bogaert)
January 4–7. *Journey Into Mohawk Country*,
2006.

MICHAEL AVON OEMING AND IVAN
BRANDON
The Cross Bronx, 2006.

PAUL POPE
Fun!! Comics. *THB: Comics from Mars*
no. 1.

NATE POWELL
Please Release, 2006.

BRIAN RALPH
Daybreak no. 1.

KEVIN SCALZO
Sugar Booger no. 2.

STAN SAKAI
Usagi Yojimbo no. 101.

B.J. AND FRANK SANTORO
Cold Heat, 2007.

ARIEL SCHRAG
Shit. *Stuck in the Middle*, 2007.

GRANT SHAFFER
Thirty Kinds of Passion. *Blurred Vision* no. 2.

DASH SHAW
The Mother's Mouth, 2006.

JASON SHIGA
Bookhunter, 2007.

BISHAKH K. SOM
Come Back to Me, 2007.

MICAH SPIVAK
Pissed on Another Planet. *Human Being
Lawnmower* no. 1.

LESLIE STEIN
Fun Time with. . . . *Eye of the Majestic
Creature* no. 2.

MALCOLM SUTHERLAND
Oola Dug, 2007.

JILLIAN TAMAKI
Gilded Lilies, 2006.

JAMIE TANNER
The Patron. *The Aviary*, 2007.
War Atrocity Love Song. *The Aviary*, 2007.
Always in Love. *The Aviary*, 2007.
Barry Pago, Crime Scene Photographer. *The
Aviary*, 2007.

MATTHEW THURBER
1-800-MICE no. 1 and 2.

SARAH VARON
Robot Dreams, 2007.

ESTHER PEARL WATSON
Unlovable no. 5.

LAUREN WEINSTEIN
Horse Camp. *Stuck in the Middle*, 2007.

MATT WIEGLE
Seven More Days of Not Getting Eaten, 2007.

BRIAN WOOD
DMZ, Volume 2: Body of a Journalist, 2007.

JEFF ZWIREK
Burning Building Comics no. 1.

THE BEST AMERICAN SERIES®

THE BEST AMERICAN SHORT STORIES® 2008
Salman Rushdie, editor, Heidi Pitlor, series editor

ISBN: 978-0-618-78876-7 $28.00 CL
ISBN: 978-0-618-78877-4 $14.00 PA

THE BEST AMERICAN NONREQUIRED READING™ 2008
Edited by Dave Eggers, introduction by Judy Blume

ISBN: 978-0-618-90282-8 $28.00 CL
ISBN: 978-0-618-90283-5 $14.00 PA

THE BEST AMERICAN COMICS™ 2008
Lynda Barry, editor, Jessica Abel and Matt Madden, series editors

ISBN: 978-0-618-98976-8 $22.00 POB

THE BEST AMERICAN ESSAYS® 2008
Adam Gopnik, editor, Robert Atwan, series editor

ISBN: 978-0-618-98331-5 $28.00 CL
ISBN: 978-0-618-98322-3 $14.00 PA

THE BEST AMERICAN MYSTERY STORIES™ 2008
George Pelecanos, editor, Otto Penzler, series editor

ISBN: 978-0-618-81266-0 $28.00 CL
ISBN: 978-0-618-81267-7 $14.00 PA

THE BEST AMERICAN SPORTS WRITING™ 2008
William Nack, editor, Glenn Stout, series editor

ISBN: 978-0-618-75117-4 $28.00 CL
ISBN: 978-0-618-75118-1 $14.00 PA

THE BEST AMERICAN TRAVEL WRITING™ 2008
Anthony Bourdain, editor, Jason Wilson, series editor

ISBN: 978-0-618-85863-7 $28.00 CL
ISBN: 978-0-618-85864-4 $14.00 PA

THE BEST AMERICAN SCIENCE AND NATURE WRITING™ 2008
Jerome Groopman, editor, Tim Folger, series editor

ISBN: 978-0-618-83446-4 $28.00 CL
ISBN: 978-0-618-83447-1 $14.00 PA

THE BEST AMERICAN SPIRITUAL WRITING™ 2008
Edited by Philip Zaleski, introduction by Jimmy Carter

ISBN: 978-0-618-83374-0 $28.00 CL
ISBN: 978-0-618-83375-7 $14.00 PA

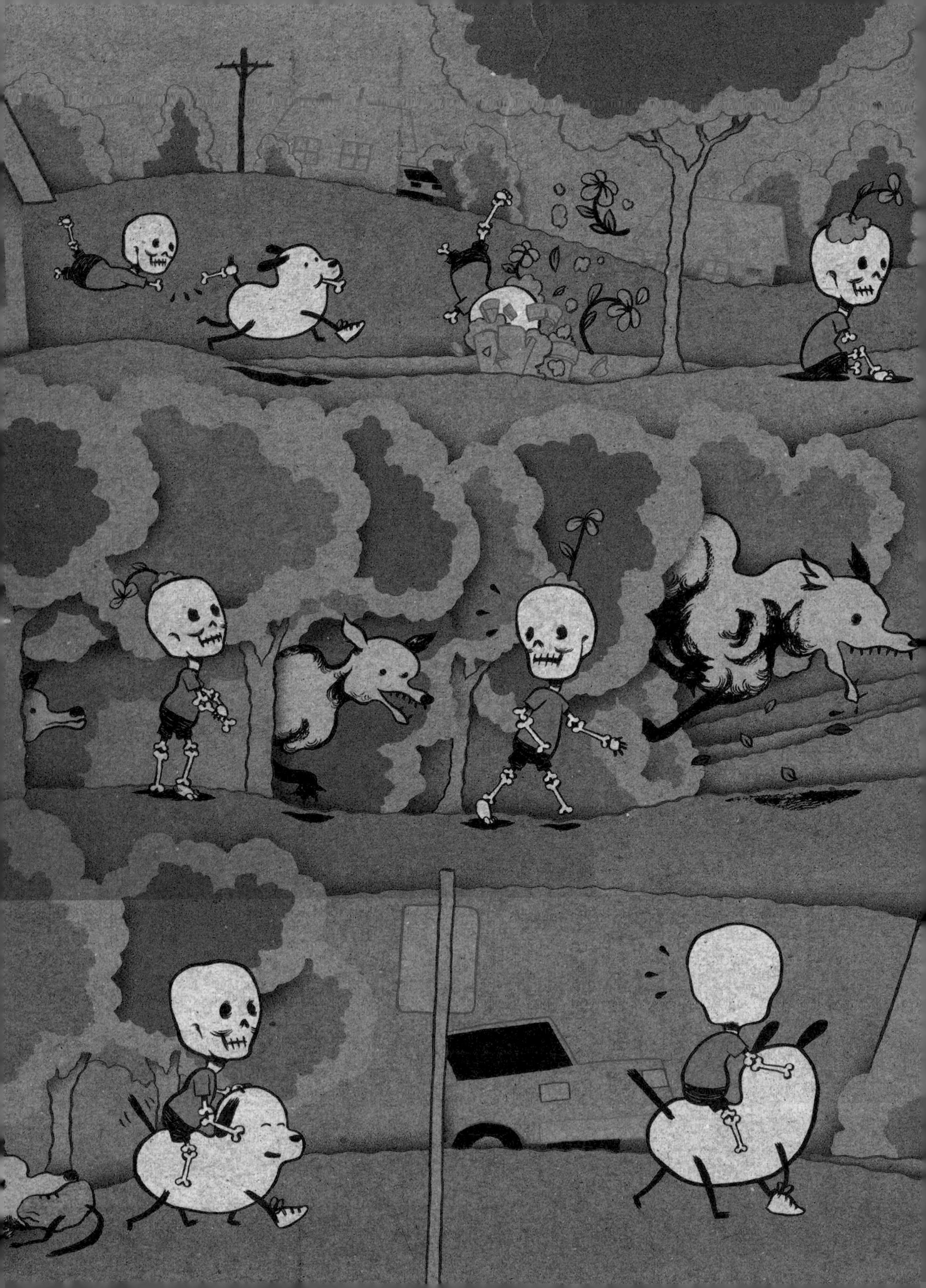